Organisational Behaviour and Analysis

Visit the *Organisational Behaviour and Analysis, third edition* Companion Website at **www.pearsoned.co.uk/rollinson** to find valuable **student** learning material including:

- Multiple choice questions to help test your learning
- Chapter resource sheets providing additional support material
- A guide to working with case studies
- A brief overview of organisational research
- An online glossary to explain key terms

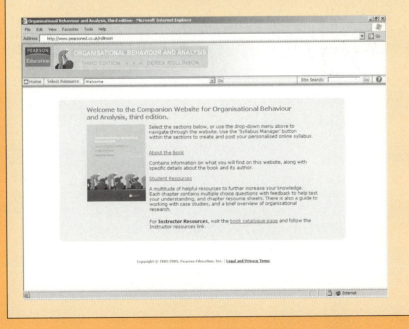

We work with leading authors to develop the
strongest educational materials in business,
bringing cutting-edge thinking and best learning
practice to a global market.

Under a range of well-known imprints, including
Financial Times/Prentice Hall, we craft high quality print and
electronic publications which help readers to understand
and apply their content, whether studying or at work.

To find out more about the complete range of our
publishing, please visit us on the World Wide Web at:
www.pearsoned.co.uk

DEREK ROLLINSON

Organisational Behaviour and Analysis

An Integrated Approach

THIRD EDITION

Prentice Hall
FINANCIAL TIMES

An imprint of **Pearson Education**

Harlow, England • London • New York • Boston • San Francisco • Toronto • Sydney • Singapore • Hong Kong
Tokyo • Seoul • Taipei • New Delhi • Cape Town • Madrid • Mexico City • Amsterdam • Munich • Paris • Milan

Pearson Education Limited
Edinburgh Gate
Harlow
Essex CM20 2JE
England

and Associated Companies throughout the world

Visit us on the World Wide Web at:
www.pearsoned.co.uk

First published 1998
Second edition published 2002
Third edition published 2005

ISBN-10: 0-273-68578-3
ISBN-13: 978-0-273-68578-4

British Library Cataloguing-in-Publication Data
A catalogue record for this book is available from the British Library

10 9 8 7 6 5 4 3 2
09 08 07 06 05

Typeset in 9.5/12pt Sabon by 35
Printed and bound by Ashford Colour Press, Gosport

The publisher's policy is to use paper manufactured from sustainable forests.

To my wife Victoria, whose tolerance and help enabled this book to be written, and my daughter Sara, who kept my feet on the floor.

Brief Contents

Contents

Supporting resources

Visit **www.pearsoned.co.uk/rollinson** to find valuable online resources

Companion Website for students
- Multiple choice questions to help test your learning
- Chapter resource sheets providing additional support material
- A guide to working with case studies
- A brief overview of organisational research
- An online glossary to explain key terms

For instructors
- Complete, downloadable Instructor's Manual
- PowerPoint slides that can be downloaded and used as OHTs

Also: The Companion Website provides the following features:

- Search tool to help locate specific items of content
- E-mail results and profile tools to send results of quizzes to instructors
- Online help and support to assist with website usage and troubleshooting

For more information please contact your local Pearson Education sales representative
or visit **www.pearsoned.co.uk/rollinson**

OneKey: All you and your students need to succeed

OneKey is an exclusive new resource for instructors and students, giving
you access to the best online teaching and learning tools 24 hours a day, 7 days a week.

OneKey means all your resources are in one place for maximum convenience, simplicity
and success.

A OneKey product is available for *Organisational Behaviour and Analysis, third edition* for use with Blackboard™,
WebCT and CourseCompass. It contains:

- Interactive Study Guide
- Glossary of key terms
- Weblinks and further reading
- Case studies and assignments
- Testbank of assessment questions

For more information about the OneKey product please contact your local Pearson Education sales representative or visit
www.pearsoned.co.uk/onekey

Acknowledgements

We are grateful to the Financial Times Limited for permission to reprint the following material:

Investing in China: Beijing sows seeds of conservation, © *Financial Times*, 5 November 2003; Wildcat industrial action returns with a roar, © *Financial Times*, 6 November 2003; Manager wins payout after boss's 'prejudiced middle-class' slur, © *Financial Times*, 28 November 2002; Fighting its risky reputation, © *Financial Times*, 23 March 2003; Unhappy staff burden Singapore economy, © *Financial Times*, 21 October 2003; Half of on-the-job training fails, say inspectors, © *Financial Times*, 18 November 2003; Profit machines that put people first, © *Financial Times*, 26 September 2003; A safe way to hold on to staff, © *Financial Times*, 28 November 2003; GKN sizes up locations for R&D centre, © *Financial Times*, 27 November 2003; Stress used as 'excuse to skive', © *Financial Times*, 21 October 2003; Army tactics are the business, © *Financial Times*, 26 November 2003; Barclays University: taking the lead in staff training, © *Financial Times*, 23 June 2004; Campaigning to win war of words, © *Financial Times*, 13 November 2003; Cadbury cuts 10% of jobs in restructuring, © *Financial Times*, 28 October 2003; Nokia model targets 3G, camera markets, © *Financial Times*, 26 September 2003; Leading directors exit in shake-up at Boots, © *Financial Times*, 29 October 2003; Culture change: how it works, © *Financial Times*, 1 September 2003; Microsoft offers reward to catch virus writers, © *Financial Times*, 6 November 2003; Birth of the Living Company, © *Financial Times*, 21 August 2003; Champion of the individual, © *Financial Times*, 7 August 2003.

We are grateful to the following for permission to use copyright material:

Five ways for British companies to raise their game, from *The Financial Times Limited*, 12 November 2003, © Will Hutton; Figure 3.8 from *Fact and Fiction in Psychology*, copyright © H J Eysenck 1965, published and reproduced by permission of Penguin Books Ltd (Eysenck, H J 1965); Figure 3.9 from *The Structure of Human Abilities, 2nd Edition*, published by ITPS Limited (Vernon, P E 1961); Figure 4.2 from *Organizational Behaviour, 5th Edition*, © 1989, reprinted with permission of South-Western College Publishing, a division of Thomson Learning: www.thomsonrights.com. Fax 800 730-2215 (Hellriegal, D, Slocum, J W and Woodman, R W 1989); Figure 4.10 from *Perceptions*, published by ITPS Limited (Gregory, R L 1986); Figure 7.3 after Figure in *Motivation and Personality, 2nd Edition*, reprinted by permission of Pearson Education, Inc. (Maslow, A H 1970); Figure 8.4 from Goal Setting: A motivational technique that works from *Organizational Dynamics*, Autumn, copyright 1979, reprinted with permission from Elsevier Science (Latham, G P and Locke, E 1979); Table 10.1 'The social readjustment scale' from *Journal of Psychosomatic Research*, August, reprinted with permission from Elsevier Science (Holmes, T H and Rahe, R H 1967); Table 13.2 developed from *New Approaches to Effective Leadership*, published by John Wiley & Sons, Inc., reprinted by permission of the authors (Fiedler, F E and Garcia, J E 1987); Figure 19.4 from *The Character of a Corporation*, copyright © 1998 by Rob Goffee and Gareth Jones, reprinted by permission of HarperCollins Publishers Ltd and HarperCollins, Inc. (Goffee, R and Jones, G 1998)

In some instances we have been unable to trace the owners of copyright material, and we would appreciate any information that would enable us to do so.

Chapter 3

Personality, Intelligence and Aptitude

LEARNING OUTCOMES

After studying this chapter you should be able to:

- define personality, describe the factors that influence personality differences and explain the relationship between personality and behaviour
- explain the differences between idiographic and nomothetic approaches to personality
- explain in outline the basic principles of psychodynamic theory and contrast psychodynamic, interpersonal and humanistic approaches
- describe, compare and contrast trait and type theories of personality and explain how personality is normally assessed
- define intelligence, explain the controversial nature of the concept and distinguish between intelligence, attitude and ability
- appreciate that personality, intelligence and aptitude can reflect the influence of cultural factors and that this has implications for interpreting the results of tests that measure these characteristics

---

WORK-RELATED ATTITUDES 149

(Iverson and Buttigieg 1999; Wood and Albanese 1995). These days it is widely assumed that in the light of the fast-moving business environment it is desirable, if not essential, to have committed employees, because commitment results in creativity and flexibility. However, flexibility and creativity tend to be products of the diversity of views and perspectives that arise in different organisational sub-units, whereas senior managers view it as something that is given to the organisation as a whole. As is noted above, it is unlikely that people are committed to the organisation as a whole. Rather, if anything, they are committed to their immediate workgroups.

CASE STUDY 5.2: Peter Larson

Peter Larson, a Swede who now lives in Great Britain, works as a junior hospital doctor in a large National Health Service (NHS) trust hospital. He originally came to Great Britain to study medicine and, after gaining his degree, he gravitated fairly automatically to his present post, which he has occupied for slightly under two years. Having recently given notice that he would be leaving in three months' time to return to Sweden, he was interviewed by his boss, a consultant surgeon, about his decision to leave. When asked whether his decision was prompted by any dissatisfaction with his duties at the hospital, Peter replied that he had no regrets about deciding on medicine as a career. He enjoyed doing what he felt was a responsible, worthwhile job that gave continuing opportunities to learn. In his view his colleagues and superiors were all dedicated people who were a delight to work with and while his pay as a junior doctor did not exactly permit a life of luxury, it was sufficient for his present needs. In any event, since he found himself working nearly 80 hours each week, even if he was paid more, he would hardly have time to spend the money.

'Then what is the problem?' his boss asked. 'Are you homesick?' 'Not really,' replied Peter, 'I have been here for nearly eight years now, and in some respects I prefer England to Sweden.' 'So what's the problem?' his boss asked again. 'To tell you the truth,' replied Peter, 'it is something to do with England. Working for the NHS is so far from my idea of what practising medicine should all be about that I would rather give up the profession than remain in the NHS. You seem to forget that I was brought up in a country where healthcare is available as a right to all who need it, whenever they need it. In Great Britain, however, it seems to me that the chronic under-funding of the NHS is rapidly moving things to a situation in which free healthcare is rationed. As such, before long the poor and needy will get nothing more than a second-rate service, and only those who can afford private healthcare will get what I believe is the basic right of everybody.'

Questions

1. To what extent do you feel that Peter Larson gets satisfaction from doing his job?

2. What do you feel is Peter's level of organisational commitment?

3. In your view what is it that has prompted him to leave – lack of job satisfaction or lack of organisational commitment?

Case Study
Short, European case studies with associated questions, challenge you to apply organisational studies principles to real people in real situations.

Learning Outcomes
Listed at the start of each chapter, highlighting the knowledge and skills you should acquire after studying the chapter.

APTITUDE AND ABILITY 95

- **Manual dexterity**   This covers abilities such as hand–eye coordination, which could be vital in a number of manual jobs. With greater use of computers and keyboards, this is also increasingly important for white-collar work.
- **Numeric ability**   In its simplest form numeric ability means that arithmetic calculations can be completed accurately. However, at a more advanced level there are also tests of this type which assess the potential for more abstract mathematical manipulations.
- **Spatial and diagrammatic ability**   These can be extremely important in creative or design work, for example, being able to mentally rotate an object and imagine what it would look like from a different position.

OB IN ACTION: Misusing Psychometric Tests

An advertising manager has won compensation after her boss gave her a psychometric test that suggested she was a 'prejudiced middle-class girl'.

Ana Stamenkovic had worked at the City company for four years, selling jewellery and watch advertising space and she reached a settlement for constructive dismissal after being forced out of her job with Cru Publishing last year when Eddie Prentice, managing director at the business publisher, gave her a psychometric test and told her the results showed she was just a 'middle-class girl who is prejudiced and only able to get on with people of her own category,' she told an employment tribunal.

Mrs Stamenkovic launched a £50,000 claim for sexual discrimination and unfair dismissal but the tribunal ruled that, although she had been constructively dismissed, she was 75 per cent to blame for her sacking while her bosses were 25 per cent culpable. Her sexual discrimination claim was rejected and the two sides had been due to return to the tribunal to finalise compensation when the company agreed to pay her an undisclosed sum.

Mrs Stamenkovic, who now works as a freelance advertising executive, recently said, 'Everything is so weighted in favour of companies. The tribunal system is impossible for the employee. In my case the company had insurance and could fight the case. I did not have any legal representation until the day when I took a barrister friend along.' At the tribunal, Mrs Stamenkovic said she was bypassed for promotion to a new post of advertising director and was forced to take the psychometric test after being stripped of her responsibilities. She said Mr Prentice went through the test results 'in excruciating details, departing from the computer-generated answer with his own amateur psychological diagnosis' and the strain of being hounded out of her job brought on stress-related illnesses.

Source:

Brun-Rovet, M (2002) Manager wins payout after boss's 'prejudiced middle-class' slur, *The Financial Times*, 28 November.

OB in Action
'Real Life' examples, many sourced from the Financial Times, illustrate application and context of theoretical concepts.

Further reading
Annotated further reading encourages you to read more widely around the subject and provides a shortlist of recommendations

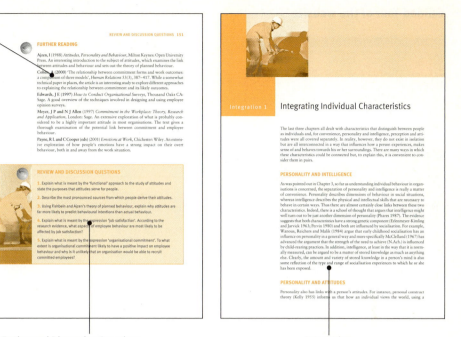

FURTHER READING

Ajzen, I (1988) *Attitudes, Personality and Behaviour*, Milton Keynes: Open University Press. An interesting introduction to the subject of attitudes, which examines the link between attitudes and behaviour and sets out the theory of planned behaviour.

Conlon, J (2000) 'The relationship between commitment forms and work outcomes: a comparison of three models', *Human Relations* 53(3), 387–417. While a somewhat technical paper in places, the article is an interesting study to explore different approaches to explaining the relationship between commitment and its likely outcomes.

Edwards, J E (1997) *How to Conduct Organisational Surveys*, Thousand Oaks CA: Sage. A good overview of the techniques involved in designing and using employee opinion surveys.

Meyer, J P and N J Allen (1997) *Commitment in the Workplace: Theory, Research and Application*, London: Sage. An extensive exploration of what is probably considered to be a highly important attitude in most organisations. The text gives a thorough examination of the potential link between commitment and employee behaviour.

Payne, R L and C Cooper (eds) (2001) *Emotions at Work*, Chichester: Wiley. An extensive exploration of how people's emotions have a strong impact on their overt behaviour, both in and away from the work situation.

REVIEW AND DISCUSSION QUESTIONS

1. Explain what is meant by the 'functional' approach to the study of attitudes and state the purposes that attitudes serve for people.

2. Describe the most pronounced sources from which people derive their attitudes.

3. Using Fishbein and Ajzen's theory of planned behaviour, explain why attitudes are far more likely to predict behavioural intentions than actual behaviour.

4. Explain what is meant by the expression 'job satisfaction'. According to the research evidence, what aspects of employee behaviour are most likely to be affected by job satisfaction?

5. Explain what is meant by the expression 'organisational commitment'. To what extent is organisational commitment likely to have a positive impact on employee behaviour and why is it unlikely that an organisation would be able to recruit committed employees?

Review and Discussion Questions
Encourage critical reflection on the main topics and issues covered in each chapter, either individually or in a group.

| Integration 1 | Integrating Individual Characteristics |

The last three chapters all dealt with characteristics that distinguish between people as individuals and, for convenience, personality and intelligence, perception and attitudes were all covered separately. In reality, however, they do not exist in isolation but are all interconnected in a way that influences how a person experiences, makes sense of and behaves towards his or her surroundings. There are many ways in which these characteristics could be connected but, to explain this, it is convenient to consider them in pairs.

PERSONALITY AND INTELLIGENCE

As was pointed out in Chapter 3, so far as understanding individual behaviour in organisations is concerned, the separation of personality and intelligence is really a matter of convenience. Personality describes dimensions of behaviour in social situations, whereas intelligence describes the physical and intellectual skills that are necessary to behave in certain ways. Thus there are almost certainly close links between these two characteristics. Indeed, there is a school of thought that argues that intelligence might well turn out to be just another dimension of personality (Phares 1987). The evidence suggests that both characteristics have a strong genetic component (Erlenmeyer-Kimling and Jarvick 1963; Pervin 1980) and both are influenced by socialisation. For example, Wanous, Reichers and Malik (1984) argue that early childhood socialisation has an influence on personality in a general way and more specifically McClelland (1967) has advanced the argument that the strength of the need to achieve (N.Ach.) is influenced by child-rearing practices. In addition, intelligence, at least in the way that it is normally measured, can be argued to be a matter of stored knowledge as much as anything else. Clearly, the amount and variety of stored knowledge in a person's mind is also some reflection of the type and range of socialisation experiences to which he or she has been exposed.

PERSONALITY AND ATTITUDES

Personality also has links with a person's attitudes. For instance, personal construct theory (Kelly 1955) informs us that how an individual views the world, using a

Integration
Five integrating sections enable you to establish links between topics and chapters.

Replay
Situated at intervals throughout the text, a brief review of the main concepts covered in the preceding sections.

88   CHAPTER 3 • PERSONALITY, INTELLIGENCE AND APTITUDE

REPLAY

- An individual's personality characteristics are influenced by four main groups of factors: genetic, social, cultural and situational (experience).
- The connection between personality characteristics and behaviour is influenced by the situation in which behaviour occurs.
- Idiographic personality theories deal with the individual as an integral whole and are of two main types: psychodynamic theories, which focus on the development of personality, and interpersonal theories, which are more concerned with mapping the personality of the individual as it is.
- Nomothetic theories of personality focus on the description and assessment of personality in terms that could be applied to all people, either by describing personality along a number of dimensions (trait theory), or by personality types.
- Most personality assessment in organisations is conducted using a nomothetic approach.

INTELLIGENCE

Many topics in psychology are controversial but the concept of intelligence, and in particular the testing and measurement of intelligence, is so controversial that it tends to arouse quite passionate feelings. Some scholars, such as Hernstein (1973), hold that the measurement of intelligence is psychology's most telling accomplishment to date. Others point out that while intelligence testing is often portrayed as a highly rigorous branch of psychological science, it is riddled with circularities and inconsistencies that it would embarrass any respectable scientist (Heather 1976). There are those who go even further and claim that intelligence testing has adverse social consequences, which make the practice unethical (Kamin 1977). Much of this debate arises from what is meant by the expression intelligence, a word that tends to be used in an ill-defined way, even by some psychologists (Miles 1957). The first step must therefore be to explore the meaning of the word intelligence and to define how it will be used in this chapter.

TIME OUT

Think of a number of people you know well. Try to identify some you would classify as intelligent and some who are less intelligent. What evidence have you used to classify the people in this way?

The Concept of Intelligence

Like many psychological concepts, intelligence is an abstract construct based on the tenet that mental activity of some sort precedes all physical behaviour. In common

Time Out
Exercises enable you to draw on your own experiences to apply a concept or theory.

Guided Tour of the website

Multiple choice questions

Resource sheet

Case studies

Glossary

Like the first and second editions of the book, this one provides a comprehensive introduction to the study of Organisational Behaviour (OB) and Organisational Analysis (OA). It has been written to make it suitable for students with no prior exposure to these subjects. However, it also gives an initial exposure to some of the more advanced knowledge in the area, which makes it of use to those who wish to commence studying the subjects at a higher level. The text is directed at undergraduate and diploma students where OB and OA are core or optional subjects, and also at postgraduate and post-experience students, where an exposure to knowledge of human behaviour in organisations is an essential part of their programme of studies.

Organisational Behaviour and Organisational Analysis are both subjects that deal with the behaviour of people in organisations, and together they contain a wealth of knowledge about this matter. Nevertheless, each one has a somewhat different focus. The traditional concern of OB is at the micro level of organisation and so it normally has a heavy, if not exclusive focus on the characteristics and processes of individuals and groups. Conversely, OA is much more heavily focused on the organisation as a whole and deals with characteristics such as structure, effectiveness, goals and culture and also with processes such as control, communication and change.

To some extent this is a matter of academic convenience. It allows what is a broad and extensive body of knowledge to be broken down into two manageable parts for the purposes of instruction. In addition, because OB is sometimes considered an essential prerequisite to the study of OA, it is also a matter of necessity. This, however, can result in two unfortunate tendencies. First, OB is often regarded as a less advanced topic than OA and, second, the two bodies of knowledge can come to be regarded as discrete and separate; indeed, they are often taught by different people, using totally unrelated teaching materials.

This book sets out to avoid these pitfalls. It purposely avoids treating OB and OA as two separate bodies of knowledge. Both are regarded as two parts of a single subject that deals with the matter of human behaviour in organisations and how that behaviour affects, and is affected by, the behaviour of the organisation as a whole. The rationale for adopting this approach is quite simple. In practice, the two levels do not exist in isolation and they are in continuous interaction. The behaviour of individuals and groups in an organisation is inevitably affected by the organisational context within which the behaviour occurs and if we wish to understand why individuals and groups behave as they do, account needs to be taken of the influence of these wider organisational factors. Similarly, the behaviour of a whole organisation is strongly influenced by the actions of its individuals and groups, which means that account has to be taken of lower-level factors to understand the behaviour of an organisation as a whole. In summary, therefore, understanding behaviour at either the macro or the micro level requires an integrative approach, where attention is directed at the effects of one level on the other.

This does not mean that OB and OA cannot be taught separately, or in a sequence in which one follows the other. Indeed, because of time constraints in many institutions, together with the extensive nature of both subjects, this will probably continue to be a matter of necessity. Nevertheless, it still remains important that students of OB are made aware that OB is only part of the story, and the same is true for OA. For this reason both subjects need to be taught in a way that demonstrates the complementary nature of their respective concerns, rather than as separate subjects in which the body of knowledge in one is allowed to override or contradict that in the other.

This can be difficult to achieve when teaching the subjects from two separate textbooks. For example, many OB texts tend to focus exclusively on micro level issues, or pay lip service to the existence of OA and in the same way, texts in OA frequently ignore the body of knowledge in OB. The remedy adopted here has been to produce a text in which both subjects are brought within the same cover. Therefore, if OB and OA are taught separately for the sake of convenience, integration is made easier because both are covered in a similar way and with integration in mind.

Another feature of either OB or OA texts that this book seeks to avoid is the way that topics within each subject are sometimes treated as discrete parcels of knowledge. Most books cover different topics in different chapters in order to break down the subject into manageable parts that can be easily digested by the reader. However, this is sometimes done in a way that leaves the reader with an impression that they are unrelated topics. Clearly this is not the case, and for this reason the book purposely cross-links the different topics in OB or OA, as well as integrating OB and OA with each other.

Like most texts this book also has its own philosophical approach to dealing with the subject matter. For example, in most American texts a strongly managerialist stance is adopted and this is also the case with several British books. These texts are addressed primarily to a management (or would-be management) audience, and the subject matter of OB and OA is put over as being part of the managerial tool-kit that helps managers to be in control. While OB and OA are subjects that are often included in courses taken by people who see themselves as managers, or the managers of the future, this book is at pains to avoid a managerialist perspective. Indeed, the underlying philosophy is that both subjects are, or should be, neutral. Thus, the approach adopted is that of informing the reader rather than trying to equip him or her with the knowledge to manipulate or control others.

DEVELOPMENTS FROM THE SECOND EDITION

Readers familiar with the second edition, published in 2002, will notice a number of changes to the text. One that is immediately apparent is that this edition has only a single author.

For the most part all other differences between the second and third editions are a matter of progressive refinement, rather than a fundamental change in direction. In deciding what these should be the author has been greatly aided by many helpful comments and suggestions from reviewers, colleagues and many other lecturers and students. The aim has been to retain features from the second edition that people found particularly useful and to add features and content that these people felt would add to the utility of the book. Examples of the former are: the comprehensive nature of the book; specific learning objectives; margin notes; self-study exercises; summary points and further readings. Features that have been amplified are: an increased emphasis on the practical applications of OB and OA; and a certain amount of case material set in a non-British context. To summarise, while the format of the book remains much the same as the second addition, all chapters have been updated and some have been extensively revised.

Derek Rollinson
April 2004

THE STRUCTURE OF THE BOOK

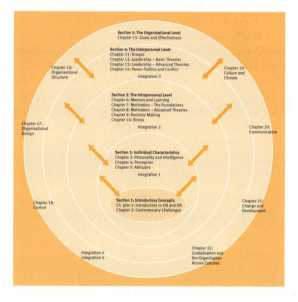

Section 5: The Organisational Level
Chapter 15: Goals and Effectiveness

Section 4: The Interpersonal Level
Chapter 11: Groups
Chapter 12: Leadership – Basic Theories
Chapter 13: Leadership – Advanced Theories
Chapter 14: Power Politics and Conflict
Integration 3

Chapter 16: Organisational Structure

Chapter 19: Culture and Climate

Section 3: The Intrapersonal Level
Chapter 6: Memory and Learning
Chapter 7: Motivation – The Foundations
Chapter 8: Motivation – Advanced Theories
Chapter 9: Decision Making
Chapter 10: Stress
Integration 2

Chapter 17: Organisational Design

Chapter 20: Communication

Section 2: Individual Characteristics
Chapter 3: Personality and Intelligence
Chapter 4: Perception
Chapter 5: Attitudes
Integration 1

Section 1: Introductory Concepts
Chapter 1: Introduction to OB and OA
Chapter 2: Contemporary Challenges

Chapter 18: Control

Chapter 21: Change and Development

Chapter 22: Globalisation and the Organisation Across Cultures

Integration 4
Integration 5

The above diagram, which indicates the contents of the book, has two main uses. First, it is a conceptual model that stresses the need to integrate the subjects of Organisational Behaviour (OB) and Organisational Analysis (OA). As will be explained in greater detail in Chapter 1, although these subjects are often taught separately, there are powerful arguments that they are just two halves of a single, bigger subject. Therefore, a full understanding of human behaviour in organisations only comes from taking account of both bodies of knowledge.

The model divides an organisation into different levels, and the important point to note is that straddling the boundaries of each level there are a pair of double-headed arrows. This reflects the idea that whatever the issue or topic on which we focus and whatever the level in the organisation at which it exists, we need to recognise that it is affected by matters at the level above and also exerts an influence in return.

The second use for the model is as a navigational aid that helps the reader steer him or herself through

the book. For this reason it will reappear in a slightly modified form in the short introductions that precede the five sections into which the book is divided. Each of these sections deals with topics that are focused at a particular level of organisation and are briefly described in what follows.

Section 1: Introductory Concepts

This section contains two chapters that are introductory in nature. The first gives a general introduction to the subjects of Organisational Behaviour and Organisational Analysis, based on the assumption that the reader has no prior exposure to either of them. The second chapter outlines some of the more pressing challenges currently facing organisations. Since these will almost certainly exist into the foreseeable future, they resurface fairly frequently in subsequent chapters of the book, and so their nature and the problems they pose for organisations are outlined in some detail.

Section 2: Individual Differences

This section commences the study of the micro aspects of human behaviour in organisations and all three chapters focus on the way that people differ as individuals. Chapter 3 covers personality, intelligence and aptitude, Chapter 4 deals with perception and Chapter 5 attitudes. At the end of the section there is a short integrative sub-section, which is shown on the model as Integration 1. This traces links between the three characteristics covered in the preceding chapters.

Section 3: The Intrapersonal Level

The five chapters in this section also deal with matters at an individual level, but since they cover processes that occur within (intra) people, they have a more dynamic focus. Chapter 6 deals with the processes of memory and learning and Chapters 7 and 8 cover work motivation. Chapter 9 deals with the matter of individual decision making and Chapter 10 with stress and stress management. Again an integrative sub-section (Integration 2) is given, which traces links between the topics covered in the preceding five chapters. It also explains how the individual characteristics covered in section 1 of the book are related to the individual processes covered in this section.

Section 4: The Interpersonal Level

In the four chapters included in this section the focus moves to the level of the group. These chapters deal with some of the visible social aspects of organisational life, which are important in their own right, but also as a bridge with the chapters in section 5, which will be outlined presently. Chapter 11 covers the topic of groups; why they are important, their functioning, characteristics and processes. The next two chapters (12 and 13) address the matter of leadership and the processes involved. Finally in Chapter 14, the focus widens to consider three important intra- and inter-group processes: power, politics and conflict. The integrative sub-section (Integration 3) that comes after these chapters traces links between the topics covered in each one and shows how group level matters are related to the matters covered in Integration 2.

Section 5: The Organisational Level

Although it is much more difficult to distinguish between characteristics and processes at this level of an organisation, an arbitrary distinction is made in which the first three chapters are treated as characteristics and the remaining four as processes. Chapter 15 covers the apparently simple (but in reality complex) issues of organisational goals and effectiveness, and in Chapters 16 and 17 the focus moves respectively to organisational structure and organisational design.

The next four chapters all deal with macro organisational processes. The first of these, Chapter 18, addresses the issue of control and has purposely been located to this point because control systems are often part of an organisation's structural design. Depending on the way they are viewed, the topics of culture and climate, which are the subject of Chapter 19, could either be viewed as organisational characteristics or processes. However, Chapters 20 and 21, which cover respectively communication and change and development, are very firmly process-orientated.

Once again the matter of integration is covered at the end of this section. This time, however, in two sep-

arate sub-sections. The first, Integration 4, traces links between the characteristics and processes covered in Chapters 15 to 21. Integration 5 has a somewhat different and in many respects more significant aim. This traces links between all the different levels of organisation covered so far in the book and in particular emphasises two important features. First, the way in which macro level characteristics and processes have an influence on matters at the intrapersonal and individual levels and, second, how matters at the micro level have an impact on the whole organisation.

Chapter 22 deals with an important special issue in OB and OA. It focuses on globalisation and cross-national organisations, a topic that has recently received a great deal of attention in the area. The chapter explains why large multinationals and globalised organisations tend to be more complex than those that operate in a single country. It also points out that virtually all of the topics covered in other chapters of the book take on a completely new dimension when applied to organisations in other cultures.

HOW TO USE THE BOOK

General

Lecturers vary considerably in terms of the theories and concepts that they consider to be the necessary minimum when providing instruction on a particular topic and they also differ in terms of the amount of time they have available for instruction. Therefore, in the interests of providing a text that can be used by the widest possible number of lecturers, it has purposely been made comprehensive in terms of the coverage of each topic. This means that in some cases there could be more information in some chapters than a lecturer wishes to use. For this reason the chapters have been written in a way that permits some of the material to be omitted (where this is necessary) and lecturers should not hesitate to be selective about the concepts and theories they use from each chapter.

Each chapter in the book deals with a separate topic and since each one has a clear set of learning outcomes that can be met by covering the contents, it is not vital to use the chapters in the order in which they appear in the book.

The material reflects teaching styles which have now become more common in higher education in Great Britain. These have a focus on *learning* rather than teaching, which tends to mean that there is less emphasis on formal, in-class instruction, and students are required to take an increased level of responsibility for their own learning outside the classroom. For this reason instruction periods often have a stronger focus on checking that learning has taken place, and applying the concepts in exercises and/or case studies. To facilitate this, the book has been written as a complete vehicle of instruction in its own right, rather than just background reading. Each chapter contains a full explanation of the concepts and theories it contains, together with associated exercises and/or case studies that can be used to apply the material. There are two main reasons for doing this. First, to produce a text in which students and instructors have confidence. Second, the aim has been to *eliminate the need for an additional workbook to support the text*. This latter point reflects the difficulty of persuading students to buy *any* book, let alone an additional one, at a time when their income has been progressively reduced by cutbacks in funding.

Activities Featured in the Text

A set of **Learning Outcomes** is given at the start of each chapter, which tell the reader what he or she should be able to understand or to accomplish after covering the chapter's contents. To some extent these can also be used by students to measure their progress.

LEARNING OUTCOMES

After studying this chapter you should be able to:

- define organisations and name the five key features that qualify an entity as an organisation
- explain why it is important to study organisations
- define Organisational Behaviour and Organisational Analysis and understand their origins
- understand the traditional difference in approach to the study of organisations adopted by OB and OA and the case for their integration
- describe the characteristics of contemporary Organisational Behaviour and Analysis
- compare and contrast the major conceptualisations (metaphors) for organisations and contrast them with the postmodernist perspective

---

A small number of **Time Out** exercises are included in each chapter. These are very short exercises that confront the reader with questions that encourage the application of concepts and theories covered in the text, but in a way that prompts the person to draw on his or her own experience. While these are primarily designed to be an aid to learning, which allows students to complete exercises outside the classroom,

they can, if required, be used in the classroom as discussion topics or as illustrative exercises. Students are also provided with **Margin Notes**, which define new concepts as they are introduced and are also brought together at the end of the book in a **Glossary**.

TIME OUT

1. Think about a university or college as an organisation. Describe ways in which it qualifies as an organisation in terms of the five characteristics given above. That is: is it an artefact?; does it have goals and what do you feel they are?; are there many people involved and who are they?; does it have a structure and coordinating mechanisms and, if so, what are the signs that these exist?; can you place nominal boundaries on the institution and, if so, where would you place them?
2. Now do the same for your immediate family; how easy is it to conceptualise this as an organisation?

From Chapter 2 onwards each chapter contains two short **Case Studies**, which give students the opportunity to apply a single concept or theory. In addition, the companion Instructor's Manual and associated Student Website contain a longer, supplementary case study for each chapter which brings together several concepts or theories. Sometimes cases are of the unfolding or rolling scenario type, in which the second case builds on information given in the first one, and so on. Because this removes the necessity to examine a new situation from scratch for each case, it allows more time to apply concepts and theories as they are introduced in the text, thus saving valuable time for students and lecturers.

Most cases are drawn from real-life situations, some from the author's own experience of encountering these conditions within an organisational context,

---

CASE STUDY 1.1: Apprentice Training at Servco

Servco is a large organisation, active throughout Great Britain, which sells, installs and services domestic appliances. It has a large workforce of skilled service engineers and, nationally, takes on approximately 400 school leavers as apprentices each year. Until four years ago, the apprenticeship scheme was a traditional one. That is, it lasted four years, during which time apprentices spent four days per week assisting a skilled and qualified service engineer and were given release for one day each week to attend a local technical college to study for the recognised craft qualification, a City and Guilds certificate. However, four years ago the scheme was completely revised and an apprenticeship now lasts three years. Apprentices spend three months each year studying full-time at a technical college, three months at a national apprentice training school, where they are taught practical skills by instructors, and the remainder of their time with skilled tradesmen, but not in the role of a helper to a tradesman. They now perform the work tasks and their work is assessed by the skilled man.

The management of Servco has given you the task of evaluating changes brought about by the introduction of the new scheme. You will be undertaking this task with a view to writing up the study as a dissertation which will count towards your degree. In order to gain a preliminary overview of the matter, you have conducted short interviews with several interested parties in the organisation and identify a number of themes, each of which could become the focus of the study.

First, there is the question of whether the new scheme is as cost-effective as its predecessor. Second, it seems possible that craftsmen trained under the old scheme consider the current one as not being a 'proper' apprenticeship that produces a skilled tradesman. Third, there is the question of the views of customers, who see two people arrive at their home to do a job, but only one of them actually works, while the other just seems to sit there and watch.

Questions

1. Which organisational metaphor is likely to be most appropriate for each of these issues?
2. Is there a single metaphor which could embrace them all. If so, which one?

OB IN ACTION: How Not To Be Seen as a Stakeholder Organisation

In response to criticisms in the City that it has been slow to cut costs and improve returns to shareholders, in late 1999 Barclays Bank announced a future programme of branch closures, ultimately involving the shedding of approximately 6,000 jobs. As part of this initiative, in April 2000 it closed 171 small, rural branches. At a stroke this left 63 villages and small towns without any banking facilities, which in rural areas can be essential for paying bills, etc. As a result, many customers, including some that were elderly or infirm, were faced with the prospect of having to travel to the nearest town to gain access to a branch. This move occurred in tandem with a widely circulated rumour that under a new performance-related remuneration package, top executives of the organisation would be due for bonuses that would run into millions of pounds.

The whole matter prompted a wave of protest from a number of quarters, including rural protection groups and church leaders. Charles Kennedy, the leader of the Liberal Democratic Party, joined in the debate by saying that the closure of rural branches would go down like a 'lead balloon' when taken together with what he described as 'the megalomaniac scale of top executive pay increases'. In addition, the government's environmental minister, Chris Mullin, was said to have publicly advised Barclays' customers to 'vote with their feet' in protest at the moves, by taking their business elsewhere. In the face of this protest, however, Barclays remained unrepentant about its decision, arguing that the closures were necessary in order to improve the bank's financial performance and to avoid it ending up defunct, like Rover or the NatWest bank.

Sources:

Treanor, J and P Heatherington (2000) Bank ignores protests and shuts branches, *The Guardian*, 8 April.

Treanor, J (2000) Big boss, big fees and big trouble, *The Guardian*, 8 April.

REPLAY

- The machine metaphor likens an organisation to a machine that is designed to serve a specific purpose.
- The organism metaphor likens an organisation to a biological system that exists in conjunction with, and must adapt to, its environment.
- The political systems metaphor views an organisation as a system of subsystems, all of which have their own aims and goals, which means that there is always some potential for conflict between subsystems.
- The cultural systems metaphor views an organisation primarily as a system of values, beliefs and understandings that guide the behaviour of its members.
- The postmodernist perspective is not a metaphor but a philosophical standpoint that strongly questions current assumptions about the nature of organisations.

perhaps when collecting research data. Others were reported to the author by students or colleges and were subsequently written-up into cases.

Although primarily intended for in-class use, the cases can also be used as material around which assignments or examination questions can be based. Because case studies will sometimes be a new learning vehicle for students, a guide to using cases has been provided in the companion website to this book.

OB in Action boxes will also be found dispersed throughout the text in a chapter. These are not case studies in the accepted meaning of the expression, although they can be used to illustrate a point or to stimulate discussion. Rather, they are real-world examples of the application of concepts or theories covered in the text. Sometimes they supplement a point already made in the chapter. Their main use, however, is to bring home the idea that the theories and concepts in OB and OA are not abstract pieces of knowledge constructed for the amusement of academics, but things that find real-world applications in organisations.

Replay lists will also be found at the end of each major section of a chapter. Each one consists of a list of bulleted summary points that re-emphasise concepts, theories, ideas and themes contained in the section.

At the end of each chapter there is a block of **Review and Discussion Questions**. These can be used for a final review of its contents, or to re-emphasise its major points. They can also be used for separate tutorials, or as a check on learning. Finally, for those who may wish to delve deeper into a particular topic or issue, each chapter also contains a short list of **Further Reading** at its end.

Supporting Materials

The book is supported by its own dedicated website www.booksites.net/rollinson and an **Instructor's Manual**. The website, which is organised chapter-by-chapter and is freely accessible to students, provides:

- a short summary of the major points covered in a chapter;
- definitions of new concepts introduced in the chapter;
- hints for completing Time Out exercises;
- the supplementary case study association with the chapter;
- a short battery of multiple-choice questions, which can be used by students for self-assessment purposes;
- answers for the multiple-choice questions;
- a list of potentially useful additional literature references, over and above those given in the main text;
- a list of potentially useful websites that provide additional information.

The instructor's manual, access to which is restricted to lecturers who adopt the book, provides in addition:

- session running guides for each chapter;
- model answers to the cases and exercises in the book;
- additional tutorial questions and answers;
- specimen assignment and examination questions;
- a short battery of multiple-choice test questions and answers for each chapter;
- OHP slide masters for the diagrams in the book.

Introductory Concepts

The diagram, which was first introduced on page xvi, tells you that this section of the book contains two chapters. Both of these are introductory in nature and the first introduces the subjects of Organisational Behaviour and Organisational Analysis. Chapter 2 is rather different. It gives an explanation of a number of contemporary challenges facing organisations that will resurface from time to time in different chapters of the book.

Section 5: The Organisational Level
Chapter 15: Goals and Effectiveness

Section 4: The Interpersonal Level
Chapter 11: Groups
Chapter 12: Leadership – Basic Theories
Chapter 13: Leadership – Advanced Theories
Chapter 14: Power Politics and Conflict

Integration 3

Section 3: The Intrapersonal Level
Chapter 6: Memory and Learning
Chapter 7: Motivation – The Foundations
Chapter 8: Motivation – Advanced Theories
Chapter 9: Decision Making
Chapter 10: Stress

Integration 2

Section 2: Individual Characteristics
Chapter 3: Personality and Intelligence
Chapter 4: Perception
Chapter 5: Attitudes

Integration 1

Section 1: Introductory Concepts
Ch pter 1: Introduction to OB and OA
Chapter 2: Contemporary Challenges

Chapter 16:
Organisational
Structure

Chapter 17:
Organisational
Design

Chapter 18:
Control

Chapter 19:
Culture and
Climate

Chapter 20:
Communication

Chapter 21:
Change and
Development

Chapter 22:
Globalisation and
the Organisation
Across Cultures

Integration 4
Integration 5

Chapter 1

An Introduction to the Study of Organisations

LEARNING OUTCOMES

After studying this chapter you should be able to:

- define organisations and name the five key features that qualify an entity as an organisation

- explain why it is important to study organisations

- define Organisational Behaviour and Organisational Analysis and understand their origins

- understand the traditional difference in approach to the study of organisations adopted by OB and OA and the case for their integration

- describe the characteristics of contemporary Organisational Behaviour and Analysis

- compare and contrast the major conceptualisations (metaphors) for organisations and contrast them with the postmodernist perspective

INTRODUCTION

This chapter has two purposes: first, to introduce organisations as a field of study and, second, to explain how this book will deal with the subject. Because the word organisation is often used in a very loose way that means different things to different people, the chapter starts by defining how the word is used in this book. The next section of the chapter deals with the subjects of Organisational Behaviour (OB) and Organisational Analysis (OA).

Traditionally OB and OA focus on different levels of organisation. The former usually focuses on the micro level and deals with the behaviour of individuals and groups within organisations, whereas the latter focuses on the macro level and deals with the behaviour of whole organisations. Since the book covers both levels of organisation, OB and OA are defined, their respective approaches to understanding behaviour in organisations and by organisations are compared and their origins are described. The chapter then argues that while the distinction between macro and micro levels is convenient, it is artificial. That is, to understand behaviour at the micro level requires taking account of factors at the macro level, and to understand the behaviour of a whole organisation requires that due account is taken of how individuals and groups behave at the micro level. The characteristics of contemporary Organisational Behaviour and Organisational Analysis are described and the chapter closes with an explanation of a number of different perspectives, each of which consists of a different way to conceptualise an organisation.

WHAT IS AN ORGANISATION?

Although our lives are dominated by organisations, like many things we take them for granted. Since this book deals with the behaviour of organisations and the people in them, before entering the subject matter it is necessary to define the entities on which the book is focused. As will be seen later in the chapter, there are several ways of conceptualising an organisation but here a simpler approach will be used to illustrate that organisations have a number of important features, which are set out in the following list:

- **Organisations are artefacts**   They do not exist in nature but are brought into existence by humans.
- **Goal directed**   Organisations are created to serve some purpose. However, this does not mean that everyone in a particular organisation has the same common goal and neither does it follow that everybody is aware of the goals pursued by the organisation.
- **Social entities**   Organisations usually consist of more than one person and although a one-person business (such as the corner shop) can be conceived of as an organisation, and in legal terms it might well be classified as one, this is not normally what we mean by the word.
- **Structured activity**   Achieving the purpose or goals for an organisation normally requires that human activity be deliberately structured and coordinated in some way, thus there will usually be identifiable parts or activities.

● **Nominal boundaries**   It is usually possible to identify nominal boundaries for an organisation, which give a degree of consensus about who or what is part of the organisation and who or what belongs elsewhere. However, this does not mean that the organisation is, or can be, completely sealed off from what is outside.

With these simple features in mind a basic definition which would encompass all major conceptualisations of an organisation is:

a social entity brought into existence and sustained in an ongoing way by humans to serve some purpose, from which it follows that human activities in the entity are normally structured and coordinated towards achieving some purpose or goals.

TIME OUT

1. Think about a university or college as an organisation. Describe ways in which it qualifies as an organisation in terms of the five characteristics given above. That is: is it an artefact?; does it have goals and what do you feel they are?; are there many people involved and who are they?; does it have a structure and coordinating mechanisms and, if so, what are the signs that these exist?; can you place nominal boundaries on the institution and, if so, where would you place them?

2. Now do the same for your immediate family; how easy is it to conceptualise this as an organisation?

WHY STUDY BEHAVIOUR IN ORGANISATIONS?

Although organisations are extremely complex entities that are not easily understood without conscious effort, this in itself is no reason why they should be studied. However, there are two main reasons why an understanding of organisations and the behaviour of people in them is, or should be, important to all of us.

First, it takes but a moment's thought to realise that, in one form or another, organisations are the dominant institution in the modern world. The nature of society is shaped (some would assert badly shaped) by them, and in return they are shaped by the world. Some things in life can only be accomplished if people come together to apply collective physical and mental effort, and in many cases this enables tasks to be completed in a more effective way. Although organisations exist in many forms, for the last 400 years they have tended to become larger, more complex and more specialised in what they do. The days have long gone when a family could itself do all that needed to be done to remain self-sufficient, and most people today would be incapable of performing all these activities because they have been taken over by organisations. Thus we all occupy specialist niches in a huge jigsaw of roles that makes up a modern society, in which organisations have become the institutions that shape the conditions under which we live, and we are all dependent on them. In addition, they have huge amounts of power. Their decisions about where to locate and the activities in which they engage have a huge impact on individuals, communities and even nation states. They wield immense power with governments, and in certain cases there is more than a suspicion that they control government decisions. Therefore, the life of everyone in modern society is affected by the existence and behaviour of organisations, and this alone is sufficient reason to try to understand them better.

Second, throughout our lives we are inevitably involved in organisations of some sort. In our early years we are members of an immediate family (a special type of organisation), and from then on we are members of other organisations for the remainder of our lives. We are educated by organisations and our livelihoods depend on them, as does a large part of our social contact with other people, and when we approach the end of our lifespan and can no longer care for ourselves, we gyrate to other organisations to live out our remaining years. However, this book is mainly concerned with work organisations, in which we probably spend well over half of our lives. For most of this time we try to come to terms with how an organisation functions, how it affects our behaviour and how, in turn, we affect the behaviour of others. To understand this context is part of understanding the world in which we live, and this is also sufficient reason for knowing about the behaviour of organisations and the people in them.

In addition to these two reasons, which apply to everyone, there is a third, which applies to a smaller population: those who manage, or even aspire to manage, organisations or parts of them. For these people, a vital part of performing their roles effectively is understanding human behaviour in an organisational context. Organisations are social collectivities and whatever is done in or by them is ultimately the result of human action. Even in the abstract, robotic world of science fiction, it is humans who decide to create and switch on the robot, and so even machine activity is ultimately traceable to some human action. Therefore, if we are concerned about the effective functioning of organisations, or whether they should become a force for good rather than evil, the human element must be considered. In this sense, understanding the behaviour of organisations and the people in them goes to the very heart of the process of management. However, these subjects are not lessons in how to manage. Neither do they seek to show managers how to manipulate others, or to bend them to their will. This cannot be emphasised too strongly. There is a tendency to treat these subjects as part of a tool kit that equips the manager to 'be in charge'. This view can be detected in some European texts, but is much stronger in those published in America, and is probably linked with the American view of organisations, which is strongly functionalist and instrumental. That is, they are not seen as social entities, but in terms of tasks that need to be completed, functions that need to be performed and objectives that must be achieved. This view gives rise to a highly managerialist perspective, in which managers are seen to have an almost divine right to decide the goals and objectives of other people and, perhaps more significantly, a right to be obeyed. Thus anything which is official in organisational terms, or is laid down by a manager, is that which is correct, and while American texts are full of platitudes about the need to understand human behaviour, they leave a strong impression that the main purpose of understanding is to enable managers to get their own way.

However, the managerialist perspective is not one that is universally held. Neither is the belief that human behaviour can be easily controlled by the use of structures and rules. Over 40 years ago Philip Selznick (1957) drew attention to the idea that an organisation is first and foremost a collection of human beings. Therefore, while organisations do have formal and officially sanctioned structures, these can never account

REPLAY

The main reasons for studying organisations and the behaviour of people in them are:

- everyone in modern society is affected by the existence and behaviour of organisations;
- we are all members of organisations of one sort or another for most of our lives;
- since all that happens in organisations is ultimately traceable to human action, those who manage organisations need to take account of those factors that affect human behaviour; not, however, to control or manipulate humans, but to better understand their behaviour.

for the full range of human behaviour. In practice, individuals interact as people who bring their personalities, problems and interests with them into the work situation, and this influences how well they fit into the neat boxes we call work roles.

TIME OUT

Reflect on an organisation of which you are or have been a member, preferably not your family or the university or college at which you study, but perhaps one where you have worked. Now re-examine the three reasons given in the Replay section for studying organisations and try to answer the questions below.

1. In what ways did the organisation or the people in it affect your behaviour? How did you feel about this?
2. In what ways did you affect the behaviour of the organisation or that part of it in which you were located? How did you feel about this?
3. If you aspire to manage an organisation or a part thereof, how could the conclusions you have drawn by answering questions 1 and 2 be useful to you in the future?

ORGANISATIONAL BEHAVIOUR AND ANALYSIS

Opening Definitions

Since the terms were first coined a number of competing definitions for Organisational Behaviour and Organisational Analysis have existed. As will be seen later, the argument advanced in this book is that both are really part of a wider subject concerned with understanding human behaviour in organisations, and the behaviour of organisations themselves. Nevertheless, it needs to be recognised that in practice, organisations tend to be studied at one or other of two levels and it is this which gives rise to what are apparently two different subjects, one called Organisational Behaviour and the other Organisational Analysis.

Organisational Behaviour can most succinctly be defined as:

the study of individuals and groups in organisations.

(Schemerhorn *et al.* 2000, p 3)

The subject is primarily concerned with examining organisations at the micro level and deals with the cognitive and emotional differences between individuals and how individuals interact with each other. To a large extent the subject relies on knowledge drawn from individual psychology, social psychology and, to a far lesser extent, sociology, and in this book these matters are dealt with in Chapters 3 to 13, and to some extent Chapter 14.

Organisational Analysis is much harder to define, mainly because it is still an evolving subject in which there is an ongoing debate about what an organisation is, how it can most appropriately be viewed, and what methods should be used to study organisations. The reader should also be aware that some authors in this subject do not even use the title Organisational Analysis, but instead prefer the older expression Organisation Theory. This can be defined as:

the macro level examination of organisations, which uses the whole organisation as the unit of analysis.   **(Daft 1996, p 26)**

The subject is primarily concerned with differences in structure and behaviour at this level of analysis. Since it views the organisation itself (rather than its component parts) as the social system to be examined, it draws heavily on sociological work. This perhaps is the reason for the ongoing debate about what the nature of the subject should be: different schools of sociology can be notorious in 'going their own ways' and distancing themselves from others who approach a phenomenon from a different perspective. In this book Chapters 14–22 cover topics that would normally be considered part of Organisational Analysis.

THE EVOLUTION OF ORGANISATIONAL BEHAVIOUR AND ANALYSIS

While humans have worked together in organisations for thousands of years the serious study of behaviour in organisations is less than 100 years old, and what we know today is just one stage in an evolving body of knowledge. Until the 1940s Organisational Behaviour and Organisational Analysis tended to be regarded as part of a somewhat ill-defined subject, variously called Management or Administrative Studies. This dealt almost exclusively with formal aspects of organisations, but had a strong influence on thinking about behaviour in them. However, some of the theories that have had an abiding influence on the subject are much older than this. Therefore, it is convenient to trace the historic emergence of OB and OA as occurring in a number of phases: first, early formative work; second, for OB and OA separately, a precursor phase followed by a maturity phase; and finally, for OB and OA together, the current phase. This is shown in outline in Figure 1.1 and for convenience the account that follows will deal with matters in historical order.

Early Formative Work

Long before people began to focus explicitly on the study of organisations and the behaviour of people in them, scholars were addressing topics that subsequently shaped

Figure 1.1 An outline of the evolution of contemporary Organisational Behaviour and Analysis

YEAR	
	EARLY FORMATIVE WORK – work having a subsequent influence on OB and OA, e.g.: Smith (1776) – division of labour Ricardo (1817) – distinctive competences Marx (1870s) – capitalism
1900	Weber (1890s) – bureaucracy Marshal (1891) – industrial economics Taylor (1916) and others – scientific management
1920	

ORGANISATIONAL BEHAVIOUR

PRECURSOR PHASE

1930 — Hawthorne Studies

1940 — Human Relations School

1950

MATURITY PHASE

1960 — Body of knowledge concerning a wide variety of topics at the individual and group levels of organisation, e.g.: personality; perception; attitudes; motivation; decision making; memory; learning; job design; stress; groups;
1970 — leadership; gender, etc.

ORGANISATIONAL ANALYSIS

PRECURSOR PHASE

Classical (Administrative) Management School e.g.: Fayol (1916), Barnard (1938), Parker-Follet (1926), Urwick (1943)

MATURITY PHASE

Body of knowledge concerning a wide variety of topics at the whole organisation level, e.g.: power; politics; conflict; goals and effectiveness; organisational structure and design; control; culture and climate; communication; change; the organisation–environment relationship; gender, etc.

1980

CONTEMPORARY/ORGANISATIONAL BEHAVIOUR AND ANALYSIS

1990 — Ongoing study and further refinement of the body of knowledge in both areas, but with:
• concern for comparative (cross-national) studies;
• integration of OB and OA

the thinking of later workers. The list of these people is almost endless and space precludes mentioning more than a few of the most influential scholars. Among the earliest was an economist, Adam Smith (1776), whose classic description of pin making in Redditch illustrated the effects of specialisation of labour on the economic efficiency of production and this had a lasting impact on theories of organisational structure and the design of jobs. A little later another economist, David Ricardo (1817), expanded on the work of Smith and developed the concept of 'distinctive competences', that is, the skills and capabilities that an organisation has over and above its competitors.

Later still, another economist, Alfred Marshall (1891), developed Ricardo's ideas even further to explore the competitive advantages of organisations under different market conditions and shortly before this, Karl Marx (1894) had explained how organisational structures and work designs were used as the primary mechanisms for subjugating and exploiting workers.

In addition to economic theories, there were early social scientists whose work had a lasting impact on thinking about organisations. One who had a great influence on the next (precursor) phase in the development of OA was the German sociologist Max Weber (1948), who documented the characteristics and workings of bureaucracy, which was influential in later thinking about organisational structure.

All the above work originated from academic sources but, in terms of its enduring impact, the most significant set of ideas came from another source altogether. This appeared early in the twentieth century and, since its effects are still very much in evidence, it deserves a more lengthy description.

Scientific Management

Well before the turn of the nineteenth century the increasing size and complexity of industrial organisations had started to make it more difficult to organise human effort in an effective and efficient way. A diverse but informal collection of American industrial managers, the so-called 'systematic management movement', was formed, which reached the conclusion that the (then) current methods of organising large-scale production were no longer appropriate. The most influential set of ideas to emerge from this movement became known as *scientific management*, a term coined by Frederick Winslow Taylor (1911), but it is also associated with others who later developed his ideas.

Scientific management: a set of techniques for organising work methods to give managers greater control over the labour process, i.e. the exchange of effort for rewards

Scientific management is very different from anything that we would now call Organisational Behaviour. Strictly speaking it is a technique for organising or reorganising work methods to give managers greater control over the labour process; that is, the exchange of effort for rewards. Nevertheless, in management circles, Taylor's ideas were, and still are, very influential, and his work contains a number of behavioural assumptions. Taylor was an engineer and, to judge from his writings, he had a limitless faith in the application of the principles of physical science and engineering to identify the 'one best way' for an organisation to function. As applied to the matter of obtaining maximum productive effort, this was enshrined in his four key principles: that managers should

1. gather together all of the traditional knowledge (the essence of skills, techniques, etc.) which had been acquired and held by workmen in their minds, record and tabulate this information and, wherever possible, reduce it to laws, rules, or even mathematical formulae;

2. scientifically select workpeople and progressively train and develop them to do the jobs that are required;

3. bring the scientifically designed job and the scientifically selected workers together;

4. divide up the actual work of the organisation between management and workers (according to their capabilities and training).

Soldiering: working at a much slower pace than the one of which a person is capable

Taylor had an obsession with combating *soldiering* – the practice of working at a much slower pace than the one of which a person is capable – and he reasoned that there were two basic ways to address this issue. Either close and constant supervision could be given (which adds to the cost of the job), or some incentive to work faster could be provided. The second of these was his preferred option, and his proposed solution is reflected in the first of his four principles, which removes all responsibility for the design and planning of work from the hands of those who perform it, and allows work to be designed by managers to extract the maximum amount of effort from the worker. Taylor recognised that this did not necessarily mean continuous effort, for example, obtaining the best effort for a full day would mean that rest pauses would be needed, to permit a measure of recuperation. However, this brought into play the second of his four principles. He openly acknowledged that maximum effort would result in boring and repetitive tasks, which in turn required careful selection of operators with the required physical attributes, but a corresponding lack of aspiration for anything more mentally stimulating. More significantly, he stressed that the most effective way to induce people to follow the laid-down design was to make payment contingent on output. Thus, in basic terms, his theory rests on the assumption that high pay is the main (and perhaps only) thing that people seek to obtain from work.

Taylor's ideas contain a great deal that would be considered controversial, if not downright patronising, today. For instance, he asserted that everyone is first class at something, and that being less than first class could only arise for one of two reasons: either the person had been badly selected or trained for the task, or the person was just plain lazy. He also reasoned that since some people are better endowed with mental abilities, and others with physical attributes, efficiency required the separation of 'thinking' from 'doing', with each task allocated to the appropriate people. In Taylor's view, since managers were the (superior) thinking part of an organisation they should provide the mental effort, with the operatives performing the (more menial) physical tasks. Taylor could also be accused of being naive in his thinking. He was convinced that because both parties get the rewards they most desire – for workers, more pay, and for managers a more productive and efficient workforce – scientific management would bring huge benefits to both parties, and lead to a community of interest with an in-built force for cooperation. The truth, of course, turned out to be somewhat different. Managers tended to use the techniques to grind the last ounce of effort from employees, and later, when applied to mass production, they simplified and deskilled work so that cheaper labour could be used. Thus it is not surprising that trade unions saw scientific management as a device to denigrate workers and hasten a return to 'sweated labour' conditions and, as a result, in 1911, there was a wave of strikes against its use in America. Nevertheless, by the 1920s the principles were in widespread use on both sides of the Atlantic and it has become the most widely used set of general principles for organising production.

Although scientific management is a long way from having the same concerns as either Organisational Behaviour or Organisational Analysis, it became the starting point for many fruitful lines of enquiry. For example, it contains an implicit if somewhat oversimplified and crude theory of motivation, an issue which is important in Organisational Behaviour. In the emphasis on task specialisation it also has an outline prescription for the structural design of organisations and this is an important topic in both Organisational Behaviour and Analysis.

Organisational Behaviour

The Precursor Phase: The Hawthorne Studies and Human Relations

Scientific management has attracted a measure of criticism from quite early on, mainly because it seemed to result in an element of dehumanised working conditions, together with physical and psychological strain. A study that did much to highlight its shortcomings, and which became a major turning point in thinking about people in organisations, emerged from a series of investigations in the late 1920s and early 1930s in the Hawthorne plant of Western Electric Company in America. This work, which subsequently become known as the Hawthorne Studies, can be thought of as the first, founding step in Organisational Behaviour, and it also gave rise to a new school of management thought, the *human relations movement*.

The original work, undertaken by industrial engineers in the company, started in the early 1920s and studied female employees engaged in light assembly work, with the aim of uncovering the intensity of lighting conditions that gave the highest level of output. Workers were divided into two groups: an 'experimental' group, where lighting conditions were systematically varied, and a comparison 'control' group, where no changes took place. The experiments took place over a two-year period and resulted in two major findings. First, whenever the intensity of lighting was changed output increased in the experimental group, even when conditions were restored to those pertaining at the start. Second, and perhaps more puzzling, although lighting conditions were only changed for the experimental group, whenever they were changed, output rose in both groups. From this it was concluded that it was probably the change rather than the actual amount of light that influenced output. Moreover, since the control group also responded to the change, it was obviously not the lighting conditions alone that caused the rise in output. There had to be some other factor. Word of these results soon came to the attention of a group of industrial psychologists at Harvard University who, together with employee relations research staff at Hawthorne, conducted experiments for several more years (Mayo 1933; Roethlisberger and Dickson 1939). Since the work is far too extensive to be covered in full, two major experiments, from which significant conclusions were drawn, will be described.

The first is what is now known as the **Relay Assembly Test Room (RATR) Experiments,** in which six female workers engaged in assembling relays for telephone switchboards first had their baseline output accurately measured on the production line, and then were moved into a specially constructed experimental room. The studies on this group took place over a five-year period, and a large number of changes to working conditions were introduced, either singly or in combination. For example, changes were made to working hours, rest periods and physical conditions such as temperature and lighting and also the use of a group financial incentive scheme. These workers were also allowed to make suggestions about conditions in the experimental room, in which a member of the research team was located permanently as an observer, and who virtually took on the role of their supervisor.

Over the five years, output rose to its highest ever recorded level: a 30 per cent increase on the baseline. However, other significant changes were observed in the group. Since the people had much more freedom to control the way that work was done and could interact socially, they welded together as a social entity with its own standards of behaviour and a strong team ethos. Two general conclusions were drawn from this

Human relations movement: a view of the employment situation which holds that employees respond primarily to the social context of the workplace, an important part of which is interpersonal relations at work

experiment. First, that work satisfaction is strongly dependent on informal social factors, for example, friendliness, cooperation between group members, the feeling they were doing something worthwhile and, importantly, relations with the supervisor. Second, that these social factors had a far greater impact on output than physical conditions.

The second set of experiments are generally referred to as the **Bank Wiring Observation Room (BWOR) Studies,** in which fourteen men engaged in wiring, soldering and inspecting banks of telephone switchgear were subject to detailed observation. In time, the men came to ignore the observer, who was able to record several interesting features about the group, one of the most important of which was the existence of a distinct group structure. In practice, there were two sub-groups or cliques: one at the back of the room and one at the front, and each had slightly different patterns of behaviour. In addition, there was a certain amount of rivalry between the groups, with the one at the front considering itself to be of slightly higher status, because it was engaged in more difficult work. However, as a whole the fourteen men had developed a code of conduct, which was enforced by workers putting pressure on each other, and the most significant item in the code seemed to be a norm about the level of output. No matter what management and supervision deemed to be the required output, the group had established its own criteria for what it considered to be a 'fair day's work'. Therefore, even though management introduced a payment-by-results bonus scheme to boost output, the group made no attempt to maximise production, but aimed for the figure that they had decided was fair. If by chance they did overproduce, this was kept secret from management and used to restore the balance on some future day when there was underproduction. Moreover, this output norm was actively policed by group members, who exerted pressure to conform on the 'chisellers' (those who underproduced), or those who overproduced (the 'rate busters'). This pressure usually took the form of unpleasant but not harmful physical blows, which the men called 'bingeing', together with mild social isolation of the offending colleague. However, the pressure was clearly experienced as significant by those concerned, because there were cases of individuals asking to be transferred to other work.

Output restriction of this type is not unknown and so the Bank Wiring Room results are important in drawing attention to one of the limitations of scientific management. In theory, it is possible to create a formal system of work in which jobs are carefully designed to eliminate non-productive effort. However, alongside, or even as part of, the formal system there exists an informal organisation, which has its own norms, values and expectations, and these informal codes of conduct are sometimes more influential on day-to-day behaviour than the formal rules.

TIME OUT

Look closely at the conclusions drawn by the Hawthorne researchers and compare these with the major assumptions associated with scientific management.

1. To what extent are the two sets of ideas compatible, or does one contradict the other?
2. Can you identify an organisation or an industry in which the principles of scientific management could still be in use?

While the results and conclusions of the Hawthorne Studies have been criticised in terms of the rigour of the research (Yorks and Whitsett 1985), they have had a major impact on the understanding of behaviour in organisations. The most important inference is that people have social needs to be satisfied at work, which can be equally as important as monetary needs. This, it can be noted, is a direct contradiction of one of the tenets of scientific management. Ideas such as this gave rise to the **human relations** school of thought which heralded the emergence of what has eventually become the subject of Organisational Behaviour. As will be seen in Chapters 7 and 8, some of the assumptions of human relations theory have a strong influence on certain theories of work motivation. Human relations theory also gave rise to much of the work on groups and leadership, which will be covered in Chapters 11 to 13.

The Maturity Phase of Organisational Behaviour

From the 1950s onwards OB rapidly emerged as a mature field of study in its own right. Psychologists were the first in the field, but shortly after this other academic disciplines became involved and it is probably true to say that virtually every aspect of human behaviour in organisations has received some attention, often from several different disciplinary perspectives. Since a great deal of this work is covered in the different chapters of this book, it would be inappropriate to single out any one in particular here.

Organisational Analysis

The Precursors: Classical Organisation Theory

Shortly after scientific management came into widespread use a complementary set of ideas began to emerge, which subsequently became known as *classical organisation theory*. However, while scientific management initially focused on the micro level issue of job design, organisation theory attempted to lay down guiding principles for the design and functioning of a whole organisation. In some respects the ideas that emerged are similar to those put forward by the German sociologist Max Weber (1948), whose classic study of bureaucracy laid the foundations for the serious scientific study of formal organisation (see Chapter 17). However, unlike Weber, whose ideas were based on empirical investigation and focused on the large public sector bureaucracies of Germany, classical management theorists were largely practising managers, who derived their ideas from the practical experience of running large industrial organisations, and who set out what they believed to be guides to good practice. Although these writers differ in detail, they are remarkably similar in terms of basic approach. All give highly prescriptive guidelines, which they claimed were universally applicable. Perhaps the best known is Henri Fayol, who derived a set of fourteen principles of organising. Because these will be considered in Chapter 17, the details need not concern us here. Suffice it to say that these guidelines set out a highly prescriptive recipe for the design of organisational structures that Fayol claimed was universally applicable, and for this reason the whole approach has been much criticised. For example, it takes no account of interactions between people, and because it underestimates their mental capacities, it has a very naive view of the way they think; in addition it understates the potential for conflict in organisations (March and Simon 1958). Indeed, so prescriptive and mechanical is the approach that it has been called a description of 'organisations

Classical organisation theory: a diverse group of theories which set out to derive universal rules and guidelines for the design and functioning of organisations without people' (Bennis 1959). Nevertheless, the ideas give a very clear and unambiguous set of guidelines that are easy to understand and apply, and the approach is remarkably resilient in management circles; dressed up in different words it is still common to find the ideas espoused in current management textbooks. So far as current thinking is concerned, the strongest criticism of this school is the assumption that a valid set of universally applicable design principles can be derived from it.

The Maturity Phase of Organisational Analysis

Shortly after OB entered its maturity phase, what has now become known as OA began to emerge as a mature field of study, although the term Organisational Analysis was coined somewhat later. For the most part the first workers in the field were essentially management theorists, many of whom were dissatisfied with the prescriptions of classical management theory with respect to structure and organisational design. As such, they abandoned the search for universal prescriptions and, instead, sought to locate structural forms that best fit the specific circumstances of an organisation. In addition, scholars from other academic backgrounds entered the area and, if anything, OA emerged as a more eclectic field than OB. However, it is relevant to point out that some of these developments, particularly in terms of work that originated in the USA, are somewhat controversial. Until the early 1960s the development of organisation theory was mainly located in sociology departments of universities, but from then on in America it was increasingly concentrated in business schools. When this occurred the purer concerns of social science tended to be replaced by highly managerialist concerns that were almost exclusively focused on promoting the design of more efficient and effective organisations. As such, many interesting and vital lines of enquiry about the nature and functioning of organisations had a tendency to be regarded as irrelevant (Hinings and Greenwood 2002). This, it can be noted, parallels an earlier change that had occurred in OB, in which the Harvard Business School had effectively hijacked the findings and conclusions of the Hawthorne Studies, to evolve a highly managerialist version of Human Relations Theory (O'Connor 1999). Once again, since much of this work is covered in chapters of this book, it would not be appropriate to single out anything for a special mention here.

REPLAY

- Organisational Behaviour and Organisational Analysis originate from two different sources that were focused respectively on micro and macro level aspects of organisations.
- While not in itself Organisational Behaviour, there are assumptions about factors that influence micro level aspects of behaviour contained in scientific management theories. However, the more identifiable origins of Organisational Behaviour lie in the findings of the Hawthorne experiments that gave rise to the human relations movement.
- Organisational Analysis traces its roots to the classical management school of theorists, who attempted to formulate universal principles for the design and functioning of organisations.

The Case for Integration

At first sight it is all too easy to conclude that Organisational Behaviour and Organisational Analysis are two completely unconnected subjects. They have different names, they are often taught and researched by two different sets of people and, sometimes, these people keep well away from each other. However, since both subjects deal with the behaviour of people in organisations, the author of this book views the distinction as more apparent than real. Why then is the distinction so frequently made? To some extent, it is the result of different academic disciplines imposing their own definitions of the most important features of organisations that should be studied. For example, when applied to organisations and the people in them, the word behaviour can refer to a number of different levels:

Level 1: Individual   Where the focus is on matters (such as values, attitudes, beliefs, aptitudes, intelligence and motivation) that influence how people behave as individuals.

Level 2: Group   Which is more concerned with social and interactive features such as group dynamics and leadership.

Level 3: Organisational   Where the main concern is the behaviour of an organisation as a whole, for example its relationship with the environment and its structure, culture and processes.

This rather arbitrary classification is only possible because different academic disciplines focus their efforts at these different levels. For instance, level 1 exists because this is what individual psychologists do; level 2 because this is where social psychologists and, to a lesser extent, sociologists focus their endeavours; and level 3 because this is the area of interest to writers on management, sociologists and economists. This has regrettably led to two distinct views of organisations: the **macro** (level 3) view and **micro** (levels 1 and 2) view. However, the separation could be very unreal and even downright misleading.

Academically, placing micro level features in one box and calling it Organisational Behaviour and macro level matters into another box and calling it Organisational Analysis is very convenient. It permits the whole body of knowledge to be cut up into manageable chunks and written down as syllabi for courses. However, it also permits different academic disciplines to claim territorial rights over the boxes and sometimes results in an element of unhealthy criticism between the disciplines. The net result of this is that there is almost an inbuilt force that conspires to treat Organisational Behaviour and Organisational Analysis as different bodies of knowledge. However, if we look at one of the first attempts to define the subject of Organisational Behaviour – which, despite its age, is more in keeping with the arguments expressed in this book – we can see that this was never intended:

> the study of the structure, functioning and performance of organisations and the behaviour of groups and individuals within them.   (Pugh 1971, p 9)

Note that in addition to the behaviour of people in organisations at the micro level it also refers to the behaviour of an organisation as a whole. However, it is important to sound a note of caution here. While people regularly speak of the behaviour of an organisation, organisations can never be said to behave in the same sense that people behave. The word organisation refers to something that is an abstract phenomenon.

Reification: to treat an abstract idea as something that actually exists

Therefore, to refer to the behaviour of a person and an organisation in the same sense is *reification*; that is, to treat an abstract idea as something that actually exists. Nevertheless, because this is part of the way that they conceive the world, people customarily talk of organisations 'behaving', and to some extent it is meaningful to do so. For example, an organisation behaves as a whole towards its environment, and although this is usually the result of a decision by an individual or group of individuals, since it is a social collectivity, it is meaningful to speak of the behaviour of the collectivity as a whole. This, more than anything else, explains why Organisational Behaviour and Organisational Analysis cannot sensibly be considered as two separate areas of study. Without behaviour by people within an organisation there would be no behaviour of the organisation, thus we need to understand how the behaviour of people influences its actions. Similarly, if we want to know why people behave as they do, we not only need to understand how individual and group factors shape behaviour, but also how the organisation and its interactions with the outside world result in pressures for people to behave in certain ways. Indeed, a recent review article notes that the single most significant failure of Organisational Behaviour (OB) over the last 40 years is to ignore the 'O' and to overemphasise the 'B'; that is, to pay insufficient attention to the impact of the organisational context on the behaviour of individuals and groups (Porter 1996). For this reason it is worthwhile examining what the two approaches have in common, and to do this a way of thinking about organisations that is widely used in Organisational Behaviour and Organisational Analysis will be used: the organisation as an *open system*.

Open system: a system not sealed off from its environment and, therefore, subject to the intrusion of environmental influences

In its simplest form, an open system can be portrayed as in Figure 1.2 and the principles can be translated into something that is more easily recognised as a commercial organisation in Figure 1.3. Complex systems have a host of interdependent parts, which contribute to the well-being and survival of the whole, and they all exist in environments to which they must adapt to survive. Thus an organisation as a system can be thought of as a set of subsystems, all of which interact with each other, with the whole existing in an environment with which it interacts. This is shown in Figure 1.4, where the subsystems labelled groups A–D can be thought of as departments or functions although, for convenience, they are simply called groups here. Also note that each group is made up of sub-subsystems, which can be regarded as individuals.

The first and most obvious point that can be made relates to the focus and concerns of the two levels of study. At the micro level the focus is on parts (or subsystems) of an organisation, and so the unit of analysis is the individual or group. The macro level perspective has a focus on the organisation as a whole, that is, the total system made up of all the subsystems.

A second, highly important, point that emerges from Figure 1.4, is the idea of system, subsystem and sub-subsystem. Therefore, at any level, a feature or process that is under consideration can usually be viewed as a system in its own right. Each of the groups in Figure 1.4 is a subsystem made up of individuals who interact with each

Figure 1.2 Basic open systems model

Figure 1.3 Simplified open systems model of a commercial organisation

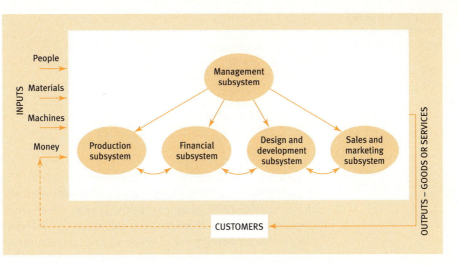

Figure 1.4 The organisation as a system of subsystems and sub-subsystems

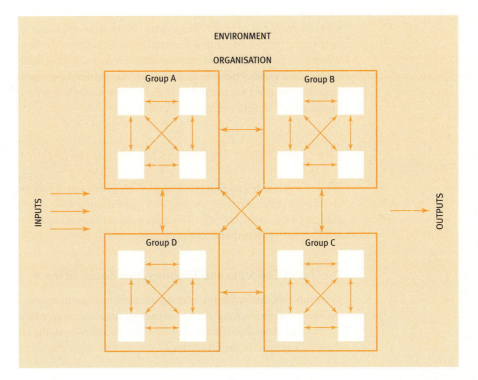

other, so its characteristics and properties are not simply the sum of its parts, but it will have emergent properties that only arise because the individuals interact. If we reduced one of the groups from four people to three it would behave differently. Therefore, an individual in one of the groups is affected by being part of the subsystem, the behaviour of the subsystem is affected by his or her presence, and it will be affected if he or she leaves. This principle can be applied in the same way at the next

Figure 1.5 Interaction of macro and micro levels of organisation

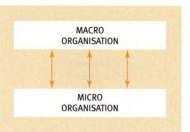

level upwards. The system itself (organisation) is made up of interacting subsystems, and some of its characteristics only exist because subsystems A–D interact. Moreover, each one is affected by being part of the system, the system is affected because it is there, and the system's characteristics and behaviour will change if it is removed.

This rather elementary use of systems principles illustrates the idea that if we wish to gain a fuller understanding of the behaviour of people in organisations, or the behaviour of an organisation as a whole, there is a need to integrate micro and macro approaches. Since the behaviour of component subsystems and sub-subsystems is a result of being part of a bigger system, to comprehend behaviour of groups and individuals, account needs to be taken of the forces exerted on these systems by the organisation as a whole. Similarly, the behaviour of the organisation as a whole is dependent on the way individuals and groups behave and we can only understand the behaviour of the whole organisation if we take account of behaviour at the lower level, and this is portrayed by the simple diagram given in Figure 1.5.

CONTEMPORARY ORGANISATIONAL BEHAVIOUR AND ANALYSIS

While Organisational Behaviour and Organisational Analysis have largely remained apart until comparatively recently, it is now more widely recognised that they are two aspects of the same overall subject. For this reason it is now relevant to examine the characteristics that they have in common.

The Use of Concepts and Theories from Social Science

Both subjects deal with the human element in organisations, with the aim of understanding and explaining the behaviour of organisations and people within them. To do this they draw heavily on concepts and theories from the social sciences and apply these to an organisational setting.

A Multidisciplinary Focus

There are a number of different social science disciplines and they all tend to focus on slightly different aspects of the social world. Therefore, the same phenomenon is sometimes studied by more than one discipline, each bringing its own unique concepts and theories, and so there are often several competing explanations of the same phenomenon. However, this does not mean that the findings and explanations stay separate in discrete compartments. Sometimes scholars working in the area integrate the work, to

Table 1.1 The major social science disciplines involved in Organisational Behaviour and Analysis

Social science discipline	Organisational phenomena of interest
Individual psychology	Individual differences, intelligence, personality, aptitude, motivation, learning, perception
Social psychology	Group dynamics, attitudes, leadership
Sociology	The organisation as a social system, socialisation of organisational members, structures, cultures, communication
Social anthropology	Culture and its effects on behaviour
Politics	Power, decision making, conflict, the behaviour of interest groups, coalitions, control
Economics	Labour markets, product markets and their influence as part of organisational environment

produce a more comprehensive explanation and, occasionally, a phenomenon will be studied by a multidisciplinary team. The major disciplines involved and their primary areas of focus are shown in Table 1.1.

Theoretical Orientations with Practical Implications

The use of theory to understand organisational phenomena is seldom a matter of 'knowledge for knowledge's sake'. Usually the aim is to inform a wider audience so that its members will better understand what goes on in organisations. This audience includes other scholars and teachers in the area and specialist staff and managers in organisations. However, this knowledge is not targeted at any one group in particular. While the subject is more frequently taught to students of business and management than to anyone else, it is most definitely is *not* the aim that managers should become better equipped to control or manipulate the actions of others in a way that takes away their freedom.

A result of the dual emphasis is that knowledge gives rise to technologies; that is, pure knowledge (science) results in a technology for applying the scientific knowledge. At the risk of giving a rather oversimplified picture, see Figure 1.6 where macro and micro levels of theory and technology are compared.

Note that all four cells in Figure 1.6 are connected, which means that the theories at one level need to take account of those at the other level. Starting at the macro level, organisational development is an organisation-wide strategy for change, which is covered in Chapter 21 and will not therefore be discussed here.

At the micro level, a great deal of the knowledge which emerges gets incorporated into the practice of human resource management. However, to speak of a 'human resource manager' is somewhat confusing. Most managers deal with human resources and they need to know something about human behaviour. Nevertheless, in many organisations there are specialists in this area who advise and guide functional managers.

Open Systems Perspectives

Either consciously or unconsciously, both subjects adopt an open systems perspective. Systems ideas were described in outline earlier and will not be elaborated on again.

Figure 1.6 Relation of macro and micro level of theory and practice

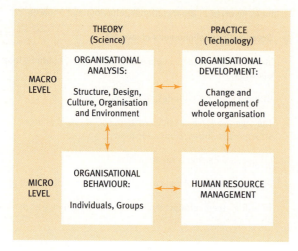

However, it can be noted that because it contains a recognition that anything on which we focus is influenced by its environment, and this can affect the behaviour of the system, the concept of an open system can be usefully applied at any level of analysis.

Contingency Perspective

Although the precursors of Organisational Behaviour and Analysis sought universal principles and often tried to identify the 'one best way' of addressing problems, this is only possible if there is absolute certainty about what influences a particular piece of behaviour. To some extent this is possible in the physical sciences, because they deal with things rather than people. For example, we know that if we heat an iron bar it will expand and so, if we carefully measure its length before it is heated, then raise its temperature by a known amount, we can determine its expansion per degree celsius. From then on we can with certainty assume that if the temperature of the bar is raised by a given number of degrees we can predict its exact length. However, human beings are not like iron bars. They react differently to the same factor and what motivates one individual might not have the same effect on another. For this reason it can be very hard to predict behaviour. Therefore, almost all current work abandons any pretext of being able to derive universal rules that apply everywhere. It usually adopts a *contingency perspective*, which acknowledges that the solution to a problem has to fit the situation in which the problem exists. This, in turn, requires very careful examination of the situation to see what factors are at work, and an equally careful selection of a solution that addresses these factors.

Contingency perspective: an approach to problem solving which assumes that there is no universally applicable solution to a particular type of problem and so remedies have to be tailored to the situation in which the problem exists

Research Orientated and Unprescriptive

Concepts and theories in Organisational Behaviour and Analysis invariably arise out of extensive research. Although this does not mean that students of the subjects need to be experienced researchers, to grasp the strengths and weaknesses of a theory it is sometimes necessary to have an elementary knowledge of the research process. For those who wish to look a little deeper into this matter, the associated website to the book gives a very brief outline of the nature and methods of organisational research, and for the present it is sufficient to note that there are two important features of the theories that result.

First, as theories, they are much more descriptive than predictive. The function of a theory in social science is usually to specify whether there is a relationship between two or more variables and, if possible, to explain the nature of this relationship. However, this does not mean that we can predict with any degree of certainty what change will take place in one variable if there is a change in another. The subject is rich in results that tell us a great deal about the complex nature of behaviour in organisations and also alerts us to the idea that if one variable should change, changes can be expected in others. In some cases it also provides highly plausible explanations of why these changes occur, but the explanations are seldom strong enough to enable us to predict behaviour with certainty.

Second, although the subject provides information that gives us a better understanding of human behaviour in organisations, no attempt is made to say what the behaviour should be. This is often a source of acute frustration to students of the subject, particularly if they are managers who feel that they should be able to obtain precise remedies for problems. However, because there is a reluctance to be prescriptive, this does not mean that scholars in the area are evasive, or that they have no opinions. Social scientists are only too painfully aware that when someone asks for prescriptive advice it is because he or she has a reason. All too often this reason is connected with the person's desire to manipulate the behaviour of others to his or her own advantage. Quite simply, social scientists do not see their purpose in life as serving a particular constituency of interests in this way, and they can be highly critical of those of their number who do. In addition, it is part of a social scientist's training to recognise that he or she has values and to be on guard, lest they influence the way that a social situation is perceived. A natural extension of this is to avoid making prescriptions, because these are almost bound to reflect what the prescriber thinks is right, rather than give an unbiased picture.

Cross-national Perspectives

Organisational Behaviour and Analysis both orginated in America and while considerable contributions have been made by scholars from European nations and elsewhere, overall there has traditionally been a strong bias towards the Anglo-American conceptualisation of organisations and their employees. In recent years, however, perhaps because of the growing prominence of internationalised organisations, there has been a growing awareness that the body of knowledge based on American and British studies should not be regarded as the last word on matters. Thus it might be necessary to accept that matters could be different in other countries. Therefore, wherever possible, there is an increasing tendency to try to incorporate an element of comparative work into topics that are studied, and a cross-cultural perspective is fast becoming an important dimension of the subject in its own right. However, this work is still in its infancy and much remains to be uncovered. To a large extent this is because it is much more difficult to undertake comparative work than studies in a single country. To start with the costs incurred in replicating a study of the same phenomenon in several different countries can be significant. In addition, unless the work can be undertaken as a collaborative venture, for example by several universities around the world, the sheer volume of work for a single research team is prohibitive.

REPLAY

- Contemporary Organisational Behaviour and Analysis reflect a trend towards integrating the two subjects, which is based upon the premise that micro and macro levels are so strongly interconnected that events and behaviour at one level cannot be understood without taking account of matters at the other level.

- Organisational Behaviour and Analysis both use concepts and theories from social science; they usually take an interdisciplinary perspective, have strong practical implications, use open systems perspectives, adopt a contingency (rather than 'one best way') approach and are research orientated and unprescriptive.

DIFFERENT PERSPECTIVES ON ORGANISATIONS

The definition of an organisation given at the start of this chapter is a very general one that purposely avoids singling out anything as the most important characteristic of an organisation. This is only one way of viewing matters and it is often the case that the perspective used to view a particular organisational phenomenon depends on what the person investigating the phenomenon considers to be the most appropriate way to view an organisation. For this reason it is fitting to conclude this chapter by making the reader aware that there is no single right way of conceptualising an organisation. Rather, the conceptualisation used tends to depend on what are considered to be the most important characteristics of an organisation, or the reasons for examining a particular phenomenon.

Morgan (1997) draws attention to the idea that there are a number of competing metaphors for organisations. A *metaphor* is a figure of speech in which a term is transferred from the object it ordinarily designates to another object it can designate by an implicit analogy. For example, to refer to the world of business as a jungle implies that it operates on the basis of Kipling's first law of the jungle: 'kill or be killed'. Because metaphors provide a distinct way of perceiving an object and make us aware that some features are considered more important than others, they can be very useful devices. However, because each metaphor provides a different and sometimes competing insight or perspective, none of them is inherently right or wrong. Each one is only a partial view that draws attention to those features of organisations that the user of the metaphor considers to be the most important or interesting. Nevertheless, they can be useful and the four metaphors described by Morgan (he calls them different images of organisations) are: the machine metaphor; the organism metaphor; the (political) systems metaphor; and the cultures metaphor. Each of these is now discussed separately.

Metaphor: a figure of speech in which a term is transferred from an object it ordinarily designates to another object it can designate by implicit analogy

Machine metaphor: organisations regarded as analogous to a machine that is designed for a purpose

The Machine Metaphor

Machines are constructed to do something specific, for example, a kettle turns cold water into hot water. Thus the *machine metaphor* focuses on the purpose and goals of an organisation and how these are achieved by combining its component parts. This view draws attention to such matters as:

- **Purpose or goals**   What is to be achieved.
- **Organisational design**   How the overall task is split down into a set of structured sub-tasks and how these are coordinated.
- **Methods, rules and procedures**   What is done, what behaviour is permitted and what is prohibited.
- **Effectiveness and efficiency**   Whether goals are achieved and whether this is done in a way that is economic in use of resources.

If it is inappropriate for the job, or when a part malfunctions, a machine can fail to serve its purpose. Thus the metaphor is useful if the main reason for studying an organisation is to define what it does and how well it does it. Nevertheless, this view has its shortcomings. Everything is evaluated in terms of technical efficiency and only the functional aspects of organisations are considered. Indeed, people tend to be viewed as merely components of the total machine, which contains two implicit assumptions: that the people have a common purpose; and that they should all behave in a predictable way. Since both of these are highly questionable, the metaphor tends to ignore the complexity and diversity of motives that underlie human behaviour.

The Organism Metaphor

Organism metaphor: organisations regarded as analogous to biological organisms

Organisms are living entities and so the *organism metaphor* is based on a biological analogy. It also makes use of a concept which in one form or another has come to dominate most current views of organisations – the organisation as a system, which draws attention to:

- **Interaction with environment**   That an organisation exists in, interacts with and is affected by its environment.
- **Subsystems**   Organisations are systems made up of subsystems.
- **Interconnectedness**   The way that all parts of an organisation are connected, either directly or indirectly.
- **Human element**   Implicit recognition that humans are an important organisational component.

Reductionist: the belief that complex systems can be understood completely by understanding their constituent parts

The word system is familiar to everyone and most of us use it almost every day. However, it also refers to a whole way of thinking about the world, which originated in biology. Together with physics, biology shares the distinction of being highly *reductionist*, because it advances knowledge by studying progressively smaller components of an organism to examine how they work. For example, by progressing from organs down to cells and, these days, down to the fundamental building blocks such as DNA and RNA. This is an extremely powerful approach, but in the 1930s a rather different way of thinking began to emerge in biology. This was the *holistic* perspective which, expressed in the simplest way, pointed out that cells do not exist in isolation, but as parts of organisms. Thus, to understand how cells work in an organism or, indeed, how the organism itself affects the functioning of cells, it is necessary to think in wholes.

Holistic: the belief that reality is made up of unified wholes that are greater than the simple sum of their parts

Providing certain criteria are met, almost anything can be regarded as a system. For example, we can think of the human body as a total system composed of many subsystems, all of which interact together: the digestive system, the respiratory system, the nervous system, to name just three. Many people would assert that 'all' systems are open systems, which interact with their environments by taking in inputs and transforming them into outputs. For instance, the human body takes in food and transforms this into usable energy to maintain the body and also exports waste products. Deciduous trees take in nutrients from the ground and their leaves convert sunlight into energy; they also shed their leaves in the autumn and shut down for the winter. The fallen leaves decay, which provides food for a host of smaller organisms that convert the leaves into nutrients so that they can be reingested by the plant. A parallel can be drawn with organisations. Just as a tree absorbs water, nutrients and the sun's energy, organisations take in inputs and use them to survive; and just as a tree sheds its leaves in autumn to protect itself against the harsh winter, an organisation must be managed and controlled to enable it to respond to its environment in an appropriate way. An example of the use of this conceptualisation is given earlier in the chapter where it was used to explain the case for integration of micro and macro level perspectives on organisations.

Since the organism metaphor accepts that all the parts of an organisation are interconnected and have to function in a way that contributes to the whole, it recognises the importance of the human element. However, it still tends to assume that all the component parts of an organisation have a unified, common purpose and, so far as the human element is concerned, this is an oversimplification.

The (Political) Systems Metaphor

Political systems metaphor: organisations regarded as analogous to a political system composed of diverse groups, all of which have their own objectives

The *political systems metaphor* marks a fundamental break with an assumption held by those described above, and draws attention to:

- **Subsystem aims and objectives**   Recognition that different parts of an organisation can have their own aims and objectives that they seek to fulfil, rather than all of them subscribing to a single set of organisational goals.
- **Potential for conflict**   The possibility of competition or conflict between subsystems is acknowledged.

The machine and organism metaphors both assume that an organisation has a common purpose or goal, whereas this perspective draws attention to the idea that organisations consist of diverse groups that pursue their own aims, some of which are common to all groups, but others can be unique to a particular group. This means that there is always some potential for conflict. However, it does not mean that the metaphor endorses the idea of conflict, merely that a hierarchy of authority and a structure that brings people together into departments and functions will result in groups that have different viewpoints and interests, some of which can give rise to a degree of competition or even conflict. The perspective also focuses on how conflicts are pursued.

The great strength of this metaphor is its recognition of the complex nature of human behaviour in organisations. Instead of assuming a common purpose for everybody, it regards this state of affairs as something that occurs for very special reasons. It also recognises that conflict is not always pursued in an open way, and so political behaviour is regarded as a natural part of organisational life, not just an aberration. Nevertheless, it has its limitations. It all too easily overplays the conflictual aspects of organisations and neglects the idea that, if the circumstances are appropriate, there is also potential for cooperation.

Organisations as Cultural Systems

Cultural systems metaphor: organisations regarded as analogous to cultural systems in which members have common beliefs, values and shared assumptions

The *cultural systems metaphor* also takes a systemic perspective, but this time the focus is on one of the less tangible features of an organisation: its culture. This metaphor draws attention to such features as:

- **Values and beliefs**   Organisational members usually share a number of values and beliefs that they use to make sense of the world.
- **Effects of culture on behaviour**   The ways in which deep-rooted and largely unstated patterns of belief and values have a pervasive influence on behaviour in an organisation.

In broad terms, a culture is a system of values and beliefs shared by a group of people. The culture has a very pervasive effect on their behaviour. For instance, it helps them to understand why they do certain things and establishes desired patterns of behaviour. Few of us would deny the existence of different national cultures and their influence on behaviour, and in much the same way different organisations can also have distinctive cultures. Indeed, in some ways, exploring the culture of a firm can involve viewing it as a society in miniature. However, to identify a culture and its effects it is usually necessary to delve well beneath the surface to try to uncover the social significance that procedures and practices have for organisational members.

In terms of explaining behaviour this can be a very penetrating perspective, but for those not used to this way of thought it has its problems. To start with, each of the three previous metaphors has its own logic or rationality, which is applied to explain organisational activities. For example, the machine analogy uses an engineering logic to decide whether sensible rules have been followed to design and maintain an effective and efficient organisation. The organism metaphor applies its own criteria of rationality to examine whether an organisation is able to adapt internally, to adjust to changing environmental conditions. Finally, the political systems metaphor seeks to explain behaviour by applying the logic of competition for scarce resources. Therefore, if we accept that any of these metaphors is a useful tool for its intended purpose, with practice we can see how each one can be used to explain how certain actions can lead to certain outcomes. However, the cultural metaphor has no over-arching rationality, and it casts doubt on whether the word rational can be used to explain human behaviour. It holds that if a person behaves in a certain way because this is the normal way to behave in a certain context, he or she may not even be aware of behaving in that way. Thus there are probably no universal criteria that can be used to evaluate whether the culturally induced patterns of behaviour are more appropriate in one organisation than another. Indeed, to analyse an organisation it is usually necessary to accept the culture as what it is, and simply try to identify how it affects behaviour.

A second problem stems from the use of the word 'organisational' in conjunction with the word 'culture'. This is sometimes used to imply that everybody in an organisation has the same set of cultural norms. However, different parts of an organisation usually have some differences in outlook, and it is these differences and their behavioural outcomes that give rise to the political systems metaphor. Thus, rather than view an organisation as a cultural system, it might make more sense to think of it as a system of subcultures. Finally, as will be seen in Chapter 19 (which explores culture in greater depth), although the concept started out as a penetrating way of examining the nature

Table 1.2 Comparison of organisational metaphors

Metaphor	Analogy	Main focus	Strengths	Weaknesses
Machine Metaphor	Organisation as a machine that is designed to serve a specific purpose	Technical efficiency or fitness for purpose	Strong focus on organisation as a whole and how efficiently it functions	Neglects the human element
Biological System	Organisation as an organism existing in, interacting with and influenced by its environment	Relationship with environment Interrelation of subsystems in organisation and influence this has on the behaviour of the organisation as a whole	Acknowledges that organisations have a wide variety of component parts (including the human element) which have to play their respective parts if the whole organism is to function well	Tends to assume that all the component parts have a common purpose
Political System	Organisation as a system composed of diverse subsystems, all of which have their own aims and objectives	Conflict and competition between subsystems	Accepts that organisations contain different groups whose interests need to be reconciled. Thus conflict and competition are everyday features of organisational life	Some tendency to focus on conflict to the exclusion of all else, and underplay the idea that there are also cooperative features of organisations
Cultural System	Organisations as cultures	Beliefs, values and shared meanings of organisational members and how these result in identifiable patterns of behaviour	Goes well beneath the surface to try to uncover some of the less tangible features of organisations, and their effects on human behaviour	Has a tendency to regard culture as the only important factor, which underplays the impact of factors external to the person

of organisations, certain popular writings have trivialised and watered it down to the extent that it is now almost worthless.

In summary, each of the four metaphors has its distinctive uses, strengths and weaknesses, and for comparative purposes these are shown in Table 1.2.

TIME OUT

Think about the organisation where you work. If you are not in employment, think about your own university or college as an organisation. Identify those aspects and features of the organisation (and the way that it functions) if you were to examine the institution by using:

the machine metaphor;
the organism metaphor;
the political systems metaphor;
the cultural systems metaphor.

A More Recent Development: The Postmodernist Perspective

Postmodernist: either (i) a new era in which the fundamental nature of organisations will be different from hitherto, or (ii) a philosophical stance which questions current assumptions of the nature of reality

Epistemology: a branch of philosophy dealing with the nature and origins of knowledge

Over the last fifteen years a more radical view of organisations has emerged: the so-called *postmodernist* perspective. However, the word is used in two very distinct ways. The first defines a new era in which there will be a radical change in the fundamental nature of organisations (Cooper and Burrell 1988), and this will be considered briefly in Chapter 2. The second use of the word involves epistemological considerations. *Epistemology* is a branch of philosophy dealing with the nature and origins of knowledge. Postmodernist thought goes to the very root of how an organisation and its activities are conceived, and this results in something much more radical than a new metaphor. Postmodernists are highly critical of conventional ways of conceiving organisations and they would probably reject all four of the metaphors described above as unreal and false. In essence, they argue that current thinking is based on a false notion of scientific rationality, which emphasises rigorous investigation and communication of results to expand the boundaries of knowledge. This is said to hinge on the practice of viewing the world as a set of static, discrete entities and trying to identify causal links between them. For example, phenomena such as individuals, organisations and structures are treated as things which can be separated from the rest of the world, and conventional thought tends to focus on such questions as 'Is there a link between culture and structure?' or 'Is culture caused by structure or vice versa?' Postmodernists point out that, because nothing is static, features such as culture and structure have no reality, but are merely temporary states that are treated as fixed and static. This ignores the most important matter of all: the social processes that result in the movement from one state to another. Some postmodernists, for example Bauman (1992), argue that this search for causality is a futile endeavour, based on the false assumption that reality exists and consists of certainty about entities, or what Whitehead (1985) calls the 'fallacy of misplaced concreteness'. Thus the key idea is that everything is in motion, and that what traditional thought views as an object or an entity is only a transitional state, which means that anything that seeks to establish the ultimate truth about entities is a search for the impossible.

Postmodernists argue that to pretend that there is a truth about anything is to deny the essential nature of the world. Their remedy is to regard everything as being in a state of motion, and to reject the idea that anything is real and tangible. So far as studying organisations is concerned, they believe we should shed the intellectual tyranny of thinking in terms of objects, and direct attention to more important issues. Indeed, they argue that the very term 'organisation' is problematic, because it is not a real entity, simply a label we attach to a very fluid and mobile social configuration (Chia 1995).

Nihilism: a now discredited doctrine that nothing really exists and thus there can be no knowledge of anything and hence knowledge cannot be communicated

These, of course, are very deep philosophical questions, but for anyone who aspires to do more than retreat into a cave and contemplate his or her own navel they are full of problems. For someone who is trying to grasp what makes an organisation tick, postmodernist thought results in more paradoxes than helpful insights. For instance, if nothing is concrete, people can only describe things to each other in terms of their own experience, but postmodernism also asserts that meaning is so personal that it cannot really be communicated. Taken together, these points lead to the inevitable conclusion that it is simply not worth conducting enquiries to try to understand organisations, because we cannot communicate our findings. Therefore, what is portrayed as the leading edge of analytical thought can all too easily start to look like the long-discredited doctrine of *nihilism*: that nothing exists, is knowledgeable or can be communicated.

REPLAY

- The machine metaphor likens an organisation to a machine that is designed to serve a specific purpose.
- The organism metaphor likens an organisation to a biological system that exists in conjunction with, and must adapt to, its environment.
- The political systems metaphor views an organisation as a system of subsystems, all of which have their own aims and goals, which means that there is always some potential for conflict between subsystems.
- The cultural systems metaphor views an organisation primarily as a system of values, beliefs and understandings that guide the behaviour of its members.
- The postmodernist perspective is not a metaphor but a philosophical standpoint that strongly questions current assumptions about the nature of organisations.

Discourse: the idea that language is more than just a useful tool of communication. Indeed, what is said can convey what seems like the essential truth about how things are, and this has the effect of disarming challenges to an argument, suppressing alternative meanings and supporting particular interpretations or conclusions

Deconstruction: a method used in postmodernist analysis to reveal underlying assumptions (in discourse) and challenge them with counter-arguments or alternative interpretations

Perhaps the greatest problem is the postmodernist conception of scholarship. Many self-proclaimed postmodernists reject the value of empirical work, favouring instead a seemingly endless stream of *post hoc* criticism of the empirical work of others. This is a rather particular definition of scholarship, which is less concerned with explanation and verification than with vilifying the explanations produced by other people. Thus postmodernists probably spend more time convincing other postmodernists of the correctness and sanctity of postmodernism than they do in advancing the frontiers of knowledge. Indeed, one observer has remarked that 'postmodernism may well end up being nothing more than writers who write about other writers, and address what they write to even more writers: a rather dangerous approach that comes near to turning social science into literary criticism rather than empirical enquiry' (Alvesson 1995).

Therefore, while the postmodern approach may eventually turn out to be something which is both revolutionary and useful, it is doubtful whether it has reached that stage yet and in some respects it is far too complex to be of practical use in an introductory text such as this. Conversely, Organisational Behaviour and Analysis have long sought to increase our understanding of the behaviour of people in organisations, and to do this in a way that makes the knowledge usable by people interested in improving organisations. To date, postmodernism has probably only opened up a debate that could eventually increase our understanding. Indeed, while it gives academics something new to talk about, it does precious little else, and it could even be no more than a new bandwagon that presents an opportunity for them to become the gurus of the future. If so, it risks committing the same crime of which it accuses prior systems of thought: that is, of becoming a new intellectual tyranny that creates its own truth effects (Alvesson 1995). For all this, the reader is urged to beware of condemning postmodernism out of hand. With its emphasis on the importance of *discourse* (an idea much older than postmodernism) and the allied technique of *deconstruction*, it opens up new possibilities for the way in which we conceptualise organisational phenomena. Therefore, for those who might wish to explore the topic further, some suggestions are included in the list of further readings at the end of the chapter.

FURTHER READING

Appignanesi, R and C Garratt (1995) *Postmodernism for Beginners*, Cambridge: Icon Books. An informative, but difficult-to-read book that contains a useful commentary on the use of language to describe reality.

Bauman, Z (1992) *Intimations of Postmodernism*, London: Routledge. Not an easy book to read, but an essential text for those wishing to explore postmodernist thought.

Carey, A (1967) 'The Hawthorne studies: a radical criticism', *American Sociological Review* 32(2), 403–16. As the title suggests, a critique of the findings and conclusions that were drawn from the Hawthorne studies.

Hatch, M J (1997) *Organisation Theory, Symbolic and Postmodern Perspectives*, Oxford: Oxford University Press. An interesting and clear guide to organisation theory that explores and contrasts three perspectives on organisations: modernist, social constructivist and postmodern.

Hinings, C R and R Greenwood (2002) 'Disconnects and consequences in organisation theory', *Administrative Science Quarterly* 47(3), 411–21. A review article that traces the origins of organisation theory and how it has been co-opted by American business schools in a way that serves managerial ends.

Kvale, S (ed.) (1992) *Psychology and Postmodernism*, London: Sage. A book of readings that explores the implications of postmodernist thought for psychology.

Mayo, E (1933) *The Human Problems of Industrial Civilization*, New York: Macmillan. A work by one of the founding fathers of Organisational Behaviour, which contains ideas that by now read as highly patronising and full of elitism.

Morgan, G (1997) *Images of Organisation*, London: Sage. A very readable book that develops and fully explains the different metaphors for organisations.

O'Connor, E S (1999) 'The politics of management thought: a case study of the Harvard Business School and the Human Relations School', *Academy of Management Review* 24(1), 117–31. Gives a useful insight describing how early developments in Human Relations theory were hijacked by the Harvard Business School, to serve managerialist ends.

Whitehead, A N (1985) *Science and the Modern World*, London: Free Association Books. An essential, but rather technical, text for those wishing to explore postmodernist thought.

REVIEW AND DISCUSSION QUESTIONS

1. Explain what you take the word 'organisation' to mean and compare your answer with the five key features (given at the beginning of the chapter) which qualify an entity as an organisation.

2. Explain the case for integrating knowledge from OB and OA. To what extent do you feel that failing to integrate knowledge from both areas can result in an incomplete or inaccurate explanation of behaviour in and by organisations?

3. Debate the following statement and state whether, in your collective view, the assertion is a valid one.

Social science seldom, if ever, produces definitive, irrefutable laws that enable behaviour to be predicted with certainty. Therefore, it is highly questionable whether Organisational Behaviour and Analysis can add much to our understanding of organisations, and even more questionable whether they can provide information that is useful in making organisations more effective.

4. Compare and contrast the main foci and strengths and weaknesses of the following organisational metaphors: the machine metaphor; the organism metaphor; the political systems metaphor; and the cultural systems metaphor. Compare the use of these metaphors with the 'postmodernist' approach to organisations. What do you feel is the practical utility of the postmodernist approach?

CASE STUDY 1.1: Apprentice Training at Servco

Servco is a large organisation, active throughout Great Britain, which sells, installs and services domestic appliances. It has a large workforce of skilled service engineers and, nationally, takes on approximately 400 school leavers as apprentices each year. Until four years ago, the apprenticeship scheme was a traditional one. That is, it lasted four years, during which time apprentices spent four days per week assisting a skilled and qualified service engineer and were given release for one day each week to attend a local technical college to study for the recognised craft qualification, a City and Guilds certificate. However, four years ago the scheme was completely revised and an apprenticeship now lasts three years. Apprentices spend three months each year studying full-time at a technical college, three months at a national apprentice training school, where they are taught practical skills by instructors, and the remainder of their time with skilled tradesmen, but not in the role of a helper to a tradesman. They now perform the work tasks and their work is assessed by the skilled man.

The management of Servco has given you the task of evaluating changes brought about by the introduction of the new scheme. You will be undertaking this task with a view to writing up the study as a dissertation which will count towards your degree. In order to gain a preliminary overview of the matter, you have conducted short interviews with several interested parties in the organisation and identify a number of themes, each of which could become the focus of the study.

First, there is the question of whether the new scheme is as cost-effective as its predecessor. Second, it seems possible that craftsmen trained under the old scheme consider the current one as not being a 'proper' apprenticeship that produces a skilled tradesman. Third, there is the question of the views of customers, who see two people arrive at their home to do a job, but only one of them actually works, while the other just seems to sit there and watch.

Questions

1. Which organisational metaphor is likely to be most appropriate for each of these issues?

2. Is there a single metaphor which could embrace them all? If so, which one?

Contemporary Organisational Challenges

LEARNING OUTCOMES

After studying this chapter you should be able to:

- identify some of the developments which, over the last two decades, have given rise to the contemporary challenges faced by organisations

- identify the three main sources (levels) of challenge and the specific challenges associated with each one

- describe the concept of the stakeholder organisation and contrast this with traditional perspectives on corporate governance

- describe and explain the imperatives to cope with the specific challenges at each level

- explain the interrelated nature of the specific organisational challenges

INTRODUCTION

The conditions an organisation encounters can be likened to a set of forces that require it to make an appropriate response if it is to survive and prosper. Since the early 1970s many organisations have faced increasing competition from international competitors and in the 1980s and 1990s this was so severe that many of them came to view survival as their major challenge. In some respects they sought to deal with this situation by draconian measures; for example, many of them restructured and/or reduced the scale of their activities, and the remaining jobs were redesigned to extract greater effort from employees. Although the resulting organisations became leaner and were able to obtain the short-term benefit of survival, what emerged in many cases were firms that are now described as 'lean and mean' (Berggren 1993). As such, there are doubts about whether, in this form, these organisations will be able to cope with the next generation of challenges that are now starting to appear. Many of the steps taken by firms in the last two decades have themselves given rise to some of the new challenges. Moreover, since many of the conditions that prompted firms to take these steps will exist in the foreseeable future, they will continue to be forces and pressures to which they need to respond.

Although nobody knows for certain what the future will bring, current trends have led some people to predict that changes in the new millenium will have a significant impact on people in organisations. Since this book is about organisations and, in particular, the role of people in them, the main purpose of this chapter is to identify some of the ways in which organisational challenges are likely to have an impact on human resources. In subsequent chapters attention will be drawn to the challenges identified here, together with the ways in which they impact on the topic under discussion. These challenges can be conceptualised as pressures and forces that are primarily experienced at one of three levels: the macro (whole organisation) level; the micro (workplace) level; and the intermediate (mixed macro and micro) level. These are set out in Table 2.1, and for convenience a start will be made at the macro level.

THE CHALLENGE OF GLOBALISATION

Globalised economy: the 'one-world' economy, in which large firms compete for business on a worldwide scale

Whether or not they operate internationally, competing in a *globalised (one-world) economy* currently affects many large organisations, and it is said that it will affect almost everyone in the new millennium. Since the international organisation is a topic in its own right, which is considered in more detail in Chapter 22, the aim here is simply to describe globalisation and to explain why it is a significant challenge for all organisations.

As things stand, there are three very large trading regions: the so-called golden triangle of North America, which embraces Canada and Mexico; the Pacific Rim countries of Japan, South Korea, Taiwan, Singapore, Hong Kong and Australasia; and the European Union (EU), which at present embraces 25 European nations. However, the position is fluid and other countries are likely to emerge as part of one of these regions in the near future. For example, countries such as China, Malaysia, Indonesia and Thailand are industrialising rapidly and could become part of the Pacific Rim group. Some of the Latin American countries are also making great strides in industrialisation and, in addition, the EU is likely to expand even further in the future.

Table 2.1 Challenges facing contemporary organisations

Level and origin of challenge	Specific challenges
Macro: The Organisation–Environment Relationship	The globalised economy Other economic and competitive challenges • the state of the economy and changes in markets • size reductions • the quality revolution • technological challenges • organisational ownership and rewards distribution
Intermediate: Mixed Organisation–Environment and Intra-organisational Issues	Corporate social responsibility The stakeholder organisation Organisational learning
Micro: Intra-organisational Issues	Ethics Workplace issues • changed workforce composition • workforce diversity • changed working practices • employment relations/employee voice • the psychological contract

The Effects of Globalisation

Globalisation has had a dramatic effect on organisations. For example, the USA was relatively unaffected by foreign competition until the 1970s, but by 1980, 70 per cent of the goods and services produced by American firms faced competition from imported products (Astley and Braham 1989). In terms of relative size, American firms also ceased to dominate the world. In 1960, 70 of the world's 100 largest firms were American, but by 1985 the number had dropped to 45 and by 1990 it was down to 33.

Large firms often have no choice but to adopt a global perspective. To target only the home market is to compete against larger firms that can draw on global finances, and which often have better design competencies and technologies that give production advantages. The moral is stark and simple: compete on the same basis or lose the ability to compete at all. Indeed, Porter (1990) argues that it was the lack of competitive pressure within America that made it an easy target for Japanese firms.

In Great Britain globalisation has had a huge effect on the nation's manufacturing base. Rather than manufacture something themselves, many smaller firms simply sell foreign products. Indeed, an increasingly large proportion of British industry is foreign owned, often by Japanese or American companies. In addition, some large British companies are now seeking to become global organisations. Until the late 1980s, for example, British Gas (now Transco) was a nationalised industry almost exclusively concerned with providing fuel and services in Great Britain, but it now derives an increasingly large proportion of its revenues from foreign operations. Changes like this immeasurably alter the face of an organisation. It has to learn to deal with a more diverse and heterogeneous customer base, and the new structures and processes needed for international operations.

TIME OUT

Bearing in mind what you have read about the globalised economy and, in particular, the nature of the globalised company:

1. Identify the likely effects on the working population of an industrialised country.
2. What do you feel would be the effect on a small- or medium-sized company that is not large enough to contemplate becoming a globalised organisation?
3. What do you feel would be the major differences in working for a globalised organisation compared with one that is not globalised?

REPLAY

- In the last two decades markets have become far more globalised; three very large trading regions (North America, the Pacific Rim and the European Union) have emerged and these will almost certainly grow in the future.
- Globalised organisations tend to have significant competitive advantages and so large organisations have little alternative but to move in this direction, which poses a strong challenge for all organisations, irrespective of whether they are large enough to contemplate this step.

OTHER ECONOMIC AND COMPETITIVE CHALLENGES

With or without globalisation, there are a number of pressures that would probably still exist, all of which are worth noting because they affect a wide variety of organisations: the state of the economy, together with changed markets; size reductions; the quality revolution; technological challenges; organisational ownership and rewards distribution.

The State of the Economy and Changed Markets

An organisation is strongly influenced by the demand for its products and services and this is often a reflection of the buoyancy of the whole economy, a factor which is beyond an organisation's control. In countries such as Great Britain national prosperity is also acutely dependent on trade with other countries, and so British firms are particularly affected by conditions elsewhere. From 1997 onwards there have been economic crises in the Far East, notably in Japan, and several South American countries that prompted renewed fears of a world recession, which has affected business confidence worldwide. In many countries firms cut back the level of their activities, and this resulted in large-scale unemployment, which in turn reduced consumer spending power and made the recessionary effects even worse. In Great Britain, however, the level of unemployment has declined steadily over the past few years. To some extent this has been the result of a consumer boom prompted by falling rates of interest and so it could be a temporary rather than permanent recovery. Moreover, it is also necessary to remember that there is still a psychological legacy in the minds of many employees of having lived through prior recessionary periods and this could have a profound effect on organisations for some time to come.

A recent survey conducted by the Economic and Social Research Council (ESRC 2002) confirms patterns of attitudes found in an earlier survey by the Central Statistical Office (CSO 1996). It reveals that the population of Great Britain is extremely dispirited about working conditions in organisations, and pessimistic about the future. This seems to apply equally to people who are back in employment after prior recessionary conditions as well as those who have, so far, managed to avoid becoming unemployed (Donnelly and Scholarios 1998). This pessimism also has its effects on managers of organisations, many of whom are reluctant to expand capacities in order to take advantage of a permanent economic upturn.

Human capital approach: a recognition that the contribution made by human skills and knowledge to the production of goods and/or services is a vital ingredient in an organisation's success

In addition, products and services can rapidly become obsolete in the globalised marketplace, and this means that markets for many products become more volatile, more competitive and product life cycles tend to be shorter. For this reason it is very hard to plan for the future and, in order to survive, firms need to become more innovative, flexible and adaptable. The key factor here would seem to be the use of a more flexible and versatile workforce. At the very least this is likely to require a greater investment in the training and development of employees, by adopting a *human capital approach*, where the workforce is viewed as a valuable resource whose skills and abilities are nurtured and developed to obtain a competitive advantage, rather than something that is discarded once it has served its useful purpose. Thus, the challenges facing organisations are:

- to find ways of being able to respond to increased demand, if and when it occurs;
- to find ways of reinvigorating and remotivating employees, many of whom still feel insecure, apprehensive and dispirited;
- to recruit and retain employees who are able to deliver the skills needed and invest in their continued training and development;
- to create conditions in which they feel committed enough to use their skills and abilities.

Downsizing: a reduction in the size of an organisation or the scale of its activities, theoretically to attain the appropriate size for its volume of sales

Size Reductions

As noted earlier, since the early 1980s there has been a huge amount of retrenchment in industrialised countries. While new names such as *downsizing*, *rightsizing*, *delayering* or even simply cutbacks have been invented to gloss over what has occurred, the results are remarkably similar. Plant closures, redundancies, wage cuts, capacity reductions and the replacement of people with machines have all been commonplace, and while some firms have survived and even regained a competitive position, this resulted in a great deal of unemployment. Some firms have done their best to help those leaving, perhaps by providing counselling or helping people to locate new employment. Nevertheless, when a downsizing initiative is in progress people are understandably apprehensive and so commitment and loyalty are inevitably lowered (Savery *et al.* 1998). In addition, for those who are not made redundant, working life is frequently more stressful, insecure and often more physically demanding due to longer hours. Indeed, conditions have been described by one author as 'working with pain' (Berggren 1993).

Rightsizing: see downsizing

Delayering: a reduction of the number of levels in an organisation's hierarchy, usually by removing one or more levels of supervision and/or middle management

The survivors are sometimes demotivated, dispirited, lack a sense of security and their loyalty to an employer can be severely reduced because they feel that they work for an organisation that treats people as a commodity rather than as humans who deserve consideration (Cooper 1998). Indeed, evidence suggests that one of the most strongly affected groups of survivors consists of managers who, because they have had to make other people redundant, have subliminal fears that what they have done to others could be done to themselves (Kets de Vries and Balazs 1997). The need to address these psychological effects on those who remain has only recently been recognised (Doherty and Horsted 1995) and research in some of these slimmed-down organisations has revealed that organisational commitment can be much lower and intentions to leave much higher (Allen *et al.* 2001). Thus, the challenge for organisations is to:

- develop new employment relationships and conditions of work in which these feelings no longer exist.

The Quality Revolution

The current view of quality is that it is not simply a matter of a product or service being more durable than an available alternative. Rather, it consists of a bundle of attributes that ensure that the needs of customers are satisfied. In the last two decades the greater degree of competition for business is often said to have led to consumers becoming much more demanding (Grey and Mitev 1995), and quality has become extremely important in giving a firm its competitive edge. However, price has not been totally eclipsed by quality as the basis of competition, and where there are two substitute products of equal quality, customers will usually buy the cheaper one. Thus, it is usually important to achieve high quality while keeping the price low and *productivity*, which can be defined as the quantity of outputs obtained from a given level of inputs, is therefore a very important consideration. The traditional view is that quality can only be obtained if an element of productivity is sacrificed, but a broader view is that a more effective and efficient use of resources can often be obtained if quality is built in during the production process.

A number of approaches to this issue have been put forward, one of which is *Total Quality Management* (TQM), which theoretically consists of an organisation-wide strategy that focuses on achieving or exceeding customer expectations. Most texts on TQM argue that realising its promised advantages is crucially dependent on using human resources in an appropriate way (Schonberger 1982). Here there is very strong evidence that the firms who get the best from TQM are those that also have a compatible set of human resource practices, such as empowering the workforce and eliciting its cooperation and commitment (Macduffie 1995). However, there is also evidence that TQM often sets up a number of workplace tensions. For instance, work is sometimes deliberately organised to put pressure on employees to produce for every second and worker autonomy is actually reduced because people are forced to achieve tight work targets. In addition, people are usually organised in teams, in which they have to cover for an absent colleague; this results in peer pressure being used as an instrument of management control to minimise absence (Parker *et al.* 1993). Employees are not blind to these effects (McCabe 1996) and so the challenge for firms is to:

- develop ways of using these methods that elicit cooperation and commitment, and avoid workplace tensions.

Productivity: a measure of efficiency consisting of the ratio of inputs to outputs

Total Quality Management (TQM): an organisation-wide strategy that focuses on achieving or exceeding customer expectations

Technological Challenges

Technology influences the way that inputs are transformed into outputs and this has become a major factor in achieving a competitive position. Prior to the 1980s the main reason for introducing new technology was to replace human labour with machines, but in the last two decades newer information technologies, which can perform many of the monitoring and control tasks formerly undertaken by supervisors and middle managers, have appeared. Thus, the elimination of whole layers of management and supervision has been commonplace.

Unfortunately, because they see this as an end to the traditional notion of career, and to many people the idea of a career is very important, it demoralises employees. The idea of a career implies that hard work, diligence and loyalty can lead to later rewards, which gives people hope for the future and research shows that in many organisations this hope is fast disappearing, to be replaced by strong feelings of demoralisation and frustration (Holbeche 1995). Thus, the organisational challenge is to:

- build a new relationship with employees, which contains something as effective as the traditional notion of career in eliciting commitment and loyalty.

Organisational Ownership and Rewards Distribution

The last half-century has seen a significant change in the structure of organisational ownership. Mergers and acquisitions have resulted in the control of a significant proportion of firms now being concentrated in the hands of a small number of large companies. Perhaps more importantly, the share capital of these large organisations is increasingly in the hands of large financial institutions (Blackhurst 1996). Institutional investors have only one duty: to produce the highest possible return for those people whose investment portfolios they manage, and this puts heavy pressure on firms to produce high short-term returns, which sometimes means that they have to forego long-term opportunities (Hutton 1995).

In the last decade another phenomenon has appeared: the growing inequalities in rewards between those at the top of an organisation and those lower down; for example, the 75 per cent pay rise for the chief executive of British Gas, awarded at the same time that the firm put forward proposals to reduce pay and conditions for its retail staff. More will be said about this later when the topic of ethics is introduced, but for the moment it is sufficient to note that at least part of the responsibility for this state of affairs can be traced to the pressures for short-term results that are inherent in patterns of share ownership. If anyone has the power to intervene and call a halt to the practice of executive greed it is institutional fund managers, who seem to be all too willing to stand to one side and allow chief executives to acquire exorbitant rewards packages. Organisations desperately need to find a way out of both of these dilemmas. One proposal has been for firms to spread share ownership more widely among the firm's employees, perhaps by using save-as-you-earn (SAYE) share option schemes in which employees can acquire shares on advantageous terms (see Smethurst 2003). However, the idea that employees might actually acquire enough shares to exercise effective control of the organisation would probably alarm many managers. Thus, where firms do have a scheme of this type the extent of employee share ownership may be restricted to a small proportion (usually below 10 per cent) of the total share capital of the organisation (Baddon *et al.* 1989).

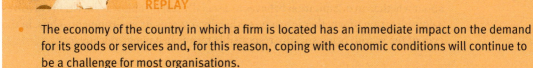

REPLAY

- The economy of the country in which a firm is located has an immediate impact on the demand for its goods or services and, for this reason, coping with economic conditions will continue to be a challenge for most organisations.

- Because rapid change in market conditions and quality as a basis of competition both require a flexible, skilled and committed workforce, a challenge for organisations is to find ways of counteracting the demoralisation and lowered motivation in their workforces.

- Another significant challenge for organisations will be to overcome the after-effects of the size reductions and the introduction of new technologies in the last two decades, which has seriously affected the morale of employees.

- Two significant challenges for large firms will be to find ways of resisting the pressures to take a purely short-term view of organisational performance, which arises because these organisations are largely owned by institutional investors, and to tackle the problem of excessive levels of executive remuneration.

TIME OUT

Reflect on the challenges and conditions that have been described so far in the chapter. Assuming that an organisation identifies that it needs to address every one of the challenges, to what extent do you feel that this would be possible, and what steps might have to be taken to do so?

THE CHALLENGE OF ETHICS AND SOCIAL RESPONSIBILITY

Ethics: an individual's moral beliefs about what is right and wrong, or good and bad, that provides a guide to his/her behaviour

The study of ethics and the study of the social responsibilities of organisations are both fairly recent additions to Organisational Behaviour and Analysis, and modules on ethics are now offered by some universities and colleges as part of a Business Studies curriculum. Strictly speaking, there is a sense in which ethics and social responsibility cannot be divorced but, because they concern behaviour at different organisational levels, here they will be considered separately.

The scope of the topic of *ethics* has been described as:

dealing with moral issues and choices and concerning an individual's beliefs about what is right or wrong and good or bad.   (Garrett and Klonoski 1992)

(Corporate) social responsibility: an organisation's obligation to contribute to, or protect, the environment of which it is a part

(Corporate) social responsibility is somewhat harder to define, but with respect to organisations it can be described as:

**concerning the relationship of an organisation to its social environment and the obligation to protect or contribute to that environment of which it is a part.
                  (Donaldson and Preston 1995)**

As can be seen, ethics is essentially an individual matter, whereas social responsibility is a macro level concept, and if reification (see Chapter 1) is to be avoided, organisations cannot be treated in the same way as individuals. Nevertheless, any judgement about whether an organisation behaves in a socially responsible way inevitably involves a consideration of whether it behaves ethically towards its environment. Thus, in the eyes of the world, being socially responsible means behaving ethically.

Ethics

Standards of behaviour in organisations, and in particular the behaviour of those who own or manage them, have been a matter of public concern since the industrial 'robber barons' of the nineteenth century first attracted public criticism. This was largely because they were widely perceived to have amassed vast personal fortunes at the expense of the public and to be ruthless and corrupt in their dealings with anyone who stood in their way. Much of the current concern for ethics in business has been prompted by a resurfacing of similar concerns; for instance, the recent 'fat cats' scandals in which senior executives of companies are widely perceived to be in receipt of exorbitant remuneration packages, including overgenerous severance terms. Another issue which hit the headlines was the unauthorised futures dealings of the Singapore-based financial broker Nick Leeson, which resulted in the collapse of Barings merchant bank. Although these are very dramatic examples, it has been argued that ethical dilemmas arise in business more frequently than it is convenient to recognise (Walton 1988). However, since ethical standards are essentially relative rather than absolute, they vary from place to place and change with time (Carlisle and Manning 1996). Thus it is important to recognise that there are a large number of factors that influence a person's behaviour, some of which are not always conducive to the individual behaving in a way that is ethical in a particular organisational context. These are outlined in Figure 2.1.

Figure 2.1 Factors influencing individual behaviour

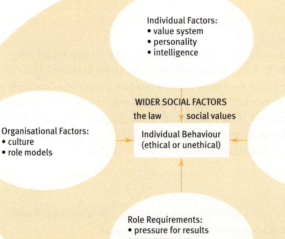

Individual Factors

Personal characteristics such as personality, intelligence and values play a part in the ethics of individual behaviour. Some of these, for example, authoritarianism and Machiavellianism, will be described in Chapter 3 and for the present it is sufficient to note that they have a bearing on what individuals with these characteristics consider to be the acceptable limits of behaviour.

Upbringing and Social Background

Socialisation has a huge influence on a person's ethical standards. What he or she learns in early socialisation in the family, at school or in peer groups can have dramatic effects later in life. As will be seen in the next chapter, Freudian theory (Freud 1940) stresses that a person's superego (an aspect of personality that can loosely be equated with conscience) is acquired as part of his/her upbringing. In addition, the works of Kohlberg (1968) and Wright (1971) show that moral responsibility is strongly influenced by early social experience.

Role Requirements

As will be seen in Chapter 11, a person's work role often results in pressures to behave in certain ways. Most of us are subject to a number of these competing pressures, for instance, from the boss, from peers, from subordinates, and pressures to produce results. All of these can exert an influence on the person to deviate from standards that are part of his or her personality, or those that have been learned outside the organisation.

Organisational Factors

Most organisations expect certain patterns of behaviour from their members and an organisation's culture usually gives clear signals about the behaviour expected. For example, a culture in which senior figures clearly have high ethical standards and act as role models can help an individual to be ethical, whereas one in which the individual's personal code of ethics is ridiculed can make it much harder for him or her to behave ethically (Trevino and Bart 1992).

Wider Social Factors

A number of factors in the outside world also directly impinge on organisational life and have a bearing on individual behaviour. Certain standards are enshrined in law, and some originate in the basic values of society. In certain parts of the world, for example in Arab states, business is conducted in a different way from the West. Hiring relatives in preference to others, using family contacts to influence and expedite events and paying money for favours do not have the unethical connotations of nepotism or bribery that most people would associate with these practices in the West (Muna 1980).

All of these groups of factors interact, and because the demands of a particular situation can overwhelm other considerations, people can sometimes act out of character. For example, if the culture of an organisation permits people to be treated harshly in a time of crisis then someone who is normally humane and considerate can behave in a highly cavalier fashion towards others.

Current Areas of Ethical Concern

Since the list of issues about ethical standards is continually growing, a convenient way to consider matters is to examine two relationships: the internal relationship between an organisation and its employees and the relationship between an organisation and its external stakeholders. As well as being influenced by some of the matters covered above, the first of these is strongly affected by the workplace challenges that will be described presently, which have a huge impact on what will be described later in the chapter as the 'psychological contract'. For this reason it is more convenient to put them aside for now and move on to the organisation's relationship with its environment. This brings us to the matter of corporate social responsibility.

Corporate Social Responsibility: The Relationship with Environment

An organisation's relationship with its environment often poses a considerable number of ethical dilemmas, but until comparatively recently the dominant view has been that a profit-making organisation's responsibility to its owners should be set above all other responsibilities. However, in the last half-century, British governments have introduced an increasing amount of legislation to emphasise organisational responsibilities to wider society and three examples are: the Companies Acts from 1948 onwards, Consumer Protection legislation from the 1960s onwards and the Health and Safety at Work Act 1974. While opinion is still divided on this matter, a consensus has emerged in the last decade that business owes some form of duty to a wider set of interests than those of its shareholders. More recently this has been prompted by a number of corporate scandals such as the demise of giant US corporations such as Enron and WorldCom, together with the activities of companies such as Shell (the Brent Spar episode) and Union Carbide (the Bhopal disaster). For this reason the expression corporate social responsibility (CSR) is now familiar in most boardrooms, and it is also one that has attracted a great deal of public attention.

However, it is always difficult to tell whether a business that behaves ethically towards its environment is prompted by altruism or something else. The sceptical view expressed by writers such as Roberts (2003), Parker (2003), Arthur (2003) and Doane (2003) is that talk of ethics in CSR is talk and little else; a cheap and easy way for the corporation to manufacture an image of its own goodness. Conversely, there are others who point out that the pressures to improve CSR performance are real, albeit prompted by self-interest as much as anything else. For instance, it could well be a matter of sound business sense because a host of groups such as customers, employees and shareholders have developed tendencies to disassociate themselves from companies that fail to behave responsibly (Cook 2003).

This begs the question of how organisations could (or should) approach the matter of CSR. Since this of necessity involves considering the interests of a wide variety of internal and external groups, the most convenient perspective to adopt is that of the 'stakeholder organisation', which is considered next.

The Stakeholder Organisation

Stakeholder: people or groups with an interest in the activities of an organisation and the outcomes of those activities, whether or not the organisation has an interest in them

In the last seven years the word *stakeholder* has attracted an increasing amount of attention when discussing organisations. No one who followed the run-up to the 1997 General Election in Great Britain (and how could anyone avoid it!) could help becoming aware that New Labour had adopted the concept of a *stakeholder economy* in its manifesto, within which it also embraced the idea of the stakeholder organisation. In organisational terms, stakeholders can be defined as:

> **people or groups with an interest in the activities of an organisation and the outcomes of those activities . . . they are identified as people who have an interest in the organisation, whether or not the organisation has an interest in them.**
>
> **(Donaldson and Preston 1995, p 67)**

TIME OUT

Stakeholder economy: an economy which is theoretically run for the benefit of all participants who have an interest in the performance of the economy

Bearing in mind that all organisations have stakeholders:

1. Who would you identify as the different stakeholder groups of a university or college?
2. What are your grounds for stating that the groups you have identified are relevant stakeholders?
3. What are the interests of these stakeholder groups?
4. Are the interests of the different stakeholder groups compatible, that is, is it possible to satisfy them all or are the interests so opposed that if one group is satisfied, some other group could not be satisfied, and what would be your suggested remedy to this situation?

There is nothing new about the idea that organisations have stakeholders, and in academic circles the term has been in use for some time. However, Donaldson and Preston (1995) point out that the word has been used in three different ways. First, it is used descriptively, to advance the idea that there are many groups of people who have a vested interest in the actions of an organisation, and there is strong evidence that many managers now view matters in this way (Merrick 1997). Second, it can be used in an instrumental way, usually by academic researchers to explore the idea that there is a link between organisational performance and considering the interests of a wide constituency of stakeholders. For example, there is said to be strong evidence that the most successful firms adopt a stakeholder perspective (Greenley and Foxall 1997). Finally, there is what Donaldson and Preston call the normative use, which is essentially a moral and philosophical argument that firms should be managed in a way that takes due account of the interests of all stakeholders.

Currently the normative use of the word dominates the debate, and this is in sharp contrast to the traditional view that since shareholders are the owners of the business, the primary (if not sole) consideration should be to maximise their return. However, Donaldson and Preston argue that the traditional view is morally untenable, because society now demands that organisations should adopt a wider perspective of their responsibilities, that is, one in which each group of stakeholders merits consideration for its own sake.

One of the most visible signs that this view is taking root in Britain was the appearance in 1995 of a report entitled *Tomorrow's Company* (RSA 1995). This strongly advocates a style of corporate governance that is fast becoming known as a *stakeholder management perspective*, the key attribute of which is a simultaneous attention to the legitimate interests of all appropriate stakeholders. While a strong rearguard action is being fought by traditionalists, there are encouraging signs that the report has had some impact. For instance, to explore ways of implementing the report's proposals, a permanent 'think tank' – the Centre for Tomorrow's Companies – now exists, and in 1996, Kleinwort Benson Investment Management launched its 'Investment in Tomorrow's Companies' fund, which will invest only in companies that take an inclusive approach to business relationships. In addition, in late 1996, British Telecom announced that it will become the first large, mainstream, commercial organisation in the UK to undergo a regular, independent social audit of how it treats stakeholder groups (Cowe 1996).

Nevertheless, the stakeholder approach is not straightforward. In legal terms, the directors of a company owe a primary duty to protect shareholders' interests, and while this does not prevent other interests being considered as well, it still leaves the problem of defining whose interests should legitimately be considered (see Mitchell *et al.* 1997). The most interesting and comprehensive approach to this matter is to adopt what could be described as the *potential harms and benefits approach*, that is, to define relevant stakeholders as 'those who potentially benefit or are potentially harmed by the actions of an organisation' (Donaldson and Preston 1995). With this in mind, Figure 2.2 portrays stakeholder constituencies to whom this duty of consideration could be argued to be held.

Stakeholder management perspective: simultaneous attention to the legitimate interests of all the appropriate stakeholders of an organisation

Potential harms and benefits approach: a way of identifying the relevant stakeholders of an organisation as those who potentially benefit or are potentially harmed by its actions

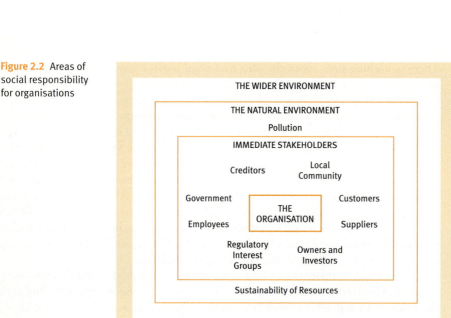

Figure 2.2 Areas of social responsibility for organisations

OB IN ACTION: How Not To Be Seen as a Stakeholder Organisation

In response to criticisms in the City that it has been slow to cut costs and improve returns to shareholders, in late 1999 Barclays Bank announced a future programme of branch closures, ultimately involving the shedding of approximately 6,000 jobs. As part of this initiative, in April 2000 it closed 171 small, rural branches. At a stroke this left 63 villages and small towns without any banking facilities, which in rural areas can be essential for paying bills, etc. As a result, many customers, including some that were elderly or infirm, were faced with the prospect of having to travel to the nearest town to gain access to a branch. This move occurred in tandem with a widely circulated rumour that under a new performance-related remuneration package, top executives of the organisation would be due for bonuses that would run into millions of pounds.

The whole matter prompted a wave of protest from a number of quarters, including rural protection groups and church leaders. Charles Kennedy, the leader of the Liberal Democratic Party, joined in the debate by saying that the closure of rural branches would go down like a 'lead balloon' when taken together with what he described as 'the megalomaniac scale of top executive pay increases'. In addition, the government's environmental minister, Chris Mullin, was said to have publicly advised Barclays' customers to 'vote with their feet' in protest at the moves, by taking their business elsewhere. In the face of this protest, however, Barclays remained unrepentant about its decision, arguing that the closures were necessary in order to improve the bank's financial performance and to avoid it ending up defunct, like Rover or the NatWest bank.

Sources:

Treanor, J and P Heatherington (2000) Bank ignores protests and shuts branches, *The Guardian*, 8 April.

Treanor, J (2000) Big boss, big fees and big trouble, *The Guardian*, 8 April.

Immediate Stakeholders

Immediate stakeholders are groups of people or organisations that are directly affected by the actions of a firm. Some of the issues that concern the interests of these groups have been mentioned earlier, and others will be dealt with in more detail presently, when considering workplace challenges.

The Natural Environment

Responsibility to the natural environment is an area of increasing concern, and there are two particular issues. The first is pollution where, in the past, the record of commercial undertakings has been abysmal. Although there is legislation to outlaw pollution, this does not stop it happening, largely because doing so costs money, and this affects profits. Moreover, those who create the pollution seldom have to live with its consequences, for example, atmospheric pollution creates acid rain, but this tends to fall on another country. Another example is the depletion of the ozone layer and the resultant global warming, the results of which are more likely to be felt by subsequent generations.

The second area of concern is the depletion of the world's natural resources, where there is much debate about moving towards development that is sustainable, that is, development that avoids exploiting natural resources to provide a fast stream of income, which rapidly withers as resources disappear. One example is the problem of deforestation, which is proceeding at an alarming rate in some tropical countries. Trees take a long time to grow and cannot be replaced quickly, even where replanting takes place (which is all too rarely the case). Moreover, the felling of trees reduces the planet's capability to absorb carbon dioxide, a greenhouse gas which contributes considerably to global warming.

The Wider Environment

Theoretically, wider society takes in the whole world and in the past this responsibility has been regarded as the preserve of government. However, there are now suggestions that firms should look beyond their immediate environments, a trend which started in the 1980s, when a number of organisations in America and Europe withdrew from all activities in South Africa as a protest against apartheid. More recently the British charity Oxfam has urged retailers to band together and sign up to a code of practice that would preclude them buying from highly exploitative, overseas producers, many of whom use child labour (Littlefield 1996). Some of Europe's biggest companies have also formed the European Business Network for Social Cohesion and pledged themselves to such measures as bringing socially disadvantaged people into the labour market, creating new jobs and promoting social integration (Overell 1996). More recently, the retailing chain Littlewoods has announced that it will require all of its international suppliers (and their subcontractors) to guarantee that they adopt ethical human resource practices (Prickett 1998).

An important challenge for firms that concerns both ethics and social responsibility is the issue of so-called *whistle-blowers*. Many firms that like to think of themselves as ethical and socially responsible also have employee 'gagging' clauses as a condition of employment. Procedures that allow employees to bring ethical issues to the surface internally are also uncommon and this places employees in an impossible position. While an employee who discovers something unethical can ignore the matter and keep silent, this makes a mockery of having a policy on ethics in the first place. Alternatively, he or she can try to highlight the concern internally, which raises the risk of being considered a troublemaker. In the last resort, if the person makes the matter public outside the organisation, he or she risks dismissal (Smith 2002). However, legislation in the form of the Public Interest Disclosure Act (1998), which became effective in 1999, now gives employees some safeguards in this respect. For instance, in appropriate circumstances it gives a victimised whistle-blower the right to claim unfair dismissal and compensation (Williams 1999). However, by this time an employee would have been dismissed, which begs the question of whether legislation can ever adequately protect people who inform on their employers in this way.

Whistle-blowers: people (usually employed by an organisation) who make public the unethical or questionable activities of an organisation

Evidence from America, which has had laws to protect whistle-blowers in the public sector for several years, would suggest not (Miceli *et al.* 1999). For example, although legislation seems to have encouraged people to 'blow the whistle' if they actually observe wrongdoing, the numbers who say that they have observed something worth reporting tend to have declined. In addition, the number of whistle-blowers who report that they have been subjected to a degree of employer retaliation has increased significantly, as has the number who say they are only prepared to inform on their employer if their anonymity can be protected (Rothschild and Miethe 1999). For these reasons Kenyon (2003) infers that genuinely progressive firms, those that wish to put ethical policies into practice, should develop clear whistle-blowing policies.

OB IN ACTION: Sustainable Development in China

The Chinese government is to cooperate with the World Wide Fund for Nature (WWF) in a drive to reduce imports of illegally logged timber from countries such as Russia and Indonesia. Analysts have said that if successful, the efforts of the Chinese government, WWF and furniture companies such as Ikea and Kingfisher could have a real influence, not only on the worldwide trade in timber and the sustainability of forest resources, but also on propagating the idea of corporate social responsibility in China.

China is the world's second largest importer of wood, with imports of unprocessed wood estimated to reach 100 million cubic metres by 2010 and total demand to reach 200 million cubic metres by the same year. The problem is that currently much of Chinese demand is satisfied by illegal logging operations in countries such as Indonesia and Russia, where primary forests are being felled at an alarming rate for quick profits. The WWF, along with China's State Forestry Bureau and companies, have agreed to implement a system of 'forest certification', in which a certificate is issued by an independent auditor attesting that a shipment of timber comes from a forest that is being well managed. Kingfisher and Ikea, which each sourced roughly $500 million in timber from China last year, have agreed to cooperate with the programme in China and Chinese companies are planning to improve their corporate social responsibility in this way. 'As the world's second largest importer of wood, China must take full responsibility for global forestry conservation,' says Claude Martin, director-general of WWF international. 'China's efforts so far in forest restoration and forest-sustainable management are a good start.' For instance, in 1998 China undertook significant changes to its forestry policies following devastating floods along the Yangtze river that were partly caused by the lack of forest cover. Since then the forest area in China has been increasing and the 'WWF hopes that China will become a model for promoting the legal timber trade,' says Martin.

Source: Kynge, J (2003) Investing in China: Beijing sows seeds of conservation, *The Financial Times*, 5 November.

REPLAY

- Organisations are likely to come under increasing pressure to meet the challenge of ensuring that they behave in a socially responsible way towards an ever-widening constituency of external stakeholder groups, possibly by becoming stakeholder organisations.

CASE STUDY 2.1: Ballast Ltd – The External Environment

Ballast Ltd is a well-established quarrying company that is located in the Peak District, an area of outstanding natural beauty in the centre of England. It produces limestone ballast which is mainly used for roadworks and, while it operates on several sites, its main source of production is the Blunt Tor quarry. This has been in operation ever since the company acquired the mineral rights to a site of 100 acres (virtually the right to remove a whole mountain) over 40 years ago. Since the cost of purchasing the site has long since been recovered, it is a highly profitable company that pays good dividends to shareholders. However, the quarry is situated in a national park and because the company's operations are a blot on the landscape, there is constant pressure on the planning authority to withdraw the firm's licence for mineral extraction. The company has a large fleet of lorries which are used to remove crushed stone from the site and the planning authority constantly complains to the firm about the way that these vehicles damage what would otherwise be quiet country lanes and create excessive noise in villages. One solution to this problem, which has been proposed by a railway company, is for Ballast Ltd to pay towards the cost of constructing a spur from the branch line that runs along a nearby valley. This would have the dual advantage of keeping the branch line open, thus ensuring a public rail service to the area. To date Ballast has resisted moving to rail transport because this would be slightly more expensive and less flexible.

Nevertheless, the firm makes a large annual donation to the National Trust, a charitable organisation devoted to safeguarding sites of historic and archaeological interest and areas of natural beauty. In business circles, however, this is regarded somewhat cynically as an attempt by the chairman to 'buy his way on to the New Year's Honours List'.

Questions

1. Who are the relevant stakeholders of Ballast Ltd?

2. Would you describe the firm as a stakeholder organisation?

WORKPLACE CHALLENGES

While everything discussed so far in this chapter has some impact at the level of the workplace, there are five workplace issues that are likely to pose significant organisational challenges in the future. These are: the changing composition of the workforce, which results in challenges of a more diverse workforce and more diverse working arrangements; changes in working practices, including structural changes; employment relations/employee voice; organisational learning; and the psychological contract.

The Changing Composition of the Workforce

Until comparatively recently, different occupations were filled by people who were similar in certain respects; for instance, the higher professions were largely staffed by middle-class males who were mostly educated at a small number of (elite) schools and universities. Since some jobs were regarded as male occupations, and others as more suitable for females, people tended to get channelled into occupational streams quite early in life and stay there until retirement. Indeed, it was often assumed that women would enter the workforce direct from school, marry at an early age and leave to have a family, perhaps never to return. Thus women were not expected to embrace the idea of a career and tended to be confined to a restricted range of junior occupations, usually jobs with common, transferable skills (such as typing or retail sales), where little physical effort was required.

Conversely, males were conditioned to think of themselves as family breadwinners who entered work after full-time education and remained in continuous employment until retirement age. Nevertheless, there was a high degree of segregation, even among men. Those with low educational attainment tended to gravitate to the ranks of the unskilled or semi-skilled, where physical effort dominated their jobs. Others, with a slightly higher level of education, could become craftsmen or technicians, which involved further study, and those with a good education would perhaps enter jobs with real prospects of advancement.

In the last four decades a number of changes have altered these historic patterns. Traditional industries that were largely staffed along gender lines have declined and changed technologies and production methods now allow jobs that were once physically arduous to be undertaken by women. Wider access to further and higher education has also resulted in a larger number of women who are well qualified, and the population now contains an increased number of well-educated people from diverse ethnic origins, who (rightfully) seek equality of opportunity with other citizens. Declining birthrates and longer life expectancies have also produced a population where people have longer active lives, and some of them have no desire to leave the world of work early. The net result of all these trends is a heterogeneous working population and, for most firms, a need to cope with two different but interconnected workplace challenges: a more diverse workforce and more diverse working arrangements.

Workforce Diversity

A challenge facing firms and the country as a whole is how to avoid the sensitive, unpleasant and potentially volatile behaviour that can arise when groups or individuals who differ in some respect come into close contact. Individuals have the same prejudices,

Table 2.2 Male and female employment expressed as percentages of total UK workforce

	1971 (%)	1994 (%)	2003 (%)
Female employees			
Full-time	25.2	26.6	27.6
Part-time	12.7	23.0	20.9
Male employees			
Full-time	59.4	45.1	46.7
Part-time	2.7	5.3	4.8

contract employees, to provide cover for absent full-time employees. In Great Britain, until the Employment Protection (Consolidation) Act 1978 was amended by the Employment Protection (Part-time Employees) Regulations of 1995, many such employees were treated as an underclass in terms of employment rights. Moreover, while permanent part-timers often get a comparable rate of pay to full-time workers, they seldom qualify for enhanced rates for working overtime and are often excluded from certain important benefits such as sick pay and pensions. Indeed, they often have lower access to training and development to enhance their skills, which perhaps explains why many employers tend to view them as a resource that underperforms. However, the tendency for non-standard workers to be employed on conditions that verge on being exploitative is unlikely to be tolerated indefinitely. There are several items of impending European legislation that are explicitly designed to give equal or pro-rata rights to non-standard workers in a number of areas; for example, in rates of pay, social security entitlement and vocational training.

Clearly there is a huge paradox in the current situation. While employers see these working arrangements as advantageous, at the same time they perceive that they are not getting the best out of these employees. Although non-standard working has always existed, very little is known about these working arrangements and even less about non-standard workers. There is, for example, evidence which suggests that full-time and part-time workers have different job-related attitudes (Fenton-O'Creevy 1995), but as things stand there is an imperfect understanding of why such differences exist. Some job-related attitudes arise from the degree of match between a person's needs, wants and expectations of work and the extent to which these are met; for instance, some might only wish to work part-time, while others would rather be in full-time employment. If part-time and full-time workers have different needs and wants, but the work only caters for the needs of full-time employees, some degree of under-performance by part-time workers could be expected. Thus, if organisations are intent on making greater use of non-standard workers, and wish to obtain a real advantage from doing so, they are faced with three challenges:

1. to fully understand what these employees seek to obtain from work;
2. to design the work experience accordingly;
3. to find ways of complying with new legislation when it appears so that non-standard workers are not treated as an underclass.

OB IN ACTION: The Return of Wildcat Industrial Action?

Wildcat industrial action has made an unexpected comeback. There have been three high-profile outbreaks since mid-summer 2003 and observers are now beginning to wonder whether the infection is becoming contagious.

It was not meant to be like this. Tory legislation was supposed to fetter union activists, to prevent them from such impromptu shows of strength and for unions temped to ignore this tortuous ritual, there was the prospect of heavy fines and asset sequestration. So why have firefighters, postal workers and airport staff all recently taken unofficial action? If ringleaders have weighed up the risks against the potential benefits, their behaviour could make sense. Although any worker who strikes can be dismissed for breach of contract, people who strike en masse know that employers rarely sack large cohorts of workers for striking. Those who have taken action over the past few months know this and, faced with a pressing problem, workers may not be prepared to wait before deploying the strike weapon. For example, the Fire Brigades Union was not informed that its members would not receive the full pay rise they wanted until exactly a week before it was due, while postal workers belonging to the Communication Workers' Union claimed their working conditions were being altered without notice. As Lionel Fulton of the Labour Research Department says, 'If people feel badly treated they are always inclined to try to do something as soon as possible.' Union members are also aware that wildcat industrial action can be devastatingly effective. The summer BA dispute was the classic example. Trade union negotiators had succeeded in breaking the iron link between pay and productivity improvements because the prospect of cancelled flights and serious damage to BA's reputation was too terrifying for management to contemplate.

But this does not explain the sudden bunching together of three separate, significant cases of wildcat action. Wildcat breeds wildcat, argue some observers. Unofficial action by postal workers spread across the country like wildfire. Working-to-rule by firefighters followed the next day and as one analyst of the union movement observes, 'Firefighters must have thought, the postal workers have done it and the sky hasn't fallen in.' So what does the future hold? Carolyn Jones of the union-financed Institute of Employment Rights says the solution is to remove the straitjacket imposed by union laws: 'Sound industrial relations depend on the law offering workers the freedom to express discontent through organised industrial action. The complicated nature of the present system limits this freedom.' Others are more relaxed. David Yeandle of the EEF manufacturers' organisation regards the three recent high-profile cases as isolated incidents 'with no connection to each other'.

However, Mr Fulton is more ambivalent: 'If unofficial action is seen to be successful it may become more common. But if it fails, the opposite lesson will be learned.'

Source: Turner, D (2003) Wildcat industrial action returns with a roar, *The Financial Times*, 6 November.

Changes in Working Practices

Business Process Re-engineering (BPR)

Business process re-engineering: a fundamental rethink and, if necessary, radical redesign of business processes, with the aim of making dramatic improvements to critical aspects of performance, such as cost, quality, service and speed

According to its foremost advocates, Hammer and Champey (1993), re-engineering involves a fundamental rethink and, if necessary, radical redesign of business processes, with the aim of making dramatic improvements to critical aspects of performance such as cost, quality, service and speed. This goes well beyond other initiatives such as TQM and in its pure form could mean starting with a clean slate and redesigning the organisation (including its structure) from scratch.

Any new business technique that has a catchy, with-it name seems to be attractive to managers these days, particularly if it promises economic salvation. Indeed, new techniques are often so 'talked up' that managers feel uncomfortably outdated until they have embraced the latest fad. Re-engineering emerged in just such a way in the early 1990s and was quickly embraced by many organisations. However, far from delivering the enhanced performance it promised, in many organisations profits, effectiveness and efficiency actually declined (Grey and Mitev 1995). While the reasons for this are often very complex, there seems to have been at least one common mistake. Many of these firms appeared to have neglected an elementary, but very important, point: that the changes inherent in BPR are often so radical and upsetting to employees that the commitment, loyalty and teamwork that an organisation has taken years to build up is virtually destroyed overnight. This was not really due to a flaw in the original conception of BPR and in many respects the blame can be laid at the door of organisational managers, many of whom had interpreted its principles in a highly selective way. A large number of them equated BPR as being synonymous with labour shedding, which became a must, even in highly profitable firms. So strong was this trend that Davenport, one of the early advocates of BPR, stated that re-engineering had gone seriously awry and had become a 'fad that forgets people' (Davenport 1992).

A penetrating analysis of this pattern of failure by Mumford and Hendricks (1996) notes that while there is nothing inherently wrong with the design principles suggested by BPR, if these are to work in practice the design must be compatible with prevailing human values in an organisation, otherwise people will find ways to undermine what takes place. Mumford and Hendricks argue that where a firm embraces BPR it must either work around existing cultures, or try to modify cultures to suit BPR. Since cultural modification can be a long, drawn-out process, the first option is the most feasible, but this is precisely what firms had failed to do. No doubt BPR will continue to be adopted by many more firms, and the challenges for these organisations are threefold:

- to recognise that successful BPR requires a willingness by employees to put the changes in place, and make them work;
- to anticipate the potential effects on human resources;
- wherever possible, to adapt the initiative to match existing value systems rather than expect values to change automatically to meet the requirements of what is proposed.

Empowerment

Empowerment: giving people the authority to make decisions in their own area of operations without the approval of someone above

Like re-engineering, empowerment is a buzzword in management circles and, as a practice, it also has distinct structural implications. Claydon and Doyle (1996) point out that much of its appeal to managers lies in two features:

- its promise to offer a way of obtaining a higher level of performance from employees without the use of strict supervision and control;
- its humanistic rhetoric, which allows managers to feel that they are doing the right thing by giving employees autonomy and opportunities for self-development and personal growth.

Theoretically, empowerment gives employees the authority to make decisions in their own areas of activity, without getting the approval of someone above, and while this sounds much the same as delegated authority, it is much more. It is intended to be results-orientated, which means that people are not only allowed to make decisions but they are also encouraged to use their initiative and, given the necessary resources, to implement their decisions. This, however, is empowerment in theory, and while saying that employees have been empowered is one thing, empowering them in practice is another.

Almost inevitably, empowerment occurs in a delayered or downsized organisation, and while there is often initial enthusiasm among employees, this can quickly turn to disillusionment when they start to ask where all this is leading. For example, managers tend to assume that the more interesting work is sufficient reward in itself, and so employees find themselves working much harder for the same remuneration (Cunningham *et al.* 1996), and many of the things that employees hoped for in the future, such as promotion and security, become far less accessible. The challenge for organisations is to avoid these pitfalls, which often occur because empowerment has been introduced for reasons of fashion, in conditions where it is unsuitable or cannot possibly work. Here it has been powerfully argued that empowerment is not advantageous in all circumstances, nor is it suitable for all employees (Bowen and Lawler 1992). It could be advantageous in a dynamic, unpredictable environment, where technology is complex and non-routine, to develop long-term relationships with customers and, above all, where employees have high needs for personal growth. However, if the conditions are the reverse, there are few, if any, advantages.

Employment Relations/Employee Voice

Employment relations, or rather a lack of some of the traditional employment relations mechanisms, could well become one of the most significant challenges facing organisations in the future. Prior to the late 1970s trade unions were extremely powerful and well over half of the British workforce was unionised. Most firms were therefore acutely aware of an industrial relations challenge, if only because *collective bargaining*, in which employee interests were represented by a trade union, was the dominant way of setting the terms and conditions of the relationship between an organisation and its employees. However, there have since been two major recessions, a growth in the service sector of the economy, which is not widely unionised, and eighteen years of anti-union legislation that has severely restricted trade unions in representing their members' interests. The net result is that trade union membership is now only a little over half of what it was in 1979, only one-third of the workforce is unionised and firms that do not recognise unions for collective bargaining are far more commonplace. While the legislation mentioned above would have enabled most organisations to de-recognise trade unions quite easily (had they wished to do so), many continue to recognise trade unions, and it must be assumed this is because they perceive that

Employment relations: the relationship between an organisation and its employees, which includes the full range of interactions and communications between the two parties and the processes through which they adjust to each other's needs and wants

Collective bargaining: a way of setting and modifying the terms and conditions of employment in which employees are represented collectively by a trade union or other association that speaks for them with 'one voice'

the advantages outweigh the disadvantages. Nevertheless, in many organisations these changes have resulted in ambiguity. While the earlier system of industrial relations has probably been dismembered for good, it cannot be said that a clear replacement system has emerged in its place, and what tends to exist in many firms is a host of *ad hoc*, piecemeal practices.

Whether it is good or bad, close or distant, every firm has a relationship with its employees and, while the prior way of constructing and modifying the relationship has largely disappeared, there are four important trends that make it essential that firms address this matter. First, some of the evidence cited earlier in the chapter suggests that much of the British workforce is apprehensive about future conditions in organisations.

Second, a survey conducted by National Opinion Polls revealed that the vast majority of the British public is far from being anti-union. Indeed, there is a widespread belief that the legislative restrictions placed on trade unions between 1979 and 1997 went much too far (Kellner 1996). Thus there are now tentative signs that the decline in union membership may be about to be reversed (Walsh 1999).

Third, trade unions have changed tremendously and many now embrace a philosophy of working in partnership with employers to create an environment within which employee needs for security and fair treatment can be met by a prosperous organisation (Monks 1999).

Finally, the EU directive on information and consultation, which is due to be implemented in Great Britain by 2005, is likely to have an important impact. The draft proposals require organisations with more than 50 workers to consult with representative employee bodies and even in non-union firms an employer could be forced to set up a works council if petitioned to do so by 10 per cent of the workforce. Clearly, therefore, there is an intention that organisations should establish firm provisions for *employee voice*.

Employee voice: a two-way dialogue that enables employees to have a say, or influence, on matters that affect them

Whatever is said against the industrial relations system of earlier years, it is difficult to deny that it allowed employees some say in matters that affected their daily working lives. This has been conspicuously absent in the 1980s and much of the 1990s and so the challenge for organisations and their managers is to recognise the new importance of employment relations and employee voice. People are always far more committed to decisions that they have had a hand in shaping, and so if a firm wants a committed and loyal workforce, the challenge is to establish methods and procedures that enable employees to have a say in matters that affect them (Luchak 2003).

The Learning Organisation

It is widely acknowledged that firms who compete in the globalised marketplace need to be more proactive in their stance and dynamic in their response to market changes. While advances in the new information technologies and initiatives such as the total quality approach can all help in this respect, it can be argued that this is not enough, and that firms must adopt a radically different philosophy about sensing and adapting to the environment. The concept which currently embraces this way of thinking is that of the learning organisation, an idea that was first put forward by Argyris and Schön (1978, 1996), who distinguished between single- and double-loop learning.

Single-loop learning: learning how to improve performance in achieving goals and objectives when the goals and objectives remain fixed and unchanging

Single-loop learning is concerned with improving performance in achieving a fixed and unchanging goal or objective. For example, although it might be difficult to achieve,

CASE STUDY 2.2: Ballast Ltd – Workplace Matters

During the last year there have been a number of workplace developments in the company. Quarrying stone and crushing it down into small ballast is a dirty and sometimes dangerous operation. However, it is heavily mechanised and is nowhere near as labour intensive as in bygone days, when quarry owners often relied on convict labour. The company mainly uses local people, of whom there is a plentiful supply. For this reason, and although the company pays minimum wage rates because there is little in the way of alternative employment in the area, the workforce is relatively passive. With an eye to increasing its profitability, significant changes to operations are in the process of consideration. The most radical proposal is to outsource the transportation of materials from the Blunt Tor site. The management of the company have proposed that existing drivers would effectively become owners of their lorries, thus becoming self-employed contractors to the firm. To facilitate this the firm would loan drivers the money to purchase the vehicles, and the loan would be repaid out of what the firm pays them for transporting the crushed stone. By doing this it would save on the indirect costs of employing these people, and all the maintenance work and running costs for the vehicles would become the responsibility of the new owners. In announcing this proposal the chairman stated that the board of directors strongly believed in empowering employees and could think of no finer way of putting this into practice than by giving them the opportunity to become businessmen in their own right.

Questions

1. Using the above information and where appropriate that from Case Study 2.1, how would you describe Ballast's approach to its internal stakeholders?

2. If implemented, is the proposal likely to make relationships with external stakeholders easier or more difficult?

Double-loop learning: a style of learning that goes beyond learning how to achieve existing goals and that involves questioning whether the assumptions that underpin the goals are appropriate for the organisation

Adaptive learning: learning how to adapt to environmental change

an annual goal of increasing sales by 10 per cent involves no change in the basic assumption that an annual 10 per cent increase is an appropriate goal. *Double-loop learning*, however, is rather different. A firm that functions in this way will constantly re-evaluate its goals and objectives and examine whether the values, beliefs and assumptions that underpin them are valid. This is not just a matter of changing the way it thinks about the market, but instead of simply asking the question 'are we doing things right?' it addresses the more basic question of 'are we doing the right thing?' This probably requires a change in the whole culture of an organisation, otherwise it is difficult to bring matters into the open to challenge existing assumptions. According to Argyris and Schön, only when this is possible has the organisation truly learned how to learn.

More recently Senge (1991) has elaborated on these ideas and distinguished between two types of learning: adaptive and generative. *Adaptive learning* consists of learning how to adapt to environmental changes, something that many firms are forced to do or go out of existence. For example, the latest generation of micro-computers are so powerful that they have taken over many of the functions that could once only be performed by a mainframe, and this has prompted huge changes in computer

Generative learning: a constant re-evaluation of the environment, together with the creative adaption that enables anticipation of environmental changes and the development of appropriate responses

manufacturers such as IBM. The more advanced *generative learning* style is usually what is meant by a fully developed learning organisation. It involves a constant re-evaluation of the way that the environment is experienced and a style of learning that goes well beyond simply adapting to changes. Rather, the organisation becomes highly creative and innovative and tries to anticipate what is likely to occur.

While an organisation of this type is likely to be far more resilient and successful in today's dynamic, fast-moving environmental conditions, examples of the fully developed learning organisation are comparatively rare, and so it is essentially a view of 'what might be' rather than 'what is' (Pedler *et al.* 1997). For this reason McGill and Slocum (1993) point out that the journey to become a fully developed learning organisation can be a long one that takes place in four distinct stages.

Stage 1: The knowing organisation is one that fully understands its current environment. It aims to be highly efficient and in control of events by making small, adaptive, incremental changes. However, if the environment remains stable and predictable there is little need for the organisation to change, and so long as the need to learn does not arise, it is perfectly capable of being successful.

Stage 2: The understanding organisation whereby the firm seeks to understand more clearly what is happening in its environment and relies on its strong cohesive culture and customer loyalty to pull it through any changes.

Stage 3: The thinking organisation recognises the problematic nature of environmental changes. However, its actions tend to be reactive and, while it constantly scans the environment, its focus is on identifying potential problems and developing a fast reaction.

Stage 4: The learning organisation whereby change is viewed as a way of life and there is some emphasis on getting ahead of the game. Every experience is regarded as a learning opportunity, nothing is sacred and anything that stands in the way of improvement is open to challenge. Thus experimentation or trying new methods as a way of enhancing relationships with customers and other environmental elements is actively encouraged.

As can be seen, the fully developed learning organisation would be radically different from what is found in most places. In conventional firms, vision is deemed to be the prerogative of top managers, who also decide what has to be done, with everyone else following instructions. Senge (1993) points out that a learning organisation requires a totally different ethos. Since vision is assumed to be capable of emerging from anyone, the top management role is to encourage and nurture vision in others. Moreover, putting the vision into practice becomes everybody's responsibility, which means that highly collaborative working, with little emphasis on status differences, must become the norm.

There seems little doubt that if a firm becomes a learning organisation it could have a strong competitive edge in the fast-moving globalised economy, and this poses a significant challenge for many organisations and their managers. Becoming a learning organisation means unlearning established patterns of behaviour that most people have come to accept as the appropriate way for an organisation to function. Here the

REPLAY

- A significant workplace challenge that will confront many organisations is to provide equality of opportunity for a workforce of a more diverse ethnic and gender composition.
- Organisations will also be faced with the challenge of catering for the needs and expectations of people employed in more diverse working patterns, e.g. non-standard patterns of attendance.
- Another significant challenge will be to overcome feelings of employee demoralisation arising from significant structural changes and to empower employees in a real (rather than cosmetic) way.
- Constructing new and appropriate systems of employee relations will also be a significant organisational challenge for the future, particularly in the light of impending European Union social legislation.
- To cope with ever more volatile and fast-moving environments, a major challenge for many firms will be to become learning organisations.

greatest challenge is for managers, many of whom have learned their craft in organisations where being in charge, being the person who has the ideas and being the one who directs and controls the activities of others is the real meat of a manager's job.

The Psychological Contract

Legally the relationship between employer and employee is expressed in the contract of employment. The terms of the contract come from many sources including those expressly agreed by the parties at the point when employment first commences, i.e. salary, hours, etc. Its content is also affected by laws conferring basic rights and obligations on the parties, for example those covering Health and Safety.

Formal contract: the formally agreed terms of the employment relationship, i.e. the legal concept as reflected in the 'contract of employment'

Important though it is, the legal view of the relationship is somewhat oversimplified. It ultimately rests on the idea that the relationship can be reduced to an economic contract, the terms of which can be exactly specified. Although the employment relationship does include a contract to exchange service for rewards, it is notoriously difficult to be specific about some of the things exchanged. For example, the relationship is not a one-off transaction, but something that extends into the future, and it can be impossible to state precisely what terms of exchange will be needed then. These features add a whole new dimension to the contract and the nature of the exchange process that it involves. Fortunately, there is a framework that is capable of capturing some of the potential complexity and subtlety of the relationship. This is the concept of the psychological contract, which was originally articulated by Schein (1980) and recently there has been a reawakening of interest in the idea (Guest and Conway 2002; Rousseau and Parks 1993).

Informal contract: a less formal expression of the employment relationship that reflects a degree of give and take between the parties

Schein draws attention to the idea that in the employment relationship there are really three types of contract. The *formal contract* largely reflects the economic aspects of the exchange and is normally embraced by the legal conception of a contract of employment. In addition there is always an *informal contract*, some of the

Table 2.3 The psychological contract – possible expectations of employees and employers

Employee expectations (of employer)	Employer expectations (of employees)
• Working conditions will be safe and as pleasant as possible	• Acceptance of the main values of the organisation
• Jobs will be interesting and satisfying	• Recognition that diligence and conscientiousness in pursuit of objectives are important to the organisation
• Reasonable efforts to provide job security	• To avoid abusing the trust and goodwill of superiors
• Involvement or consultation in decisions that affect them	• To have concern for the reputation of the organisation
• Equality of opportunity and fairness in selection and promotion	• Loyalty and willingness to tolerate a degree of inconvenience for the good of the organisation
• Opportunities for personal development and progression	• Trustworthiness and honesty
• To be treated with consideration and respect	• To conform to the accepted norms of behaviour in the organisation
• Fair and equitable remuneration	• Consideration for others

components of which are derived from wider social norms about how people should treat each other, while others are more specific to a particular organisation; for example, how much give and take there will be about timekeeping and working late. Usually the contents of formal and informal contracts are well understood and discussed by the parties to the relationship.

The third type of contract, the *psychological contract*, has contents that are seldom, if ever, explicitly stated. These largely consist of the unvoiced expectations and obligations of the parties, neither of whom could be consciously aware of their expectations until they are not met. Therefore, the psychological contract reflects intangible needs, wants and expectations that vary widely, and its details can be very difficult to specify. Nevertheless, some idea of what it might embrace can be seen in Table 2.3.

Psychological contract: an (unvoiced) set of expectations that the parties have of each other and obligations that they feel towards each other

All three of these contracts have an impact on the nature and shape of the relationship between employers and employees. For the relationship to come into existence the formal contract has to be seen by both parties as acceptable. By putting in place convenient variations through which the parties accommodate each other, the informal contract acts as a lubricant to the formal one. Finally, the psychological contract goes to the very heart of the exchange by expressing emotional aspects of the relationship, and if either organisation or employee views the psychological contract as unacceptable, the exchange is likely to seen as unequal and weighted in favour of the other party. Nobody likes to feel that they are being cheated and, as the OB in Action box on page 53 indicates, where this happens the relationship deteriorates, there is less likelihood that the other party will be treated with consideration, and there will probably be no desire for the relationship to continue.

Virtually everything that has been covered in this chapter has implications for the state of the psychological contract in an organisation. In responding to the challenges of the last two decades, notably the imperative to safeguard survival, many organisations had to take steps that were, to say the least, unpleasant for employees and, in so doing, damaged the psychological contract. Having emerged from this process, however, many of them now find that they have a strong need for the loyalty, perseverance, commitment and emotional attachment of their employees, otherwise future survival could be placed in jeopardy. The challenge, therefore, is for organisations to take decisive steps to rebuild their relationships with employees in a way that results in psychological contracts that are seen by employees and managers alike as fair and equitable.

CONTEMPORARY CHALLENGES: AN OVERVIEW AND PREVIEW

Although the challenges described in this chapter have been considered separately, they are not discrete issues; many are strongly interconnected, and some indication of this has been given at various points in the text. To reinforce this, it is now relevant to highlight some of the more important connections, which are brought together in the influence model given in Figure 2.3.

Since the environmental forces are not only challenges in their own right, but are also the ones that have prompted many of the internal challenges, it is more convenient to start at this level and work inwards. As can be seen, the **globalisation** of world trade has two primary effects: first, an effect on a **domestic economy** and second, by creating **changed market characteristics** in a country. These two outcomes are interconnected. For instance, if organisations within a particular national economy are less able to compete in the global marketplace, balance of payments problems can arise, the country's currency is less valued abroad and this makes it even harder for firms to compete globally. Changed market conditions often result in a **changed basis of competition**, and when this was coupled with the poor state of the economy in Great Britain, the outcome was **organisational size reductions**. This does not necessarily mean

Figure 2.3 The interconnected nature of contemporary organisational challenges

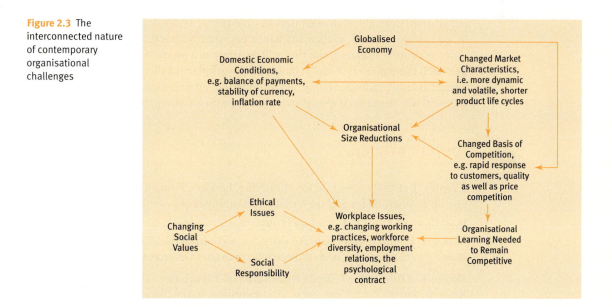

that firms produce less in terms of volume or value of outputs, although initially, when the effects of the global economy were first felt, the sheer inability to compete often had this effect. In the longer run, however, the firms that survived usually did so by becoming more efficient, which in turn gives rise to some of the **workplace issues**, for example changed working practices and employment relations. The changed basis of competition also creates pressures to modify internal processes, cultures and structures, and this is shown by the arrow leading to the **learning organisation**, which in turn connects to workplace issues.

However, these market-related challenges are not the only ones that can arise. To some extent the nature of the domestic economy also creates pressure for changes in workforce composition; for example, increased numbers of women might seek to enter the labour market to help out with the family budget. In addition, **changing social values** about the role of women in society play a part; for instance, the increasing desire on the part of women to be something more than a housewife who stays at home. Importantly, it is also the changing social values that give rise to some of the **ethical issues** and **social responsibility** issues with which firms have to contend.

Although all of these pressures have some degree of connection, they tend to result in challenges that have greater significance for some aspects of organisational life than others. This book deals with both macro and micro aspects of organisations and some of the challenges tend to be felt more strongly at a micro level, while others are distinctly macro in nature. Therefore, while all of the challenges discussed in this chapter will resurface somewhere in the book, their significance tends to depend on the topic covered in a particular chapter. Certain of them have a pervasive effect at both macro and micro levels, notably the ethical, social responsibility and diversity challenges, all of which become very important when international influences impinge on an organisation.

Other challenges are more significant at specific levels; for instance, the challenges of globalisation and the learning organisation are essentially macro level issues. As such, they will resurface more frequently in chapters that deal with different aspects of macro organisational behaviour, as will certain of the workplace issues that have implications throughout an organisation. Conversely, workforce diversity and the ethics of some organisational practices can have a particularly strong impact where individual differences are considered, and they will resurface in a prominent way in chapters that deal with these matters. Finally, most of the workplace challenges have their greatest impact at either individual or group levels within an organisation, which means that they will re-emerge in chapters covering these aspects of organisational behaviour.

FURTHER READING

Cannon, T (1994) *Corporate Responsibility*, London: Pitman. A serious but readable text on business ethics and the social responsibilities of organisations.

Davidson, M J and C L Cooper (1992) *Shattering the Glass Ceiling: The Woman Manager*, London: Chapman. An extensive account of the difficulties facing females wishing to have careers, and of those who manage to overcome the barriers.

Doyle, C (2003) *Work and Organisational Psychology: An Introduction With Attitude*, Hove: Psychology Press. An interesting, easily digested text that examines (often critically) current trends and likely future developments in organisations.

Dunning, J N (1993) *The Globalisation of Business*, London: Thompson. Globalisation and its development is explained in an easy-to-understand way, together with informed speculation about possible future trends.

Hutton, W (1995) *The State We're In*, London: Vintage. A penetrating account of the economic and political developments over the last two decades which gives a good background to many of the challenges facing organisations.

Legge, K (1995) *Human Resource Management: Rhetorics and Realities*, London: Macmillan. A good exploration of the major debates about human resource management and its potential contribution in British organisations.

Rollinson, D J (1993) *Understanding Employee Relations: A Behavioural Approach*, Wokingham: Addison-Wesley. A readable and comprehensive introduction to British employee relations.

Rousseau, D and J Parks (1993) 'The contracts of individuals and organisations', *Organisational Behaviour*, 15(1), 1–43. An article which gives a sound and extensive exploration of the concept of the psychological contract.

Senge, P (1991) *The Fifth Discipline: The Art of Organisational Learning*, New York: Doubleday.

Stein, H (2001) *Nothing Personal, Just Business: A Guided Journey Into Organisational Darkness*, Westport: Quorum Books. Although a difficult read in places, a penetrating book that exposes the interior of many current organisations to reveal how they operate on the assumption that everyone is made disposable in the name of organisational survival.

Wilkinson, A, M Marchington, T Redman and E Snape (1997) *Total Quality Management: Organisational Change and Human Resource Management*, London: Macmillan. A critical examination of TQM that draws on recent research to assess it as a vehicle for organisational change.

REVIEW AND DISCUSSION QUESTIONS

1. Explain how the organisational size reductions that took place in the 1980s and 1990s have resulted in significant challenges for organisations now and for the future. What steps do organisations need to take to address these challenges?

2. Define ethics and social responsibility and explain why there is likely to be an overlap between ethics and social responsibility on the part of an organisation. Illustrate your conclusions by explaining how ethical considerations apply to other areas in addition to the interests of immediate stakeholders.

3. Reflect on the challenges and the conditions giving rise to them that have been described throughout the chapter and in particular the challenges arising at the workplace level. Assuming that an organisation identifies that it has a need to address every one of the challenges, to what extent do you feel that this would be possible, while still pursuing the aim of being a stakeholder organisation?

Individual Characteristics

As the diagram indicates, this part of the book consists of three chapters, all of which deal with important ways in which people can be distinguished as individuals. These characteristics have a bearing on a person's behaviour in an organisation and, among other things, they are likely to have a strong impact on whether the individual is more suitable for some roles rather than others. However, it is important to realise that while these characteristics exist in everyone, they are abstract constructs that are used as 'expressions of convenience' to summarise what are presumed to be certain mental activities. Although they all have different names they are not 'stand-alone' characteristics, and so the short integrative section that follows Chapter 5 traces links between them.

Section 5: The Organisational Level
Chapter 15: Goals and Effectiveness

Section 4: The Interpersonal Level
Chapter 11: Groups
Chapter 12: Leadership – Basic Theories
Chapter 13: Leadership – Advanced Theories
Chapter 14: Power Politics and Conflict

Integration 3

Section 3: The Intrapersonal Level
Chapter 6: Memory and Learning
Chapter 7: Motivation – The Foundations
Chapter 8: Motivation – Advanced Theories
Chapter 9: Decision Making
Chapter 10: Stress

Integration 2

Section 2: Individual Characteristics
Chapter 3: Personality and Intelligence
Chapter 4: Perception
Chapter 5: Attitudes

Integration 1

Section 1: Introductory Concepts
Chapter 1: Introduction to OB and OA
Chapter 2: Contemporary Challenges

Chapter 16:
Organisational
Structure

Chapter 17:
Organisational
Design

Chapter 18:
Control

Integration 4
Integration 5

Chapter 19:
Culture and
Climate

Chapter 20:
Communication

Chapter 21:
Change and
Development

Chapter 22:
Globalisation and
the Organisation
Across Cultures

Chapter 3

Personality, Intelligence and Aptitude

LEARNING OUTCOMES

After studying this chapter you should be able to:

- define personality, describe the factors that influence personality differences and explain the relationship between personality and behaviour

- explain the differences between idiographic and nomothetic approaches to personality

- explain in outline the basic principles of psychodynamic theory and contrast psychodynamic, interpersonal and humanistic approaches

- describe, compare and contrast trait and type theories of personality and explain how personality is normally assessed

- define intelligence, explain the controversial nature of the concept and distinguish between intelligence, attitude and ability

- appreciate that personality, intelligence and aptitude can reflect the influence of cultural factors and that this has implications for interpreting the results of tests that measure these characteristics

INTRODUCTION

By definition all individuals are different and ways that are commonly used to distinguish between them are their personalities and their intelligence. Starting with personality this chapter deals with these differences. The concept is defined and the two major approaches to the study of human personality are briefly explained. Some of the factors that can shape personality are then considered, followed by an explanation of several major personality theories. Finally, we look at the significance of personality characteristics in the work context and describe the ways in which personality can be assessed.

Intelligence, which is the next topic to be considered, is one of the most controversial subjects in the field of psychology and, for this reason, the meaning of the concept is discussed at some length. The major theories concerning the structure of human intelligence are explained and its measurement discussed. Finally, to consider its practical implications in a work context, the chapter briefly explores two concepts closely allied to intelligence: aptitude and ability.

PERSONALITY

The Importance of Personality

Just as people can be distinguished in terms of physical characteristics, individuals think in slightly different ways, and experience their environments in unique fashions. Most of us recognise this in others and routinely use words to distinguish people in terms of their mental characteristics, saying, for example, that someone is moody, lively, morose or bookish. In doing this we are using words that describe what we see as the essence of a person's mental make-up or, to put it another way, his or her personality. These descriptions are also used to predict the behaviour of people, and at some time we have all probably said something like: 'Of course he does that; what do you expect? He's that type of person.' However, these are only implicit personality theories; in psychology, personality has a much more rigorous meaning than that used in everyday conversation. It is an all-embracing concept that reflects how individuals interpret and react to the world, and this goes to the very heart of the way that people differ as individuals. Although there are many different psychological theories of personality, for the purposes of discussion the definition used here is:

> **those relatively stable and enduring aspects of an individual that distinguish him/her from other people and at the same time form a basis for our predictions concerning his/her future behaviour.** **(Wright *et al.* 1970)**

This represents the mainstream view in psychology and, while there is some debate about how stable and enduring a person's characteristics are, it has two important implications:

- stability and permanence imply that it is possible to identify an individual's personality characteristics, and
- that if the characteristics are identified they can be used to predict the person's behaviour.

The Origins of Personality

Personality is probably one of the most misused terms in the English language (Terborg 1981). Evaluations are often made without any real evidence, and people often over-simplify matters by referring to what they believe to be an individual's single most important characteristic; for example, Bill is aggressive or Mary is timid. Considerably more evidence than this is required fully to describe an individual's personality. In scientific psychology there are two main approaches: the **nomothetic** approach, which is mainly concerned with identifying the basic dimensions of human personality and devising ways to measure it; and the **idiographic** approach, which focuses on the uniqueness of the individual and treats him or her as an integrated whole. One of the main differences between these two approaches is the extent to which an individual's personality is regarded as fixed, which is a reflection of an even more fundamental controversy in psychology: the *nature versus nurture debate*.

Naturists hold that mental and physical characteristics are largely determined by genetic make-up. Conversely, the nurture school regards mental characteristics as being strongly determined by interaction with the environment, for example by upbringing and the experience of mixing with others.

Although there are extreme positions in either school, most psychologists adopt a middle-of-the-road *interactionist perspective* and assume that, while mental characteristics predispose us to behave in set ways, when we do so the environment exerts a counter-force in return. This force is experienced by the person as either rewarding or punishing, which in turn brings about slight adjustments to our psychological characteristics.

Within this general interactionist view there is a bewildering array of theories that explain personality but, for the present, discussion will centre on the general factors that can shape the personality of all people. These fall into the four groups which are shown in Figure 3.1.

Genetic Factors

There is a great deal of evidence that our inherited genes play some part in the formation and development of many of our mental characteristics, including that of personality. Children of the same family, for example, often have some aspects of temperament in common and identical twins (who of course are also identical in genetic

Nature vs nurture debate: the question of whether hereditary factors or the environment has most effect on behaviour

Interactionist perspective: that hereditary factors and environment interact to determine behaviour

Genetic factors: inherited factors that influence physical and mental characteristics

Figure 3.1 Sources of personality

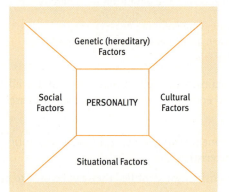

make-up) have even stronger similarities. For example, the incidence of schizophrenia tends to be significantly higher in children of schizoid parents (Gottesman and Shields 1972); and so certain psychoses could have a strong genetic component. In addition to these direct effects, it is also possible that genetics could have an indirect influence on personality. Height, build and physical attractiveness are all genetically determined and have a bearing on how others behave towards us in social settings. This can influence how we view ourselves and impact on our personalities.

One very extreme theory of genetic determinism is that of Sheldon (1954), who associates three body shapes with personality types. The **endomorphic** person has a soft, round, stocky body, a large trunk and short legs and is said to have a relaxed, easy-going sociable temperament and a fondness for bodily comforts. **Ectomorphic** people, those with a delicate, slender build, tend to be aesthetic, inhibited and socially withdrawn. Finally, the **mesomorph** is the muscular, athletic type and is said to be highly energetic, assertive, boisterous and possibly aggressive. While some degree of stereotyping based on visual appearance is commonplace, ideas such as these are now regarded as naive and simplistic. Although most psychologists acknowledge that personality has a genetic component and there is convincing evidence that approximately 40 per cent of personality is genetically determined (Plomin 1994), the idea that it is totally determined by genes has largely been discounted. Even identical twins reared together have slight personality differences, and these differences become greater if they are reared apart, which tells us that environment plays some role in shaping personality (Pervin 1980).

Social Factors

Social factors: factors that influence personality that arise from interaction with other people

Humans are social animals and their psychological characteristics are in part a reflection of their interactions with other members of the species. Therefore early *socialisation*, which includes interaction with parents, siblings and peers, has an effect on personality and behaviour in later life. Indeed, the *behaviourist* school of psychology, which views all human behaviour as environmentally determined, regards personality as little more than a set of accumulated learning experiences (Skinner 1974), although this is a rather extreme view. Nevertheless, the literature on socialisation strongly supports the idea that early experiences carry over into adult life and that to some extent we are socialised and resocialised throughout our lives (Wanous *et al.* 1984).

Socialisation: the process of being taught how to behave and how to feel by other (influential) people within a specific social setting

Behaviourism: the branch of psychology which holds that all human behaviour is determined by factors outside the person

Cultural Factors

Cultural factors: wider social beliefs, values and motives that are absorbed by an individual and guide behaviour towards that which is acceptable within a particular social context

In many ways *cultural factors* can be viewed as an extension of socialisation. A culture embraces patterns of belief, values and motives that are acceptable in a particular society, and these give individuals a general set of predispositions to behave in certain set ways. However, what is acceptable can vary dramatically between different cultures. In Western society, and particularly in America, a high value is placed on individualism and achieving worldly success. As will be seen in Chapter 7, it has been powerfully argued that this results in a socially induced personality trait, the 'need to achieve' (McClelland 1967). Conversely, in Japan individualism takes second place to being a good team player, and the success of the group comes first (Hofstede 1980). Thus, while it is an exaggeration to state that there is something as far-reaching as a Japanese or American personality, these value differences are almost bound to have some effect on the personalities of people in each country, which has important implications for the testing and measurement of personality.

Situational Factors

Situational factors: the effect of a specific experience or situation on a person's feelings and behaviour

Different experiences can also affect personality, for example, the trauma of losing a parent or a loved one can sometimes change a person in a dramatic way. In addition, certain situations can bring out hitherto unrecognised aspects of personality that could have been repressed in the past. An example that dramatically ilustrates these situational effects is provided by Zimbardo (1973), who conducted a series of experiments in which ordinary people were required to act out the roles of warders and prisoners. So strongly did they immerse themselves in their allotted roles that those who were playing the parts of warders confessed to having feelings verging on hate for the prisoners. Indeed, at one point the behaviour of warder subjects became so violent and aggressive towards the prisoner players that the experiment had to be terminated.

TIME OUT

Try to take a dispassionate look at what you perceive to be your own personality characteristics by answering the questions below.

1. Using single words or short expressions, try to think of six characteristics that accurately reflect your own personality.
2. To what extent do you feel that these characteristics are similar to those of your parents?
3. To what extent do you feel that these characteristics have been influenced by your upbringing?
4. Do your personality characteristics always show through whatever the situation, or are there some situations in which they remain largely hidden?

The Stability of Personality and Behaviour

From the foregoing we see that genetic, social, cultural and situational factors all play a part in shaping personality. Thus, to some extent, personality development is an ongoing process. For this reason an important issue is whether personality characteristics are stable and unchanging, because unless this is the case, it becomes immensely difficult to develop valid ways of evaluating personality, and it could even be pointless to try, as measures of personality would be of little use in predicting behaviour and, so far as most people in organisations are concerned, this would negate the whole value of the concept.

Although the evidence suggests that after 30 years of age the adult personality is relatively stable and unchanging (McCrae and Costa 1990), this does not mean that it is an infallible guide to a person's behaviour. A number of psychologists, such as Epstein (1980), point out that the association between personality measures and expected behaviour is often very weak, mainly because personality characteristics are essentially predispositions to behave in a certain way and these can sometimes be overwhelmed by situational factors. For this reason, Mischel (1977) cautions that there is a need to

Figure 3.2
Stability of personality
characteristics (after
Mischel 1977)

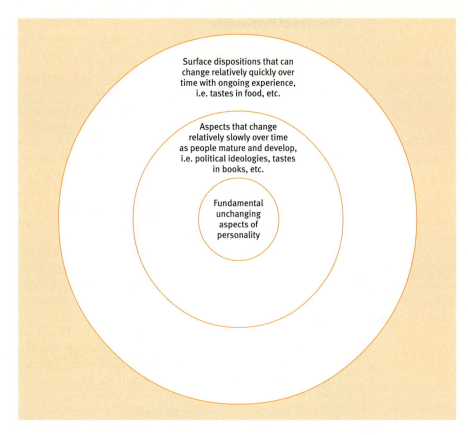

Surface dispositions that can
change relatively quickly over
time with ongoing experience,
i.e. tastes in food, etc.

Aspects that change
relatively slowly over time
as people mature and develop,
i.e. political ideologies, tastes
in books, etc.

Fundamental
unchanging
aspects of
personality

**Strong situations:
those where
personality
characteristics are
good predictors of
behaviour**

**Weak situations:
those where
personality
characteristics are
poorer predictors
of behaviour**

take account of situational effects by distinguishing between two types of situation
that affect the predictive value of a personality measure. *Strong situations* give people
easily discernible cues about what behaviour is appropriate. These are usually interpreted in the same way by most people, and so the incentive to behave in a predictable
way is very strong because the situation itself is strong enough to overcome any minor
personality differences. In these circumstances personality measures are likely to be
good predictors of behaviour. Conversely, in *weak situations* the cues about what
constitutes an appropriate response are more ambiguous. People are likely to have
different interpretations of the circumstances, which means that it is much harder for
someone to draw on prior learning as a guide to what is appropriate. Thus there is a
much weaker incentive to behave in a predictable way and in these circumstances the
finer nuances of personality can take over and personality measures can become poor
predictors of behaviour.

   To take account of these matters perhaps the safest way to view the stability of
personality and its effects on behaviour is shown in Figure 3.2, which portrays the
structure of personality as something akin to an onion, made up of an infinite number
of layers. On the surface are those aspects of personality which are most amenable to
change; as we get deeper we reach those aspects that are much more likely to be fixed
and unchanging.

Theories of Personality

Idiographic vs Nomothetic Approaches

Idiographic: theories which describe personality in terms that are unique to the person

Earlier it was noted that a distinction can be drawn between two major approaches to the study of personality: idiographic and nomothetic. *Idiographic* theories view personality as an integrated whole. They attempt to capture the essence of an individual's total personality and, from this, draw inferences about how the person will react in different situations. Theories of this type tend to avoid the assumption that personality is fixed and often focus on the way that it develops and changes as a result of ongoing experience. For this reason idiographic theories seldom categorise people according to fixed personality dimensions, but produce a description or explanation of an individual's personality that is highly idiosyncratic, which makes it hard to compare people in like terms. In contrast, the *nomothetic* approach is concerned with identifying basic personality characteristics that are common to all people, but which can vary in degree from person to person. They are based on an underlying assumption that personality is relatively fixed and resistant to change. The aim is usually to evolve schemes that can be used to describe personality along a number of dimensions or as a number of types and, from this, develop ways of accurately measuring the personality characteristics of individuals.

Nomothetic: theories which describe personality in terms of set dimensions that could be applied to all people

Neither approach is inherently right or wrong. They approach personality with different sets of underlying assumptions. Assessment and description of personality is also undertaken in different ways and, usually, the information obtained is put to a different use. Needless to say adherents of one approach often conflict strongly with those of the other school. For example, the idiographic approach is often criticised for being too subjective, imprecise and lacking in scientific rigour, while the nomothetic approach probably overemphasises the separate dimensions, and sometimes draws rather glib conclusions about subsequent behaviour from scores on a personality test (Lazarus 1971).

Idiographic Personality Theories

The Psychodynamic Perspective

While most people associate the psychodynamic approach with the work of Freud, it is really a very broad, diverse group of theories with some assumptions in common, but distinct differences on some issues. Since Freud was the founding father of the approach, and his name is better known than many others, it is Freudian theory that will be outlined here. Before doing so, however, it is important to highlight common assumptions that underpin all psychodynamic theories and these are given below.

- **Psychological determination of behaviour**, which holds that all human behaviour is psychologically driven, with mental activity preceding physical activity.
- **The unconscious** has a prominent role in determining behaviour. It is constantly at work and is the dynamic source of energy that drives behaviour.
- All behaviour is **goal directed**. However, because some goals are located in the unconscious, humans are not always aware of them.
- Most psychodynamic theories lay a strong emphasis on **personality development** in which the roots of personality lie in childhood experiences. In Freud's view,

CASE STUDY 3.1: Psychological Testing

Dr Major, a psychologist who lectures in Organisation Behaviour in the Department of Management Studies in one of the new universities returned from his summer vacation to find a note from the Head of Department (HOD) awaiting him. This simply said 'please see me urgently about psychological testing'. On doing so he discovered that the HOD had 'volunteered' his services to the Personnel Department to test and give advice about candidates for a senior non-academic post. Dr Major had encountered problems of this nature before with the HOD, who, it was sometimes remarked, would volunteer his staff as a direct replacement for the SAS (see note below) if he thought it would enhance his own prestige. Therefore, he firmly pointed out that he had made it quite clear in the past that he did not engage in consultancy work of this type. Nevertheless, since a promise had been made, he agreed to see the personnel manager to give what advice he could.

At his meeting with the personnel manager, Dr Major was informed that a preliminary trawl for candidates for the post in question would be conducted by a firm of recruitment consultants, who would identify what were felt to be the four most promising applicants. The university would then handle the selection process and, as an aid in this, the personnel manager was desirous of having details of candidates' personalities. Dr Major then enquired about the details of the job, for example, whether there were any indications from the present incumbent about personality characteristics that might be important. To this the personnel manager replied that because it was a completely new post, created at the behest of the head of the university (the Vice Chancellor), no job description yet existed and the exact nature of the job would largely be shaped by whoever was appointed.

Questions

1. What should Dr Major's advice to the personnel manager be?

2. From (1), what should Dr Major do now?

NOTE the Special Air Services Regiment (SAS) is an elite and highly specialist branch of the British Army that engages in a wide range of (sometimes covert) duties such as counter-terrorism and 'behind enemy lines' activities during wartime.

therefore, the child is the father of the man. Thus, rather than simply seeking to describe and measure personality, the psychodynamic approach is the only one that seeks to explain in a detailed way how an individual's personality comes to be what it is.

The Freudian Conception of Personality Structure and Dynamics

In Freud's (1901a) theory a person's psyche consists of three components, which develop from birth onwards. They do not coincide with any physical parts of the brain, but are abstract concepts, used to describe the driving forces behind behaviour. These forces reside at different levels of depth in the mind, an idea which is portrayed diagrammatically in Figure 3.3.

Figure 3.3 Freud's conceptualisation of the structure of personality

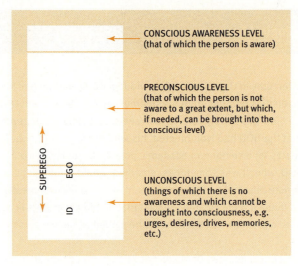

CONSCIOUS AWARENESS LEVEL
(that of which the person is aware)

PRECONSCIOUS LEVEL
(that of which the person is not aware to a great extent, but which, if needed, can be brought into the conscious level)

UNCONSCIOUS LEVEL
(things of which there is no awareness and which cannot be brought into consciousness, e.g. urges, desires, drives, memories, etc.)

Id: the biologically driven component of personality that consists of inherited drives etc. and which demands immediate gratification of its pleasure-seeking drives

The ultimate driving force of all behaviour is the *id*, which is present at birth and consists of the biological element of personality that contains all our inherited instinctual drives, desires and urges. The id is irrational, impulsive and demands immediate gratification of all that is pleasurable. Thus it makes no distinction between right or wrong but acts as a powerful driving force to seek pleasurable experiences no matter what the consequences.

Ego is absent at birth and eventually develops out of the id. In the early stage of development the infantile ego is narcissistic and seeks to gratify the demands of the id by taking from the outside world. However, as the person progresses into early childhood, ego gradually recognises that the outside world is immensely powerful and that if the id is given a free rein, conflict with the outside world will become inevitable. For this reason, ego develops into that part of the psyche which tries to protect the person from the potentially destructive forces of the id by attempting to balance the id's demands against the reality of the external world, thus becoming the force that holds the individual together as a whole.

Ego: a component of personality that grows out of the id and which strives to reconcile the demands of the id, superego and the realities of the outside world

The *superego* consists of the learned values and demands of culture and society, which are absorbed in childhood as part of a person's upbringing. Superego eventually gives rise to two psychological substructures: the **ego ideal**, which informs the person of that behaviour which is appropriate, and **conscience**, which allows a person to recognise that certain behaviour is not permitted.

In Freudian theory, adult personality dynamics are viewed as a three-cornered conflict between id, ego and superego, as shown in Figure 3.4.

Superego: a component of personality that reflects the learned rules of society which are absorbed in upbringing

In a normal, well-adjusted person, effective functioning occurs when these conflicts are resolved, a task undertaken by the ego. The id will always seek to drive the person to gratify instinctive desires without regard to the consequences; at the same time, superego is working in the opposite direction to restrict any gratification whatsoever. This means that there are two powerful psychological forces in opposition. In addition, the person is confronted with the external reality of the situation, which can tip the scales in favour of either id or superego. Neither id nor superego is a part of the psyche that has any inclination to compromise and, since external reality is all powerful, any resulting behaviour is likely to have longer-term consequences. Thus

Figure 3.4 Freud's concept of the conflictual dynamics of personality

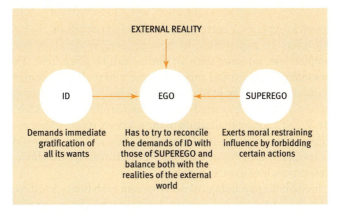

ego has to absorb the demands of both id and superego and find a compromise solution that matches the short-term and long-term reality of the outside world. To the extent that ego is well developed and powerful enough to undertake this task, the person is said to be well adjusted. However, if either id or superego is more dominant than ego, permanent anxieties can be present. **Neurotic anxieties**, for example, are said to result from an id-dominated personality. Where superego dominates, **moral anxieties** arise, and if the external world dominates then the person experiences **objective anxieties** (Freud 1940).

In the well-adjusted person ego will be able to resolve these conflicts by coordinating internal and external forces. However, if the conflict places extremely severe demands on the ego, it can protect itself (and the person) by bringing defence mechanisms into play (Freud 1901b). These operate at the unconscious level and are:

- **Repression**   where the ego protects itself (and the person) from damage by denying the existence of a problem, perhaps by removing disturbing thoughts into the unconscious.

- **Suppression**   occurs in a situation where id exerts an extremely powerful demand to satiate a potentially harmful desire and ego urges the person to exercise conscious control.

- **Projection**   where a person protects him or herself from feelings that cause discomfort by attributing the motive giving rise to the feelings to another person; for example, a person who has a subconscious desire to steal can become acutely suspicious about the honesty of others.

- **Fixation**   occurs where the prospect of doing something creates anxiety, and ego protects itself by finding a reason for not doing it.

- **Regression**   is said to occur when ego is confronted with a threat, which it resolves by taking the person back to a form of behaviour that was successful earlier in life, to cope with a similar situation or divert attention from it. For example, when told off for a minor misdemeanour, such as being late, a person might break down into tears.

- **Reaction formation**   occurs when ego copes with an undesirable, id-driven impulse or desire by doing the exact opposite. For example, a person who enjoys staying in bed and has a tendency to want to arrive late for work may go out of his or her way to be the first one into the office in the morning.

Freud's Theory of Psychosexual Development

As well as explaining current personality and behaviour, the psychodynamic approach also offers an explanation of how personality develops but, since the theory is a complex one, no more than an outline can be given here. The three components of personality – id, ego and superego – are said to develop sequentially. In Freud's view all interactions in the psyche involve energy, and the only source of energy available is *libido*. This is associated with instinctual drives, of which the sexual drive is just one. Freud's conceptualisation of the sex drive is something more comprehensive than simple sexual gratification, because it embraces the life instinct and preservation of the species. It is therefore extremely powerful and, since libido is connected with very basic drives, it originates in the id.

Libido: the source of all psychological energy, including the sex drive

Freud links psychological development with biological development, which occurs as libidinous energy and is redistributed in stages from one erogenous (sexually stimulating) zone to another, the zones being mouth (oral), anus (anal), phallus (phallic) and genitals (genital). However, the stages are not completely separate, and none of them ever disappears completely. This idea is shown in Figure 3.5; note that while there is agreement about the sequential development of the three components, the age at which they emerge is only approximate.

The form in which libido is gratified depends on the erogenous zone on which attention is focused at the time. With very small babies almost all gratification comes via the mouth through feeding and suckling, but later on other zones become more prominent. While these changes in focus are partly determined by physical development, shifts in the focus of gratification can also be prompted by external factors, such as social relationships. Events in early life handled in a way that is disturbing to the child can have an emotional impact later on, for example, an over-severe emphasis on toilet training is said to give rise to id domination in adult life.

Figure 3.5
Developmental aspects of Freud's theory

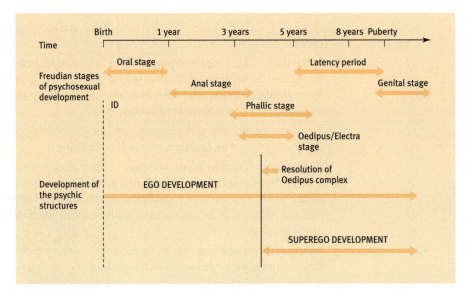

It is important to note that while other psychodynamic theorists agree with the idea of staged development, there are many who strongly disagree with Freud's belief that personality development is sexually driven. Jung (1960), for example, accepted that development takes place in stages, but considered Freud's emphasis on the sexual influence far too strong. In addition, he believed that the influence of personality on current behaviour is not just a carry-over from the past, but is orientated to the future. Similarly, Adler (1928), another disciple of Freud, while broadly endorsing the idea of sequential development, focused on how, in development, infants overcome their feelings of powerlessness and inferiority, that is, to a one-year-old child, even a four-year-old seems like a giant. In addition, another psychodynamic theorist, Eric Fromm (1942), placed a much stronger emphasis on the effects of the social context as a determinant of behaviour, which to some extent acknowledges cultural influences.

Psychodynamic Theory: An Overview

For the most part, psychodynamic theory is little used outside clinical settings, for example in psychoanalysis. With the exception of certain aspects of Jung's work, which has been applied to develop a scheme of personality types that can be used for selection or counselling, it is not well known or used in organisations. Nevertheless, in terms of organisational research it has been used to penetrating effect to analyse neurotic behavioural styles in managers (Kets de Vries and Miller 1984) and has been argued to be an extremely powerful tool for exploring unconscious processes that affect behaviour in organisations (Amado 1995). It should also be noted that it is much criticised by nomothetic personality theorists such as Eysenck (1970) as being unscientific and untestable, mainly because some of the concepts are almost impossible to define in terms of observable behaviour and so it is hard to design experiments to test the theory. Among psychologists, psychodynamic analysis of personality is considered to be a highly specialised area. However, it should never be underrated. It is the one and only branch of personality theory that goes beyond descriptive schemes and attempts to explain how an individual's personality comes to be what it is.

Interpersonal Theories

Although interpersonal theories of personality are idiographic, they are very different from those in the psychodynamic tradition. They primarily map perceptions rather than personality characteristics and focus on how people respond to what they believe to be the objective reality of their world. As will be explained in Chapter 4, because perceptions are strongly influenced by personality and prior experience, they can be a powerful way of gaining insights into personality. Like most idiographic theories, those using an interpersonal approach have their origins in clinical work such as psychotherapy and counselling but, rather than trying to uncover hidden or repressed emotions, these theories are more sharply focused on the everyday implications of personality.

Kelly's Personal Construct Theory

Kelly's (1955) view of the human personality assumes that functioning on a day-to-day basis requires that people need to be able to anticipate events, rather than just react to them. To do this they seek to bring meaning and order into what they encounter by developing a set of criteria (constructs) that are used to interpret the world. Clearly constructs are only usable in a practical way if they give a person accurate and useful guides to action, and for this reason people revise their constructs in the light of experience.

Two important points should be noted about Kelly's use of the word constructs: first, they are assumed to be bipolar and thus have extremes; for example, a person might use two constructs, 'a' and 'b', to evaluate other people, the extremes of which are:

'a' HAPPY ————————————— SAD

'b' TALL ————————————— SHORT

Second, there are no universal constructs. People develop their own and use those that are meaningful in terms of distinguishing between outside objects (people being considered as one class of outside objects).

Each construct is a dimension along which objects are evaluated and each dimension has two poles, one of which is the opposite of the other. A person's constructs are not universally applicable to all events, objects or people, and each one has what Kelly calls a range of convenience. However, some can be applied quite widely; for example, tall or short could be applied to people, buildings or trees. Most, however, can only be used selectively; for instance, evergreen or deciduous can only be applied to trees. Therefore constructs are often nested together hierarchically, which means that if we spot one characteristic of a person, this can lead us to making evaluations at a more general level (Bannister 1970). This is illustrated in Figure 3.6, which shows a set of hierarchically arranged constructs that a person might use to evaluate his or her supervisor.

Note that this hierarchy also gives us some clues about how the *halo effect*, which will be discussed in more detail in the next chapter, can occur. For instance, if this was

Halo effect: the assumption that because a person has a certain trait he or she automatically has other traits

Figure 3.6
Hierarchical arrangement of bipolar constructs

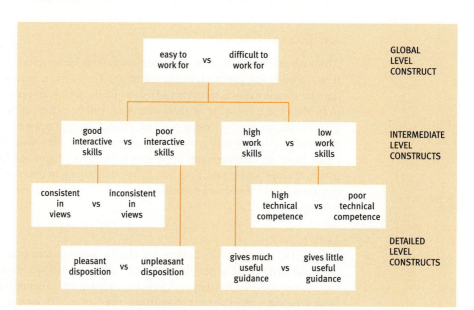

a set of personal constructs that you used to evaluate your supervisor in a job to which you had just been appointed, you could notice that he or she gives useful guidance (detailed level construct). Without further evidence you might then proceed to ascend the hierarchy, to infer that he or she has high work skills (intermediate level) and is, therefore, easy to work with (global level).

Kelly explicitly assumes that people often have to revise their personal construct systems in the light of experience and so one way to view a person's construct system is as a set of working hypotheses. Like hypotheses, they are tested and, if found valid, are retained, but if shown to be false they are modified or discarded. In addition, Kelly acknowledges that because construct systems are part of personality, they can give rise to behavioural problems. For example, when an individual's personal construct system is applied to events that have never been encountered before, it might turn out to be inadequate and the person becomes racked with anxiety. Similarly, if a construct system is used to evaluate another person and the evaluation turns out to be totally inaccurate, hostility can occur. For example, I might use a particular set of constructs to predict that a job applicant will fit nicely into my work team but subsequently find that he or she does not. Instead of revising my construct system I could become hostile and aggressive towards the person and try to coerce the individual into fitting in. As such, people can feel threatened if they discover that their construct systems do not work accurately.

Humanistic Perspectives: Carl Rogers' Person-centred Theory

Like most idiographic theories, Rogers' (1951) ideas emerged in the light of his clinical experience as a therapist. In some respects they are similar to Kelly's work because the theory is informed by a belief that, to understand people, it is necessary to understand how they view themselves and the world around them. This can be tremendously important in therapy, where the therapist often has to find a way of resolving a person's inner tensions or difficulties in social relationships, because how we view ourselves has a huge impact on how we relate to others.

Unlike Freud, whose emphasis on the dark forces of the id gives a negative view of humanity, Rogers has a highly optimistic and positive view of humans. He believes that their most enduring tendency is to seek to self-actualise, that is, to try to move in the direction of greater independence, self-responsibility and self-determination. The central plank of Rogers' theory is an individual's *concept of self*. He believes that all individuals have what can be called a *phenomenal field*, that is, a set of perceptions and meanings that the person attaches to all external events. Included in this is the individual's view of him or herself, that is, the *actual self* of 'me' or I, what and who I am and what I stand for. Alongside this actual self the individual also has a concept of *ideal self*, which can loosely be described as the self that the person would most like to become.

According to Rogers, most people behave in a way that tries to maintain congruence between what they do and their concept of self, and this has an important implication for personality. If someone sees him or herself as a compassionate, caring person, then this is how he or she will behave and a corollary of this is that if an accurate picture can be obtained of a person's concept of self, this provides some basis for predicting his or her behaviour. According to Rogers, people always try to bring the actual self closer to the ideal self, because this is what self-actualisation consists of and,

Concept of self: a person's view of what he or she is

Phenomenal field: the perceptions and meanings people attach to external events which result in them experiencing the world in a particular way

Actual self: the self as the person currently views him or herself

Ideal self: the self as the person would like it to be

as will be seen in Chapter 7, this also has very important implications for motivation. For instance, because a person's needs largely arise from the desire to bring the actual self nearer the ideal self, a motivator is something that offers a realistic prospect of doing so.

The Idiographic Approach: Concluding Comments

The idiographic approach takes a highly idiosyncratic view of personality. It seeks to understand the uniqueness of individuals and to capture the essence of their personalities, which has a number of advantages. Because people are accepted as unique, the approach is relatively free of preconceived notions of how personality can be most appropriately described, and this is likely to produce a very rich picture of individual characteristics. In addition, the approach directly links personality and behaviour, and so it fits well with other psychological constructs such as attitudes and perceptions that have behaviourial implications.

Notwithstanding these advantages, there are criticisms of the approach:

- because it takes a highly individualistic perspective, it ignores situations where it can be important to compare the personalities of different individuals;
- while the approach infers that there are dimensions along which personality could be categorised, it stops short of actually developing measures that could be used to differentiate individuals along these dimensions;
- since most idiographic theories have their origins in clinical work, they have a tendency to be more concerned with the abnormal than the normal;
- in particular, the psychodynamic view has been subject to much criticism because its ideas and concepts are not amenable to experimental investigation and many psychologists regard it as implausible, unscientific and unverifiable mumbo-jumbo.

In summary, while idiographic theories are useful in explaining poor adjustment to everyday conditions, they are of less use when it comes to describing personality in a way that can be applied to a wider range of day-to-day situations. This requires a completely different approach, and it is to this that attention is now directed.

The Nomothetic Approach

The word nomothetic means legislative or appertaining to the formulation of general or scientific laws. Thus, theories using this approach aim to identify regular, measurable aspects of personality and relate them to human behaviour. They are based on the assumption that an individual's personality is relatively stable and unchanging, and the theories fall into two main groups. Trait theories describe people in terms of a number of personality dimensions, whereas type theories categorise people as falling into one of a number of personality types.

Traits: individual characteristics of thought or feeling that result in tendencies to behave in specific ways

Trait Theories

Traits are individual characteristics of thought or feeling that give rise to tendencies to act or react in certain ways (Drever 1964). However, even if someone has a particular trait, this is not an infallible guide to their actions; it merely indicates that the individual has a predisposition to behave in predictable ways in certain circumstances. Nevertheless, trait theories usually assume a strong association between traits and behaviour. For instance, a trait theory would not accept that conscientious people are conscientious simply because they persevere in what they do; rather, the assumption would be that they are perseverant because their behaviour is driven by the personality trait of conscientiousness.

There are many different types of trait, for example: motive traits are those that guide behaviour; ability traits relate to specific skills and abilities; temperament traits are those that refer to mood etc.; and stylistic traits refer to visible aspects of behaviour. However, in personality theory the most important distinction is between surface traits and source traits. *Surface traits*, such as assertiveness, can be observed in behaviour, while *source traits*, such as self-discipline, can only be inferred. Theories in this tradition all use traits in a very similar way. They derive a scheme of universal traits (those that all people have in some degree) that are then used to classify people according to their combination of trait strengths, and it is how they are organised that gives a person a unique personality (Allport 1961).

Cattell's Sixteen Personality Factor Scheme

Cattell (1965) distinguishes between patterns of observable behaviour (surface traits) and source traits, which he calls *primary factors*. These, he claims, are the fundamental factors, or building blocks, that make up personality.

In Cattell's original results, twelve primary factors (source traits) are identified and these were said to be the fundamental dimensions of personality, from which all visible behaviourial tendencies (surface traits) originate. Subsequent work led to an upward revision and currently the most widely used scheme has sixteen factors, which form the basis of the Cattell Sixteen Personality Factor Questionnaire (16 PF for short). These are shown in Figure 3.7.

Although at first sight some of these factors might appear to hang together, Cattell's view is that they do not, but are, in fact, independent dimensions. Also note that the sixteen factors are bipolar dimensions of personality. Therefore, although a person can be located somewhere between Reserved and Outgoing, these are two opposing characteristics, not a scale which measures how reserved or outgoing the person is. It is possible to reduce Cattell's sixteen primary dimensions to a smaller number (five) of second-order factors. However, since it is Cattell's view that these can only influence behaviour through the source traits, they will not be considered further here.

As noted earlier, Cattell claims to have identified the fundamental building blocks of personality. This is a highly controversial claim and one that has been disputed by many other psychologists. For example, Peck and Whitlow (1975) suggest that his analytic assumptions result in a grossly oversimplified picture. Nevertheless, Cattell's theory is extremely robust. It has stood the test of time and the 16 PF test, which has been revised and refined a number of times, is widely used in an organisational context.

Type Theories

Type theories place people into predetermined categories (personality types) on the basis of characteristics that are said to give rise to certain patterns of behaviour.

Surface traits: those that are directly observable in behaviour

Source traits: those that cannot be observed directly and whose existence can only be inferred

Primary factors: the factors which, in Cattell's personality theory, are the fundamental building blocks of personality

Figure 3.7 Cattell's sixteen personality factors

Low score description	Factor	High score description
Reserved, detached, critical, aloof *sizothymia*	A	**Outgoing**, warmhearted easygoing, participating *affectothymia, formerly cyclothymia*
Less intelligent, concrete thinking *lower scholastic mental capacity*	B	**More intelligent**, abstract thinking, bright *higher scholastic mental capacity*
Affected by feelings, emotionally less stable, easily upset *lower ego strength*	C	**Emotionally stable**, faces reality, calm, mature *higher ego strength*
Humble, mild accommodating conforming *submissiveness*	E	**Assertive**, aggressive, stubborn, competitive *dominance*
Sober, prudent, serious, taciturn *desurgency*	F	**Happy-go-lucky**, impulsively lively, gay, enthusiastic *surgency*
Expedient, disregards rules, feels few obligations *weaker superego strength*	G	**Conscientious**, persevering, staid, moralistic *stronger superego strength*
Shy, restrained, timid, threat sensitive *threctia*	H	**Venturesome**, socially bold, uninhibited, spontaneous *parmia*
Tough minded, self-reliant, realistic, no-nonsense *harria*	I	**Tender-minded**, clinging, over-protected, sensitive *premsia*
Trusting, adaptable, free of jealousy, easy to get along with *alaxia*	L	**Suspicious**, self-opinionated, hard to fool *protension*
Practical, careful, conventional, regulated by external realities, proper *praxernia*	M	**Imaginative**, wrapped up in inner urgencies, careless of practical matters, bohemian *autia*
Forthright, natural, artless, unpretentious *artlessness*	N	**Shrewd**, calculating, worldly, penetrating *shrewdness*
Self-assured, confident, serene *untroubled adequacy*	O	**Apprehensive**, self-reproaching, worrying, troubled *guilt proneness*
Conservative, respecting established ideas, tolerant of traditional difficulties *conservatism*	Q_1	**Experimenting**, liberal, analytical, free thinking *radicalism*
Group dependent, a 'joiner' and sound follower *group adherence*	Q_2	**Self-sufficient**, prefers own decisions, resourceful *self-sufficiency*
Undisciplined self-conflict, follows own urges, careless of protocol *low integration*	Q_3	**Controlled**, socially precise, following self-image *high self-concept control*
Relaxed, tranquil, unfrustrated *low ergic tension*	Q_4	**Tense**, frustrated, driven, overwrought, *high ergic tension*

Most type theories use a very small number of categories into which people must be slotted, but since people seldom fit neatly into one type or another, one criticism is that the theories oversimplify matters. Nevertheless, some type theories are quite sophisticated in terms of their conceptualisation of personality, and the best known is described next.

Figure 3.8 'Eysenck's personality types' from Eysenck, H J (1965) *Fact and Fiction in Psychology* (pub Penguin Books Ltd), copyright © H J Eysenck 1965

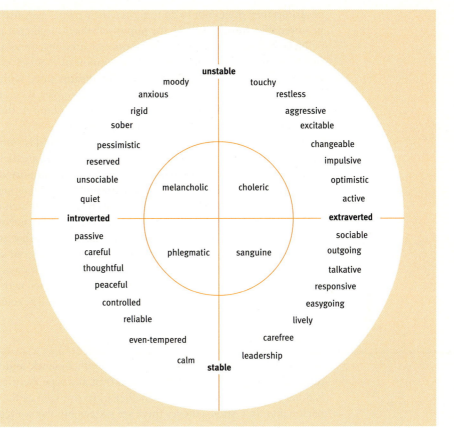

Eysenck's Type Theory

Eysenck's interest in personality theory developed in the Second World War when he was involved in treating neurotic soldiers at Mill Hill Emergency Hospital. Like Cattell, his theory is based on extensive empirical work, and, in its original form, the theory is based on two fundamental dimensions of personality: *extroversion–introversion* and *neuroticism–stability* (Eysenck 1947). This gives four general personality types, which are sometimes identified by the same names used by Hippocrates in naming the four human temperaments: stable extroverts – the sanguine type; unstable extroverts – the choleric type; stable introverts – the phlegmatic type and unstable introverts – the melancholic type. However, it is rare to find that someone is an extreme example of any single type. Each type is also associated with a number of specific personality traits, and Figure 3.8 shows Eysenck's well-known diagram relating the traits to the personality types.

A great deal of work has been undertaken to identify the behavioural correlates of extroversion–introversion and neuroticism–stability. **Extroverts** are usually found to be tough-minded, impulsive, quick-tempered and visibly emotional. They are often aggressive, crave strong external stimulation and excitement and are sociable, care-free and active. Since extroverts like to be the centre of attention and are fond of social

Extroversion–introversion: one of the two fundamental dimensions of personality used in Eysenck's type theory

Neuroticism–stability: the second fundamental dimensions of personality used in Eysenck's type theory

occasions they prefer not to do things on their own. They also have some tendency to be unreliable. **Introverts** have the opposite behaviourial characteristics.

Neurotics are usually unstable, emotional, anxious, obsessive, over-conscientious, finicky people. They often have a low opinion of themselves and feel that they are unattractive failures. Thus they are usually disappointed with their lives and tend to be persistent worriers. Neurotics are also easily upset when things go wrong. They tend to be annoyed by a lack of order and easily submit to those with greater formal power. Once again, **stable** people are the opposite.

In Eysenck's view personality is largely inherited and is associated with the physiology of certain parts of the brain. In the lower brain there are parts which contain groups of cells that have been shown by research to have an important role in regulating the level of arousal of the higher brain. In neurophysiological terms, Eysenck suggests that introverts are people who are generally over-aroused, which means that the level of excitation in the upper brain centres is high. To correct this imbalance they tend to avoid all possible outside stimulation, which accounts for their behaviourial characteristics. Conversely, extroverts are under-aroused and so they seek out all that they can possibly obtain in terms of additional outside stimulation. Later Eysenck added a third dimension, psychoticism (Eysenck 1970), which when combined with the other two results in an extremely complex theory, discussion of which is well beyond the scope of this book.

Traits vs Types: Cattell and Eysenck Compared

Since traits play a part in the theories of both Eysenck and Cattell it is sometimes difficult to grasp the difference between trait and type theories. However, the matter is quite simple and depends on whether traits are seen as the determining factors in personality. In Cattell's theory there are sixteen bipolar source traits. To some extent all people exhibit these traits and, since any combination of them is theoretically possible, it is the way they combine that gives an individual his or her personality. Thus, in trait theories, traits are the fundamental building blocks that determine personality. With Eysenck's theory, personality is said to fall into one of a number of types, and certain traits flow automatically from being a particular type. Thus it is the type which defines a person's personality, and traits are just visible manifestations of the type.

There is also a difference between Eysenck and Cattell in terms of the role that heredity plays in determining personality. Eysenck believes that while people become more diverse and individualistic as they gain a wider experience of the world, their reactions to the experience depend upon their personality type. Therefore, hereditary factors are assumed to have a strong enduring influence. While Cattell also acknowledges that genetic inheritance shapes traits, he believes that socialisation and experience play a more prominent role in determining the position on each particular trait dimension. Thus he leans more towards the idea that personality is changeable, albeit slowly.

A Recent Development: The 'Big Five'

As can be seen above, in one form or another the psychology of personality and, in particular, personality assessment relies heavily on the trait concept. At the current time, however, the debate is not so much about whether the trait or type approach is most appropriate, but about the structuring of traits and, in particular, how many traits are needed to give a comprehensive description of an individual's personality. Eysenck

Table 3.1 The Big Five personality dimensions and associated traits

Dimension	Associated traits	
	Desirable (representative of the characteristic) traits	Undesirable (opposite of the characteristic) traits
I Extraversion	outgoing, sociable, assertive	introverted, reserved, hostile
II Agreeableness	kind, trusting, warm	hostile, selfish, cold
III Conscientiousness	organised, thorough, tidy	careless, unreliable, sloppy
IV Emotional Stability	calm, even-tempered, imperturbable	moody, temperamental, nervous
V Intellect or Openness	imaginative, intelligent, creative	shallow, unsophisticated, imperceptive

(1991) expresses a strong preference for four personality types, from which clusters of traits flow automatically, and Cattell remains strongly committed to sixteen source traits, of which one is intelligence. The rapidly emerging winner in this debate is, however, a five-factor structure, the so-called 'Big Five' (Digman 1990). This expresses what are said to be the five basic dimensions of personality and these, together with representative trait descriptions, are shown in Table 3.1.

In one sense, the Big Five scheme is a halfway house between trait and type theory. Taken together, the five dimensions allow personality profiles to be derived in a similar way to Cattell's scheme. However, by using only five dimensions, each of which is associated with certain traits, a profile that is easier to read is derived and, importantly, evidence suggests that the profiles derived integrate well with older theories (Barrick *et al.* 2003; Lord and Rust 2003).

Personality in the Workplace

The definition of personality given earlier in the chapter assumes that personality results in predictable patterns of behaviour, and for this reason the personality concept has some significance for organisations. Most organisations have their own cultures and accepted patterns of behaviour, which means that some people are likely to fit into a culture better than others. In addition, jobs differ in terms of the personal characteristics they require and so an individual's personality could have an impact on his or her suitability for certain roles. These features give rise to two associated issues: the key personality characteristics for organisational members and how to determine whether people have these characteristics. In practice these are closely connected but, for the sake of convenience, each will be considered in turn.

Locus of control: whether a person believes outcomes and events are under his or her control, or whether they are determined by external factors that cannot be controlled

The Issue of Key Characteristics

Organisations differ in what they consider to be important and, within most organisations, different roles tend to require different characteristics. There is no single personality that is ideal everywhere; at best, attention can be directed to those personality variables that are currently of great interest in organisations.

Locus of control is one aspect of personality that currently attracts some attention. Work in this area originates in Rotter's (1966) theory of social learning, which holds that people differ in terms of the extent to which they believe they can shape and control their own environments. In this respect individuals are said to be of two types. Those with an *internal orientation* (locus of control) feel that they can exert a great deal of influence on events around them and have a strong desire to play a prominent part in these events. For example, 'internals' believe that what happens to them is mainly the result of their own actions (DeBrabander and Boone 1990). Conversely, those with an *external orientation* are more likely to believe that they are swept along by events, and that what happens is determined by fate or luck. This aspect of personality has significant implications for organisations and their managers. For instance, those with an internal orientation are much more likely to shoulder responsibility for goal achievement, with all that this means in terms of adaptive behaviour. In addition, they are perhaps more likely to have confidence in their abilities to cope with ambiguous situations. Some evidence to support these ideas is given in a study by Anderson, Hellriegel and Slocum (1977) of the reactions of managers when their businesses were devastated in a hurricane. Externally orientated people tended to wallow in self-pity, while internals, who recognised that the event was a severe setback, immediately set about coping with the problem. It is also worth noting that because internally orientated people tend to regard a reward as something that has been acquired by their own efforts, they respond more positively to the use of incentives, particularly if they can play some part in setting their own goals (Kren 1992).

Authoritarianism is also a personality characteristic in which there is ongoing interest. The idea of an *authoritarian personality* has a long pedigree in social science and the first serious study, which was something of a landmark in social psychology, was reported shortly after the end of the Second World War (Adorno *et al.* 1950). Although controversial, the results give a very strong indication that some people have a personality that places a high value on power and status differences. Authoritarians are often strong advocates of a highly ordered and regimented environment, and so they tend to be unadaptable and prone to seeing others in a stereotypical way. However, as employees they seem to enjoy working for managers who have a highly directive style. Indeed, those with an authoritarian personality take orders from above in a very willing way, and embark on courses of action in which they have little faith or belief, simply because they have been ordered to.

Machiavellianism describes a 'strategy of social conduct that involves manipulating others for personal gain, often against their self-interests' (Wilson *et al.* 1996). Somewhat unjustly, the trait is named after Nicolo Machiavelli, an adviser to Italian Renaissance noblemen, who wrote a classic treatise on political behaviour, *The Prince* (Machiavelli 1958). People of this type are said to be rational, unemotional and willing to go to extreme lengths to achieve their personal goals, even if this means lying and subterfuge. Machiavellians are said to be loners who put little emphasis on friendship and loyalty and, while they enjoy manipulating others, they are extremely wary of being manipulated themselves. What seems to have awakened interest in this characteristic is the increasing awareness of political behaviour in organisations (see Chapter 14).

The Issue of Assessing Personality

Where personality is a factor that could significantly influence job performance, there could be an advantage in having this information available when making selection and promotion decisions. In addition, details of an individual's personality can be useful for vocational guidance purposes.

A number of tests that assess personality are available, usually based on the nomothetic approach. Most are self-completed, pencil-and-paper questionnaires, in which the person responds 'Yes' or 'No' to a forced choice statement that describes him or herself. Although these tests are widely used in organisations, their use has been criticised on the grounds that they are prone to giving an inaccurate picture of personality. This is not necessarily because the tests themselves are at fault; rather, there is a regrettable tendency on the part of those completing the tests to lie to themselves, by ticking boxes in a way that is more indicative of what they would like to be, rather than what they are (Furnham 1990). While it is possible to overcome this to some extent by incorporating lie scales into the questionnaire, it is virtually impossible to eliminate it altogether.

To be useful as a method of assessing personality a test requires a number of features. First, it must possess what is technically known as *reliability*; that is, there should be little possibility of getting different personality profiles if a person takes the test on two successive occasions. Because they have been subjected to extensive investigation to produce standardised score profiles, reputable personality tests are extremely reliable. Tests also need to possess the property of **validity**. In the context discussed here, the essential requirement is for *predictive validity*, which means that the personality of the individual, as revealed by the test, should be a good predictor of performance in a specific role. For selection purposes, the most widely used personality tests measure traits (Deary and Matthews 1993); for them to be useful in this role there should be some evidence that a certain trait profile will result in a predictable job performance. The problem is that while personality tests are increasingly in vogue as a selection tool, particularly for management jobs, there is little evidence that they accurately predict job behaviour (Epstein 1980; Gray 2003; Monson *et al.* 1982; Robertson 2001). This can be most easily understood by reference back to two types of situation distinguished by Mischel (1977), described earlier in the chapter. These days many jobs, particularly management jobs, consist of dealing with uncertainty. Because there are no cues about what is the right thing to do, the person needs to be able to 'think on the hoof' and act in an appropriate way, and this is usually what is meant by good job performance in these circumstances. However, the circumstances are also what Mischel describes as a 'weak situation', and good job performance might well require the individual to act in a way that goes against the grain of his or her personality. Thus, personality is likely to be a poor predictor of good job performance.

This is not to say that personality tests have no role in selection. When used in combination with other techniques such as exercises and role play, which provide information on behaviour in a wider variety of situations, they can help to provide a well-rounded picture of a person. This is generally referred to as the **assessment centre** method, and is a growing trend in selection. What is perhaps a more worrying feature is one that applies to psychometric tests of all types. There is no such thing as a culturally neutral test and so unless great care is taken, psychometric tests can introduce an element of unfair discrimination into a selection or assessment procedure. Since this applies to intelligence and aptitude tests as well as those that assess personality, it is more convenient to defer further discussion until later in the chapter.

Reliability: whether a test produces the same results when applied to the same person on two separate occasions

Predictive validity: whether tests scores are good predictors of behaviour or job performance

REPLAY

- An individual's personality characteristics are influenced by four main groups of factors: genetic, social, cultural and situational (experience).

- The connection between personality characteristics and behaviour is influenced by the situation in which behaviour occurs.

- Idiographic personality theories deal with the individual as an integral whole and are of two main types: psychodynamic theories, which focus on the development of personality, and interpersonal theories, which are more concerned with mapping the personality of the individual as it is.

- Nomothetic theories of personality focus on the description and assessment of personality in terms that could be applied to all people, either by describing personality along a number of dimensions (trait theory), or by personality types.

- Most personality assessment in organisations is conducted using a nomothetic approach.

INTELLIGENCE

Many topics in psychology are controversial but the concept of intelligence, and in particular the testing and measurement of intelligence, is so controversial that it tends to arouse quite passionate feelings. Some scholars, such as Hernstein (1973), hold that the measurement of intelligence is psychology's most telling accomplishment to date. Others point out that while intelligence testing is often portrayed as a highly rigorous branch of psychological science, it is so riddled with circularities and inconsistencies that it would embarrass any respectable scientist (Heather 1976). There are those who go even further and claim that intelligence testing has adverse social consequences, which make the practice unethical (Kamin 1977). Much of this debate arises from what is meant by the expression intelligence, a word that tends to be used in an ill-defined way, even by some psychologists (Miles 1957). The first step must therefore be to explore the meaning of the word intelligence and to define how it will be used in this chapter.

TIME OUT

Think of a number of people you know well. Try to identify some you would classify as intelligent and some who are less intelligent. What evidence have you used to classify the people in this way?

The Concept of Intelligence

Like many psychological concepts, intelligence is an abstract construct based on the tenet that mental activity of some sort precedes all physical behaviour. In common with other constructs it is plagued by our inability to see mental activity directly, and so the only indication of intelligence is observable behaviour. In a broad sense intelligence is revealed by adaptation to environment, and since humans are the most adaptable species in the animal kingdom, it is generally accepted that we are the most intelligent animal of all. No other species has yet been able to bridge the quantum gap that exists between itself and humans. Thus, it is fair to assume that there must be an inherited component in intelligence, which means that, in simple terms, it can be defined as 'an innate, general, cognitive ability' (Burt 1955).

The idea of a genetic component to intelligence is much older than Burt's definition, and disputes about the size of the component are still very much alive today. In an attempt to sidestep this controversy and progress towards a more precise definition it is important to note that Hebb (1949) distinguishes between two meanings that can be attached to the word. Vernon (1955) later added a third, and all three will be used hereafter. They are:

- **IA** the potential intelligence of an individual as determined by his or her genetic make-up, which is neither observable nor measurable directly;
- **IB** the level of ability an individual actually shows in his or her behaviour in everyday life (quickness and depth of thought, understanding, insight, practical judgement etc.), which is a product of the interplay between genetic potential and the stimulation provided by environment;
- **IC** an expression of a person's intelligence as measured by standardised tests which attempt to give a sample expression of the skills involved in intelligent behaviour.

Note that the three uses of the word neatly distinguish between what is measurable and what is not. A move from IA to IC gets further and further away from a pure expression of intelligence towards ways of assessing and measuring it, and this contains inherent problems. By definition, IA is not measurable, and to get a true evaluation of IB it would be necessary to know the individual's reactions to every experience that he or she has encountered – a difficult, if not impossible, task. This leaves IC, which relies on 'sampling' from what it is hoped is the whole repertoire of a person's intelligent behaviours, which contains a risk that something important will be omitted from the sample of repertoires chosen, with the corresponding risk that an individual's potential will be wrongly estimated.

Moreover, intelligence IB acknowledges an interaction between environmental experience and genetic potential, and so anything measured in IC could be partly the result of learning. For example, if there are two people with the same level of intelligence IA, and one has wider experiences of the world than the other, they will almost certainly be different in terms of intelligence IB. Since intelligence IC only takes a sample of IB, if both people are compared on this, in all likelihood one will be evaluated as more intelligent than the other, whereas in fact both have the same potential.

Since IA cannot be observed or measured directly, any definition of intelligence is bound to be controversial, which is why all three definitions are given. All this poses difficult problems for organisations, and unfortunately there are no easy answers. Clearly, intelligent behaviour is important in employees, but what do we mean by intelligence, and how can we tell whether a potential recruit is intelligent? Leaving aside the actual testing of intelligence IC, which will be considered presently, by definition,

IA cannot be evaluated and so, at best, an organisation can try to assess intelligence IB in job applicants. In most cases this comes down to judging them in terms of qualifications and other attainments. However, this has its own problems. Some people might have had better teachers than others and might have worked harder at school or university, although arguably this could be taken as a sign of intelligent behaviour in terms of adapting to the academic environment. With lower-level qualifications (those below first degree level) there could also be the problem of social background. For instance, some people could have been sent to a boarding school by their parents, where classes are smaller and there are fewer distractions. On their own these problems are bad enough, but there is the additional matter of the other indicators that selectors use to evaluate intelligence, which will be considered later.

The Genetic Component of Intelligence

The three-part definition given above alerts us to the idea that there is a strong genetic component in intelligence, the evidence for which is overwhelming. For example, the incidence of retarded children born to retarded parents is much higher than with non-retarded parents (Reed and Reed 1964). However, it is much more difficult to be precise about the degree of genetic influence, both in terms of size and the effects that it has. The most thorough work to date is derived from studies of identical twins. One such study used standardised tests to compare the intelligence of identical and non-identical twins, either reared together since birth or reared apart. From this it was estimated that somewhere between 60 and 80 per cent of intelligence is associated with genetic factors (Erlenmeyer-Kimling and Jarvik 1963). Although this was a very rigorous study, there are still problems in generalising too widely from the results. One problem is that we know environment has some effect, and child-rearing practices vary between the social classes. For instance, middle- and upper-class children tend to be brought up in environments where, in their early years, they receive a great deal of stimulation and attention from their parents, and the work cited above gives evidence of these effects: identical twins in socially advantaged families have much closer intelligence levels than those of non-identical twins or siblings. However, when children from disadvantaged families are compared, the intelligence of identical twins is not much closer than that of non-identical twins or other siblings. Thus, while genetics play a considerable part in intelligence, environmental factors such as child-rearing practices also have an important effect. For this reason, it is safer to assume that genetics merely sets a limit on a person's intelligence, and whether the individual ever comes near to realising his or her full potential depends on environmental effects. Indeed, the interaction between genetics and environment is extremely complex, so complex that it is nearly impossible to unravel. While it is probably safe to assume that 60–80 per cent of a person's intelligence is genetically determined, it is impossible to be precise about which 60–80 per cent this is.

General intelligence (g): an individual's overall intelligence level as measured by a test

Verbal:educational intelligence (V:Ed): that part of an intelligence test which assesses verbal, numeric and educational skills and abilities

Models of Human Intelligence

The controversy over the testing and measurement of intelligence has its counterpart in the debate about how the structure of intelligence can best be described. Most tests are based on Spearman's (1904) theory. In this, *general intelligence (g)* is determined by two major subsidiary factors: *verbal:educational intelligence (V:Ed)* and

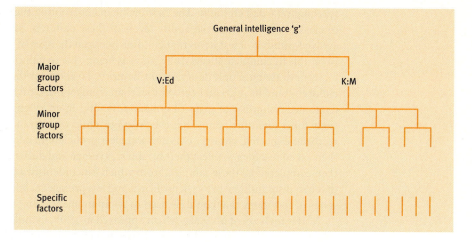

Figure 3.9
Spearman's hierarchical conceptualisation of the structure of intelligence

Figure 3.10
Thurstone's primary mental abilities

Kinaesthetic:motor intelligence (K:M): that part of an intelligence test which assesses practical, mechanical and spatial skills and abilities

kinaesthetic:motor intelligence (K:M), and these in turn are determined by minor and specific 's' factors, which are the skills associated with each type of intelligence. This is shown in Figure 3.9.

Somewhat later Thurstone (1938) developed a rather different model. His position is that there is no such a thing as general intelligence. Instead there are eight primary abilities, all of which are comparatively independent of each other, which means that any measure of intelligence needs to evaluate all eight separately. This idea is shown in Figure 3.10.

A more recent move in thinking about the concept of intelligence is represented by what is often referred to as the **information-processing** approach. This is very much the province of cognitive psychology and aims to understand the mental processes that are at work in humans when they are engaged in complex mental activities. Much of this work has been undertaken within an *artificial intelligence* framework, in which computer models of processes that could be at work are developed. One example of this is Simon's (1976) work to map out the mental process involved in solving the problem of a complex series of moves in a game of chess.

Artificial intelligence: a branch of cognitive psychology which uses computer models to try to simulate the activities of mental processes

The real foundations of modern intelligence testing can be traced to the work of Alfred Binet (Binet and Simon 1908) who, in 1904, was appointed by the French Minister for Public Instruction to a commission which examined the problems associated with teaching retarded children. The first problem confronting the commission was how to classify and measure the ability levels of these children. Binet's approach was to evolve a number of test items that children between the ages of three and twelve ought to be able to complete successfully, such as being able to name objects in pictures correctly or drawing simple designs from memory. To allow for the probability that older children could have greater capabilities than younger ones, each one of these test items contained a number of tasks of graded difficulty. In an extensive series of investigations Binet identified items that the 'average' child of a given age could answer correctly; as expected, younger children were less proficient in addressing these tasks. He then asked teachers to select their brightest, average and dullest pupils. The tests were then completed by these samples, from which Binet identified the questions and tasks that best distinguished between proficient and less proficient children. This gave a robust series of test items that could be used to compare mental abilities.

A later revision of his scale, which appeared in 1908, included an innovative (some people would say infamous) feature. This was a method for calculating a child's mental age, the *intelligence quotient (IQ)*, which is defined as:

Intelligence quotient (IQ): mental age (as indicated by an intelligence test) divided by actual (chronological) age

$$\frac{\text{mental age}}{\text{chronological age}}$$

Using this measure, a child of six who can correctly answer the same items (and achieve the same score) as the average child of eight has an IQ of 133.3, i.e. $\dfrac{8 \times 100}{6}$

After the Binet–Simon scale was translated into English in 1910 the testing of intelligence grew rapidly in popularity. The tests that resulted were individually applied and required the services of a trained and qualified practitioner. This means that they are somewhat inconvenient and expensive in mass-testing situations, and the main growth area in intelligence testing has therefore been in the use of group tests, usually self-administered 'pen-and-paper' tests. The best known in the UK are the AH2 to AH6 series devised by Alice Heim, which are based on (or at least expressed in terms of) Spearman's model of intelligence.

Although 'pure' tests of this type are sometimes applied in organisations, they are by no means used for all job applicants. They would probably be used most as part of a battery of other tests when selecting from school-leavers for trainee positions. Nevertheless, it is probably fair to say that, in one way or another, an evaluation of the intelligence of every applicant is made as part of a selection process, and one set of criteria that are used – qualifications and other attainments – has already been mentioned. Unfortunately, subjective evaluations are also made, sometimes on the flimsiest of evidence, perhaps on the basis of how quickly questions are answered in an interview, or how lively and outgoing the applicant seems to be. Not only are these poor predictors of intelligence (an applicant might be shy), if anything they are more an indication of personality, and poor indicators at that. One thing the models of intelligence given earlier tell us is that intelligence is multidimensional. Since few of us can be intelligent about everything, if we want an intelligent person for a job we have to be more specific about what type of intelligence is required. To a large extent, this is a matter of aptitude or ability, which is covered next.

- There is no single valid definition of intelligence, and in the interests of accuracy three separate definitions are required: intelligence IA – potential intelligence as determined by genetic factors; intelligence IB – intelligence as displayed in everyday life which arises from the interplay between genetic potential and experience; intelligence IC – intelligence as measured by standardised tests.

- Structural models of intelligence fall into one of two main types: the two-factor model (Spearman), which portrays general intelligence as made up of two primary factors: V:Ed and K:M; the eight primary abilities model (Thurstone).

Emotional Intelligence: A Recent Development

Emotional intelligence: ability or competence in managing one's own feelings and recognising (and dealing effectively with) other people's feelings

A concept that has recently enjoyed a meteoric rise in popularity (or, according to the viewpoint adopted, notoriety) is that of *emotional intelligence* (EI). Daniel Goleman (1998), who did much to popularise EI in America, describes the emotionally intelligent person as someone who can manage his or her own feelings and recognise and deal effectively with other people's feelings.

Dulewicz and Higgs (1999), the foremost British proponents of EI, argue that it can be measured in a valid and reliable way. It consists of three components, each of which is a group of traits:

Drivers (motivation and decisiveness) are traits that energise people and give them the motive force to achieve their goals (people high in EI normally set themselves fairly high goals).

Constrainers (conscientiousness, integrity and emotional resilience) are traits that curb the excesses of drivers.

Enablers (sensitivity, influence and self-awareness) are traits that enable people to perform well and achieve their goals.

All of these traits are what would normally be regarded as dimensions of personality and, for this reason, the word 'intelligence' needs to be interpreted with some caution. Its use might be little more than a repacking of personality theory or competences to make the idea more marketable (Woodruffe 2000, 2001; Chapman 2001). Indeed, there is an increasing number of consultants who offer training in EI and there seems to be no shortage of organisations eager to embrace the idea. Nevertheless, most experts agree that some of these traits, for instance the drivers and the enablers, are enduring dimensions of an individual's personality and there is an obvious need to be cautious in condemning new concepts too readily. For instance, work in this area shows that a combination of IQ and EI can be a highly effective way of predicting the future performance of individuals (Dulewicz and Higgs 1999). In addition, a longitudinal study using abstracted data collected across a 50-year time span, which included personality and IQ measures, shows that there is an enduring relationship between personality traits, general intelligence and career success (Judge *et al.* 1999).

Gravitational hypothesis: over the course of their time in the labour market people with certain mental characteristics sort themselves into jobs compatible with their interests, values and abilities, to achieve a good person–job fit

Similar results over a shorter time span are also revealed in a study by de Fruyt and Mervielde (1999). Both of these studies provide support for what is known as the *gravitational hypothesis*, which suggests that over the course of their time in the labour market people with certain mental characteristics sort themselves into jobs compatible with their interests, values and abilities, to achieve a good person–job fit Most of the prior evidence to support this idea has rested on measures of IQ, that is, people with high general intelligence gravitate to positions of high organisational status, because they tend to be bored with more menial work. However, recent work shows that the additional use of personality variables adds considerably to the ability to predict success.

Although work of this type is still in its infancy, the organisational implications are highly significant. For example, by using appropriate personality and intelligence measures in combination, it might be possible to inject a higher degree of accuracy into selection decisions.

APTITUDE AND ABILITY

Aptitude: the facility or potential to be able to do something (the latent ability)

Learning: a relatively permanent change in behaviour, or potential behaviour, that results from experience

Achievement tests: tests that assess what a person can currently do

Aptitude tests: tests that assess what a person will be able to do if given the required training

While the only practical way of assessing intelligence is with reference to observable behaviour, structural models of intelligence reveal many different skills and abilities that could be used to do this. One of the things that makes intelligence testing controversial is that although intelligence has a genetic component, most abilities are the result of an interaction between innate factors and experience. Thus intelligence IA gives someone an *aptitude* (latent ability) to do something, but the actual skills to do it are acquired through *learning* (experience).

However, many people have a limited range of experiences, and so in an organisational context tests of aptitude and achievement can sometimes be of more interest than tests of intelligence; that is, an organisation would probably be more interested in what a person can do, or even what he or she would be able to do, given appropriate training. In this situation tests of achievement or aptitude come into their own, but there is a difference between the two. *Achievement tests* are designed to reveal what a person can do now, whereas *aptitude tests* give an indication of what a person should be able to do with training. Both types of test are very similar in terms of the questions or problems they use and the real difference is in the way that the resulting answers or scores are interpreted (Atkinson *et al.* 1987).

Depending upon the circumstances, either type of test has a potential use in employee selection. Most jobs require a range of connected skills, and one way to assess a person's suitability is to use tests that are representative of the requirements of the job. For example, a keyboard operator could be given a practical achievement test, which assesses speed and accuracy. Alternatively, an aptitude test could be used to determine whether a person has the manual dexterity and hand–eye coordination to become a proficient keyboard operator. Since the ability and aptitude approaches to testing are not mutually exclusive, in some situations both can be used together. This is sometimes done in selecting management trainees, where it can be reasoned that managerial aptitude consists of a complex combination of mental and analytical skills, together with a personal ability to express oneself lucidly. So far as more specific skills are concerned, a wide range of tests have been developed and some of the more important areas in which aptitudes can be assessed are given below.

- **Manual dexterity**   This covers abilities such as hand–eye coordination, which could be vital in a number of manual jobs. With greater use of computers and keyboards, this is also increasingly important for white-collar work.

- **Numeric ability**   In its simplest form numeric ability means that arithmetic calculations can be completed accurately. However, at a more advanced level there are also tests of this type which assess the potential for more abstract mathematical manipulations.

- **Spatial and diagrammatic ability**   These can be extremely important in creative or design work, for example, being able to mentally rotate an object and imagine what it would look like from a different position.

OB IN ACTION: Misusing Psychometric Tests

An advertising manager has won compensation after her boss gave her a psychometric test that suggested she was a 'prejudiced middle-class girl'.

Ana Stamenkovic had worked at the City company for four years, selling jewellery and watch advertising space and she reached a settlement for constructive dismissal after being forced out of her job with Cru Publishing last year when Eddie Prentice, managing director at the business publisher, gave her a psychometric test and told her the results showed she was just a 'middle-class girl who is prejudiced and only able to get on with people of her own category,' she told an employment tribunal.

Mrs Stamenkovic launched a £50,000 claim for sexual discrimination and unfair dismissal but the tribunal ruled that, although she had been constructively dismissed, she was 75 per cent to blame for her sacking while her bosses were 25 per cent culpable. Her sexual discrimination claim was rejected and the two sides had been due to return to the tribunal to finalise compensation when the company agreed to pay her an undisclosed sum.

Mrs Stamenkovic, who now works as a freelance advertising executive, recently said, 'Everything is so weighted in favour of companies. The tribunal system is impossible for the employee. In my case the company had insurance and could fight the case. I did not have any legal representation until the day when I took a barrister friend along.' At the tribunal, Mrs Stamenkovic said she was bypassed for promotion to a new post of advertising director and was forced to take the psychometric test after being stripped of her responsibilities. She said Mr Prentice went through the test results 'in excruciating details, departing from the computer-generated answer with his own amateur psychological diagnosis' and the strain of being hounded out of her job brought on stress-related illnesses.

Source:

Brun-Rovet, M (2002) Manager wins payout after boss's 'prejudiced middle-class' slur, *The Financial Times*, 28 November.

- **Socialisation**   This results in people being taught what is acceptable and not acceptable by the groups of which they are members. There is a well-documented stream of evidence that this has an abiding influence on what people come to accept as appropriate or inappropriate ways of thinking, speaking and behaving (Berry 1969).

- **Language**   Our native language has a huge influence on the way that we think. It acts as a filter, through which our thoughts pass, and dictates the way in which we organise, analyse and interpret our external world. Therefore, two groups of people whose languages differ widely in terms of lexicon (vocabulary) and grammar usually go well beyond using different labels for the same phenomena – they tend to hold fundamental differences in the way they view the world (Whorf 1940).

These are very powerful forces and, when taken together, they often result in some cultures placing a higher value on certain skills and behaviours than others. For this reason cultures usually develop practices to foster what they regard as the most important skills and behaviours in their members, and a culture becomes something that tells its members what is acceptable and what is not acceptable. Since what is acceptable in one culture may be highly inappropriate in another, it is only to be expected that there can be differences in the personality characteristics of members of different cultures. The same is true of patterns of aptitude and skills and some of these differences are underpinned by deeper mental characteristics, about which more will be said in Chapter 22. However, it would be very wrong to think that any culture produces a better personality profile, or more intelligent people, than others; they are just different.

An employer is entitled to seek to employ staff with characteristics that give a reasonable assurance that they will perform well in a job, or be able to benefit from training. However, when it comes to the matter of comparing the personalities or aptitudes of people from different cultures for these purposes, there can be significant problems. People from different cultural groups are likely to have had different opportunities to build up the mental frameworks called for by a personality or aptitude test. Since a test only samples from a whole range of skills and abilities, there is a danger that a test constructed for one cultural group only samples the skills and behaviours valued in that culture. In other words, the test could be culturally biased.

Psychological testing is a particularly Western invention. Older personality tests often have a distinct gender bias and tests of specific abilities or aptitudes can discriminate against some ethnic minorities, albeit unwittingly. There is probably no such thing as a culturally unbiased test. The best we can hope for is that a test is culturally fair, and this is often a function of the test situation, that is, the test itself and the people who are tested. Unfortunately, it is all too easy to incorporate items in a test that unwittingly discriminate against certain ethnic groups. Vernon (1969) gives an example to illustrate this by pointing out that intelligence, aptitude and some personality tests often make use of pictures or drawings of humans. This is quite acceptable in most Western cultures, but in the Moslem religion, pictorial representation of the human form is discouraged. Thus, even allowing for the unfamiliarity of these pictures to an Arab, a test item could inhibit the person from recognising the principle that the picture sets out to illustrate.

CASE STUDY 3.2: Dr Major's Dilemma

Dr Major thought deeply about a meeting he had just attended with his Head of Department (HOD). Emboldened by a request some three months ago for advice on psychological testing from the Personnel Department of the university, the HOD, who was extremely ambitious, saw an opportunity for earning additional income for the Department. He had been approached by a large financial services organisation that was about to embark on a programme of management development and had sold them the idea of providing a psychological testing service. In general terms, what he had agreed with the firm was that each of its managers would undergo personality profiling, which would be used as a basis for counselling the person and to draw up individual development plans. After his meeting with the firm he had called in Dr Major, who pointed out to the HOD that this would virtually mean that he would have to be taken off all teaching and administrative duties for the foreseeable future. 'Nonsense,' replied the HOD, 'all you need to do is administer a quick personality test and the firm will do the rest.' Dr Major, who knew full well that the HOD was not a psychologist, then asked two questions: 'What personality test do you recommend and who is going to score the test and interpret the results?' 'I have told you,' said the HOD, 'the firm will choose the test, you will administer it and they will also counsel their own employees.' Dr Major then pointed out that almost anyone could be trained to administer a test and score it, but the part that requires psychological knowledge is the interpretation of the results. Thus, if the firm felt it was able to interpret the results, why did it need his services to administer and score the test? At this point the HOD said, 'You know very well why. Since they do not have a qualified occupational psychologist on the payroll, they can't even buy copies of the test, whereas you can.' To this Dr Major asked a final question before leaving the room: 'Let me get this straight then, what you are suggesting is that, as a qualified test user, I act as a conduit for an unqualified test user to purchase tests so that people unqualified and probably inexperienced in psychology can counsel employees on a psychological basis?'

Question

What should Dr Major do now?

REPLAY

- While aptitude and ability are two concepts that are allied to intelligence, they are more strongly focused on the measurement of intelligent behaviour in terms of usable skills.
- Aptitude reflects a person's potential to be able to do something and aptitude tests assess a person's capability to do something if given the necessary training.
- Ability is a product of aptitude and learning and ability tests measure what a person can do at the current time.
- Allowance should be made for the effects of cultural factors when comparing scores of individuals on tests of intelligence, aptitude and ability.

Chapter 4

Perception

LEARNING OUTCOMES

After studying this chapter you should be able to:

- define perception

- in outline, describe the perceptual process

- explain perceptual selectivity and attention, perceptual organisation and object recognition, and perceptual interpretation and inference

- explain some of the problems associated with social perception, including stereotyping, halo effects and self-fulfilling prophecy effects

- explain the ways in which perception can influence the performance appraisal process and processes for dealing with poor employee performance

INTRODUCTION

This chapter deals with perception, another important way in which people differ as individuals. Since perception results in people having highly individualised ways of viewing their surroundings, it can mean that two people could perceive the same situation differently, and behave towards it in different ways; something that has strong implications for organisations.

The chapter commences with a brief explanation of human sensory processes which culminates in a definition of perception. Because perception is a very complex matter, the first step in exploring the process is to consider it in its simplest form, the perception of static objects. This is followed by a consideration of a more complex version of the process that relates directly to organisational life: the perception of people and social situations. Differences in perceptual ability and accuracy are then considered and this is followed by an explanation of some of the outcomes of social perception: the self-fulfilling prophecy, the effects of perceptions on performance appraisal, and the way that managers deal with poor employee performance. A brief consideration of cross-cultural differences in perception is given, and the chapter closes with a short overview section that brings together its contents.

THE HUMAN SENSORY PROCESS

To function in the world, we all have to take in information from our surroundings and use it to regulate our behaviour. We do this through the five traditional senses of hearing, sight, touch, smell and taste, plus two more that are now currently accepted: pain and proprioception – our sense of body and limb position. Each one is a different channel for importing information about 'what is out there', and each channel has its own *sensor organs* (the eye for visual data and the ear for auditory information), but there are limits on what a receptor can sense. After having sensed something 'out there', the information is transmitted to the brain via the appropriate nervous pathways; in the case of visual information, via the optic nerves and from the ear via the auditory nerves. While a certain amount of preprocessing of information takes place along these nervous pathways, the major and most important processing functions are performed in the appropriate cortex of the brain.

In everyday life most situations are so rich in information that there is probably too much to handle. For instance, if you look at a crowd scene on television you will probably be aware of several hundred people, but you will only register details of facial features and clothes for a few of them. Therefore, we attend to some features and not to others and this can happen with any of the receptor channels. The example given above illustrates features of perceptual processes at work. The process is highly individualised, and two or more people confronted with the same external situation can experience matters in different ways. Humans seldom see or hear reality; they infer or construct personalised versions of reality from the stimuli to which they are exposed. While a simplistic and very naive view of this is that some people are more observant than others, this assumes that people are simply passive recipients of information. However, the reality is that we all process information in an active way and with this in mind, *perception* is defined as:

Sensor organs: organs that detect information about stimuli in the environment, i.e. the eye for visual information

Perception: a mental process involving the selection, organisation, structuring and interpretation of information in order to make inferences and give meaning to the information

an active mental process which involves the selection, organisation, structuring and interpretation of information in order to make inferences and give meaning to the information.

In organisations our perceptions are usually of people, and we make judgements about them and how they respond to what we say or do, on the basis of our perception. However, our perceptions are inferences rather than a faithful reproduction of what is there. Therefore, before dealing with the extremely complex matter of social perception it is important to understand something of the limitations that the perceptual process places on us by considering it in a basic way: the perception of static objects.

THE PERCEPTUAL PROCESS

The following discussion will deal mainly with visual perception. However, it is important to recognise that we use all our senses to perceive, and so other channels have their own equivalents of many of the phenomena that will be described.

The Basic Perceptual Model

Although perceiving something depends on the stimuli that register on a particular sensor, perception is more than simply sensing 'what is out there'. The idea that perception is just a one-way, data-driven process will be referred to here as the *bottom-up processing* conception. This is now regarded as rather simplistic, because it implies that identifying something such as a triangle simply means that information about external stimuli is passed to the brain, where it is processed and matched up with some sort of stored template with the label triangle attached to it. However, triangles come in all shapes and sizes, and we are able to recognise them all as triangles. Therefore, perception is more than recognising distinctive shapes and, because we can identify all three-sided figures in which the sides connect as triangles, it must also involve the use of concepts. Thus, higher-order brain processes are at work and a certain amount of *top-down processing* occurs as well. Without going into detail, it is known that incoming sensory data is refined a great deal along the nervous pathways between the sensory receptor and the brain, and in all probability the brain instructs the pathways how to process the data. One way to portray the idea that bottom-up and top-down processes are at work together is by using the simplified model shown in Figure 4.1. Somewhat artificially, the model divides the perceptual process into three stages, in which incoming sensory data is gradually transformed into a perception. For convenience, the process will be described in three main stages and each one will be explained separately.

Bottom-up processing: perceptual processes driven by incoming data imported through sensor organs

Top-down processing: perceptual processes driven by the higher brain

Stage 1: Attention and Selection

People are often confronted with more stimuli than they can comprehend at the same time. Some are outside the range of their sensory apparatus and some are screened out to enable attention to be focused on others. This is not a random event and people usually attend to stimuli that are the most salient (noteworthy) at that point in time. In general terms, two sets of factors influence salience: first, the characteristics of the

Attention and selection: the tendency to acknowledge some stimuli and ignore or mask out others

Figure 4.1 The basic perceptual process

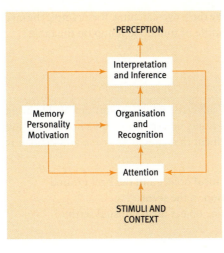

Figure 4.1 The basic perceptual process

stimulus itself, which are registered via bottom-up processes and, second, internal, higher-order mental processes, which come into play through top-down aspects of processing.

External (Bottom-up) Factors

All other things being equal, the **size** of a stimulus, its **intensity** and the **contrast** between stimulus and background all influence the degree of attention. An example of contrast is given in Figure 4.2: even though both of the dark, inner circles are the same size, the one on the right probably seems slightly larger.

People also attend more to an object in **motion** than to one that is static and within limits; **repetition** or repeated exposure to a stimulus has the same effect. An allied principle is that of **novelty** and **familiarity**, in which new objects in a familiar setting attract our attention.

These characteristics of the perceptual process are well known and used by the advertising industry. Monster advertisements on a hoarding, for example, attract our attention more than small fly-posters on a wall. Bright colours in an advertisement are likely to grab the attention more than those that are drab, particularly if there is a strong element of contrast between a focal object and its background. Because over-exposure to a particular advertisement weakens its impact over time, advertisements for a product often run in a series, containing a unifying theme. Novelty is also used in

Figure 4.2
The contrast principle from *Organizational Behaviour, 5th Edition* by D Hellriegal, J W Slocum and R W Woodman, © 1989. Reprinted with permission of South-Western College Publishing, a division of Thomas Learning. Fax 800 730 2215

advertisements to make them eye-catching, for example the medieval lord sitting down to a banquet with a bottle of tomato ketchup on the table.

TIME OUT

Try to think of a 'still' advertisement that you can readily bring to mind that you have seen recently in a magazine, newspaper or on a hoarding. Now try to analyse what it is about the advertisement that caught your eye and made it memorable. Was it:

intensity of colours
contrast between the focal object and the background
an impression of **motion** in the scene
the **novelty** of a familiar object in an unusual setting?

Internal (Top-down) Factors

Personality variables predispose people to pay attention to certain stimuli more than others; indeed, the recognition of certain features in an ambiguous picture or scene is one way of assessing personality. **Motivations** also have an impact on attention. An unsatisfied need has a motivating effect and so people can be highly sensitive to stimuli that offer a route to needs satisfaction. For instance, a cool stream or a refreshing drink in an advertisement would probably attract the attention of someone who was thirsty and some advertisements, notably those for cars, come uncomfortably close to awakening our needs for status symbols. Because prior **learning** and **experience** create expectancies that some things are more important than others, these also influence attention. For instance, the experience and training of a policeman would make him sensitive to an open window on the ground floor of a house because it is an easy access point for a burglar. Finally, a person's **perceptual set,** that is, the mental predispositions that make some stimuli more interesting than others, can also play an important role in selective attention. For instance, if you know that you have to let your boss have a particularly important item of information, the very presence of a computer on your desk might attract your attention because e-mail is a means of conveying the message.

Stage 2: Stimulus Organisation and Recognition

Stimulus organisation and recognition: the organisation of stimulus information into meaningful patterns that form identifiable wholes

When certain features of a stimulus attract attention, they are then organised into a meaningful whole. There is a great deal of ongoing research in this area, but the basic principles were uncovered many years ago and are given in what follows.

Figure-to-ground Effect

Figure-to-ground effect: the tendency to organise data so that all figures are seen as existing against a background

This is the most basic form of perceptual organisation. It simply means that figures are always seen against a background – the most readily available example is this text. What registers on your eyes is a set of irregular black and white shapes. Your mind organises the stimuli into recognisable black figures (letters, words and punctuation marks) on a white background. However, things are not always as simple as this. In some situations figure and ground can seem to switch. In Figure 4.3, what do you see? A white vase against a dark background, or two faces silhouetted against a white background?

Figure 4.3 Figure-to-ground effect

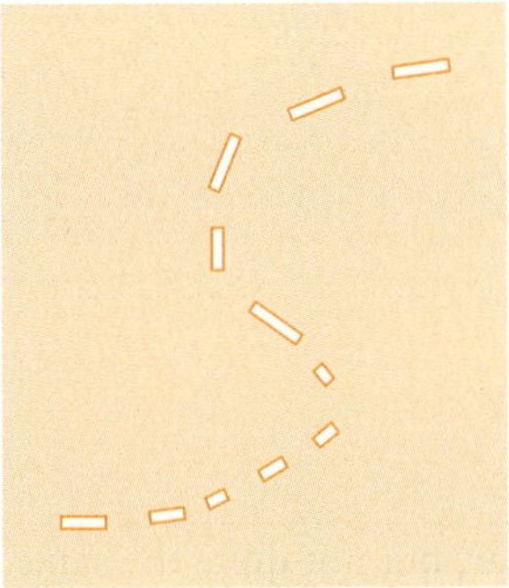

Figure 4.4 Closure principle

Grouping effect: the tendency to organise data into meaningful groups or patterns

In organisations people can be made more aware of particularly important pieces of equipment by the use of bright colours to increase the figure-to-ground effect. For example, fire alarm switches are normally painted bright red.

Grouping Effects

Closure principle: gaps between stimuli are filled in so that discrete stimuli are perceived as connected

This principle reflects the tendency to organise stimuli into meaningful groups and patterns, by either closure, proximity, continuity or similarity. In *closure*, top-down processes fill in any gaps in the incoming sensory stimuli, and a whole is inferred where one does not exist. An example of closure is shown in Figure 4.4, where the blobs are usually interpreted as the number 5 or the letter 'S'.

Proximity principle: objects are perceived as related because of their closeness

The *proximity principle* results in a group of objects being perceived as related because of their physical closeness to each other. For instance, in Figure 4.5, some people find it more meaningful to perceive the three groups of blocks in (b) as a larger group of nine, as shown in (a). In addition, it is probably easier to recognise that a string of digits that you have written down is a telephone number if it is presented as 0161 729785, rather than 0161729785.

Figure 4.5 Perceptual grouping

Figure 4.6 Continuity principle

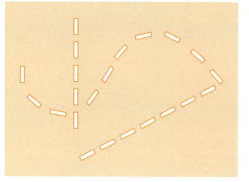

Figure 4.7 Similarity principle

DOB102
BOD2O3
AOX33O

Continuity principle: the existence of missing stimuli is inferred, resulting in a perception of links between unconnected stimuli

The *continuity principle* is similar, but not quite the same. Because the mind has a tendency to disregard changes in shape or direction, missing stimuli are supplied where none exist to result in the perception of a continuous line. An example of this is shown in Figure 4.6, where a number of separate lines tend to be seen as one which traces an irregular shape.

Similarity principle: the tendency to infer that two objects alike in some respects are alike in other ways

With the *similarity principle*, because an object is alike in some way to another one, it is perceived as being identical in several other respects. An example of this is given in Figure 4.7, where the first line contains the capital letters 'D', 'O', 'B', followed by the digits one, zero, two. Here, there is usually a tendency to see the digits in the second and third lines as also containing zeros, but they actually contain the capital letter 'O'.

Constancy effect: the perceiver is able to make adjustments for distance etc. so that the object is experienced as the same size irrespective of its distance

Constancy Effects

Constancy effects enable us to organise incoming stimuli in a highly sophisticated way. In much the same way that the size of a photographic image depends on distance between camera and object, the size of an image on the retina depends on the distance between the object and the eye. Thus, if someone walks towards us, the retinal image gets larger and so we could expect to see the person increasing in size. However, we do not experience things in this way because, somehow, top-down processing compensates for the size of the retinal image.

Context effect: the use of information from the context of the object to infer its identity

Context Effects

The features surrounding a stimulus can also have a profound effect on the way that incoming information is organised. This also involves top-down processing, in which the deeper recesses of memory are used to make sense of the stimuli. According to the surrounding context, the same stimulus clues can be interpreted as quite different objects

Figure 4.8 The effect of context

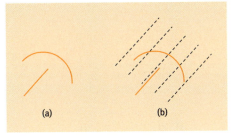

(a)   (b)

and an example of this is given in the apparently meaningless object in Figure 4.8(a), which might possibly be interpreted as a badly drawn letter 'T'. Compare this with Figure 4.8(b), where a context of diagonal hatching has been superimposed, which makes it much easier to infer that the object could be an umbrella.

In organisations that have large, open plan offices, furniture is sometimes arranged as a context that makes it easier to locate certain people. For example, sections or departments can have their desks laid out in a triangle arrangement, in which the section leader or head is always located at the apex of the triangle.

Perceptual Defence

Perceptual defence: the resistance to acknowledging a stimulus because doing so would contradict a person's deeply held values or what he or she already believes

This is an organising principle which has some similarity to the use of contextual information. Sometimes defences are built against acknowledging certain stimuli. For instance, Bruner and Postman (1947) show that people erect barriers to recognising words that threaten their concepts of self, and McGinnies (1949) notes that people have a strong emotional resistance to the recognition of critical, taboo words. Another study shows that people have a remarkable resistance to acknowledging something that clashes with a preconceived notion – in this case the idea that manual factory workers could be characterised as intelligent (Haire and Grunes 1950). Defences such as these can be strongly related to the phenomenon of stereotyping, which is discussed in greater depth later in the chapter.

Stage 3: Interpretation and Inference

In the two prior stages certain stimuli receive attention while others are largely ignored, and those that are accepted are organised into meaningful patterns. However, a perception does not take place until a decision is made that the pattern means something. All that has happened so far is that processes such as continuity and closure supply information which is absent, but in this stage much more significant events take place. The philosopher Wittgenstein (1953) observes that all seeing is 'seeing as'. We do not just observe shapes and sounds, but see the shapes as recognisable objects such as chairs and tables and hear noises as bangs, tunes or shrieks. Thus an identity and nature is imputed and, since sensory data is usually insufficient to provide unequivocal evidence about identity, we make *inferences*, that is, we reach a conclusion about something based on incomplete evidence, and make assumptions about what the missing evidence is. For example, if you look in a mirror and see someone standing behind you, your knowledge of elementary optics enables you to infer that the person is there, even though you cannot see through the back of your head and you cannot see the light rays

Perceptual inference: a conclusion about an object is reached on the basis of incomplete evidence

Figure 4.9 Ambiguous shapes

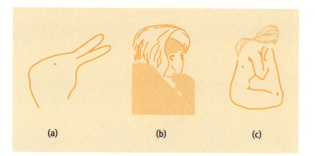

(a)   (b)   (c)

carrying the person's image. By thinking things through you can make a conscious inference, and similar processes are at work in perception. However, they are unconscious and bring together the various pieces of evidence to infer both that something is out there and that it has an identity.

Schema

Although it is fairly easy to accept that we make these interpretations and inferences, this still begs the question of how they are made. It seems likely that each person has a repertoire of *schema*. These are structured mental representations of what the world is like, or what it contains, that are used to bring the evidence together and draw conclusions about an object's identity. Look at the line drawings in Figures 4.9(a), (b) and (c). What objects do they represent?

As you have probably spotted, each picture could represent two objects: Figure 4.9(a) is either a duck or a rabbit; Figure 4.9(b) is an old crone or a sophisticated young woman; and Figure 4.9(c) is a kneeling woman or a man's face. With practice you can possibly switch between the two interpretations, but note that it is impossible to see both together. Thus, at any point in time, the information has to be structured in a particular way to infer what the object is, and this is related to a mental picture (schema) of how an object of this type should look. This is a very important idea. Schema tell us what to expect and are vital in recognising that something is impossible. Now look closely at the object shown in Figure 4.10. What do you notice?

Clearly the object in Figure 4.10 is a triangle, but a very odd one. If you look closely, you will see that it could never exist in practice, because a flat surface cannot be behind and in front of another flat surface at the same time. Very complex mental processes are at work in recognising this and, unless we assume that schema of some sort exist, it is difficult to see how we could do it. While schema tell us what to expect, where do they come from and, more importantly, how do we use them? Our accumulated knowledge

Schema: a structured mental representation of what the world is like or what it contains

Figure 4.10

Figure 4.11 Analysis by synthesis (after Neisser 1976)

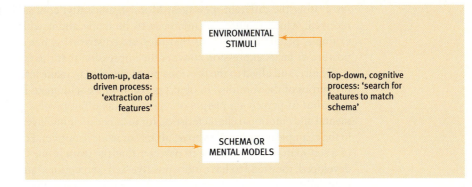

Analysis by synthesis: a self-adjusting cycle in which an estimate of the identity of an object is derived from incoming sensory data. This is compared with a schema for the object and if the initial inference is confirmed, a search for confirmatory information is made

and expectations probably provide the schema, and how they are used is addressed by Neisser's (1976) *analysis by synthesis* model, which is shown in Figure 4.11.

Neisser suggests that there is a self-adjusting cycle, which starts when receptor cells and nervous pathways give a preliminary representation of the stimulus on the basis of its properties such as figure-to-ground relationships and proximity. At this point the person is not actually attending to the stimulus but nevertheless extracts some of its important features. If this results in an initial indication that the stimulus could be salient, attention is triggered, followed by a preliminary best guess or working hypothesis about what the stimulus could be. At this point other top-down processes are activated. An appropriate schema is selected and compared with the bottom-up sensory input and, if there is a match, the cycle is repeated to search for additional confirmatory evidence. Where there is no match, an alternative working hypothesis is constructed and this prompts a further search until a match is found.

SOCIAL PERCEPTION

Perception in social situations reflects all of the basic processes described above. However, there are at least four significant differences between perceiving objects and perceiving social scenes.

First, in object perception the stimuli are relatively unchanging. If you look at the ambiguous objects in Figures 4.9(a), (b) and (c), your perceptions are likely to be the same tomorrow, because the drawings will not have changed. In social situations the stimuli keep changing and, because the ground shifts under the perceiver's feet, he or she probably needs to make constant revisions and refinements.

Second, in social perception the stimulus is another person or people. We don't just perceive other people, we interact with them, and our perceptions influence our interactions. Thus how I experience somebody else is often a function of how he or she experiences me. To give an example, there is strong evidence that individuals who perceive that they have a good relationship with their immediate superior tend to put increased effort into doing their work well, in order to cement this relationship. Because this effectively rewards the supervisor, he or she also tends to put more into the relationship and so it is likely to become even stronger (Wayne *et al.* 1997).

Third, social perception involves the use of several sensory systems together. Therefore, the processing centres in the brain have a much more complicated task to perform in integrating the different messages. More significantly, contradictory signals can be received, which requires an inference to be made about which one is correct; for example, people might tell us that they are trustworthy, but something about their posture or facial expression conveys the impression that this is not true.

Finally, and allied to the previous point, we tend to make inferences about abstract properties of the stimulus. In object perception we seldom go beyond deciding 'what it is', but in perceiving people our perceptions often involve inferences about their mental and emotional characteristics, for instance their intelligence and personality, or in the example immediately above, about someone's motives. For example, if members of a self-managed team come to perceive that the team is one that is mature and well developed, they tend to have more positive 'self-perceptions' and, if they feel this way, they develop positive self-images, which seems to result in the team becoming a more highly effective unit (Neck *et al.* 1999).

Perceiving People

Social perception plays an important part in organisational behaviour. Some people are immensely proud of what they believe is their ability to make accurate judgements about others, and the assumption that some individuals have special skills of this type is quite widespread. Ideas such as this have long fascinated psychologists, and they give rise to two separate but interconnected questions. First, do people differ in terms of their abilities to perceive the characteristics and attributes of others? Second, to what extent are people able to make accurate assessments of other people? Since both are important, they will be considered separately.

Differences in Perceptual Abilities

In object perception, a factor that can influence whether a stimulus attracts a person's attention is its salience. Therefore one explanation of differences in perceptual abilities could lie in the salience of other people's characteristics. Tagiuri (1969) suggests that the impressions we form fall into basic classes, each of which represents a group of attributes of other people, such as their:

- intentions
- ideas
- traits
- attitudes
- abilities
- thoughts
- emotions
- purposes
- memories

Each of these basic classes splits down further, to give more specific dimensions along which we make perceptual judgements about other people. For example, the dimensions for abilities might include:

- creativity
- physical
- imagination
- musical
- intelligence
- literary etc.

TIME OUT

Look closely at Tagiuri's (1969) nine basic classes for evaluating other people. For each of these classes write down two or three dimensions that you would use to evaluate other people. For example, in what three ways do you evaluate their emotions?

We also know from object perception that people differ in what they attend to, and in social situations it is possible that they differ in terms of the dimensions that attract their attention (Dornbusch *et al.* 1965). For instance, Jane and Fred both tend to focus on the abilities of other people, but creativity and intelligence attract Jane's attention, while Fred notices musical and literary abilities. What, then, makes some dimensions more salient than others? Tajfel (1969) suggests that an individual's most salient dimensions are those that have the highest *functional significance*, that is, those that the person finds most useful in ordering and making sense of his or her particular world; for example, to a clothes designer the physical attributes of a person might be all important, but for a busy manager a person's reliability and initiative could be the most salient.

Functional significance: the dimensions of evaluation used by a person because they are useful in making sense of the world

One of the most important things we know about the use of categories is that some individuals differ in terms of the size of their repertoires of dimensions. This is known as a person's *cognitive complexity*, which reflects his or her degree of sophistication in perceiving the world, usually the number of **independent dimensions** the person employs. For instance, if I evaluate someone as happy because he or she is outgoing, I am not differentiating between happiness and being outgoing as two independent dimensions; whereas if I work on the assumption that the two things are not the same, I would be using a more complex system of dimensions.

Cognitive complexity: the number of independent dimensions used by a person to evaluate objects and people

A word of caution is necessary about the concept of cognitive complexity. Although people with high cognitive complexity find it easier to make sense of apparently conflicting information about others (Little 1969), there is no relationship between cognitive complexity and intelligence (Cook 1971). Nevertheless, people with complex systems of categorisation are much less likely to make the 'stereotyping' or 'halo effect' errors that will be discussed shortly.

It is also important to remember that context plays a significant part in social perception. If someone is wearing a white coat in a laboratory setting we might well assume that he or she is a scientist and make favourable inferences about intelligence and skills, whereas the same person in the same white coat emerging from the back room of a restaurant could attract a far less complimentary judgement.

TIME OUT

Try to think of someone you know, or have known in the past, about whom your initial evaluation turned out to be incomplete, misleading or inaccurate when you came to know the person better. Now try to analyse why there were differences between your initial impression and the more accurate one you built up over time. Was this because you:

assumed that the person had certain attributes or qualities because he or she fell into a certain class of person that you believe normally has those attributes, or

was it because you assumed that since the person had a certain characteristic he or she automatically had other definable attributes?

Accuracy in Perceptions of Others

Although the perceptual process results in inferences rather than in a faithful reproduction of reality, the idea of perceptual accuracy implies that some people produce more faithful representations than others. A great deal of research has been carried out in this area and while people do differ in their evaluation of others, the idea that this is connected with the accuracy of their evaluations is an oversimplification.

The current view is that while people differ in the way that they perceive others, this is not linked to accuracy. Rather, some people are good at perceiving some attributes, but not so good at perceiving others, and nobody is likely to be perfect at perceiving everything (Cook 1971). For instance, person 'A' could be an accurate judge of 'impulsiveness' in others, but a poor judge of 'kindliness', and the reverse could be true of person 'B'. Thus, accuracy could come down to whether the most appropriate person is asked to make the judgement. For this reason accuracy could well depend on the perceptual judgement that an individual has to make. One way of guarding against perceptual errors of this type is by having different individuals evaluate whether or not a particular person has certain attributes. This is a widely adopted practice in organisations in the selection process, where an interview panel made up of several different people, each one of which is looking for something different, is used to assess the suitability of applicants for a job.

To summarise, in social situations some individuals use relatively simple schemes to make inferences about other people, while others have highly complex and detailed sets of categories. This is very important because an organisation is a context in which individuals perceive other individuals all the time, and their perceptions are likely to influence the nature of their interactions. Two phenomena that can sometimes give rise to problems are considered in what follows.

Stereotyping

Stereotyping: attributing a person with qualities assumed to be typical of members of a particular category (e.g. age, sex etc.) because the person falls into that category

A stereotype is a convenient, pre-assembled block of text used by printers because that particular combination of words occurs frequently. The word is also used in perception to describe:

> **the general inclination to place a person in some category according to some easy and quickly identifiable characteristic such as age, sex, ethnic membership, nationality or occupation, and then attribute the person as having qualities believed to be typical of members of that category.**
> **(Tagiuri 1969)**

Almost any characteristics can be used to make stereotyped judgements, for instance: age – older people are resistant to change; sex – women are too swayed by their emotions; nationality – Scots are mean about money; occupation – all engineers are good at maths; physical appearance – blondes are dumb; social background – upper-class people are all snobs; interests – artistic people are badly organised.

People use stereotypes to reduce the amount of information processing necessary to reach a perceptual judgement. Instead of using an elaborate system of dimensions to categorise people, they use a smaller, more restricted framework that assumes that some attributes go hand in hand. Since all individuals are unique, this can result in wildly inaccurate generalisations. Although not all stereotypes are negative, research into stereotyping has usually focused on its negative side, often in the study and analysis of prejudice. In organisations, its greatest danger is that something important about a person will be overlooked; for example, in the selection situation, incorrect assumptions can be made about candidates which result in an inadequate exploration of their skills and abilities. The same point could be made about the performance appraisal process. This

OB IN ACTION: Perceptions of Doing Business in Russia

Russia faces an uphill struggle to convince the Anglo-American business elite that it is ready to receive Western capital. That is the tough message delivered by SRU, a market research and consultancy group, and Expert Information Group, a Moscow consultancy, whose joint survey of 30 business leaders found that the former superpower is still viewed as a 'wild west' frontier state that has made little progress. Peter Wallis, SRU's managing director says that Russia remains 'off the investment map' and tended to be regarded as a 'no-man's land'. Even BP's purchase of a 50 per cent stake in a new oil joint venture, TNK-BP, did not herald a sea change in Western perceptions of Russia. Although Vladimir Putin, Russia's president, was admired for stabilising the country there is concern that the 'Putin effect' is too reliant on his political survival. Indeed, Russia's regime was compared unfavourably to China's – at least for the purposes of investment.

Potential investors seem to have perceptions of lack of respect for the rule of law and a corrupt society dominated by criminals, which has acted as a major disincentive to every kind of possible involvement in the country. One chief executive of a UK manufacturer said, 'We wouldn't touch Russia with a ten-foot pole and it's physically unsafe for Western managers.' A UK investment banker said, 'If you're doing business in Russia, you have to check your partners out very carefully. You can't take anything on trust: they could be gangsters.' Yet, for all the wariness, leading members of the Anglo-American establishment believe that Russia does – or, rather, must have – long-term potential. Its key attraction is its population and there is a widespread view that the country's people are well educated – particularly in science and technology. Its natural resources are also seen as a plus – although not universally so. However, in the eyes of respondents, to realise its potential Russia needs to strengthen its institutions and ensure that no one stands above the law. 'The real test for the government is seen as its ability to restrain the Russian mafia and the business oligarchs. That won't be easy and it explains why investors and companies are playing "wait-and-see" with Russia. Why go to Russia,' said the chief executive of a UK retailer, 'if you can get everything you want in Hungary or Poland?'

Source:

Targett, S (2003) Fighting its risky reputation, *The Financial Times*, 23 March.

not only wastes an organisation's resources but can result in unfair and unjust evaluations about people that run foul of the law on racial or sexual discrimination.

The Halo Effect

This occurs when a person who has one behaviourial trait is automatically credited with having other traits. At first sight this might seem to be the same as stereotyping,

OB IN ACTION: Mental Health Discrimination

Albeit in a mild form, it has been estimated that 25 per cent of the population will experience some form of mental illness in their working lives. Unfortunately many people have a deeply ingrained fear of those who are mentally ill and a survey by the mental health association MIND found that almost 40 per cent of sufferers had been either denied employment or dismissed because of their condition. The problem seems to be that the mentally ill tend to be viewed in a highly stereotyped (or negative halo effect) way, and the mere mention of schizophrenia or depression conjures up a vision of someone who could run amok in the workplace, which is far from being the truth.

A case that illustrates the point is that of Andrew Watkiss, who had successfully held down the senior position of assistant company secretary at the dairy products group Unigate for several years. Watkiss applied for and was offered the higher-paying post of company secretary at the construction company John Laing. However, the offer was withdrawn the following month when it was discovered in a medical examination that he had a history of schizophrenia, and he was told by the company that the new post would be too stressful for him. Eventually the case came before an employment appeal tribunal, where it was ruled that Watkiss had been subject to disability discrimination within the meaning of the Disability Discrimination Act (1995). Thus, in terms of employment law, the issue is one of increasing significance because it has been estimated that 12 per cent of the cases heard in employment tribunals are brought by people with mental health problems who complain of discriminatory treatment. Therefore, wise employers are making attempts to combat stereotyped thinking about mental health. For example, British Telecom (BT) is said to be moving in this direction, as are a number of local authorities.

Sources:

Welch, J (2000) Mental block, *People Management*, 20 January: 30–5.
Pawsey, V (2000) Landmark settlement for schizophrenic job seeker, *People Management*, 20 January: 15.

Halo effect: the assumption that because a person has a certain trait he or she automatically has other traits

and in the final analysis the end result is often the same: an inaccurate evaluation of a person. However, in stereotyping, the judgement is made because all people in a certain category are assumed to have common characteristics, whereas with the *halo effect* a particular trait is taken to be an indication that a person also has a number of other traits. The halo effect can lead to generalisations that are either positive or negative. For instance, a cooperative subordinate, who is receptive to a manager's ideas, could also be evaluated by the manager as perceptive and intelligent, whereas one who is not so cooperative might be condemned as blinkered and unintelligent. In reality, of course, the first person might just be trying to ingratiate him or herself with the manager, while the second has genuinely spotted a flaw in the manager's ideas.

The most worrying thing about the halo effect is its seemingly all-pervasive nature. This is well illustrated in an early study by Asch (1946), in which subjects were shown lists describing the personality traits of two imaginary people. Only one word was different on the lists; person 'A' was described as warm and person 'B' as cold. However, the subjects seemed blind to all other words but warm and cold and inferred that 'A' and 'B' had completely different personalities.

Two areas of organisational activity in which the halo effect can have potentially adverse consequences are selection and performance appraisal. While it has been known for some time that the phenomenon is commonplace, and despite all the effort that is put into training interviewers and appraisers, the problems are still very much in evidence. Indeed, a recent review of the literature indicates that it is still an extremely common phenomenon in appraisal (Murphy *et al.* 1993).

THE OUTCOMES OF SOCIAL PERCEPTIONS

One of the most important things about social perception is that it influences the way that people interact with each other. In organisations almost everything that takes place involves human interaction, which means that the effectiveness of organisational processes can be strongly influenced by perceptions. To illustrate this point, in addition to stereotyping and the halo effect, two additional areas are worthy of particular attention: the self-fulfilling prophecy effect and the effects of perception on performance evaluations.

The Self-fulfilling Prophecy

Self-fulfilling prophecy: a prophecy that comes true solely because it has been made

Merton (1957) is usually credited with inventing the term '*self-fulfilling prophecy*', which broadly means a prophecy which comes true solely because it has been made. It is now widely accepted that it is a common feature of all social interaction, and is important because our perceptions of other people can unwittingly influence their behaviour and their perceptions of themselves.

The best-known account of the phenomenon is a study conducted in an elementary school in the USA (Rosenthal and Jacobsen 1968), in which psychological tests that were said to be able to predict intellectual growth were given at intervals over a year to more than 600 pupils. The fine details of the study, while interesting, are less important than the results and conclusions drawn by the researchers. Early in the academic year, the researchers selected the names of a number of children randomly. Teachers were then told that these children would be academic 'fast developers'. At the end of the year, what the teachers reported about these children tied in absolutely with this, while other children, who had actually developed as much (or even more), were reported in far less favourable terms.

Rosenthal and Jacobsen largely attributed these differences to the way that teachers had behaved towards the children during the year. Those expected to show intellectual growth were treated in a way that encouraged them to grow intellectually; for example, if one of them raised a query, the teacher tended to answer in a way that gave the child the impression that he or she had asked a profound or intelligent question. Conversely, a pupil branded as less intellectual who asked the same question might receive an answer that conveyed the impression that the teacher viewed the child as

CASE STUDY 4.1: Judgements about John McTavish

National Chemical Industries (NCI) employs approximately 40 graduate trainees each year. For the first ten months, these trainees spend two months in each of the five major functions of the organisation, and managers in each one complete a report on each trainee. Given below are comments extracted from five different reports on John McTavish, who joined NCI after graduating from Cambridge University with first-class honours in Chemistry.

1. A highly competent, intelligent and creative person, as would be expected from someone who has obtained first-class honours in a degree at Cambridge.
2. Mr McTavish is an articulate and confident person. Clearly, therefore, his intelligence and imagination are beyond question.
3. Mr McTavish's timekeeping while in this department left much to be desired. Although he worked well enough when present, this raises some doubts about his keenness, self-discipline and commitment.
4. Like many people with an academic training in the physical sciences, Mr McTavish tends to be hidebound by rules and formulae. As such, he tends to look for ready-made solutions to problems and is rather lacking in creativity and innovation.
5. Mr McTavish has an inquiring mind and although he is seldom fast in solving problems, this tends to be because he has explored every possible alternative and for this reason, his solutions are often imaginative and creative.

Questions

1. The five managers reporting on John McTavish have identified a total of eight different characteristics. What are these characteristics? Why do you feel that the managers differ in terms of the characteristics on which they focus?

2. Are stereotyping or halo effects evident in the above statements? Classify each one according to whether it contains stereotyping or the halo effect.

rather backward. As a result, the predicted bloomer was rewarded and the other child punished. Teachers also tended to reward fast-track children in other ways; for instance, by giving them more time and attention, or asking them questions that allowed them to shine.

There is much support for the existence of the self-fulfilling prophecy effect, which has also been observed in organisational settings. For instance, Word *et al.* (1974) provide convincing evidence that in job interviews black candidates get fewer encouraging non-verbal signs of approval from white interviewers than do white candidates. Therefore, they tend to give less confident answers to questions and have a poorer interview performance. It is not hard to extrapolate these findings to many situations in organisations, and a process something like the one shown in Figure 4.12 could be at work.

Figure 4.12 Model of self-fulfilling prophecy effect

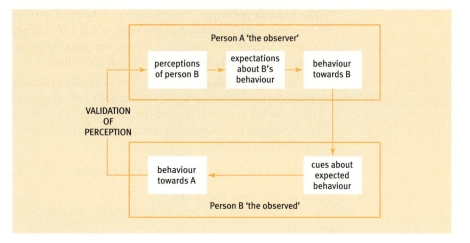

To illustrate the model, assume that a manager has just appointed three new employees, 'A', 'B' and 'C', who joined his department directly from university. In the selection process he gained an impression that 'A' is the sharpest, most enthusiastic and ambitious. After a short assimilation period he starts to take this person under his personal wing, perhaps by giving 'A' special instructions, accurate feedback and jobs that allow the person to grasp rapidly the full intricacies of the work and show his or her full capabilities. Unless 'B' and 'C' have been lucky enough to attract the attention of someone else who gives them similar advantages, 'A' will probably soon outstrip them. Indeed, even if they do progress to a similar extent, this may not be recognised by the manager because he will be far more familiar with 'A' than with the other two.

Perception and Performance Appraisal

In one way or another everybody in an organisation has their performance evaluated at some time. In a formal sense the most visible evaluation is the appraisal of subordinates by managers, which normally occurs annually or twice-yearly and is commonly applied to all employees (Long 1986).

Most texts on performance appraisal stress that managers should avoid subjective evaluations. However, management work is full of diverse, fragmented activities and interruptions, which makes it unlikely that a manager will be able to observe subordinate behaviour in a systematic way. Thus managers can be forced back into relying on memories of isolated incidents that are put together to build up a picture of the subordinate. This is described in graphic terms by Feldman (1981), who argues that managers construct *prototypes* to categorise subordinates.

In Feldman's terms, prototypes are schemes used to label people according to their perceived attributes. Since there is no universal system of prototypes, managers construct their own on the basis of convenience. For example, a university head of department might use a three-part system of prototypes to classify lecturers as follows:

Prototypes: mental schemes which categorise people into types based on the assumption that each type has distinctive attributes

- **The administrator prototype** someone who likes to be in charge of running a course and likes contact with students, not necessarily in the classroom, but in solving their problems and advising them on which classes to take.

- **The research prototype**   a person more concerned with adding to the body of knowledge than teaching it to students, a little self-indulgent and easily bored with the routine of classroom teaching, but proud of being up to date in the latest information in his or her particular specialism.
- **The dedicated teacher prototype**   very devoted to teaching, would prefer to avoid administrative work and sometimes a little sloppy with these duties, often content to teach out-of-date subject knowledge because this consists of well-tried principles that he or she has learned to put over well, so that students find the material easy to grasp.

There are two important points about prototypes:

- almost everybody uses them;
- prototyping involves a process similar to the halo effect.

To categorise someone as conforming to a prototype, evidence is not collected that he or she has all the traits, but if one or two are recognised then the others are assumed to be there. Having categorised someone, in appraisal the manager has a strong predisposition to recall only those characteristics and pieces of behaviour that fit the particular prototypes. For instance, for university heads of departments, if someone is classified as a dedicated teacher, the person's administrative contribution will probably be overlooked. In addition, a single item of administrative work that was done badly will be recalled and magnified out of all proportion. Indeed, any work of this type done well will probably be attributed to other people doing their jobs well, which leaves the person with nothing out of the ordinary to handle. Thus a prototype not only influences what is selectively recalled, it tends to stand in the way of the appearance of contradictory evidence.

Feldman argues that many managers do this because they are forced to gather information about subordinates in a fragmented way, by picking up random pieces of information as and when they can. The information is then stored temporarily in the memory, but because the capacity for short-term storage is limited, the memory store has to be emptied periodically. The information then gets shunted into the manager's long-term memory, where the prototype acts as a sort of magnet that attracts only some of the data. Thus, having categorised someone in a certain way, information consistent with the prototype is more likely to be remembered, and the non-prototypical behaviour forgotten or suppressed.

The implications of this reliance on hasty and incompletely informed impressions are all too clear. Instead of being a process that can potentially benefit both individual and organisation, appraisal can come to be viewed by subordinates in a cynical way. Moreover, the subordinate can come to perceive the manager as not only inaccurate in his or her judgements, but unfair and unjust, which can sour the relationship between the two people.

PERCEPTION AND ATTRIBUTIONS

Attribution:
imputing a cause for
an observed action

Attributions can be thought of as a special class of perceptions that we use to make sense of our own and other people's behaviour. When we perceive a certain action we seldom leave matters at that, but subconsciously impute a reason for it. In the

Figure 4.13 Criteria for inferring causes of behaviour

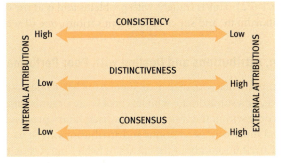

Internal attribution: the cause of a person's behaviour is assumed to be connected with his or her psychological characteristics, e.g. attitudes, personality etc.

External attribution: the cause of a person's behaviour is assumed to be connected with a factor in his or her environment

Behaviourial consistency: whether a piece of behaviour is typical of the way that the person normally behaves

Behaviourial consensus: whether a person's behaviour in a particular situation is typical of other people in the same situation

Behaviourial distinctiveness: whether a person behaves in the same way in several different circumstances

Fundamental attribution error: the tendency automatically to attribute internal causes for behaviour

original formulation of attribution theory (Heider 1958) the person who observes a particular piece of behaviour in someone else will attribute its cause to factors associated with one or other of two sources: those internal to the person who behaves in a certain way (his or her abilities, attitudes, intentions etc.) or those external to the person (task-related factors, luck, environment etc.).

This distinction, which is fundamental in attribution theory, has some important implications for judgements made about other people. An *internal attribution* contains an assumption that the person's behaviour is under his or her control, whereas in an *external attribution* it is assumed that the person is under the influence of circumstances which cannot be controlled. For instance, if I make an internal attribution about one of my colleagues who is persistently late for work, I might infer a lack of self-discipline, but an external attribution could involve an assumption that the lateness is due to a poor bus service.

What then prompts us to make an internal or external attribution? Kelley (1967) suggests that we observe a person's behaviour within a particular context and that three factors influence the type of attribution that is made. These are shown in Figure 4.13.

In everyday language *behaviourial consistency* means that a particular piece of behaviour is 'in character' for the person, because this is the way that he or she normally behaves in the same situation. The more consistent the person's behaviour, the more likely is an internal attribution.

Behaviourial consensus is the extent to which other people behave in the same way within a particular context. The more a person's behaviour is in line with that of other people, the more likely is an external attribution.

Behaviourial distinctiveness concerns whether the person tends to behave in the same way in several different situations. The more a person's behaviour is unique to one context, the more likely we are to assume that the behaviour is a result of the specific circumstances and to make an external attribution.

The problem is that to use these factors we need prior knowledge of the person's behaviour. What happens when we do not have this? A great deal of evidence suggests that people make what is known as the *fundamental attribution error* (Ross 1977) and impute an internal cause, particularly where the other person's behaviour has an impact on the beholder (Chaikin and Cooper 1973). When people attribute a cause to their own behaviour, however, they take a much more charitable view and display a pervasive tendency to attribute their own actions to situational factors; and attribute the cause of the same behaviour in another person to his/her personal disposition (Jones and Nisbett 1972). This is fraught with problems and is at the root of many difficulties between subordinate and superior in organisations, one of which is considered next.

Perception, Attributions and Dealing with Poor Performance

There are times when a manager or supervisor has to deal with a poor subordinate performance, or a subordinate who has broken an organisational rule. Matters of this type often come within the confines of the disciplinary process and, almost inevitably, manager and supervisor perceptions and attributions are at work, notably perceptions of guilt and attributions about the causes of behaviour. Using Kelley's (1967) attributional model, a study of disciplinary judgements by Mitchell *et al.* (1981) revealed some interesting outcomes. Using the criterion of **consistency**, their results strongly suggest that an employee who has transgressed in the past is much more likely to have his or her behaviour attributed to an internal characteristic, for instance low ability or lack of effort. Similarly, using the criterion of **consensus**, the results show that an employee whose behaviour is dissimilar to that of other workers is also more likely to attract an internal attribution. A number of studies have shown that other factors also affect whether an internal or external attribution is made. External attributions are more likely if the manager has personal experience of a subordinate's job (Mitchell and Kalb 1982) and also where the person about whom the judgement is made holds a senior position (Rosen and Jerdee 1974). Internal attributions are more likely if the supervisor or manager is personally affected by the employee's transgression (Greenberg

CASE STUDY 4.2: Kurt Marks

Eric Hauber, the manager of the customer accounts department at Alvo Stores, gathered his thoughts about the conduct of Kurt Marks, a subordinate he had called to a meeting that was due to commence in an hour's time to review Kurt's attendance record. Kurt had only been with the department for a little over a year, having worked in other departments of the firm for the previous three years. After an unblemished record for the first six months in the department he had started to show an escalating degree of absence from work, most of which he had reported as due to various types of sickness. On making informal enquiries with managers in the departments in which Kurt had previously worked, Eric obtained no concrete information other than subjective estimates that his level of absence was no worse or better than average. Although Eric had only been with the firm since shortly before Kurt joined the department, he suspected there could be a culture of absenteeism among employees. Therefore, he felt obliged to tackle matters in a firm way with Kurt, lest he become the same as other people. Therefore, Eric's purpose for the meeting was to tackle him about his absence and give him a formal warning under the firm's disciplinary procedure in order to send a signal to other employees that absenteeism would not be tolerated.

Questions

1. Using an appropriate theoretical framework, explain Eric Hauber's conclusions about Kurt Marks.

2. What is the nature of the judgement he has made about Kurt and is Eric being fair and just?

1996) and, in addition, female subordinates are much more likely than males to attract an internal attribution for the same transgression (Larwood *et al.* 1979). Moreover, because an internal attribution contains an assumption that the person concerned has acted 'in character', it is hardly surprising that these attributions are associated with disciplinary sanctions that are much more severe (Mitchell and Wood 1980).

These features of the disciplinary situation can have a huge impact on subsequent employee behaviour. In discipline, sanctions can be taken against an employee and so it would be hoped that managers would err on the side of caution in making attributions about the causes of poor performance or rule breaking. However, the evidence suggests that is not the case. The fundamental attribution error seems to be just as commonplace in discipline as in other situations and, if a manager has pre-judged matters in some way, it can be very hard to conceal this from the employee. Moreover, if an employee undergoes a disciplinary interview and perceives that the manager has pre-judged the issue, or is using the process merely to justify imposing a sanction, the outcome is likely to be the exact opposite of encouraging acceptable behaviour from then on. For example, a study by Rollinson *et al.* (1997) shows that where the disciplined subordinate has perceptions and attributions of this type, there is a strong tendency for the employee to rationalise him or herself as a victim. This in turn has the rather predictable consequence that the tendency to flout the rule in the future is increased rather than lowered.

CROSS-CULTURAL EFFECTS ON PERCEPTION: A BRIEF NOTE

The perceptual process is a highly individualised one and since it is invisible, it is near impossible to draw hard-and-fast conclusions about how it could be influenced by cross-cultural factors. Nevertheless, in the previous chapter it was pointed out that personalities can be shaped by the beliefs and values inherent in the cultures in which people are reared. In addition, there are almost certainly differences between cultures in terms of what are taken to be the signs of 'intelligent' behaviour. For these reasons there are strong grounds for suspecting that the three stages of the perceptual process – attention and selection, organisation and recognition, interpretation and inference – are all influenced by cultural factors. One way to understand these potential effects is by applying Tagiuri's (1969) explanation of perceptual dimensions given earlier.

Different cultures are likely to place greater value on certain dimensions of a particular class of attributes than others, because people reared in a particular culture are taught as part of their upbringing that certain attributes and behaviours are acceptable or unacceptable, and they become highly sensitised to the presence or absence of them. There is nothing inherently right or wrong with these attributes. Since people are prisoners of the culture in which they are reared, the behaviour that results seems normal to other people who have absorbed a particular culture. However, because there can be significant differences between cultures in this respect, stereotyped images of people in cultures other than our own can be all too common and a fairly obvious example of this is the attribute class of emotions.

In Great Britain people tend to be rather reserved and taciturn, because many of them are reared with a caution of 'not showing their feelings'. In other cultures, however, notably in some of the Latin countries such as Italy and France, there is far less inhibition about giving a visible display of emotion. An unfortunate side-effect of this is that people in one culture can develop stereotyped images of the characteristics of people in other cultures, and also make attributional judgements about what causes these characteristics. People in Latin countries can sometimes interpret British reserve as being prompted by 'aloofness' or 'coldness', and in return, British people are sometimes wont to regard Latin emotional expression as 'volatility' or 'lack of self-control'. Needless to say there is often insufficient evidence to come to these conclusions, and it is only when we come to know people from other cultures better that we find that the conclusions can be highly inaccurate. What is perhaps more disturbing is that these judgements have a habit of resulting in self-fulfilling prophecy effects. Because British people have a tendency to regard Latin people as somewhat volatile, they keep their distance in interactions. This probably exasperates Latin people, and perhaps prompts them to try to be warmer and more demonstrative. However, this only confirms the British view that Latins are volatile and makes them keep their distance even more, which further strengthens the Latin opinion that the British are cold and reserved.

This has important implications for organisations. As pointed out in Chapter 1, international organisations are becoming far more common and there is an increasing need for people from different cultural backgrounds to work with each other. Even where an organisation does not operate on an international basis, its members probably come into contact with people from other cultures far more frequently these days. Thus, unless people can make allowance for and, if necessary, guard against cultural influences on their perceptions, their interpersonal interactions can be impaired.

REPLAY

- Perception is an active mental process in which features of the environment are selected as a focus of attention and the incoming information about these features is organised to make inferences and give meaning to what is there.

- Because perception involves both data-driven, bottom-up processes and higher brain functions (top-down processing) that guide selection and inference, it is much more than simply being observant.

- Object perception can take place through any of the five senses, but it is normally studied through one sense in isolation to reveal basic laws. For example, in visual perception the effects of size and intensity on stimulus selection and attention, and figure-to-ground relationships on object recognition.

- Social perception – the perception of people in social situations – follows the same basic process as object perception, but is a much more complex phenomenon. All five senses are usually at work together and individuals not only perceive characteristics of other people, but they also behave towards those people according to what is perceived. Therefore, the process is highly dynamic, and how we behave towards other people shapes their perceptions of us.

- In organisations, social perception has the added hazard of having a potential for impaired interactions or misjudgements about people. Therefore, it is important to remember that judgements about people are based on perceptions and perceptions are not necessarily the reality of a situation, but merely a personal inference about what reality is.

OVERVIEW AND CONCLUSIONS

Perception is an important way in which people differ as individuals and can influence the way that they behave in organisations. It is a complex mental process in which we filter out some of the incoming information from the environment and attend to only part of what is available. Information is then organised into meaningful patterns and recognisable wholes, which allows us to make an inference about what is there. The factors affecting this are external (the nature of the object perceived and its surrounding context) and internal (our higher mental processes and personalities). These processes are also at work in perceiving people and social situations, but matters often go one stage further. We not only perceive people and what they do, but also attribute reasons for their behaviour. Judgements such as these often contain errors and misunderstandings, and so some account needs to be taken of the idea that our evaluations of others are seldom based on hard facts, but on what we perceive to be the facts. Perhaps most important of all, it is necessary to recognise that in a social situation perceptions give rise to chain effects in behaviour. How we perceive people has a strong influence on how we behave towards them and this, in turn, has a strong effect on how they behave towards us. For this reason we need to guard against snap judgements which can give rise to halo effects and self-fulfilling prophecies.

FURTHER READING

Goldstein, E (1998) *Sensation and Perception*, San Francisco: Brooks Cole. A very comprehensive, but easy-to-read introduction to the psychology of perception and sensations.

Gordon, I E (1997) *Theories of Visual Perception*, 2nd edn, Chichester: Wiley. A comprehensive text which fully explores the seven major approaches to understanding visual perception.

Hewstone, M (1989) *Causal Attribution: From Cognitive Processes to Collective Beliefs*, Oxford: Blackwell. A rather technical and scholarly book, but nevertheless one that is easy to read and gives a comprehensive introduction to attribution theory.

Laing, R D (1972) *Knots*, Harmondsworth: Penguin. A rather old but nevertheless penetrating description of the way that we interact with others and how this can be influenced by our perceptions and attributions.

Rosenfeld, P, R A Giacalone and C A Riordan (1995) *Impression Management in Organisations*, London: Routledge. A scholarly but straightforward and entertaining account of how people in the workplace are able to manipulate the judgements that others make of them.

REVIEW AND DISCUSSION QUESTIONS

1. Define perception, distinguish between 'bottom-up' and 'top-down' processing and explain the significance of these for the assertion that perception is an 'active' mental process.

2. To what extent is it useful to divide the perceptual process into three distinct stages for the purposes of explanation and what misconceptions can arise from using this three-stage model?

3. Explain the ways in which social perception differs from the perceiving of simple objects. What are the implications of these differences for the accuracy of perceptions of people?

4. What is meant by the term 'cognitive complexity', what is its significance in perceiving other people and is it true that some people are much more accurate than others in their perceptions of other people?

5. Explain two prevalent perceptual errors that people can make, and also how the self-fulfilling prophecy effect can influence the perception of people.

6. What is an attribution and what is the difference between an external and an internal attribution? Explain the three factors that influence whether a particular piece of behaviour by a person will attract an internal or external attribution.

Chapter 5

Attitudes

LEARNING OUTCOMES

After studying this chapter you should be able to:

- define attitudes and distinguish between attitudes, beliefs and values

- describe the three components of an attitude

- explain the functions of attitudes and describe factors influential in their formation

- explain the association between attitudes and behaviour and define the conditions under which attitudes are good predictors of behaviour

- discuss the principles of attitude change and the extent to which attitude change can realistically be achieved

- discuss the nature of the work-related attitudes of job satisfaction and organisational commitment

Figure 5.1
Implications of
attitude dimensions
for behaviour and
attitude change

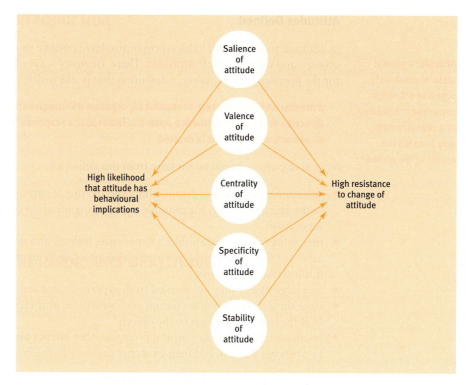

Valence: the degree
of positive or negat-
ive feelings about an
attitude object

Centrality: the extent
to which an attitude
is part of a person's
concept of self

Interrelatedness:
the extent to which
an attitude is related
to a person's other
attitudes

Stability: the
attitude's resistance
to change

Specificity: the extent
to which the attitude
is specific to some
attribute of the
attitude object

Salience: the
degree of conscious
awareness of holding
the attitude

Valence is the degree of positive or negative feelings about an attitude object, which
is what attitude scales normally measure.

Centrality is the extent to which an attitude is part of a person's self-concept and
reflects his/her identity.

Interrelatedness is the extent to which an attitude is related to a person's other
attitudes; for instance, someone with a positive attitude to religion could also
have a negative attitude to promiscuity.

Stability is simply an attitude's resistance to change.

Specificity is the extent to which the attitude is differentiated from other attitudes.

Salience is a person's conscious awareness of the attitude – a dedicated pacifist, for
example, could be totally preoccupied with a strong negative attitude to war.

These dimensions are not independent of each other and their importance will become
apparent later. For now the point can perhaps most easily be made with the use of
the simple model given in Figure 5.1 and two observations can be made about the
relationships it portrays:

● high valence, centrality and specificity all give an attitude stability, and resistance
to modification;

● the link between attitude and behaviour is sometimes rather precarious but, all
other things being equal (and sometimes they are not), the greater an attitude's
salience, valence, specificity, centrality and stability, the more likely it is that it
will have predictable behaviourial outcomes.

THE FUNCTIONS OF ATTITUDES

Functional approach: the assumption that attitudes are held because they serve a useful purpose for the holder

Almost all attitude theory adopts what is known as the *functional approach*, which assumes that attitudes serve a useful purpose. Unlike other individual differences, which probably have a genetic component, attitudes are man-made. They are part of an individual's psychological make-up and develop and change in response to the person's current needs (Rosenberg 1960). While a number of ways of categorising these functions have been derived, the most widely used is still the classic framework developed by Katz (1960), which has four functional categories.

The Adjustment Function

Adjustment function: helps the person adjust to his or her world

This helps an individual to adjust to the world and to obtain rewards and avoid punishments from the environment. It is sometimes referred to as the instrumental or utilitarian function and explains why most people have positive attitudes to objects that provide rewards and negative attitudes towards punishing objects.

The Ego-defensive Function

Ego-defensive function: helps the person to defend his or her self-image

Attitudes help people to defend their self-image, and this function can take many forms. People who feel their abilities are unrecognised sometimes develop positive attitudes towards status symbols, as a way of bolstering their self-image.

The Value-expressive Function

Value-expressive function: allows the person to derive satisfaction from expressing attitudes that reflect his or her central values

This allows an individual to derive satisfaction from expressing attitudes that reflect his or her central values and concept of self. This goes much deeper than the two previous functions and reflects a need present in most people to express their central values and demonstrate to the world that they are what they believe themselves to be.

The Knowledge Function

Knowledge function: helps the person mentally to structure and organise his or her world so that it is more understandable

As Katz points out, not everybody avidly seeks after knowledge, but most people want to be able to understand events which impinge upon them. The *knowledge function* helps a person to do this, by mentally organising and structuring the world so that it is more understandable. Managers and union officials, for example, often seem to hold negative attitudes towards each other. The union official will perhaps assume that a manager will always try to take away hard-won concessions, and a manager will tend to assume that union officials will always try to get new concessions. However, while their attitudes are over-generalised and stereotyped, these people represent conflicting interests and their attitudes help them make sense of the task at hand.

One implication of these functions, particularly the last one, is that they have a potential effect on perceptions. As noted earlier, a perception imposes order on incoming information to give it meaning and allow inferences to be made; since attitudes are dispositions towards objects, they are likely to play some part in how objects are perceived.

- Attitudes are held towards specific situations and objects (people being a special class of object) and they reflect how the attitude holder experiences and reacts to that part of his or her world.
- While attitudes are related to a person's beliefs and values, they are not the same thing.
- Attitudes are formed as a result of experiences of objects, people and social situations.
- Attitudes have three components: cognitive, affective and behaviourial, and they have a number of functional purposes for their holders, all of which relate to the holder's world.
- Attitude formation takes place as part of a person's mental and emotional development, which is affected by his or her direct experience, exposure to objects, socialisation and social learning, development of self-image and the need to express values.

ATTITUDE CHANGE

Consistency principle: that people attempt to maintain consistency between the three components of an attitude: cognitive, affective, behaviourial

Cognitive dissonance: the unpleasant mental feeling that arises when behaviour towards an object is not consistent with the attitude towards the object

Attitudes usually change for the same reasons they are formed: because it is useful to do so. The prevailing view is that change follows the *consistency principle*, in which people strive to maintain a consistency between the affective, behaviourial and cognitive components of an attitude. Thus, if one component changes, and this gives rise to feelings of inconsistency, a person has two alternatives:

- to reverse the change to the single component; or
- change the other components to fall in line.

The best-known consistency theory is Festinger's (1957) theory of *cognitive dissonance*, which assumes that consistency is sought between a consciously held attitude and the behaviour towards an object. Festinger's basic propositions are:

- where inconsistencies exist between attitude and behaviour, an individual will develop a feeling of dissonance, i.e. that something is not quite correct;
- the experience of dissonance is unpleasant and so the person is strongly motivated to remove or avoid it, and the stronger the dissonance, the greater the urge to do so;
- where dissonance is present, as well as attempting to reduce it, the person will actively try to avoid situations and information that create awareness that dissonance exists.

To give an example of how this works, suppose that I am so fond of dogs that I try to make friends with them in the street, but I do this once too often and get badly bitten. Naturally I tend to be more wary in future, but this is inconsistent with my feelings about dogs. Therefore, to remove inconsistency, my attitude changes, perhaps by rationalising that dogs are nice, but also unpredictable. Now when I see a dog in the street I avoid the inconsistency of liking dogs and at the same time being wary of trying to make friends by crossing over to the other side of the road.

CASE STUDY 5.1: Alex's Attitudes

Richard Edwards, a manager in a medium-sized firm had been approached over the telephone by one of his colleagues to give an informal opinion about one of his subordinates, Alex Wilson, who had applied for a promotional vacancy in another department. His first comments were that Alex was a conscientious and diligent worker who could always be relied upon to give of his best. In addition, Alex had a very flexible approach to his duties, was always ready to try something new and was quite innovative in finding novel solutions when a problem needed to be solved. However, Richard also added that one aspect of Alex's performance left something to be desired: he seemed to have an attitude problem. For example, it was quite difficult to give him feedback about his performance because he seemed to find it hard to take constructive criticism. Indeed, he gave a distinct impression that he was resentful of authority, and had what Richard jokingly called a 'David and Goliath complex'. Richard also commented that Alex's handwriting was virtually illegible. Apparently he was by nature left-handed but, early in his schooldays, he had been forced to write with his right hand and had continued to do so from then onwards.

Questions

1. Do you feel that it is plausible that Alex could have formed an anti-authority attitude?

2. How could you explain this attitude?

The consistency principle underpins most serious attempts to change attitudes. However, in organisations, it is difficult to contrive something as dramatic and extreme as the equivalent of being bitten by a dog. Nevertheless, there are occasions when attitude change is considered desirable. This is usually as part of an organisational change initiative, where radically new working practices or totally different structural arrangements are to be put in place, and it is realised that existing patterns of attitudes and culture will not be compatible with the new situation. Organisational change is covered in detail in Chapter 21 and so this matter will surface again there. Here it is sufficient to note that most attitude change initiatives rely on techniques of persuasion to create dissonance. For instance, communication techniques are used to try to change patterns of belief, which in turn creates dissonance so that behaviourial change will follow. For this reason, it is important to examine factors that influence the effectiveness of the persuasive process.

The Source of the Message

The source of the message has a huge impact. Credible sources – those we admire and respect – are much more influential than those that lack credibility, which is why health food advertisements often use athletes to endorse the products. In organisations it is clearly better if managers who have to convey these messages have a high degree of credibility, perhaps because their expertise is highly regarded by subordinates.

However, it must be remembered that persuasion is seriously undermined if a manager's motives are suspect.

The Nature of the Message

If a message is perceived as balanced and unbiased, it reinforces the sender's credibility, because he or she is seen to be someone who does not underrate the intelligence of the audience (Murphy and Davey 2002), but where the message is seen to be biased and one-sided, the reverse is often the case. In addition, the evidence suggests that because it arouses strong emotions that stiffen defences to the message, attempts to use fear can be counter-productive (Janis and Feshback 1953).

 OB IN ACTION: A Quiet Revolution in Management Attitudes

In response to the competitive pressures of the last fifteen years, many organisations have been downsized and/or delayered and for those employees who remain, work has become more hectic and intensified. At the time, managers in many of these organisations adopted an attitude towards employees of 'either you buy in to the changes or you go'. In return, perhaps prompted by fears for their security, many employees became resigned to having to put the job before anything else, irrespective of the personal cost. However, in more enlightened companies there are now signs that the tide is beginning to turn, and there seems to be a growing recognition that people are unlikely to be innovative and productive unless they are also able to have a life away from work. For example, the pharmaceutical giant Glaxo Welcome is reported to have taken a long, hard look at itself and set out to discourage 'presenteeism' (an attitude of compulsive attendance). A policy of flexible working has been adopted that allows many employees to choose their own patterns of working, so long as they work the contracted hours. In addition, managers are instructed to take a firm line with employees who have tendencies towards presenteeism, to the extent that they are told to go home. Similar policies are said to be in place at the accounting and consultancy group Pricewaterhouse Coopers. At British Telecom (BT) there are definite attempts to adopt practices that allow employees to achieve a better work–home balance, by allowing them to propose and negotiate their own patterns of attendance. Interestingly, this seems to have done BT no harm, and employee attitude surveys show that these steps have had highly beneficial outcomes in terms of increased morale and motivation and more positive attitudes of enthusiasm and loyalty.

Sources:

Cooper, C (2000) Choose life, *People Management*, 11 May: 35–6.
Caulkin, S (2000) The new way is not quiet desperation, *The Observer*, 14 May.

The Recipients

People vary in their receptiveness to persuasive arguments: those low in self-esteem seem to be highly susceptible to persuasive messages, while those who hold extreme attitude positions tend to have a great deal of resistance (McGinnies 1949). Any discrepancy between a person's current attitude position and the one advocated by the message can also have an effect. A small difference will often mean that the message is interpreted as concordant with the person's current attitudes, but where the difference is wide the recipient can exaggerate the gap even more, which reduces the credibility of the source.

The Boomerang Effect

An attempt to change attitudes can sometimes result in a change that is opposite to the one desired. One explanation is that where people feel that a message threatens their personal freedom they become aroused to take steps to maintain the freedom (Brehm 1972). Therefore, if the persuasiveness of the message is low compared to the importance of the freedom, the person is likely to do the reverse of what has been requested. This also explains why attempts to change attitudes that are central to a person's concept of self are often met with a fierce reassertion of individuality and strong resistance to change. Nobody likes to feel easily manipulated, and if a great deal of visible pressure is put on us to change our attitudes we are likely to exert pressure in return, perhaps by doing the opposite (Heller *et al.* 1973).

The possibility of a boomerang effect, which can include increased antagonism towards the source of the message, raises the question of whether attitude change should be attempted, or even whether it is possible. Although persuasive messages might prompt people to think about their attitudes, they are only changed if there is a good reason to do so. Ultimately, the only person who can change an attitude is the attitude holder, and this seldom happens because artful manipulation or quick-fix communication exercises have been used.

ATTITUDES AND BEHAVIOUR

The most comprehensive exploration of the link between attitudes and behaviour is contained in a theory developed by Fishbein and Ajzen (1975). This incorporates the role of beliefs and values and is expressed in the general equation:

$$A_o = \sum_{i=1}^{n} b_i \, e_i$$

where: A_o is the attitude towards some object 'o'
b_i is the belief that i is an attribute of 'o'
e_i is the evaluation of attribute i
n is the number of beliefs about 'o'

Although it looks complicated, the equation simply means that an attitude is the sum of the positive and negative feelings about the different attributes of an object. To give an example, suppose that we want to identify an individual's attitude to cars and determine that he has five identifiable beliefs about them, i.e. that cars:

Table 5.1 Calculation of attitudes to Cars

Beliefs that cars are:	'b' subjective probability that belief is true	'e' goodness or badness of attribute	b × e
Convenient	0.9	+3	2.7
Pollutants	0.7	−2	−1.4
Dangerous	0.5	−1	−0.5
Costly	0.6	−1	−0.6
Make owners lazy	0.3	−2	−0.6
			−0.4

- are a convenient means of personal transport;
- pollute the air;
- are dangerous;
- are costly;
- make their owners lazy.

It is unlikely that the person believes that all of these attributes are equally true. Therefore, a subjective probability value between 0 (untrue) and 1 (true) can be placed against each one. In terms of evaluations, 'e' represents the general goodness or badness of the attribute, which is usually estimated as somewhere between +3 (good) and −3 (bad). Thus we have the attitude shown in Table 5.1. Overall, a weak negative attitude.

TIME OUT

Think about the experience of your life at college or university. Using the Fishbein and Ajzen method illustrated above, do the following:

1. Set down your beliefs about university life and estimate your subjective probabilities that these are true.
2. Set down the goodness or badness of each one of these beliefs.
3. Now calculate your overall attitude to university life.

Two important points can be noted about this conceptualisation of attitudes.

1. It acknowledges that a person can have positive and negative feelings about an attitude object at the same time, and that this is likely to have an effect or behaviourial outcome of an attitude (a point that will be explained shortly).
2. To obtain an accurate picture of a person's attitude to an object, it is also necessary to know a person's most important beliefs about the object, and these are bound to vary in some degree between individuals. For instance, I might consider the two most important attributes of dogs to be the companionship they offer and their watchdog role, while someone else could view their inconvenience

Figure 5.2 The theory of planned behaviour (after Ajzen 1991)

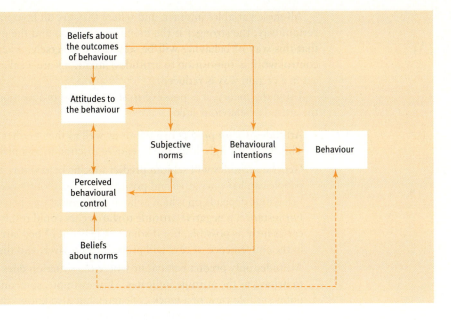

and hygiene implications as the most important attributes. This clearly has strong implications for constructing measures of attitudes that can be applied to a wide number of people.

The Fishbein and Ajzen theory has found its most significant use in tracing the link between attitudes and behaviour. This idea was originally expressed as the theory of behaviourial intentions and, more recently, as the revised theory of planned behaviour (Ajzen 1988). A diagrammatic representation of the latter is given in Figure 5.2.

The main idea underpinning the model is that behaviour is more predictable if we focus on the specific behaviourial intentions rather than attitudes in isolation. In general terms, a positive attitude gives a predisposition to behave towards an object in a positive way, and a negative attitude a predisposition to behave negatively. This results in what is shown in the model as the **attitude to the behaviour**. However, this is influenced by **beliefs about the outcome of the behaviour**. For instance, people usually have positive attitudes to any behaviour they believe will help them achieve their goals, and negative attitudes to behaviour that blocks achievement of their goals (Rosenberg 1960). Therefore, the stronger the attitude, the stronger the intention to behave in a certain way. Nevertheless, intentions are mediated by **subjective norms**: the socially accepted rules of behaviour in the person's group or context. If these social pressures conflict with the attitude, the intention to behave in the way suggested by the attitude will be weakened, but where the norms support the attitude, the behaviourial intention is strengthened. Similarly, a person's actions are influenced by their degree of **perceived behaviourial control**. This is the estimate of how easy or difficult it will be to behave in a particular way, which arises from past experience and also reflects a view of current impediments or obstacles to behaving as intended (Orbell 2003). As can be seen, this is influenced by **beliefs about norms,** and these reflect the person's perceptions of how other people expect him or her to behave – a very powerful set of constraints on most people.

All these variables interact, and where they are all favourable towards acting in a certain way, the stronger is the intention to do so and the greater is the probability that this way of behaving will be selected. Conversely, where norms and perceived control work in opposition to attitudes, intentions are weakened and the tendency to act in a certain way is reduced.

Using the theory, it is possible to state general propositions about the strength of the attitude–behaviour link.

- **Attitudes do not predict behaviour as well as they predict behaviourial intentions** This flows strongly from the foregoing discussion and little more need be said.

- **General attitudes will seldom predict specific behaviours accurately** Since people can have negative and positive feelings about an object at the same time, behaviour depends on which belief is uppermost in a person's mind at the time. For instance, a negative attitude towards cars could result in a resolve to use the car as little as possible, but if someone gets out of bed late one morning, a belief in the convenience of cars will probably take over, and the car will be used.

- **Attitudes only predict behaviour where the situation does not limit the freedom to behave as the attitude indicates** For example, someone who has a highly unfavourable view of a work colleague, but also knows that the boss has a high regard for this person, will probably keep his or her mouth shut.

- **Until activated, attitudes can remain latent** Until confronted with the object of an attitude, the attitude probably remains at a subconscious level. For instance, a person could have a strong attitude about racial or sexual discrimination, but if he or she works in an environment where there is no discrimination, the person may not even be aware of holding the attitude.

The theory of planned behaviour has been extensively tested in empirical studies. This has resulted in a great deal of independent evidence that if it is applied correctly, it is capable of predicting a wide range of intentions and behaviours (see Conner and Armitage 1998). Current work in the area mostly focuses on refining the model. For example, Armitage and Conner (1999) suggest that *self-efficacy*, which can broadly be described as a person's belief in his or her ability to act in a certain way (see discussion in Chapter 10), is a readily available way of evaluating a person's 'perceived behavioural control'. In addition, Terry *et al.* (1999) suggest that the 'subjective norms' variable in the model needs to take account of self-identity, because the behaviour of some people is much more strongly influenced by their own self-images than the views of their peers.

The great value of a theory such as this is that if it is applied carefully to tap people's attitudes, it gives a useful way of predicting how they will behave. Thus the theory finds widespread application in certain aspects of organisational life, such as market research and in employee opinion surveys (to obtain a picture of employee attitudes, and likely behaviour, towards various aspects of organisational life, or impending change) (see Chapter 21). For this reason it is necessary to explain something of how attitudes can be measured, which is covered next.

Self-efficacy: a person's belief in his or her ability to act in a certain way

ATTITUDE MEASUREMENT

Since attitudes play an important part in explaining behaviour, a great deal of time and effort has been devoted to developing ways of measuring them. While this could be done by simply asking someone a question, single questions are seldom reliable because they tell us very little about the strength of an attitude. The usual way to resolve this problem is to develop a multiple-item, pencil-and-paper test that attitude holders complete themselves, which gives a scale that reflects the strength of the attitude. The most widely used scaling techniques at present are Likert scaling and the semantic differential test, and these will now be outlined.

Likert Scales

This method (Likert 1932) is very widely used. It is basically very simple and involves considerably less time and effort than earlier methods to produce a usable scale. Space precludes an extensive definition of the methods used to design scales of this type but, for those who wish to know more, suggestions are made in the Further Reading section at the end of the chapter.

An example of the first six items of a scale developed by the author to examine attitudes to work for public sector employees is shown in Figure 5.3. The figures in circles at the top of the scale are the scores used for each column.

Figure 5.3 An example of a Likert scale

SECTION A: VIEWS ON WORK

GIVEN BELOW ARE A NUMBER OF STATEMENTS OF OPINION ABOUT WORK, SOME ARE CONCERNED GENERALLY WITH WHITE-COLLAR WORK – THAT IS SALARIED STAFF OR NON-MANUAL OCCUPATIONS; OTHERS REFER MORE SPECIFICALLY TO FEELINGS THAT COULD EXIST ABOUT DOING A PARTICULAR JOB OR WORKING FOR A SPECIFIC EMPLOYER. PLEASE INDICATE HOW MUCH YOU AGREE WITH EACH ONE BY TICKING THE APPROPRIATE BOX.

	5	4	3	2	1
	I definitely agree	On balance I agree	Neither agree nor disagree	On balance I disagree	I strongly disagree
1. I would always want to stay in the white-collar field because of its better promotion opportunities.					
2. So far as I can see manual jobs are now far better paid than white-collar work.					
3. I would be quite happy to remain in this organisation for the rest of my working life.					
4. Here the only people who get promoted are those who toe the line and don't make waves.					
5. You can't really supervise people in white-collar work too tightly because the jobs vary so much.					
6. Management and supervisors here are very bad at dealing with the people beneath them.					

Figure 5.4 Example of a semantic differential scale

Semantic Differential Scales

Research by a group of American psychologists (Osgood *et al.* 1975) resulted in another method of scaling which is, if anything, even easier to use than the Likert approach. The original research addressed the thorny problem of the measurement of meaning and involved asking literally thousands of people to rate an array of objects and concepts in terms of several attributes. The analysis of this data revealed three main dimensions that are used by people to make judgements about objects:

- **evaluative** which rates the object or concept on a good–bad (or something similar) dimension;
- **potency** which rates the object or concept on a strong–weak, hard–soft etc. dimension;
- **activity** which corresponds to an active–passive or fast–slow dimension.

The analysis revealed that the most important of these dimensions is the evaluative one, and this is exactly what is required to tap attitudes. A semantic differential scale looks very similar to a seven-point Likert scale. However, since the scale taps the three main dimensions of judgement (evaluative, potency, activity), it not only tells us how an object is evaluated but also something about the way a person conceives the object. An example of a scale is shown in Figure 5.4.

Note that there are four 'evaluative' lines (numbering from the top 1, 4, 7 and 8) and three each for potency (2, 5 and 9) and activity (3, 6 and 10). The extremes on either side of the scale (e.g. good and bad) are normally assigned values of 7 and 1 respectively, and the average of each dimension is used to assess the person's judgement. The important point to note is that the evaluative dimension tells us whether a person likes or dislikes an object, while the other two give some indication of how he or she could behave towards it. An example given by Osgood *et al.* (1957) is a comparison of two subjects who rated the concept Negro. The first rated Negro as unfavourable, strong and active, while the second produced ratings of unfavourable, weak and passive, and Osgood suggests that these ratings would be likely to lead to different behavioural outcomes. For example, the first person would probably avoid all contact with black people, and if contact was unavoidable he or she would behave warily. Conversely, the second might simply ignore them or even regard black people as exploitable.

EMPLOYEE OPINION SURVEYS

As noted earlier, employee opinion surveys are widely used to assess employee attitudes and perceptions about work-related issues (Edwards 1997). For reasons of convenience, speed, economy and ease of analysis the usual way to do this is with pencil-and-paper questionnaires, which are completed by a sample, or even all of a particular workforce. Most questionnaires utilise the Likert format to tap opinions (see Figure 5.3), because this allows the person completing the questionnaire to express a degree of agreement or disagreement with the statements.

Where scales of this type have been well designed, thoroughly pilot tested before use and are completed by a representative cross-section of organisational employees, they are capable of providing a great deal of useful information about employee attitudes. However, there are two inherent (but not insurmountable) difficulties in using attitude questionnaires for this purpose: first, designing an appropriate questionnaire and, second, interpreting the data when the instrument has been used.

Designing an attitude questionnaire may look simple, but it is full of pitfalls for the unwary. For this reason, organisations often seek expert help, perhaps by importing the services of a consultant occupational psychologist on a temporary basis. To some extent this can also help with the second problem by providing expertise to interpret the results. Nevertheless, an error that is commonplace even with experts is the treatment of 'non-responses', that is, people who have been asked to complete the questionnaire but have not done so.

To give an example, suppose that we want to evaluate the levels of job satisfaction and commitment among employees in a firm. Well-validated, published scales are obtainable to tap these attitudes, and this solves the design problem. To obtain a well-rounded picture of these attitudes everybody in the organisation (say 500 people) is given a questionnaire to complete, but despite appeals and reminders to the workforce, only 300 completed questionnaires are obtained. This is only 60 per cent of the workforce and, in surveys of this type, even lower response rates are commonplace. In order to obtain frank and honest responses to questions, the questionnaire would purposely have been designed to protect the anonymity of individual employees. Thus there is no way of identifying the people who failed to complete the instrument and we would probably have to accept that a 60 per cent sample is the best we can obtain.

What usually happens in this situation is that an assumption is made that those who failed to respond have broadly similar attitudes to those who did. Thus the 60 per cent of employees whose attitudes we have successfully tapped would be treated as representative of all the employees in the organisation. However, very recent evidence suggests that there is often something very distinctive about people who choose not to take part in an employee opinion survey, particularly where it seeks to tap attitudes such as job satisfaction or commitment. Thus a very misleading picture of attitudes is likely to emerge. This information comes from a study reported by Rogelberg *et al.* (2000), who deliberately set out to compare the attitudes of people who complete an employee survey questionnaire with those who do not. Those who 'opted out' were found to be much lower in all aspects of job satisfaction and commitment to the organisation. In addition, and despite any assurances they were given, they had very negative and suspicious beliefs about how the survey data would be used. This raises the possibility that those who do not respond are often disaffected in some way, and that they fail to take part as a way of not cooperating with the organisation.

Thus allowances for this need to be made in any decisions that are based on the survey evidence.

WORK-RELATED ATTITUDES

There are many work-related attitudes that could be of interest to an organisation. While some are highly specific, for example attitudes towards a particular process or a technology, there is usually more interest in generalised attitude patterns. Traditionally the one that has been explored is job satisfaction; the one that currently attracts a great deal of attention is employee commitment.

Job Satisfaction

Job satisfaction:
a pleasurable or positive emotional state resulting from a person's appraisal of his or her job or job experience

Job satisfaction can be defined as:

> **a pleasurable or positive emotional state resulting from the appraisal of one's job or job experience.**
>
> **(Locke 1976, p 1300)**

For many years this was viewed as a single, unified concept, but it is now widely recognised as a more complex cluster of attitudes towards different aspects of a job, arising from a person's expectations of work and his or her actual experiences (Clark 1996). Since people differ widely in what they expect, this is likely to be a highly individualised attitude cluster, but research suggests that there are five major dimensions to the attitude, all of which reflect affective responses to particular aspects of a job.

The Work Itself

This dimension reflects the match between expectations and experience in terms of whether the job provides interesting tasks, a measure of responsibility and opportunities for learning. To the extent that there is a good match, this aspect of job satisfaction is likely to be rated positively.

Pay

There seem to be two connections between pay and satisfaction; first, whether the financial reward for a job is regarded as adequate and, second, whether it is considered to be equitable compared to that received by other people. While most people need a certain minimum level of income to live on, the relationship between pay and satisfaction is a very complex one. To some people pay is a reflection of how much their efforts are recognised, which means that it has an intrinsic component as well as the purely extrinsic effect of cash in hand. In addition, many other rewards have a financial equivalent, for example fringe benefits such as medical insurance and pensions.

Promotion

To some extent this speaks for itself and reflects perceived possibilities for an increase in status. However, promotion is not desired by everybody and so satisfaction in this respect is very strongly influenced by the match between expectations and receipts. Indeed, since promotion usually brings an increase in pay, for some people this is the major satisfaction it provides, while for others it is more connected with self-image and ego.

Supervision

This dimension reflects the extent to which a person derives satisfaction from the relationship with his or her immediate superior. As will be explained in Chapters 12 and 13, satisfaction with supervision is usually connected to two aspects of supervisor behaviour:

- **interpersonal support**   the supervisor's interest in the person's welfare;
- **technical support**   the extent to which the supervisor provides technical and task-related help and guidance.

Again, satisfaction tends to be a highly personalised matter that is closely connected with the match between expectations and receipts. Not everybody welcomes a close personal interest and some people interpret a high level of technical guidance as a sign that the supervisor has a lack of trust in their work.

Co-workers

Satisfaction in this respect has similar effects to supervision and reflects the extent that members of an individual's workgroup are perceived to be socially supportive and competent in their own tasks. Once again, this can acutely depend on the match between expectations and receipts. While most people find group membership is psychologically rewarding, they also vary in their sociability and the need for peer support.

The Importance of Job Satisfaction

The interest in this cluster of attitudes dates from **human relations theory**, a basic assumption of which is that a satisfied worker is automatically effective and productive. However, since the relationship between job satisfaction and performance is now acknowledged to be much more complex (Staw and Barsade 1993), it is important to examine what the research evidence tells us about the potential effects of satisfaction.

Employee Turnover

There is convincing evidence that where job satisfaction is high labour turnover is reduced (Tett and Meyer 1993). However, because there are many other things that affect turnover, it is unwise to draw a conclusion that this is a direct relationship. For instance, the longer a person stays with a firm, the greater is the wrench involved in leaving, and in a recession, when jobs are harder to find, people tend to stay where they are. Therefore, job satisfaction is probably one of those experiences of work that make it less likely that someone will think about leaving even if there are available opportunities, but if it is absent and the opportunities are there, turnover could well increase.

Employee Absenteeism

The effects of satisfaction on absenteeism seem to be much stronger. When job satisfaction falls absenteeism tends to rise (Steele and Rentsch 1995), and since absenteeism is an alternative to leaving when the possibility of finding a suitable job elsewhere is low, this is understandable. As such, satisfaction probably has a similar influence on absenteeism as that which it has on quitting.

Employee Productivity

There has long been a debate about whether satisfaction leads to high performance. The idea that it does has a great deal of intuitive appeal to managers, because it implies that rewards play a relatively minor part in obtaining high performance. However, a review of a large number of studies indicates that, if a relationship exists at all, it is a rather weak one. What seems more likely is that rewards have a far more important effect on productivity than was once thought to be the case, and that satisfaction only has a mediating role; that is, rewards result in satisfaction, which then leads to greater effort (Podsakoff and Williams 1986). It should also be noted that there is an ongoing, but as yet unresolved, debate about whether satisfaction leads to good performance, or whether good performance leads to satisfaction.

Organisational Commitment

Organisational commitment: an attitude towards the organisation as a whole, reflecting the individual's acceptance of its goals and values, his or her willingness to expend effort on its behalf and an intention to remain with the organisation

Whereas job satisfaction refers to attitudes to specific aspects of a job, *organisational commitment* is normally regarded as a global attitude to the organisation as a whole. Nevertheless, there is a connection between the two concepts in that people who have job satisfaction are often found to have higher levels of commitment (Eaton 2003; Mulinge 2001). The most explicit definition of commitment is provided by Mowday, Steers and Porter (1979), who define it as a three-part construct embracing an individual's:

* acceptance of the goals and values of the organisation;
* willingness to exert effort on behalf of the organisation;
* intention to stay with the organisation.

Note that these three constructs correspond very closely to the three components of an attitude that were given earlier:

* **Cognitive component**   normative acceptance of organisational goals and values.
* **Affective component**   attachment to the organisation.
* **Behaviourial component**   exertion of effort on behalf of the organisation and intention to stay.

The outcomes of commitment are generally taken to be the same as for job satisfaction: increased employee effort and lowered tendencies to undesirable behaviour such as absenteeism and quitting (Mathieu and Zanjoc 1990). While these are clearly advantageous for an organisation, there is some confusion about what prompts employees to become committed. The current view is that commitment emerges from a process of social exchange (Morris *et al.* 1993). Imagine that you have just joined

OB IN ACTION: Employee Attitudes in Singapore

Singapore may have a highly skilled and well-educated workforce, but surface appearances are deceptive: the city-state's employees are an unhappy lot, according to a recent Gallup poll, which found employees to be 'actively disengaged and disaffected' with negative attitudes to their work and employer. The poll estimates that the general level of unhappiness among the workforce is a heavy cost for the Singapore economy to bear. Ashok Gopal, regional practice coordinator of the Gallup organisation, says the survey (the third exercise of this type in Singapore) illustrates that there are deep issues and significant problems within the Singapore workforce, which have to be addressed. These results raise eyebrows – especially as it reflects on a workforce that has generally been seen in positive terms in the global marketplace. A 'highly disengaged' workforce, in which only 6 per cent of workers are seen as loyal, satisfied and productive, is an embarrassment to a country which has developed the status of a first-class economy.

Observers say the poll's findings may be a reflection of the current social and economic conditions. In the last three years many companies had to go through restructuring and the rising unemployment could affect workers' sentiments. However, it does not explain another fundamental problem the survey highlighted. Twenty-five percent of the workers have no clear idea of what their duties are at work, and only one in three feels that his or her potential is fully recognised or has been exploited. Thus, observers say the lack of managerial skills – such as handling employee needs and keeping staff motivated – are to blame. Leadership usually smacks of top-down management and in most corporations there is no two-way channel of communication, which leaves very little room for feedback or constructive criticism. Observers also say that as the work environment in Singapore becomes more demanding, there is a greater need for managers within organisations to develop new mechanisms to encourage employees to exchange ideas. Communication seems to be the key to driving a workforce forward, because if your message is 'You do what I say', then your workers are not going to contribute.

Recognising the problem is essential, especially if Singapore wants to reduce the financial burden the issue of disenchanted workers is having on its economy. A strong, highly motivated and healthy workforce is necessary for the city-state to emerge from the deeper structural problems it is currently facing and for it to be able to continue to march ahead. But being aware alone is not enough – action is necessary. We're talking about changing the mindset of a nation, and that's not going to happen overnight.

Source:

Unhappy staff burden Singapore economy, *The Financial Times*, 21 October 2003.

an organisation. In all probability your subjective feelings about your future relationship with the organisation will be something like these:

- I expect that the relationship will result in rewards for myself, specifically something near to the combination of intrinsic and extrinsic rewards that I desire.
- In return I expect that the relationship will cost me something in terms of the effort I expend and the inconvenience of not having complete freedom of choice over what I do.
- This gives me a ratio of costs to benefits, and so long as my benefits at least equal my costs the exchange will be a fair one.
- If this ratio is maintained in the future, the organisation is being fair with me and I will be fair in return.

TIME OUT

Use the four statements of subjective feelings about a social exchange relationship given above and apply them to the relationship between yourself and the organisation you work for. If you have no direct experience of paid employment, complete the exercise for the relationship between you and your college or university.

1. What rewards do you expect to obtain from the relationship, i.e. how do you expect to be treated?
2. What costs do you expect to incur to obtain these rewards, i.e. how do you expect to treat the organisation?

These expectations give rise to three very interesting points:

- Unless people feel that there is some commitment to satisfying their needs and meeting their expectations, they are unlikely to be committed in return.

- Where commitment exists, it is because it has grown out of the relationship and is only likely to be obtained if steps have been taken to win this attachment from an employee; thus it would be impossible to select new entrants who are already committed.

- Perhaps most important of all, it is doubtful whether sentiments of this type are held towards an organisation as a whole; it is much more likely that people have these feelings about the immediate context in which they work, and the evidence suggests that commitment is expressed towards departments and sub-units, rather than a whole organisation (Becker *et al.* 1996; Cohen 2000; Belanger *et al.* 2003).

Taken together, these points lead to the inevitable conclusion that there are two huge paradoxes in current management thinking about employee commitment. The first of these revolves around the management assumption that commitment only consists of something that employees give to the organisation. As can be seen, this is only one side of the exchange, and something has to be given in return. The second is connected with the part commitment plays as a pivotal aim in formulating human resource strategies

(Iverson and Buttigieg 1999; Wood and Albanese 1995). These days it is widely assumed that in the light of the fast-moving business environment it is desirable, if not essential, to have committed employees, because commitment results in creativity and flexibility. However, flexibility and creativity tend to be products of the diversity of views and perspectives that arise in different organisational sub-units, whereas senior managers view it as something that is given to the organisation as a whole. As is noted above, it is unlikely that people are committed to the organisation as a whole. Rather, if anything, they are committed to their immediate workgroups.

CASE STUDY 5.2: Peter Larson

Peter Larson, a Swede who now lives in Great Britain, works as a junior hospital doctor in a large National Health Service (NHS) trust hospital. He originally came to Great Britain to study medicine and, after gaining his degree, he gravitated fairly automatically to his present post, which he has occupied for slightly under two years. Having recently given notice that he would be leaving in three months' time to return to Sweden, he was interviewed by his boss, a consultant surgeon, about his decision to leave. When asked whether his decision was prompted by any dissatisfaction with his duties at the hospital, Peter replied that he had no regrets about deciding on medicine as a career. He enjoyed doing what he felt was a responsible, worthwhile job that gave continuing opportunities to learn. In his view his colleagues and superiors were all dedicated people who were a delight to work with and while his pay as a junior doctor did not exactly permit a life of luxury, it was sufficient for his present needs. In any event, since he found himself working nearly 80 hours each week, even if he was paid more, he would hardly have time to spend the money.

'Then what is the problem?' his boss asked. 'Are you homesick?' 'Not really,' replied Peter, 'I have been here for nearly eight years now, and in some respects I prefer England to Sweden.' 'So what's the problem?' his boss asked again. 'To tell you the truth,' replied Peter, 'it is something to do with England. Working for the NHS is so far from my idea of what practising medicine should all be about that I would rather give up the profession than remain in the NHS. You seem to forget that I was brought up in a country where healthcare is available as a right to all who need it, whenever they need it. In Great Britain, however, it seems to me that the chronic under-funding of the NHS is rapidly moving things to a situation in which free healthcare is rationed. As such, before long the poor and needy will get nothing more than a second-rate service, and only those who can afford private healthcare will get what I believe is the basic right of everybody.'

Questions

1. To what extent do you feel that Peter Larson gets satisfaction from doing his job?

2. What do you feel is Peter's level of organisational commitment?

3. In your view what is it that has prompted him to leave – lack of job satisfaction or lack of organisational commitment?

- Theories of attitude change are usually based on the assumption that people strive to maintain consistency between the three components of an attitude, and methods of attempting to bring about change usually rely on creating inconsistency by using techniques of persuasive communication.
- While attitudes have a strong impact on the intention to behave in a characteristic and consistent way towards an attitude object, the existence of an attitude is not an infallible guide to the behaviour that will occur.
- Attitudes are usually measured by the use of self-administered, multiple-item attitude scales, the most commonly used techniques being Likert scales and the semantic differential scale.
- Because of the behaviourial implications of attitudes, work-related attitudes are of some interest to managers in organisations and the two that are currently of greatest interest are job satisfaction and organisational commitment.

There is a great deal of extremely muddled thinking about commitment. While it is easy to see why the concept appeals to managers, commitment is not an attitude that people bring into the organisation. It is one they acquire from their experience of the exchange between organisation and employee and this begs the question of whether employee commitment can be managed. One argument is that commitment, like any other attitude, is amenable to change, which, as was explained earlier, is normally attempted by communication initiatives. However, because it arises out of what is exchanged, rather than what is said, it is unlikely to be an attitude that is amenable to easy modification using persuasive communication techniques. Indeed, as Guest (1992) notes, the very idea of managing commitment is based on the assumption that employees are passive recipients of a manager's attempts to manipulate their feelings. Needless to say they are not, and they almost certainly resent being told what to think.

OVERVIEW AND CONCLUSIONS

Attitudes are patterns of feeling and emotion towards objects, persons, ideas and events. They give rise to persistent tendencies to behave in characteristic ways and have three components: emotional, cognitive and behaviourial. Attitudes have positive functions: they facilitate adjustment to what people encounter, allow them to define their own self-images, express their basic values and react to the world in a consistent way. However, while attitudes have some stability over time, they are not an infallible guide to a person's behaviour. Although an attitude usually gives rise to an intention to behave in a particular way, many other factors can influence actual behaviour. Work-related attitudes are of importance to many organisations and, because they have potential outcomes that could be beneficial, the two that are usually considered the most significant are job satisfaction and organisational commitment.

FURTHER READING

Ajzen, I (1988) *Attitudes, Personality and Behaviour*, Milton Keynes: Open University Press. An interesting introduction to the subject of attitudes, which examines the link between attitudes and behaviour and sets out the theory of planned behaviour.

Cohen, A (2000) 'The relationship between commitment forms and work outcomes: a comparison of three models', *Human Relations* 53(3), 387–417. While a somewhat technical paper in places, the article is an interesting study to explore different approaches to explaining the relationship between commitment and its likely outcomes.

Edwards, J E (1997) *How to Conduct Organisational Surveys*, Thousand Oaks CA: Sage. A good overview of the techniques involved in designing and using employee opinion surveys.

Meyer, J P and N J Allen (1997) *Commitment in the Workplace: Theory, Research and Application*, London: Sage. An extensive exploration of what is probably considered to be a highly important attitude in most organisations. The text gives a thorough examination of the potential link between commitment and employee behaviour.

Payne, R L and C Cooper (eds) (2001) *Emotions at Work*, Chichester: Wiley. An extensive exploration of how people's emotions have a strong impact on their overt behaviour, both in and away from the work situation.

REVIEW AND DISCUSSION QUESTIONS

1. Explain what is meant by the 'functional' approach to the study of attitudes and state the purposes that attitudes serve for people.

2. Describe the most pronounced sources from which people derive their attitudes.

3. Using Fishbein and Ajzen's theory of planned behaviour, explain why attitudes are far more likely to predict behavioural intentions than actual behaviour.

4. Explain what is meant by the expression 'job satisfaction'. According to the research evidence, what aspects of employee behaviour are most likely to be affected by job satisfaction?

5. Explain what is meant by the expression 'organisational commitment'. To what extent is organisational commitment likely to have a positive impact on employee behaviour and why is it unlikely that an organisation would be able to recruit committed employees?

Integrating Individual Characteristics

The last three chapters all dealt with characteristics that distinguish between people as individuals and, for convenience, personality and intelligence, perception and attitudes were all covered separately. In reality, however, they do not exist in isolation but are all interconnected in a way that influences how a person experiences, makes sense of and behaves towards his or her surroundings. There are many ways in which these characteristics could be connected but, to explain this, it is convenient to consider them in pairs.

PERSONALITY AND INTELLIGENCE

As was pointed out in Chapter 3, so far as understanding individual behaviour in organisations is concerned, the separation of personality and intelligence is really a matter of convenience. Personality describes dimensions of behaviour in social situations, whereas intelligence describes the physical and intellectual skills that are necessary to behave in certain ways. Thus there are almost certainly close links between these two characteristics. Indeed, there is a school of thought that argues that intelligence might well turn out to be just another dimension of personality (Phares 1987). The evidence suggests that both characteristics have a strong genetic component (Erlenmeyer-Kimling and Jarvick 1963; Pervin 1980) and both are influenced by socialisation. For example, Wanous, Reichers and Malik (1984) argue that early childhood socialisation has an influence on personality in a general way and more specifically McClelland (1967) has advanced the argument that the strength of the need to achieve (N.Ach.) is influenced by child-rearing practices. In addition, intelligence, at least in the way that it is normally measured, can be argued to be a matter of stored knowledge as much as anything else. Clearly, the amount and variety of stored knowledge in a person's mind is also some reflection of the type and range of socialisation experiences to which he or she has been exposed.

PERSONALITY AND ATTITUDES

Personality also has links with a person's attitudes. For instance, personal construct theory (Kelly 1955) informs us that how an individual views the world, using a personal set of evaluative dimensions, is strongly connected to how the person behaves towards objects in the world (Orbell 2003). Attitudes are also evaluative frames of reference that influence how people behave towards objects and one of their most important functions is to protect an individual from information that contradicts his or her self-image (Katz 1960). Self-image, it should be noted, is a fundamental part of personality, and its defence by an attitude means there are also connections between personality and object recognition in perception. Indeed, there is evidence to show that people erect strong mental barriers to recognising objects or symbols that are threatening to the concept of self (Bruner and Postman 1947; Haire and Grunes 1950; McGinnies 1949).

PERCEPTION AND ATTITUDES

There is almost bound to be a strong connection between attitudes and perception and some hint of this is given above. Although attitudes only reflect the way that people feel about their surroundings, whether a person likes or dislikes an object, person or event that he or she encounters is virtually certain to impact on the way that it is perceived, which in turn can influence behaviour towards the object.

PERSONALITY, PERCEPTION AND ATTITUDES

Since perceptions and attitudes both have behavioural implications, each one probably has some connection with personality. It should be remembered, however, that unlike personality and intelligence, both of which are widely acknowledged to have a direct hereditary component, perceptions and attitudes are much more the result of social, cultural and developmental experiences. Nevertheless, this raises the possibility (although it is probably very slight) that there is a genetic influence on perception and attitudes.

In summary, therefore, personality seems to have a pervasive link with all other individual characteristics. However, because personality is unique to the individual and, by definition, there are as many personalities as there are people, this means that personality is not a foolproof way of predicting a person's intelligence, perceptions or attitudes; they are all merely connected. These links are shown in Figure I1, the first integrative diagram in the book. This is just the first of several building blocks that will be used throughout the book to integrate its contents. As you progress through the different sections of the book you will encounter further integrative subsections that make links between the topics covered in a particular section, and between different book sections.

Figure I1 Interactions between individual characteristics

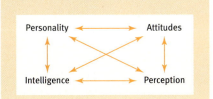

The Intrapersonal Level (Individual Processes)

As indicated by the diagram, this section of the book consists of five chapters, all of which deal with important individual processes. These have a strong influence on the way that people behave and an impact on whether an individual is likely to be considered more suitable for some organisational roles than for others. Because a person's behaviour is a reflection of his or her mental characteristics, there is clearly a connection between this section and the one that precedes it. For this reason, the integrative subsection that follows Chapter 10 not only traces the links between processes, it also traces links between individual characteristics and processes.

Section 5: The Organisational Level
Chapter 15: Goals and Effectiveness

Section 4: The Interpersonal Level
Chapter 11: Groups
Chapter 12: Leadership – Basic Theories
Chapter 13: Leadership – Advanced Theories
Chapter 14: Power Politics and Conflict
Integration 3

Section 3: The Intrapersonal Level
Chapter 6: Memory and Learning
Chapter 7: Motivation – The Foundations
Chapter 8: Motivation – Advanced Theories
Chapter 9: Decision Making
Chapter 10: Stress
Integration 2

Section 2: Individual Characteristics
Chapter 3: Personality and Intelligence
Chapter 4: Perception
Chapter 5: Attitudes
Integration 1

Section 1: Introductory Concepts
Chapter 1: Introduction to OB and OA
Chapter 2: Contemporary Challenges

Chapter 16: Organisational Structure

Chapter 19: Culture and Climate

Chapter 17: Organisational Design

Chapter 20: Communication

Chapter 18: Control

Chapter 21: Change and Development

Integration 4
Integration 5

Chapter 22: Globalisation and the Organisation Across Cultures

Chapter 6

Memory and Learning

LEARNING OUTCOMES

After studying this chapter you should be able to:

- define memory, understand its importance in the learning process and, in outline, explain the 'two-store' model of memory

- define learning and explain the concept of 'levels of learning'

- distinguish between classical and operant conditioning and understand the limitations of behaviourist explanations of learning

- describe the cognitive approach to learning and explain the major tenets of social learning theory

- explain the concept of experiential learning, the concepts of the learning cycle and learning styles, and understand their significance for organisations

INTRODUCTION

This chapter deals with memory and learning; mental processes that are used by everyone. Since all human behaviour is influenced by these processes, they have a strong impact on the way people function in organisations, and while both are usually treated as separate topics in psychology, they are two complementary processes. If knowledge is available in a person's memory it must have been learned at some time, and learning how to perform a certain action has little purpose if the information is not stored somewhere to be recalled when needed.

The chapter commences by considering the topic of memory. A definition is given and this is followed by a description of what has come to be the most widely accepted model of human memory, 'two-store' theory.

The remainder of the chapter deals with the subject of learning, which opens with a definition and a short overview of the different approaches that have been used to try to explain the learning process. This is followed by a description of the three main theoretical approaches to understanding learning: behaviourist theory, cognitive theory and experiential learning theory. These are brought together to compare and contrast the different approaches, and the chapter closes with a brief consideration of knowledge management and an overview section that integrates the topics of memory and learning.

MEMORY

Memory: the ability of an organism to retain information internally and demonstrate this retention through behaviour

Memory performs many functions and it is involved in virtually every aspect of our lives. Nevertheless, it tends to be something we take for granted, and we are usually more aware of forgetting things than remembering them. Thus we often fail to recognise how accurate our memories can be. All that we do or experience involves a contribution from memory and every time we react to something new, we interpret it in relation to past experience. Indeed, we can usually only make an inference about what an object is by interpreting it within the context of what we already know.

There are many definitions of memory, but here it is defined in a general way as:

the ability of an organism to retain information internally and to demonstrate this retention through behaviour.

Two important points can be noted about this definition, both of which imply a connection between learning and memory:

- to retain information it is necessary to be exposed to it and acknowledge its existence;
- the acid test of memory is whether retention of information can be demonstrated by behaving in a certain way.

As will be seen later in the chapter, a potential change in behaviour is also the acid test of whether something has been learned, which could not take place unless we are able to recall what has been learned. Thus, the important connection between memory and learning is that while learning has a potential impact on behaviour, the proof that learning has taken place is the capability to demonstrate that behaviour is changed in some way. Nevertheless, the reader needs to be aware that learning and memory are regarded as two separate topics in psychology, and they address two different questions. With learning the question is, 'How and why does an organism learn?' and memory research asks, 'How, when something has been learned, is the information represented, stored and retrieved?'

The academic study of memory is a very complex area. It comprises many different theoretical approaches and it would be impossible to cover them all in a book such as this. Many of the basic principles of the memory process were uncovered nearly 50 years ago and since then work in the area has become increasingly more specialised and complex so that the study of memory is near to becoming a branch of psychology in its own right. This poses a problem for an introductory text such as this. Grasping the implications of recent developments requires an understanding of basic models and principles, which is difficult enough for students of pure psychology. Because this is not a book on pure psychology, this chapter confines itself to covering only the basic principles of memory, because going beyond this might confuse, rather than inform, the reader. Thus the explanation mostly draws on the older, more basic studies and is largely confined to a description of what is by now the most widely accepted approach for portraying the human memory: 'two-store' theory.

A Model of Human Memory

The naive view of memory is that it is simply a repository for storing information. However, since memory plays an important part in the way we experience the world, it is a highly active process. The basic question addressed in memory research is, 'In order for it to be remembered and recalled when required, what happens to information as it arrives from the outside world?' This results in what can broadly be described as the 'information processing' approach to memory, in which the most widely accepted model is 'two-store theory'. In some respects, however, the expression 'two-store' is misleading. While the name reflects the idea that the overwhelming body of evidence suggests that humans have two memory stores, it underplays the equally important point that there are several important processes associated with these stores. To explain this, the two-store model will be developed in stages, but before doing so it is important to sound a notion of caution. The two-store model is a theory derived from experimental evidence, and it explains how memory *could* work and nothing more. It is not a model of the physical parts of the brain and although it portrays different memory stores that have different functions, these stores do not work in isolation; they are strongly interdependent.

Sensory registration: the memory stage in which environmental stimuli are first registered for onward transmission into memory

Stage 1: Sensory Registration

For material to get into the memory at all, it must be sensed in the organism's environment and its presence registered. What is sensed and registered is clearly connected with the perceptual process described in Chapter 4 and it is important to note that we do not experience reality, but infer it from our perceptions. This is a fleeting process and so it is more convenient to describe the stage as one that uses a register, rather than a store.

In order for the information to be transmitted along neural pathways, it needs to be encoded in some way. Here the evidence suggests that this occurs in a way that is specific to the sensory receptor cells involved: visual coding for visual signals and

Figure 6.1 Sensory registration

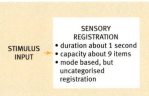

STIMULUS INPUT →

SENSORY
REGISTRATION
• duration about 1 second
• capacity about 9 items
• mode based, but
  uncategorised
  registration

acoustic coding for acoustic signals (Coleheart *et al.* 1974). However, the information is not retained in a mode-specific way in the register, but is just registered 'as there'. The capacity of the register is very limited and once information is registered, it fades rapidly. For instance, Sperling (1960) provides convincing evidence that the capacity of the register is only about nine characters for visually encoded information. Although all nine characters can usually be recalled immediately, the number that a person is able to recall reduces drastically if recall is delayed for as little as one second. Because people are exposed to many different signals at the same time in a work situation, this can sometimes pose problems. If we want to make sure that a particularly important piece of information is registered so that it will pass onwards into memory, it is often necessary to try to get a person to focus on that signal and nothing else. For example, in a process in which an article is heat-treated in a furnace, there will probably be a gauge that indicates the temperature and, in addition, a flashing light that draws attention to the temperature if it exceeds a safe level.

To summarise, matters at this stage of the memory process are portrayed in Figure 6.1.

Stage 2: Short-term (working) Memory

Short-term (working) memory: the stage in which information from the sensory register enters a short-term memory store

From the sensory register information is passed to a short-term memory store (STS). This also has a fairly limited capacity, but the duration of retention is somewhat longer. Miller (1956), for example, suggests that it can hold about seven chunks of information (names, words etc.) and that these are retained for something between six and twelve seconds for the average person. However, there is a crucial difference between the sensory register and short-term memory. The short-term store is not just a simple repository for information, but a functioning component of memory that undertakes a host of tasks. For this reason, some psychologists (e.g. Baddeley 1976) refer to the STS as 'working memory'. It is the centre of a control system that directs the flow of information and probably also attaches additional information that helps with retrieval from long-term memory. Therefore, to enter the short-term store, it seems inevitable that incoming information is re-coded after it leaves the sensory register.

Short-term memory appears to use an abstract verbalised code (Conrad 1964). One of the more interesting control functions performed in the short-term store is rehearsal – the repetition of information to retain it in the STS – so that it can be fixed as a trace for onward transmission into long-term memory. For example, if at work I look up a telephone number in a directory, I tend to repeat this to myself as I pick up the telephone and dial, and if I do this enough times, I soon find that I no longer have to look up the number again.

To summarise, Figure 6.2 represents the memory stages covered so far.

Figure 6.2 Sensory registration and short-term memory

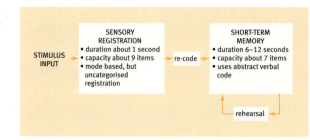

Stage 3: Long-term Memory

This is the (relatively) permanent memory store and, potentially at least, its capacity and duration are limitless. It has been recognised for some time that the way information is stored in a *long-term memory* is different from that in the STS. Thus further encoding or re-coding must take place between short-term and long-term stores. Tulving (1974) suggests that there are two types of long-term memory. These are not only connected with the type of information being stored, but also with how it has been acquired.

The first of these is called *episodic memory*, which receives and stores information about episodes and events in our lives in autobiographical terms. This allows us to draw on experience; for instance, in a work situation it allows me to recall such details as the procedures to be followed for evacuating the building in the event of the fire alarm bell ringing, which I practised in a safety drill some six months ago. One way that information of this type can be stored is by the use of schema. These were described in Chapter 4. They consist of structures developed through experience, which organise incoming information in relation to previous experience, and this tells us what to expect. Another way is by developing scripts, which can be thought of as elaborate schema, which in a single word or phrase gives a repertoire of behaviour appropriate to a particular situation (Gleitman 1991). For example, the cinema script (a sequence of actions involved in seeing a film at a cinema) can be: buy ticket, buy popcorn on the journey from the kiosk to the auditorium, locate a suitable seat in the auditorium, relax and wait for the film to start.

The second type of memory, *semantic memory*, is much more abstract and contains our accumulated knowledge about things we may never have experienced first-hand, but nevertheless know, or believe that we know. Essentially this is information of a conceptual nature, together with knowledge of how the concepts relate to each other. For instance, this could be knowing that there are 100 centimetres in a metre, or knowing the meaning of the word 'aggressive'.

This still begs the question of how abstract, conceptual information can be stored and integrated. The best-known theory about this is the hierarchical model of Collins and Quillian (1969), who suggest that we develop hierarchical taxonomies of ideas or concepts, which enable us to relate them to each other. An example of such a taxonomy relating to the animal kingdom is given in Figure 6.3. Note, however, that this does not mean that we have a picture similar to Figure 6.3 stored in the memory. The idea is that we recognise that birds and fishes are both part of the animal kingdom and that canaries and ostriches are both types of bird, with their own distinctive characteristics.

In summary, the memory process so far is portrayed in Figure 6.4.

Long-term memory: the relatively permanent store in which information and knowledge is retained

Episodic memory: a memory store containing information about episodes and past events in our lives

Semantic memory: a memory store recording information of an abstract, conceptual nature

Figure 6.3
Simplified example of a hierarchical semantic taxonomy (after Collins and Quillian 1969)

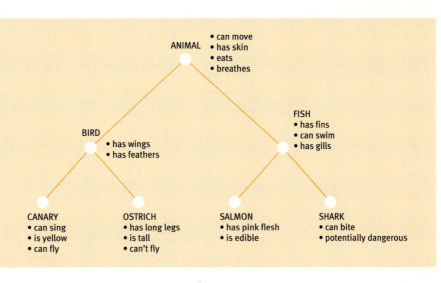

Figure 6.4 Sensory registration, short-term and long-term memory

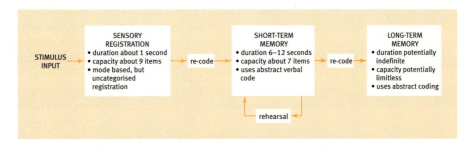

Stage 4: Retrieval

Strictly speaking this is not part of a memory store, but unless we can retrieve information and demonstrate this in behaviour, it is hard to show that the material has been assimilated and retained in memory. Although most of the discussion here centres on retrieval from long-term memory, it is important to recognise that we also retrieve from the short-term store.

Problematically, there are few cast-iron explanations of how the retrieval process works, because most of the experimental evidence deals with forgetting – the inability to remember. One explanation of failure to remember is the 'levels of processing hypothesis' (Craik and Lockheart 1972), which argues that retention is a function of the level at which information processing occurs; for example, that superficial processing only leads to a shallow, short-term retention and a high level of forgetting. However, Taylor *et al.* (1979) argue that retention is connected with depth of processing (processing effort). For instance, if, fairly soon after having learned something, we retrieve the information from the long-term store and re-learn it, we are more likely to fix it in memory.

Theoretically, there could be a number of reasons why we forget information: inefficient search procedures in long-term memory, a poor storage system for information, poor retrieval cues, or a decayed memory trace. However, the strongest evidence

Retrieval: the processes used to recall information or knowledge from the long- (or sometimes short-) term memory store

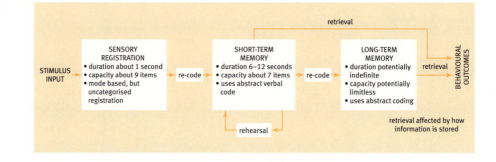

Retroactive interference: the most recent material learned interferes with recall of material that has been learned earlier

Proactive interference: recall of material learned earlier interferes with recall of material that has been learned later

is for a phenomenon known as interference (Waugh and Norman 1965). This can occur in two ways. The first is *retroactive interference*, in which material that is learned later interferes with the recall of something learned earlier. For example, suppose you have an important meeting at work tomorrow and rehearse what you need to say at the meeting immediately before falling asleep. This gives you a greater likelihood of remembering it, because while you are asleep there is no new incoming material to interfere with what has been learned; that is, unless you dream (Ekstrand 1972). The second type of interference is *proactive interference*, in which material learned earlier interferes with attempts to recall subsequent material. To use the meeting example again, although you have memorised what you need to say, someone might give you some important additional facts just before the meeting starts and this message is swamped out by the earlier material. However, it is also possible that there are other reasons why we forget things. We could have repressed the information, because we have a subconscious desire to avoid retrieving something associated with an unpleasant event; for instance, it can sometimes be convenient to forget a dental appointment. Similarly, emotions could render retrieval processes ineffective, for example nervousness in examinations.

To bring all these stages together, a simplified model of the complete memory process is given in Figure 6.5.

TIME OUT

Make a list of all the things that you did last Saturday, from the time you got out of bed in the morning until the time you went to bed that night.

1. How complete is your memory of the whole day? Are there any parts of the day where, although you are generally aware of doing something, you cannot recall the full details? Why do you think this is the case?
2. Now from what you can recall, try to analyse the different ways in which doing all these things involved you in drawing on your memory.
3. In which of these activities was memory essential to its completion?
4. Was there any time at which your inability to recall something from memory made an activity more difficult?

Memory: Concluding Comments

Memory plays an important role in our day-to-day, minute-by-minute functioning. It is much more than a crude, static repository for information, but a set of highly active mental processes. There are at least three crucial interconnected sets of processes at work: input processes, which provide appropriate encoded representations of environmental stimuli that can enter the memory; retention processes that maintain information in the store; and, finally, retrieval processes that seek out information from the store as and when it is needed.

These processes do not store information in a random fashion and, like any efficient storage system, there tends to be a place for everything and everything has its place. Memory is more than a passive recording of events. In order to aid understanding, the mind actively associates new inputs with knowledge already stored so that new material is integrated into a framework that already exists. Therefore, enlarging the memory is rather like expanding a well-designed filing system. This search for meaning also has a huge impact on the capacity to learn new information, and so the importance of the link between memory and learning should never be underestimated.

REPLAY

- Current approaches to understanding memory adopt an information-processing perspective.
- The 'two-store' model dominates current explanations of the memory process.
- Memory consists of three interconnected sets of processes: input processes to sense and register environmental stimuli; retention processes to store information about stimuli; retrieval processes to reactivate information from memory stores.

LEARNING

Learning: a relatively permanent change in behaviour, or potential behaviour, that results from experience

Although there are many definitions of *learning*, it is defined here as:

> **a relatively permanent change in behaviour, or potential behaviour, that results from experience.** **(Hulse *et al*. 1980)**

A number of important points flow from this definition:

- It excludes changes in behaviour that result purely from maturation.
- Learning cannot be observed directly, but only inferred from behaviour.
- Because a person is unlikely to perform better until he or she has learned to do so, there is clearly a relationship between performance and behaviour, but a lack of performance is not an infallible sign that no learning has taken place. This is emphasised in the definition by use of the phrase 'potential behaviour'.
- For the behaviour that provides evidence that learning has taken place to be exhibited, there often has to be a motivation or incentive to do so.

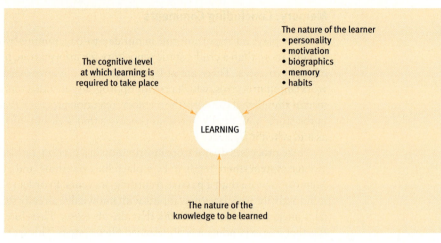

As with memory, the principles of some of the older (conditioning) theories of learning were laid down many years ago. Since then they have not substantially changed and, in the interests of simplicity, with these theories reference is made to the original work. Nevertheless, while they can explain some aspects of learning, these theories cannot explain everything. Thus, other theories have been evolved to clarify other facets of the learning process and these will be presented in the order in which they appeared.

Learning is a complex process that could take place in many ways and the four points made above imply that it is not a discrete process, but has connections with other mental processes. Bruner (1973) draws attention to the idea that to understand learning, account needs to be taken of the three important groups of variables that are shown in Figure 6.6.

We will return to two of these factors later in the chapter when discussing experiential learning but, for the present, it is more important to focus on just one of them: the nature of the knowledge to be learned.

Unfortunately, there is no all-encompassing theory that can cover all types of learning, or the learning of all types of material. This is made clear by Bloom's (1956) discussion of the six levels at which learning can take place, which is summarised in Table 6.1. As we ascend the hierarchy, the nature of what is to be learned gets progressively more complex and so the mental activities involved also increase in complexity. It should also be noted that learning at any level subsumes the use of all lower levels. That is, learning at level 4 also involves learning at levels 1 to 3. Most psychologists would argue that methods of learning that are adequate for levels 1 to 3 would be unlikely to result in learning at the levels above this. These higher levels require more than simply rote learning of information that has been produced by other people and involve reasoning, or the ability to uncover the underlying logic in a situation and make links between different items of knowledge. For this reason, if we want to understand the nature of learning, it is important to understand that it can take place in many different ways and that some of these only facilitate learning at the lower levels in Bloom's hierarchy. As such, the next section of the chapter considers different theoretical approaches to the process of learning and these are presented in an order that roughly equates to an ascent of the levels of the hierarchy shown in Table 6.1. Conditioning

Table 6.1 Levels of learning and their associated behavioural outcomes (after Bloom 1956)

Level	Cognitive domain	Example
6	Evaluation	The ability to judge the value of the material using explicit, coherent criteria. For example, that if we have a set amount of voltage available, delivered at a set current, we can derive the maximum resistance that the circuit must have in order to be able to deliver the voltage along an electrical conductor, which would enable us to select appropriate material to construct the circuit.
5	Synthesis	To be able to reassemble the parts into new and meaningful relationships forming new wholes. That is, to be able to transform the equation above into R = V divided by I, which tells us what the resistance of the circuit is when the voltage and current are known.
4	Analysis	The ability to break down the material into its constituent parts and see the relationship between them. That is, if the resistance of the circuit and the current are known, the voltage that needs to be available to drive electricity around the circuit can be ascertained.
3	Application	The ability to apply the knowledge. That is, to calculate V if I and R are known.
2	Comprehension	Understanding the meaning of the knowledge. That is, that V represents power in Volts, I is current in Amperes, R is Resistance in Ohms.
1	Knowledge	Simple knowledge of facts in terms of theories, actions etc. That is, that Ohm's law for an electrical circuit is $V = I \times R$.

theories, which are the first to be described, explain learning at up to level 3, while those that come afterwards explain higher levels of learning.

THEORIES OF LEARNING

Behaviourist (Conditioning) Theories

Classical Conditioning

Classical conditioning evolved from the work of Ivan Pavlov (1927), who uncovered the concept of the conditioned reflex, which is the main component of classical conditioning.

A reflex is a predictable, unlearned, involuntary response to a stimulus. However, it is not a response that occurs as a result of a conscious decision to do something, but usually has the function of protecting the organism in some way, or helping it to adapt to its environment. For instance, if someone waves a fist in my face, I blink automatically to protect the eye. A reflex of this type is known as an unconditioned reflex (UR) but Pavlov's work showed that it is possible to condition a reflex so that it is elicited by a new and completely different stimulus. Perhaps the easiest way to explain this is to describe Pavlov's experiment, the main stages of which are shown in Figure 6.7.

In Figure 6.7(a) the *unconditioned stimulus* (US) is the sight of food, which elicits an *unconditioned response* (UR) of salivation by the dog. This is a natural, automatic response (reflex) on the part of the animal and, if a *neutral stimulus* (NS), in this case the sound of a bell, appears on its own, as in Figure 6.7(b), the dog does not salivate. However, if the bell is rung in the presence of food, as in Figure 6.7(c), once again the

Unconditioned stimulus: a naturally occurring stimulus to which there is an inbuilt response in an organism's nervous system

Unconditioned response: a reflex response built into the nervous system of an organism

Neutral stimulus: a stimulus which does not evoke a reflex response on the part of an organism

Figure 6.7 Classical conditioning

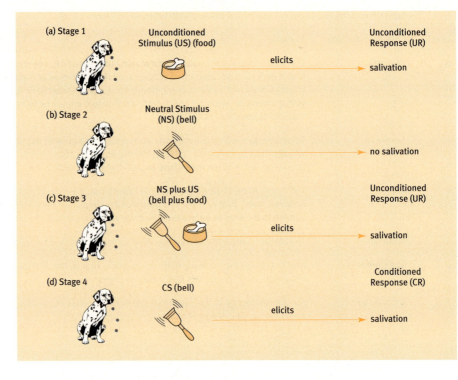

Conditioned stimulus: a relatively artificial trigger to the production of a reflex response in an organism

Conditioned response: a reflex behaviour elicited by pairing a neutral stimulus with an unconditioned response

dog produces the unconditioned response of salivation. Initially, it is the food that elicits the salivation, but if Figure 6.7(c) is repeated enough times, the animal builds up an association between the neutral stimulus and the unconditioned stimulus and the two stimuli become 'paired' in its mind. This permits moving to the final stage shown in Figure 6.7(d), where the sound of the bell alone is sufficient to excite the nervous system of the animal. The bell becomes a *conditioned stimulus* (CS), that is, it elicits salivation and salivation is now a *conditioned response* (CR).

In classical conditioning learning has occurred when the conditioned stimulus becomes paired with the unconditioned response and for this to happen, there must first be an association between the unconditioned stimulus and the unconditioned response. However, once the pairing has taken place, it is possible to substitute a new neutral stimulus and turn it into a conditioned stimulus. For instance, with the animal that has learned to salivate in response to the sound of the bell, a flashing light could be paired with the bell, and eventually the dog will salivate in response to the light. When an animal is conditioned in this way the association can remain intact for a considerable period, but over time some deterioration tends to occur. For example, the dog might continue to salivate, but less saliva would be produced. Indeed, the conditioned response can be removed altogether by introducing an inhibitory force to induce extinction. For instance, if the bell is rung enough times and the dog never receives food in its presence, it will eventually cease to salivate at the sound of the bell.

While classical conditioning can only explain reflexive or passive learning, it still has a number of prominent effects in our everyday lives. It is quite widely used in advertising; for example, in advertisements that convey the message that using a particular brand of aftershave results in a man becoming more attractive to beautiful women. Here the unconditioned stimulus is probably an imagined liaison with the highly attractive woman, which produces an unconditioned response of a degree of sexual arousal and pairing the use of aftershave with the unconditioned stimulus eventually produces the same effect. However, as an explanation of learning there are limitations to classical conditioning. While it can account for how we learn to associate a new stimulus with a reflex response, it only explains how involuntary reflex responses can be triggered. Therefore, it cannot explain how behaviours that are not already built into the nervous system are learned. The next theory to be covered gives an insight into this matter and although this still involves conditioning, it is a very different type of conditioning.

Operant Conditioning

Skinner (1974), the originator of the term 'operant conditioning', distinguishes between the two types of behaviour: respondent and operant. Respondent behaviour follows the pattern of classical conditioning, in which an organism learns to associate an innate, reflexive response with a new stimulus. In operant behaviour, however, the organism emits a new behaviour to deal with new environmental conditions and the behaviour is strengthened by its consequences. This idea has its origins in much earlier work by Thorndike (1911), who believed that all learning is a question of stimulus–response (S–R) bonds and that in lower animals at least, learning occurs through a trial-and-error process. Thorndike's law of effect states that learning only occurs if it has some effect on an organism and, if the effect is a pleasant one, it strengthens the connection between a stimulus and response but, if it is unpleasant, the connection is weakened.

Using Thorndike's law of effect as a starting point, Skinner proceeded to try to answer such questions as why does an organism repeat (or not) a particular behaviour and what factors affect the rate of response? Through a series of carefully controlled laboratory experiments, he discovered much about what influences operant behaviour and formulated the concept of operant conditioning, which is most easily explained by describing Skinner's technique with the aid of the diagram shown in Figure 6.8.

In the first phase of the experiment a hungry pigeon is placed in a box that contains an illuminated button. Pigeons tend to peck at anything that attracts their attention and, eventually, the pigeon pecks the button and a trap door opens in the wall of the box to expose a container of grain. The pigeon eats for a few moments, after which the trap door closes.

The pigeon again begins to strut around the box pecking randomly and eventually it pecks the lighted button again, at which the trap door opens for a brief while and it eats. As time goes by, the pigeon will cease to strut and peck in a random way, and will peck the button more often. Eventually, each time the trap door closes, it will immediately peck the lighted button to open the trap door again. Note that what has happened in this experiment is that the pigeon has learnt to peck at a button to obtain food. Moreover, access to the food container has been reinforced (made more likely) by the behaviour of pecking the button. Thus access to the food makes it much more likely that the button-pecking behaviour will be repeated on future occasions. The important point is that unless the organism emits the correct response, no reward is

Figure 6.8 Operant conditioning

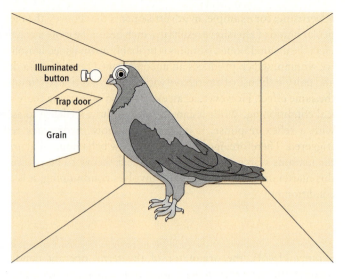

forthcoming. Therefore, the reward, which is only given after the desired response, becomes contingent on the occurrence of the response.

This is a very simple example. However, a wide variety of behaviour can be shaped in this way, some of which can be quite sophisticated. For example, pigeons have been taught to knock skittles down by bowling a ball and, in America, the technique has been widely employed in organisations in behaviour modification techniques, which are described in Chapter 8. To understand how this is possible, it is necessary to know a little more of the principles of using reinforcement.

Reinforcement

Positive reinforcement: an outcome occurring after a behaviour that tends to maintain repetition of the behaviour

A reinforcer is only a reinforcer if it increases the probability that the organism will respond in the desired way. For this reason, operant conditioning is sometimes called 'instrumental' conditioning. In *positive reinforcement* the organism is rewarded for a particular piece of behaviour (a response). However, positive reinforcers can be of two types: primary and secondary. Primary reinforcers satisfy a primary need, usually one that is physiological, such as hunger or thirst. Therefore, their rewarding properties are automatic and do not have to be learned. Secondary reinforcers, however, acquire their reinforcing value through learning, often because they have become paired with a primary reinforcer. An obvious example is money, which gives us the ability to acquire a primary reinforcement. Indeed, behaviourists argue that there can be whole chains of secondary reinforcement. For example, praise or congratulations from the boss can have a positive reinforcing effect because it engenders a hope that promotion and/or higher pay will eventually be forthcoming.

Negative reinforcement: the removal of an aversive stimulus as a result of an organism exhibiting a desired behaviour

Negative reinforcement refers to a situation in which the removal of an aversive stimulus increases the likelihood of a particular behaviour. For example, if I start a new job, I may be told that the first six months' service is a probationary period and a permanent appointment is contingent on good performance in this period. This creates a situation of uncertainty, which for most people is an aversive stimulus. However, the uncertainty can be removed by performing well.

Punishment

This is often confused with negative reinforcement, but they are quite different. *Punishment* is intended to eliminate a particular behaviour, whereas a negative reinforcement aims to strengthen a behaviour by removing an aversive stimulus. Punishment can be applied in two ways. *Punishment by application* consists of using an aversive stimulus immediately following a particular act of behaviour, for instance, spanking a child for misbehaviour. Another way of applying punishment is *punishment by removal*, which occurs when a positive reinforcement is removed after a particular behaviour. An example here could be the loss of certain privileges for persistent lateness at work.

Schedules of Reinforcement

If they are to have the desired effects in operant conditioning, rewards and/or punishments should not be used in a haphazard way and so it is necessary to give some thought as to how they will be applied. Reinforcement can be given in a continuous or intermittent way. In *continuous reinforcement* a reward is given each time the desired behaviour occurs. This is a useful technique in the early stages of the conditioning procedure because it quickly establishes a strong link between the desired behaviour and the reinforcing stimulus. However, the person who is conditioned only by continuous reinforcement tends to have a low tolerance to frustration on the task and low perseverance when things go wrong. *Intermittent reinforcement* occurs when a reinforcer is not given every time the desired response occurs. It has a variety of forms and each one has its own associated behavioural outcomes.

In a *fixed interval schedule*, reinforcement is given at regular, fixed intervals of time. For instance, reinforcement can be given once per minute, hour or day, irrespective of how often the desired behaviour occurs. Problematically, the organism soon seems to learn how often the reinforcement arrives and adjusts its own rate of exhibiting the desired behaviour accordingly.

A *variable interval schedule* makes the reinforcement available in a less predictable way, sometimes after a short interval and sometimes after long intervals. Because the organism is less able to predict when the reward will occur, this leads to a certain degree of persistence in exhibiting the behaviour. That is, because reinforcement can occur at any time, it becomes worthwhile for the organism to exhibit the desired behaviour continuously and this is probably one of the most useful forms of reinforcement to maintain a behaviour once it has been learned.

In a *fixed ratio schedule*, reinforcement occurs when a single reinforcement is given for a fixed number of desired responses, for example, 1 in 10, or 1 in 20, and so on. To some extent the organism can predict when reinforcement will be given and so this tends to result in a pause in activity immediately after reinforcement, followed by a rapid burst of activity leading up to the next reinforcement. Perhaps the most readily available organisational example of this schedule is the use of piecework payment systems, in which pay is contingent on the amount of work done. That is, a machine operator can see how much bonus (the reward) has been earned by simply counting the number of pieces of work he or she has completed. However, with this payment system people can slow down as soon as they have earned as much reward as they desire, and so instead of maximising output, they might work very hard in the morning and take things easy in the afternoon.

Variable ratio schedule: reinforcements which are delivered after a random number of desired responses

A *variable ratio schedule* is the most difficult one for the organism to predict. Sometimes reinforcement occurs after a few responses and sometimes after many. Because the organism can never accurately judge when the reward will be given, this tends to result in a more continuous level of persistence in behaviour. This perhaps explains why people show persistence when playing gambling games, for instance, fruit machines or roulette.

Extinction: a decrease in the occurrence of a behaviour arising from its non-reinforcement

Extinction

Withdrawal of reinforcement from an operant behaviour usually has the result of extinguishing the behaviour. Paradoxically, extinction is much faster when continuous reinforcement has been used to shape a pattern of behaviour than where it has been shaped with intermittent reinforcement. Nevertheless, it is easy to see why this happens if we imagine ourselves using two vending machines. The first one, machine A, produces what we desire (say a cup of coffee) every time we insert the correct money. Machine B is far less reliable and sometimes it produces nothing, although when this happens, it does allow us to get our money back. If, on a particular day both machines are broken down, it is far more likely that we would persevere longer with machine B than machine A. Why? Probably because machine B is less predictable than machine A, and so we would have to try to use it many more times before we realised that it was broken down.

A Comparison of Classical and Operant Conditioning

Although they can both be classified as conditioning techniques, classical and operant conditioning are quite different. This can be seen in Table 6.2.

Table 6.2 Classical and operant conditioning compared

Characteristic	Classical conditioning	Operant conditioning
Behaviour involved	Involuntary, reflex behaviour	Voluntary behaviour
How behaviour obtained	Elicited (drawn-out) by use of relevant stimulus	Emitted by organism for instrumental reasons, i.e. to obtain rewards, or to avoid aversive stimuli
Procedures used	Organism passive, with no control over US or CS	Organism active. It cannot obtain reward or avoid aversive stimulus until it emits desired behaviour, and can obtain repeated rewards for doing so
Selection of desired behaviour	Only innate responses can be selected for conditioning	Any natural behaviour emitted by the organism can be selected for conditioning
Changes in behaviour possible	Only to the extent that an innate response is made to occur to different stimuli	Since organism learns that certain behaviours result in it obtaining reinforcement, whole new repertoires of behaviour can be learned
Reinforcement	Reinforcement not contingent on response. Reinforcement elicits the response, i.e. $$S \longrightarrow R$$	Reinforcement contingent on response, i.e. $$R \longrightarrow S$$

The Limitations of Behaviourist Theories of Learning

While behaviourists tend to explain all human behaviour in terms of stimulus and response links, it is difficult to see how this can explain all types of learning. For instance, if you look back at Table 6.1 it is quite likely that with sufficient patience, levels 1 to 3 (factual knowledge, comprehension and application) could be learned with some form of operant conditioning. For instance, the material to be learned can be broken down into small increments, and appropriate reinforcements can be used to reward successful learning. Indeed, this is the way new staff are trained in some call centres using computer-based techniques. Working at a computer screen a trainee deals with a simulated customer call and is prompted with a message on the screen about what should be said to the customer. The computer analyses the operator's responses, reinforces those that are correct and discourages those that are not. In this way the trainee learns how to parry time-wasting or tangential customer questions that could disrupt the smooth flow of the process of dealing with the query (Whitehead 1999). In addition, there is strong evidence that conditioning can be used to ensure that people adopt patterns of behaviour, such as consistent attendance that is desired by organisations (Stajkovic and Luthans 1997).

However, these examples only require people to exhibit fairly simple behaviour, which involves learning at low levels. Beyond these levels learning requires more than mere knowledge of what is or is not acceptable. For anything above level 3 in Table 6.1 higher brain processes, such as memory and reasoning, are required. For example, Adam (1972) shows that it is relatively easy to condition people to produce a certain quantity of output, but it is much harder to get them to pay attention to quality. To use quantity as a criterion of performance only requires the learner to learn to count, whereas quality is a much more abstract concept that involves learning to analyse and evaluate. Useful as they are in explaining some learning, behaviourist theories cannot deal with many of the ways in which we learn the more complex information that better enables us to cope with daily life. For this reason, the next section considers some of the approaches that take a more complex view of learning.

TIME OUT

Carefully consider the subjects you study at university or college. If you examine matters closely, you will probably be aware that lecturers attempt to get you to behave in certain ways and dissuade you from other patterns of behaviour. Focus on just one of the subjects you study and answer the questions below.

1. What is the pattern of behaviour that the lecturer seems to want you to adopt?
2. What specific behaviours does the lecturer seem to want to discourage?
3. Does the lecturer use inducements of some sort to try to get you to behave as he or she wants and, in particular, are there any reinforcements that he or she gives when you or others behave in this way?
4. Does the lecturer use particular methods of dissuading you from behaving in certain ways and, in particular, does he or she use punishments (either by application or withdrawal) to induce you to avoid these behaviours?

- Classical conditioning theory explains how an organism can be induced to learn to emit a reflex response to a new environmental stimulus.

- Operant conditioning theory explains how an organism can be induced to learn how to behave in a set way by reinforcing (rewarding) the desired behaviour after it has been emitted and/or extinguishing undesired behaviour using punishment, after it has been emitted.

- The different schedules of reinforcement and/or punishment that can be used in operant conditioning have different behavioural outcomes in terms of the learning process. Thus different schedules each have their own uses at different stages in the process of shaping behaviour.

- Conditioning theories only explain relatively simple levels of learning, beyond which account needs to be taken of the role played by cognitive processes in learning.

CASE STUDY 6.1: A Consideration of Industrial Discipline

Wheeler (1976) observes that most industrial discipline consists of a rather crude use of operant conditioning techniques. Guides to good practice for the handling of discipline (for example, ACAS 2000) stress that 'the main purpose of the process is to encourage an improvement in employees whose standard of work or conduct is unsatisfactory', which suggests that the use of discipline should be 'a learning situation'.

Most disciplinary cases involve employees who have repeatedly transgressed in a minor way, for instance, by poor timekeeping, absenteeism or low work standards. Early stages in the process are usually handled informally, but with repetition of the offence each incident is dealt with in a progressively more formal way (i.e. first and final verbal warnings then first and final written warnings) until eventually a formal disciplinary hearing is held. At this, evidence is produced about the employee's past conduct, and if he or she is found guilty, a sanction up to and including dismissal can be taken against the person concerned.

Questions

1. Using your knowledge of the principles of operant conditioning, explain how the disciplinary process could be used to encourage an employee to observe an organisational rule that he or she has a history of breaking.

2. To what extent do you feel that managers use the process to achieve this aim?

3. To what extent do you feel that the process is likely to be successful in achieving this aim?

The Cognitive Approach to Learning

A revolt against the behaviourist explanation of learning had started to occur even in the heyday of behaviourism. Hebb (1949), for example, who was himself a behaviourist, argued that it is impossible to describe behaviour as simply an interaction between sensory processes and motor processes and that central brain processes, such as thinking, must also be at work.

The cognitive approach has a strong emphasis on change in what a learner knows, rather than simply what he or she does. Most work in this area assumes that people participate actively and consciously in order to learn; for example, by drawing on past experience to make decisions about the present. These ideas were first put forward by other behaviourists (Tolman *et al.* 1946), who conducted a series of experiments in which rats were allowed to wander at random around a laboratory maze, in order to find a roundabout route to gain access to food. Tolman and his colleagues noted that when the most obvious route to the food was blocked off, the rats seemed to know their way around the maze and quickly located an alternative pathway. From this it was concluded that the rats had probably developed some sort of cognitive map of the maze in their earlier explorations, which means that central brain processes, including memory, could be at work.

More recent cognitive theories all expand and develop these ideas. There are two broad strands in work of this type. The first, the latent learning approach, emphasises the use of what has been learned on a prior occasion (sometimes without realising it) and using the knowledge later. The work of Tolman *et al.* (1946), described above, is an example of this and another development in this tradition will be explained presently. The second strand is the learning by insight approach, which has an emphasis on the organism understanding what it has learned and thinking about it, so that the learning can be generalised to cope with new situations. Work in this tradition will also be described presently when dealing with experiential learning.

Social Learning Theory

While social learning theory (SLT) has its roots in behaviourism, it uses behaviourist terms in a revised and more liberated way. In general SLT holds that a vast amount of human behaviour is learned in interpersonal situations. Although it does not deny the effect of classical and operant conditioning, it holds that these processes cannot adequately account for every aspect of behaviour, particularly the use of appropriate behaviour in novel situations that have never before been encountered.

In SLT prominence is given to two main ways of learning from social situations: observation and imitation, both of which can result in learning without the learner setting out to learn something. For example, Bandura *et al.* (1961) show that, to some extent, aggression is a behaviour that can be learned by imitation. However, not all behaviour is learned by imitating others and there is a difference between learning from others and directly imitating them. For instance, people can learn and absorb the behaviour of others, but not display a behaviour until it is rewarding for them to do so (Bandura and Walters 1963). This is sometimes called vicarious learning, because it involves learning a pattern of behaviour without actually doing it. It can also result in learning to avoid the mistakes that other people make. For example, if we see someone behaving in a certain way and he or she is punished for this act, we can learn not to replicate the person's behaviour (Manz and Simms 1981).

Self-efficacy: a person's belief in his or her ability to act in a certain way

Perhaps the most interesting development in SLT is the use of the concept of *self-efficacy*, which is a person's belief in his or her ability to act in a certain way. Bandura (1982) describes it as perception of self, in which a person positively evaluates how well he or she has coped with a task. People high in self-efficacy tend to persevere and perform better without becoming stressed than those low in self-efficacy (Gist and Mitchell 1992), and there is a stream of research work that shows a strong relationship between high self-efficacy and high work performance. Social learning theory shows that as well as learning by responding to external reinforcement, people also develop new patterns of behaviour acquired through self-reinforcement and, to some extent, this explains why people with high self-efficacy perform well. They could well reward (reinforce) themselves for high performance, which leads to greater perseverance to continue to do well.

Experiential Learning

With the exception of social learning theory, the approaches covered so far in this chapter can only explain how learning in its simpler forms takes place. This is not to deny that learning by conditioning is a significant influence on behaviour, and we are all conditioned as part of our upbringing. However, learning by conditioning can only

OB IN ACTION: On-the-Job Training

Almost half of on-the-job training has been branded a failure by the most recent annual report of the Adult Learning Inspectorate, which found that 46 per cent of schemes were failing – although this represented an improvement on the 60 per cent found to be failing in the previous year. Some 40 per cent of organisations that provided training at work, in prisons, for the unemployed and in adult education were 'blighted' by poor leadership and management, said David Sherlock, chief inspector of adult learning. 'Too many unlucky learners unknowingly join an organisation which is never going to give them the teaching and support that they deserve.' His report also criticised 'a confusing array of syllabuses, awards and awarding bodies' and called for the government to devise a simpler system.

Sixth form colleges were singled out for 'impressively high' standards, and the report said Learn Direct and the University for Industry had 'almost eliminated poor provision'. However, 95 providers of work-based learning for young people or contractors for Jobcentre Plus were awarded the lowest grades by inspectors – 'a matter of real concern', according to Mr Sherlock. The Learning and Skills Council, the agency charged with delivering the government's £8bn skills strategy, was praised for withdrawing contracts from providers who were not delivering high standards.

Source:

Green, M (2003) Half of on-the-job training fails, say inspectors, *The Financial Times*, 18 November.

explain the acquisition of very basic items of knowledge and their associated behaviours; for example, the rote learning of facts and fairly simple codes of behaviour that we learn in order to fit in with society. Unfortunately these theories cannot explain some of the more abstract facets of learning, such as how people learn in an ongoing way by building on experience, or how they integrate what they have learned so that they can generalise from one situation to another and generate solutions to problems that they have never before encountered. This aspect of learning can be particularly important in organisations, where people are expected to be able to learn from their day-to-day experiences.

Senge (1994) distinguishes between two types of learning, both of which were discussed briefly in Chapter 2. The first is **adaptive learning**. This involves an ongoing development of understanding and the capacity to cope with new situations, by reflecting and analysing what has been done in the past, with a view to improving ways of dealing with fairly familiar situations. To do this people can ask themselves such questions as: What did I do then? Did it work? What could I have done better? How does it help solve the current problem? Almost everybody does this in some degree and, for the most part, it is the mode of learning that will be dealt with here.

The second form of learning, **generative learning**, is a different process that consists of developing new ways of viewing the world. This type of learning is essentially directed at the future and involves speculation, creating possibilities and redefining standards of performance. It is an approach that receives a great deal of attention when considering the 'learning organisation', which was also discussed in Chapter 2 and we will return to the topic at the end of this section. In the meantime, because it applies to most adults, it is more important to consider the other topic, adaptive learning. To do this we must return to two of the groups of factors that affect learning, which were mentioned earlier and which are shown in Figure 6.6, that is, the nature of the learner and the nature of the learning process.

The Nature of the Learner

Here there are many factors that could influence whether effective learning takes place. For example, if people are racked with *anxiety*, this can inhibit the learning process. If they can see that the knowledge to be learned has a practical use in achieving their goals, people who are *highly motivated* tend to learn easily. To some extent, *age* also has a bearing on effective learning. Very young children tend to have difficulties in handling abstract concepts, but in organisations, learners are usually adults, and by this stage of their development most people can deal with abstract concepts in some degree. A person's *memory* is another factor that can affect his or her learning process. For instance, the more a person can recall from past experience, the more likely it is that he or she will use this recollection for integrating new knowledge.

The Nature of the Learning Process

Gangé (1974) suggests that the act of learning involves a chain of seven events, some of which are internal to the learner and some are external. Moreover, he argues that failure to learn will take place if any of the eight links shown in Figure 6.9 do not operate effectively. It can be noted that the whole sequence of seven steps is highly dependent on relating the past to the present. Thus the sequence specifically acknowledges

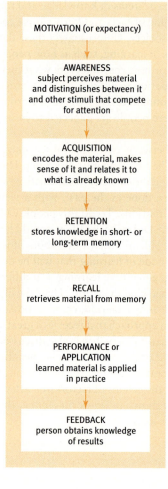

Figure 6.9
The sequence of events in learning (after Gangé 1974)

that higher-order brain processes, such as motivation, perception and memory, are involved, and these are highly specific to the person.

Without delving into this matter too deeply, it is sufficient to note that individuals tend to have their own cognitive styles, that is, preferred ways of organising information to give it meaning. As part of his or her cognitive style, an individual will also have a learning style or a learning strategy, which is used by the person to integrate new knowledge with that which has already been acquired, and to develop strategies for putting the knowledge to use as and when it is required. There are two useful models for describing the effects and implications of these ideas, and these will be considered in turn.

The Kolb and Fry Learning Cycle

Kolb and Fry (1975) argue that learning, and for that matter personal development, occur through an integrated process. This is based firmly on experience and its four stages are shown in Figure 6.10.

Figure 6.10 The Kolb and Fry learning cycle

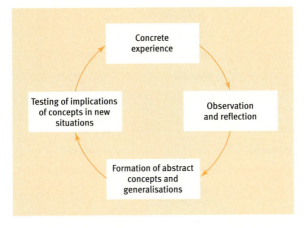

Figure 6.10 The Kolb and Fry learning cycle

A **concrete experience** occurs when a person experiences something new and (perhaps subconsciously) collects information on the phenomenon. If, for example, I have heard of something called a 'ratchet screwdriver', but as yet have never seen one, the first time that I encounter this tool I might note that it is like any other screwdriver, except that it has a 'slide switch' just below the handle.

In the **reflective observation** stage, the person moves beyond merely collecting information on the phenomenon and begins to analyse its implications. With the screwdriver, for example, I might reason that the switch on the screwdriver must have a purpose, probably that of locking the handle, according to whether I want to turn a screw clockwise or anti-clockwise.

Abstract conceptualisation involves going even further into generating abstract concepts and mental models. With the screwdriver, I already know that if I turn a screw clockwise, it screws into a piece of wood, and if I turn it anti-clockwise the screw comes out of the wood. From this I conceptualise a situation where I only need one hand and not two (one to steady the screwdriver and one to turn it) to tighten or loosen a screw.

In the **active experimentation** stage the abstract model I have developed is tested and, lo and behold, the ratchet screwdriver works with only one hand.

There are two very important implications of the Kolb and Fry model:

- It views learning as a cyclical process, in which each stage impacts on the next one, and the end of each cycle becomes the start of a new one. For example, I might think of other jobs where a 'ratchet' tool would be useful, for instance a 'ratchet spanner'.
- The model firmly places learning within the context of our everyday experience of life, not something that only occurs in formal learning or training sessions.

Kolb and Fry (1975) further argue that individuals vary in their preferences for using one of the stages in the cycle – usually the one with which they are most 'at ease'. While a person's style can be modified over time with a great deal of persistence and effort, he or she has a natural inclination to use the dominant style in preference to others. Indeed, people can find that trying to learn in the style that corresponds to another stage in the cycle is difficult, stressful or even unpleasant.

A practical outcome of Kolb and Fry's ideas is a questionnaire, the 'Learning Styles Inventory', which can be used to identify an individual's dominant learning style.

Figure 6.11 The
Honey and Mumford
learning cycle and
associated learning
styles

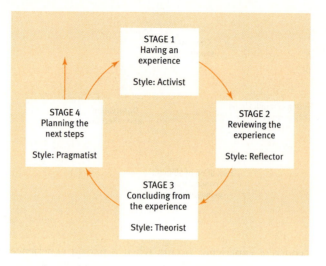

Figure 6.11 The Honey and Mumford learning cycle and associated learning styles

However, this has been criticised on statistical and methodological grounds (see Allinson and Hayes 1988) and research into learning styles now tends to centre on a broadly similar typology, which is considered next.

The Honey and Mumford Model

Like Kolb and Fry, Honey and Mumford (1992) also identify four learning styles, each of which is associated with a preference for a particular stage of a learning cycle, which is shown in Figure 6.11. While Honey and Mumford argue that none of the stages is fully effective on its own (and so all styles are needed), they also acknowledge that people tend to be more at ease with, and focus more strongly on, one style rather than others. However, their ideas differ from those of Kolb and Fry in one important respect. They do not regard it as inevitable that after a person has completed the cycle, he or she will revisit the stages to improve learning on the current issue. That is, the person might veer away from a straightforward repeat of the cycle and enter a completely new learning activity. Honey and Mumford also describe the patterns of behaviour that are associated with each style, summary descriptions of which are given in what follows.

Activists are people who enjoy the here and now. They throw themselves into immediate experiences and are open minded, which tends to make them enthusiastic about anything new. Because they will try anything once, they tend to act first and consider the consequences afterwards. However, as soon as the excitement from one activity has died down, they look for the next. As such, they thrive on the challenge of new experiences, but are bored with implementation and longer-term routine.

Reflectors prefer to stand back and ponder experiences. Thorough collection and analysis of data about experiences and events is all-important to them, and so they try to observe experiences from many different perspectives. Because they are thoughtful and introspective, they try to consider all possible implications before making a move, and tend to postpone reaching definite conclusions for as long as possible. They prefer to take a back seat in meetings and discussions and enjoy observing other people in action and listening to their views. Thus, when they act, they adopt a low profile, consider the past as well as the present, and take other people's knowledge into account.

Theorists adapt and integrate their observations into complex but logical theories. They think problems through in a step-by-step way and assimilate disparate facts into coherent theories. However, they tend to be perfectionists who prefer to analyse and synthesise. Above all, they prize rationality and logic and are dedicated to rational objectivity rather than anything subjective or ambiguous. They prefer to maximise certainty and feel uncomfortable with subjective judgements, lateral thinking and anything flippant.

Pragmatists are keen to try out ideas, theories or techniques to see whether they work. They search out new ideas and take all available opportunities to experiment and get involved with the application of ideas they find attractive. As such, they respond to problems and opportunities as challenges and are often impatient with long, open-ended discussions. They are essentially practical people, who like making practical decisions and solving problems.

TIME OUT

Carefully examine the outline descriptions of Honey and Mumford's four learning styles.

1. Which of these do you feel most closely resembles your own dominant style and what evidence can you offer that this is the case?

2. What do you feel are the main implications of this learning style for successfully studying the subjects that you take at university or college? For example, do you find that some subjects seem easier for you to learn than others? Could this be because the methods that need to be used to acquire knowledge in the subject fit well with your dominant learning style?

3. To what extent do you feel that you complete the full learning cycle when studying something new in this subject? Or do you seem to get locked into one stage in the cycle? What implications does this have for your proficiency in the subject?

The Implications of Learning Styles

One of the most important implications of learning styles is that they influence how people prefer to learn, and this is likely to have a huge impact on how well individuals work with each other. For instance, a person whose natural style is that of a pragmatist will probably be impatient with discussions about possibilities and options. Indeed, such people may well find these activities irrelevant and frustrating. They also have a need for clear guidelines and prefer to avoid the ambiguity inherent in some tasks. If they are subject to training or retraining, they will probably prefer a conventional mode of instruction where they are 'talked at', rather than working in a group that reaches conclusions through discussion. In contrast, the very nature of activists is that they are gregarious people. However, although they enjoy social contact and have few problems in interacting with others, they can sometimes try to centre all activity on themselves. Thus while pragmatists and activists are both 'activity orientated', they are different enough for them to clash if they are both members of the same team. As will be seen in Chapter 11, this might not be a huge problem in a permanent group, where people learn to keep some of their natural tendencies in check to preserve group harmony. However, as is often the case these days, when forming teams and groups on a temporary basis, some account needs to be taken of different learning styles of people in the group so that they work well together.

Another important implication of experiential learning is in terms of organisational change and development, which is considered in detail in Chapter 21. As was pointed out in Chapter 2, there is a strong emphasis on firms transforming themselves into what has become known as 'learning organisations', which involves a move from 'single-loop' to 'double-loop' learning. Although this is normally taken to mean learning by the organisation as a whole, for an organisation to learn, it is necessary for individuals to learn. Therefore, no matter how the 'learning organisation' is defined, it is impossible to conceive it existing without a high degree of learning by individuals, most probably by becoming 'generative' rather than 'adaptive' learners, and this gives rise to two interconnected issues.

First, individuals are likely to be far more comfortable with their own natural learning styles and in a firm that has not yet become a learning organisation, there will probably be a fair degree of accommodation for people with different styles. This means that there is little incentive for people to break away from relying on their single dominant style to become people who complete each stage of the learning cycle with equal ease. However, if the descriptions of adaptive and generative learning are examined closely, it can be seen that a generative learner is probably someone who completes several journeys around a complete cycle for a single issue. Thus, the first problem is to devise ways of encouraging people to shed reliance on a single style, to become individuals for whom completing the full cycle becomes second nature. Although this is not impossible, it takes a great deal of time and perseverance on the part of the people concerned.

The second matter, which is strongly connected with the first, is that individuals are affected by the nature of the organisations in which they are located. They can

REPLAY

- Cognitive theories of learning, which first arose as a reaction to the restrictions of behaviourism, emphasise changes in what the learner knows, rather than simply what the learner does.
- In the cognitive approach to learning, account is taken of the role of brain processes, including perception, memory and reasoning.
- Social learning theory, which had its origins as an application of behaviourist principles, has now emerged as part of the cognitive approach and lays stress on the (sometimes unconscious) learning that takes place in social situations, through the process of modelling.
- Experiential theories stress the idea that people differ in the ways that they learn, that is, in terms of their dominant styles of learning.
- Experiential learning theories also stress that effective learning of something involves the completion of a sequence of learning activities, in which the learner uses all of the different learning styles in turn.

CASE STUDY 6.2: Industrial Discipline – A Further Consideration

An empirical study by Rollinson *et al.* (1997) reveals some interesting outcomes of the disciplinary process. Less than 50 per cent of the people who undergo formal disciplinary hearings subsequently observe the rule, the breaking of which led to them being disciplined. Those who subsequently fail to observe the rule often emerge from the formal hearing with strong feelings of resentment about:

- visible assumptions of guilt on the part of the manager conducting the hearing;
- the summary nature of the hearing in which anything said by the employee in his or her own defence seems to be discounted;
- unfairness in treatment compared to other employees who have been disciplined for the same or similar offences;
- widespread flouting of the rule by other employees, whose conduct seems to be ignored;
- not being informed beforehand about the seriousness of the rule;
- supervisors who, after the formal hearing, shun the employee and fail to give any positive help in observing the rule.

Questions

1. Using the information above, together with that given in Case Study 6.1, explain why the use of conditioning techniques could be less than successful in persuading an employee to abide by the rule in the future.

2. Explain what other approaches to learning, such as social learning theory and experiential learning, can offer in the way of insights into why discipline is largely unsuccessful.

either be helped or hindered in their efforts to become complete learners by the cultures and climates of the organisations in which they work. In a conventional firm, the person who is a generative learner is probably likely to be considered, at best, as a time-wasting perfectionist and, at worst, an oddball or a maverick. Therefore, moving to a situation where generative learning becomes the norm probably means that considerable attention has to be devoted to changing cultures and climates, in order to encourage people to be generative learners.

KNOWLEDGE MANAGEMENT

As noted above, learning at an individual level has strong implications for learning by the whole organisation, which can result in what is referred to in Chapter 2 as a 'learning organisation'. While there seems little doubt that if an organisation is able to do this, it will be better equipped to cope with the fast-moving nature of the globalised economy, it is likely to require new ways of operating to take advantage of the outcomes of individual learning by organisational members. Thus, the burning

Knowledge management: a process or practice of creating, acquiring, capturing, sharing and using knowledge wherever it resides, to enhance learning and performance in organisations

Explicit knowledge: knowledge available to everybody that is easy to codify, articulate and express

Tacit knowledge: individualised, personal knowledge and understanding, which, although understood by the person, is difficult to describe, articulate and disseminate because it embraces the person's experience and intuitions

question is how does it do this or, to put matters another way, how can it translate the advantages of being a learning organisation into competitive advantage?

In the eyes of many people, the answer is to utilise a system of *knowledge management*, which is loosely defined by Scarbrough and Swan (1999) as a process or practice of creating, acquiring, capturing, sharing and using knowledge wherever it resides, to enhance learning and performance in organisations.

In many respects knowledge management has acquired the status of the latest 'must have' in many organisations, and its popularity relies as much as anything else on the idea that the one thing that it is impossible to have too much of in any organisation is management.

Problematically, knowledge itself is tremendously hard to define. However, Nonaka and Takeuchi (1995) draw an important distinction between two types of knowledge: explicit and tacit. *Explicit knowledge* is knowledge that is easily communicated, codified and expressed and is available to anyone within a particular context. For instance, this is the type of knowledge and understanding that most people in organisations have about what to do or how to function in certain circumstances. *Tacit knowledge*, however, is much more personal and individualised. It is difficult to articulate and communicate to others because it is part of a person's experience and know-how. Thus it includes his/her intuitions and insights, or what he or she has found is something that works. For example, if you are particularly good at a sport such as soccer, this is probably what enables you to send the ball just where you want it to go; but just try explaining how you do this to somebody else.

According to Nonaka and Takeuchi, both explicit and tacit knowledge complement each other and they are both required in an organisation if it is to be creative and innovative. Taken together they are the accumulated wisdom of the organisation or, to put matters another way, part of its intellectual assets, and so an organisation that knows how to use both is likely to have a significant competitive edge. For this reason, steps are being taken in some organisations to capture knowledge of both types, often by using information technology to develop databases of organisational specialists (and their prospective expertise) which can be used as and when necessary (Rajan *et al.* 1999). However, a system of knowledge management that attempts to ensure that people's knowledge is made available for others to use can reduce the emphasis on becoming a learning organisation. In addition, knowledge management can give rise to a number of other problems. First, personal knowledge and expertise is what gives an individual his or her personal market value, which can prompt people to self-censor any creative ideas that they might have (Williams 2002). Second, it can be noted that one of the fundamental principles of scientific management is that managers should try to make themselves the central repository for all knowledge in organisations (see Chapter 1). To a large extent managers have been unsuccessful in this, simply because employees are not naive and quickly become aware that an invitation to share knowledge and expertise can become the fast route to redundancy. As such, there are grave reservations in some quarters about the extent to which knowledge can actually be managed (Harrison 2000).

OB IN ACTION: Knowledge Management in Practice

In any large, complex organisation there is usually a great deal of knowledge which is absolutely crucial to its effective functioning but which resides in people's minds rather than in formal documents. This represents the 'taken-for-granted' accumulated wisdom of the organisation that is sometimes never passed on, and, if it is, only by word of mouth. In many cases it is what enables the organisation to run smoothly, and if someone who possesses knowledge of this type leaves, the organisation can lose something extremely valuable.

One such organisation is the Post Office, which, with 210,000 employees, is one of the largest and most complex in Great Britain. In recognition of the vital importance of information of this type it has recently set up a 'knowledge management' team to try to capture this tacit or implicit learning that accumulates in people's minds. To do so the team has developed two novel methods. First, what it calls 'after action reviews' are used when someone has completed a novel task or special project. These seek to identify the aims of the project, what actually occurred, why things happened as they did and whether matters could be improved if something similar arose in the future.

The second and perhaps most important tool is the 'knowledge interview'. In an attempt to become aware of important insights that the person has gained and which might otherwise be lost, this is used when a senior member of staff moves on. It is also used with people who are recognised as having particularly important knowledge that should be more widely disseminated, and sometimes for new employees who could have gained relevant and useful information in other employment. Interestingly, the Post Office explored the use of computerised knowledge-capturing packages for this task, but these turned out to be nowhere near as effective as face-to-face, in-depth interviewing techniques.

By learning about itself in this way and spreading best practice more widely throughout the organisation, the Post Office is reported to have become more efficient and saved a considerable amount of expenditure.

Source:

Whitehead, M (1999) Collection Time, *People Management*, 28 October: 68–71.

OVERVIEW AND CONCLUSIONS

Memory and learning are both crucial processes in everyday life. For most people, the world changes from day to day, albeit in very small increments. Thus, most of us encounter something that is new in our personal environments at fairly frequent intervals, and it is through the learning processes that we adjust to what is new and discover how to cope with it. Without a memory where we can store this information until it is needed again, there would probably be little point in learning how to cope, and this is as true of our lives outside the workplace as it is about our time at work. For this reason, the first and perhaps most important conclusion that can be drawn is that the processes of memory and learning are highly interdependent and in constant interaction. The second major conclusion that can be drawn is that learning can take place at several levels. At one extreme it can consist of a simple awareness that a new phenomenon exists and, at the other, a sophisticated understanding of what that phenomenon means, and how this knowledge can be put to practical use. This is made clear in the discussion of Bloom's (1956) levels of learning, explored earlier in the chapter.

The third conclusion is allied to the previous one. Just as there are different levels of learning, so there are many explanations of how learning takes place. These range from the simpler behaviourist explanations of learning by conditioning to much more sophisticated accounts of the cognitive processes at work contained in the theories of experiential learning cycles. Because behaviourist theories take no account of cognitive processes such as perception and memory, they give a somewhat mechanical explanation of learning that ignores the meaning the learner attributes to what is learned. To explain learning of more complex information and, in particular, how we make sense of what we learn and come to be able to apply it to new situations, cognitive approaches to learning are required. These theories all take note of the roles of higher-order brain processes such as perception and memory. For this reason, recent developments that focus on experiential learning are those that are most interesting to organisations. These not only give an explanation of the different learning styles that come naturally to individuals, but they also reflect the idea that to become a learning organisation it can be desirable to foster a more versatile range of styles in individuals, so that they complete full learning cycles.

FURTHER READING

Argyris, C (1982) *Reasoned Learning and Action*, San Francisco: Jossey-Bass. By now this has come to be regarded as a classic book about the nature of individual and organisational learning.

Bandura, A (ed.) (1997) *Self-efficacy in Changing Societies*, Cambridge: Cambridge University Press. A book of readings, most of which use a social learning theory perspective to analyse the diverse ways in which beliefs of personal efficacy shape life events. It contains interesting perspectives on the influence of cross-cultural factors.

Dixon, N M (2000) *Common Knowledge: How Companies Thrive by Sharing What They Know*, Boston: Harvard Business School Press. The book effectively argues for the use of knowledge management techniques. It advances the idea that organisations need to deal with different types of knowledge, each of which needs to be managed in a different way, otherwise people will not share the knowledge.

Honey, P and A Mumford (1992) *The Manual of Learning Styles*, Maidenhead: Peter Honey. The definitive text on experiential learning that contains an extended description of different individual learning styles and their implications.

Pedler, M, J Burgoyne and T Boydell (1997) *The Learning Company: A Strategy for Sustainable Development*, 2nd edn, London: McGraw-Hill. Although having a very strong managerialist stance, the book gives a well-rounded if somewhat theoretical account of the learning organisation.

Rubin, D C (1995) *Remembering Our Past: Studies in Autobiographical Memory*, Cambridge: Cambridge University Press. A scholarly but readable account of cognitive theories of memory.

REVIEW AND DISCUSSION QUESTIONS

1. For the purposes of study, learning and memory are regarded as two specialist areas in psychology. Explain the limitations of this perspective in terms of gaining a practical understanding of the learning process.

2. Using practical examples from work or your place of study to illustrate your answers, explain the role of the following in learning:

- positive reinforcement;
- negative reinforcement;
- punishment by application;
- punishment by withdrawal.

3. While it has its roots in behaviourist psychology, social learning theory (SLT) has a very different conception of the process of learning. Using practical examples to illustrate your answer, explain what SLT tells us about the learning process that is not explained by behaviourist ideas.

4. Critically examine the idea that understanding his or her own learning style can help a person become a more effective learner.

Chapter 7

Work Motivation:

Basic Concepts and Theories

LEARNING OUTCOMES

After studying this chapter you should be able to:

- define motivation and describe the basic motivational process

- understand the role of needs and expectations of work in the motivational process, together with some of the barriers to work motivation

- describe the origins of motivation theory and understand, discuss and integrate four major content theories of work motivation

- understand and describe the implications of individual job design for work motivation

INTRODUCTION

Humans seldom accept their surroundings in a passive way. They seek to make use of contextual circumstances to pursue their aims and objectives. For this reason work motivation is a topic of enduring interest in the field of Organisational Behaviour and, in general terms, motivation theory seeks to explain how hard people strive to undertake their work tasks, together with the factors that can affect their efforts.

This chapter, which deals with basic theories of motivation, commences by examining the importance of motivation in an organisational context, and then gives a general description of the motivational process. This is followed by a consideration of some of the barriers to work motivation and human reactions to the barriers. Since needs and expectations play a fundamental part in all motivation theories, the discussion then considers human needs and expectations of work and the next part of the chapter explains four of the simpler theories of work motivation. These are content theories, which deal with human needs and their role in motivation, and this part of the chapter concludes with a section that integrates the four theories.

The nature of the jobs that people do has a strong impact on work motivation. This is considered in the next section of the chapter, which deals with the design of individual jobs and the implications of job design for work motivation. As a prelude to the next chapter, which deals with more advanced theories of work motivation, this one closes with a short overview section.

MOTIVATION IN A WORK CONTEXT

Although motivation is fascinating to social scientists as an abstract topic, it has a much stronger practical significance to managers. Ultimately everything achieved in or by an organisation depends on human activity. Therefore, managers want subordinates who will willingly channel their energies into their allotted tasks (Child 1984). However, people usually join an organisation to satisfy their own needs and wants, which gives a possibility that they will be more interested in achieving their own personal aims than the objectives laid down by a manager. For this reason, any interest that managers have in motivation tends to be highly instrumental; by understanding what motivates people, managers hope to be able to control their work performance so that they work harder and more willingly. However, performance does not depend on motivation alone and this is pointed out by Vroom (1964) who argues that task performance is a function of the three factors given in the following symbolic equation:

$P = f(E, A, M)$ where:

Performance (P) is how well the task is performed

Environment (E) is the context of equipment etc., in which the task is to be performed

Ability (A) is the skills and knowledge to perform the task well

Motivation (M) is the motivation to perform the task

Here it should be noted that:

- managers have direct control over the selection process, which has some influence on employees' skills and knowledge;

OB IN ACTION: Invest in Motivation as well as New Technology

These days, managers can come to see investment in new technology, particularly information technology, as something they must do, and sometimes feel compelled to invest in the latest developments for fear that they will fall behind competitors in the race into e-commerce. Inevitably they also expect to see concrete results for the investment, for example, faster response times, higher output from the same workforce, or even more output from less people. However, because employees come under greater pressure, stress levels rise, turnover or absenteeism can increase and output falls – and so the results are in the reverse direction.

In the light of this it is all the more interesting to note that Alan Thompson, the UK managing director of Toshiba Computer Systems, one of the major manufacturers and suppliers of new information technology, urges managers to think matters through very carefully before rushing into changes of this type. Thompson points out that new technology is only likely to be beneficial if it is introduced in a careful way and argues that as well as enabling employees to work more effectively, it should improve the work environment and raise their levels of motivation and enthusiasm. This does not happen of its own accord simply because new equipment has been provided, but only where its impact on people has been carefully considered and it is introduced in a way that is sensitive to human needs. As an example he cites the recent modernisation of Toshiba's call centre, in which more money was invested in psychological research and human change management methods than in the new technology itself. The aim was to make work a more stimulating and enjoyable experience, and thus raise motivation, morale and commitment. The results, he argues, speak for themselves. Employee turnover has fallen by 30 per cent since the change. This, it can be noted, is the opposite of trends in many call centres.

Source:

Thompson, A (2000) Put people before machines, *Professional Manager*, July: 6.

- in addition, these things can be improved with training and development, which is also under management's control;
- however, motivation comes from inside an employee, it is unobservable and cannot be altered at will by a manager.

One of the most enduring myths about motivation, however, is that managers 'motivate' their subordinates. It is commonplace to hear them refer to motivation as if it is some sort of medicine that can be dispensed in variable quantities to those who need it most. This is an impossibility, and Vroom's equation draws attention to several basic points:

- motivation is an invisible process;
- the nearest a manager is likely to come to being able to motivate people is to control the circumstances that surround them, in order to bring about a situation that they find psychologically stimulating;

- in itself this is a difficult task, because people must be equipped with appropriate skills and abilities, and placed in surroundings that offer a strong likelihood that some of their most important needs and wants will be satisfied;
- only then will they want to use their skills in a willing way that also achieves some of the manager's aims.

MOTIVATION: A DEFINITION AND EXPLANATION

The first step in understanding how the points made earlier can be satisfied is to examine the motivational process in a very basic way. However, because the word is used by different people in different ways, it can be very difficult to find a universally acceptable definition of motivation. In this chapter, motivation is taken to mean:

a state arising in processes that are internal and external to the individual, in which the person perceives that it is appropriate to pursue a certain course of action (or actions) directed at achieving a specified outcome (or outcomes) and in which the person chooses to pursue those outcomes with a degree of vigour and persistence.

In psychology, motivation is essentially an explanatory concept used to explain why a person behaves in a certain way. It describes three components of behaviour that have an impact on performance:

- **direction** of behaviour, which is greatly influenced by what a person most desires to do;
- **intensity** of behaviour, which roughly equates to how hard the individual strives to go in that direction;
- **persistence**, which consists of the individual's willingness to stay with the direction when obstacles are encountered.

The Basic Motivation Process

Figure 7.1 shows the basic process of motivation and expresses the idea that there is a driving force within individuals that prompts them to achieve some goal or other. The process is triggered by comparison between **self** and **ideal self**. As explained in Chapter 3, all humans have a self-identity (Rogers 1961) which consists of their view of what they are in terms of strengths and weaknesses, abilities, beliefs and feelings. An individual also has a conception of ideal self – the person he or she would like to be – which is usually somewhat different from the actual self. Even small differences usually give rise to a desire to bring actual and ideal selves into closer alignment (Leonard *et al.* 1999) and this has strong motivational implications.

Needs are the experienced differences (deficiencies) between ideal and actual self. For example, a person can perceive a difference between the skills and abilities that he or she has and those that other people acknowledge. This can give rise to a need for recognition, which prompts the next stage in the model.

Goals are milestones that a person believes will lead to satisfaction of needs. *Expectations* also come into play, because humans have a strong tendency to anticipate that certain behaviours will result in predicable outcomes, that is, achieving the goals. *Motives and drives* are the energisers of action to achieve the goal. In the

Needs: experienced deficiencies between what someone is or has and what he or she wants to be or have, which result in a desire to remove the deficiency

Goals: milestones that are perceived to lead to satisfaction of needs

Expectations: an anticipation that certain behaviours will result in achieving goals

Motives and drives: subconscious processes that provide the energy to engage in the goal-directed behaviour

Figure 7.1 Basic motivation process

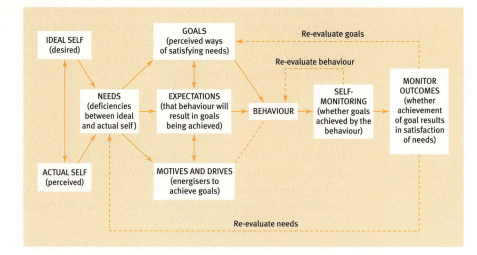

example given earlier, there could be an expectation that a position of higher status would be a mark of recognition, and so promotion could become a goal. This might suggest to the person that he or she displays a pattern of behaviour that induces other people to see him or her as suitable for promotion and all this results in the next stage of the model.

Behaviour is directed at achieving the goal and in the example used here the person could be expected to engage in actions calculated to show superiors that he or she is capable of things beyond the present role. Because these acts are intended to achieve something, the person will normally engage in the next stage, *self-monitoring*, in which he or she evaluates whether the desired outcome has been achieved; for example, whether the new pattern of behaviour actually impresses the boss. For this reason there is a feedback loop shown in Figure 7.1, which indicates that behaviour can be modified if necessary.

Monitoring of outcomes enables the person to evaluate whether the behaviour originally perceived as appropriate achieved the intended outcome, in this case recognition as reflected in promotion. This is one of the main ways in which humans learn appropriate repertoires of future behaviour, because achieving a goal reinforces similar behaviour in the future. In some cases, however, it leads to the person re-evaluating the goal itself. In the example used so far, the person could find that promotion is not achieved. If the goal is no longer seen as attainable, the person will probably search for another one to satisfy the need. As will be seen later, the idea that there is an almost unlimited reservoir of needs just waiting to be awakened is embodied in at least one significant theory of work motivation. It is therefore important to examine needs and expectations in the work context.

Behaviour: activity directed at achieving something

Self-monitoring: examining one's own behaviour to see whether it has had the desired result

Monitoring of outcomes: examining whether the behaviour used has resulted in needs satisfaction

NEEDS AND EXPECTATIONS OF WORK

Work is not the only place where a person can engage in activities that satisfy needs, and although being an employee essentially involves exchanging labour for rewards, humans usually have more needs than money. They come to expect that at least some of these will be satisfied in the work situation and so it is useful to have a way of classifying the various ways in which rewards can be obtained.

**Extrinsic rewards:
rewards conferred
from outside the
individual**

- *Extrinsic rewards* are those tangible benefits such as pay, fringe benefits, pensions, conditions of work and security that individuals receive in return for their efforts. Because these are provided by the organisation, how much is received is largely beyond the control of the individual.

**Intrinsic rewards:
psychological
rewards that come
from inside the
person**

- *Intrinsic rewards* are the psychological rewards that come from the experience of work, or from being part of an organisation; for example, having an opportunity to use skills and abilities, having a sense of challenge or achievement, or having one's efforts recognised and appreciated. These rewards come from inside the person and are given by people to themselves, which can only occur if the conditions they experience allow them to feel this way.

**Social rewards:
psychological
rewards obtained
through interaction
with other people**

- *Social rewards* are obtained by being with other people, often by having a sense of common purpose with them and obtaining reassurance or confirmation of identity. These also have a substantial psychological content.

Humans have very strong social impulses. As will be seen in Chapter 11, a large part of the human 'sense of self' comes from being able to test our ideas of who and what we are on other people, and from obtaining some confirmation that we are correct: the so-called 'looking-glass self' (Cooley 1964).

Whether or not something at work is experienced as rewarding, and, if it is, how it rewards a person, is a highly individualised matter. What is seen as an extrinsic reward by one person can sometimes be an intrinsic reward for someone else, and while people vary enormously in the relative mix they expect, most individuals expect rewards of all three types, which is portrayed diagrammatically in Figure 7.2.

Since the motivation to engage in a particular piece of behaviour is triggered by the expectation that the behaviour will lead to a reward that satisfies a need of some sort, it is important to note the following:

Figure 7.2 Rewards
and satisfaction
of needs and
expectations

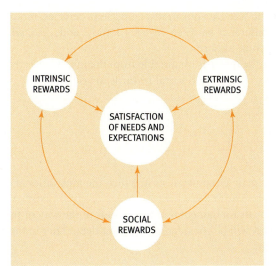

- extrinsic motivation comes from an expectation of receiving an extrinsic reward and intrinsic motivation from the expectation of obtaining an intrinsic reward;
- because social rewards emanate from outside the person, but their rewarding effects are largely psychological, they are a combination of extrinsic and intrinsic factors;
- in practice it is very difficult to ensure that people receive some types of reward rather than others; for instance, the opportunity for people to interact can be provided, but nobody can make people give and receive social rewards;
- because intrinsic motivation is generally assumed to be a more powerful driving force, most managers focus on intrinsic and extrinsic rewards;
- since motivation is a highly personalised process that depends on a person's mix of extrinsic, intrinsic and social needs, providing intrinsically motivating circumstances requires a good understanding of an individual's pattern of needs, but for a variety of reasons this is seldom convenient or possible;
- thus, there is often a general reliance on extrinsic motivators.

However, relying on extrinsic motivators alone seldom results in motivated employees. It tends to make people feel that their behaviour is primarily driven by external factors rather than their own motives, and evidence suggests that too high a level of extrinsic rewards tends to damp down intrinsic motivation (Jordan 1986).

TIME OUT

Carefully consider the experience of your job to date and try to answer the questions below. If you are in full-time or part-time employment, this should be your present job. If you have never been an employee, answer the questions in terms of your experience of university or college life.

1. What do you feel were your needs, goals, expectancies, motives and drives when you started the job?
2. What do you feel are your needs, goals, expectancies, motives and drives now?
3. Is there a difference between answers 1 and 2 and, if so, why and how did this difference come about?
4. In terms of the rewards obtainable from the job, what is the relative importance of extrinsic, intrinsic and social rewards to you?

BARRIERS TO WORK MOTIVATION

Job-related barriers:
features of the job
that remove the like-
lihood that it can
satisfy a person's
needs

There are two main circumstances in which the motivational chain described earlier can break down. The first is where *job-related barriers* exist – where something about the job itself or its fundamental nature stands in the way of the individual becoming motivated. This will be considered in greater detail later in the chapter when dealing with job design.

Goal blocking: a state where motivations are aroused but goal attainment is thwarted

The second set of circumstances, *goal blocking*, occurs when a person's motivations have been aroused but attainment of a goal is thwarted in some way. This tends to result in **frustration** which, if severe enough, can result in one or other of two basic reactions that some writers (e.g. Mullins 2002) call positive and negative reactions. However, the idea that some behaviour is positive and other behaviour is negative is a very one-sided and simplistic view. It looks at the situation totally through the eyes of an outsider, and takes no account of the idea that so-called negative behaviour could have the positive function of relieving inner tensions for the individual concerned. For this reason, the responses will be described in neutral terms as adaptive or non-adaptive behaviours.

Adaptive behaviour: that aimed at removing or circumventing a situation where goal blocking occurs

The first alternative is to engage in *adaptive behaviour* of some sort. One way to do this is for the person to try to remove or circumvent the barrier. Someone with a strong need for recognition of a job well done could, for example, make a definite request for feedback.

Non-adaptive behaviour: that which is directed at shutting out the realisation that goal attainment is blocked

Non-adaptive behaviours are the other possible reaction. They are a way of shutting out the goal-blocking conditions and most of them, such as repression, suppression, projection, fixation, regression and reaction formation, were described in Chapter 3 when discussing Freud's (1901b) explanation of defence mechanisms.

Because there are usually several factors at work when goal blocking occurs, it is often extremely difficult to predict whether a person's behaviour will be adaptive or non-adaptive. The individual's personality, the strength of his or her needs, how firmly the person is attached to a particular goal, the strength of the motivational force and whether he or she perceives that the barrier can be circumvented can all be pertinent. Where only one of these is involved, things are not too complicated, but it is far more likely that there will be several, and this results in a highly complex situation, the remedies for which are well beyond the scope of this book.

REPLAY

- Motivation is an inner mental state that prompts a direction, intensity and persistence in behaviour.
- It is triggered by a desire to bring the actual self closer to the ideal self, which results in needs, goals, expectancies, motives and drives, which result in motivated behaviour.
- Needs and expectations of work are highly individualised and consist of the desire to obtain some combination of extrinsic, intrinsic and social rewards.
- Barriers to motivated behaviour can exist in the work situation and these can be classified as two main types: job-related barriers and barriers that block individual goal attainment.

CASE STUDY 7.1: Working at Tyreco

Jerry is in his early thirties and is a tyre moulder at Tyreco. He services a bank of 40 presses, which are the final stage in the production of automobile tyres. These presses cure (a combination of heat and pressure) raw cases (the made-up tyre consisting of fabric and rubber) into the finished product. The curing time is pre-set and so Jerry's basic task is to unload a cured tyre from the press when it opens, load an uncured tyre into the press and then press a button which closes the press and the curing cycle commences. He does this continuously for an eight-hour shift, five days a week. The work is tedious and the building is extremely hot and noisy so that Jerry frequently feels near to the point of collapse at the end of a shift. Jerry has two special mates in the shop: Alec, who works the line of presses that back on to those that Jerry operates, and Bill, who works back-to-back with Jerry. There is little time for them to chat and in any event it would be near impossible because of noise levels in the shop. However, they usually manage to take their meal breaks together. The work is very well paid but, since it is classified as semi-skilled, there is little or no prospect of advancement.

Questions

1. What do you feel would be Jerry's likely motivational state?

2. Do you feel that Alec and Bill would be similarly motivated?

THEORIES OF WORK MOTIVATION

The Precursors of Work Motivation Theory

All motivation theories make assumptions about what is popularly called 'human nature' – the idea that all people have inner driving forces that prompt them to do certain things. This is a very old idea, in use long before the appearance of what we now call theories of motivation. However, the beginnings of motivation theory as we know it today can most easily be traced to the work of Frederick W Taylor (1911), the originator of **scientific management**, whose work and its assumptions were described in Chapter 1.

While scientific management is not a theory of work motivation, but a technique for obtaining more efficient use of labour, it is highly influential with managers and contains assumptions that have strong motivational implications. The most important of these is the assumption that the main (and perhaps only) thing that people seek to obtain from work is high pay. This ignores situations where people exhibit highly motivated behaviour where economic rewards are low and the next major development took a different perspective.

This was the **Hawthorne Studies** (Roethlisberger and Dickson 1939) (described in greater detail in Chapter 1), which gave rise to a new school of management thinking: the **human relations movement**. This left its own mark on ideas about work motivation, the most important of which is that people have social needs that are as important as the economic imperative. As will be seen presently, the assumptions inherent in human relations theory have had a strong influence on the major group of motivation theories which were the next development in the area. To put them into context, however, it is important to stress that work motivation theory has tended to split into two major streams, each of which deals with a different aspect of the subject.

The group covered in this chapter is generically known as *content theory*. These theories focus on the needs, wants and desires of people, which are taken to be the main impetus for motivated behaviour. The second group, which are covered in the next chapter, are called *process theories*. These do not discount the importance of needs as a driving force and explicitly acknowledge that it is the compulsion to satisfy a need at any given time that provides the motivational impetus. However, theories of this type recognise that needs are highly personalised and can vary for each individual over time. As such, there is a much stronger focus on matters that influence the strength of the motive force and the ways in which a need gets translated into a particular pattern of behaviour.

Content theories: focus on the needs of people as the prime impetus for motivated behaviour

Process theories: focus on mental processes which transform the motive force into particular patterns of behaviour

CONTENT (NEEDS) THEORIES OF MOTIVATION

Theories of this type assume that people strive to satisfy a range of deep-rooted needs. While they differ in terms of their assumptions about the relative importance of different needs, it is the desire to satisfy them that is said to energise behaviour.

Maslow's Needs Theory

Maslow's work (1954) dates from the late 1940s and is based on the assumption that human needs are inexhaustible: as one set of needs is satisfied another arises in its place, which means that needs are arranged in a hierarchy. The usual way of portraying Maslow's theory is as a pyramid of five levels, as shown in Figure 7.3, where the bottom three consist of more basic needs and the top two are the so-called higher-order needs.

Figure 7.3 Maslow's need hierarchy. After Figure 'Hierarchy of Needs' in *Motivation and Personality, 2nd Edition* by A H Maslow. Reprinted by permission of Pearson Education, Inc., Upper Saddle River, NJ

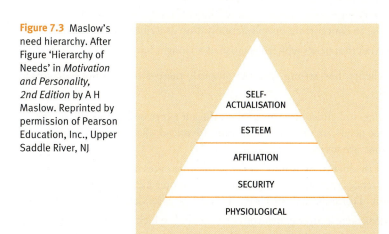

- **Physiological needs** are the most basic of all and arise from internal physical imbalances such as hunger, thirst, warmth and shelter; they need to be satisfied at fairly frequent intervals.
- **Security needs**, which are at the next level, consist of security, freedom from pain or harm, emotional security and well-being, fairness, predictability and order.
- **Affiliation needs** are prompted by the strongly social nature of humans. Most people enjoy feelings of belonging, friendship or being loved, which can only be satisfied through social interaction. Needs of this type provide the motivation to be part of a group, an experience that gives us the opportunity to form meaningful relationships and to gain (and give) support from (and to) others.
- **Esteem needs**, which are sometimes called 'ego' needs, are located at the next level upwards and are often split down into two sub-types. Needs for **self-esteem** concern an individual's view of him or herself, for instance having a sense of self-respect, self-confidence or of doing something that is meaningful and worthwhile in a competent way. **Esteem by others** is needed because a considerable part of our self-concept is obtained from signals about ourselves that we get from other people (Cooley 1964), and if other people indicate that their view of us is as favourable as the one that we hold of ourselves, it is a highly rewarding experience.
- The topmost level consists of the so-called **self-actualisation needs**. These are virtually inexhaustible and are concerned with a person's need to realise his or her full potential, and it is these that are said to drive humans to do things that have never been done before.

Maslow's theory contains a number of highly important assumptions, two of which have significant implications for work motivation:

- He argues that the different levels of need are universally addressed sequentially, which means that needs at one level will not normally play a significant part in motivation until those at the level immediately below have been satisfied. However, in rare cases an individual will bypass one or more levels altogether. For example, if someone is deprived of love and affection in childhood, the person will sometimes lack affiliation needs later in life. Similarly, there are people with very high moral ideals who willingly forgo satisfaction of everything else to concentrate on self-actualisation as a mystic or aesthetic.
- Maslow assumes that needs which are satisfied no longer have a motivational effect.

Although the theory has strong intuitive appeal, there are a number of strong criticisms:

- It is patronising and elitist in terms of the values it expresses. For example, the idea that some needs are primitive and some advanced, that some are higher order and some are lower order (Lazarus 1971).
- The idea that the hierarchy is universally applicable takes no account of cross-cultural differences, which will be discussed in Chapter 22, where the matter of motivation in different cultures is examined in greater detail.
- Maslow's ideas have a mystic, metaphysical quality, which is largely the result of armchair theorising and often contradicted by research evidence. For example,

the assertion that needs are arranged hierarchically has been contradicted by a five-year longitudinal study by Hall and Nougain (1968), which examined changes in the needs of a group of people. In addition, there is little empirical support for Maslow's explanation of the way that different levels of needs trigger different motivations. He suggests, for example, that a satisfied need no longer has a motivational effect and empirical work (Wahaba and Bridewell 1976) has failed to find any evidence for this. Moreover, an investigation by Alderfer (1972), which explored the relative importance of several needs for over 2,000 managers, showed quite clearly that unless people were actually conscious of non-fulfilled lower-level needs, those at the very highest level were always considered important.

- Perhaps most damning of all is the criticism that the assumptions underpinning Maslow's ideas are seriously flawed. The ideas are the result of armchair theorising from his very early anthropological studies of dominance in groups of monkeys. He not only assumed that it is safe to generalise across species, which is itself a highly questionable assumption, but he generalised from animals held in captive conditions, who behave in far less subtle ways than those existing in the wild (Cullen 1997).

In the light of all this evidence there must be grave doubts about the practical utility of Maslow's theory. Every individual is unique, and so it is extremely difficult to make generalisations about needs and need strengths. This means that the theory is too simplified and imprecise to be used successfully as a way of influencing employee motivation. However, this is not to say that it has no value at all. It gives a general framework for categorising needs of different types, and if nothing else, it makes an important contribution as a descriptive tool.

TIME OUT

Carefully reflect on your life to date and, using the description of needs at each level in Maslow's hierarchy, try to answer the questions below.

1. What level of needs satisfaction do you feel you have reached?
2. Is it true that in reaching this level you have satisfied all of your needs at the levels below? If not, what needs remain unsatisfied?
3. Assuming that needs at the next level upwards are now your motivators, what are your particular goals at this level and how does this affect your behaviour in terms of its direction, intensity and persistence?
4. Now try to repeat questions 1 and 3 for someone else that you know well, for example a friend or parent.

Alderfer's ERG Theory

Alderfer (1972) also uses the idea of hierarchical ordering, but this has only three levels: Existence (**E**), Relatedness (**R**) and Growth (**G**), from which comes the theory's name.

- **Existence needs** are those necessary for human survival and are roughly equivalent to Maslow's bottom two levels.
- **Relatedness needs** are concerned with needs to interact with others and approximate to Maslow's affiliation category, together with some of his esteem needs.
- **Growth needs** are at the highest level and take in some of the esteem needs in the Maslow scheme, plus self-actualisation.

While there is some similarity between the Maslow and Alderfer models, the categories do not match up exactly and there are also other very important differences:

- in Alderfer's scheme the different levels are viewed more as a continuum than as discrete categories;
- Alderfer does not assume a sequential progression up the hierarchy, but allows for more than one level (or even all levels) to be active at the same time;
- although he suggests that satisfaction of needs at one level will normally lead to someone seeking satisfaction at the level above, he also deals with the important issue of what happens when needs are not satisfied.

In Maslow's theory it is assumed that a person remains at one level until all needs are satisfied, whereas Alderfer argues that continued frustration of satisfaction at one level can result in a person regressing to the level below and refocusing attention there. This is shown schematically in Figure 7.4.

Unfortunately, Alderfer's theory has received little empirical testing beyond that done by its author. Despite this, he argues that the theory could be a more powerful, but simpler explanation of the effects of needs than Maslow's ideas (Alderfer 1972).

Figure 7.4 Alderfer's ERG theory Outcome of Need Satisfaction or Frustration

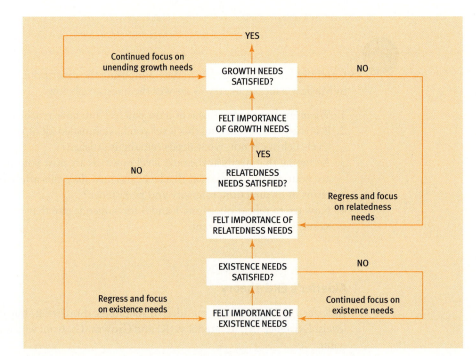

In some academic circles the theory has been well received and is considered to be an important contribution to needs theory because it gives a plausible explanation of a person's likely reactions when needs are not satisfied (Hodgetts 1991).

Herzberg's Two-factor Theory

A departure from the idea of hierarchically ordered needs is given in the theory of Frederick Herzberg and his co-workers (1959). Herzberg avoids using the word 'need' and, instead, divides features of the work environment into two major groups: hygiene factors and motivators. His theory hinges on the idea that people are motivated by things that make them feel good about work, but have aversions to things that make them feel bad. In his theory, motivators are the factors that produce good feelings about work, while hygiene factors, if not present, can result in feelings that the work situation is unsatisfactory. However, it is important to note that the two sets of factors are not opposites. They have different roles and, in Herzberg's view, these are equally important, as shown in Figure 7.5.

Hygiene factors:
features of the work
environment which, if
present, help avoid
dissatisfaction with
work

Hygiene factors are features of the work environment rather than the work itself, for example, working conditions, status, company procedures, quality of supervision and interpersonal relations. The word 'hygiene' indicates that they have a role similar to preventative medicine, that is, they stop illness (in this case dissatisfaction) from occurring. However, their presence does not motivate because the absence of dissatisfaction is not satisfaction. All the hygiene factors do is ensure that a state of **no dissatisfaction** exists.

Motivators: features
of the job itself that
people find enjoyable
and that have a
motivational effect

Nevertheless, unless this is the case, the other set of factors cannot come into play. These are the *motivators*, which are mainly intrinsic in nature, for instance, a sense of achievement, recognition, responsibility, the nature of the work itself and prospects of growth and advancement. Once again, if the motivators are absent, this will not actually result in dissatisfaction, so long as the hygiene factors are adequate, because the opposite of satisfaction is not dissatisfaction, it is merely **no satisfaction**.

Herzberg's original study has been replicated many times, both by himself and by others (Hodgetts and Luthans 1991). While the results usually support his original findings there are still some worrying criticisms of the theory.

Almost inevitably these are criticisms of his research methodology, which used what is technically known as a 'critical incident' technique, in which people were asked to

Figure 7.5 Herzberg's
two-factor theory

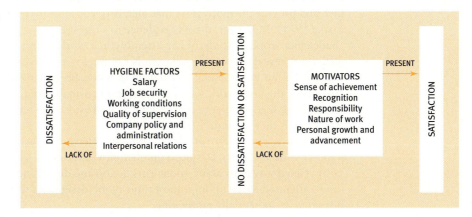

recount incidents that had made them feel exceptionally good or bad about their jobs. Criticisms here are that:

- Answers to this type of question are all too easily contaminated by respondent self-images, for instance, people commonly attribute something that made them feel good to their own behaviour and shift the blame for feeling bad on to the organisation. Thus, hygiene factors and motivators could be incorrectly classified.
- There is always some tendency for the answer to a question to depend on how the question is put, which means that researcher biases can enter the data collection process, and these can be reinforced in the way that the researcher interprets the answers.
- The technique also tends to push things into bipolar (good or bad) categories of evaluation and this takes no account of a situation where someone dislikes one aspect of a job but, overall, likes the job a great deal.

While these criticisms do not really detract from the idea that satisfaction and dissatisfaction could be different dimensions of the work experience, people are unique. Thus, what are motivators for one person could well be hygiene factors for another.

A second set of criticisms centres on the way that Herzberg classifies organisational features of the work situation as hygiene factors or motivators, and even more controversial is his assertion that the two sets of factors have distinctly different functions. A replication study by Wernimont (1966), for example, indicated that both motivators and hygiene factors are capable of giving feelings of satisfaction or dissatisfaction. Indeed, House and Wigdor (1967) argue that the theory grossly oversimplifies the sources of job satisfaction and dissatisfaction and this could be particularly true if the potential effects of different national cultures are considered. Just as Maslow's theory can be criticised for its assumption of universal applicability, so can Herzberg's work. What are hygiene factors in one culture could be motivators in another and vice versa.

The theory has also been criticised in terms of its very limited range of application. Herzberg's original work and a great many of the replication studies have been conducted on samples of professional or quasi-professional employees, people who tend to regard job interest and enrichment as the most important features of work. In other jobs, for instance unskilled manual work, there is usually far less scope to enlarge the task and provide the motivators that Herzberg considers so essential (Schneider and Locke 1971). Moreover, there is evidence to suggest that not everyone wants highly challenging work. A study of car assembly line workers in the 1960s (Goldthorpe *et al.* 1968) revealed a considerable number of employees who had what the researchers identified as an instrumental orientation to work. Because their central life interests lay outside the firm, work was merely a means to an end and seldom seen as a route to satisfying higher-order needs, so long as it provided the remuneration to support the lifestyles they desired.

Nevertheless, in the face of all these criticisms Herzberg's theory has remained highly popular with managers. Despite a number of weaknesses it has the virtue of giving a fairly refined way of thinking about satisfaction and dissatisfaction at work, and also draws attention to the all-important topic of job design as a way of providing conditions that are potentially motivating.

TIME OUT

Reflect on your experience as an employee in your current job (either full-time or part-time) and answer the questions below. If you have never been an employee, answer the questions in terms of your experience of the university or college. Using Herzberg's two-factor theory:

1. Identify what you consider to be the hygiene factors that are present in your work situation.
2. Identify any important hygiene factors that you consider to be absent.
3. From your answers to questions 1 and 2, what do you consider to be the overall balance with respect to hygiene factors?
4. Now repeat questions 1–3 for the motivators.
5. Overall, to what extent do you feel that work or university/college is a situation that you experience as motivating?

McClelland's Theory of Learned Needs

McClelland's (1967) theory assumes that certain individual needs are a reflection of society's cultural values and are acquired in childhood, which makes the behaviour associated with satisfying needs in adult life something akin to a culturally induced personality trait. Three very powerful needs are acknowledged by McClelland, each of which will be described in turn.

The Need for Achievement (N.Ach.)

Need for achievement (N.Ach.): the need to succeed or excel in areas of significance to the person

This prompts a person to try to succeed or excel in areas that have significance to the individual. McClelland (1971) cites evidence that themes in children's literature, together with other child-rearing practices in a particular country, promote high levels of N.Ach., and that these correlate strongly with the economic prosperity of a particular nation. A theory as bold as this clearly has strong implications for selecting people to fill organisational roles. Therefore a great deal of research (e.g. Cassidy and Lynn 1989) has been devoted to identifying the characteristics of people with a high need for achievement. In general terms this has revealed that high N.Ach. people:

- have a major preoccupation with succeeding in whatever they do;
- find the prospects of failing highly depressing, and so they tend to choose tasks of only moderate difficulty with clear but attainable goals, because with goals that are too ambitious there is a risk of failure and too modest a goal gives no sense of accomplishment;
- tend to prefer to work on their own so that they take full responsibility for what they do;
- like to receive regular, clear and unambitious feedback;
- tend not to value money for itself but more as a symbol of success.

In the light of these characteristics it is not surprising to find that people high in N.Ach. are more frequently found in some occupations than in others. Entrepreneurs, for example, tend to have high N.Ach. scores, whereas scientists' scores are low. However, although people high in N.Ach. are often successful (because the behaviour of trying to achieve probably helps them to rise fairly rapidly to a certain level), very senior organisational roles often require very different attributes. For instance, delegating work to others is not likely to appeal to someone high in N.Ach., but senior executives who do not learn to delegate and avoid personal involvement can quickly collapse under the strain. Moreover, top managers tend to be involved in long-term decision making about the future, a situation in which the risks are high and there is little prospect of clear and immediate feedback, which could be distasteful to the high N.Ach. person. A more controversial research finding is that women generally have lower N.Ach. levels than men, one explanation being that women are said to have a fear of success because it is largely incompatible with traditional female roles (Horner 1970). However, whether this is still true today, when women have a far greater tendency to take control of their own lives, is a highly debatable point. Since the needs which a person acquires are not necessarily connected with work, McClelland has also suggested ways in which adults can be retrained to increase their N.Ach. levels, and he claims a great deal of success for these methods.

The Need for Power (N.Pow.)

Need for power (N.Pow.): the need to control the activities of other people

Because power is almost inevitably associated with prestige and social standing, people who have this need and are able to satisfy it probably obtain a sense of psychological fulfilment which boosts their self-concept. Indeed, he argues that for managers in large, modern organisations, the need for power is a more important attribute than N.Ach. and his research indicates that successful managers tend to have moderately high levels of N.Pow., coupled with low needs for affiliation (McClelland and Boyatzis 1982).

The Need for Affiliation (N.Affil.)

Need for Affiliation (N.Affil.): the need to interact with, and be liked by, other people

This results in a tendency for the person to want reassurance and approval from others. People high in N.Affil. frequently seek work that has a strong element of interpersonal contact. They are strongly influenced by what they perceive other people want them to be and tend to accommodate themselves to the will of other people.

Although McClelland's theory is generally accepted as valid, there are some criticisms. McClelland's assertion that adults can be easily retrained to have higher levels of N.Ach. is debatable. For this to occur a fairly radical shift in personality would need to take place and the idea that this is easily done flies in the face of a wealth of contrary psychological evidence. To some extent it also contradicts McClelland's own argument that traits such as N.Ach. are permanently acquired in early childhood. Personality characteristics are relatively fixed by the time a person becomes an adult, and so while intensive training could have a short-term effect, there are strong reservations about effecting permanent changes (Stahl and Harrell 1982).

CONTENT THEORIES: INTEGRATION AND OVERVIEW

All content theories assume that motivation is best understood by focusing on the structure of innate or learned needs. However, each theory explains matters in a slightly different way, and has its own view about which needs are most important. To the

Figure 7.6
Relationship between
content theory
categories

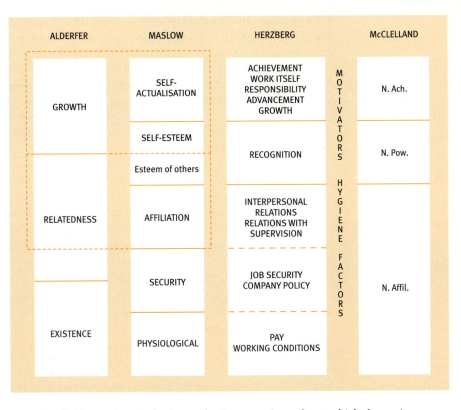

Figure 7.6
Relationship between
content theory
categories

uninitiated this can be perplexing and raises questions about which theory is correct. The simple answer is that none of them is inherently right or wrong. None should be regarded as a definitive picture of human needs, and neither should any one, on its own, be used as the sole basis for explaining behaviour. The theories do not contradict each other and, since each one emphasises a different pattern of needs, it is more appropriate to view them as complementary. This idea is reflected in Figure 7.6, which compares the theories.

As can be seen:

- The Maslow and Alderfer theories have a strong affinity: both view needs as structured hierarchically and where they differ is that Maslow sees the order of needs as fixed, while Alderfer views them in a much more flexible and dynamic way.

- In Herzberg's work, hygiene factors roughly correspond to Maslow's physiological, safety and affiliation needs (existence and relatedness in the ERG scheme), and Herzberg's motivators are roughly equivalent to Maslow's esteem and self-actualisation needs (growth in ERG theory).

- McClelland's theory does not take specific account of lower-order needs, but the need for affiliation embraces some of Herzberg's hygiene factors, which means that it has some correspondence to the security and relatedness categories in Maslow and Alderfer schemes.

- Similarly, N.Pow. is strongly related to Herzberg's recognition factor, and thus to Maslow's esteem needs.

- Finally, the need for achievement has some similarity to Maslow's self-actualisation needs and Alderfer's growth needs.

To some extent, all of the theories are known and have an appeal to managers (Hollyforde and Whiddett 2002). However, their popularity probably rests on the fact that they are simple and easy to understand, which tends to confirm the no-nonsense, commonsense folk wisdom that managers use to explain employee behaviour (Salancik and Pfeffer 1977). Managers often feel distinctly uncomfortable, suspicious and possibly insecure about explanations which are too obviously the output of social science research (Staw *et al.* 1986). Therefore, Maslow's theory, which is the simplest of all, is probably the best known because it is very easy to grasp and probably gives managers a feeling of 'being in control' by knowing how to motivate employees.

If Maslow's theory is the most popular, Herzberg's work comes a close second. Again, it is easy to understand, explains things in terms managers are likely to find intuitively appealing, and offers something they probably feel that they can apply. McClelland's work tends to be far less widely known, at least among managers in the UK.

Despite their appeal, none of the theories is above criticism, but most of their weaknesses are conveniently ignored by managers. They all ignore some potentially important features of human motivation, for example:

● Maslow ignores individual differences and the effect of a change in needs;
● Alderfer's model could well simplify the structure of needs far too much;
● Herzberg's use of hygiene factors and motivators tends to assume that everybody has similar needs to be satisfied;
● McClelland's assertion that needs can be permanently changed by training is far from proven.

The theories all adopt a psychologically universal view that assumes that everyone has a common set of needs, which conveys the impression that people are predictable in terms of what motivates them. This not only ignores the crucial issue of individual differences, but also the potentially powerful effects of different national and organisational cultures as factors that can shape human needs. The effects of national and organisational cultures are considered elsewhere in this book and will not be elaborated on here. Suffice it to say that to many people work is a means to an end, and just one of many ways they can use to satisfy their needs.

REPLAY

● Content (needs) theories assume that motivation is best understood by understanding the needs that people seek to satisfy.
● Maslow's and Alderfer's theories assume that needs are structured in a hierarchy and are addressed in ascending order.
● Herzberg's theory describes two groups of needs, hygiene factors and motivators, which have different roles in motivation.
● McClelland identifies three important needs which are said to be culturally induced.
● While needs theories, particularly those of Maslow and Herzberg, are well known by managers in organisations, at best they tell us about needs that could trigger motivation, but nothing about the process of motivation itself.

OB IN ACTION: The Key to Motivation – Treating People Well

For over 40 years students of management have been collecting data to show that treating people well leads to improved productivity and profits and, according to Jeffrey Pfeffer, Professor of OB at Stanford Business School, over 100 studies show that a 30 to 40 per cent productivity and profit advantage is obtainable by treating people in the right way. In his book *Competitive Advantage Through People*, published 1994, Pfeffer argues that many traditional sources of competitive advantage – market share, technology etc. – were becoming less powerful, and warned that, as other sources of competitive success have become less important, the crucial differentiating factor to the organisation is its employees and how they work. Moreover, 'organisational learning' and 'knowledge management', two of the biggest ideas of the 1990s, were based on the notion that intangible assets such as skills, experience and the ability to adapt were becoming the overriding sources of competitive advantage.

So why do companies continue to treat people in ways that are not only painful for individuals but also damage their own long-term performance? The fundamental reason, according to Pfeffer, is that if you look for success in the wrong places, you will not find it. The obsession of managers with quick fixes, such as mergers and acquisitions, downsizing and strategy prevents them from seeing the more sustainable gains from managing human capital. Fortunately, however, it is still possible to find companies that pay more than lip-service to the idea that people are their most important asset and two that are cited as outstanding examples are:

Xilinx, a California-based maker of microchips, which has bent over backwards to create a culture of openness and trust and last year consulted employees before instituting a pay cut across the board rather than make forced redundancies.

SAS Institute, the largest privately held software company which has continued to hire through the downturn on the grounds that dismissals at other companies represent a once-in-a-cycle opportunity to recruit good people; in addition, the company provides staff with on-site childcare, healthcare and an 'elder-care' programme to help employees deal with the burden of elderly relatives.

Source:

London, S (2003) Profit machines that put people first, *The Financial Times*, 26 September.

JOB DESIGN AND MOTIVATION

As noted at the start of this chapter, management's interest in motivation is sharply focused on its outcomes rather than the processes at work, and managers probably hope that if they understand something of what motivates people, employees can be induced to work more diligently. It was also pointed out that employees have their own needs that they seek to satisfy at work, and as the OB in Action box above indicates, they have expectations about whether their jobs will provide these satisfactions. As such, jobs that are designed to permit satisfaction of important employee needs are likely to be those in which people become motivated to give of their best (Griffin and McMahan 1994). Job design (or redesign) can be defined as:

> **a set of activities that involve alteration of specific jobs or interdependent systems of jobs with the aim of improving the quality of employee job experience and on-the-job productivity.** **(Bowditch and Buono 1985, p 210)**

This is a very broad definition and its reference to the employee work experience can be taken to mean the satisfaction of needs which, for convenience, can be classified as extrinsic, intrinsic and social. Much of the thinking and research into job design has focused on how jobs can be made more intrinsically rewarding, which will be the main concern of what is covered here. Nevertheless, social rewards are also important and these are also experienced intrinsically. In recognition of this, some of the more recent ideas about job design are focused at group, rather than individual, level. Since these are more easily grasped if the reader has some appreciation of the internal dynamics of groups and teams, which is covered in Chapter 11, consideration of these initiatives will be deferred until then.

The Traditional Approach to Job Design

Job simplification: the breaking down of a job into its simpler constituent elements

This relies heavily on *job simplification*, in which the overall task is broken down into combinations of its smallest possible elements, and these become the jobs of individual people. This does not necessarily mean that each person only completes a single element, such as putting a nut in place, while someone else tightens the nut. Using work study techniques, the details of which need not concern us here, the aim is usually to identify the optimum degree of simplification so that the overall task can be completed in the cheapest way. Nevertheless, this usually results in a whole task being broken down into a set of much simpler sub-tasks, which are completed in a set order. This is illustrated in Figure 7.7(a).

The most widespread application of this approach is found in mass production industries, for example in the manufacture of cars and domestic appliances. However, its use is not confined to manufacturing and if you visit a fast-food restaurant such as McDonald's you can observe the principles in action. The task of serving customers is broken down into taking the order, grilling the burgers, putting them in rolls, adding condiments and wrapping, all of which are completed on a form of assembly line.

Job simplification has significant economic advantages and its widespread adoption was responsible for much of the dramatic rise in output in the first half of the twentieth century. Its most important advantages for an employer are:

- a significant increase in productive efficiency and economy when compared to multi-task methods;
- because job occupants are only required to master a very limited range of skills, training costs are low;
- job occupants work faster because they do not have to stop doing one thing to focus on something else;
- special purpose machines that speed up the operation can be used;

Figure 7.7
(a) Job simplification;
(b) Job enlargement;
(c) Job rotation

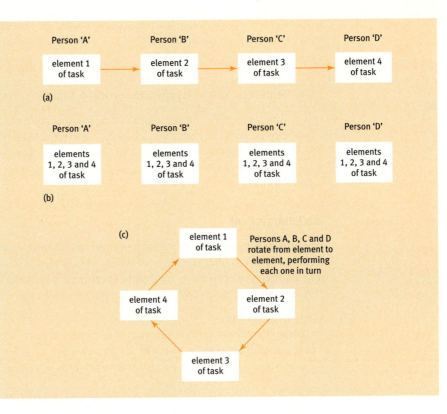

- unskilled labour, which is cheaper and more easily replaced, can be used;
- the operation is more predictable and easily controlled.

However, nothing in this world is for free, and a number of disadvantages have been identified:

- employees often experience the jobs as monotonous, boring and repetitive;
- employees tend to have no feelings of accomplishing anything meaningful;
- many types of problem behaviour tend to appear, for example, carelessness, low quality, absenteeism, high turnover, industrial unrest and occasionally sabotage.

Probably the best documented account of the dysfunctional effects of job specialisation comes from a study of car manufacture by Walker and Guest (1957), who identified that while workers were reasonably satisfied with pay and non-monetary benefits, they were extremely dissatisfied with the work itself. In particular there were six aspects of work that gave rise to discontent:

- the machine-paced nature of jobs;
- lack of control over how the job was done;
- low skill requirements;
- the repetitive nature of jobs;
- the meaninglessness of jobs – workers could not see how their efforts related to the whole;
- few opportunities for social interaction.

In summary, it is possible that job simplification might only create an illusion of efficiency. Its drawbacks could mean that the theoretical advantages of lower costs and increased productivity are not fully realised.

Early Remedies for the Dysfunctions of Job Simplification

It is doubtful whether any firm could completely abandon the economic advantages of job simplification. Nevertheless, when taken too far, it has its problems and, prompted by research such as that of Walker and Guest (1957), there was a search for alternatives to counter the demotivating conditions it creates, three of which are described in what follows.

Job enlargement: horizontal expansion of a job to provide variety for the individual

Job Enlargement

By horizontally expanding a person's job and introducing a greater range of tasks, this technique aims to alter the scope of work. This is shown in outline in Figure 7.7(b), where instead of persons A, B, C and D performing separate elements, each of them performs all four tasks. This has the theoretical advantages of:

- greater task variety;
- workers are more versatile in what they can undertake, which can be useful in coping with temporary absences due to sickness;
- it can be used as the first step in a move towards obtaining a wider degree of flexibility in the workforce;
- to some extent it results in a greater degree of job satisfaction;
- work motivation could be greater.

Nevertheless, job enlargement can have its own drawbacks:

- it sacrifices some of the advantages (e.g. speed) obtainable from simplification;
- since the workforce is more versatile, workers could ask for more pay;
- except in the very short run, it does little to increase motivation and satisfaction because a large boring job is no less boring than four small boring jobs;
- workers can feel threatened and vulnerable by the new arrangements because versatility could make them easier to replace.

Job rotation: the systematic rotation of workers from one job to another to reduce boredom

Job Rotation

Job rotation also consists of increasing the scope of a job by using horizontal enlargement. This time, however, it is done by systematically moving people between different elements in a cycle, as shown in Figure 7.7(c). This tends to have the same advantages and disadvantages as job enlargement.

Job enrichment: enlargement of a job both horizontally and vertically to give the employee more responsibility and control over how the job is performed

Job Enrichment

It is generally assumed that motivation is sustained by the job itself and in particular the level of intrinsic rewards it provides. In essential terms this is the main argument that underpins Herzberg's two-factor theory explained earlier. Herzberg argues that raising motivation requires a lot more than simply expanding a job by horizontal enlargement – it requires the job to be 'enriched'. In this sense the technique of *job enrichment* is

Figure 7.8 The principles of job enrichment (after Herzberg 1968)

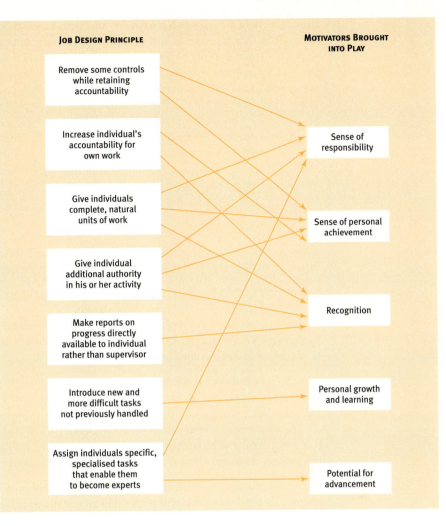

a direct outcome of Herzberg's work and it results in something quite different from either job enlargement or job rotation, both of which only expand a job horizontally. Crucially, it also involves a measure of vertical expansion so that the person has some authority over the planning, execution and control of the work. This, Herzberg (1968) argues, will bring into play the more powerful intrinsic motivators. His recommendations about how this can be achieved are shown in Figure 7.8.

Theoretically the advantages of job enrichment are:

- it is easy to apply, that is by simply enlarging the job vertically as well as horizontally;
- it is broadly in line with currently fashionable ideas about empowerment;
- it almost certainly increases job satisfaction;
- adding task complexity and responsibility should have a positive effect on work motivation.

Notwithstanding these arguments, the research evidence on job enrichment is extremely mixed. Some firms have embraced the idea and report enthusiastically on the effects, whereas others have tried it and withdrawn very quickly. While there is little doubt that it results in higher levels of job satisfaction, this is only a desirable outcome from the point of view of employees and managers might expect to see something additional, for example increased productivity. In this respect job enrichment is something of an act of faith. Herzberg merely assumes that a more satisfied worker is more productive and this is also an assumption that is present in most of the evaluation studies of enrichment (see House and Wigdor 1967). For this reason there may well be an important limiting condition that affects whether job enrichment gives improvements that satisfy both managers and employees. It might only produce results that satisfy everybody if it is applied to those employees who positively value the increased autonomy that results. Not everybody does.

The Comprehensive Approach to Job Design

While job enrichment as proposed by Herzberg is a step in the right direction, it is a 'broad brush' approach that has a number of inherent problems:

- since it is underpinned by a universalistic (content) theory of motivation, it has an equally universal approach to job design;
- it defines enrichment purely in terms of providing Herzberg's motivators;
- it assumes everybody wants an enriched job in these terms, and that everyone wants his or her job enriched in the same way.

Like the content theories on which it is based it takes no account of individual differences and these could be crucial. For instance, some people might only want certain aspects of their jobs enriched and others might prefer mundane jobs that are not enriched at all. There have been attempts to address these issues, the first of which was a pioneering study by Turner and Lawrence (1965), the results of which show that different types of people respond to different aspects of complexity and challenge in different ways. Thus:

- there is probably no such thing as a universally valid prescription for enriched jobs, to which everyone will respond in an equally positive way;
- individual differences could be an important determinant of the job characteristics that people prefer.

Ideas such as these have been tested by other workers, for example Blood and Hulin (1967) who drew the conclusion that individual differences could be an important moderator of the way that people respond to the design of jobs. This led to a search for ways of allowing for these differences, which gave rise to what is generally acknowledged to be the most successful comprehensive theory of job design. This is job characteristics theory (Hackman and Oldham 1980), the essentials of which are shown in Figure 7.9.

The job characteristics model sets out to identify two important causal links:

- the connection between the key features of a job (its core characteristics, which are shown in the left-hand column of Figure 7.9) and the way that a person doing the job experiences these characteristics (shown in the middle column);
- the link between these experiences and the probable outcomes in terms of intrinsic motivation, satisfaction and work performance (shown in the right-hand column).

Figure 7.9 The job characteristics model (after Hackman and Oldham 1980)

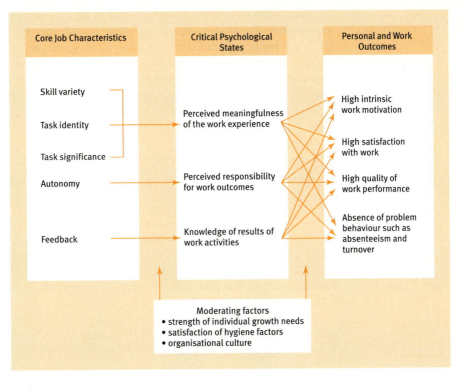

The five core job characteristics are:

1. *Skill variety*: the extent to which the job requires a mix of skills, the exercise of which is valued by the job holder.
2. *Task identity*: the extent to which the job is a 'whole' one, that is, it has a beginning and an end and results in completion of a tangible, identifiable outcome.
3. *Task significance*: the extent to which the job occupant perceives that the job 'matters', in terms of affecting the work or lives of other people inside or outside the organisation.
4. *Autonomy*: the extent to which the job gives its occupant the freedom and discretion to plan the work and decide how it is carried out.
5. *Feedback*: the extent to which doing the job gives its occupant clear information about the effectiveness of his or her efforts.

To the extent that these features exist, they are said to influence the critical psychological states that are shown in the central column of the model. These arise from the person's perceptions of:

- *Meaningfulness*: the degree to which the person experiences the job as one that makes a valuable and worthwhile contribution.
- *Responsibility*: the extent to which the person perceives that he or she is personally responsible for the successful completion of the work.
- *Knowledge of results*: the extent to which the person has clear understanding and evidence of how effectively he or she performs the job.

It is important to note that different core characteristics trigger different psychological states. For instance, it is skill variety, task identity and significance that result in the job being experienced as meaningful. However, according to Hackman and Oldham, meaningfulness on its own is not sufficient to trigger the other critical psychological states and high motivation only occurs if these are triggered as well; that is, when the person feels that he or she is responsible for completing the work (triggered by job autonomy), and has knowledge of results, which comes from having feedback built into the job. This is reflected in the equation:

$$\textbf{Motivating Potential Score (MPS)} = \frac{(\text{Variety} + \text{Identity} + \text{Significance})}{3} \times \text{Autonomy} \times \text{Feedback}$$

MPS is fairly easy to measure and a return will be made to this shortly. For the present, however, it is more important to note that at the bottom of the model there is a box containing three moderators: individual growth needs, satisfaction of hygiene factors and organisational culture. The presence of these spells out that there are limits on the extent to which the core job characteristics will necessarily result in the critical psychological states, which also limits the extent to which the states will result in the attitudinal and behavioural outcomes shown. The need for personal growth broadly corresponds to Maslow's self-actualisation needs and even if the job has the three required characteristics, the individual is unlikely to regard it as meaningful unless he or she values the opportunity for self-actualisation. The important point here is that so far as work motivation is concerned, the model explicitly recognises that the presence of growth needs cannot be taken for granted. Some people prefer boring jobs and others might seek to satisfy their growth needs by engaging in (what are to them) meaningful activities outside work.

Even if this condition exists and the person has high growth needs, the second moderator, hygiene factors, is important because Herzberg's two-factor theory tells us that motivators only come into play if hygiene factors are satisfied. Finally, certain organisational cultures can give rise to contextual circumstances that are not supportive of the causal chain suggested by the model. For example, a highly bureaucratic culture that has a strong emphasis on rules and formal procedures would probably result in a situation where people experienced some of the core job characteristics, such as increased autonomy, as highly 'unnatural'.

Returning now to the motivating potential score, this can fairly easily be measured by using a questionnaire called the Job Diagnostic Survey developed by Hackman and Oldham (1975). This taps employee perceptions of the characteristics of the job, employee psychological states and personal work outcomes. Therefore, as well as being a theory, the job characteristic approach has a great deal of practical applicability. For instance, it would enable an organisation to estimate whether a job has the potential to be intrinsically motivating and, if not, whether conditions are favourable for a redesign initiative.

In general terms there is a great deal of empirical support for the Hackman and Oldham model. This indicates that people who score high on the Job Diagnostic Survey are more highly motivated, have higher job satisfaction and perform better than those who score low (Glick *et al.* 1986; Renn and Vandberg 1995). Note, however, that there are no universals in terms of designing jobs with the required characteristics – the people who do these jobs have to be asked how they experience things.

Like most theories, there are also criticisms of the Hackman and Oldham model. Some studies, for example, suggest that the critical psychological states are in serious need of refinement and revision (Kelly 1992). In addition, there are some doubts about whether the job characteristics actually predict the critical psychological states and whether the psychological states faithfully predict the personal and work outcomes (Algera 1983). Nevertheless, the model is not so easily dismissed. The balance of evidence is in its favour, and this shows that people who work in jobs that contain core dimensions that are thoughtfully designed are usually more highly motivated, satisfied and productive.

The Work Context and Motivation

Perhaps the most important feature of Herzberg's two-factor theory of motivation is its distinction between hygiene factors and motivators, which is acknowledged in the Hackman and Oldham model by including hygiene factors as a moderating variable. This tells us that in terms of enhancing motivation, job redesign can be a futile exercise unless satisfaction of hygiene factors is also catered for. While the usual view of hygiene factors is that they are part of the context in which work takes place, some of them can be part of the job itself. Since these can affect motivation, before closing the chapter it is important to briefly consider some that can be influential. These are shown in Figure 7.10 and are described in what follows.

The Physical Working Environment

Any student who has tried to concentrate in an ill-ventilated, overheated examination room, or attempted to study in a library where other users persist in chattering, will understand the demotivating effects of poor physical working conditions. The number of factors that can result in poor physical conditions is potentially endless, but four (temperature, noise, lighting and air quality) can be powerful sources of discomfort and reduced motivation (Bell *et al.* 1990).

Figure 7.10
Contextual factors affecting work motivation

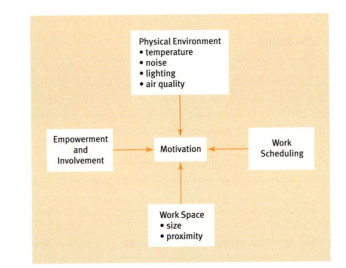

Temperature can have a noticeable effect on motivation and performance although the tolerance to either low or high temperature varies considerably between individuals.

In terms of *noise*, the human auditory system is fairly limited in its capabilities. While noise levels of up to about 85 decibels can be tolerated so long as the noise level is fairly constant, unpredictable variations in pitch or level can seriously interfere with concentration, become nerve racking and reduce job satisfaction and motivation (Baron 1994; Bell *et al.* 1990).

The intensity of *lighting* required for work to take place depends heavily on the task that needs to be undertaken, for example, on the degree of accuracy and precision that is required (Baron 1994). Insufficient illumination puts a strain on the eyes and can result in tension, headaches and the long-term deterioration of sight, and the same is true of extremely harsh lighting.

Air quality sometimes has unseen effects. To function well we all need to breathe, and breathing polluted air can have long-term effects on health. However, people seem to adjust to air contamination but, without actually being aware of it, their performance can deteriorate.

Work Space

Unfortunately the strongest correlate of the *size* of work space a person occupies is not what he or she needs to do the job, but status. Here we should note that highly visible differences of this type can have a demoralising effect on people, particularly where they have insufficient 'elbow room' to do their jobs effectively.

Proximity refers to the distance between people in a work situation and how far they are from the facilities necessary to do their jobs. We all need some degree of personal space, but if people are too distant from each other, social contact becomes difficult and most people need a degree of social interaction. Thus the layout of a workplace can have either a motivating or demotivating effect. Because it permits them to complete complex, demanding tasks that require concentration, many people also need a degree of privacy (Baron 1994) and, if this is absent, it can sometimes lead to frustrations and demotivation.

Work Scheduling

Irrespective of the content of a job, there are a number of ways that work can be scheduled. Some of these have strong implications for motivation because they can allow people to achieve a more convenient balance between home and work life (Curran 2003). It is important to note, however, that operational considerations often mean that few of them can be used everywhere.

In organisations that experience wide seasonal fluctuations in the volume of business activity, one scheduling alternative is *annual hours contracts*. Under this arrangement people might work a shorter working week at some times of the year, balanced by longer hours in other seasons. Something which is similar in principle is the *compressed working week*, for example, four ten-hour days in place of five eight-hour days.

Another popular arrangement is *flexitime*, in which people attend for a standard working week (say 37 hours), and so long as they are present for a specified core period in each day (often 10 am to 3 pm), they have the discretion to start early or finish late. Clearly this can be a very convenient arrangement for employees who have a need to balance home life with work, for example people with young children. However, flexitime arrangements are difficult to use in some industries; in retailing, for example, where stores have to remain open late for the convenience of customers.

Telecommuting refers to a situation where people avoid the physical journey to and from a place of work, by performing their duties at home on a computer, with the results sent electronically to the firm. This was once forecast to be the fastest area of growth in terms of changed working arrangements, but to date any increase has been relatively modest. While those who work at home often appreciate the convenience and lack of interruption that this brings, it can be a lonely life and is probably not for those people to whom the social interaction opportunities of conventional working arrangements are important. In addition, homeworkers can come to realise that there are hidden costs, for example, the heating and lighting expenses that are normally borne by the employer are shifted on to the homeworker.

Empowerment and Involvement

If implemented in an appropriate way, and unfortunately it seldom is, these are methods of providing some degree of enrichment to jobs, by giving employees more autonomy, discretion and responsibility.

In today's conditions, where competing in globalised markets means that a fast response to changing conditions is needed, it can be argued that something that not only harnesses the talents and skills of employees, but also their commitment can be vital. One way to do this is to allow people a greater say in making decisions that affect their daily working lives and, where they are used properly, both empowerment and involvement seek to do this.

REPLAY

- The work motivation of individuals is influenced by the nature of their jobs and the traditional approach to designing jobs relied on job simplification techniques.
- While job simplification has significant economic advantages, it tends to result in a number of human problems.
- Early remedies for these dysfunctions were the introduction of variety into jobs, using designs that expanded job content horizontally, i.e. job enlargement and/or job rotation.
- These initiatives had limited impact and were superseded in some firms by attempts to introduce an additional measure of vertical expansion using job enrichment.
- More recently, comprehensive theories of job design have appeared that take account of individual differences, for example Hackman and Oldham's job characteristics model.
- Job satisfaction and motivation are not only affected by the design of jobs, but also by a host of contextual factors that can influence whether the needs of the employee, as well as those of the employer, are satisfied.

OVERVIEW AND CONCLUSIONS

The theories covered in this chapter have all had a strong influence on the body of knowledge concerned with the motivation of people at work. Evidence for this can be found in the theory and practice of job design, most of which draws heavily on content theories of motivation. Two of these theories are well known in management circles and this is testament to their influential, if somewhat simplistic, ideas. Although all of these theories have their own strengths and weaknesses, they all have something to offer to our knowledge of work motivation. However, while the theories tell us something about work-related factors that could trigger motivation, they have nothing to say about the mechanisms of motivation itself. They cannot explain why two people with identical needs could pursue them with different degrees of intensity and persistence. Thus, they only tell us something about needs that could give rise to motivated behaviour, and have little capability of explaining how a particular individual can be motivated (Arnold *et al.* 1998). This is the province of process theories, which are considered in the next chapter.

FURTHER READING

Kanfer, R (1992) 'Work motivation: new directions in theory and research', in I Robertson and C L Cooper (eds) *International Review of Industrial and Organisational Psychology*, Vol. 74, Chichester: Wiley. An interesting but technical account of the ongoing development of motivation theory.

Petri, H L (1996) *Motivation: Theory, Research and Application*, London: Thompson. A specialist, but nevertheless readable, text that gives a comprehensive coverage of all the major approaches to motivation theory.

Pfeffer, J (1996) *Competitive Advantage Through People: Unleashing the Power of the Work Force*, Boston: Harvard Business School Press. The book gives a damning critique of scientific management and goes on to explain a range of techniques for increasing employee motivation and enhancing employee performance.

Robertson, I, M Smith and D Cooper (1992) *Motivation: Strategies, Theory and Practice*, 2nd edn, London: IPD. A very easily read analysis of the strengths and weaknesses of theories of work motivation.

Spector, P (1995) *Industrial and Organisational Psychology: Research and Practice*, Chichester: Wiley. A wide-ranging text that has good coverage of motivation, and discusses it within in a wider psychological context.

Weiner, B (1992) *Human Motivation: Metaphors, Theories and Research*, London: Sage. A comprehensive book that gives an interesting integration of the different theoretical perspectives on motivation.

REVIEW AND DISCUSSION QUESTIONS

1. Explain the difference between needs, goals, expectations, motives and drives and their respective roles in the process of motivation.

2. In outline terms, describe Maslow's theory of human needs. What are the two major assumptions that underpin Maslow's theory and what implications do these have for work motivation?

3. Since Herzberg does not use the word 'needs' in his two-factor theory, to what extent can it be regarded as a content theory and what are the respective functions of hygiene factors and motivators in the theory?

4. Describe the three needs dealt with in McClelland's work and state his assumptions about the way that humans acquire their needs.

5. What do you feel are the particular strengths vs weaknesses and advantages vs disadvantages of content theories of motivation?

Chapter 8

Work Motivation:

Advanced Concepts and Theories

LEARNING OUTCOMES

After studying this chapter you should be able to:

- distinguish between content and process theories of work motivation

- understand and discuss two alternative expectancy theories of work motivation

- understand and discuss the equity theory of work motivation

- understand and discuss the goal-setting theory of work motivation

- understand and discuss the concept of Organisational Behaviour Modification and how it differs from motivation theory

INTRODUCTION

As was pointed out at the end of the previous chapter, content theories tell us a great deal about human needs that could give rise to motivated behaviour, but tell us virtually nothing about the process of motivation, or how a particular individual comes to be motivated.

The latter is the province of cognitive psychology, which is concerned with the mental processes that underpin complex human behaviour. Theories that approach motivation in this way are known as process theories. Rather than simply cataloguing what people do, or why they do it, these theories focus strongly on variables that account for the direction, intensity and persistence of behaviour and the way that these variables interact. An important feature of them all is that they recognise that because most individuals have preferences for certain outcomes rather than others, motivated behaviour is usually a result of conscious choices.

The chapter presents four of the best-known and most highly developed process theories. These are presented separately, after which there is a short section that compares and integrates them. This is followed by a consideration of behaviour modification. In some American texts this is portrayed as another theory of motivation, but as will be seen, it is not and can more accurately be described as an application of operant conditioning (see Chapter 6). A brief consideration of how motivation is assessed in organisations and organisational responses to motivational problems is then given. The chapter closes with an overview of motivation theories given in this and the previous chapter, which identifies a number of important general considerations, together with implications for managers in work organisations.

EXPECTANCY THEORY

This is currently the most influential process theory in academic circles. However, it is not a single theory, but a group of theories, all of which have three common assumptions:

- in choosing between different courses of action people are influenced by their expectations of whether the action will result in a favourable outcome for themselves;
- people are capable of weighing up the odds about whether acting in a certain way will result in a favourable outcome;
- other things being equal, people will try to behave in a way that gives the maximum return to themselves.

To set the scene, assume that an employee has been asked to take on a new and unfamiliar task by a manager, who infers that if the task is done well, the employee will benefit in some way, perhaps by being promoted. Applying the three assumptions above, the employee will evaluate:

- whether he or she values the prospect of promotion enough to make it a desirable end;
- what is involved in being able successfully to perform the new task;
- whether successfully performing the new task is likely to improve his or her promotion prospects.

Figure 8.1 Vroom's valence–expectancy model

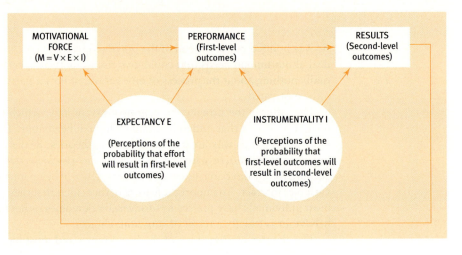

The basic principle underlying expectancy theories is that the motivation to take on the task will only be strong where the employee values promotion and promotion is seen as the likely outcome of performing well. There are, however, different ways of explaining the strength of the motivation and the way that the motivated state arises, and these in turn depend on which expectancy theory is used.

Vroom's Valence–Expectancy (VIE) Model

Vroom (1964) is usually credited with the first articulation of expectancy theory and his ideas are shown diagrammatically in Figure 8.1. To understand the model, it is necessary to explain the terms used.

Valence

Valence: the strength of preference for a particular outcome

Valence is the strength of an individual's preference for a particular outcome, which can be positive or negative. In the example given above, if the employee desired promotion it would have positive valence, and if promotion was not wanted it would be negative. Valence only expresses the feelings about the outcome and Vroom's theory allows for values (say from −10 to +10) to be put on valence.

Outcomes

First-level outcomes: the immediate results of behaviour

Second-level outcomes: those that flow in the longer term from first-level outcomes

Outcomes are the things that result from behaviour and can be expressed at two levels:

- *first-level outcomes* are the immediate results of behaviour. In the example given earlier, the first-level outcome would be performing the new task (hopefully in a successful way);
- *second-level outcomes* are those that flow from the first-level – for example, gaining promotion.

Expectancy

This is the person's perception that his or her behaviour will result in the first-level outcome – in this instance, whether he or she will be able to perform the new task successfully. Note that the word 'perception' is used. Since the event has not yet occurred, a person's expectancy can only ever be a subjective estimate.

Instrumentality

Instrumentality: the perceived strength of the connection between first- and second-level outcomes

Instrumentality consists of the perceived strength of the connection between first-level and second-level outcomes. Again note the word 'perception'. Any preference for the first-level outcome (successfully performing the task) not only depends on the extent to which the second-level outcome (promotion) is valued, but also on whether the first-level outcome is perceived to lead to the second-level outcome; that is, the likelihood that promotion will be forthcoming if the new task is successfully performed.

Vroom acknowledges that outcomes at the second level are usually multiple. For example, while promotion can be valued for its own sake, it normally brings other valued outcomes such as status and higher salary as well. For this reason, what Vroom calls 'motive force' or effort is the sum of the different outcomes and their valences.

Like most motivation theories, Vroom's has been subjected to a degree of empirical testing. An early study by Pritchard and DeLeo (1973) demonstrates powerful effects on performance when conditions are changed to those where instrumentality is higher. Nevertheless, like most innovative theories, the original model is open to some criticism, in this case because it can be very hard to apply in a practical way. However, the concept of expectancy is generally considered to be too useful to discard, and this has led to further developments, the best known of which is considered next.

TIME OUT

Using the instructions below, apply Vroom's model by working out your own 'motive force' for working hard on an assignment in order to pass this module with flying colours.

1. Work out your valence (V) for getting a good final mark for the module. Assuming that this will always have a positive value, give valence a score between 0 (you don't care whether or not you get a good mark for the module) to 10 (it is very important for you to get a good mark).

2. Now give a score for expectancy (E), your estimate of the probability that if you work hard for the assignment this will result in a good grade. This should be between 0 (there is no connection between working hard and getting a good assignment mark) and 1.0 (there is a very strong connection between working hard and getting a good assignment mark).

   Note: the assignment mark corresponds to the first-level outcome in Vroom's model.

3. Now work out your instrumentality (I) score, that is your estimate of the probability that if you get a good mark for the assignment this will result in you getting a good mark for the module as a whole. This should also be 0 (no probability) to 1.0 (high probability).

Note: the mark for the module as a whole corresponds to the second-level outcome in Vroom's model.

4. Now work out your motive force by using the formula M = V × E × I. This should be somewhere between 0 and 10.

5. What conclusions do you draw from your motive force score?

The Porter and Lawler Expectancy Model

This model (Porter and Lawler 1968) is a development of Vroom's ideas and has a number of important additional features that enhance the explanatory power of the expectancy concept. The most significant development is Porter and Lawler's treatment of Vroom's 'motive force'. Porter and Lawler note that a criticism of Vroom's model is that even where the valence of second-level outcomes and instrumentality are both high, other factors can influence the success of a person's actions. Figure 8.2 shows the Porter and Lawler model. The terms are explained below.

Value of reward (1) is the extent to which a person values an outcome, and it has a similar role to valence in Vroom's model. However, Porter and Lawler note that value is highly individualised, and so an outcome valued by one person might have no value to another person. They also note that the value placed on an outcome can be strongly influenced by prior experiences, for example, whether a reward obtained on an earlier occasion was found satisfying. This is indicated by the feedback loop to value from another variable (9) further on in the model, about which more will be said presently.

Perceived *effort to reward probability* (2) is almost identical to Vroom's expectancy concept, that is, the perceived likelihood that rewards will follow from successful performance.

Value of reward: the extent that a person values a reward

Effort to reward probability: the perceived likelihood that a reward will follow successful task performance

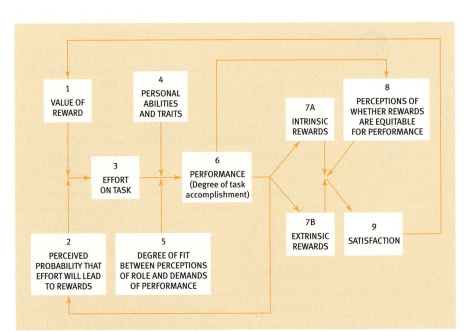

Figure 8.2 The Porter and Lawler expectancy model (*Source*: Porter and Lawler 1968)

Effort on task (3) indicates something rather different from Vroom's use of the word. It is not a motive force, but simply how hard someone tries to perform the task and, important as it is, effort alone does not ensure successful task performance. Two other variables are likely to have mediating effects:

- **Personal attributes and traits** (4), which are the skills, aptitudes and mental dispositions of the person, which facilitate or inhibit task performance.
- **Fit between perceptions of role and demands of performance** (5), which corresponds to the person's views on whether performing the task is compatible with his or her current role. For instance, if the new task requires dealing with more ambiguous situations and decisions have to be made on incomplete information, this might make the task more stressful, or even distasteful.

Performance (6) is the final outcome of engaging in the task and includes whether it is successfully accomplished or not.

Rewards are the outcomes for the person performing the task. They fall into two groups:

- **intrinsic rewards** (7A) are the inner feelings of accomplishment and sense of challenge;
- **extrinsic rewards** (7B) are tangible items such as pay and promotion.

Note that there is a connection between both types of reward so they must be considered together. Porter and Lawler stress that it should not be assumed that doing a job well is a reward in its own right, particularly if special efforts have been made to perform it. Nor should it be assumed that extrinsic rewards are the ones most desired, because extrinsic incentives can merely serve to incentivise people to demand even more extrinsic incentives. Also note the feedback loop from the reward variables to variable 2. This reflects the idea that, on a future occasion, a person's perception of whether it will be worthwhile expending effort is likely to be affected by the rewards that he or she receives now.

Perception of equitable rewards (8) equates to the person's judgement about whether the intrinsic and extrinsic rewards obtained on this occasion are fair and just in terms of the successful performance that has been delivered.

Satisfaction (9) is influenced by intrinsic and extrinsic rewards, largely the extent to which they are perceived as equitable, and this is one of the most significant features of the Porter and Lawler theory. Merely giving rewards does not ensure job satisfaction. This is crucially dependent on whether the rewards are perceived as equitable for the effort that has been expended in performing the task.

Finally, note that there is a very important feedback loop from satisfaction (9) to value of reward (1), which reflects the point made earlier – what happens now is likely to influence the future. In the example of the employee who has been asked to take on a new task, the manager inferred that this could lead to promotion. If the employee finds that promotion turns out to be little more than a job with greater responsibility and a new title but with no increase in pay, the word promotion is unlikely to act as an inducement in the future.

The Porter and Lawler model has been extensively tested, both by its authors and others. While it stands up well to the rigours of empirical examination (Wanous *et al.* 1983), there are still criticisms. It is one of the most comprehensive models yet devised,

CASE STUDY 8.1: The CAD Project

Mario and George are both section leaders in a design department and each is in charge of half of the staff in the office. They have recently had separate interviews with the Chief Design Engineer to discuss the introduction of computer-aided design (CAD) into the activities of the department across the next twelve months. He has asked Mario and George to take on the additional responsibility for introducing CAD into his respective area of activity. In these meetings the Chief Design Engineer, who everyone expects will be promoted within the coming year, stressed that CAD is a pet project of one of the directors and also intimated that anyone who takes it under his wing is likely to find himself well placed when the job of Chief Design Engineer becomes vacant.

Mario is 26 years old, single, extremely ambitious and very conscious of status. George is 40, married and devoted to his family. Both of them value the idea of promotion but for different reasons. Mario because the Chief's job would be a rise in status and a stepping stone to the high executive position to which he aspires; George because it would bring more money and a better standard of living for the family. Both of them consider that the boss has every right to ask for this additional responsibility to be taken on. However, Mario values it as an opportunity to manoeuvre himself into a position where he is the obvious candidate for the Chief's job in twelve months' time, whereas George is much more sanguine about the future and discounts the promotion prospect because, as he puts it, 'I have had carrots dangled in front of my nose before'.

While Mario is well educated, very keen and hardworking, he has only been with the firm for about one year and knows very little about how it functions beyond his immediate area. Moreover, he knows nothing about computers. George, on the other hand, has been with the firm for fifteen years since leaving university and computing is his hobby outside working hours.

Questions

1. Which of the two people do you feel will give the higher performance?

2. Using the Porter and Lawler expectancy model, justify your answer to question 1.

but this is something of a mixed blessing, because it is hard to apply in a practical way. It also assumes that people make decisions in a rational, objective and well-considered way when, in practice, they are sometimes more intuitive. Finally, the theory ignores some of the more unpleasant features of organisational life, which still result in effective task performance, for example coercion and insecurity. Despite these criticisms, and the fact that outside academic circles the theory is less well known than others, it makes some very important points. These are that it:

- draws attention to the important point that extrinsic and intrinsic rewards are not substitutes for each other; both need to be provided;
- directs attention to the importance of employee traits, skills and abilities, particularly those which are needed in order to be able to perform well;

- draws attention to the idea that incentives for good performance only have a practical use if they are valued by employees;
- stresses that employees need to be able to see that rewards are realistically obtainable.

EQUITY THEORY

Equity: the fairness of treatment of a person compared to the way that another person is treated

The concept of *equity* has a long pedigree in social science as a factor that affects work attitudes and behaviour (Runciman 1966). It has a pivotal role in social exchange theory, which acknowledges that, since there are no absolute criteria of fairness, people normally evaluate how fairly they are treated by making comparisons with others in similar circumstances (Blau 1964). The equity theory of motivation (Adams 1965) uses these principles and incorporates a very simple idea: that an individual's motivation to put effort into a task will be influenced by perceptions of whether the rewards obtained are fair in comparison to those received by other people. To explain the theory, the process involved is shown in Figure 8.3.

The process starts with a **comparison** stage, in which someone evaluates the inputs and outputs associated with performing a task, and these are compared with the inputs and outputs of another person's task. This is usually someone in close proximity, with

Figure 8.3 Equity theory

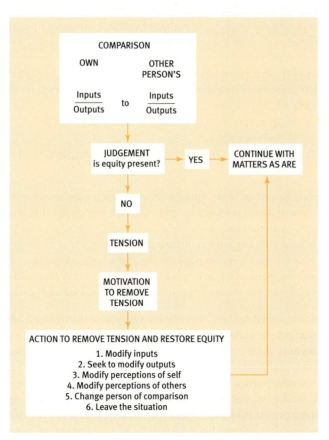

whom a direct comparison can be made because he or she does similar work. Inputs are the things that a person brings to the job, such as education, skill, experience and effort. Outputs are the rewards received for the job, such as pay, promotion, praise etc. Inputs can be viewed as costs and outputs as benefits and, to make a comparison, a person mentally constructs two subjective cost–benefit ratios: one for him or herself and one for the other person. Although these comparisons are almost bound to contain a high element of subjectivity, they are nevertheless the 'reality' of the situation to the person concerned, and this brings the next stage of the model into play.

A **judgement** is made about whether the person's own ratio is the same or near to that of the 'comparison other'. If it is, then all is probably well, but if it is not, feelings of inequity can arise and this triggers the next stage in the process.

Tensions, or feelings of psychological discomfort, arise from perceived inequity. For example, someone who perceives that he or she brings more skill and experience to a job than the other person can feel that inequity exists until pay is raised above the other person's level. The greater the degree of tension, the greater is the motivation to do something that eases it.

This results in **action** to lessen the tension, invariably by restoring equity to the situation. Here Adams lists six basic options for action:

- modifying inputs; for example, where a person feels under-rewarded effort can be reduced, and in the case of perceived over-reward it can be increased;
- seek to modify outputs, perhaps by demanding more pay if there is a feeling of being under-rewarded, although it is hard to see how a person would deal with a situation of perceived over-reward;
- modify perceptions of self; for example, the person could re-evaluate his or her inputs and outputs and come to the conclusion that equity does exist after all;
- modify perceptions of the 'comparison other', which has much the same result as the previous option;
- change the person or persons used as the 'comparison other';
- leave the situation.

Exercising one of these options (or possibly a combination of them) is said to result in restored feelings of equity and, when this occurs, tension is eased and the person accepts the situation.

Adams's theory is straightforward, and elegant in its simplicity. It has been tested empirically on a number of occasions, which shows that the theory has good predictive powers, particularly in conditions where under-reward could exist (Cosier and Dalton 1983). Thus, the theory has a number of important implications:

- when designing jobs and reward systems, it is extremely important to recognise that people make comparisons;
- because these comparisons are subjective and seldom precise, care should be taken to relate similar jobs in terms of the inputs they require and outputs they provide, particularly if they are in close proximity;
- if managers want to avoid inaccurate conclusions about equity, it is necessary to keep people informed about the basis on which rewards are made, particularly where the quality of what is produced is as important as its quantity.

TIME OUT

Carefully reflect on your own work situation, on the job you do and on those of two other people you work with who do similar jobs to yourself. If you are not in employment, either part-time or full-time, reflect on your own situation and that of fellow students you know well and with whose work you are familiar. Now answer the questions below.

1. What inputs do you bring to work (e.g. skills, knowledge, diligence, persistence, extent of private study outside the classroom, care in assignments and contribution in class)? How many of these things do the other people bring as inputs?

2. What outputs do you receive for your efforts (e.g. pay, praise, understanding, good grades etc.)? How do these compare with the outputs received by the other people?

3. Do you feel there is equity of treatment compared to these other people and, if not, do you feel under-rewarded or over-rewarded? Why?

4. If you feel there is inequity, go back and carefully check that you have not omitted an important input or output for yourself or the other people.

5. If you still feel there is inequity, do you feel inclined to take steps to restore the equity balance? What steps will you take?

GOAL-SETTING THEORY

Most people have goals or objectives of some sort and the idea that motivated behaviour is a function of a person's conscious goals and intentions is the basis of Locke's (1968) goal-setting theory. His major concern is the way that performance is affected by the process of setting goals and, for this reason, he acknowledges that his model, which is shown in Figure 8.4, is more a motivational technique than a theory of motivation.

Figure 8.4
Goal setting
(*Source*: Latham and
Locke 1979)

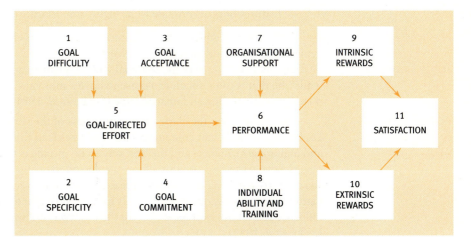

CASE STUDY 8.2: Piecework Payments

Unbeknown to themselves, two groups of workers ('A' and 'B') took part in a field experiment to test equity theory. Both groups were paid on a 'piecework' basis and both were in close proximity, performing similar, but not identical, tasks. Rates of pay for both tasks had been fixed in secret beforehand and the allowed time (time to produce 1 unit of output) for each task was 10 minutes. Initially, however, both groups were told that the allowed times had only been estimated, and that any over or underpayment would be corrected after the trial.

For phase 1 of the experiment, which lasted two weeks, group 'A' was told that the allowed time was 9 minutes for its task and group 'B' was told its allowed time was 10 minutes. Measures of quantity (output level) and quality (defect level) were taken for each group across the two weeks and at the end a short questionnaire was administered. The questionnaire tapped opinions of pay levels, allowed times and comparisons with other groups of workers.

In phase 2, which also lasted two weeks, group 'B' was withdrawn from its task, group 'A' was set an allowed time of 10 minutes, and similar measurements were taken as in phase 1.

For phase 3, group 'A' was withdrawn, group 'B' was set an allowed time of 11 minutes, and similar measurements were taken as for the earlier phases.

Questions

Using equity theory, what would your predictions be with respect to:

quantity and quality for groups 'A' and 'B' in phase 1?
quantity and quality for group 'A' in phase 2?
quantity and quality for group 'B' in phase 3?

Two basic features of goals are said to be highly important:

Goal difficulty:
how challenging
and demanding the
goal is

- *Goal difficulty* (1), which is the extent to which a goal is challenging and demanding for the individual. Up to a certain point motivated effort rises as goal difficulty increases – a very modest goal will not challenge the person enough, while one that is too difficult can cease to have a motivational effect because it is seen as frustrating and unattainable (Locke *et al.* 1981).

Goal specificity: how
clear and explicit the
goal is

- *Goal specificity* (2) is the clarity and explicitness of the performance target. In Locke's view, goals that contain specific outcomes lead to much greater effort and higher performance, and the best way to be specific is to express the goal in quantitative terms because this allows the person to evaluate how close he or she has come to achieving it. There is a great deal of support for Locke's view in this matter. For instance, quantifiable goals have been shown to have a far stronger influence than those expressed in a 'do the best you can' way (Locke 1968; Locke *et al.* 1981).

In the model, goals give rise to **goal-directed effort** (5), that is the direction and persistence of behaviour. However, this is influenced by two additional factors:

- **goal acceptance** (3), the extent to which someone accepts a goal as a legitimate and appropriate one for him or herself;
- **goal commitment** (4), which is a person's vested interest in achieving the goal.

Neither acceptance nor commitment happen by themselves, and so they should not be taken for granted. Therefore, it is important to recognise that they can be influenced by a number of other factors. To start with, the person must be able to see that achieving the goal will lead to the receipt of valued rewards (Latham and Steele 1983). There is also evidence to suggest that if a person participates in selecting the goals, he or she will have a higher commitment to achieving them (Arnold *et al.* 1991; Erez *et al.* 1985). However, commitment is one thing and achievement is another and it should be noted that the evidence on whether participating in goal setting actually leads to better performance is very mixed. To enhance future commitment, Locke also considers it important to give people accurate feedback on performance, which is said to increase a person's sense of achievement and accomplishment as well as indicating that his or her efforts have been noticed (Latham and Locke 1979).

Performance (6) is an indication of whether, and to what extent, the goal is actually achieved, and the theory recognises that this can be strongly influenced by two additional factors:

- **organisational support** (7), which is the extent to which adequate resources (staffing, budgets, physical resources etc.) are available to the person who has to achieve the goal;
- **individual ability and training** (8), which need to be commensurate with achieving the goal; for example, achieving some goals may require special or rare skills and other goals can be so novel that considerable training may be necessary to help people tackle them.

Where goals are achieved the person should then be rewarded and, like Vroom, Locke explicitly states that **intrinsic** and **extrinsic rewards** (9 and 10) are both important. He also recognises that a person's eventual level of **satisfaction** (11) will crucially depend upon whether the rewards are seen as equitable for what has been achieved.

Locke's ideas have been extensively researched and most studies strongly support the model (Locke *et al.* 1981). Moreover, the principles embodied in the theory have been widely applied in performance appraisal and schemes of management by objectives, both of which are dealt with elsewhere in this book. Like all theories, however, Locke's ideas have attracted a number of criticisms. One of these is related to Locke's own admission that the model is not really a theory of motivation, but a motivational technique. For instance, Arnold *et al.* (1991) note that its greatest deficiency is that it simply accepts that goals are motivators, but fails to explain why they should have such a pronounced effect. In addition, Austin and Bobko (1985) note three circumstances where the effects are much more uncertain than those predicted:

- The quality of a person's performance is often as important as quantity of output, but unless this can somehow be translated into a quantitative measure, the theory tends to break down.

- Organisations increasingly emphasise group effort by using techniques such as team working, which runs counter to Locke's basic theory that goals and responsibility for achieving them should be assigned to individuals.

- Rather than having one goal to achieve, an individual usually has several, which inevitably results in a degree of conflict between some goals and could mean that one goal probably has to be sacrificed to achieve the others (Yearta *et al.* 1995). As will be seen in Chapter 18, sub-optimisation of goals can sometimes result in even more significant difficulties in the matter of organisational control.

PROCESS THEORIES: AN INTEGRATION AND OVERVIEW

All process theories have certain similarities and differences, but they also differ in terms of:

- the degree of importance they attach to factors internal or external to the individual;
- the role that rewards play in the motivational process.

In spite of these differences, the theories can all be reconciled to some extent. For example, it has been suggested that goal-setting and equity approaches are both capable of being integrated into a more comprehensive version of expectancy theory (Mitchell 1982). As such there are three important points emerging from these theories:

- all process theories stress the need to establish clear links between performance and rewards;
- they all show that, if motivation is to be aroused, it is important to pay attention to work environments; for example, employees need to feel that work organisation and group sentiments are not barriers to successful performance;
- since the theories all acknowledge that successful performance can crucially depend on individual attributes, there is a clear need to match employees and jobs.

What emerges from these points is a highly significant general implication. People bring a whole range of skills and abilities to a job, and in this respect equity theory has a particularly significant point to make. Even when the job only calls for some skills to be used, individuals are still likely to build all of their skills into evaluations of equity. The moral of this is all too clear: it is important to use the full range of talents of each employee, and reward the person accordingly.

OB IN ACTION: Motivation – the importance of the psychological contract

Since January 2003, when William Morrison set out to acquire its rival, the 85,000 people who work for Safeway, the British food retailer, have lived with uncertainty. So far, however, Safeway's trading performance has not suffered and the predicted haemorrhage of staff has not materialised; staff turnover has even fallen by 8 per cent in its stores division. Safeway was fortunate in having a loyal workforce but, even so, their loyalty to a retailer that does not pay the best wages in its industry has been surprising and after Morrison launched its bid, Safeway's HR team faced the challenge of trying to maintain morale among a large workforce worried about the fate of the company. The response involved a series of measures, including training, information and incentives. Senior managers attended a leadership programme to enable them to reassure staff in the absence of long-term job security, the company evolved new ways of communicating with staff in an effort to prevent unsettling rumours and retention bonuses linked to achieving have been made available.

Valerie Garrow, principal researcher at Roffey Park Management Centre, comments that 'this is an impressive example of the benefits of managing the psychological contract during change'. While the future is still not clear and the company could not make promises, it has been able to be open in communication, listen to its employees and fulfil obligations.

Safeway already knew from internal research that many employees stayed with the company out of loyalty to colleagues, but people had lots of questions: some wanted to know the bid timetable, and others to understand the impact on their own financial situation. Jim White, HR director, and Fiona Bailey, director for culture, made a weekly 'state of the nation' report to the board on how employees are responding to developments and the state of their morale. The HR team also realised that people needed a different kind of training to enable them to gain new skills; for example, training to help managers understand the impact of the changing situation, encourage open discussion and maintain people's commitment to the business.

Ms Garrow points out that Safeway kept the relationship with employees alive and that mutual expectations were still clear, in spite of the ambiguity of the situation. This illustrates the importance of not ignoring or breaking the psychological contract because if this happens, employees can react in a variety of ways. They may cut back on what they give to the organisation, for example by keeping good ideas to themselves, or they may try to get more from the company by taking sick days, arriving late or even resorting to petty theft. If they feel the contract has been violated, they may react emotionally by walking out, bad-mouthing the organisation externally or engaging in sabotage, and negative reactions such as these can seriously damage a newly combined company.

Source:

Maitland, A (2003) A safe way to hold on to staff, *The Financial Times*, 28 November.

REPLAY

- Process theories focus on the cognitive processes at work that account for the direction, intensity and persistence of motivated behaviour.
- Expectancy theories are based on the assumption that people choose between different courses of action according to which one results in the most favourable outcome for themselves.
- Equity theory focuses on the way that people are motivated to adjust their behaviour, according to their perceptions of the fairness of their own inputs and receipts from performing a task compared to the inputs and receipts of other people performing comparable tasks.
- Goal-setting theory assumes that the goals set for a person are the source of motivation rather than the needs that prompt people to derive their own goals. As such, it is more a motivational technique than a theory of motivation.

ASSESSING MOTIVATION AND DEALING WITH MOTIVATIONAL PROBLEMS

At the start of Chapter 7 it was noted that high motivation results in a direction, intensity and persistence of behaviour. For this reason there are clear advantages for an organisation if it has employees who are highly motivated to perform their tasks. Indeed, it is fair to say that unless employees have high enough levels of motivation to see jobs through to completion without the need for direct supervision, the word 'empowerment' is nothing more than wishful thinking on the part of management. This gives rise to two important issues, which can be expressed as questions:

- how can it be determined whether (or not) motivation is at a high level, and
- where it is not, how can it be raised?

Any answers to these questions are bound to be strongly connected, but for convenience, the issues will be examined separately.

The Issue of Evaluating Motivational States

Because motivation is an inner mental state, it cannot be observed directly and any evaluation of motivation involves a judgement about a person's psychological state. There are psychological tools for doing this, one of which is the Job Diagnostic Survey questionnaire, which is used in the Hackman and Oldham (1980) job redesign method described in Chapter 7. Another method is to use well-designed attitude questionnaires (see Chapter 5). These, however, are more often used to conduct employee opinion surveys and, in the interests of obtaining frank responses to questions, respondents usually remain anonymous, which tends to rule out their use for assessment of individuals. Nevertheless, they can be useful in identifying general trends in a workforce, for example, whether people are conscious of features of the organisation such as poor hygiene factors that could stand in the way of high motivation.

An opportunity to evaluate individual motivation occurs regularly in most organisations in the form of the annual 'performance appraisal' interview but making accurate assessments of these things requires special skills, which not only involves asking appropriate questions, but asking them in an appropriate way. Thus, unless they have received special training, managers can draw highly inaccurate conclusions about subordinates.

This is not to say that these evaluations are never made. Despite the availability of psychometric tools to assess motivation, it is likely that most managers evaluate it in a very subjective way, and draw conclusions that are based on the flimsiest of evidence. Usually this will be done on the basis of some aspect of subordinate behaviour, for example, whether the person exhibits what the manager believes are the signs of job satisfaction or commitment, and the whole practice is fraught with problems. Since many managers (incorrectly) assume that motivation is something they directly bring about in subordinates, few managers would want to admit that they could have failed in this respect. Thus, there can be a high element of self-deception in any evaluation that a manager makes about the motivational state of an employee. Even where this is not the case and the manager is scrupulously honest with him or herself, there is still a strong possibility that the actions of employees can result in inaccurate evaluations. If they want to safeguard their future prospects, it is not in the interests of employees to make it obvious that their work motivations are low, and this can result in a great deal of behaviour designed to demonstrate keenness, enthusiasm and commitment.

Addressing Motivational Problems

As noted in the previous chapter, management's interest in motivation is seldom in the process itself, but in the prospects it offers for bringing employee behaviour under tighter control. Managers can hardly be blamed for believing that motivation theory offers this opportunity, because content and process theories both imply that if we know a person's needs, the person can be motivated (Hancock 1999). Thus, what interests managers most is behaviour and not motivation. Nevertheless, when dealing with performance that does not reach the level that a manager requires, there is an inbuilt tendency to assume that motivation is the culprit. In the absence of concrete evidence to the contrary, people have a tendency to make a 'fundamental attribution error' when seeking to explain the behaviour of others, by making an internal attribution (e.g. low motivation as the cause) to explain poor performance, rather than seeking an explanation in the surrounding circumstances (external attribution). If this error is to be avoided, the first place to look for a remedy to poor performance should always be in the context of a task.

In addressing a situation of low motivation the most common approach for the last four decades has been through job redesign. Since this is covered at an individual level in Chapter 7, it will not be repeated here. However, in cases where work redesign is considered there is a danger of searching for a universal solution that raises the motivation of everybody, often by an exclusive reliance on content theories. It must always be remembered that motivation is an individual matter and so it is often necessary to search for individual solutions using process theories. For example, Ganzach (1998) convincingly demonstrates that there is an interaction between intelligence and the jobs that people find satisfying. Thus, not everybody wants a complex, challenging job.

The most recent remedy for trying to influence motivation is through a programme of culture change. However, culture is a complex topic in its own right and coverage of this is deferred until Chapter 19.

BEHAVIOUR MODIFICATION: AN ALTERNATIVE TO USING MOTIVATION THEORY

So far, motivation has been discussed in a rather detached way and it has been repeatedly stressed that if it has an appeal to managers it is because it is seen as a way of increasing control over employee behaviour, so that management objectives will be achieved. Using motivation theory to achieve this end is just one way of applying behavioural science knowledge, and is a uniquely European way of looking at things. European social scientists are somewhat wary of being seen to serve managerial interests too closely, whereas their counterparts in America seldom have these inhibitions and they are far less reluctant to advocate practices that serve management aims. A case in point is behaviour modification, which is often described in American textbooks as a theory of motivation but, as will be seen, is nothing of the sort. Rather, it is an application of one of the theories of learning described in Chapter 6. Nevertheless, it has some capability to shape employee behaviour and for this reason managers can make use of it to achieve control over employee behaviour.

In essence, behaviour modification – the full title is organisational behaviour modification (OB Mod.) – is a form of Skinnerian operant conditioning described in Chapter 6 and the technique is applied to humans in work situations with the aim of shaping and fixing behaviour into a pattern that is desired by a manager. In technical terms, it has been defined as:

the systematic reinforcement of desirable organisational behaviour and non-reinforcement of unwanted organisational behaviour.

(Luthans and Kreitner 1985, p 303)

In this definition lies the crucial difference to motivation theories. Whereas motivation is concerned with internal factors that influence behaviour, reinforcement principles are concerned solely with external matters. Conditioning theory assumes that the primary determinant of an organism's behaviour is the consequence (for the organism) of behaving in a certain way. Therefore OB Mod. is only concerned with shaping, and any psychological causes of behaviour have little significance.

In theory, although not necessarily in practice, the principles applied are very simple. The fundamental idea is that behaviour can be learned, shaped and maintained by the judicious use of rewards and punishments. Before describing how the techniques are used, you may wish to briefly refresh your memory of the principles of operant conditioning given in Chapter 6.

When the principles of operant conditioning are incorporated into a well-designed, systematically applied plan in a work organisation, the process is known as OB Mod. (Luthans and Kreitner 1975). Figure 8.5 gives a simplified model of the steps involved and a description of the method follows.

To illustrate the method, assume that a bank wishes to engender loyalty in customers by getting them to feel that the bank really cares about them and considers them important. Customer opinions have been researched and this has revealed that the two features

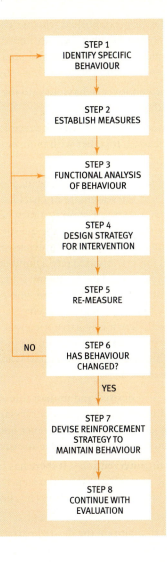

Figure 8.5 Simplified model of behaviour modification process

most associated with a caring attitude by the bank are the friendliness and helpfulness of counter staff.

Step 1: identify the employee behaviours that need to be changed   Here, assume that the research has identified that customers are conscious of three behaviours on the part of counter staff associated with friendliness and helpfulness. These behaviours are for counter staff to: greet customers in a cheerful way; serve them and answer queries promptly; wish customers a cheerful goodbye as they leave.

Step 2: take baseline performance measures for the three behaviours indentified
These are the three behaviours identified in step 1 and the aim is to establish the current frequency of these behaviours for each member of counter staff, together with the current frequency of undesirable behaviour. This is a vital step and, as will be seen presently, the information is used later to evaluate whether the behaviour-shaping intervention has been a success.

Step 3: functional analysis   Here it is established whether employees know how management wants them to behave, whether there are impediments to them behaving in this way and what outcomes (such as rewards and punishments) can be used to reinforce the desired behaviours and eliminate those that are undesirable.

Step 4: devise methods to shape employee behaviour into the desired patterns
To do this, two matters need to be addressed:

- to choose the range of rewards that are available to reinforce desired behaviours;
- to select those that will be used, together with punishments that will be applied for undesirable behaviours.

To establish a basis for applying rewards and punishments, the bank might get counter staff to give customers a very short questionnaire or checklist that evaluates friendliness and helpfulness. This has a code number on it somewhere, which identifies the member of staff who dealt with the customer, and the questionnaire is deposited in a box as the customer leaves. Thus a weekly or monthly customer evaluation of each member of staff is obtained and this is translated into a number of points for each individual staff member. Points can be accrued over time and traded for the reward, a cash bonus or perhaps additional holiday days, while those who get adverse ratings from customers are admonished. In addition, schedules of reinforcement can be selected to reward or punish staff behaviour. Here it is worth noting that it is much harder to use punishment as a conditioning stimulus than to use positive reinforcement. Indeed, since punishment often has undesirable side-effects (Arvey and Ivancevich 1980), wherever possible positive reinforcement is used.

Step 5: re-measure the frequency of desired and undesirable employee behaviours
Strictly speaking, in this example this would be unnecessary because behaviour is measured continuously by using data from customer questionnaires. However, this is not always possible, and sometimes a distinct re-measurement stage is required.

Step 6: evaluate the success of the intervention   If there has been little or no improvement, it may then be necessary to return to step 1, and possibly step 3, to redesign the intervention strategy. Where success has been obtained, matters proceed to steps 7 and 8.

Step 7: devise ongoing strategy to maintain the desired patterns of behaviour
This would be done by selecting methods of reinforcement that would be used in the long term, and since no system of rewards has an indefinite shelf life, this leads to step 8.

Step 8: ongoing re-evaluation

What then is the potential usefulness of OB Mod.? As noted above, it is not a motivation theory, or even an application of one. In Great Britain it tends to be considered a highly controversial technique, not least because it has unpleasant connotations of Orwell's 'Big Brother' watching everybody. Advocates of motivation theory are likely to condemn these methods strongly and argue that people are far too complex to be treated like white rats in a laboratory experiment. Indeed, to many psychologists operant conditioning does not even qualify as psychology, but should rightfully be classified as a mere technique. Behaviourists, of course, argue otherwise. Nevertheless, the research evidence suggests that OB Mod. can be effective in shaping behaviour, at least in the short term (Stajkovic and Luthans 1997).

As usual, however, there are criticisms, and these cannot be ignored. Locke (1977), for example, considers that the effects are likely to be too short-lived to be useful. The effects quickly wear off and, even if steps are taken to maintain the behaviours, in the long run these can quickly come to be regarded by employees as a routine part of the organisation's rewards package. Other criticisms focus on the idea that OB Mod. takes no account of individual differences in personality. What is a reinforcer for one person is not for another and this makes it hard to identify rewards that are likely to have the same effect on all employees. Yet another criticism is that OB Mod. takes no account of whether group norms and peer pressures run counter to the behaviours that managers want to obtain.

Perhaps the most significant criticisms of all centre on the ethical considerations alluded to above. Most British psychologists would be reluctant to use techniques that give managers even more power over employees. To do so is to subscribe to the idea that managers are infallible and have an unquestioned right to exercise control over everything. Since psychology likes to consider itself an ethical discipline, it is possible that these feelings are more connected to psychologists' self-images than anything else. Their objection is not so much to OB Mod. itself but to the uses to which it can be put, for example to induce a slavish following of management instructions. Paradoxically, few people (and this includes psychologists) would find anything reprehensible about conditioning employees to avoid accidents by working more safely. This, after all, is doing good and can easily be reconciled with our self-images. Indeed, almost everybody is conditioned to some extent during their upbringing and most managers probably use crude conditioning techniques on a day-to-day basis without realising it. For the present, however, OB Mod. is, and will probably continue to be, a relatively unused technique in Great Britain.

REPLAY

- OB Mod. is not, as it is sometimes portrayed, a theory of motivation that explains the process which results in motivated behaviour.
- It is an application of operant conditioning techniques in a workplace setting that aims to induce workers to behave as managers want them to behave.
- As such, OB Mod. is an alternative to using motivation theory.

OVERVIEW AND CONCLUSIONS

Since there are strong connections between this chapter and the one that precedes it, this section will review the contents of both. The major approaches covered in the two chapters focus on different aspects of motivation, and it might appear that there is an element of contradiction in what they say. However, they are complementary rather than opposed. Content theories deal with the needs that give rise to motivated behaviour, but perhaps oversimplify matters because they tend to portray human beings as having a homogeneous set of needs. Nevertheless, as long as due allowance is made for individual differences, this does not detract from their potential usefulness. Process theories have a different emphasis: they seek to explain the dynamics of the motivation process and so much greater account is taken of individual differences. Problematically, this results in theories that are more complex, which means that they are more difficult to apply in practice. Although behaviour modification is not a motivation theory, it is potentially useful to explain how motivation can be sustained once a person has become motivated. Thus, while none of the theories should be regarded as the whole story, when taken together they all have something useful to offer. Therefore, it is fitting to conclude by highlighting a number of important conclusions that can be drawn from the motivation theories covered in this and the previous chapter:

- When an employee becomes motivated, this is the outcome of a psychological process.

- It is not possible directly to observe this process at work, nor can managers apply or supply motivation directly to employees.

- Nevertheless, it is still possible to influence an employee's level of motivation to some extent, by creating conditions that the individual finds stimulating and encouraging.

- It is unlikely that stimulation and encouragement can be provided for all employees in an identical way and so there is a need to be sensitive to variations in individual needs, goals, preferences and abilities (Lucas 2002).

- Conditions can change, both inside and outside an organisation, which means that the needs of individuals can change and so can the organisation's capability to meet them. For this reason the provision of a stimulating and encouraging work environment should never be taken for granted, nor should it be regarded as a once-and-for-all exercise, but rather as a matter which should be kept under constant review.

- It is important to recognise that work is not the only vehicle that individuals can use to satisfy their needs and wants.

- Nevertheless, if work has the capability to result in outcomes that are highly valued by employees, the first and perhaps most important step in the motivational process has been taken.

- The people most likely to be able to ensure that this step is taken are the managers of an organisation, and this can be done in two ways: by seeking to discover what conditions are required by individuals in order to satisfy their needs, and by providing a work experience that gives sufficient diversity, opportunity and challenge to satisfy the needs.

FURTHER READING

Locke, E A and G P Latham (1990) *A Theory of Goal Setting and Task Performance,* New York: Prentice Hall. A comprehensive account of the authors' views which, by their own admission, result in more of a technique for applying motivation theory rather than a new theory in itself.

Petri, H L (1996) *Motivation: Theory, Research and Application*, London: Thompson. A specialist, but nevertheless readable, text that gives a comprehensive coverage of all the major approaches to motivation theory.

Porter, L W and E E Lawler (1968) *Managerial Attitudes and Performance*, Homewood Ill: Irwin. A very clear explanation of the authors' expectancy theory that is widely cited in academic circles.

Sarafino, E P (1997) *Principles of Behaviour Change*, Chichester: Wiley. Again a specialist book, but one that gives an up-to-date coverage of behaviour modification techniques and practices.

Spector, P (1995) *Industrial and Organisational Psychology: Research and Practice*, Chichester: Wiley. A wide-ranging text that has good coverage of motivation, and discusses it within in a wider psychological context.

Steers, R and Porter L (1991) *Motivation and Work Behaviour*, New York: McGraw-Hill. The book gives a very detailed but highly managerialist view on the application of motivation theory from an American perspective.

Weiner, B (1992) *Human Motivation: Metaphors, Theories and Research*, London: Sage. A comprehensive book that gives an interesting integration of the different theoretical perspectives on motivation.

REVIEW AND DISCUSSION QUESTIONS

1. Define the terms 'valence', 'expectancy' and 'first-level outcomes' as used in Vroom's (VIE) expectancy model. Explain how these are connected to demonstrate a person's motive force.

2. Describe any important additional features that the Porter and Lawler model has beyond those contained in Vroom's version of expectancy theory. Explain whether, in your view, these additional features result in a more plausible explanation of the process of motivation, that is, of practical utility to people in organisations.

3. In equity theory, what is assumed to be the factor which most influences a person's motivation to expend effort on a task? Explain in outline the basic sequence of mental processes that are said to influence motivation.

4. To what extent are goal setting and organisational behaviour modification (OB Mod.) theories of motivation?

5. What do you feel are the advantages and shortcomings of OB Mod.? Explain the extent to which you feel that it is a technique that can be practically applied by managers.

| Chapter 9 | # Individual Decision Making |

LEARNING OUTCOMES

After studying this chapter you should be able to:

- define decision making and distinguish between decision making and problem solving

- distinguish between bounded and unbounded problems and trace the implications of each type for the nature of the decision making process

- compare and contrast the three decision making models described in the chapter: rational choice, bounded rationality and the garbage can model

- describe the phenomenon of escalation of commitment to a failing course of action and the factors that explain its existence

- describe the three main groups of factors that influence the way in which decisions are made by individuals in organisations

INTRODUCTION

The decision making process has long been of interest to Organisational Behaviour and Organisational Analysis and it is usually studied at one of three levels. First, strategic decision making, which affects the whole organisation, is concerned with decisions that establish an appropriate relationship between the organisation and its environment. Since this is the major concern of the subject of business policy, it is beyond the scope of this book.

Second, decision making by groups, which usually focuses on the internal dynamics of the decision process and how this has an influence on the way that decisions are made. To understand this it is first necessary to understand something of how groups function, which is covered in Chapter 11 and so the topic will be deferred until then. Finally, there is decision making by individuals, which is the focus of this chapter, where the aim is to understand how individuals handle information in order to select alternative courses of action.

To address this topic the chapter commences with a definition of decision making and how it relates to the broader process of problem solving. To set the scene for the remainder of the chapter, two types of problem that can be encountered by people in organisations are contrasted – bounded problems and unbounded problems – each of which normally requires its own approach to decision making. The remainder of the chapter explores a number of models of decision making and the first to be considered is the 'rational choice' model, which is a theoretical prescription for how decisions *should* be made. Since this model is based on a number of underlying assumptions that mean that its use in a pure form is comparatively rare, the next model to be considered is the theory of 'bounded rationality', which gives a more realistic description of how decisions are made in practice. The last model to be covered is the theory of 'garbage can' decision making, which presents a picture of how decisions are made in more ambiguous circumstances.

The next section of the chapter considers the matter of post-decision behaviour. This is explored by considering the phenomenon of 'commitment to a failing course of action', in which a decision maker persists in implementing a decision in the face of evidence that the decision is inappropriate. This is followed by a section that pulls together the material covered in the chapter into a model of the three main groups of factors that can shape the behaviour of decision makers, and the chapter closes with an overview section that reviews its contents.

DECISION MAKING IN PERSPECTIVE

Decision making: the process of making a choice between alternatives

Problem solving: the process of producing a solution to a recognised problem

Decision making is widely defined as 'choosing between alternatives', which reflects the idea that if there is only one alternative to choose from, there is no decision to take. However, the term is sometimes used synonymously with the expression *problem solving*, and some authors (e.g. Lang *et al.* 1978) refer to problem solving as part of the decision making process. In practice, problem solving can never be completely isolated from making a decision; at a conceptual level, the two things are different. This can be seen in Simon's (1960) conceptualisation of the decision making processes as something consisting of the three main activities (Figure 9.1).

Figure 9.1 The three basic activities involved in decision making (after Simon 1960)

INTELLIGENCE ACTIVITY	DESIGN ACTIVITY	CHOICE ACTIVITY
Searching the environment for conditions that call for decision making	Inventing, developing and analysing possible courses of action	Selecting a course of action from among the alternatives

OB IN ACTION: The Politics of Decision Making

In the near future GKN will decide whether to base a key research and development centre in the fast-growing aerospace materials field in the UK or in the US. The UK engineering group's decision comes at a sensitive time for the British government following recent criticism from other manufacturers for failing to invest in the country's high-technology skills base. Moreover, Rolls-Royce, the aero-engine maker, hinted recently that it could consider moving more R&D work abroad unless the government overhauls its science spending, to put industrial applications before pure research. In addition, Ford has warned the government that the UK will fall behind competitors in manufacturing if it does not focus on training more engineers.

The GKN decision comes against the backdrop of two government reviews of its innovation policy. Lord Sainsbury, Science Minister, is looking at ways of halting the exodus of manufacturing abroad by focusing on high-tech industries such as aerospace. The Treasury is also expected to publish the Lambert Report in the near future, which will call on industry to play a greater role in forging links with universities. Kevin Smith, GKN's Chief Executive, said in an interview with the *FT* that 'it felt right' for GKN to have the new centre in Britain, because this is where most of the company's expertise in aerospace materials has been developed. 'But we have a duty to shareholders to examine other alternatives and to make a financial case for either option,' he said, adding that he had 'some sympathy, with Rolls-Royce's view.' GKN is considering building the centre in the US at its composite manufacturing site in Tallahassee, Alabama, and if it chooses Britain, it will almost certainly build the centre on the Isle of Wight, where the company has existing aerospace activities.

GKN is a world leader in carbon fibre-based materials. Their low weight and strength means composites are playing an increasingly important role in aircraft manufacturing. The company is planning to invest about £10m ($16.8m) in the centre, which will employ some 20 scientists and, although the numbers are relatively small, ministers will be monitoring GKN's decision making process anxiously.

Source:

Odell, M and P Marsh (2003) GKN sizes up locations for R&D centre, *The Financial Times*, 27 November.

Strictly speaking, only the final activity in Figure 9.1 involves making a decision, but the first two are necessary prerequisites for the third and can rightly be considered part of the process. However, taking the third step does not necessarily mean that a problem has been solved. The decision might only be one of a series that all contribute to solving the problem, and even where only a single decision is involved, the chosen alternative might be incorrect and another needs to be tried. As such, problem solving embraces other activities, for example implementing the decision and monitoring its appropriateness. Since these take place after a decision has been made, the essence of a decision is that a number of alternatives are considered before one is chosen. Note, however, that evaluation of alternatives on its own is not decision making, which only happens when a choice is made. For these reasons, decision making is taken to be an activity that focuses on the central issue of choosing between alternative courses of action, and problem solving is a much broader process, of which decision making is a part (Cook and Slack 1991).

TYPES OF DECISION

Not all decisions are the same. Some are relatively simple and others involve a more complex range of considerations. Even though they can be extremely complex, engineering problems often involve only hard, tangible considerations, whereas if human factors are concerned, decisions may involve softer, intangible aspects of organisational life. Some writers, for example Cook and Slack (1991), suggest that it is possible to distinguish between decisions in terms of 'good' and 'bad'. This, however, is misleading, if only because what is perceived to be good by one person can just as easily be perceived by someone else as bad. For this reason, decisions will be distinguished in terms of their 'effectiveness', which ultimately comes down to whether a decision is focused on the matter about which a decision is required. Decisions are usually made in the hope that they will solve problems, and to decide whether a decision is effective in this sense it is necessary to consider the nature of the problem on which it is focused.

As with many things, problem types cannot be distinguished on the basis of a single criterion and so a multidimensional perspective is required. These dimensions can be brought together to distinguish between what will be referred to here as *bounded* and *unbounded problems*, the major characteristics of which are shown in Table 9.1.

To illustrate a bounded problem, imagine the case of an organisation considering the purchase of a new machine. Because this is a one-off issue of whether to replace a single machine, its implications are small and although the existing machine probably requires an increased level of maintenance, it is not completely defunct. Thus the decision could be put off and, in terms of time scale, it is a short-term problem that is not really serious. The relative costs and benefits of replacement can easily be determined and, since these give a clear set of priorities to guide decision making, it is clear what information needs to be obtained to make the decision. Finally, the problem can be treated as discrete from any others in the firm, and it has few associated human problems.

Compare this with the highly unbounded problem of a firm that has some worries about its ageing product line. The scale of the problem is much larger, it has potentially serious implications for the whole organisation, and these stretch well into the

Bounded problems: problems that can be more easily defined and treated as separate from the context in which they exist

Unbounded problems: ambiguous problems that are harder to define and which cannot easily be separated from the context in which they exist

Table 9.1 Bounded and unbounded problems

Characteristics	Bounded problems	Unbounded problems
Scale of problem	Usually small, or can be broken down into a series of smaller discrete problems	Large and if there are multiple problems, they usually need to be solved simultaneously
Implications of problem	Usually less serious	Serious implications
Time scale	Usually exists over a limited time scale	Longer and uncertain time scales
Clarity of problem	It is usually clear what the problem is	Uncertainty about what the problem is; there are often several candidates
Potential solution	Even though the actual solution to a problem has not yet been identified, it is known what a solution would be	There is, as yet, no known solution to the problem
Priorities	Clear priorities exist to determine a satisfactory solution	Priorities are uncertain
Knowledge	A solution to the problem is known, which means that relevant information can be collected	It is not certain what information needs to be obtained to solve the problem
Discreteness	The problem can be divorced from the context in which it exists and solved separately	The problem is part and parcel of the context in which it exists
People	Usually few people are involved	Often many people are involved

future. However, although the firm has apprehensions about the age of its products, there is little clarity about whether a problem actually exists, or what its nature might be. Neither is there a clear solution, merely a realisation that at some time in the future a replacement range of products will be needed, but not, however, what the products will need to be. As such, priorities are very unclear. For instance, the cost, sales and production implications are not known and, at this stage, the firm does not know what its information requirements are in order to solve the problem. Neither can it treat the problem as discrete from a host of other problems. For example, what are its competitors doing about the future and are customer tastes changing? Perhaps most worrying of all, as well as the people in the firm who may be affected, external stakeholders are likely to be concerned, for example shareholders, customers and banks.

The nature of each of these problems is quite different. It is not just the size of the issue that is significant. What makes life difficult with an unbounded problem is the degree of inherent risk, uncertainty and ambiguity. For this reason, each type of problem needs to be handled in a different way. If, for example, a bounded problem is treated as one that is unbounded, a great deal of time and effort could be wasted in searching for solutions. Even worse, if the complexities of an unbounded problem are not recognised and it is treated as one that is bounded, the range of possible solutions developed could be inadequate.

TIME OUT

Carefully consider what you feel your ideal job would be. Try to list your preferences for particular types of work, your goals in terms of salary, location and so on, and what you estimate to be your chances of obtaining the sort of job that you want.

Now look at the characteristics of bounded and unbounded problems given in Table 9.1. Is the matter of making a decision about your future career at this point in time a bounded problem or one that is unbounded?

REPLAY

- Decision making, which can be defined as 'choosing between alternatives', is part of the wider process of problem solving.
- The complexity of a problem that requires a decision can be expressed by the extent to which it is either bounded or unbounded.
- Decisions associated with unbounded problems tend to require a different approach from those that are bounded.

MODELS OF DECISION MAKING

Decision making models fall into two broad categories: normative (prescriptive) models and descriptive models. Normative models express how decisions 'should' be made, whereas descriptive models set out to explain how decisions are made in practice. Most normative models have a heavy emphasis on rationality, and in decision making this hinges on knowing the link between doing something (cause) and what happens when we do something (effect). In many organisational situations this link is tenuous, to say the least, and we will return to this point later. For the present, however, it is more important to set out the first model – the model of rational choice.

Rational Choice: decision making as it is supposed to be

Rational choice: the assumption that decisions are taken with full knowledge of all the relevant facts and that the option chosen maximises expected utility

The *rational choice* approach to decision making is firmly in the normative category. It gives a prescriptive set of steps that describe what decision makers should do if they behave in a rational, detached way. Its origins lie in the economic theory of expected utility (Von Neuman and Morgenstern 1947), which is underpinned by the idea that a rational economic decision maker will always seek the optimal solution to a problem. Here 'optimal' is defined as the solution with the greatest economic utility. The model has a number of assumptions. That:

- the decision maker recognises and has knowledge of all the possible alternative solutions to a problem;
- he or she has complete knowledge of the consequences of each of these alternatives;

CASE STUDY 9.1: Compco

Compco was founded in the mid-1970s by two computer programmers, Rick Arthur and Graham Black. For the first three years of its life it operated as a two-man consultancy, specialising in the provision of programming solutions for mainframe computers. However, with the advent of personal computers (PCs) in the early 1980s, it branched out into the small-scale design and manufacture of PCs, by which time it had approximately fifteen employees. The firm's location was in Cornwall and by the mid-1980s it was faced with two significant decisions. It was fast becoming clear that in the next decade the market for PCs could explode and this would be a huge opportunity to develop application programs for PCs that could be sold through retail outlets. The first decision, therefore, was whether to focus its efforts on the development of software (application programs) or to try to become a major manufacturer of PCs. The second decision concerned the location of the company. Although its partners were happy in Cornwall, the location was too far off the beaten track. As such, whatever the result of the first decision, the firm needed to relocate to somewhere nearer the centre of the UK, where the infrastructure was better developed. The problem was, where?

Questions

1. Other than the fact that they concern different facets of the firm's development, is there anything different about the nature of these decisions?

2. Would it be possible to use the same general approach to making these decisions, or are they so different in nature that each one requires a different approach, and if so what approach would be most appropriate to each decision?

- the decision maker has a well-developed and perfectly organised set of preferences for outcomes, so that the alternatives can be evaluated;
- he or she will have unlimited resources, including skills and abilities, in order to process data to compare the utilities of these outcomes and to determine the one that is optimal.

The model gives a logical set of steps that should be followed in order to arrive at the optimal decision. These are shown in Figure 9.2.

Step 'A': Problem identification and definition   Normally a problem is acknowledged when there is a shortfall between a planned or desired state of affairs and what happens in practice. After this the model splits into two parallel sets of activities, which can occur simultaneously, or as a set of four steps in sequence.

Step 'C1': Goal formulation   In this step the clear goals are established, achievement of which will result in removal of the problem. This usually consists of identifying why there is a gap between targets or goals and the actual state of affairs.

Figure 9.2
The rational choice
model

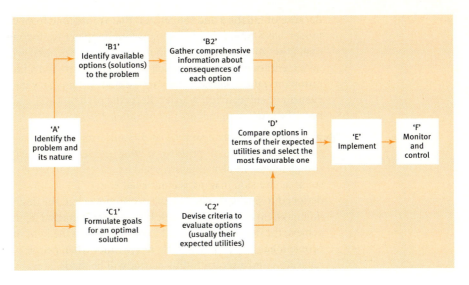

Step 'C2': Devise criteria to evaluate alternatives   Since the aim is to maximise
   expected economic utility, the most common criterion used is contribution to
   profit, which means that the costs and expected benefits of each alternative
   need to be known. Although this sounds simple, gathering the information
   can be quite complex. To start with, costs occur in the present, whereas benefits
   might be spread over several years, which adds an element of uncertainty to the
   decision. Thus criteria such as associated risk and the timing of the payback
   come into play. Almost inevitably, information of this type consists of estimates
   and for this reason, while the method is called 'rational choice', an element of
   subjectivity tends to be injected into the process, the results of which can be
   seen in the description of the next step.

Step 'B1': Identifying or generating solutions   This step is the essence of the
   rational choice model. It consists of developing a range of feasible alternative
   solutions to the problem and usually there are several alternative ways of
   achieving the desired goal. While it can be relatively easy (but time-consuming)
   to do this for a bounded problem, it is clearly a much more difficult step for
   one that is unbounded, because there is often a lack of clarity about what the
   problem is.

Step 'B2': Information gathering   Here the decision maker gathers precise,
   detailed information about the outcomes of each alternative solution, for
   example investment costs, expected returns and so on.

Step D: Compare options and select one   In a truly rational decision, if all of the
   options are compared, the one that ranks highest in terms of expected utility
   should be chosen. Suppose, for example, that three alternatives 1, 2 and 3
   have been identified, the costs and benefits of which are as follows:

	Costs	Benefits (profits per annum)
1	£15,000	£5,000 for 5 years
2	£20,000	£6,000 for 6 years
3	£30,000	£8,000 for 8 years

Because of inflation and the interest that is foregone from risk-free investments, money has a time value and so it is commonplace to discount the value of future cash flows to their equivalent in net present values, after which a decision is taken. Although techniques such as this appear to add a greater degree of rationality, the assigned values are estimates. Thus they inevitably contain an element of subjectivity, which reflects the preferences for safety or risk on the part of the decision makers (Weber *et al.* 1992).

Steps 'E' and 'F': Implementation and monitoring   Strictly speaking, these are part of the broader issue of problem solving and so they are only described here for completeness. Implementation speaks for itself, and the more significant issue so far as decision making is concerned is step 'F', monitoring, which should be designed to evaluate whether the decision has had the desired effect and has no unanticipated consequences. If necessary, remedial action is then taken to achieve the desired outcomes. However, even in the light of evidence that a problem has not been solved there are times when people simply press on regardless and a return to this matter will be made later.

Criticisms of the Rational Choice Model

There are three main streams of criticism of the idea of rational choice, all of which are concerned with its underlying assumptions. These are:

- in terms of uncertainty, while the model assumes that decision makers have complete information about the consequences of alternatives, this is rarely the case, and the use of hunches and intuition is probably far more prevalent than people would care to admit (Fagley and Miller 1987);

- the model assumes that decision makers have fixed and consistent preferences, whereas they are probably far more pragmatic; their preferences are seldom set in tablets of stone, but in many cases evolve gradually in the light of experience (Singh 1986);

- there is an assumption that decision makers have unlimited resources at their disposal and an unlimited capacity to process information, which can be far too optimistic a picture in many organisations (Simon 1978).

The second and third points are probably the most damning. In terms of preferences, there are times when people are not completely sure of what they want until they know what is available and, in the meantime, until fixed preferences can be expressed, the only options considered are those which are currently politically and socially accept-able. In terms of information processing capacities and resources, decisions sometimes have to be taken quickly, and so the long, drawn-out process of the rational choice model would be unworkable or inappropriate (Perlow *et al.* 2002). Indeed, the one resource that is frequently not available to a decision maker is time. Thus March (1982) suggests that being a rational decision maker can come down to taking short-cuts, and aiming for a decision that is 'good enough' rather than optimal, because this optimises the use of time, which is sometimes the most precious resource of all. For these reasons, the conditions in which rational choice methods can be used are probably the excep-tion rather than the rule.

In addition there is a more recent stream of criticism that points out that even when the right conditions exist, the use of rational choice methods can be extremely unlikely for cultural reasons. This is a matter that will be explored in more detail in Chapter 22, which deals with cross-cultural factors and here it is sufficient to note that there are strong arguments that every step in the rational choice model can be handled in a different way according to the cultural context in which decisions are made (Adler 1997).

In summary, although the rational choice model is often portrayed as the most appropriate way to make decisions, few people would seriously argue that it represents an accurate picture of what always occurs in practice. Simon (1978), who was awarded a Nobel Prize for his research on decision making, notes that the assumptions underpinning the idea of perfect rationality are far from being an account of the processes that people use in everyday situations. As an alternative, he proposes a descriptive model, which identifies processes actually used by decision makers, and this is considered next.

Bounded Rationality

The rational choice model tends to portray decision making in stark terms. Either the decision maker behaves rationally by adopting an optimising approach, or accepts a sub-optimal solution, in which case the person is deemed to have behaved irrationally. However, as Simon (1957) pointed out, there are several types of rationality:

- objective rationality, which in decision making means that the person seeks to maximise given values in a given situation;
- *post hoc* rationality in which a decision is made quickly, and is legitimised after the event by developing an argument that it was rational in the prevailing circumstances;
- subjective rationality, where an attempt is made to maximise the outcomes within the constraints of limited information.

The rational choice model only deals with the first of these and *post hoc* rationality will be dealt with later in the chapter, when considering what can happen after a decision is made and it fails. Therefore, it is important to examine the matter of subjective rationality, which is dealt with in Simon's (1957) model of *bounded rationality*.

Bounded rationality: the recognition that a person's ability to take a position of perfect rationality in decision making is constrained by limited time, limited information, or a limited capacity to process information

The basic premise underpinning Simon's ideas is that, in most circumstances, decision makers are subject to a huge variety of constraints that limit their capabilities to make decisions in the way envisaged by the rational choice model. For example, they have a limited capacity to process information (Jones 1995) and are often confronted with unbounded problems that are inherently so complex and full of uncertainty that they have only the vaguest idea of what information needs to be collected. In addition, there is often a shortage of information, a lack of knowledge concerning how critical the decision is and, above all, pressing time constraints. In these circumstances, which are often triggered by signs of a shortfall in some aspect of organisational performance, decision makers have a strong imperative to simply 'do something'. This is often because they have a much wider range of matters to which they must attend, which precludes an exhaustive consideration of all the possible alternative actions, in order to make the best use of time. As such, they tend to reduce the information processing demands involved in the rational choice model and find a solution that largely relies on past

Figure 9.3 The bounded rationality model of decision making

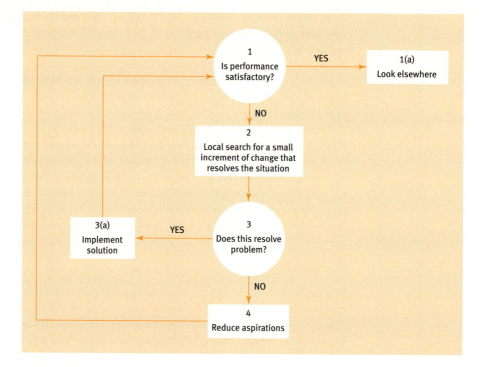

experience. Any search for remedies tends to be very limited and local, and this makes use of decision heuristics, which will be considered presently. All this, however, introduces potential biases into decisions, the net result of which is that decision makers are not really able to *optimise*, and instead they have to *satisfice*. They do not seek a perfect or best solution, but one that is satisfactory or 'good enough' in the circumstances (Bowen and Qui 1992). To put matters another way, decision makers tend to accept a solution that makes the problem 'go away'. Thus, in searching for solutions, they will usually accept the first alternative that is good enough, without any comparison of alternatives. These ideas are reflected in the model shown in Figure 9.3.

In step 1, there is a recognition that decision makers are usually too busy to go looking for problems to solve and that, unless one appears, their attention falls on a host of other matters to which they must attend (step 1a). If however, a significant problem comes to light, a local search for a solution is made, which involves the use of heuristics (step 2). If a solution is located that makes the problem go away (step 3), it is implemented (step 3a) and this prompts a return to step 1, where monitoring to verify that the problem no longer exists is undertaken. Should the solution fail to resolve the problem, the decision maker then has two alternatives: to keep repeating the cycle until a satisfactory solution is found, or to reduce his or her aspirations, for example, by choosing a solution that is good enough and which produces results that the person can 'live with'.

In this model the first and last steps illustrate an interesting facet of organisational life: the 'if it ain't broke, don't fix it' point of view. In most organisations where things

Slack: unexploited opportunities or undiscovered economies such as surplus resources

function without apparent problems, there is virtually no search for alternative or better ways of doing things. This means that *slack* (unexploited opportunities, undiscovered economies and underutilised resources) tends to accumulate. It is only when performance falls below the standards set by goals that there is an imperative for a search for alternatives. When one is found, it results in slack being taken up.

However, step 4 draws attention to the idea that when a decision maker conducts a search for an alternative, he or she sometimes becomes aware that there are limits to what can be achieved and, if reserves of slack have been used up, it is more than likely that the person will reduce the goals to match what is actually achieved. For instance, the easiest and quickest way to reduce the defect level is to lower the standards of inspection.

Simon's bounded rationality model is generally accepted as far more realistic than the rather abstract concept of rational choice, but it is important to recognise that the difference between the two models is one of degree. While they are both theories that make use of the concept of rationality, the rational choice model assumes that objective rationality is possible, whereas Simon recognises that rationality is usually subject to severe constraints. Thus the main difference between the two models is in terms of how much attention is allocated to a particular problem.

The Use of Heuristics

Heuristics: rules-of-thumb or simplifying strategies that help a decision maker cope with information overload in the search for solutions

Heuristics are rules-of-thumb, or simplifying strategies, that help a decision maker to cope with information overload in the search for solutions (Tversky and Kahneman 1974). Essentially, heuristics tell people where to look for a solution or something about the potential utility of a solution, and they are usually derived from three sources:

- a (mental) summary of past experience, which provides an easy way of evaluating the current situation;
- subjective rules that guide information collection and interpretation;
- using techniques that reduce mental activity and effort in processing information.

The use of heuristics is likely to reduce the range of solutions that are examined, which in turn means that systematic bias can be introduced into decisions. Some evidence on this matter is given by Bazerman (1994), who takes bounded rationality one step further by identifying the heuristics that are used in search procedures and how these produce biases that influence judgement. Three major heuristics are identified by Bazerman and these are described below.

The availability heuristic

Availability heuristic: a rule-of-thumb used by a decision maker to assess the probability of the outcome of a decision

The *availability heuristic* is used by a decision maker to assess the probability of the outcome of a decision, which is done by recollecting the outcomes of a similar decision in the past. The problem here is that for most people the past events that are most accessible in the memory are usually those that are vivid and easily recalled because they evoke an emotional reaction. For example, if a decision maker has used a particular solution to a problem in the past and it backfired, causing some embarrassment, the person would probably avoid taking a similar step in the present, even though it could be appropriate.

Representativeness heuristic: a rule-of-thumb used by a decision maker to judge the likelihood of the outcome of a current decision option by using a stereotyped similarity to something in the past

Anchoring or judgement heuristic: a decision maker arrives at a final judgement by starting at an initial position and then making adjustments to reach the solution that is eventually chosen

The representativeness heuristic

The *representativeness heuristic* is used by a decision maker to judge the likelihood of the outcome of a current option by using a stereotyped similarity to something in the past. In the case of decision making, for example, it might well be assumed that the successful solution to every decline in sales is to increase advertising.

The anchoring or judgement heuristic

With the *anchoring or judgement heuristic* the decision maker makes a judgement by starting at an initial position which is then adjusted to reach the solution that is eventually chosen. Usually the initial position is chosen on the basis of historical precedent, or by the way the problem is presented. If, for example, the decision maker has used a similar option in the past, which resulted in unanticipated consequences, he/she would probably avoid the same option again. However, if the problem is an urgent one and something needs to be done quickly, he or she might reason that given certain precautions the same thing will not happen again.

Although Bazerman's explanations are complex, his work tells us a great deal about how decision makers conduct localised searches for solutions under conditions of bounded rationality. Moreover, there is an emerging body of research evidence to show that the heuristics he identifies are widely used (Allinson *et al.* 1992).

The Garbage Can Model

This model (Cohen *et al.* 1972) was also derived because the rational choice model is unable to explain how many decisions are made in practice. However, unlike the models presented so far, it avoids the assumption that decision making follows an orderly sequence of steps and instead argues that some decisions are taken in a haphazard, random fashion.

Essentially, Cohen *et al.* argue that the decision making context in many organisations is so complex that it becomes impossible to specify the steps used in a decision process. Rather, problems, their solutions, the opportunity to take decisions and decision makers coexist in a turbulent state of flux. This being the case, there is no neat, orderly set of decision steps, but a disordered collection of circumstances, that is:

- problems looking for a solution;
- solutions looking for issues to arise to which they can become the solution;
- decision makers looking for decisions to make;
- opportunities for making a decision that are looking for a problem about which to make a decision.

At first all this might seem contradictory, but matters can be more easily explained with the aid of the so-called garbage can model shown in Figure 9.4.

Event Streams

Figure 9.4 portrays the idea that problems, solutions to problems, participants and participants' choice opportunities are all independent entities that flow into the organisational decision situation as streams of events. This is metaphorically regarded as a garbage can in which these things get dumped until, by chance, they become connected

Figure 9.4
The garbage can model of decision making

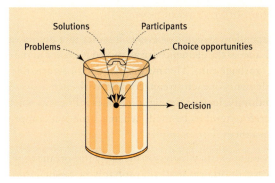

and then interact. For this reason problems can exist independently of solutions and the existence of a particular problem does not mean that a solution will be found.

Problems

In this model problems are a shortfall of some sort in organisational performance.

Solutions

These are the answers to problems and they sometimes exist before a problem is identified, because ideas constantly flow through an organisation and these can remain unused until a problem arises. Therefore, solutions are not always identifiable courses of action that are put into effect, but often consist of available, but as yet unused, ideas about how to handle a particular problem if it arises. Thus the essential point is that problems often go unrecognised until people are confronted with a solution. To give an example from everyday life, you might not recognise that you have run out of some essential household item such as toilet paper, until you go shopping for food on Saturday and a shelf full of toilet paper reminds you.

Participants

These are the organisational members concerned with making decisions, all of whom bring different priorities, attitudes, values and prior experiences to the decision making situation. Some of them will have solutions to problems of which they have not yet been made aware and others will be aware of problems to which their prior backgrounds contain no clue of a solution.

Choice Opportunities

While these occur frequently in organisations, this happens in an irregular and unpredictable way (Cohen *et al.* 1972). There are the occasions when a decision *can* be made, but there is no guarantee that this will happen. For instance, some opportunities occur regularly in terms of regular meetings, but others are unique because a crisis might well prompt a special meeting.

The Interaction of Streams of Events

The four independent streams of events interact in a highly random fashion in most organisations and so the elements are all mixed together in the organisation's decision environment (garbage can). This means that decisions are only taken as and when the appropriate elements of each stream connect with each other. Since these connections also occur randomly, luck or timing sometimes influences whether a decision is taken. Decisions therefore tend to be made when a situation comprises a certain combination of circumstances. For example:

* when a problem exists which is sufficiently important to warrant the attention of those concerned, otherwise it will probably be pushed into the background;
* when a potential solution is known and brought to the attention of someone who has the authority and energy to make a decision;
* most important of all, when a problem and a solution both surface in sequential order, and this state of affairs coincides with a choice opportunity.

There is fairly strong evidence that the model is an accurate, but complex, picture of the way that decisions are made in organisations (Levitt and Nass 1984) and it has a number of far-reaching implications. These are:

* some decisions will only be made when the streams coincide and this introduces an element of randomness into the decision process;

* because some decision makers are guided by political motives and have their own personal agendas to pursue (see Chapter 14), the timing of connections between the four streams of events is open to manipulation, which can delay the making of decisions;

* the whole process of decision making is likely to be extremely volume sensitive because if people are extremely busy, they are likely to absent themselves from events that constitute choice opportunities;

* flowing directly from the previous point, as the number of problems in an organisation rises, people can find that the time they have available to attend

REPLAY

* Decision models can be divided into two main groups: normative and descriptive.
* Normative models (e.g. the model of rational choice) give prescriptions for what decision makers should do and strongly endorse the aim of 'rational' procedures to achieve an 'optimal' solution.
* Descriptive models explain how decisions are made in practice.
* The (descriptive) model of 'bounded rationality' explains how decisions are made under conditions where only a limited degree of rationality can be applied, because of pressures on time and other resources.
* The 'garbage can' model describes how decisions are made in conditions of greater uncertainty, i.e. unbounded problems.

CASE STUDY 9.2: Compco – Further Developments

By the early 1990s Compco had moved to Coventry, in the West Midlands, and was firmly established as a mass producer of PCs, most of which were sold to retailers. For several years market conditions had been highly favourable and the firm took pride in being a progressive employer. For example, vending machines that gave employees a free and unlimited supply of tea and coffee were installed in the offices and on the factory floor. The firm also provided free health insurance for its employees and a great deal of attention was paid to training and retraining, to promote flexibility and innovation. In addition, development of special machines for some of the more intricate manufacturing operations was successfully undertaken. Because the market was extremely buoyant, most management effort went into solving distribution problems and developing customer service procedures.

By the mid-1990s, however, other problems had begun to surface. Foreign competition became a serious problem and because they had a huge range of different manufacturers to choose from, large retail customers became much more aggressive in negotiating low prices. For these reasons Compco made strong efforts to reduce costs, initially by economising on labour usage, reducing defect levels and any wastage of materials. Although this achieved significant economies, there was no respite in external pressures and matters became progressively worse. The firm was therefore forced to review its priorities and, as a result, training expenditure was cut back, charges were introduced for vending machines and medical insurance and there was a greater sense of urgency in developing methods of producing PCs more cheaply, but of a higher quality.

QUESTIONS

1. Compare the early 1990s and the mid-1990s for Compco and identify one example in each time period of:
   - search for solution
   - raised or lowered aspirations
   - reduction of slack.

2. Which decision making model best characterises the way that Compco addressed the problems it faced in the mid-1990s?

3. To what extent would it have been possible for Compco to have anticipated its problems of the mid-1990s much earlier, say in the early 1990s, and if it had tried to do so, what type of problem would it have faced?

meetings declines, and so the opportunities to make decisions that could solve problems tends to decrease;

- this means that important and novel problems are more likely to be solved than those which are mundane and routine, particularly if they are problems experienced by power holders, who can create choice opportunities, perhaps by calling special problem solving meetings.

POST-DECISION BEHAVIOUR

Both rational choice and bounded rationality models contain implementation and monitoring stages which occur after a decision is taken. Hopefully, most decisions will resolve problems, but in the face of evidence that this has not happened it is reasonable to suggest that a decision maker would seek another solution. In some situations, however, a decision maker can become so enamoured of the chosen course of action that he/she disregards signals that the decision was an inappropriate one. There are many examples of this and one that hit the headlines a few years ago was the decision to build the Millennium Dome.

This phenomenon has been labelled '*escalation of commitment to a failing course of action*' (Staw 1980) and the question of why and how it happens has been addressed by Staw and Ross (1989), who identify four primary reasons for escalation: psychological factors, social factors, project factors and organisational factors.

Escalation of commitment to a failing course of action: a decision maker's tendency to persist with a failing course of action in the face of clear evidence that the decision taken is an inappropriate one

Psychological Factors

If a decision goes wrong the threat to self-image and ego can be significant and one result of this is that a decision maker can ignore the negative signs of failure and 'press on regardless'. In addition, he or she can interpret incoming information in a biased way, for example, by underplaying the risk of complete failure and emphasising the necessity of recovering the costs of implementing the decision.

Social Factors

Because people are naturally reluctant to advertise the fact that they have made a poor decision, it can be extremely difficult for a decision maker to reverse a decision that he or she strongly advocated. This is particularly the case if other people rallied round the decision maker to give public support, which can become a silent pressure on the decision maker to stay with the decision, otherwise he or she 'lets the team down'.

Project Factors

Because most projects have a delayed return and benefits do not appear for some time, project factors usually have the greatest impact on escalation. In this situation there is an almost inbuilt tendency to regard any sign that the decision was incorrect as temporary, or something that can be remedied with a little more expenditure (Garland 1990). For these reasons there is little sense of urgency to seek an alternative course of action.

Organisational Factors

In many organisations once a decision has been taken, there is a sense of relief that the matter is now in the past, and this can be particularly strong when the search for a solution has been an extensive one. In addition, there can be vested interests at stake in a particular solution, and this sets up political pressures to stay with the course of action.

TIME OUT

Carefully reflect on your past and try to identify a decision that you made that went wrong, but you still tried to see things through despite evidence that the decision was an inappropriate one. If this has never happened to you (be honest with yourself) try to complete the exercise for someone that you know well. How do you account for your commitment to the failing course of action?

Reducing Escalation Tendencies

Staw and Ross (1987) suggest a number of measures that can be put in place to reduce tendencies towards escalation. These receive support from empirical work (Simonson and Staw 1992) and are:

- set minimum targets for performance and insist that the decision maker compares performance with the target;
- ensure that the people who make the initial decision and those who evaluate its success are different;
- try to ensure that decision makers do not become too ego-involved with a project;
- provide more feedback about project completion and costs;
- reduce the risks or penalties of failure;
- try to ensure that decision makers are aware of the consequences of persistence.

FACTORS AFFECTING DECISION MAKING

So far the chapter has treated the decision making process in a rather abstract way, as something that can be separated from everything else in an organisation. However, this is not how things take place in the real world and it is important to recognise that the nature of decision making is affected by the surrounding context and, in return, the resulting decisions have an effect on this context. With this in mind it is now time to bring together some of the matters covered in the chapter and add some detail which gives a more comprehensive picture of the factors that can shape the nature of the decision process. To structure the discussion Figure 9.5 portrays three major groups of influential factors and these are considered in what follows.

Individual Factors

Individual differences can have a profound influence on how people approach the matter of making decisions and, in particular, four differences can be significant.

Personality Variables

As can be seen from the OB in Action box below, these can have an impact on a person's preferred behaviour in a particular decision context. For instance, people with strong *machiavellian* tendencies (see Chapter 3) can view the decision situation

Figure 9.5 Factors affecting the decision making process

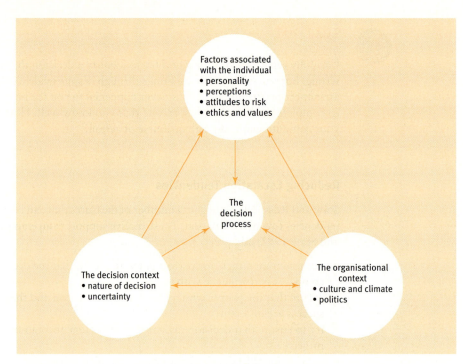

Figure 9.5 Factors affecting the decision making process

as an opportunity to manipulate others for their own personal gain. Thus they might have a tendency to keep decisions to themselves, or withhold vital information to maintain control over other people. Depending on their status in an organisation, individuals with an *authoritarian personality* can behave in one of two ways. Since authoritarians have a low tolerance to ambiguity and endorse the idea of a highly ordered environment, this can prompt them to rely on precedents and rules to guide decision making. If people of this type occupy positions of high status, they may also view decision making as something that should not be shared with subordinates, but as the prerogative of their rank.

Perceptions

Perceptions can strongly influence the way that people view a problem and so they are likely to interact with personality variables to shape preferred decision strategies (MacCrimmon 1974). For instance, if a person's prior experience has been confined to a restricted range of situations involving only bounded problems, he or she will probably have a tendency to see most new problems as similarly bounded. Depending on the person's occupational history, he or she can develop a bias towards seeing all problems in a particular way and to seek solutions accordingly (Beck and Kieser 2003).

Attitudes towards Risk

People vary in their acceptance of risk (Bass 1983) and, in general terms, individuals can be placed along a continuum, the extremes of which are 'risk-takers' and 'risk-averters'. According to where they are located on this continuum, people tend to

OB IN ACTION: Emotions and Personality in Decision Making

Because strategic decisions concern the fundamental nature of a whole organisation, it tends to be assumed that decisions of this nature are taken in a cool, rational and detached way by people whose actions are uncontaminated by moods or emotions. However, all decision making involves the processing of information by individuals. This is a cognitive activity and recent research reveals how, like all cognitive activities, it can be strongly influenced by emotions, particularly anxiety and/or depression.

Anxiety influences the factors on which decision makers focus their attention and highly anxious people attend more to what they perceive to be the threatening aspects of a situation. In addition, anxious or depressed people tend to give greater prominence to negative information. For instance, while all decision options probably have both negative and positive possibilities, people of this type seem more predisposed to see only the negatives. To some extent this can be a function of certain personality characteristics and people high in *negative affectivity*, for example, are naturally pessimistic and focus very strongly on the negative aspects of work and life. Thus, in a strategic decision making situation, they are likely to have strong preferences for decision options that offer a defensive organisational posture in the face of what could be perceived as an extremely hostile business environment.

What can be just as problematic is that people of this type can have a huge impact on other members of a decision making team. The pessimistic perceptions associated with negative affectivity can be highly contagious and this can establish biases for defensive strategies in other people. Thus organisational strengths and environmental opportunities can be overlooked, while organisational weaknesses and environmental threats can be magnified out of all proportion.

Source:

Daniels, K (1999) Affect and strategy in decision making, *The Psychologist*, 12(1): 24–8.

display characteristic patterns of behaviour in decision making (MacCrimmon and Wehrung 1986) and the behaviours associated with the extremes are summarised in Table 9.2.

Ethics and Values

As noted in Chapter 2, ethical behaviour is not solely determined by individual predispositions, but is usually the result of an interaction between individual factors and contextual variables. Since concern about ethics injects a degree of uncertainty into a decision, and for most people uncertainty can be uncomfortable, this can have a huge impact on the decisions that are taken. At one extreme, people can try to shield their core values by either not making a decision or behaving with excessive ethical zeal. At the other extreme, they can try to shut out their values by rationalising that anything goes so long as they 'put the good of the organisation before their own feelings'.

Table 9.2
Characteristics of
risk-averters and
risk-takers (after
MacCrimmon and
Wehrung 1986)

Characteristics of the decision	Risk-averters tend to look for	Acceptable to risk-takers
Conditions of possible loss	a low maximum loss, with low probability of loss	higher maximum loss, with higher probability of loss
The context in which decision is taken	a familiar environment, a high provision of information and higher degree of control over decision implementation	higher degree of unfamiliarity with environment, less information, higher uncertainty and less control over the decision and its implementation
Decision style	shared responsibility, consensus contingency planning, easy exit when risk arises	sole responsibility, tolerance to conflict, less contingency planning, risk

The Decision Context

The Nature of the Decision

This has been covered earlier in the chapter when discussing bounded and unbounded problems and a glance at Table 9.1 shows that it is much easier to grasp the nature of a bounded problem than one that is unbounded. Providing there are sufficient resources and time is not pressing, something akin to the rational choice method can be used for many bounded problems; for example, a decision about where to locate a new factory might be made in this way. This, however, does not mean that all the assumptions of rational choice decision making, such as complete information about alternatives, apply. Rather, it is far more likely that with the importance of the decision and the considerable expenditure that is involved, people will feel far more comfortable with acting in a way that looks as though it is completely rational. These situations are comparatively rare in organisations and the vast majority of decisions made at middle levels, where there is an imperative to respond quickly to a shortfall in performance or 'to be seen to be doing something' about a problem, will be made using a 'bounded rationality' method. Finally, at both middle and upper levels in an organisation the garbage can mode of decision making can come into play. This is particularly the case where unbounded problems are encountered and, although decision makers are likely to have preferences for certain courses of action, in unbounded problems preferences are seldom set in tablets of stone. The sheer ambiguity of this type of problem sometimes means that preferences only emerge in the light of experience, and in some cases it is not a matter of identifying the best way to achieve goals, but of deciding what the goals should be.

Uncertainty

The degree of uncertainty surrounding the outcomes of a decision can shape how the decision is made. In most organisations risk is usually regarded as a reflection of the likelihood that a particular decision option will succeed in resolving a problem, whereas uncertainty is a characteristic of the problem itself; for example, the clarity of the problem, incomplete information, or whether the alternative courses of action are clear. If these circumstances exist, it makes the problem an unbounded one and work by Lipshitz and Strauss (1997) indicates that decision makers tend to treat unbounded problems as bounded; for example, by trying to reduce uncertainty by collecting additional information, relying on experts, making assumptions, or even by suppressing information about the degree of uncertainty.

The Organisational Context

Organisational Culture and Climate

The culture and climate of an organisation can have a profound influence on decision making by its members. A somewhat cryptic definition of culture is 'the way we do things around here' (Deal and Kennedy 1982). In certain organisations the culture is highly risk aversive and in some, decision making is regarded as a matter for shared responsibility, while in others it is strictly the responsibility of individuals (Ouchi 1981). Climate, which is a shorter-term phenomenon, also has an impact on decision making. In some organisations, for example, behaviour is strongly governed by formal rules and regulations, which results in a strong tendency to make decisions according to past precedents and, wherever possible, rules are formulated to remove the necessity for decisions to be taken.

Organisational Politics

This facet of organisational life can also shape the nature of decision making. The topic of organisational politics will be explored in depth in Chapter 14, where it is explained that certain types of decision situation provide unrivalled opportunities for organisational politicians to manoeuvre to pursue their own personal goals (Mintzberg 1985). This means that decision making can become a matter of 'game playing' and when this happens the whole process can be shaped and reshaped as power bases are built up and alliances made.

OVERVIEW AND CONCLUSIONS

Decisions come in all shapes and sizes and, in organisations, they are all taken in an attempt to resolve a problem, real or anticipated. However, decision making and problem solving are not the same thing, and the decision process is more correctly viewed as part of the wider process of problem solving. In this respect, a distinction can be made between two main classes of problem: bounded and unbounded. Each type has its own characteristics and the decision making methods appropriate for one type are not necessarily appropriate for the other.

In many organisations decisions are the prerogative of managers, most of whom prefer to think of themselves as taking decisions in a rational way. However, the evidence suggests that this is not always the way that decisions are made and a number of decision making models have been evolved to explain the process. These fall into two broad types: normative and descriptive. Normative models, the best known of which is the rational choice model, give a highly prescriptive recipe for how decisions 'should' be made. Problematically, the assumptions that underpin the model mean that very grave reservations exist about whether it can be used in its pure form for many decisions.

Descriptive models, which are usually based on substantial research evidence, seek to explain how decisions are made in practice and, since they recognise the limitations of the normative models, they tend to give a far more realistic picture of decision making.

When decisions are made and implemented, they sometimes turn out to be inappropriate. In these circumstances decision makers do not always recognise their mistakes and instead doggedly stick to the initial decision and become embroiled in 'escalation of commitment to a failing course of action'. Finally, it is worth remembering that decision makers are individuals, with all that this means in terms of personal idiosyncrasies. It is rare to find two decisions that are identical and the way that decisions are made can vary considerably and be influenced by three important groups of factors: those associated with the individual decision maker, the nature of the decision itself, and the organisational context in which the decision is made.

REPLAY

- The phenomenon of 'escalation of commitment to a failing course of action' explains why, when a decision has been implemented and found to be wanting, the decision maker does not abandon the chosen course of action but persists with implementation of the original decision.
- There are three major groups of factors that shape the nature of the individual decision making process: individual factors, decision context factors and factors associated with the organisational context.

FURTHER READING

Bazerman, M N (1994) *Judgement in Managerial Decision Making*, 3rd edn, New York: Wiley. A very comprehensive and penetrating exploration of the judgemental heuristics used by managers, as identified in the research of Kahneman and Tversky.

Beach, L R (1997) *The Psychology of Decision Making*, London: Sage. The book gives a comprehensive introduction from a psychological perspective of the way individuals make decisions in organisations. It also gives a useful description of how contextual factors in organisations shape the decision process and decisions that are made.

Cook, S and H Slack (1991) *Making Management Decisions*, 2nd edn, London: Prentice Hall. A useful book that is now regarded as a standard text on the subject of organisational decision making.

Harrison, E F (1994) *The Managerial Decision-making Process*, 5th edn, Chicago: Haughton Mifflin. This book has a focus on middle and top management levels to explain organisational decision making.

Kahneman, D and A Tversky (eds) (2000) *Choices, Values and Frames*, Cambridge: Cambridge University Press. A book of readings that gives an account of some of the more recent research evidence on decision making and, in particular, that concerning biases and the use of heuristics.

Schick, F (1997) *Making Choices: A Recasting of Decision Theory*, Cambridge: Cambridge University Press. A penetrating and scholarly analysis of decision theory, but written in a very readable and non-mathematical way.

Shapira, Z (1997) *Organisational Decision Making*, Cambridge: Cambridge University Press. A book that brings together contributions from scholars who approach decision making from a cognitive perspective, together with those who study organisational aspects.

REVIEW AND DISCUSSION QUESTIONS

1. Describe the differences between bounded and unbounded problems. Explain what could happen in an organisation if what was thought to be a bounded problem turned out to be one that is unbounded. Give examples of when this could occur.

2. Describe the types of problem in which it would be possible to make successful use of the rational choice method of decision making, giving examples to illustrate your answer.

3. Consider each stage of the rational choice model of decision making and identify what 'irrational' things could happen in each one that could call into question a decision that is made. Give examples to illustrate your points.

4. At which levels in an organisation – supervisory, middle, top – are the following modes of decision making likely to be most prevalent: rational choice, bounded rationality, garbage can?

5. Describe the circumstances in which escalation of commitment to a failing course of action could occur, the factors responsible for it occurring, and what could be done to prevent escalation in organisations.

Chapter 10 | Stress

LEARNING OUTCOMES

After studying this chapter you should be able to:

- define stress, explain its importance and describe the stages of the General Adaptive Syndrome

- define workplace stress, how it arises and, in outline, describe a model of the important variables in workplace stress

- describe the four main groups of stressors that can impinge on people in the work situation: contextual, organisational, social and individual

- describe the four outcomes at which stress can manifest itself: physiological, psychological, cognitive and behavioural

- describe the six important groups of moderators of stress: individual characteristics, lifestyle, social support, appraisal of stressors, life events and biographic and occupational factors

- describe approaches to the management of stress at individual and organisational levels

INTRODUCTION

A degree of work-related stress has probably always existed in organisations, but in the last three decades, there has been a considerable acceleration in the pace of life, together with a radical change in the nature of many organisations. In the light of these changes, some of which are described in Chapter 2, it is not surprising to find that work-related stress is commonplace and most people experience it at some time.

Nevertheless stress is poorly understood and our knowledge of how to cope with it is far from perfect. Therefore, the chapter starts by defining stress and tracing its increasing importance to organisations and this is followed by an examination of stress as a psycho-physiological process. The remainder of the chapter focuses more explicitly on stress at work. To structure the discussion, a model of the stress process is presented, the first feature of which is the factors that can give rise to stress. This is followed by a description of the four major effects that stress can have on a person and since stress is a highly individualised reaction to workplace conditions, the next matter to be considered is the factors that can moderate how a person reacts to a particular set of stressors. Managing workplace stress is discussed next and the chapter closes with a section that reviews and integrates its contents.

STRESS: BASIC CONSIDERATIONS

Stress: an adaptive response to external stimuli that place excessive physical or psychological demands on a person

Stress is as old as mankind itself and in one way or another, all animals are susceptible to it. While there are many ways of defining stress, the definition adopted for this chapter is:

> **an adaptive response, mediated by individual differences and/or psychological processes, that is a consequence of any external action, situation or event that places excessive physical and/or psychological demands on a person.**
> **(Ivancevich and Matteson 1993, p 244)**

The idea underpinning this definition is very simple. When humans are subject to an external pressure, there are two alternative reactions: to try to withstand the impact of the pressure (fight) or move away from it (flight). Stress usually arises when an attempt is made to withstand the pressure, and a number of important points should be noted:

- stress is a reaction to an external force or demand and while anything physically or mentally demanding or burdensome can create stressful conditions, this does not necessarily mean that it occurs;

- for this to happen the situation must have sufficient impact on the person to attract his or her attention, perhaps because it evokes feelings of disappointment, annoyance, anger or hostility, or simply because the individual feels that the situation should not exist;

- more importantly, the pressure needs to be experienced as something of such magnitude that the person finds it difficult to cope with;

Stressors: external factors that impinge on a person and potentially result in stress

- while stress can be debilitating, it is an adaptive response to the *stressors*, and not simply a state of anxiety or nervous tension; both of these can result from stress, but they are purely emotional or psychological reactions, whereas stress often has physical effects as well;

Figure 10.1
The relationship between performance and level of stress

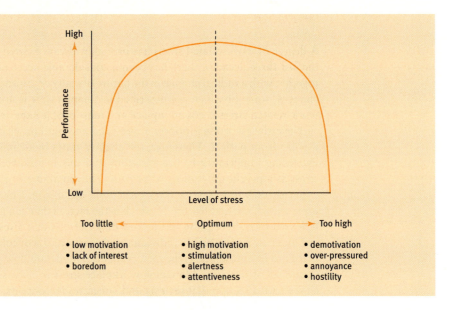

- when subject to stressors, the amount of stress experienced is a highly individual matter and, as Lazarus (1966) points out, there are no objective criteria that can be used to define whether a situation will be stressful;

- individuals vary considerably in the way that they experience stressors, and no two people are likely to experience the same stressor in the same way;

- people also vary considerably in terms of their capabilities to cope with different stressors and the only person who can accurately define whether and to what extent a situation is stressful is the person on the receiving end.

To some extent everyone encounters stressors and in some degree stress inevitably follows or, as Selye (1974) puts it, 'a complete absence of stress is death'. Although it is almost universally thought of as something bad, stress has a potential positive aspect. Many people find a mild degree of pressure stimulating and they often report that it seems to make them more alert, attentive and clear-thinking, so that they function better (Cavanaugh *et al.* 2000). Therefore, it seems likely that each person has an optimum level of stress and this idea is portrayed in Figure 10.1.

The Importance of Stress

Stress is now acknowledged to be a very widespread phenomenon. For example, survey evidence (Natvaney 1996) suggests that over 50 per cent of European employees experience some degree of occupational stress, and in America, mental stress insurance claims in California alone have been estimated to be in the region of $400 million each year (Beehr 1995). In Great Britain, work-related stress has reached record levels with an estimated 13.4 million days lost each year due to stress-related absence, at an estimated annual charge to the economy of £3.8 billion (Revil 2003).

While these figures illustrate the importance of stress in economic terms, there is another reason why it has become significant to organisations. A number of landmark personal injury cases for stress have been brought against employers in the last few years and these have resulted in high levels of compensation for employees. Perhaps more significantly, The Health and Safety Executive (HSE) has recently announced its intention to prosecute any employer failing to provide a safe working environment, which became a reality when it issued an improvement order against West Dorset Hospitals NHS Trust for not tackling workplace stress (Roberts 2003).

Unlike many topics in Organisational Behaviour, stress has implications that directly translate into costs, or loss of reputation for organisations. In addition, there are more humane reasons for being concerned about occupational stress. Stress-related illnesses, for example coronary disease, psychoses, alcohol dependence and tension-related disorders, are all on the increase (Arnold *et al.* 1998) and the personal costs for those affected can be enormous.

Stress as a Psycho-physiological Process

In everyday language stress normally indicates that a person has a distressed state of mind, possibly accompanied by physical symptoms, and that this makes it hard for the individual to function normally. While there is nothing inherently wrong with this conception, it glosses over the complexity of what occurs and infers that stress only results from unpleasant circumstances, whereas pleasant stimuli can also result in stress. The description is also rather one-sided. Its main focus is on a person's performance, which implies that the matter is relatively unimportant if the individual can cope or adapt to the stressors. Finally, the description implies that there is a one-way direction of causality, in which stressors give rise to stress, which in turn affects performance, whereas high performance can often be a stressor in its own right and in the long run it can result in severe stress. For these reasons, it is necessary to explore the processes at work that result in someone experiencing stress.

In the late 1950s a substantial body of work was undertaken by Professor Hans Selye (Selye 1976) who set out to determine whether exposure to unpleasant or noxious environmental conditions resulted in stimulus-specific responses, or in a generalised response to all stimuli. This resulted in the discovery of what Selye called the *General Adaptive Syndrome* (GAS), which provides a physiological explanation of the way in which a state of stress arises. The GAS describes a three-stage defence reaction to a stressor that:

General Adaptive Syndrome: a three-stage physiological process that takes place when an organism is subject to a stressor

- is *general* because the reaction occurs to all stressors and affects several different parts of an organism;
- is *adaptive* because it involves stimulation of defence mechanisms which help the body adjust to, or deal with, the stressor;
- is a *syndrome* because all three stages occur together, or in very close succession (see Figure 10.2).

Stage 1: Alarm

In this first stage, the person becomes aware of being subject to the effects of a stressor, which can be any environmental stimulus that has a disruptive effect on the individual; for example, something that physically attacks the body such as a virus, or even another person who threatens bodily harm. It could also be a set of conditions, such as overwork, that disrupts psychological well-being. There is an initial reaction to this,

Figure 10.2
Selye's General
Adaptive Syndrome

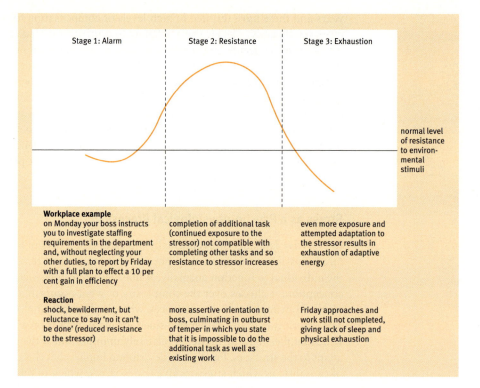

in which the body tries to meet the challenge, and this sets up a non-specific response via the body's endocrine system. This commences with activity in the pituitary gland, which sends a chemical messenger (the hormone ACTH) to the adrenal glands, which in turn triggers increased activity in the autonomic nervous system. The autonomic nervous system is divided into two parts: sympathetic and parasympathetic. The presence of the stressor induces dominance by the sympathetic system, which triggers a host of physical changes, such as increases in the heart rate and blood pressure. This prepares the body for action, but does not initiate activity, so at this stage the body is in a state of temporary retreat, which involves a minor loss of efficiency until it has rallied its reserves. If the influence of the stressor continues, this then leads to the next stage.

Stage 2: Resistance

Here the person starts to fight the effects of the stressor. The adrenal glands secrete their own hormones into the bloodstream (adrenaline and non-adrenaline) and this triggers action in several organs. The liver releases sugar, the heart beats faster and adrenaline reaches the brain, which stimulates an increase in the level of activity. All this enables the body to isolate the effects of the stressor in order to minimise damage to the organism as a whole. Thus there is a degree of adaptation to the stressor. However, since the body has a finite capacity to adapt, resistance cannot continue indefinitely and if the body is subject to an environmental stressor of sufficient strength for sufficient time, its reservoir of adaptive energy becomes depleted. The problem is that the endocrine system, in which the adrenal glands are strongly involved, gives the body an ability to resist other agents, such as germs and microbes, which are also threatening. When the system is overloaded it cannot cope with everything, which explains why stress is so often accompanied by physical illness. If there is prolonged exposure to the stressors, the depletion of adaptive energy makes it almost inevitable that the third stage of the process will be entered.

Stage 3: Exhaustion

On entering this stage, all reserves of easily available adaptive energy are nearly exhausted, and in order to try to replenish its short-term store, the body shuts itself off from the stressful stimuli. Before long all resistance to the stressor(s) has virtually disappeared and the immune system is seriously affected (Kiecolt-Glaser and Glaser 1987). In addition, there are usually attendant psychological effects, such as mood changes, emotional problems and feelings of helplessness, and these can be accompanied by significant behavioural changes, for example, a clenching of hands, fidgeting, finger tremors and weak legs. Unfortunately, because the long-term energy store also has finite reserves, any attempt to draw on it to replenish the short-term store tends to be a debt that can never be repaid and so a stressor can cause irreversible harm.

Although all this paints a somewhat dismal picture, it must be remembered that stress is essentially an adaptive process, at least in the physiological sense. Unpleasant as it may be, the final stage should be viewed as what it is – the body protecting itself from even greater harm by shutting itself off from further exposure to the stressor(s).

TIME OUT

Many students report that they find examinations result in a degree of stress. If you feel this way, carefully consider the last time that you took examinations and answer the questions below.

1. What is it that you found stressful about the examination situation?
2. Did you find yourself going through the three stages set out in the description of the General Adaptive Syndrome, that is, alarm, resistance and exhaustion?
3. If the answer to question (2) is yes, what actions or outcomes on your part coincided with each stage?

REPLAY

- Stress is an adaptive response to external factors that put physical and/or psychological demands on a person.
- It is possible that each person has an optimum level of stress, that is, a slight amount of stress could help him or her to function more effectively, whereas higher levels are detrimental to performance.
- Stress has important economic, humanistic and legal implications for organisations.
- The way in which an organism reacts to external forces that can result in stress can be explained in general terms of conformity to the General Adaptive Syndrome.

Workplace Stress

Workplace stress:
stress that arises
from an interaction
between people and
their jobs

So far, while stress has been considered in a very general way, this book is concerned with matters within organisations, and it is necessary to sharpen the focus on to *workplace stress*. However, there are dangers in compartmentalising human behaviour in this way. While a great deal of stress has its origins in organisations, there are also sources beyond the organisation and because people seldom leave the outside world behind them when they come to work, the effects of stressors outside have a habit of spilling over into the work situation and, in the same way, work-related stress can prompt stress outside work. Thus, the effects of stress inside and outside work can be cumulative. With this in mind, and to distinguish the topic from stress in a more general sense, workplace stress is defined here as:

> **conditions arising from the interaction of people and their jobs, which are characterised by changes within people that force them to deviate from their normal functioning.**
>
> **(Beehr and Newman 1978, p 666)**

A WORKING MODEL

Figure 10.3 gives a general working model, which will be used to structure the discussion in the remainder of this chapter. It portrays the dynamics of workplace stress as a process that has three stages:

- stressors, which are shown on the left, are conditions that have the potential to result in a person experiencing a situation as stressful;
- the middle stage, experienced stress, is a reflection of the individual's reaction to the potential stressors;
- experienced stress then results in a set of outcomes which are shown on the right of Figure 10.3.

Figure 10.3 A working model of stressors, outcomes and moderators

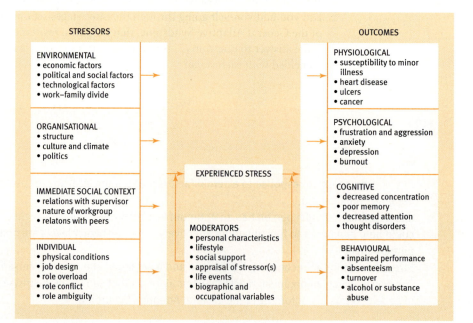

The degree of stress experienced and the ways in which a person reacts to it can be influenced by a number of other factors, and these are shown lower down as the moderator variables.

Before exploring the model it is important to note that stress is such an individual matter that there can be no hard-and-fast rules about what happens. The effects of everything shown on the model are relative rather than absolute, and this is particularly true of the potential stressors. What one person experiences as stressful, other people often regard as normal and the effects of potential stressors can be considerably amplified or reduced by cultural factors. As will be seen in Chapter 22, in some national cultures people have a very low tolerance to ambiguity, whereas in other cultures it is regarded as part of everyday life. Thus ambiguity is not likely to have the same (stressful) effects everywhere.

STRESSORS

For convenience, stressors are brought together into four major groups, according to the level at which the potential source of stress originates, and these will be described in turn.

Environmental Stressors

Environmental stressors: forces external to the organisation that can be potential sources of stress for individuals

Environmental stressors consist of forces that can become worrying or potentially disturbing to individuals and they are located in the environment of an organisation.

Economic Factors

In Western society work is a central feature of our lives and anything that threatens the stability or certainty of future employment can become a stressor. Rising unemployment figures, news of decreased national competitiveness and rising interest rates are all potential threats to a person's economic security, news of which evokes feelings of uncertainty and helplessness.

Political and Social Factors

A new government can have different priorities from its predecessor and so political changes always bring a degree of uncertainty. While some of the changes associated with a new government are likely to appear as economic factors, uncertainty can also be brought about simply because there has been a change in political ideology.

In addition, certain social factors can also induce feelings of insecurity. An element of racial discrimination is still widespread in society and this undoubtedly creates a degree of apprehension for ethnic minorities.

Technological Factors

If a technology exists, someone will find a use for it and the tremendous rate of technical change in the world has a significant impact on people's lifestyles. Keeping pace with new technological developments can be a problem for almost everybody, and technical change establishes a requirement for individuals to adapt, all of which makes for potentially stressful situations. Information technologies, which speed up information transfer, make the pace of life faster and the volume of information that can be transmitted in these ways tends to put people at risk of information overload. In addition, increased traffic and population density in urban areas makes travelling a more frustrating experience.

The Work–family Divide

Paradoxically, although the family can be one of the most significant sources of support to help people cope with stress (Fryer and Payne 1986), an increased pace of life can often result in tensions and divided loyalties between work and family responsibilities. There seems little doubt that the wave of downsizing described in Chapter 2 has resulted in most people having to work harder and for longer hours, and downsizing has been described as 'a constellation of stressor events' (Shaw and Barret-Power 1997). In a downsized organisation it often becomes the norm for people to have to take work home, which makes it much harder for them to juggle the different roles of employee, spouse and parent to the satisfaction of all concerned. This problem can be particularly acute in so-called 'dual career families', which seem to be very prone to home–work conflicts (Lewis and Cooper 1987), and there is some evidence that one stressed-out partner can quickly transmit his or her stress to the other (Jones and Fletcher 1993).

Organisational stressors: characteristics of the whole organisation that can be potential sources of stress for individuals

Organisational Stressors

Organisational Structure

Structure can have a considerable effect on emotions and feelings. In structures that are too rigid, people can feel that there are few opportunities for growth and personal development, whereas very loose, ill-defined structures can give rise to feelings of role ambiguity and anxiety. Thus, either of these extremes can be stressful to some people. Of equal importance is the effect of structural changes that have become commonplace in the last decade. As noted in Chapter 2, measures such as downsizing, rightsizing and delayering, all of which involve size reductions and changes to structure, have left many survivors with jobs that are more physically demanding and feelings that life is less secure. So pronounced are these effects that one author describes the situation as 'working with pain' (Berggren 1993) and others actually describe conditions as 'management by stress' (Parker and Slaughter 1988). As such, there is some evidence of demoralisation and anxiety in organisational workforces that have been through this experience (Green 2001; Kets de Vries and Balazs 1997). So intense are these pressures in some cases that people find it hard to 'shut off' from the sources of stress.

Culture and Climate

As will be seen in Chapter 19, one definition of culture is 'the way we do things around here' (Deal and Kennedy 1982). If a highly pressurised work environment is part of the culture, there can be heavy work demands on employees which creates highly stressful conditions (Schaunbroeck and Ganster 1993). Conversely, there is empirical support for the idea that cultures and climates that incorporate a strong element of participative management reduce the stressfulness of conditions (Ivancevich *et al.* 1990).

Organisational Politics

People in organisations tend to be interdependent and have to rely on each other, but if cooperation from others cannot be obtained, this can bring an element of resentment and frustration to the person concerned. In addition, if it is found that these people are going one step further and manoeuvring behind the scenes for their own ends, the effects can be even more devastating. For example, in a survey of 2,500 managers by Kiev and Kohn (1979), respondents rated a poor political climate as one of the most frequent sources of stress.

Immediate Social Stressors

Immediate social stressors: features of a person's immediate (social) work context that can be stressful

The social aspects of work are as important for most people as the opportunity to earn money. Thus certain immediate social conditions can result in stress, and three in particular can be important: relations with one's immediate superior; the nature of a workgroup; and interpersonal relations with group members.

Relations with Immediate Superior

It is all too easy for the behaviour of an inconsiderate or thoughtless supervisor or manager to create stressful conditions for an employee. As can be seen from the OB in Action box below, this can sometimes be so extreme that it verges on being the act of a tyrant. A study by Fox *et al.* (1993) shows that a number of behaviours can be particularly stress-provoking. These are:

- inconsistent instructions;
- failure to provide physical and emotional support;
- lack of concern for employees' well-being;
- lack of adequate direction;
- too strong an emphasis on productivity;
- focusing only on isolated incidents of sub-standard performance;
- ignoring good performance.

Nature of a Workgroup

Being a member of a group is an important feature of work for most people, and later in this chapter it will be seen that a person's workgroup can be an important source of social support to resist the effects of stressors.

In current conditions temporary groups and teams tend to be used a great deal. Thus individuals sometimes find that they have to move in and out of new groups, and each time this happens people have to adjust to the personal idiosyncrasies of a new set of people and find a role within the group. A newly formed group is full of unresolved ambiguities and if it is not given enough time to work through the necessary processes of formation (see Chapter 11) these ambiguities can turn into conflicts that persist for some time, all of which creates a highly stressful set of conditions.

OB IN ACTION: Bullying at Work

It has now been recognised that harassment and bullying is all too common in the workplace and a recent survey by the TUC, the coordinating body for British trade unions, suggests that over 5 million people have been subjected to bullying at work. Employees treated in this way often exhibit the classic signs of stress, such as physical illness, acute anxiety, depression and sometimes a complete mental breakdown. Some estimates suggest that bullying accounts for over one-third of all stress-related absence, costing the national economy £1.3 billion each year.

Bullying seldom involves physical abuse, but usually consists of severe psychological pressures by someone in authority, for example, ridicule, scapegoating, constant fault-finding and blame, which has a highly demoralising effect on the victim. It has largely been attributed to the increasingly pressurised work environment that exists in many organisations, where people are expected to achieve more and more with fewer and fewer resources. In these conditions managers are themselves under greatly increased pressure and handle the situation by passing on the pressures. Problematically, once habits like this take root in an organisation, they can quickly be absorbed into its culture.

One organisation that has made a positive attempt to tackle this matter is the large retail chain Littlewoods, which, in a determined attempt to create a positive working environment for its 27,000 employees, launched its 'dignity at work' policy. This sets out steps that employees can take if they feel that they have been subject to bullying or harassment and, if necessary, can involve the use of an independent internal investigator, although most employees seem to prefer to use less formal methods. In addition, about 90 employees have been trained to act as 'supporters' – people who give emotional support to others who are considering making complaints. In the interests of natural justice, managers or supervisors also have guidance and support services available, and 'dignity at work' issues have now become part of the training received by every manager and supervisor in the organisation.

Source:

Lucas, E (1999) The new breeding ground for bullies, *Professional Manager*, July: 10–12.

Interpersonal Relations with Group Members

To some extent this flows from the point above. Good personal relationships between group members can be a central factor in individual well-being (Argyris 1964) and the major stressors in this respect can be:

- conflictual relations with other group members;
- a lack of interpersonal trust;
- unsympathetic co-workers.

Individual stressors: features of a person's job that can give rise to stress

Individual Stressors

Certain features of an individual's role can be stressful, and five in particular can be highly significant: physical conditions; job design; role overload; role complexity/conflict; and role ambiguity.

Physical Conditions

The effects of physical conditions on individual well-being are covered in some detail in Chapter 6, where it is noted that the physical conditions in which work takes place can have a significant impact upon individual productivity. Many of these have an impact because they are potential stressors and Shostak (1980) notes five that have this effect:

- temperature extremes;
- bright or harsh lighting;
- too little illumination;
- a dusty or dirty atmosphere;
- loud noise.

Job Design

A number of features of an individual's job can have the potential to induce stress. Machine-based, repetitive work gives a person low task control or personal responsibility, whereas a job with a high degree of autonomy has the opposite effect and acts as a buffer to the effects of other stressors (Makin *et al.* 1996). Repetitive work that under-utilises a person's skills can result in a degree of anxiety, depression and boredom, all of which can lead to stress (Reeves 2003).

Long working hours or intensified working conditions can be highly stressful (Green 2001; Sparks *et al.* 1997) and shift work disrupts bodily rhythms, levels of blood sugar and mental efficiency. A shift worker's body clock is permanently in disarray and there can be a lack of alertness at work and because the person attends work while friends and family are asleep and vice versa, there can also be a sense of social isolation, all of which can give rise to a potential for stress and stress-related diseases (Monk and Tepas 1985).

Working with a computer screen for prolonged periods can result in 'repetitive strain injury' from adopting the same posture for long periods and become a significant source of stress (Mackay and Cox 1984).

Role Overload

Most people have some idea of what constitutes a reasonable level of work and from time to time almost everybody has to exceed this, by working long hours or to extremely tight deadlines, to cope with an emergency. If it is temporary people can usually cope with a *quantitative* overload of this type and some individuals actually like working under pressure in this way. However, if the situation persists it can become highly stressful.

Qualitative overload, in which the requirements of the job are beyond the skills of its incumbent, is a more difficult situation, even in the short term. This occurs for most newcomers, and it is usually accepted that they will underperform until they 'find their feet'. However, the situation can also occur for people who have been redeployed in an organisational restructuring and, because they are familiar faces in the firm, there is sometimes no tolerance to their inexperience in a certain task.

Variety overload can occur when someone has a very wide range of different tasks to perform, which demands a constant shift in attention and concentration. Since downsizing and delayering are often quickly followed by empowerment initiatives, in which employees have to take on some of the tasks hitherto performed by supervisors and managers (Claydon and Doyle 1996), these circumstances can result in all forms of overload.

Role Complexity/Conflict

This occurs when two or more different roles held by the same person have competing demands. Thus, complying with one set of demands makes it difficult or impossible to meet demands of the other set(s). It has long been recognised that role conflicts of this type result in a highly stressful situation and Kahn *et al.* (1964) note that these circumstances are associated with:

- high levels of interpersonal tension;
- decreased job satisfaction;
- poor interpersonal relations;
- decreased confidence in the organisation;
- decreased commitment to the organisation.

Moreover, this state of affairs is not confined to conflict between roles within an organisation; there can also be significant effects if competing pressures exist between work and family roles.

Role Ambiguity

This occurs when someone is uncertain about:

- what he or she should accomplish in a job;
- the expectations of other people;
- what needs to be accomplished to meet their expectations.

Ambiguities of this type can be uncomfortable and highly stressful and, although some degree of role ambiguity is probably inevitable in today's fluid, downsized organisations, individuals vary considerably in their capacity to live with the situation. Thus, individual differences have a strong bearing on the degree of stress experienced. In general, the following can all result from role ambiguity and they can all be precursors of stress (French and Caplan 1973):

- low job satisfaction;
- low self-confidence;
- low self-esteem;
- a sense of futility;
- low motivation;
- depression.

TIME OUT

As for the previous Time Out exercise, carefully reflect on the last time you took examinations, but this time answer the following questions:

1. Were there any stressors emanating from the external environment of your university or college that you felt were impinging on you?
2. What organisational stressors do you feel were present?
3. What stressors emanating from your immediate social context at your university or college do you feel were impinging on you?
4. What individual stressors do you feel were present?

REPLAY

- Workplace stress results from the interaction of people and their jobs and, in particular, from changes that force them to deviate from their normal functioning.
- There are four main groups of stressors (forces that impinge on people and result in stress): contextual, organisational, those in a person's immediate social context and individual factors.

CASE STUDY 10.1: Nede Obuto

Nede Obuto felt tired and dispirited. For the last eighteen months he had worked as a lecturer in a new university in the south of England and prior to this he had been a research student at another institution, working towards a PhD. Unfortunately he had not completed his research at the end of the allowed three years, at which time his funding had ceased. Since neither he nor his wife had any savings, he then sought work as a lecturer and decided to complete his PhD on a part-time basis, hoping that an academic employer would actively support his studies. Although he felt that he had interviewed well for his present job, his appointment was made probationary for two years, a permanent post being made contingent on him completing his research and submitting the thesis for examination by the end of the probationary period.

Nede had always felt a strong pressure to achieve academically because education was revered in his family. Indeed, it was largely to obtain educational opportunities for the children that had prompted his parents to move from West Africa 20 years ago. As matters stood, however, he had grave doubts about whether he could complete his research on time. Despite assurances at the interview that the university was strongly supportive of research, as a newcomer he was given a full teaching load, much of which he suspected was work that other lecturers wished to avoid. To make matters worse, the work was extremely varied and a great deal of it was well outside his specialist area, which involved him in a great deal of study and preparatory work. As such, he found himself with little time to spend with his wife and children, and his guilt about this became another source of pressure.

(Box continued)

(Box continued)

What made life even harder was that he shared an office with two other lecturers, who he suspected were somewhat racist. While neither of them acted in an overtly racist way, they were always a little too polite and, at times, rather patronising. Both of them were extremely 'chatty' with each other and this seriously interrupted Nede's attempts to work. What made matters worse was that, in a shared office, he was not only interrupted by his own students, but also by those of his colleagues. As a result, he found it progressively harder to work on his PhD and he started to become apprehensive about completing it within the next six months.

Questions

1. How would you classify the state of affairs in which Nede Obuto finds himself?

2. What stressors (and of what type) do you feel are impinging on Nede?

THE OUTCOMES OF STRESS

Stress can manifest itself in many ways, but these can be divided into four main categories suggested by Beehr (1995). From the perspective of an organisation, the most significant outcomes are those that affect performance, which are included here in the behavioural and cognitive categories. However, it is important to remember that overt behaviour is just the final, most visible symptom and, if behavioural symptoms are evident, it is virtually certain that there will also be psychological and cognitive outcomes. In the long run, physiological problems will also probably appear. Historically the majority of research on stress has explored its link with physical illness and work on psychological and cognitive outcomes is a more recent development. Thus, in what follows, although the four outcome categories are discussed separately, it is vital to remember that they are all interconnected.

Physiological outcomes: the effects of stress on a person's bodily health

Physiological Outcomes

There is a substantial body of evidence to support the idea that stress has serious effects on physical health (O'Leary 1990), an early indication of which was given in the work of Holmes and Rahe (1967), which will be covered when describing the moderators of stress. The reason why stress has these effects was described earlier when covering the General Adaptive Syndrome. The endocrine system enables the body to resist agents such as germs and microbes, and plays a part in providing the adaptive energy to cope with novelty, uncertainty and conflict, the very conditions associated with stressors. If its reserves are limited and it has to try to provide the energy to cope with stressors, it simply has less energy to resist microbes.

It is also known that high levels of stress are accompanied by an increase in the level of cholesterol in the bloodstream, and with increased blood pressure. Since these phenomena are associated with heart disease, there are good reasons for suggesting that stress is a major contributory factor, and there are even arguments to suggest a link between some forms of cancer and stress (Bammer and Newberry 1982).

Psychological
outcomes:
the effects of stress
on a person's mental
health

Psychological Outcomes

Frustration and Aggression

As explained in Chapter 7, frustration occurs when goal achievement is blocked. Goal blocking is an endemic feature of organisational life and many of the stressors described earlier can give rise to frustrating experiences. Where these are fairly limited in duration all will probably be well, but if the experience is prolonged, or the limits of tolerance are exceeded, frustration becomes a driving emotional condition that can all too easily degenerate into aggression. Thus it is not surprising to find that high levels of stress are associated with aggressive actions such as interpersonal hostility, or even sabotage (Chen and Spector 1992).

Anxiety

Anxiety occurs when someone believes that he or she has no effective way of dealing with disturbing circumstances that might occur, while fear is a reaction to danger that is already perceived to exist. Many of the stressors identified earlier are associated with ambiguity and uncertainty about the future, and this is almost bound to prompt a degree of anxiety. Where anxieties are slight or moderate, however, this tends to keep people alert and ready for action, but where anxiety becomes severe, it can all too easily result in non-adaptive, escapist behaviours, including aggression.

Depression

Because it can take so many different forms, depression can be very hard to define. Nevertheless, Flach (1974) gives some of the symptoms of chronic depression as:

- disturbed sleep;
- loss of appetite;
- lowered sex drive;
- indecision;
- fatigue;
- poor concentration;
- avoidance of social contact;
- an inability to find pleasure in almost anything;
- feelings of being trapped and helpless.

At times most of us become mildly depressed and because this makes us slow down and build up our reserves of energy, it has a useful function and most people seem to pull themselves out of mild depression. However, there are others who find depression harder to shake off, and they sink deeper into self-defeating patterns of behaviour. The great paradox is that depressed people tend to feel that they have no control over events, but at the same time blame themselves for feeling depressed (Abramson and Sackheim 1977).

Clearly many of the stressors described above have the capability to induce mild depression and if several of them are present in combination and for a sufficient time, matters could become serious. Moreover, since depression is a condition that can lead to even more serious problems with mental health, it is sometimes one that needs psychiatric attention.

Burnout

Burnout: a chronic outcome of stress characterised by a general feeling of complete exhaustion, depersonalisation, disinterest and lack of personal accomplishment

Burnout can be defined as 'a general feeling of exhaustion that develops when an individual experiences too much pressure and too few sources of satisfaction' (Moss 1981). While it is more commonplace than depression, it is almost exclusively associated with work-related stressors and some of its associated symptoms are:

- emotional exhaustion;
- physical exhaustion;
- disturbed sleep;
- absence of any positive feelings about work;
- feelings of hopelessness and futility;
- a cynical perspective about almost everything associated with work.

There is general agreement that the key component of burnout is emotional exhaustion (Gaines and Jermier 1983). When this occurs the person becomes callous towards, or withdrawn from, colleagues and clients, and then develops a sense of a lack of personal accomplishment about work. It seems to be far more prevalent in people whose jobs include a large component of interaction with other people who have their own problems; for example, the police, teachers, nurses and other caring professions (Evans and Fischer 1993).

Jobs such as these often attract people with high ideals and the nature of their work places strong emotional demands on them, but if these demands cannot be met, they develop burnout through frustration. For this reason burnout can seldom be associated with a specific stressor that appears at a set point in time. Rather, it is an outcome that appears and then gets worse. This idea is cogently expressed in a review of the literature by Cordes and Dougherty (1993), from which the model shown in Figure 10.4 has been synthesised.

Cognitive Outcomes

Cognitive outcomes: the effects of stress on thought processes

The word cognitive refers to thought processes and the main cognitive problems associated with stress are:

- lowered concentration;
- impaired memory;
- lowered attention;
- distorted perceptions;
- (in extreme cases) thought disorders.

However, these are symptoms and, because the relationship between stress and thought is so complex, it can be hard to pinpoint a definite effect, because highly circular processes are likely to be at work; for instance, a person's thoughts about a stressor can give rise to an emotional reaction that becomes an additional source of stress. However,

Figure 10.4
The development of
burnout (after Cordes
and Dougherty 1993)

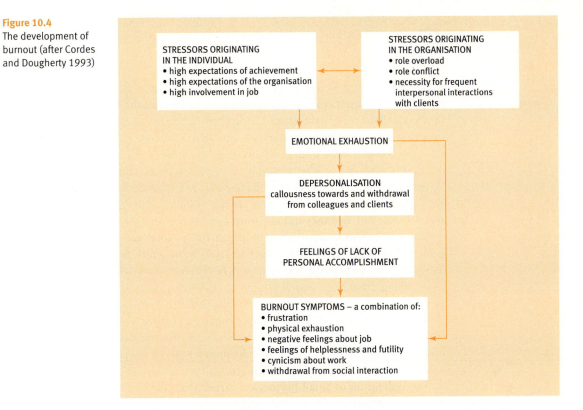

while we know that certain cognitive processes are affected by stress, we do not really
know why. What is known is that when stress occurs hormones that affect brain
functioning are released and in mild cases this increases brain activity and sharpens
thinking, alertness and concentration. Problematically, when this stress-induced
arousal reaches a certain level, more primitive reactions occur. The person becomes
less sensitive to his or her surroundings and the intake of information and its interpretation can be impaired, and this results in hasty action and mistakes.

Behavioural Outcomes

**Behavioural
outcomes:** the effects
of stress on overt
behaviour

Work Performance

Because there are moderating variables that can mitigate some of the effects of stressors,
it is hard to pinpoint the direct effect of stress on job performance. There are people
who argue that it can only have a negative effect, while others adopt the view that a
moderate degree of stress probably improves performance. Nevertheless, if the stress
is too severe performance is inevitably undermined and Cohen (1980) draws three
significant conclusions:

- in most cases stressors have no immediate effects on behaviour because, in the
  short term, the majority of people adapt in order to maintain performance;

OB IN ACTION: Employer Attitudes towards Stress

Many employers think that workers are using the excuse of 'stress' to take days off to which they are not entitled, according to a recently published survey. The revelation has added a twist to the issue of stress at work, which health chiefs say is emerging as a serious problem for employers. Although the survey provoked protest from the largest private sector trade union, it elicited evasiveness and embarrassment from business organisations, who refused to endorse employers' widespread suspicions.

Nevertheless, 51 per cent of human resource professionals believe that over half the days that employers lose to stress are not 'genuine', and 40 per cent of private sector businesses said they did not want to raise the profile of stress, in case this encouraged increased reporting of it. Roger Lyons, joint general secretary of the Amicus trade union, complained that employers were 'utterly wrong' to believe that many workers were taking sick days for dubious reasons. 'Modern living and modern working place huge stress on families,' said Mr Lyons, and 'failure to recognise this is part of the problem.' However, while Ben Willmott, of the Chartered Institute of Personnel and Development, conceded that 'we will always have a few employees who will use stress as the excuse to take the odd day off', stress is a real problem, although some managers, under pressure themselves, perhaps do not have a lot of sympathy for a stressed employee.

The Federation of Small Businesses warned that employers were 'increasingly aware of vexatious claims, and are concerned about an area which is vaguely defined at the moment'. Elizabeth Gyngell, head of 'better working environment' at the Health and Safety Executive – which has led the campaign to increase awareness of stress – said if companies tackled the causes of stress they would be 'in a stronger position to tackle the people they might think are skiving'.

Source:

Turner, D (2003) Stress used as 'excuse to skive', *The Financial Times*, 21 October.

- the adaptive process has its penalties and, while these take time to have an effect, reduced tolerance to frustration and less efficient working eventually start to appear;
- importantly, the whole process takes less time in the presence of multiple stressors and so it seems safe to conclude that a decrease in performance is a function of the aggregate number of stressors, and the time for which they are experienced.

Other Behavioural Outcomes (absenteeism, turnover, substance abuse)

A whole host of other behavioural outcomes have been linked to stress. There is evidence of a relationship between stress levels and absenteeism and staff turnover (Steers and Rhodes 1978), although some employers are sceptical about whether absenteeism is necessarily stress related (see OB in Action box on previous page). Other outcomes that have attracted increasing interest are alcohol and drug abuse but, because of the secretive nature of both practices, it is difficult to find hard evidence that they are related to stress. Nevertheless, it is more than possible that people seek solace in alcohol and drugs as a result of stress, even if this only shows up as unauthorised absence the following day.

TIME OUT

Returning to the subject of examinations used for the previous Time Out exercise, now answer the questions below about the outcomes of stress that might have been present.

1. Were there any physical symptoms and, if so, what were they?
2. Were there any psychological symptoms and, if so, what were they?
3. Were there any cognitive symptoms and, if so, what were they?
4. Were there any behavioural symptoms and, if so, what were they?

REPLAY

- There are four main outcomes of stress and, while these can sometimes appear in isolation, it is common for them all to appear together.
- Physiological outcomes have effects on the person's health.
- Psychological outcomes include frustration, aggression, anxiety, depression or burnout.
- Cognitive outcomes affect thought processes.
- Behavioural outcomes are manifested as changes in the individual's work performance, possible absenteeism and/or staff turnover.

THE MODERATORS OF STRESS

Research has revealed a number of factors that can moderate the effects of stressors, in one or both of two ways:

- by influencing the amount of stress that a person experiences;
- by influencing the person's reactions to the experience of stress, which has an impact on the outcomes he or she exhibits.

Although the effects of the moderators are well documented, our knowledge of the mental processes through which these effects are produced is still far from perfect. In what follows they will all be considered separately, but it is important to point out that there are connections between some of them, and several can act in combination.

CASE STUDY 10.2: Nede Obuto – Further Developments

For the next six months Nede threw everything into getting his PhD completed and on the second anniversary of his appointment, he posted off his thesis to his supervisor. However, this removed few of his apprehensions about the future. To start with, Nede was aware that his thesis was a rushed job, which was badly argued in places, full of typographical errors and poor English. Therefore, he was by no means sure that he would get his PhD without heavily modifying the work. Worse still, on informing his boss that the thesis had been submitted and asking for confirmation of permanent employment, the criteria changed overnight from 'submission of thesis' to 'award of PhD'. When this happened Nede immediately approached his trade union, and the case was taken up with the employer, with the result that his employment (on a probationary basis) was guaranteed until the thesis was examined. However, he became acutely aware that putting matters in the hands of the union had resulted in him annoying the Human Resources Manager for exposing the matter, which did nothing to remove his apprehensions.

Completing the thesis had also taken its toll on Nede in other ways. He became increasingly aware that the lack of support from the university while he was doing his PhD was a reflection of its lack of support for research in general. As one of his colleagues put matters, 'Yes, the university would like to see us all producing published research papers, but so far as giving us time to do the work, the most they ever give is pious rhetoric.' Therefore, Nede felt there would be no future opportunities for research at all. From then on he sank deeper into despair. He stopped talking to many of his colleagues, became extremely short-tempered with those who shared his office and had less and less patience with students. While he managed to keep on top of his work, he became aware that his memory was not what it had been, and that he had started drinking heavily at home. All in all, he had come to dislike the university and the job itself. This was made no easier by the string of minor ailments he experienced, which ranged from colds to boils, all of which culminated in a severe bout of shingles that kept him away from work for three weeks.

Questions

1. Do you feel that Nede displays any signs of suffering from stress?

2. Identify any symptoms of stress and classify them as physiological, psychological, cognitive or behavioural.

3. What could be done to help Nede with his problems?

Personal Characteristics

Self-efficacy:
a person's belief in
his or her ability to
act in a certain way

Self-efficacy

This, which is connected with personality, can be defined as an individual's perception of his or her ability to act in a certain way, which in this case means acting in a way that allows the person to remain in control of the work situation (Bandura 1982). In terms of stress, this probably comes down to the person's belief in his or her ability to withstand or adjust to change.

This is also likely to be an important determinant of a predisposition to succumb to stress, and a case study by Fox *et al.* (1993) indicates that people who are high in self-efficacy maintain a relatively low blood pressure when exposed to stressors. It is perhaps for this reason that participative decision making, which can give people a feeling of having some element of control over matters, can reduce the stress-inducing potential of work (Jackson 1983). The reverse of a feeling of remaining in control is what Seligman (1975) dubs a state of 'learned helplessness', which predisposes people to give up easily and accept that they will be stressed.

Hardiness

Hardiness:
a psychological
characteristic that
helps a person
withstand the
effects of stressors

This is a global predisposition first identified by Jackson (1983), who noticed that under stress some people tend to go to pieces much more readily than others. In an investigation of managers subject to stress, those who experienced lower rates of stress-related illnesses were classified as having what the researchers called 'hardiness' (Kobasa *et al.* 1982), which was associated with three distinct characteristics:

- **commitment**   they were highly involved in their work;
- **challenge**   they felt that change rather than stability was normal;
- **control**   they felt able to influence the outcome of events.

From these results Kobasa and her colleagues reason that these characteristics help people to resist stress by erecting a buffer between themselves and workplace stressors.

Negative Affectivity (NA)

**Negative affectivity
(NA):** a tendency to
focus strongly on the
negative aspects of
work and life

This is a tendency to focus on the negative aspects of work and life and it is a characteristic that seems to predispose people to be more affected by stress (George 1990). Those high in a negative affectivity tend to become easily angered, afraid or depressed about events in their lives, and this could well shape their appraisals of workplace stressors. Indeed, there is fairly strong empirical support for the idea that when exposed to the same stressors, individuals high in NA tend to experience higher levels of stress than those low in this characteristic (Schaunbroeck *et al.* 1992).

Lifestyle (Type A and Type B Behaviours)

Following a lengthy and exhaustive programme of research into cardiovascular (heart) disease, the scientific world was shaken by the findings of two researchers who uncovered the risks of what they identified as Type 'A' behaviour (Friedman and Rosenman 1974). Prior to this, it had been assumed that the main risk factors in heart disease were diet, high blood pressure and a genetic predisposition. However, the researchers uncovered another factor, which consists of a set of behavioural traits that dominate the lives of those most at risk. These are Type 'A' people, who display the following characteristics:

- to achieve maximum efficiency and output they strive to do a multitude of things at the same time;
- they are aggressively competitive, ambitious and forceful;

- they are impatient, so tend to do everything at a frenzied pace and consider any delay a chronic waste of precious time;
- they are highly combative with people, events and objects;
- they have a tendency to speak in a rushed, explosive way and are impatient with others who speak slowly and often try to finish other people's sentences.

In contrast, Type 'B' people, while still having drive and ambition, have a much steadier pace of doing things.

Research has amply demonstrated the inherently stressful nature of Type 'A' behaviour (Jex *et al.* 2002). Instead of condemning the pace of organisational life, these people may well have a tendency to use the circumstances as an unrivalled opportunity to behave according to their preferred pattern, which places a huge amount of stress on themselves and those around them.

Social Support

Social support: emotional support received through interaction with other people

While receiving and giving *social support* is usually advocated as a way of helping to combat stress, it also has a role in resisting stress and can be a powerful moderator of the effects of stressors. Social support is derived from the give-and-take relationships that are built up with other people, particularly those who give support at an emotional level and Williams and House (1985) argue that this helps combat the effects of stressors in three important ways:

- by creating a setting in which needs for affection, approval, security and social interaction are met;
- by reducing the likelihood that poor interpersonal relations will become a source of stress, which makes the work environment a much more pleasant place;
- perhaps most importantly, by acting as a buffer between an individual and the stressors; that is, stressors can sometimes be brought into perspective by discussing them with other people.

(Cognitive) Appraisal of Stressors

Cognitive appraisal: a person's perception of a stressor, e.g. whether it is harmful, threatening or challenging

People often evaluate the same stressor in different ways and this has a significant impact on whether it is perceived as threatening, harmful, challenging or, indeed, benign. In addition, it has some bearing on the strategies that a person might use to cope with stress. Dewe (1991) points out that if a person judges that a particular situation is likely to require resources that he or she does not possess, this poses a threat to the individual's personal well-being and stress can ensue. According to Dewe, this takes place in two stages:

- *primary appraisal*, which involves thoughts or feelings about a stressor, for example, whether it is felt to be harmful, threatening or challenging;
- *secondary appraisal*, where more detailed consideration of the stressor's characteristics takes place.

Clearly, both of these stages can have an impact on how the stressor is experienced but, according to Dewe, in terms of coping with the stressor, primary appraisal is by far the most important; a point to which a return will be made when considering stress management.

Table 10.1 The social readjustment scale (after Holmes and Rahe 1967)

Life events	Scale value	Life events	Scale value
Death of spouse	100	Son or daughter leaving home	29
Divorce	73	Trouble with in-laws	29
Marital separation	65	Outstanding personal achievement	28
Prison sentence	63	Wife begins or stops work	26
Death of close family member	63	Begin or end school	26
Major personal injury or illness	53	Change in living conditions	25
Marriage	50	Revision of personal habits	24
Dismissal from employment	47	Trouble with boss	23
Marital reconciliation	45	Change in work hours or conditions	20
Retirement	45	Change in residence	20
Major change in health of family member	44	Change in schools	20
Pregnancy	40	Change in recreation	19
Sex difficulties	39	Change in church activities	19
Gaining new family member	39	Change in social activities	18
Business readjustment	39	Very small mortgage or loan	17
Change in financial state	38	Change in sleeping habits	16
Death of close friend	37	Change in number of family gatherings	15
Career change	36	Change in eating habits	15
Change in number of arguments with spouse	35	Vacation	13
Having a large mortgage	31	Christmas	12
Foreclosure of mortgage or loan	30	Minor violations of the law	11
Changed responsibilities at work	29		

Life Events

Since stress is a reaction to the need to adapt, when people undergo significant changes, either at work or outside, stress and other health problems can occur. This idea was tested for a wide variety of life events that were mainly non-occupational in nature by Holmes and Rahe (1967), which led to the development of a test instrument called the Social Readjustment Scale. This places potential stress values on a number of life events that require people to make adjustments and is reproduced in outline in Table 10.1.

The assumption underpinning the scale is that because the life events shown in Table 10.1 are all changes that require people to adapt, they are potential stressors, and this can predispose the person to illness. The usual way of applying the scale is to identify the events that a person has encountered in a twelve-month period, and then to total the scale values of these events which are shown in the right-hand column. According to Holmes and Rahe, this can be used to predict the likelihood of illness in the following year. For a score of up to 150, people are said to be at no great risk; if the total is between 150 and 300, there is a 50 per cent probability of serious illness; if the total is above 300, the probability of illness rises to at least 75 per cent.

Depending on how it is viewed, the scale can be regarded as a warning list of potential stressors, or as a list of extra-organisational stressors that can exacerbate the effects of those in the workplace. It is in the second way that it is used here, and a high score on the scale means that there is a high potential for stress in outside events, which in turn makes it more likely that the person may succumb to workplace stressors.

Note that while a number of the events listed in Table 10.1 are what most of us would regard as pleasant events, they still require a person to undergo change and, in Holmes and Rahe's terms, they are potential stressors. This idea contradicts the popular view that stress is totally associated with aversive conditions and gives rise to one of the most frequently voiced criticisms of the scale – the assertion that aversive and pleasant events are equally important as stressors. Nevertheless, follow-up work using the scale indicates that the relationship between life events and subsequent health problems, although relatively modest, is robust (Perkins 1982). Thus the work has sufficient predictive validity to encourage other workers to develop new and improved scales. The most important inference that can be drawn from the work concerns the cumulative effect of multiple stressors. Stress outside work almost certainly lowers the ability to resist stress at work and, as a corollary, stress at work spills over into a person's private life.

Biographic and Occupational Factors

In addition to the factors covered above, there is evidence that a number of biographical and occupational factors are associated with stress. Where biographics are concerned, the sex of an individual is likely to be a moderator. All other things being equal, women seem to experience greater psychological effects of stress, while men suffer far more from physical outcomes (Geller and Hobfall 1994).

Certain occupational factors also seem to be influential. Dentists seem to be particularly prone to stress because of time and scheduling demands and negative patient perceptions (Cooper *et al.* 1988), while civil servants are particularly prone to the effects of role ambiguity (Erera-Weatherley 1996). In a study of burnout, Evans and Fischer (1993) draw attention to the idea that different occupations suffer most from different outcomes. The caring professions exhibit the symptom of depersonalisation very strongly, whereas technical occupations, such as computer hardware and software designers, are more aware of the feeling of lack of personal accomplishment that results in burnout.

TIME OUT

In the previous Time Out exercises you have noted some of the features of the stress that you felt you experienced during the time that you last took examinations. Now answer the questions below:

1. How would you classify the amount of stress that you feel you experienced: mild, medium or high?
2. Were there any moderators present that helped you either resist the effects of the stressors or cope with the stress, or made it harder for you to resist or cope? If so, try to classify the moderators into:

   (your own) personal characteristics
   (your own) lifestyle
   social support from others
   your appraisal of the stressors.

REPLAY

- There are a number of factors that can moderate an individual's reaction to workplace stressors. These are:

personal characteristics such as personality
lifestyle
availability of social support
how the person appraises the stressors
other life events
biographic and occupational factors.

OB IN ACTION: Stress Management – An Act of Faith?

A number of well-publicised court cases in which employees have been awarded large damages for work-related stress could well have resulted in a situation where large organisations feel naked without a stress management programme of some sort. However, according to occupational psychologist Rob Briner of London University, the jury is still out on whether measures of this type actually alleviate suffering.

Briner points out that stress itself is widely assumed to be a very specific and clearly defined problem, whereas it is little more than a vague umbrella term that people use to embrace anything that they find distasteful, disturbing or unpleasant in the workplace. For this reason stress management tends to throw very generalised solutions at what can be highly specific workplace problems. After discounting the efficacy of simplistic solutions used by some organisations, for example, playing calming background music, Briner comments on the three main approaches used.

The least used approach is to 'reduce exposure to potentially harmful work conditions'. This is based on the highly plausible idea that prevention is better than cure and usually involves job redesign. The evidence suggests that this achieves very mixed results; things get better for some people and worse for others. The most common approach, 'stress management training', aims to equip people with the skills and techniques to cope with harmful conditions, for example, by training them in time management, assertiveness or relaxation. Here the evidence seems to suggest a short-term improvement in feelings of well-being, which quickly fades away. Finally, 'Employee Assistance Programmes' (EAPs) treat people who have already been harmed, usually by providing counselling delivered by an external source. This, of course, is tantamount to shutting the stable door after the horse has bolted. Moreover, because people who recover are sometimes immediately returned to the situation that resulted in their problem, the evidence on EAPs is not impressive.

(Box continued)

(Box continued)

In the light of this rather depressing picture Briner cautions us not to regard stress as something that has a single, well-identified cause, like influenza, and argues for a far more strategic approach in organisations, that is, one which avoids the assumption that stress can be successfully addressed by generalised methods, but instead focuses on specific solutions to specific problems.

Source:

Briner, R (1999) Against the grain, *People Management*, 30 September: 32–41.

STRESS MANAGEMENT

The expression stress management is misleading, if only because it implies that the level of stress in an organisation can be varied at will. Moreover, a great deal of so-called stress management is more concerned with enabling people to 'learn to live with high levels of stress'. Nevertheless, it is a widely used expression and to maintain continuity with other literature, it will be used here.

A number of ways can be used to deal with stress in organisations and, in order to structure the discussion, the approaches are distinguished by locating them along the two dimensions shown in Figure 10.5.

The horizontal dimension categorises approaches according to the *level of stress management*, that is, the level in the organisation at which the matter is addressed – at the level of the individual or the organisational level. The vertical dimension reflects the timing of the approach; for example, whether it is a *reactive approach* that aims to equip people to cope with conditions that are stressful, or a *proactive approach* that is concerned with removing or minimising stressors, so that stress is no longer experienced.

Note, however, that Figure 10.5 merely portrays four theoretical categories. In practice these are not mutually exclusive and reactive approaches at either level are usually concerned with coping. Since it is far easier and less disruptive for an organisation to try to change the individual rather than itself (Cooper and Cartwright 1994), even organisational-level initiatives are largely confined to helping people to function under higher levels of stress. Thus it is convenient to commence the discussion at the individual level.

Individual Level Stress Management

Because stress is an individually experienced phenomenon, there is a sense in which all stress management approaches have some focus on the individual, because he/she is the only person who knows whether a particular technique for combating stress works.

Beehr (1995) notes that there are two ways in which an individual can try to cope with stress. By using either:

Level of stress management: whether dealing with stressors is focused at the level of the individual or the level of the organisation

Reactive approach: attempts to help people better cope with the effects of stress after it has occurred

Proactive approach: attempts to remove or lessen the influence of stressors before stress occurs

Figure 10.5
A typology of stress
management
approaches

		LEVEL OF (STRESS MANAGEMENT) FOCUS	
		Individual	Organisation
TIMING OF STRATEGY	Reactive	**Aim**: to equip specific individuals to cope with, or recover from, the effects of stressful conditions after stress has occurred **Example**: stress management techniques	**Aim**: to equip (on request) any individual in the organisation to be able to cope with, or recover from, the effects of stressful conditions as and when encountered **Example**: Employee Assistance Programmes
	Proactive	**Aim**: individuals take action to resist the effects of stressors, or remove stressors from their working environments **Example**: negotiate change to working environment or quit	**Aim**: redesign of the working environment to reduce or eradicate stressors **Example**: structural, operational and role redesign

Control strategy:
a problem-focused
attempt to tackle
the root cause of
stress by changing
the nature of the
situation, to remove
or reduce the impact
of stressors

Escape strategy:
an emotion-focused
attempt to lower the
impact of stressors,
but without trying to
change the nature of
the situation

**Symptom-
management
strategy:** an attempt
to live with, but
mitigate, the effects
of stressors

- an emotion-focused strategy, in which the person reacts to the situation by attempting to remove or lower its emotional effects without actually trying to do anything about the situation itself;
- a problem-focused strategy which attempts to tackle the root cause of stress.

If, for example, a person finds that lack of personal autonomy or the nature of the work is stressful, an emotion-based strategy can be to reconcile him or herself to living with the situation. However, Oakland and Ostell (1996) suggest that a range of other mental and physical behaviours also fall into this category, for example, fantasising, wishful thinking, substance abuse or turning to religion or mysticism. Conversely a problem-focused strategy can be to try to negotiate more interesting work with more responsibility.

A more useful typology is given by Terry (1994), who distinguishes three different strategies:

- the *control strategy*, which broadly corresponds to a problem-focused attempt to take charge of matters by anticipating a continuation of the situation and acting in a way that tries to solve the problem;
- the *escape strategy*, which is roughly equivalent to an emotion-focused approach that involves using thought processes and behaviours that involve accepting the situation in a passive way;
- the *symptom-management strategy*, which consists of using methods that alleviate the effects of the stressors.

To some extent, the strategy a person adopts will depend on prior experiences of its usefulness in similar situations. For this reason, cognitive appraisal of the situation, which was mentioned earlier when considering the moderators of stress, is all-important. The way this process works is portrayed in Figure 10.6, which is based on the ideas of Lazarus and Folkman (1984).

Figure 10.6
Cognitive appraisal and the coping process (after Lazarus and Folkman 1984)

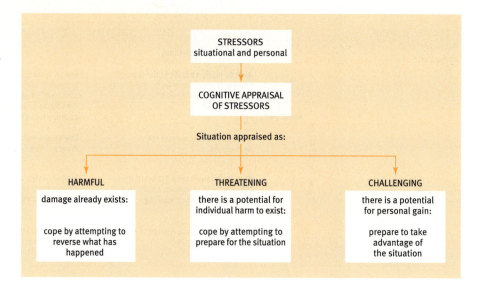

While there is quite strong evidence that individual appraisal of a stressful situation correlates strongly with the choice of coping strategy (Lowe and Bennett 2003), it is not clear which of the three coping strategies is the most effective in different situations (Dewe 1992). Since the vast majority of techniques used fall firmly into the symptom-management category, the remainder of the discussion will be focused on these. They are summarised in Table 10.2 and described in what follows.

Relaxation Techniques

One of the greatest problems for the person suffering from stress is that he or she finds it hard to relax. Thus, anything that can help in this respect is likely to be beneficial. The person could force him or herself to take a holiday, or even be ordered to do so.

Table 10.2 Some personal stress management techniques

Technique	Examples
Relaxation training	Breathing exercises, muscle relaxation
Physical exercise	Jogging, walking, workout in fitness centre
Biofeedback	Take pulse rate, check own breathing rate
Assertiveness training	Learn to reappraise stressful situations and address root causes of problems
Behavioural self-control	Learning how to manage one's own time better, learning how to recognise potentially stressful situations and making plans to cope with them
Seek social support	Discussing stressful situations with colleagues, peers and friends
Professional help	Psychotherapy, counselling etc.

In addition, there are a number of easily taught relaxation techniques that can be used, for instance, breathing exercises and muscle relaxation.

Physical Exercise

Regular physical exercise not only improves blood circulation, lowers blood pressure, muscle tension and cholesterol levels, but it also has more subtle effects. The feeling of general well-being it creates can help combat some of the symptoms of stress and when people are physically tired, they tend to sleep more soundly, which provides periods of intense relaxation and enables them to marshal reserves of energy.

Biofeedback

This is a technique of learning to monitor one's own bodily functioning, sometimes with the help of instruments. In biofeedback people are also taught elementary ways of controlling certain body functions, such as heart rate, muscle tension and blood pressure, all of which can help alleviate some of the symptoms of stress.

Assertiveness Training

Assertiveness should not be confused with aggression. The assertive person is more likely to stand his or her ground and refuse to be trampled on, whereas aggression is often an attempt to trample on someone else. Helping someone to be more assertive is perhaps the one technique that can encourage people to adopt a more problem-focused approach to stress, and there is some evidence that initiatives of this type may be highly beneficial in the long term (Bunce and West 1996). For example, assertive people are more likely to reappraise a stressful situation and try to address its root cause rather than its symptoms.

Behavioural Self-control

The aim here is usually to get people to analyse and take control of their own actions, in this case to identify ways in which their behaviour gives rise to stress. One technique is for people to learn how to manage their time more effectively and prioritise work tasks. Another is for people to learn to recognise situations that put them under stress and make plans for handling them so that the situations are less stressful.

Social Support

Social support has been mentioned earlier, when describing the moderators of stress. Here, people are usually advised to build up networks of colleagues, co-workers and friends, from whom they can receive a sympathetic ear and give the same service in return. While the link between receiving social support and the reduction of stress is complicated, there is fairly strong empirical evidence that it has beneficial effects (Schonfeld 1990) and these are greater when support comes from inside the organisation, rather than from outside (Lim 1996), perhaps because the recipient feels that these people can more readily appreciate the problems.

Professional Help

If all else fails because the level of stress has gone beyond the point where the person can bring about an improvement alone, he/she might need guidance from a clinical expert. This can involve some sort of psychotherapy and, while this might seem to be a drastic step, it must be remembered that in its severest form stress can be so debilitating that people may be incapable of working out what to do to alleviate their symptoms. In situations such as this it can be near impossible for even the most devoted friends or family members to give useful help, and these well-intentioned interventions may actually do harm. Where expert help is needed, a wide variety of techniques, such as behavioural therapies, insight-orientated approaches or even hypnotherapy, may be required. Firth-Cozens and Hardy (1992), who conducted research into the effects of clinical treatment of stress sufferers, report in highly positive terms on the outcomes of these therapies. However, a note of caution is also sounded. While anxiety tends to be lowered and people come to view their job more positively, they are no more tolerant of the organisation for allowing the stressful conditions to exist in the first place.

All of the individual techniques given above have some utility in appropriate circumstances, and the evidence suggests that they can provide a degree of help in coping with workplace stress (Ivancevich *et al.* 1990). Nevertheless, it should be noted that these methods only deal with the symptoms of stress, rather than addressing the stressors that give rise to the malady. Thus, they tend to sweep the real problem under the carpet.

Organisational Level Stress Management

Just as a distinction can be made at the individual level between reactive and proactive approaches, the same is true at the organisational level. To date, it is fair to say that the vast majority of organisational initiatives have been distinctly reactive. They deal with stress in individuals as and when it occurs, deflect responsibility away from the organisation and place it on the shoulders of individuals and, in so doing, allow stressful practices to remain (Dewe and O'Driscoll 2002). To some extent, this is tantamount to shutting the stable door after the horse has bolted – what Berridge *et al.* (1997) call the 'band aid' or inoculation approach. Thus, where they exist, organisational initiatives tend to have a highly reactive element, and the currently fashionable step is to introduce Employee Assistance Programmes (EAPs). These can be defined as:

> **a programmable intervention at the workplace, usually at the level of the individual employee, using behavioural science knowledge and methods for recognition of certain work and non-work related problems (notably alcoholism, drug abuse and mental health) which adversely affect job performance, with the objective of enabling the individual to return to making his or her full work contribution and to attaining full functioning in personal life.** (Cooper and White 1995, p 121)

From the late 1980s onwards, these programmes have increasingly been run by specialist consultancy firms, with the result that the provision of EAP services has become something of a growth industry. However, they are expensive to put in place, and it is probable that a small firm, where the potential for stress could be higher because of the hectic pace of activity, would find an EAP beyond its resources.

Table 10.3 Focal issues for EAPs (after Cooper and White 1995)

Issue	Reason for focus on issue
Decrease in job performance	Can be used to identify individuals suffering from stress
Consultative assistance	Provides help for managers who are responsible for achieving goals and identifies where manager's performance and that of subordinates is critical to achieving goals
Constructive confrontation	To get affected employees to recognise that they are experiencing stress and thus provide the motivation to become involved in EAP activities
Individual micro-level linkages	Develop planned, systematic programmes that help employees to identify how EAP can provide assistance and clarify their individual responsibilities
Macro-level (organisational) linkages	Clarify the organisation's responsibilities (towards employees) and identify how EAP can best be used by the employer
Organisational culture	The existence and use of EAP needs to be incorporated into the organisation's culture
Improved job performance	The criterion of success for the EAP is whether its use results in a sustained improvement in the performance of affected employees

A wide variety of techniques and methods can be deployed in an EAP and, to a large extent, there is a very strong emphasis on the individual methods described above. Cooper and White (1995) note that there are a number of focal issues that need to be addressed in a programme of this type, and these are summarised in Table 10.3.

Table 10.3 tells us that the reason for introducing an EAP is almost always reactive, usually because stress has become noticeable in a large number of employees. However, once installed, there is no reason why an EAP cannot be used to take remedial action at a very early stage with employees who are only just starting to experience stress.

Evidence about the success of stress management training of this type is very mixed (Cooper and Sadri 1991). Although these initiatives are well meaning, they have an inbuilt tendency to put the burden of doing something about stress on the shoulders of the individual. Usually they only provide training and facilities that can be used by individuals to try to avoid becoming stressed, or to cope with an attack of stress, and are probably underpinned by an assumption that organisations are, and will continue to be, more stressful places. Thus, they tend to focus on ways of enabling employees to function in ever more stressful environments.

Turning now to less reactive steps, there is no shortage of advocates of a more proactive organisational approach and, for example, this is the line taken by the Institute of Personnel and Development (IPD 1998). Creating a stress-free workplace is not a simple task, if only because the rapid rate of change makes it difficult to forecast whether future conditions will be stressful. Nevertheless, one of the more encouraging signs about EAPs is that some employers are reported to be looking beyond the need simply to treat stress after it has occurred, and have started to address the issue of making the organisation a less stressful place.

To this end Elkin and Rosch (1990) list a wide range of steps that can be used by organisations as part of a stress reduction strategy, the efficacy of which is well supported by the literature on Organisational Behaviour. Examples of these are:

- redesigning tasks;
- redesigning work environments;
- using more flexible work schedules;
- using more participative management styles;
- involving employees in drawing up career development plans;
- involving employees in establishing their work goals;
- providing social support and feedback;
- building cohesive teams;
- establishing fair employment and rewards practices.

A more comprehensive strategy, which potentially involves both organisational level and individual level measures is suggested in a five-step, problem solving approach given by Cooper and Cartwright (1994), which is shown in outline in Figure 10.7.

Figure 10.7 A five-step problem solving approach to dealing with workplace stress (after Cooper and Cartwright 1994)

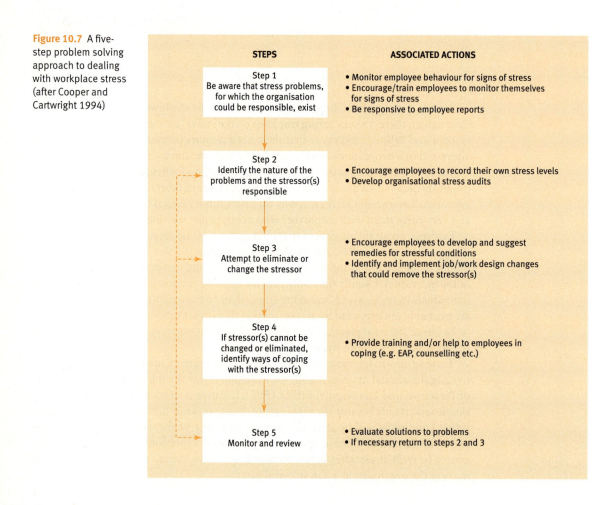

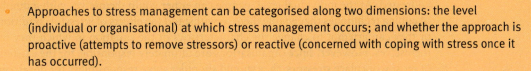

REPLAY

- Approaches to stress management can be categorised along two dimensions: the level (individual or organisational) at which stress management occurs; and whether the approach is proactive (attempts to remove stressors) or reactive (concerned with coping with stress once it has occurred).
- Individual level methods are dominated by reactive strategies.
- Organisational level approaches, for example Employee Assistance Programmes (EAPs), are also dominated by reactive methods that mainly employ individual techniques, but there are signs that some organisations have an interest in more proactive methods.

OVERVIEW AND CONCLUSIONS

Stress is a word used with increasing frequency in organisations and it is doubtful whether the phenomenon can ever be completely eradicated. It is a psycho-physiological defence mechanism through which a person tries to adapt to burdensome external pressures, and where this is not possible, he or she shuts off from the stressors to avoid greater harm. This process is known as the General Adaptive Syndrome, and it has three stages: alarm, resistance and exhaustion.

Workplace stress arises from an interaction between people and their work milieu. Stressors emanate from four main sources: contextual stressors, which are located in the environments of organisations; organisational stressors, which emanate from within the organisation as a whole; stressors in the individual's immediate work context; and, finally, stressors associated with the individual's role. Because conditions outside the workplace can either exacerbate the effects of workplace stressors or ameliorate them, there is a two-way interaction between stressors within and beyond the organisation.

Just as there are several sources of stress, the outcomes of stress can show themselves in many ways: physiologically, in terms of lowered resistance to disease and infection; psychologically, as frustration, aggression, anxiety and depression; cognitively, when thought processes become impaired; and behaviourally, in terms of changes in a person's patterns of behaviour.

Stress is an individually experienced phenomenon and it is unlikely that two people will react to the same set of stressors in exactly the same way, because a number of factors can moderate the impact of stressors, and these can also influence the way that a person tries (or fails) to cope with a stressful situation. There are six important groups of moderators: personal characteristics such as personality; the person's lifestyle and whether this predisposes an individual to stress; the extent and nature of social support available to the individual; the individual's cognitive appraisal of stressors; other life events to which the person is subject; and a number of biographical and occupational variables.

As noted above, stress can never be completely eradicated and there are arguments that a low level of stress is beneficial to humans and improves their functioning.

Nevertheless, it is important to recognise that severe stress can be highly debilitating and, for this reason, individuals and organisations need to explore ways of reducing the potential for stressful conditions to arise, and to find ways of helping people to cope with stress. In general terms there are two levels at which these matters can be addressed. At the individual level, people can either equip themselves with a number of coping techniques that enable them to withstand the effects of stressful conditions, or they can attempt to change the characteristics of the situation in which they find themselves. However, since organisations are ultimately responsible for the existence of most workplace stressors, they should shoulder some responsibility for developing solutions, perhaps with initiatives that make the work milieu a less stressful place. This approach is comparatively rare and for the most part organisations confine themselves to providing assistance for those who already show signs of stress. Thus, most organisations have a regrettable tendency to expect employees to deal with the stress that may have been brought about by the organisation.

FURTHER READING

Beehr, T A (1995) *Psychological Stress in the Workplace*, London: Routledge. A very readable account of the causes, consequences and handling of workplace stress.

Cartwright, S and C L Cooper (1996) *Managing Workplace Stress*, London: Sage. The book gives penetrating insights into stressful workplace events and happenings and explores attempts to alleviate their impact.

Cooper C L (1996) *Handbook of Stress, Medicine and Health*, Boca Raton FI: CRC Press. A book that highlights a great deal of the research that links stress with ill health.

Cooper, C L and M J Davidson (1991) *The Stress Survivors*, London: Grafton Publishing. Although the main focus of the book is on coping with stress, it also deals with many other features of stress at work.

Cooper, C L and R Payne (1988) *Causes, Coping and Consequences of Stress at Work*, Chichester: Wiley. A comprehensive book, the title of which reflects its contents.

Fontana D (1990) *Managing Stress*, New York: Routledge. A useful overview of stress and stress management from an American perspective.

Roney, A and C L Cooper (1997) *Professionals on Workplace Stress*, Chichester: Wiley. This book illustrates the problems of workplace stress that are encountered by a number of professionals, such as medical doctors, human resource managers, academics and lawyers.

REVIEW AND DISCUSSION QUESTIONS

1. It is sometimes asserted that a certain level of stress is necessary to induce high work motivation and performance. Identify the implications of this assertion and the problems associated with putting it into practice.

2. What developments in the last decade have tended to increase stress in organisations and are there any that have tended to decrease it? In the next decade what developments can you foresee as being likely to increase or decrease levels of workplace stress?

3. Which causes of stress are the easiest to identify and which are the hardest to deal with?

4. Explain why different individuals in the same situation can experience different levels of workplace stress.

5. Review the model of burnout given in the chapter and describe the circumstances leading to burnout. Explain why individuals and organisations should be concerned about burnout and what can be done to try to ensure that it does not occur.

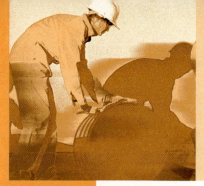

Integrating Individual Characteristics and Processes

Individual characteristics, which distinguish between people in terms of their mental and overt behaviour, were brought together in the previous integrative section, which came after Chapter 5. Since people can differ significantly in terms of their characteristics, it is hardly surprising that there can be a corresponding impact on mental processes such as memory and learning, motivation, decision making and stress that have been covered in the previous five chapters. The task of this integrative section is to trace some of these connections and because job design and its effects on motivation were covered in one of these five chapters, it is convenient to include it here. To trace these links we will follow the same method that was used in the previous integrative section, that is, the individual characteristics will be taken one by one, and some of the links with processes covered in this section of the book will be explored. Note that some of these links are 'two-way' in nature and just as individual characteristics can affect individual processes, in some cases processes can have an impact on characteristics.

LINKS BETWEEN PERSONALITY AND INDIVIDUAL PROCESSES

All personality theories have clear implications for individual motivation. For instance, Freud's (1940) theory of development tells us that whichever of the three components of personality (id, ego, superego) becomes dominant has a huge impact on a person's needs and wants, and the behaviour directed at satisfying them. In addition, research that maps the typical patterns of behaviour of people in each of Eysenck's (1947) four personality types gives strong clues about what is likely to motivate people of each type, and also some indication of their likely decision making styles.

Another link, but this time between personality and decision making, can be seen in Spector's (1982) work on 'locus of control'. To give one example, those with an internal locus like to feel in control of events and, perhaps because of this, they are more likely to be decisive people (DeBrabender and Boone 1990. This, together with Eysenck's results, clearly has implications for the organisational roles for which people of certain personality types are temperamentally most suited and, to some extent, the conditions that are most likely to motivate them. Internals, for example, work better where clear goals are set and incentives are available for good performance (Kren 1992).

There are also likely to be links in the reverse direction. According to Freud, personality is largely the result of subconsciously held memories and so the process of learning affects this important individual characteristic as well.

LINKS BETWEEN INTELLIGENCE AND INDIVIDUAL PROCESSES

As was noted, the way that intelligence is normally measured can mean that it reflects stored experiences as much as anything else, and this is precisely one of the major criticisms of intelligence testing. Moreover, what has been learned and held in the memory creates expectancies that some objects, phenomena or social situations are more likely to exist than others, and this probably has a huge impact on the object recognition stage in perception.

LINKS BETWEEN PERCEPTION AND INDIVIDUAL PROCESSES

As was explained in Chapter 4, if a person has an unsatisfied need, this has a bearing on the environmental features likely to attract his or her attention. Therefore, an individual's motivational state may well have an influence on the person's perceptions.

LINKS BETWEEN ATTITUDES AND INDIVIDUAL PROCESSES

Because attitudes are dynamic in nature and are subject to a degree of change in the light of experience, in one sense an attitude can be regarded as either a characteristic or a process. Strictly speaking, however, it is the change of an attitude that is the process and so it is more convenient to regard an attitude as a characteristic. Nevertheless, the connection between attitudes and processes is likely to be two-way.

Figure 12 Interactions between individual characteristics and processes

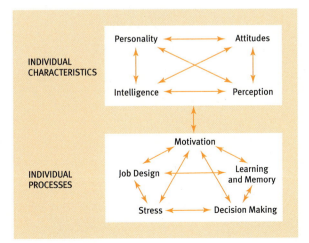

Attitudes are predispositions to behave in certain ways towards certain objects, and have a fairly clear influence on motivation. For example, the cluster of related attitudes known as job satisfaction has been shown to have clear links with labour turnover (Tett and Meyer 1993) and absenteeism (Steele and Rentsch 1995). Direct experience of an object or phenomenon also has a tremendous impact on a person's evaluation and subsequent behaviour towards it (Fishbein and Ajzen 1975). Thus there is also likely to be a strong connection between memory and attitudes.

To summarise, there are clear indications of links between different characteristics, and between characteristics and processes at the individual level. Therefore, the initial model given in Figure I1 at the end of the first integrative section can be expanded to the one given in Figure I2.

As indicated by the diagram, this section of the book consists of four chapters, all of which deal with group level processes. Important as they are, the individual characteristics and processes covered in the previous two sections of the book do not completely explain human behaviour in organisations. For the most part people work in groups and teams and a group exerts a powerful influence on the behaviour of its members. Nevertheless, it is also true that the individual members of a group play a part in deciding what the nature of this influence will be. For this reason there are strong connections between individual and group level matters in an organisation and these are considered in the integrative section that follows Chapter 14.

Section 5: The Organisational Level
Chapter 15: Goals and Effectiveness

Section 4: The Interpersonal Level
Chapter 11: Groups
Chapter 12: Leadership – Basic Theories
Chapter 13: Leadership – Advanced Theories
Chapter 14: Power Politics and Conflict
Integration 3

Chapter 16: Organisational Structure

Chapter 19: Culture and Climate

Section 3: The Intrapersonal Level
Chapter 6: Memory and Learning
Chapter 7: Motivation – The Foundations
Chapter 8: Motivation – Advanced Theories
Chapter 9: Decision Making
Chapter 10: Stress
Integration 2

Chapter 17: Organisational Design

Chapter 20: Communication

Section 2: Individual Characteristics
Chapter 3: Personality and Intelligence
Chapter 4: Perception
Chapter 5: Attitudes
Integration 1

Chapter 18: Control

Chapter 21: Change and Development

Section 1: Introductory Concepts
Chapter 1: Introduction to OB and OA
Chapter 2: Contemporary Challenges

Chapter 22: Globalisation and the Organisation Across Cultures

Integration 4
Integration 5

Chapter 11

Groups

LEARNING OUTCOMES

After studying this chapter you should be able to:

- define the term group, explain why groups are important in organisations and distinguish between formal and informal groups and the functions they perform

- explain why groups are able to influence certain aspects of the behaviour of their members, trace the stages of group development and describe the factors that influence the characteristics of the group that emerges from the development process

- explain the significance of group role structure, norms and cohesiveness

- discuss decision making in groups and explain what is meant by group effectiveness

- identify important factors that influence the relationships between groups and the factors that should be taken into consideration in managing groups

- describe group-based job designs that attempt to utilise the positive features of group functioning

INTRODUCTION

In organisations people spend most of their time in groups, and in one form or another groups are the fundamental building blocks of organisations. Being a group member can have a powerful influence on a person's behaviour, and the behaviour of a group is affected by its individual members. Thus, a knowledge of groups and how they function is vital to understanding the behaviour of people in organisations.

This chapter provides the reader with some of this knowledge. It commences by defining groups and then describes different types of group that are found in organisations. The importance of group membership to individuals is then considered, which is followed by an explanation of the influence that groups exert on the behaviour of their members. The next topic to be explored is the internal processes of groups, first by describing the process of group formation, second, by considering some of the factors that influence the nature of a group and, third, by examining group decision making processes. The matter of group effectiveness is considered next and this is followed by a consideration of relationships between groups.

In appropriate circumstances some of the effects that groups have on their members can be highly beneficial to an organisation. Therefore, the next section of the chapter describes group-based job designs and the chapter concludes with an overview section.

A DEFINITION OF GROUPS

Familiar as it is, the word group does not have a universally accepted meaning, but after Schein (1980), a group is defined in psychological terms as any number of people who:

- interact with each other;
- are psychologically aware of each other;
- perceive themselves to be a group;
- purposefully interact towards the achievement of particular goals or aims.

Three important implications arise from this definition. First, it excludes a collection of people who just happen to be together at the same time and in the same place, for instance, in a queue at a supermarket checkout. Second, since the people must all interact with, and be aware of, each other, in practical terms there is an upper limit on group size; it is very unlikely that everyone in a large department would interact with each other, and neither is it likely that every member would be psychologically aware of all the others. Third, as will be seen later, groups tend to have their own communication and role structures and to be a group, the number of people has to be small enough to permit them to interact, usually face to face. If they interact in pursuit of a common goal, group members are likely to have some sense of shared identity, but this does not mean that the group's goals are necessarily the same as the organisation's objectives. We will return to this final point later, but for the present it is more important to consider the different types of group that are normally found in organisations.

TYPES OF GROUP

Formal Groups

Formal groups:
groups brought into
existence by the
structure of an
organisation

An organisation's structure breaks down its overall task into a number of sub-tasks and makes provision for these activities to be coordinated. This brings *formal groups* into existence. These can be large departments divided into smaller sections, or small departments that are nearer to being groups as defined above. The people who make up these groups are usually allocated to them with very little choice in the matter and one way of making sense of the variety of formal groups that can exist is to classify them according to their relative degrees of permanence.

Command groups:
permanent groups
of people, all under a
single manager, who
perform like activities

Permanent formal groups arise from the relatively fixed structure of an organisation, often because people who perform similar activities are brought together under a single manager, for which the term *command groups* is sometimes used. Relatively permanent groups of people all of the same level are also commonplace, for instance, boards of directors. In most organisations, structure establishes clear connections between groups, and one interesting theory views an organisation as an elaborate set of overlapping groups (Likert 1961). In Likert's view, as well as being in charge of subordinates the supervisor or manager of a group is also a subordinate member of a group at the next level upwards, and should act as a linking pin to facilitate coordination upwards, downwards and sideways. This is illustrated in Figure 11.1.

Most current organisations have a strong emphasis on flexible structures and downsizing and delayering initiatives have resulted in a widespread use of temporary formal groups. For instance, *task groups* might be formed temporarily to tackle a specific problem or special project, and be dispersed as soon as the task is completed. While this can be a very useful device to deal with a one-off issue, its usefulness crucially depends on how quickly the people transform themselves into a well-functioning group, a matter that will be considered in some depth later.

Task groups:
temporary formal
groups formed for a
specific short-term
purpose

Teams: strongly task-
orientated formal
groups

A term that is also encountered frequently in the literature on organisations is that of '*teams*'. Indeed, these days, the virtues of teams and teamworking are extolled very widely (Katzenbach and Smith 1993). Teams can be permanent or temporary and a 'team' would conform to the definition of a group given above. The way the term is used in the organisational literature, however, makes it easier to think of a team as a distinctive class of group that is highly task orientated (Adair 1986). Thus, teams are

Figure 11.1
Overlapping structure
of groups and linking
pins (after Likert 1961)

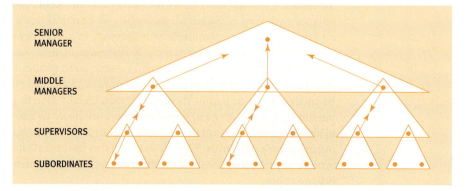

essentially formal groups that are very good at achieving the goals and objectives set for them by the organisation.

Informal Groups

Whether they are permanent or temporary, formal groups have two things in common:

- they exist because someone at a high level has decided that they are necessary to achieve specific aims and objectives;
- people are conscripted into membership.

In most organisations there is usually an informal structure that parallels the formal one, and this is made up of informal groups that exist for different purposes. While people primarily work for organisations to earn a living, they also have social needs and informal groups often play a crucial part in satisfying these social needs. Because membership of an informal group is voluntary, and only happens if existing group members consent to a new person being admitted, an informal group can often exert a far more powerful influence on a person's behaviour than a formal one. These groups often exist because a formal group does not satisfy people's psychological needs (Argyris 1964) and, sometimes, informal groups can take on a life of their own. While this can prompt the manager of a formal group to feel that he or she lacks control, the disruptive potential of informal groups is probably exaggerated and whether an informal group has a positive or negative effect often depends on whether the manager of a formal group recognises why the informal one has come into existence (Hussein 1989).

THE MEANING AND FUNCTIONS OF GROUPS

Whether it is formal or informal, group membership has a strong psychological impact on most people. From an organisation's standpoint there are certain advantages in bringing people together into groups, six of which are listed by Schein (1980):

- working on complex tasks that are not easily undertaken by an individual;
- as a means of stimulating creativity and generating new ideas;
- to act as a liaison/coordination mechanism which integrates different parts of an organisation;
- for problem solving purposes, where multiple viewpoints are important;
- to implement decisions, that is, so that a common objective or goal can be set for a number of people;
- as socialising devices, so that a common message, especially with respect to an organisation's culture, can be communicated and reinforced.

However, these are formal functions and Schein also gives a number of less formal but extremely important functions that groups perform for their members. They:

- fulfil social needs for friendship and interaction;
- allow people to develop, test and confirm their sense of identity and self-worth;
- allow people to establish and test beliefs, reality, experience and meanings;
- reduce feelings of insecurity, anxiety and powerlessness;
- allow people to achieve mutually agreed informal aims and objectives.

Although these two sets of functions might look like separate lists, they strongly complement each other. People usually have no choice about the formal group to which they are allocated, but even so, the group can fulfil some of the informal functions. Working with others on a complex task usually requires people to share their definitions and meanings, which helps them to test reality, reduce anxiety and confirm a sense of identity, and sharing ideas with other people also allows individuals to know what is going on in the organisation. To some extent working together results in people absorbing a group's culture and, providing this does not conflict with the culture of the organisation, there can be highly beneficial outcomes. For example, commitment to the aims of a local constituency (group) can bring about a degree of commitment to the organisation as a whole. In addition, the opportunity to engage in meaningful interactions with other people can be a source of stimulation that allows people to tolerate the nature of tedious, repetitive and boring work.

However, these effects are not likely to be the same everywhere. As will be seen in Chapter 22, in some countries, notably Japan, the national culture is such that people derive a great deal of their personal identity from the groups to which they belong, whereas in Great Britain or the USA, people are much more individualistic. Thus, it is only to be expected that these effects will be much stronger in collectivist cultures such as Japan than will be the case in many Western cultures.

TIME OUT

Identify at least two groups of which you are a member. One should be a formal group, for example, people you work with on a regular basis either in your employment or at college. The other should be a more informal group that only exists because its members decide to associate with each other. Now look carefully at the two lists of functions of groups given above, and answer the following questions.

1. To what extent does the formal group facilitate the formal functions being achieved?
2. To what extent does the formal group fulfil some of the informal functions?
3. Although the informal group probably has no explicit formal functions, are there any that it seems to have adopted?
4. To what extent does the informal group provide for meeting the informal functions of its members?

GROUP INFLUENCES ON INDIVIDUAL BEHAVIOUR

A group can have many influences on its members, perhaps the most significant of which is that individuals stifle their own preferences in favour of the group's code of behaviour.

The evidence about individual conformity is unequivocal and some of this will be described presently. What is not quite so clear is why people conform. One way of making sense of this phenomenon is to adopt a social exchange theory perspective (Blau

Figure 11.2 The basic social exchange process

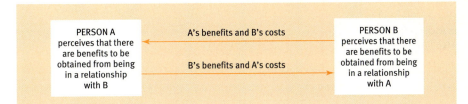

Figure 11.2 The basic social exchange process

1964) and start at a simplified level by considering a group of two people (dyad), shown in Figure 11.2.

Social exchange theory acknowledges that the basic motivation to enter into a relationship with someone else is the expectation of obtaining rewards of some sort. However, the problem is that both people expect to derive benefits and, if the relationship is to be worthwhile, each one has to provide something for the other. This means that as well as getting benefits they both incur costs and, to ensure that they continue to receive benefits, each person has to continue to meet the costs, which tells us why groups are able to exert control over the behaviour of their members.

Individuals derive several practical and psychological benefits from group membership, but to continue to receive benefits, each one has to be trusted by the others to incur his or her costs. One of the most visible ways that a person can demonstrate trustworthiness is to abide by *group norms*, that is, the rules that the group has evolved to regulate how individuals will behave towards each other. This makes everybody's behaviour more predictable, which in turn makes it easier for people to trust each other. Thus, one reason (perhaps the main reason) why a group is able to exert an influence over the behaviour of an individual is the unvoiced implication that the benefits of membership will be withdrawn unless he or she observes the group's norms of behaviour.

Group norms: the rules of behaviour adopted by the members of a group

Because any group has a vested interest in trying to ensure that the conduct of a new member is predictable, these principles are equally applicable to a larger group. Indeed, evidence shows quite clearly that groups that have developed a distinctly antisocial climate quickly induce new members to behave in the same way, and the longer a person remains within the group, the greater is the tendency for the person to adopt these patterns of behaviour (Robinson and O'Leary-Kelly 1998).

Different groups tend to evolve their own unique ways of getting new members to conform and some of these will be described later in the chapter. For the present it is more important to examine the rather surprising degrees of conformity that groups can obtain and to do this three classic, and by now venerable, research studies will be described.

The Asch Experiments

In the Asch (1951) studies groups of six people (the members of which were apparently selected at random) were shown a line drawing similar to the one illustrated in Figure 11.3. Individuals were asked to state which of the other vertical lines most closely matched the length of the reference line 'A'. Unbeknown to the one true subject in the

Figure 11.3
Line drawing used
in Asch conformity
experiments

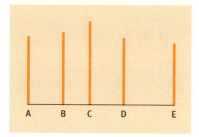

group, the other five members were confederates of the experimenter and all had been instructed to respond unanimously with a judgement that was incorrect.

The true subject either had to agree with the rest of the group or contradict them. Even when subjects were initially hesitant about giving an incorrect answer, over one-third eventually agreed in public with the group's judgement, and only where a supporting 'ally' was planted in the group was resistance continued. This illustrates the capability of a group to obtain conformity, even where conforming means making a public statement that a person knows to be untrue. In these experiments the participants were comparative strangers, which only adds weight to the conformity effect. In a close-knit group that had existed for some time, the pressures to conform would probably be even greater.

Sherif's Experiment

This work (Sherif 1936) demonstrates that a group can bring about conformity, even to the extent of shaping individual perceptions. Subjects were placed in a darkened room and asked to track a small spot of light projected on to a screen, and to report its direction of movement as either upwards, downwards, diagonally to the right or the left. This is a difficult task because 'autokinetic effects' tend to result in perceptual distortions, in which the light appears to move when it is really stationary. Thus there were often wide initial differences in what individuals reported. Where group members were allowed to exchange information before making the judgement, they all tended to report the same direction of travel. When the size of a group was increased the tendency to conform became much stronger, probably because a nonconformist finds it much harder to resist if his or her opinions conflict with many people rather than just a few.

The Milgram Studies

In the first phase of Milgram's (1965) study volunteers were asked to take part in what was described as 'an experiment to investigate the effects of punishment on learning'. They were asked to sit at a table and to converse through a microphone with an unseen individual in another room. On the table there was a control dial, and subjects were informed that this enabled them to regulate the voltage of an electric shock, which would be given to the unseen person. Using the microphone, the subject read out a printed passage of text to the other person, who then had to repeat the passage. If a wrong answer was given, the subject was instructed by the experimenter to administer an electric shock, the purpose of which was said to be 'to assist learning'. For each successive wrong answer the subject was required to increase the voltage, which was clearly labelled on the control panel as varying between 'light shock' and 'danger: extreme intensity'.

Subjects were unaware that the person in the other room did not actually receive an electric shock, but was a 'stooge' who had merely been instructed to give clear, audible signs of receiving a shock. Nevertheless, so far as the subjects were concerned, the other person received a shock which caused a great deal of distress and pain. Screams were clearly heard, and occasionally there was a period of complete silence, from which subjects inferred that the person had collapsed. Many subjects baulked at the task, particularly when there were pleas to terminate the experiment. Nevertheless, the experimenter pressed them to keep increasing the voltage, if necessary, up to the maximum and, despite their reluctance, most subjects did exactly as ordered. This phase of the studies clearly demonstrates that most people have strong tendencies to obey the instructions of an authority figure.

For a further series of experiments, there was a slight change in procedure. During the first phase subjects had been kept apart so that they could not communicate, but in the second phase they were allowed to socialise over a coffee break. Most of them had an initial reluctance to discuss what had taken place, but the longer they were allowed to mix, the more likely it was that the truth would come out. The net effect was that they became more willing to defy the authority of the experimenter and many refused to continue with the experiment. Thus Milgram's results demonstrate that conformity can extend to resisting authority and this can have important implications for organisations.

When a person conforms to a group's behavioural expectations, he or she is given the stamp of legitimacy by the group. Almost all formal groups are placed under an appointed authority figure, who is granted a degree of power by the organisation, but if a group does not legitimise this person's actions, extremely potent forces are unleashed which can result in resistance to authority.

TIME OUT

Reflect on an informal group of which you are a member. This could be a group at your place of work or at college.

1. Try to identify any rules of behaviour that the group seems to have evolved, that is, ways of behaving that it expects everybody in the group to observe.
2. What evidence have you that these norms exist? For example, what happens if somebody breaks one of these rules?
3. How do members of the group go about ensuring that someone who breaks one of these rules, either inadvertently or consciously, conforms in the future?

- A group is a number of people who interact, are aware of each other, perceive themselves to be a group, and purposefully interact to achieve goals or aims.
- The existence of formal groups is sanctioned by the organisation, whereas informal groups primarily exist to serve the needs of their members.
- Formal groups serve two main sets of functions: those concerned with achieving organisational ends and those concerned with serving the social and psychological needs of their members.
- Irrespective of an individual's personal characteristics or inclinations, groups are able to enforce a degree of conformity to the behavioural norms of the group in their members.

GROUP FORMATION AND DEVELOPMENT

It takes time for strangers to fuse together into a cohesive group and two different approaches can be used to explain this transformation. The first explains the stages of development of a group and the second maps out factors that influence what sort of group emerges. In the interests of clarity these will be presented separately, and over-all conclusions drawn afterwards.

The Stages of Development Approach

Although several different 'stage' models of group development have been proposed, the best known is Tuckman's (1965) integrative model, which suggests that groups normally pass through a number of stages before they function effectively. These are explained in what follows and while most groups develop in this way, there are exceptions, which will be discussed later. It should also be remembered that these stages seldom occur in a single meeting, and it can take weeks or even months before the final one is reached.

Forming: the first stage of group development, in which it is essentially a collection of individuals

Stage 1: Forming

People coming together for the first time are little more than a collection of individuals, particularly when they are strangers. At best they may recognise that they have come together to achieve something, but have no clear consensus about what it is, or how it will be done. As such there would be little focus on completing the task. They will probably devote more attention to getting to know each other, perhaps by testing others out, making tentative bids for the roles or positions they will like to occupy, or trying to create a personal impression. Nevertheless, they are likely to recognise that they have to achieve something, and towards the end of this stage a tentative exploration of the job that has to be done and how it will be undertaken will emerge. To reach this point, however, the social interaction and testing outlined above needs to have taken place.

Stage 2: Storming

Storming: the second stage of group development, which is characterised by interpersonal conflict

In this stage people become more aware of each other and are willing to bring their views into the open. This sometimes occurs in a very forceful way as individuals make bids for territory and position in the group and, as these personal agendas and goals surface, a degree of interpersonal hostility and conflict can emerge as people compete to get their ideas adopted. This is often a highly uncomfortable stage for everybody concerned. Sometimes the bonds and alliances made in the first stage are broken, and new ones are formed. Although it seldom seems so at the time, this stage has a highly positive function, because before convergence can take place, it is usually necessary for polarised views to come out into the open, and unless this happens, differences can remain beneath the surface as unresolved problems. This stage is vital if the group is eventually to fuse into one that can effectively accomplish its task, and if it is not skilfully handled, the group can fragment into cliques or cabals that carry on the battle afterwards. However, if the group successfully comes through this stage, it is ready to pass on to the next one, which is often much more comfortable and rewarding for those involved.

Stage 3: Norming

Norming: the third stage of group development, in which ground rules for a group's way of functioning begin to emerge

In this stage conflict and hostility subside and there is a sharper focus on the task in hand. The people start to hammer out what it must accomplish and the methods it will use. As well as having a stronger focus on the task, the nature of the interaction between members also changes. Signs of cooperation and sensitivity to others start to appear and the rules for social interaction are established. Although these are not set down in a formal way, they become the code of conduct that regulates group activities and makes future behaviour more predictable. This all helps to reduce future ambiguities and gives the group a firmer foundation that makes it ready to pass into the next stage.

Stage 4: Performing

Performing: the final stage of group development, in which the group becomes capable of effective functioning

Structures and procedures are now in place and the group is ready to get on with the job in hand. If it has successfully passed through the previous three stages, and resolved the problems and issues inherent in each one, the task aspects and the social aspects of the group complement each other. Members are not only mutually supportive and flexible, but have also learned to trust each other and the group is better equipped to perform its role effectively.

Adjourning: the group is disbanded

In a later development Tuckman and Jensen (1977) identify a further stage: *adjourning*. This refers to the disbanding of the group, perhaps because people move on, or because its task has been completed. Almost by definition, teamworking is only possible for groups that have successfully reached the fourth stage, which means that they are relatively cohesive. Because people tend to reflect nostalgically on their positive feelings about the group's achievements and other group members, adjournment is said to be characterised by sadness and anxiety, and this can be particularly relevant in today's conditions where the use of temporary groups and teams is commonplace.

The idea of a sequence of stages such as those in Tuckman's model is widely accepted but, while most new groups probably go through a similar process, there are exceptions. In some circumstances it is possible that all four stages occur together. For example, if the task in hand is so pressing that something needs to be done immediately, the group may have to pitch in and resolve task problems and its own process together. Similarly, there may be circumstances which make it unnecessary for the group to pass through the stages. An example is an airline cockpit crew. These people can sometimes be complete strangers who have never worked together before, but because they customarily come together with clear definitions of their respective roles and responsibilities, they form into a small, highly effective group in less than ten minutes (Ginnett 1990).

Tuckman's scheme gives a useful set of guidelines for anyone who is charged with starting up a new group and guiding its development. It also reveals why some groups fail to cohere and become effective. This is often because one of the first three stages has not been successfully completed, which leaves unresolved issues or emotional baggage lurking beneath the surface. Thus, it is important to allow sufficient time for each stage, and the person in charge of the group needs the patience to allow the process to run at its own pace. It is also useful if a group leader can recognise when a stage has been successfully concluded, so that matters can progress to the next one, and where

CASE STUDY 11.1: The IT Task Force

The IT Task Force is a small, *ad hoc*, multi-functional team brought together in a large retailing chain that has its headquarters just outside Paris. Senior management have appointed Pierre Blaumot to lead the team and its brief is to consider the information technology needs of the firm for the next five years and to report to senior management with a suggested IT strategy, within three months of its first meeting. The team includes representatives from all the major IT user departments, as well as computing experts in the firm. Clearly the people come from very diverse functional backgrounds and are more used to the different ways of working that exist in their own departments. Pierre is conscious of this from the start but, since their results are due within a relatively short time scale, he has adopted a working maxim at the first meeting of the group. This is that 'meetings are not the proper place at which to try to get work done, but a place where people receive jobs to do, and to which they report back with the results'. Nevertheless, before getting down to the agenda that he has drawn up, at the first meeting he allows 30 minutes for people to introduce themselves and to state the concerns of the departments they represent. For the remainder of this meeting and those that follow, there is a constant tendency for people to argue. Thus, two months into the life of the group people are still arguing about what is meant by the term 'an IT strategy for the firm'. His response to wrangles of this nature has been to impose his own definition and to keep matters moving. However, the arguments persist and, because people keep trying to thrust their own definitions forward about what the strategy should embrace, no clear definition has yet emerged, much less how to go about devising the strategy.

Question

What do you feel has gone wrong here?

Figure 11.4 Homans'
model of work group
formation

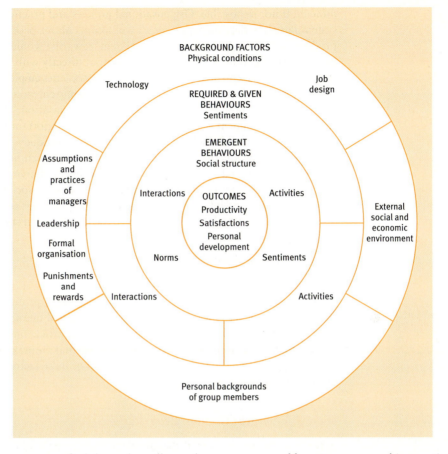

managers find themselves allocated to temporary, *ad hoc* groups or working parties,
this can be particularly important. Because it stands in the way of resolving important
social issues, too early a focus on the group's task to the exclusion of everything else
is, therefore, to be avoided.

The Outcomes of Development Approach

Some of the important characteristics of a group arise from an interplay between the
group and its environment. Since the processes at work are extremely complex and it
is not possible to give more than an overview of what occurs, a simplified version of a
comprehensive explanation, Homans' model of work group behaviour (1950), will be
used. This is shown in Figure 11.4. Starting from the outside and working inwards, the
model can be used to explain some of the characteristics that emerge. In this example,
a group of employees doing highly routine work on an assembly line will be used.

Stage 1: Background Contextual Factors

These are shown on the periphery of the model, which is divided into four segments.
Physical conditions, technology and **job design** have a huge impact on an assembly line
group because the repetitive, machine-paced nature of the job makes social interaction

difficult, if not impossible. **Organisational policies and practices** built into the work system largely reflect management's assumptions about people. For example, with production line workers, the payment system (rewards) would probably be designed to encourage maximum effort by linking output directly with pay, which says something about management's assumptions of what motivates employees. Strict rules about timekeeping and duration of meal breaks can be firmly enforced by supervisors, which says a great deal about the climate of trust in the organisation. The **external social and economic environment** of the workplace is another important factor. If the workers are employed by a firm which has a high demand for its products, managers will emphasise keeping the production line working at full pace, which has some impact on the workplace rules noted above. Finally, workers bring their own **personal backgrounds** into the workplace, for example, their values, expectations, social norms and attitudes, and these also have an influence on the nature of the group that emerges. All four groups of background factors interact to influence those in the next stage of the model.

Stage 2: Required and Given Behaviours

These consist of the behaviours and sentiments the organisation seeks to obtain from group members. In the example used here, management probably considers it essential that people's **activities** conform to tightly specified tasks, and that they confine their **interactions** with each other to passing on an article once work has been performed on it. The **sentiments** expected are probably that the maximum amount of effort will be expended on the task in hand. Again, all of these factors interact to influence those at the next stage.

Stage 3: Emergent (Actual) Behaviours

In the example used so far, if the group were observed very closely both on and off the production line, certain **sentiments** and **behavioural norms** may be seen to be at work. The work itself, together with the severe style of supervision can give rise to a tacit norm that since management views employees as motivated solely by money, then this is how they will behave. Thus, they may collectively refuse to accept any change to the job unless there is a guarantee that it will have no effect on earnings. In addition, certain **activities** and **interactions** can emerge to reinforce this cohesive spirit. The people will probably take their meal breaks together, and give each other covert support in escaping the drudgery of the line for short periods. The group is also likely to evolve a social structure. For instance, they may well have an unofficial leader or spokesperson to deal with management and, if the workforce is unionised, this may become an official union representative (shop steward) role. Perhaps most important of all, since the group has evolved a social structure as well as stable norms and patterns of behaviour, anyone joining as a new member will be quickly induced to conform. Thus the emergent behaviour on the part of a group can have a huge impact in terms of the outcomes, which are shown in the centre of the model.

Stage 4: Outcomes

In the example used here, so long as group members earn enough to satisfy their needs, **productivity** may well be the lowest level that they can get away with without attracting management attention. **Satisfaction** will largely be found in what small opportunities exist for them to interact as a group, and **personal development** will be negligible, except in finding new ways to 'beat the system'. Management and supervision will probably be aware of these things, and the paradox is that while management's assumptions play a huge part in shaping the outcomes, these assumptions are unlikely to be questioned. Instead, the outcomes are more likely to be taken as evidence by management that their assumptions are correct, and even tighter supervision and control will result.

Although the circumstances described in this example do not apply to all employees, they should not be dismissed as impossible. In industries where assembly line techniques are used, these conditions often persist (Walker and Guest 1957), which perhaps explains the ongoing interest in work methods that allow employees a degree of autonomy and decision making (see Chapter 7).

Integrating the Tuckman and Homans Perspectives

As noted earlier, Tuckman and Homans deal with different aspects of group behaviour: Tuckman focuses on the sequential stages of development that groups pass through before becoming effective as a unit, while Homans explains how contextual circumstances can affect a group's characteristics. Nevertheless, the perspectives complement each other, and there are valuable lessons to learn from considering both together. To give an example, consider the effects of the 'physical conditions, technology and job design' factors in the Homans model. These can limit member interactions, which inhibits the process of group formation. In the example used to explain the Homans model, this results in interactions away from the job, which gives a strong incentive for people to coalesce into an informal group that has norms which run counter to organisational objectives. Teamworking, which currently receives a great deal of emphasis, requires groups that are at stage four of their development in the Tuckman scheme, and for this to occur, groups need environments in which they can pass through the stages of development, and jobs that are conducive to them working with the organisation rather than against it. While these conditions are present in some organisations, they do not exist everywhere. In addition, getting the best from groups also requires an understanding of the ways in which a mature group functions, and this is explored in what follows.

REPLAY

- Most groups pass through a number of sequential stages before emerging as an effective unit.
- The characteristics of individual members influence the sentiments, norms and patterns of behaviour of a group; the context within which a group exists also has a powerful influence on these characteristics.
- Developmental factors and contextual factors both need to be considered if working groups are to be effective.

OB IN ACTION: Swarming

Swarming, a technique pioneered by the US army, is emerging as a peer-to-peer (P2P) networking technique to help civilian organisations reduce the time needed to react to new business opportunities. It was devised to enable small forces to coordinate with each other directly, rather than through a central command post, which cut the time needed to plan military operations from 10 hours to just 10 minutes, by allowing networks in the field to talk to each other and make snap decisions.

In swarming, employees use P2P collaboration tools to pull together an ad hoc team of people from anywhere in an organisation – or even outside it – to work on a specific task. When problems arise a team can add new members with the additional skills required, and the team's composition evolves until the project is successfully completed. To large companies the potential prize is worth billions of dollars. The breakthrough technology (P2P) links individuals around the world into a unit with a common focus very quickly, whereas alternative collaboration systems, which are based on centralised servers, are unsuitable because they are relatively inflexible and require too much time-consuming administration before new members can be added.

For example, when account managers at HP Services receive requests for proposals from potential customers, they invite technical architects, product specialists and other experts from all over the world into a swarm in a matter of minutes, using a P2P collaboration platform called Groove, which cuts the time needed to generate a response by up to 60 per cent. In addition, Lowe & Partners Worldwide, an international advertising agency, uses swarming to generate creative ideas for new business proposals by bringing together appropriate staff from offices around the world. Clearly security is important and while P2P technology allows traffic to pass through corporate firewalls, it uses 192 bit encryption which can't be turned off and is approved by the US government. Thus the system could be used with a Wi-Fi connection in an internet café and still be highly secure. While several armies worldwide have adopted swarming, corporate adoption of P2P technology has been slow. But as it becomes more common it seems likely that it will be used with increasing frequency as a business tactic.

Source:

Rubens, P (2003) Army Tactics are the Business, *The Financial Times*, 26 November.

GROUP CHARACTERISTICS

A group that successfully emerges from its process of development is said to have 'matured'. However, even mature groups that perform similar functions often have unique characteristics that distinguish one from another, the three most important and noticeable of which are structure, norms and cohesiveness.

Group Structure

For a group to accomplish something, individual activities have to be linked and coordinated in some way. Since individuals differ in their capabilities and inclinations, some division of labour is usually necessary and this results in a group structure. There are many ways of describing these structural arrangements, but here three different aspects of structure will be explained: role structure, status structure and communication structure.

Role Structure

Role theory uses a dramaturgical analogy to explain human behaviour and *role* is defined here as:

a set of expectations and obligations to act in specific ways in certain contexts.

Role has much the same connotations in a group situation as it has in a dramatic setting: it permits people to know roughly how others will behave, and to play their own parts in what happens. To use a dramatic analogy, imagine yourself playing Juliet and speaking 'Oh Romeo, Romeo! wherefore art thou Romeo?' only to find that the reply you get is from *Macbeth*: 'Double, double toil and trouble'. Ridiculous as it is, the analogy makes two important points:

* unless a person knows the requirements of a role, the part cannot be played properly: for example, it is Juliet's role to stand on the balcony and summon Romeo;
* the whole performance breaks down unless other role occupants play their allotted roles; Juliet's words require an appropriate response from Romeo, not the three witches in *Macbeth*.

Thus, in playing roles, people are involved in 'trading performances' (Goffman 1971).

The allocation of group roles usually occurs during the processes of formation and the role a person comes to occupy can be influenced by a number of factors, generally a combination of:

* **functional factors**   the tasks that will need to be performed in the group; the relative status that people bring with them into membership; influence or authority compared to other people; and position in the necessary communication network of the group;
* **personal factors**   the personality, attitudes, skills and abilities of the people.

In formal groups job descriptions usually lay down certain aspects of a role. However, these only specify 'what' should be done, not 'how' it should be done, and because a role is a set of expectations and obligations to act in a specific way, the *how* is as important as the *what*.

People are seldom completely free to choose their own roles and to explain this, consider a formal group of twelve people working under a manager in a design office. The office is subdivided into three sections and each section leader is in charge of a group of four subordinates. Imagine that you are one of these section leaders and that as part of the job you have to interact with a fairly large number of people:

Figure 11.5 The role set of the section leader

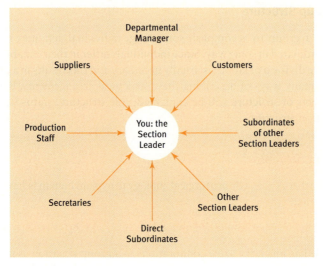

Departmental Manager

Suppliers

Customers

Production Staff

You: the Section Leader

Subordinates of other Section Leaders

Secretaries

Other Section Leaders

Direct Subordinates

Role senders: individuals who have behavioural expectations of a role occupant

Role set: the total of all role senders for a given role

Role expectations: the role occupant's expectations about what the role entails

Altercasting: the process of tacit negotiation between a role occupant and senders about behaviour which is acceptable to both

Expected role problems: a clash between role sender and role occupant about the content of their respective roles

Perceived role problems: a misinterpretation by a role occupant of a role sender's expectations

Enacted role problems: inappropriate role behaviour

- those in the design office;
- people in other departments;
- people outside the firm, for instance customers and suppliers.

All of these people will have some expectations about what you will do and how you will do it. They are the *role senders*, who make up your total *role set*. An example of a role set is shown in Figure 11.5.

Unlike an actor on a stage, you have no formal script to tell you how to behave, so how do you find out what the role is? Initially you will probably have your own opinions and your behaviour will reflect this. Your behaviour sends a signal to members of the role set about your *role expectations*. There will almost certainly be clues from other people about what is appropriate, for example, that the office manager should be shown a certain amount of deference, that other section leaders should be treated as equals and that subordinates will need to be able to approach you for advice and help. Over time, each role occupant constructs a sort of 'working agreement' about the general form of the relationship with all of these role senders. McCall and Simmons (1966) call this *altercasting*: a process in which people cast themselves and others in roles which are then tacitly negotiated and firmed up by imputation and improvisation.

Sometimes, however, things can go disastrously wrong. There can be *expected role problems*, in which there is a clash between role sender and role occupant about what is an appropriate relationship. In other cases there can be *perceived role problems* because sender and role occupant misinterpret each other's signals, and this results in *enacted role problems* of inappropriate role behaviours.

Agreeing on roles can sometimes be a long, drawn-out process and in the early stages of group development poorly conveyed and misinterpreted messages are quite common. This explains why the storming and norming stages need sufficient time to run their course. Even when these matters are resolved, if a group's task or function changes, or new people enter the group, the system of roles can be thrown into disarray and a

Role ambiguity: the role occupant is unsure of the requirements of his or her role

Role conflict: a clash between the different sets of role expectations

Task leader: the person who occupies the role concerned with ensuring that a group completes its task

Socio-emotive (group maintenance) leader: the person who ensures that group members have their social needs catered for

Guardians: group members who shield the group from external pressure

Scouts: group members who maintain contact with their environment and import information

Ambassadors: group members who represent a group with other groups

number of other problems can arise. One of these is *role ambiguity*, which occurs when a person is unsure of the requirements of a role (Katz and Kahn 1978), often because there is a lack of clarity about what is expected in terms of tasks to be performed or how to go about performing them.

Another problem is *role conflict*, which covers any situation where there is a clash between the multiple expectations of different role senders. Here a role occupant who tries to meet one set of expectations will find it difficult to meet the expectations of others. Because people usually find it stressful to perform an unclear role, this leads to very low levels of job satisfaction and job performance. Role conflict of any type can have serious consequences for both organisations and individuals (Fisher and Gitelson 1983).

Status Structure

While there is no foolproof way of predicting what roles will emerge, a feature that is almost inevitable is a hierarchy of authority, with a leader or head at the top. If the group is a formal one, this person is normally appointed by someone higher in the organisation, which gives the role occupant a degree of formal authority over other group members. Note that there are crucial differences between 'heads' and 'leaders', not the least of which is the consent of subordinates to be led. Thus, putting someone in charge of a group does not ensure that he or she will occupy a role of leadership. For this reason, it is not unusual to find that more than one leadership role emerges in a group:

- a *task leader* (or *specialist*), who ensures that the group completes its task (Bales 1950);
- a *socio-emotive* or *group maintenance leader*, who ensures that group members have their social needs catered for.

From then on, and according to the group's needs, other roles, which are seldom formally appointed, start to emerge. Three of the most noticeable and necessary roles are:

- *guardians*, who perform the role of shielding the group against external pressures;
- *scouts*, who maintain contact with the group's environment and import vital information;
- *ambassadors*, who represent the group across its boundaries and often negotiate with other groups.

Communication Structure

Another important aspect of structure is its internal communication channels. Bavelas (1950) identifies five prominent patterns of communication found in groups, and these are shown in Figure 11.6.

An investigation by Leavitt (1951) reveals that each of these has certain advantages and disadvantages:

- since the Y and wheel patterns have a focal point through which messages pass, the person in this role tends to emerge as the group's leader;

Figure 11.6 Group communication structures (after Bavelas 1950)

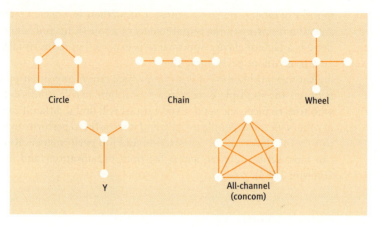

- since a single person receives and distributes all information, the wheel and Y patterns are also the fastest means of communication and give rise to fewer distorted messages;
- if a group's task is highly complex and requires a great deal of interaction between all members, the circle and all-channel structures, which involve everybody, can be the most effective and often result in the highest degree of member satisfaction;
- the chain is usually the slowest structure of all and is prone to 'Chinese-whisper' effects that distort messages.

Group Norms

These provide group members with a code of conduct to guide their actions in terms of behaviour that is important to the group. The four most important functions they serve are identified by Feldman (1984) as:

- making life more predictable, because people know what behaviour is expected of them, so that time is not wasted in continual renegotiation of roles and the group can function smoothly;
- as an expression of the central attitudes, values and beliefs of a group, which projects the group's self-image beyond its boundaries, and signals something about its nature to those outside;
- facilitating group survival, for example by ensuring that the majority subscribe to the idea that, if a member's behaviour threatens the group's integrity, he or she should be brought into line;
- avoiding embarrassing problems and issues that can disrupt the group's smooth functioning.

In general, however, norms will exist with regard to two aspects of group life:

- norms about ends, which specify what the group should achieve and give it some degree of consensus about what constitutes success or failure;
- norms about means, which signal behaviour that is considered acceptable in achieving the ends.

Although task performance is important, there are usually limits to which a group will go to achieve success and so both types of norm are necessary. For instance, while member flexibility can improve task performance, if this means that people can be made redundant, the group will probably place limits on its willingness to be flexible. Therefore, norms can work in favour of an organisation or against it, and it is unwise to assume that a group's norms necessarily coincide with organisational rules and procedures.

TIME OUT

Reflect carefully on a group of which you are a member, either at your place of work or at university or college.

1. Identify any distinct roles that have emerged in the group, for example, are there guardians, gatekeepers or scouts?
2. What is your own role in the group?
3. Does role ambiguity or role conflict ever arise for you and, if so, what type of ambiguity or conflict occurs?
4. Does the group have one leader or more than one?
5. What sort of communication structure does the group have?
6. Are there any distinct norms of behaviour for group members? Are these norms about ends or norms about means?

Group cohesiveness: the attractiveness of a group to its members and their desire to retain membership

Group Cohesiveness

The cohesiveness of a group is something that is often immediately obvious and it can be defined as:

> **the attractiveness of the group to its members, together with their motivation to remain as part of the group and resist leaving it.**   **(Piper *et al*. 1983, p 3)**

Because cohesiveness tends to have very strong effects on performance, it is a characteristic that has received a great deal of attention and it is strongly influenced by three sets of factors: those associated with the group itself; those associated with its immediate environment; and those associated with the organisation.

Group factors: characteristics of the group and its members that affect its degree of cohesiveness

Group Factors

- **Member similarity:** people who are alike in their objectives, attitudes and values will probably derive satisfaction from being in each other's company, whereas a heterogeneous membership makes it more likely that people will split into potentially competitive factions and sub-groups.
- **Past success:** gives people a sense of being part of a winning team, whereas a past record of failure lowers morale and reduces the desire to be associated with a group.
- **Frequency of interaction:** this means that there are many opportunities to identify common interests and shared perceptions.
- **Member turnover:** frequent changes in membership result in a smaller proportion of people who have been socialised into accepting the group's culture and norms.

- **Size:** also reduces cohesion, because in very large groups people can come to regard other members as unfamiliar or anonymous, from which it is but a short step to the formation of sub-groups and factions.
- **Membership criteria:** are also influential. Where it is hard to become a member of a particular group, people can feel that they are part of something exclusive, which in turn prompts them to search for other points they have in common.
- Where **dominance by focal group figures** occurs it lowers the opportunity for people to share in group decisions, which not only reduces the sense of commitment and ownership of decisions but also the need for members to interact.

Environmental factors: characteristics of a group's environment that influence its degree of cohesiveness

Environmental Factors

- **Group isolation** makes a group physically or geographically remote from other groups. Thus, its members can come to think of the group as 'something different'. While this promotes cohesiveness, it can also have negative effects, which will be described when discussing relations between groups.
- Perceived **external threats** promote cohesiveness, because people tend to put internal differences aside to deal with the 'threat'.
- **Favourable self-evaluations** can have much the same effect as past successes. Members tend to feel there is something prestigious about belonging to the group and this prompts individuals to look for similarities with other members.
- **Rewards** also have an effect on cohesion. Where the members of a group are rewarded collectively for its performance, this increases the desirability of group success and members look for ways of cooperating to achieve this.

Organisational factors: organisational features that influence a group's cohesiveness

Organisational Factors

These were all identified earlier in the chapter where the Homans model was described.

TIME OUT

In the previous Time Out exercise you identified a group to which you belong and examined its roles and structure. Now reflect further on this group and answer the following questions.

1. Would you consider the group to be a cohesive one in terms of the definition of group cohesiveness given earlier?
2. What evidence have you used to come to this conclusion about the group's cohesiveness?
3. What are the outcomes of this cohesiveness: for example, is it simply that the people like being together in a group, or is it a highly productive group in terms of completing its tasks?
4. From your point of view, can you identify any drawbacks to the cohesiveness of the group?

The Outcomes of Group Cohesiveness

A cohesive group tends to have a stable structure of roles, which brings predictability into its members' lives and increases their willingness to conform to its norms. Whether this is judged to be a satisfactory state of affairs, however, depends on the circumstances surrounding the group and who makes the judgement. In broad terms, group cohesiveness has a number of advantages to an organisation:

- cohesive groups are much better at meeting their objectives (Keller 1986);
- members have a higher degree of job satisfaction than those in non-cohesive groups, which shows up in the energy that they devote to achieving group goals (Shaw 1981);
- morale is likely to be higher and, because people will have worked through and resolved most interpersonal problems, members tend to have fewer work-related anxieties (Seashore 1954);
- there will usually be a lower degree of problem behaviour, such as absenteeism and quitting (Hodgetts 1991).

Other things being equal, therefore, cohesive groups will achieve their goals with fewer resources and a lower expenditure of energy, mainly because energy and resources are directed at the task in hand and not absorbed by internal squabbles. Nevertheless, a very high degree of cohesiveness can have its problems and whether the organisation benefits depends on several factors:

- Productivity, as the organisation would want it, is only likely when the goals that a group has for itself are the same as those of the organisation (Keller 1986). Thus, unless organisational productivity is a group norm, its potential contribution to the organisation will be limited.

- A manager can try to persuade a group to adopt productivity as a behavioural norm, but if the group is cohesive, there is the risk of a backlash, particularly where a group feels that its existing norms are the appropriate ones, in which case the manager's attempts to influence the group will be resisted (Buller and Bell 1986).

- In a cohesive group the *status quo* is comfortable and satisfying, which results in an extremely potent set of forces to resist change.

- Cohesive groups have a higher potential to generate inter-group conflict because a cohesive group is likely to view itself as unique (Dion 1973), which in extreme cases can all too easily result in a perceptual bias against outsiders.

- In certain circumstances, cohesiveness can result in strongly impaired decision making processes.

The last point is a special problem with cohesive groups and since it warrants separate consideration it is dealt with next.

Group Decision Making

Most groups in organisations need to make decisions at some time and some groups exist to make decisions rather than produce a tangible output. One of the most important issues in this area is whether a group decision is likely to be better than one reached by an individual. This has received a great deal of research attention and reviewing it

CASE STUDY 11.2: The Design Engineers

The group in question is a small team of five people in the design department of a successful manufacturer of domestic appliances. There is a highly collegiate atmosphere in the group. Everyone is on first-name terms and they are all confident of their own personal abilities and those of the other people in the team. They constantly produce highly innovative designs, both in visual and technical terms, and have never been known to miss a deadline. The people are all fairly young men in their mid-twenties, who have worked together since serving their apprenticeships. Outside work, they are all members of the same 'rock band', which, locally, is highly successful. However, although they all enjoy this, none of them has any inclination to give up the design work and pursue a music career full-time.

One of the grumbles of the manager of their department is that they are a bit too insular. As individuals they are all nice people but they tend to remain apart from others in the design office. Indeed, he suspects that they can make a far greater contribution to the department if only they will share their obvious flair with other people. However, the only time he tried to do anything positive about this situation, by dispersing the group among others in the office, this was greeted by howls of protest from the team and lightly disguised inferences that they would all leave. Another problem that occurs is that the group sometimes comes into conflict with marketing people, who don't get exactly what they want in terms of a design but what the team feels marketing should have. There are also occasional conflicts with production engineers, who sometimes complain that while the designs are probably very marketable, they are too expensive to make. When conflicts of either type occur, however, the members of the team all form a united block to stifle the complaints of either the marketers or the production engineers.

Question

How would you describe this group and, from an organisational standpoint, are the characteristics of the team desirable or undesirable?

all is beyond the scope of this chapter. However, it is worthwhile noting three general conclusions that have been drawn:

- because there is a levelling effect in groups, working together usually results in a better decision than one that would be produced by the average individual in the group; not, however, as good a result as that which would be produced by the best individual in the group working alone (Miner 1984);
- while group decision making has the advantage of involving everybody, it usually takes more time than when an individual works alone and so the advantages are only realised where time is available, or implementation requires a decision that everybody accepts (Bottger and Yetton 1988);
- groups are more likely than individuals to produce accurate, workable decisions (Michaelsen *et al.* 1989).

These points seem to suggest that there are enough advantages for group decision making to be preferred. However, the conclusion only holds good where sufficient time is available to allow the slower group process to work, and only then if nothing stands in the way of the process being an effective one. Because there is some evidence that cohesive groups are particularly prone to an impaired decision making process, the second proviso is a very important one, and two problems can arise, which will be described separately.

Group Polarisation (Risky Shift)

Risky shift: the tendency of groups to make riskier decisions than their members would as individuals

This phenomenon was first identified by Stoner (1961) and has been well documented in a number of subsequent experimental studies (Clark 1971). It describes the tendency of some groups to opt for polarised and much riskier decision alternatives than individuals, the usual explanations for which are:

- **diffusion of responsibility** a group decision is less likely to be attributed to a single individual and so blame for one that goes wrong is taken away from any single person and shared by everybody;
- **valuing risk** taking risks is sometimes associated with being macho, dynamic and adventurous; therefore, riskier alternatives have some degree of social prestige;
- **familiarisation** as the risk is discussed and people in the group become more accustomed to it, it starts to look less risky;
- **prominence/leadership effects** those most likely to speak out in group decision making meetings are often those who have most influence in the group and their suggestions are sometimes adopted without full consideration.

There is much debate about which of these explanations is the most valid and also about the circumstances in which each is most likely to apply (Clark 1971; Schein 1980). Nevertheless, there is a consensus that 'risky shift' is more likely in cohesive groups because they exert strong pressures on individuals to conform, which enables people to abandon their cautious positions and move towards those that involve greater risk.

Groupthink

Groupthink: impaired decision making by a group because the desire for unanimity overrides examining the consequences of a decision

Another process that can stand in the way of effective group decision making is particularly significant for a highly cohesive group that has a strong record of success. This phenomenon has been dubbed *groupthink* and is defined as:

> **a mode of thinking in which people engage when they are deeply involved in a cohesive group, in which strivings for unanimity override motivations to realistically appraise alternative courses of action.** (Janis 1972, p 9)

Janis's research led him to examine famous and controversial political decisions. Some of these turned out to be disastrous and highly inappropriate in the circumstances, but so far as the discussion here is concerned, the decision taken is of less interest than the process at work. Janis concluded that in each case the process was characterised by the group just 'drifting along', which gave rise to a sense of false consensus, with nobody questioning suggestions made at an early stage. In his view the signs of groupthink are unmistakable, and he identifies eight main symptoms:

- An **illusion of invulnerability** in which most or all group members overemphasise the group's strengths and play down its weaknesses. This induces a bias towards feeling that its decisions are inevitably correct, taking risks, and ignoring danger signals which should result in the assumption being questioned.

- **Assumptions of morality** where the group believes that its own aims and means are morally superior and unquestionable. This in turn results in any decision made going unquestioned.

- **Realisations** in which prior decisions, or emerging information that would necessitate the group looking again at its emerging decision, or underlying assumptions are swept under the carpet as irrelevancies.

- **Stereotyping** where its views of competing or opposing groups are distorted and simplified, which results in other groups being perceived as weak, evil, corrupt and unprincipled and enables the group to disregard any opposition from outside.

- **Self-censorship** in which members suppress any doubts, disagreements or misgivings to maintain cohesiveness and mutual support.

- **Illusions of unanimity** which occur because individuals censor any misgivings that they may have and nobody wants to be the odd one out who challenges what is perceived to be the unanimity of others.

- **Mindguarding** where some group members take it upon themselves to keep negative views or bad news from reaching others, particularly any decision leaders in the group.

- **Direct pressure** in which anyone who injects a note of questioning or caution is quickly pressured to get in line with the rest of the group.

There are several potential consequences of these symptoms:

- the group tends to curtail discussion and consider only a very limited range of alternatives;
- the search for any information that can be relevant in examining the potential consequences of its decision is limited;
- since outsiders are not given the same credibility as group members, it fails to import expert opinion when it is needed;
- it does not develop contingency plans;
- information which can indicate that the decision needs to be reappraised tends to be ignored.

The net result is a failure to audit its own decisions and their potential outcomes and suppression of dissent and self-criticism, which is sometimes very necessary. Janis argues that groupthink arises from a group's natural tendency to maintain a favourable self-image and notes certain conditions in which it is most likely to arise, for example:

- where a group is highly cohesive;
- where it has a strong record of past success;
- where it is insulated from the outside world;
- where it has high prestige with outsiders;
- where there is a strong or powerful leader who promotes his or her own preconceived solutions.

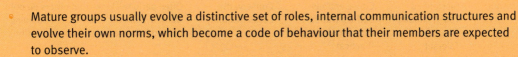

REPLAY

- Mature groups usually evolve a distinctive set of roles, internal communication structures and evolve their own norms, which become a code of behaviour that their members are expected to observe.
- The cohesiveness of a group is influenced by a number of factors particular to the group and its members, together with factors emanating in its environment.
- While cohesive groups are usually more productive than those that are not, there are potential problems inherent in highly cohesive groups, the most significant of which is the possibility of impaired decision making processes.

GROUP EFFECTIVENESS

As will be seen in Chapter 15, one way to evaluate the effectiveness of an organisation is against the criterion of whether it achieves its goals. For a group the equivalent of this is whether it accomplishes its task(s). With a group, however, task accomplishment acutely depends on member satisfaction, and with this in mind it is normal to evaluate group effectiveness against two criteria:

- **task criteria**   for example, high quantity and quality of work output, speed in completing work, economy in the use of resources;
- **member satisfaction criteria**   consisting of cohesiveness, member satisfaction with the group, wanting to be part of it and to remain a member.

These criteria make it clear that an effective group is one in which both task and socio-emotive needs are met and there seems little doubt that this occurs because individual members occupy highly compatible roles. Recent approaches that deal with the problem of developing effective management teams often use this idea as a starting point. The best known of these is Belbin's (1993) scheme, which identifies nine key roles that are present in an effective group. Belbin and his co-workers point out that effective and creative groups or teams seldom consist of people who are all of the same type, but require a balanced mix of individual characteristics, so that the positive attributes of each person complement those of others. The nine types of person needed, together with their main characteristics, are given in Table 11.1.

Independent empirical studies show strong support for Belbin's assertion that teams that are well balanced in terms of different member roles are the most effective (Senior 1997b), although there is some debate about whether the number of distinctly different roles is as high as nine (Fisher *et al.* 1998). Nevertheless, this has intriguing implications for organisations in current conditions. Conger (1993) argues that in today's delayered and downsized organisations, empowered employees are highly interdependent. This puts a strong emphasis on working in groups or teams, much of which occurs in temporary task groups and project teams. For this reason it can be vital to assemble teams that function effectively from the start. If some of the characteristics of potential team members are known before the team assembles (for example, their preferred

Table 11.1 Outline of Belbin's team role types (after Belbin 1993)

Team role type	Personal characteristics	Strengths	Potential weaknesses	Contributions to team task
Implementor (IMP)	Disciplined Tough minded Trusting Tolerant	Conscientious Self-controlled Outward looking Practical	Conservative Lacks flexibility	Often performs tasks that others do not want. Systematic and efficient planning to transform plans into practical actions
Coordinator (CO)	Calm Self-confident Trusting Outgoing Dominant	Impartial Self-disciplined Enthusiastic Positive thinker	Average ability Average intellect	Organises team operations and resources to meet its objectives. Good at evaluating and handling people and maximising team members' potential
Shaper (SH)	Highly strung Outgoing	Dynamic Achievement-orientated	Argumentative Impatient Provocative	Establishes objectives and priorities. Often has an arousing, challenging and motivating effect on others, but at times can be disruptive
Plant (PL)	Introverted Individualist Serious minded	High intellect Knowledgeable Unorthodox Creative thinker	Aloof Impractical Loner Lacks attention to detail	The ideas person who brings innovation and creativity to goals and activities
Resource Investigator (RI)	Low anxiety Sociable Extrovert Enquiring	Versatile Innovative Communicative Strong social skills	Can easily become bored	Good at creating useful contacts outside the team. Gathers useful resources and manages interactions across team boundary
Monitor-Evaluator (ME)	Sober Unemotional Detached Hard-headed	High intellect Discreet Objective	Uninspiring	Helps team analyse and evaluate objectively and prevents impulsive decisions being made
Team Worker (TW)	Gregarious Sensitive Sociable	Team player Responsive to others	Indecisive in crisis	The builder of team relationships and team spirit. Helps reduce levels of interpersonal conflict
Completer-Finisher (CF)	Conscientious Anxiety prone	Perseverance Perfectionist Attention to detail	A worrier	High contribution of effort and strong attention to detail. Good at planning and carrying through. Helps ensure team progresses the activities necessary to achieve goals and deadlines
Specialist (SP)	Single minded Self-starter	Dedicated	Dwells on technicalities	Provides knowledge and skills in rare supply. Only contributes on a narrow front

team roles) this enhances the prospects of assembling a team which knits together very quickly. To this end, Belbin and his colleagues have developed a questionnaire – the Belbin self-perception inventory – which enables people to identify their preferred team roles. While there are questions about the reliability of this instrument (Furnham *et al.* 1993), with care it can be used to slot appropriate people into a team.

RELATIONS BETWEEN GROUPS: INTERGROUP CONFLICT

Groups are not usually independent entities and so the effectiveness of an organisation often depends on smooth relationships between them. Nevertheless, each group tends to be judged on how well it performs, which can sometimes put cooperation with other groups at risk. Therefore, some degree of conflict or competition between groups may well be inevitable.

Because a cohesive group has its own norms and values, it can put its own goals before those of the organisation or another group, so cooperation between groups cannot be taken for granted. Moreover, since an organisation's structural design often creates interdependencies between formal groups, the goals and activities of one can impinge upon those of another, and from this it is but a short step to a highly competitive situation, which can turn into outright hostility.

From an organisational viewpoint intergroup conflict is clearly counter-productive, because it often results in winners and losers and the after-effects can sometimes be as disruptive as the conflict itself. Winning groups can become extremely complacent and develop feelings of superiority and invulnerability that make them susceptible to 'groupthink'. Losers can become tense and demoralised, which makes them all too anxious to pick up the cudgels again.

The structure of an organisation is often fertile ground in which intergroup conflict can flourish because it establishes different groups and gives them separate identities. Thus, each group can come to see itself as 'different' from others and become more aware of these differences. Over time, there can be a tendency for people to view their own group as the 'in group' (the one about which everything is correct) and other groups as 'out groups' (those that are nowhere near as correct), simply because they are different. Indeed, some scholars believe that when permanent groups with different identities are established, some degree of polarisation is bound to occur (Campbell 1965).

In addition, structure sometimes places groups in competition and, as a result, perceptions of the other group can become distorted, with each one perceiving the other as a distinct threat and even a potential 'enemy'. This has a number of predictable consequences. To prop up their own morale and sense of 'rightness' members tend to overevaluate their own group, its members tend to develop an increased liking for each other, and the pressure to conform to group norms gets even stronger. Further confirmation of its goodness is also obtained by denigrating the other group, which is now firmly cast in the role of 'the enemy'. The other group then has little alternative but to respond in a like way, and there is a great deal of evidence to suggest that the 'in group' and 'out group' phenomenon can arise even where there is no conflict.

Underlying all this may be extremely potent forces at an individual psychological level. Allport (1954b) notes that telling a person that he or she is better than somebody else is the easiest idea to sell in this world. Thus, when an individual devalues another person, he or she gets an immediate boost to self-esteem. Group membership gives people an opportunity to play this game on a larger scale and enhance their self-esteem in three very powerful and mutually supporting ways:

- it gives a positive value to those things which distinguish the 'in group' from the 'out group';
- as individuals, this enables them to consider themselves as different from and superior to other individuals;
- they receive signals from other people in the 'in group' that their judgement is sound.

TIME OUT

Reflect further on the group you examined in the previous Time Out exercise and answer the following questions.

1. To what extent do you consider the group an effective one in terms of the two sets of criteria given above, that is, the task criterion and the member satisfaction criterion?
2. Do you feel one set of criteria is considered more important by the group? Are both considered equally important? Or does their relative importance vary from time to time?
3. Now consider Belbin's list of nine team roles (Table 11.1). Which one do you fit most closely, and can you identify other members of the group who fit some of the other roles?
4. Does the group have any tendencies to compete or come into conflict with other groups, and what circumstances are likely to give rise to this state of affairs?

REPLAY

- From an organisational perspective, an effective group is one that achieves its goals, but this is only one criterion of effectiveness; the other is whether a group satisfies the needs of its members and unless this criterion is met, it is doubtful if the first will be achieved.
- Effective groups are likely to consist of people with different patterns of skills and abilities so that the attributes of one group member complement those of the others.
- While conflict between groups is not inevitable, there are a number of structural features in most organisations that are likely to result in groups competing with each other, and this can all too easily become outright conflict.

GROUPS AND JOB DESIGN

As noted in Chapter 7, job design can have a huge impact on the motivational state of people. For the most part, traditional approaches to job design focus exclusively on individuals, but in the last three decades there has been an increasing awareness of the need to take account of some of the positive influences that groups can have on their members. At the present time the most popular methods of trying to bring about improvements in motivation and performance are pitched firmly at the level of the work-group (Alford 1994) and over half of the manufacturing organisations in America are reportedly switching to team-based methods (Osterman 1994).

While initiatives of this type have a wide variety of names, for example, semi-autonomous work groups, high-performance work systems and, more recently, team-working, all of them are group-based job designs that aim to bring about a level of performance that is superior to that achieved with previous, individual designs. Although his description refers explicitly to high-performance work teams, Vaill (1982) nicely captures what is intended to result. That is, a workgroup which:

- has excellent performance in terms of known external standards;
- exceeds expectations by performing at a higher level than that which is assumed to be its potential best;
- strives to makes constant improvements by performing excellently in comparison to its prior level of performance;
- is judged by informed observers as having substantially better performance than other comparable groups;
- is efficient because it achieves its level of performance with fewer resources than are normally assumed to be necessary;
- is seen as an exemplar and a source of ideas and inspiration;
- is seen to achieve the ideals of the culture within which it is located.

Socio-technical Systems

Socio-technical systems: an approach to work design in which the people and the technical systems (and the relationship between them) are accorded equal importance

Group-based work designs owe much to the pioneering work of Trist *et al.* (1963) which resulted in what is now known as the *socio-technical systems* approach to work design. In outline terms, the approach holds that:

- two major organisational systems interact at the point at which work is undertaken: the technical system, which includes the task to be completed, the machinery and tools used, maintenance, location etc., and the social system, which includes the social and psychological needs of the people involved;
- it is never possible to completely satisfy the needs of one system without failing to satisfy the needs of the other;
- therefore, an effective design sub-optimises to some extent by aiming to satisfy (so far as this is possible) the most important demands of both systems.

In practice this usually means that individual jobs are deliberately clustered into groups in which people are interdependent (Cherns 1987). In addition, the group that results is often allowed a great deal of autonomy in the way that it addresses the task in hand (Cummings 1978).

Semi-autonomous Work Groups

Semi-autonomous work groups: self-managed teams that have a high degree of responsibility for their own work activities

Semi-autonomous work groups or, as they are sometimes called, self-managed work teams are an important development in job design that emerged as a natural outcome of the socio-technical systems approach. The best-known example of the use of this design started in the mid-1970s in Volvo, the Swedish car manufacturer. Hitherto, Volvo had produced cars using assembly line methods, which are widely used in vehicle manufacture throughout the world, and, in common with other mass production industries, it had experienced the usual problems associated with extreme job simplification, for example, low employee motivation, poor quality etc. On opening a new plant at Kalmar in 1974, Volvo introduced radically different work methods. Instead of a moving conveyor with workers completing very small, simple tasks, cellular manufacturing techniques were employed. The total number of tasks of the whole conveyor line was distributed between a number of work cells, each of which consisted of a team of between fifteen and twenty workers. Teams were given complete responsibility for completing an entire job, for example, the car's electrical system, its upholstery and trim, or the transmission and brakes. Within each cell, workers normally divided themselves into a number of smaller teams and, instead of a continuous conveyor, the vehicles were mounted on computer-controlled carriers that moved the car from cell to cell.

OB IN ACTION: Self-managed Teams at Vesuvius

Organisational change is never easy, particularly when it involves something as radical as moving to self-managed teams in an organisation that has traditionally been run in a hierarchical way. Nevertheless, if change of this nature can be successfully accomplished, the rewards can be high, and an example of this is provided by Vesuvius, which makes specialist ceramics and other components for the steel industry.

Vesuvius is located in Ayrshire in Scotland and is part of the Cookson group, which has a total of 74 plants located in 21 countries, with its headquarters in Brussels. Realising the competitive nature of life as part of a multinational conglomerate, Vesuvius wanted to be seen as a high performer in the group and in the early 1990s reviewed its operational policies and procedures and, in particular, those concerning the use of human resources. In the mid-1990s it embarked on a change programme built around the business excellence model derived by the European Foundation for Quality Management (EFQM). This involved building a culture in which production staff were ultimately grouped into self-managing teams that take full responsibility for all the tasks they undertake. This was a radical break with the past. Many potential barriers needed to be overcome and the changes were not accomplished overnight. For example, new working methods were necessary and to reflect the flexible, multi-skilled and more egalitarian way of working, a great deal of retraining was undertaken. Multi-skilling also required the negotiation of a completely new pay structure, which effectively resulted in a salaried workforce. Foremen, who had hitherto performed a first-line supervisory role, were initially apprehensive about job security and also needed to be retrained to become 'facilitators' rather than overseers.

Despite all this, however, the reported outcomes are impressive. Enthusiasm and job satisfaction, as measured by employee opinion surveys, has increased significantly, so much so that the teamworking concept has been extended to all other departments and functions at Vesuvius. Revenue has increased by nearly 50 per cent over a five-year period, market share has grown, the number of customer complaints has decreased and costs have been lowered, all of which are attributed to the increased competitiveness of the organisation obtained by empowering employees in self-managed teams.

Source:

Arkin, A (1999) Peak practice, *People Management*, 11 November: 57–9.

Cells were responsible for their own scheduling, planning and work allocation within the group and, in new plants opened later at Torslanda, Tuve and Uddevalla, group responsibilities were extended to include a measure of decision making responsibility for hiring and training new workers and holiday scheduling. Thus, the essential features of the work design were:

- goals (output and quality) were set for each group of workers (the cell) but the group itself decided the most appropriate way to achieve them;
- groups had a large measure of choice and discretion over allocation of jobs, planning and control of the work;
- a group policed its own activities with little or no external supervision; indeed, although supervisors still existed, they tended to become advisers to groups rather than overseers;
- any evaluation of the group was based on its performance as a whole, with evaluation of individuals being done within the group, by the group;
- to some extent the group became responsible for ensuring that it had the necessary spread of skills and abilities to complete its tasks.

Although some tensions were evident in supervisors and managers, who felt somewhat uncomfortable and threatened by the greater autonomy of workers, most reports of the Volvo experience emerged in highly positive terms, for example, enhanced job satisfaction, productivity and quality (Bailey 1983). Thus semi-autonomous work groups appeared to be a resounding success story and a number of American firms were prompted to try the method, notably General Foods at its manufacturing plant at Topeka in Kansas. Because it gave significant improvements in quality, productivity, job satisfaction, cost reductions and a lowered incidence of problem behaviours such as absenteeism, this initiative has also been widely cited as a success (Walton 1977). However, a subsequent review and analysis by Whitsett and Yorks (1983) calls some of these findings into question and points out that sufficient tensions arose in the Topeka initiative to merit a strong degree of caution about the use of the method.

Nevertheless, studies of other semi-autonomous work groups have also found that people tend to have higher levels of job satisfaction and organisational commitment than those whose jobs are designed to more traditional criteria (Cordery *et al.* 1991). Thus, it would not be surprising if these methods also give enhanced productivity. Perhaps more importantly, organisational conditions that have become widespread across the last two decades might well make something akin to semi-autonomous groups inevitable. For instance, Peters (1985) argues that this work design is entirely consistent with the increased emphasis on flatter organisational structures, quality, multi-skilling and flexibility that are required in an age of globalised competition. For this reason it is to the current version of this group-based design that the discussion turns next.

Teamworking

Teamworking: the current name for use of semi-autonomous work groups

Teamworking is by no means a new idea and in many respects it only amounts to a new and currently fashionable title for the use of semi-autonomous work groups. What is different, however, is that whereas semi-autonomous group designs were used in a small number of organisations, teamworking has caught the imagination of managers, and it is now impossible to open a management journal without finding an article that extols its virtues.

Across the last fifteen years many firms have downsized and delayered. While these steps were originally a response to economic conditions, they are fast being seen as an essential prerequisite for survival in the fast-moving, globalised marketplace. This, it is argued, requires that organisations:

- are 'lean' and have little or no surplus manpower;
- have much flatter hierarchies;
- are able to make decisions faster;
- have multi-skilled, highly adaptable workforces;
- have strong customer orientations;
- have the ability to change quickly and smoothly with minimal disruption.

To a large extent these characteristics are only likely to be obtained if responsibility for day-to-day operational problem solving and innovation is devolved to the lowest possible level (Colenso 1997). However, a lot more is required than simply telling people that from now on they will be 'teamworking'. In teamworking, a large measure of responsibility for the day-to-day running of an organisation is devolved to an empowered workforce that has to cope with a more dynamic set of conditions. Moreover, the decisions and actions of one team can have a strong impact on the performance of other teams, and this occurs in a situation where there are fewer managers to coordinate their activities. For this reason it can be argued that teams need to have a more strategic orientation to performance, and this often runs counter to the prior work experiences of team members, who were simply required to focus on working hard (Parker *et al.* 1997). Therefore, a great deal of preparatory work is needed to introduce teamworking and Holbeche (1997) sets out a number of cardinal rules for doing so:

- **communication**   employees need to be kept well informed of what is required, why it is required, why change is necessary and of the new culture, values and beliefs of the organisation;
- **leadership**   a lean organisation often needs to rely on temporary teams, which not only requires training and support for people, but also leadership to be fostered in team leaders so that they can carry people with them, without having to rely on formal authority;
- **careers**   the organisation needs to establish a career framework in which people can develop their skills and enhance their employability;
- **development**   the lean organisation is only likely to grow and retain skilled, flexible people if it invests heavily in development, which not only means training, but also creating an environment in which people continually learn;
- **reward and recognition**   an appropriate reward system that recognises performance of the team and of individuals needs to be established.

Research conducted for the Institute of Personnel and Development (see Kinnie and Purcell 1998) bears out many of Holbeche's assertions. That is, how teamworking is introduced has a tremendous impact on how well teams perform. Thus, a teamworking initiative requires a great deal of prior thought and planning before its introduction, otherwise it may well result in the opposite of what it is intended to achieve.

So far, the evidence on whether teamworking achieves the outcomes that managers desire (usually productivity and lowered costs) is very mixed. There have been a number of reported success stories, one of which, the Vesuvius case, is described above and others are set out by Banker *et al.* (1996) and Macduffie (1995). Conversely, other cases are reported in which these methods were used to drag employees into a method of working where jobs were no more interesting, enriched or empowered – merely harder and more exhausting (Delbridge *et al.* 2000).

OVERVIEW AND CONCLUSIONS

Groups are fundamental to the structure of society and have a prominent place in work organisations. Formal groups are established by the structure of an organisation, but if groups are only viewed in terms of what the organisation wants them to achieve, their role in serving a number of important social purposes tends to be ignored.

Groups often become like societies in miniature. To make life more predictable they evolve a structure of complementary roles and a set of rules (norms) to regulate the behaviour of their members and, if necessary, pressure to conform is brought to bear on people who step out of line. Self-regulation of this type is a characteristic of mature groups, but to reach this degree of maturity fairly clear role structures and behavioural norms must have emerged. For this to occur, it is usually necessary for a group to go through a number of characteristic stages of development. What emerges, however, is not simply a function of the personality and attitudes of the individuals involved; a host of important features of the work context also play a part in shaping its characteristics and subsequent behaviour.

Cohesion is an important feature of some groups and in one that is cohesive, people identify strongly with the group and its aims. Although a cohesive group is often more effective in achieving its aims, the aims do not necessarily correspond with those of the organisation. Cohesion can also have implications for the effectiveness of group processes, notably how it reaches its decisions. Too much cohesion can also give rise to the 'in group' and 'out group' phenomenon, in which a group can all too easily come into conflict with others in the organisation. For these reasons the role structure of a group can be crucial. Effective groups and teams – those that meet task requirements as well as socio-emotive needs – usually need an appropriate mixture of different roles.

Largely for economic reasons, current fashions in work design often seek to cash in on the positive outcomes of working in groups, usually under the generic banner of 'teamworking'.

FURTHER READING

Ackroyd S and P Thompson (1999) *Organisational Misbehaviour*, London: Sage. An amusing, but nevertheless serious, academic study of groups and how they often misbehave to pursue their own ends.

Adair, J (1986) *Effective Team Building*, London: Pan. A very easy-to-read book, the contents of which are based on its author's extensive research.

Belbin, R M (1993) *Team Roles at Work*, Oxford: Butterworth-Heinemann. A comprehensive description of the team roles concept and its application in organisations.

Brown, R (2000) *Group Processes*, Oxford: Blackwell. A recent and thorough review and assessment of research and theoretical developments on group processes.

Guzzo R A and W Dickson (1998) 'Teams in organisations: recent research on performance and effectiveness', *Annual Review of Psychology*, 49, pp. 307–38. A review of recent research on groups and teams. Rather technical in places, but full of useful information.

Hayes, N (1997) *Successful Team Management*, London: Thompson. A useful book that covers research and theory on groups/teams, which also makes practical suggestions for improving the performance of teams.

Hogg, M A and G M Vaughan (1998) *Social Psychology*, Hemel Hempstead: Prentice Hall. An introductory textbook containing an excellent chapter on basic group processes.

Proctor, S and F Mueller (eds) (2000) *Teamworking*, London: Macmillan. A book of readings with contributions by several prominent authors that brings together many different perspectives which reflect current views on teamworking.

Sinclair, A (1992) 'The tyranny of a team ideology', *Organisation Studies* 13(4), 611–26. The paper presents a damming indictment of managerial obsession with its latest panacea: teamworking.

Spector, P (1995) *Industrial and Organisational Psychology: Research and Practice*, Chichester: Wiley. A wide-ranging book that contains easy-to-read chapters on groups.

West, M (1994) *Effective Teamwork*, Leicester: BPS Books. A practical guide to teams and teamworking, albeit one with a 'how to do it' flavour.

Whelan, S A (1999) *Creating Effective Work Teams*, London: Sage. Another 'how to do it' book that makes practical recommendations for building high-performance teams.

Womack, J P, D T Jones and D Roos (1990) *The Machine that Changed the World: The Triumph of Lean Production*, New York: Macmillan. By now a classic that in a rather 'over-the-top' way enthuses about Japanese lean production methods, which have now been widely adopted in the West. The book has been heavily criticised in academic circles as being rampantly managerialist.

REVIEW AND DISCUSSION QUESTIONS

1. Explain the criteria that need to be satisfied in order for a number of people to be considered to be a group.

2. Explain the difference between the two types of group commonly found in organisations, and what distinguishes a 'team' from other types of group.

3. Explain why groups are able to exert such a powerful influence over the behaviour of their individual members and describe some of the aspects of individual behaviour that can be influenced by a group.

4. Describe the four stages of the group formation process and explain what occurs in each one.

5. Explain why it is that the context in which a group exists exerts an influence on its characteristics.

6. Explain what is meant by group cohesiveness, the three sets of factors that influence a group's degree of cohesion and whether cohesiveness is a good or a bad thing.

7. Describe two phenomena that can affect the quality of a group's decision making, and why and in what ways the phenomena have these effects.

Chapter 12

Leadership: Basic Concepts and Theories

LEARNING OUTCOMES

After studying this chapter you should be able to:

- define leadership
- distinguish between descriptive and functional approaches to the subject
- distinguish between leadership and management
- describe trait theories of leadership, their general assumptions and their strengths and weaknesses
- describe style theories of leadership, their general assumptions and their strengths and weaknesses

INTRODUCTION

In Chapter 11, which explored the nature of groups, it was explained that a mature group has a structured system of roles, one of which is a leader. If a group exists, a leader role of some sort is virtually certain to emerge and this chapter and the one that follows both deal with the topic of leadership, a concept that has long fascinated the organisational sciences. Because there is a wealth of information on the topic and there are many different theories of leadership, in order to avoid giving the reader too much information to digest in a single sitting, the topic is covered in two chapters. This one deals with basic concepts and theories, while Chapter 13 covers advanced theories and more recent approaches.

The chapter starts from basic principles by defining leadership and this is followed by a consideration of two very different approaches to the study of leadership: the descriptive approach and the functional approach. The next matter to be examined is whether, and to what extent, the words 'leader' and 'manager' mean the same thing, and this is followed by a brief examination of the significance of leadership to organisations. The chapter then goes on to explore two of the earliest ideas in the area, which are discussed in the sequence in which they emerged. The first to be considered is trait theory, which deals with the attributes and personal qualities that leaders are assumed to possess. This is followed by an explanation and description of style theory and its derivatives, which focuses on the behaviour that is associated with effective leadership. Finally, as a prelude to Chapter 13, traditional and contingency approaches to leadership theory are discussed.

THE NATURE OF LEADERSHIP

There are almost as many definitions of leadership as there are theories, but one that is often quoted is:

> **the process whereby one individual influences other group members towards the attainment of defined group, or organisational goals.**   **(Barron and Greenberg 1990)**

Another is:

> **the process of creating a vision for others and having the power to translate it into a reality and sustain it.**   **(Kotter 1988)**

In reality, these definitions tell us very little. The first says nothing about how the influence process occurs and would, for example, cover situations where coercion is used, which is well outside the bounds of behaviour that most people associate with leadership, while the second definition is perhaps rather too optimistic. The main problem, however, is that both definitions infer that leadership is a one-way process, in which followers passively respond to what a leader does, or what the leader is, which tends to oversimplify the processes at work. Another, but unrelated, problem that confuses matters is that the word leadership has two commonly accepted meanings. First, it is used to describe a process in which influence is used to direct and coordinate the activities of a group towards its objectives; second, it expresses the idea that followers perceive that a person has certain attributes or characteristics which enable him or her to exert influence over them (Jago 1982). Taken together, a number of important implications arise from these two meanings:

- a leader's influence is non-coercive and so followers must consent to be influenced;
- leadership is a goal-directed activity in which followers consent to a leader exercising influence with a view to achieving something;
- although this can simply mean facilitating the group completing its tasks, it is possible that they may want something else as well; in Chapter 11, for example, it was explained that group members invariably have socio-emotive needs in addition to task needs and so if they consent to be influenced by someone, it can be because they anticipate that the person will bring about satisfaction of both sets of needs;
- since followers believe, but do not know for certain, that these outcomes will be achieved, leadership is conferred on someone the followers perceive they can trust to make the desired outcomes more likely.

With these points in mind, a working definition of leadership used for this and the following chapter is:

a process in which leader and followers interact in a way that enables the leader to influence the actions of the followers in a non-coercive way, towards the achievement of certain aims or objectives.

TWO APPROACHES TO THE STUDY OF LEADERSHIP

Descriptive approach to leadership: theories that describe leadership in terms of either what a person is or his or her distinctive style of behaviour

Functional approach to leadership: theories that explain leadership in terms of the functions performed by the leader with respect to the followers

All theories of leadership adopt one or other of two distinctive approaches. The *descriptive approach to leadership* focuses on whether a leader is a special type of person and/or whether there is a most appropriate style of behaviour for a leader to adopt. For the most part this approach has dominated theory and research into leadership and the majority of theories covered in this chapter, and the one that follows, fall into this category. For this reason there is no need to elaborate further at this point, except to note that while theories of this type have much to say that is important in understanding leadership, they fail to address a fundamental question. In broad terms this can be stated as 'what functions does a person have to perform in order to be considered by others as their leader?' This matter is addressed by the *functional approach to leadership*, and since theories of this type have important implications for an issue that will be considered shortly – whether leadership and management are the same thing – it is appropriate to examine this approach in greater depth.

The Functional Approach to Leadership

As noted above, theories of this type address the question of what functions a person needs to perform in order to be considered as a leader by others. A number of different ways have been used to try to answer this question. For example, Scott and Podsakoff (1982) approach the question from an operant conditioning perspective (see Chapter 6). Starting from Bowers and Seashore's (1966) argument that leadership is 'behaviour that results in a difference in the behaviour of others', they reasoned that since leaders get psychological rewards when they successfully get followers to do something, follower behaviour prompts leaders to behave in a certain way to obtain this reward. This gives a unique perspective on the leader–follower relationship by introducing the idea of *reciprocal causality*.

Reciprocal causality: the idea that followers affect leader behaviour as well as the leader influencing followers

Most traditional models of leader behaviour simply assume that leaders affect the behaviour of followers, which treats followers as passive recipients of influence. However, this oversimplifies matters by failing to acknowledge that while the behaviour of a leader can have effects on followers, it is equally true that there are effects in the opposite direction (Green 1975). For this reason a potentially fruitful way to view leadership is from the perspective of social exchange theory. Perhaps the simplest way to express this idea is that leaders are able to be leaders if they provide something that followers want and, in return, followers provide something that the leader wants. Two models which adopt this perspective will be described in what follows, and while neither of them is explicitly framed in social exchange terms, both are capable of being interpreted in this way.

Action-centred Leadership

The action-centred theory of leadership is based on extensive research by John Adair (1984) and has subsequently been developed into a highly successful method of leadership training by the Industrial Society. Adair points out that effective leadership consists of meeting three sets of interrelated needs, which give rise to three functions that a leader must perform:

- **The task-related function**   meeting the needs of the group to complete its task by helping members to clarify the task and its nature, and enabling them to overcome barriers to completion.
- **The team-related function**   meeting the group's need to hold together as a cohesive unit.
- **The individually orientated function**   ensuring that the diverse but important individual needs of group members are met.

In terms of group performance the theory explicitly recognises that these three areas affect each other. For instance, a leader who focuses too much on the task can find that individual needs are not met, and this in turn can demoralise certain individuals to the extent that the group becomes fragmented. This is demonstrated symbolically by Adair in his overlapping circles model, shown in Figure 12.1.

In practical terms, balancing these three functions requires that the leader must have three vital skills:

- an awareness of the group's processes, which requires knowing the characteristics of people in the group and displaying some sensitivity to the finer nuances of behaviour in order to be able to diagnose how they interact and take remedial action to resolve any difficulties;
- an ability to be able to spot which of the three functional areas needs attention;
- the interpersonal skills that are necessary to bring about changes to achieve the right balance between the three functions.

From this it follows that being effective as a leader is not just a matter of choosing a specific style of behaviour, but arriving at an appropriate balance between the three

Figure 12.1
Interaction of task, team maintenance and individual needs (Source: Adair 1979)

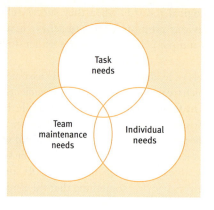

functions. What is crucially important is that one of these three functions requires the leader to serve the interests of the group as a whole. This means that leadership is a social function and essentially a process of facilitating social exchange (Barker 2001). Normally a leader is the person who is held responsible by people inside and outside the group for accomplishing the task. Thus, if he or she serves the interests of the group as a whole, and in return the team completes the task, leader and followers exchange performances that are important to each other.

The Vertical Dyad Linkage (VDL) Model

Most conventional leadership models have the same fundamental weakness. They assume that a leader uses the same behaviourial style with all group members (Danserau *et al.* 1975). However, unless people are all identical in terms of work skills and attitudes (and this is very unlikely) a leader would usually take account of the idiosyncrasies of people. Thus Danserau and his colleagues believe that it is more realistic to view leader–member relations dyadically (in pairs), in which a group consists of a set of vertical dyadic linkages, with the leader as one person in a particular dyad and another group member as the other one. Strictly speaking, this means that there will be as many dyadic relationships as there are subordinates but, to simplify matters, Danserau and his colleagues deal only with two distinct sub-groups of subordinates, each of which has a different relationship with the leader.

In-group members:
those on whom the
leader relies to go
beyond the minimum
level of performance
required

Out-group members:
people who give only
a basic level of
performance

In-group members are people who, in the leader's eyes, can be relied upon to go beyond the minimum level of effort and initiative required to undertake the group's task. They are often self-starters and obtain work satisfaction from added responsibility. The leader tacitly forms a special and more open relationship with this sub-group, in which they tend to be taken into his or her confidence and are allowed a fair amount of latitude in how they do things. Since this is often the relationship that people of this type wish to have with the leader, they respond by giving more than the minimum. *Out-group members* are people recognised by the leader as not wanting to go beyond performing at a basic level. Therefore, so long as they do what is necessary, they are not usually pressed for more, which gives another distinct type of relationship. These people are usually more distant from the leader, who uses the power of his or her position rather than person-orientated behaviour to obtain the required task performance. Therefore, expressed in terms of social exchange, there are clearly two different types of relationship at work. In-group members obtain different benefits from those people in the out-group and incur different costs in doing so. In return, the manager obtains different benefits from each sub-group and incurs different costs to reap these benefits.

There is a fairly strong body of evidence to show that leader–member relations in groups are often structured like this (Dunegan *et al.* 1992). Moreover, research indicates that appropriate patterns of leader–member exchange have positive effects in terms of member satisfaction, group effectiveness and productivity (Wayne *et al.* 1997), and this evidence has strong implications for how leadership effectiveness is conceptualised. It is all too common to find that effectiveness is viewed purely in terms of productivity or task completion, with a consequent neglect of the ways in which these outcomes are obtained. By focusing on leader–follower relations Danserau and his colleagues provide one explanation for some of the processes that may be at work, for example, an effective leader may be someone who is able to perform two vital functions *vis-à-vis* subordinates:

- an ability to identify those subordinates who have needs to perform in-group roles and those who would prefer to be in the out-group;
- to follow up with different but equally appropriate behaviours towards the two sub-groups, so that each makes its respective contribution to the group task.

The great strength of functional theories such as action-centred leadership and the vertical dyad linkage model is that leadership is treated as a negotiated role, concerned with meeting the needs of both followers and leader. This avoids the trap of dealing only with situations where a leader is endowed with formal organisational authority, and for this reason it is now time to consider the important question of whether there is a difference between being a manager and being a leader.

LEADERSHIP AND MANAGEMENT

In modern society the words 'leader' and 'leadership' carry a great deal of prestige. Thus, many managers lay claim to being leaders, and some probably believe that the positions they occupy confer the mantle of leadership upon them. Thus, it is important to examine whether leadership and management are synonymous; are they, for example, just different words that express the same idea?

One way to address this question is to examine the generally acknowledged functions of management, which are usually taken to be some combination of planning, organising, directing and controlling. Managers usually have goals or objectives to achieve and are expected to do this by the appropriate use of resources at their disposal. People are an important part of a manager's resources, and achieving objectives often requires that influence is exercised over the behaviour of subordinates. When someone is appointed as a manager the person is granted a degree of formal authority over the subordinates, which in turn gives some capability to influence their actions. All this really means is that power has been conferred from above and, in technical terms, the person occupies a position of *headship*, which means that a manager can be defined as:

Headship: the formal authority over subordinates granted as part of a manager's position

A person formally appointed to a role in the organisational hierarchy, associated with which is the formal authority (within prescribed limits) to direct the actions of subordinates. Among other things the role is concerned with some combination of planning, organising, directing and controlling the activities of human resources towards the achievement of set organisational objectives.

Most people feel intuitively that there is more to leadership than simply wielding formal, delegated authority, and several points can be noted from the discussion of the functional approach:

- Leadership is a two-way process in which both leader and followers get some of their needs satisfied.

- A person does not become a leader simply because he or she wants to take on the role, but because other people confer the authority to influence their behaviour, which means that leadership is conferred from below, not above as in headship.

- Would-be leaders will probably have their own ideas about how the role should be performed, for instance how much influence they are entitled to exert over followers, and followers will have expectations about how the leader should behave, including the amount of influence the leader should have over their behaviour.

- Whether they are prepared to concede the amount of influence that a leader wants will probably depend on whether this is felt to be an acceptable price to pay for satisfaction of their needs.

- From this it follows that the leader–follower relationship is a potentially fragile state of affairs because if conditions change, the needs of both leader and followers can change, and it is more than possible that the group will come to see the leader as an inappropriate person for the new situation. If this happens pressure is often brought to bear on the leader to change his or her behaviour, and if these moves are not successful, attempts can sometimes be made to replace the leader with someone else.

For these reasons, a leader can be defined as:

Someone who occupies a role which involves conforming to a set of behavioural norms and expectations emanating from followers, in return for which they confer on the leader a degree of power that (within prescribed limits) allows the leader to influence their actions.

Where does all this leave the manager in terms of being a leader? Because a manager has some formal authority to influence subordinate behaviour, he or she clearly has a flying start in coming to occupy a role of leadership. However, because the authority is there does not mean that subordinates will willingly assent to its use. They may simply comply with instructions, and this is far from being a situation where leadership is at work. Therefore, although managers can be leaders as well as heads, this is not an inevitable state of affairs. As such, and even though it is widely assumed that leadership can be taught to anybody (see OB in Action box below), it is probably far more realistic to regard management and leadership as two complementary activities (Kotter 1990) with each one having its own unique functions and characteristics, and both being necessary.

OB IN ACTION: Leadership Training at Barclays

When Barclays University, the training unit of the UK-based high street banking group, was looking for a way to encourage junior team leaders to adopt more of a leadership role, it turned to Epic, the quoted e-learning consultancy. It needed a programme to provide an integrated and consistent leadership proposition for everyone from junior team leaders, who may have responsibility for two to three people, up to heads of strategic business units – a total of about 5,000 potential users. 'The senior management wanted them to take a more active leadership role,' explained Donald Clark, Epic's chief executive. In partnership with Barclays University, Epic developed a training programme dubbed 'Take the lead . . .'

The training programme was built around a blended approach, integrating offline and online training resources and delivery systems. Mr Clark explains: 'A key component of this blend is the "take the lead" website, which forms a single gateway for leader development within Barclays.' The content is specifically designed to engage the 'students' by focusing on leadership issues and role models, drawn not only from within the financial organisation, but also from contemporary society and popular culture – examining Sven-Goran Eriksson's leadership style, for instance, or the dynamics of team building within the *Big Brother* house on television. The site is also the jumping-off point for a series of e-learning modules, theories, just-in-time performance support tools and online reference materials. 'Take the lead in style' is the first module to be released. Other recently introduced modules include 'take the lead' courses in performance, change, teamworking, innovation, communication, time, life and the business world. Other elements of the blended training programme include Barclays University learning 'nudges' – short pieces of 'just-in-time' learning also developed by Epic – supporting links and suggested reading, diagnostic tools, face-to-face workshops and support through telephone tutoring.

Source:

Taylor, P (2003) Barclays University: taking the lead in staff training, *The Financial Times*, 23 June.

THE SIGNIFICANCE OF LEADERSHIP TO ORGANISATIONS

Leadership is an attribute that is highly prized in most organisations and, as a result, it is an extensively studied and debated topic in Organisational Behaviour (Meindl *et al.* 1987). There is a widely held belief that leadership is one of the factors (if not the most important factor) which determines whether a group, an organisation or even a nation will be successful. As part of the positions they occupy, managers in organisations are granted a degree of power to influence subordinate behaviour and, since this can usually result in a considerable degree of employee compliance, it can be asked whether leadership is necessary. The paradox is that in today's conditions, widespread delayering has placed a strong emphasis on empowering people at lower organisational levels: so what makes leadership important? Here the answer is comparatively straightforward and can be found in the distinction between headship and leadership made earlier.

A leader can have a strong influence on the behaviour and performance of group members, and while influence is a form of authority, it is a much more subtle form of control than the naked use of power. Followers willingly consent to coming under another person's control and in so doing they become the authors of their own subordination, and because the whole situation is partly 'their idea', they are more likely to be committed to performing well. Therefore, to the extent that a manager or supervisor is able to be a leader as well as a head, it is more likely that the human effort will be deployed in exactly the way the organisation wishes. This gives us one reason why leadership is considered important in organisations; because it is likely to be a cheaper, less obtrusive and a more effective means of control than simply directing people's efforts and monitoring compliance.

There is, however, another reason why it is considered important, and this is probably more connected with the symbolic significance of the word than anything else. The word 'leader' has an almost heroic ring which conjures up an image of someone who brings order, success and triumph to a situation of potential failure or defeat; a saviour figure, without whom a group might flounder in its own lack of direction or, as one author describes matters, the CEO as an all-action superhero (Reeves 2002). This is an image firmly imprinted in our minds in the West, where our literature and childhood stories are replete with hero figures such as King Arthur or Beowulf. We are also taught that society is (or should be) a meritocracy, in which the most able people rise to positions of authority. Therefore, the concepts of leader and leadership may well have considerable appeal to managers because this is how they like to think of themselves – as those who exercise authority because all those around them acknowledge their fitness to command.

TIME OUT

Think carefully about your own experience of being a member of a group, either at your place of work, in your social life, or at college or university. Think of a situation where the group chose its own head either by formally electing the person or in a less formal way, for example, the captain of a football or hockey team is sometimes chosen this way. Now identify a situation where someone was chosen to be in charge by people outside the group, for example in a work situation.

1. Which of the two people had the most real authority with those beneath them?
2. Try to identify examples of how one person had more real authority than the other, for example, which one of them could give instructions that would most readily be followed?
3. What conclusions do you draw from this exercise about the importance of leadership as opposed to headship for organisations?

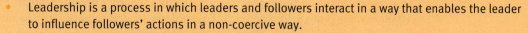

REPLAY

- Leadership is a process in which leaders and followers interact in a way that enables the leader to influence followers' actions in a non-coercive way.
- Leadership theories fall into one or other of two main approaches: descriptive or functional.
- Because they derive their authority from above, managers are not necessarily leaders but occupy positions of headship and, in leadership, authority is conferred from below by followers who willingly consent to a chosen leader influencing their behaviour.
- In organisations, leadership is important because employees are likely to work in a more committed way for someone they look upon as a leader than for someone who simply occupies a position of headship, to whom they may just give compliance.

LEADERSHIP THEORIES AND MODELS

Theorising and research into leadership has a long pedigree in the social and organisational sciences. Over the years a number of theoretical strands have emerged, each representing a different perspective on the subject. This sometimes leads to confusion about what the different perspectives have to offer. One way to make sense of this diversity is to classify the different approaches on the two-dimensional matrix shown in Figure 12.2.

The horizontal dimension shown across the top of the matrix reflects the extent to which a theory results in a universal or situation-specific view of leadership. Universal theories, which are the main focus of this chapter, claim to be applicable in all situations and normally reflect the assumption that there is a 'one best way' to lead. Conversely, situation-specific theories, which are covered in Chapter 13, draw attention to the idea that different types of leadership can be more appropriate in different circumstances. The vertical dimension reflects the extent to which a theory focuses on the leader as a

Figure 12.2 A typology of leadership theories

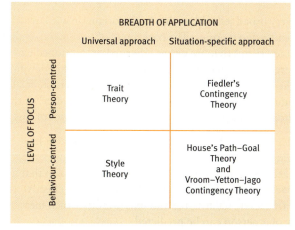

person or on the leader's behaviour. Person-centred theories deal with the leader's personal characteristics, which are usually treated as relatively fixed, while behavioural approaches focus on leader behaviour and are concerned with the way that different patterns of behaviour can affect the leadership process.

As in most fields of study, the theories appeared in a sequence because scholars perceived shortcomings in a prior approach. To enable the reader to appreciate how ideas in the area have developed, the theories will be described in the order in which they appeared. Most of the theories originate in America and focus exclusively on leadership in organisational settings. While none actually states that being a leader and being a manager are the same thing, they all focus on the manager and treat this person as someone who occupies a position of leadership: a perspective that is commonplace in most prominent leadership theorists in America.

TIME OUT

Reflect carefully on the person you identified in the previous exercise as the leader of a group to which you belong or have belonged in the past. Now identify the characteristics of the person which, in your view, resulted in him or her being chosen by the group as its leader.

1. Was this because the person had a distinctive character or personality that others looked up to?
2. Was this because the person had particular skills and/or abilities that the group found useful?
3. Was there something else about the person which resulted in him or her coming to occupy a position of leadership?
4. Bring all the information in questions 1–3 together and in one or two sentences say why you feel this person became the leader.

TRAIT THEORY

This is a very broad set of ideas that has its origins in work which pre-dates the development of leadership theories. The basic tenet of *trait theory* is that leaders have personality characteristics that are either inherited or developed early in life which result in them emerging as leaders in most situations. While this view first appeared around the turn of the twentieth century, it is a remarkably persistent idea and even today it is not uncommon to hear people speak of the 'born leader' or the 'natural leader'.

Trait theory: the assumption that certain people have inherent characteristics which enable them to be leaders

The three basic assumptions inherent in all theories of this type are:

- in order to be an effective leader, an individual must have certain personal characteristics (traits);
- traits are stable and transferable across situations so that a person who leads effectively in one situation is equally likely to be effective elsewhere;
- traits are clearly identifiable and measurable, which means that the leadership ability of a person can be predicted.

Work in this area was largely focused on attempts to identify the required traits, usually by cataloguing those people who are widely acknowledged to be good leaders, for example, great generals such as Julius Caesar, or statesmen such as George Washington and Abraham Lincoln. Like so much else in psychological research, the initial findings looked promising, but the end results are less than satisfactory. Literally dozens of seemingly important traits were identified, so many that it is impossible to find any that are common to all those people who can be identified as effective leaders. In what was perhaps the most penetrating review of the area, Stogdill (1948) pointed out that most research points to five key traits that differentiate leaders from followers: intelligence, dominance, self-confidence, high levels of energy and task-related knowledge. However, while acknowledging that these traits are important, he also noted traits are very poor predictors of who emerges as a leader; for example, some traits are also commonplace among followers. For this reason there are a number of strong criticisms of the trait approach, which can be summarised as:

- Because the list of influential traits is virtually endless, there is no real agreement about those which are the most important, and some that are said to be the most important are not even characteristics of all successful leaders.

- Even if it were possible to establish consensus about the most important traits, defining a successful leader still tends to be a matter of subjective judgement. To identify traits associated with effective leadership it is first necessary to define leader effectiveness in very precise terms. However, trait theories simply assume that someone who is prominent or successful must be a good leader, which is a highly tautological argument that effectively says 'here is a great leader, the great leader has these traits, therefore the leader is a leader because of these traits'.

- Since success or prominence can be due to many factors other than leadership, for example inherited wealth or the old-boy network, the trait approach is clearly a wildly inaccurate assumption.

- Strictly speaking, traits are personality variables whereas many of the characteristics identified as traits can more accurately be described as patterns of behaviour and a person's behaviour is partly a function of a specific situation.

Despite the above weaknesses, it would be unwise to dismiss trait theory completely. A review of the literature (Kirkpatrick and Locke 1991) suggests that effective leaders are different from other people and even Stogdill, who initially dismissed trait theory, eventually revised his stance and cautioned against the assumption that leadership is totally situational and devoid of any personal effects (Stogdill 1974). The current thinking is that, while there are probably no universal leadership traits, there are some traits that are likely to be crucially important in a selected range of situations (Judge *et al.* 2002; Taggar *et al.* 1999). In addition, Kenny and Zaccaro (1983) note that there are people who seem to gravitate to leadership positions in whatever they do, probably because they have a strong ability to predict what a situation requires and to modify their own approach accordingly. This is not the same as saying that they have important traits that guarantee their emergence as leaders, but it may indicate that they have two important characteristics:

- the ability accurately to sense the requirements of a situation;
- a repertoire of behaviours that gives a capacity to adapt to the situation.

Arguments such as these have recently given the trait approach a new lease of life in a much more sophisticated form, which suggests that certain traits have an impact on the way that someone is perceived and experienced by other people. If these traits induce other people to perceive the individual as someone who has leadership ability, then it is far more likely that he or she will be accorded the status of leader (Lord *et al.* 1986). Therefore, if the person can recognise what has happened, he or she will be well placed to manipulate the situation to ensure occupancy of a position of leadership (Smircich and Morgan 1982). Chapter 13 will return to this idea, but for the present it is more important to explore the next major development in leadership thinking.

CASE STUDY 12.1: Gordon Allbury

For the last nine months Gordon Allbury has been the manager of the personal loans department in Steadfast PLC, a savings and loan company (building society), and since taking up the post he has been somewhat perturbed about the relationship between him and his subordinates. From the outset, rather than just being the boss, he wanted to be seen as a leader who inspired his subordinates to greater effort. Therefore, he took great pains to develop patterns of behaviour that he felt were appropriate to achieving this outcome. For instance, he made a point of always being cheerful, he was energetic and had a great deal of self-confidence. If one of his staff approached him with a problem, he was careful to be seen to think deeply, so that his decision would be considered an intelligent one. He also kept himself well informed about his own boss's priorities so that he could accurately brief staff. Despite his natural inclination to put his own work above everything else, he had tried to give just as much attention to the needs of staff, and to organise their work so that nothing interfered with them getting the job done.

Despite all this, however, he felt that the staff did not see him as a leader, but were more inclined to look on one of his subordinates, a man called Ted Green, in this way. Although they were content to let Gordon make the decisions about what needed to be done, they invariably turned to Ted when they needed advice or help on how to do it. Indeed, Ted's influence seemed to extend beyond getting the job done into such matters as organising social events for the department. To be fair, Ted had never done anything to set himself up as a leader and, on reflection, Gordon realised that Ted was one of his staunchest supporters. However, Gordon could still not see why the staff looked to Ted for leadership. Although intelligent and competent, he was very quiet and had none of Gordon's self-confidence and natural enthusiasm. He held no official position of authority within the department and seemed to have no inclination to gain additional status. Moreover, he had no power to reward people materially for doing a good job and there were several other people in the department who were far more experienced than Ted. If anything, Gordon felt Ted fitted in too well with his colleagues and was a bit too considerate with them. Thus Gordon could simply not explain where Ted's apparent influence came from.

Question

Who is the leader in this department and what factors explain the patterns of leadership that exist?

STYLE THEORIES

Because trait theory failed to predict the success of leaders, but traits are generally assumed to lead to characteristic patterns of behaviour, the next development focused on a simpler question: what behaviours are most closely associated with leadership success? Work in this approach was heavily influenced by human relations theory and an early piece of research which acted as the trigger to almost everything that followed was a study of 20 eleven-year-old boys who met under adult leaders in a hobby club to undertake such activities as model building (Lewin *et al.* 1939). Lewin and his colleagues were able to place the behaviourial styles of leaders into one or other of three categories, each of which had identifiable effects on followers.

Autocratic leaders: those who strongly control subordinates and make all major decisions

Autocratic leaders made all the major decisions and exerted a high degree of control over the children. Thus, while followers were very clear about what to do, they were less sure why it needed to be done and were often unwilling to accept any responsibility when things went wrong. They also tended to have a low level of morale and some hostility towards each other and the leader.

Democratic leaders: those who involve followers in decisions

Democratic leaders involved followers in decisions and delegated much more responsibility to the group. This was said to lead to higher-quality decisions, a much stronger team spirit, commitment to implementing decisions and satisfaction among followers.

Laissez-faire leaders: those who abdicate from the leadership role

Laissez-faire leaders had a strong tendency to abdicate from the leader role. Although they did not make decisions for followers, or exercise control, this was not because of a conscious desire to delegate or stimulate participation, but simply because they had little desire to provide leadership. Thus, unless followers were competent and self-motivated, they opted out of trying to complete tasks and looked for their satisfactions in the social side of group life. This was by far the least effective style in terms of getting tasks completed.

The researchers came down heavily in favour of the democratic style, which probably reflected the dominant social values of the day. Nevertheless, the work gave a strong impetus for a shift in focus away from the trait approach, and this resulted in research of a more penetrating nature.

The milestone development in style theory came from a pair of independent studies conducted by two highly prestigious American universities: the **Ohio State Leadership Studies** and the **Michigan Leadership Studies**. Both studies focused on the behaviour of people in actual work settings and started from an explicit definition of two criteria of leadership effectiveness: task completion and follower satisfaction. The researchers examined the effects of different leader styles on subordinates' perceptions of these outcomes, and since the conclusions and assumptions are slightly different it is convenient to describe each study in turn.

Two-factor theory of leadership: that there are two independent dimensions to leader behaviour, that is, initiating structure and consideration

The Ohio State Leadership Studies

These took place in the late 1940s and resulted in what is now known as the *two-factor theory of leadership* (Fleishman 1953). Prior to the main body of work, questionnaires were developed to measure subordinate perceptions of leader behaviour and leaders' self-perceptions of their own behaviourial styles. Using these questionnaires, data was collected and two primary dimensions of leader behaviour were isolated.

- **Initiating structure**   behaviour concerned with achieving the group's formal task. Supervisors and managers scoring high on this dimension were firmly focused on completing the task and they tended to tightly structure the work of subordinates.

- **Consideration**   behaviour focused on interpersonal relations within the group, for example trying to develop mutual trust between themselves and subordinates, or showing some concern for their feelings and involving them in decisions.

The researchers drew the conclusion that these two dimensions of behaviour were unconnected. Thus a supervisor might only pay attention to one of them and, even where there was a focus on both, the score on one was independent of the score on the other. This gave four basic leadership styles:

1. High consideration and high initiating structure.
2. High consideration and low initiating structure.
3. Low consideration and high initiating structure.
4. Low consideration and low initiating structure.

Leader effectiveness was defined in terms of two group outcomes – task completion and member satisfaction – and an important finding was that the two dimensions of leader behaviour had different implications for these outcomes. Supervisors high on initiating structure were highly productive in terms of task completion but, where the focus was solely on output, grievance rates and turnover also tended to be high. Conversely, highly considerate supervisors were found to have groups with very high morale and member satisfaction but low productivity. The conclusion was drawn that both dimensions are important for leader effectiveness. Unfortunately, however, a number of later theorists over-generalised from this conclusion, by assuming that the ideal leader is someone who is high on both consideration and initiating structure. In practical terms, however, it can be extremely difficult, if not impossible, for a single person to have this dual orientation. Indeed, in many groups, these two aspects of leadership are often provided by different people.

The Michigan Leadership Studies

In terms of methodology and findings this work has strong similarities with the Ohio Studies (Likert 1961). Almost identical criteria of effectiveness were derived, supervisors and subordinates were also used as data sources, and two contrasting dimensions of leadership behaviour were identified. However, unlike the Ohio Studies where the dimensions were deemed to be independent aspects of behaviour, the Michigan researchers drew a different conclusion. The two dimensions were said to be different styles of behaviour that lay at the extremes of a continuum, stretching from production-centred leadership at one end to employee-centred leadership at the other. In the production-centred style the supervisor's primary focus was on task performance, so any interactions with subordinates were confined to briefing them on the job in hand and supervising their work. With the employee-centred style, although the supervisor still focused on productivity, this was achieved by developing a satisfied, cohesive work group.

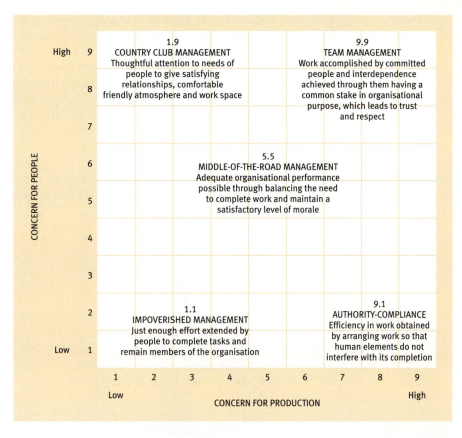

Figure 12.3 The leadership grid (Source: Blake and McCanse 1991)

Clearly there are similarities between the Ohio and Michigan studies. Both identify two similar dimensions of leader behaviour and draw similar conclusions about which of these is the most desirable. The ideas have therefore found widespread application in leadership training for supervisors and managers, perhaps the best-known example of which is the Blake and Mouton (1964) *managerial grid* (Figure 12.3).

The grid is really intended to be used as a diagnostic tool in the first stage of a more extensive programme of organisational development (see Chapter 21) which starts with managers exploring their own leadership styles. As can be seen, the terms 'concern for people' and 'concern for production' replace the expressions used in the Ohio and Michigan studies, and scores on the two dimensions can be anywhere between 1 and 9. Blake and Mouton suggest that a 9:9 style (high concern for both people and production) is the ideal. For this reason, although the grid has been widely used for a number of years – long enough, in fact, for the method to have been updated and revised (Blake and McCanse 1991) – the ideas have been strongly criticised. The assumption that the 9:9 style is universally superior has never been convincingly demonstrated (Bernardin and Alvares 1976), and since this is also a criticism of all style theories, it is relevant to conclude this section by evaluating their contribution to leadership theory.

Although style theories moved thinking about leadership out of the cul-de-sac of trait theory, they still give a universalist view of leadership, which assumes a 'one best

Managerial grid: an application of style theories of leadership used for training and development purposes

style' for all occasions; for example, the alleged superiority of the 9:9 style on the Blake and Mouton grid. Although they show that behavioural styles influence the supervisor–subordinate relationship, and that this in turn has an impact on the output of a group, the theories quietly ignore something of potential importance. This is that the circumstances surrounding the relationship can also have an impact on a supervisor's style (Tracy 1987). Even when it is not a supervisor's natural style, there can be compelling reasons why he or she behaves in a production-centred way, for instance, because the boss emphasises output above everything else. Style theory can also be criticised for the way it assumes that the supervisor or manager is a leader of some sort, and that subordinates are followers. This is a very one-sided view that underestimates the subtleties and complexities of leadership. Thus, style theories probably have more to say about differences in manager (headship) behaviour than about leadership.

REPLAY

- Style theories were an important breakthrough in leadership theory beyond trait ideas.
- They draw attention to the idea that the way a leader behaves has an important impact on the effectiveness of a group.
- Nevertheless, style theories still have significant weaknesses, the most important of which are that leaders and managers tend to be regarded as the same thing and that there is assumed to be a single style of leader behaviour suitable for all circumstances.

CASE STUDY 12.2: Comparative Supervisory Styles in the Medway Bank

Two supervisors, Jane Lewin and Allison Black, each manage a team of clerical workers in the headquarters of the Medway Bank, situated near Rochester in the southeast of England. In a recent review of the performance of the two sections it was revealed that in terms of meeting its deadlines, Jane's section consistently outperformed Allison's. In addition, the results of a recent employee opinion survey indicated that Allison's subordinates had a noticeably lower degree of satisfaction with work than the employees who work for Jane. So far as can be determined, there are no differences between the two sections in terms of the more obvious factors that might lead to differences in meeting targets. Both have adequate staffing levels and the demographic characteristics of each one (e.g. age distribution, gender composition, educational background etc.) are approximately the same. It is therefore concluded that the difference could lie in the styles of the supervisors. A more detailed description of the teams and the styles of their supervisors is given below.

Customer Enquiry Clerks

This team, which consists of ten female clerks of mixed job experience, is managed by Jane Lewin and answers queries from customers. Queries are usually received by telephone and each clerk has her own computer terminal in order to be able to access customer records. In addition, each clerk has a full set of manuals that cover the bank's product portfolio and procedures. Although most customers demand personal attention and show every sign of believing that their queries are unique, most enquiries are very routine and over 90 per cent of them can be resolved almost immediately by the clerk who receives the call. When this cannot be achieved, the clerks can consult Jane and, in more complex cases, the query is investigated and the clerk replies in writing to the customer. However, over 99 per cent of all queries are dealt with to the satisfaction of the customer within three working days.

Jane's style is roughly an equal mixture of a focus on getting the job done and supporting her subordinates. In a firm but friendly way she tends to insist that customer queries must be cleared quickly. In those instances where a decision is referred to her, she is always careful to make it a learning experience for the clerk involved, by briefing the employee on the decision that has been made before the customer is notified. To promote efficiency she encourages the ten clerks to work as three sub-teams, each of which has its own experts in different types of query. This way they can refer cases to each other within the team. She is also extremely caring about the welfare of the team members.

Account Clerks

This team consists of nine very skilled and experienced clerks of both sexes and is under the control of Allison Black. Their work consists of processing applications from customers for loans and overdraft facilities and, if necessary, this includes running a credit-worthiness check on the customer. This is highly responsible work and all the clerks are self-motivated people who take a pride in their work. Allison's style is almost identical to that of Jane. She is insistent on a three-day turnaround of customer applications and, in view of the sensitive nature of the work, she encourages clerks to consult her where there is some suspicion that a customer might be over-extending him or herself in the size of loan that has been applied for. In these cases Allison usually contacts the customer to talk things through before informing the clerk of the final decision. Like Jane, she is also very caring about the welfare of team members and strongly encourages them to share information in order to build up a good team spirit.

Questions

1. Using an appropriate style theory or a modern derivative thereof, how would you classify the leadership styles of Jane Lewin and Allison Black?

2. How do you account for the fact that Jane's team appears to perform better than Allison's and, in the light of your explanation, comment on the appropriateness of each style to the circumstances of the team.

UNIVERSAL VERSUS CONTINGENCY THEORIES

When it was realised that there is probably no such thing as a 'one best style' of leadership, research focused on identifying key situational variables that can make one style more appropriate than others. As will be seen in the next chapter, the underlying assumption of this approach is that effective leadership requires a person to use a style of behaviour that matches the conditions in which leadership is exercised. This

Figure 12.4
Continuum of
leadership styles
(after Tannenbaum
and Schmidt 1958)

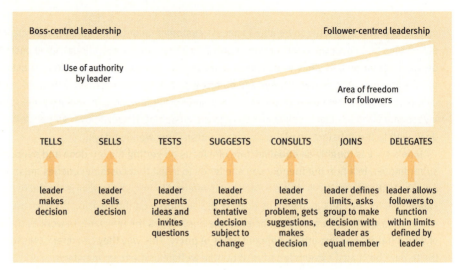

is known as the contingency theory approach and over the years many such theories have been developed. However, the precursor to this way of thinking emerged when style theories were still very much in vogue, in a theoretical model developed by Tannenbaum and Schmidt (1958), the basics of which are shown in Figure 12.4.

Tannenbaum and Schmidt's ideas were influenced by the basic distinction between job-centred (boss-centred) and employee-centred (follower-centred) behaviour, which are shown at the extremes of the continuum. However, between these extremes a variety of styles is shown, each corresponding to a different pattern of interaction between follower and manager. The appropriateness of these styles is said by Tannenbaum and Schmidt to depend on a number of factors, for example, the manager's value system, personal wants, his or her confidence in employees and the willingness of subordinates to accept responsibility. Since the authors did not develop the ideas beyond this point, no indication is given of which style is the most appropriate according to the factors at work. Nevertheless, by pointing out that there are several factors that can influence the appropriateness of different styles, it paved the way for work by others, which is covered in Chapter 13.

TIME OUT

Using the group and its leader that you identified in the earlier Time Out exercise, use the Tannenbaum and Schmidt model to answer the questions below.

1. Where would you place the leader's style on the Tannenbaum and Schmidt continuum?
2. How personally acceptable to you was/is the leader's style?
3. Why is it that you find the style either acceptable or unacceptable?
4. How acceptable do you feel the leader's style is to other group members?
5. Can you identify any reasons why they find the style acceptable or unacceptable?

FURTHER READING

Bass, B M and R M Stogdill (1990) *Bass and Stogdill's Handbook of Leadership: Theory, Research and Managerial Applications*, New York: Free Press. Almost certainly the most comprehensive text yet written on leadership theories and their application.

Bryman, A (1996) 'Leadership in Organisations', in S R Clegg, C Hardy and W R Nord (eds), *Handbook of Organisation Studies*, London: Sage. An easy-to-read critical review of leadership theory and research which, among other things, contains an excellent exploration of the links between leadership and organisational culture.

Diehl, C and M Dennelly (2001) *How Did They Manage? Leadership Secrets of History*, London: Spiro Press. To a large extent, the title is self-explanatory. Using what is essentially a trait theory approach, it has a strong 'how-to-do-it' flavour and purports to convey the essence of effective leadership by examining great leaders from history.

Koch, R (2002) *The 80/20 Revolution*, London: Nicholas Brealey. In essence the book is a testament to the persuasiveness of trait theory ideas, which according to its author are as timely today as ever.

Northouse, P G (1997) *Leadership: Theory and Practice*, London: Sage. A very readable book. It contains a brief, but sound, coverage of a wide variety of theoretical approaches to leadership and its practical applications.

Wright, P (1995) *Managerial Leadership*, London: Thomson. A very practical approach to leadership that is mainly be of interest to the manager (actual or would be).

REVIEW AND DISCUSSION QUESTIONS

1. Using the concepts of 'headship' and 'leadership' explain whether and to what extent the words 'leader' and 'manager' are just expressions that have the same meaning.

2. Why is it that most organisations give formal authority to managers to direct and control the activities of their subordinates, but at the same time stress the importance of leadership skills in managers?

3. Explain the underlying assumptions of trait theories of leadership and the extent to which these theories have a practical utility for modern organisations.

4. Explain the fundamental way in which style theories of leadership differ from trait ideas and the extent to which this results in a more realistic perspective on leadership.

5. Describe a development of style theory that has found widespread use as a vehicle for expressing leadership style and whether the fundamental assumptions of this model make it one that has practical utility for organisations.

Chapter 13

Leadership: Advanced Theories

LEARNING OUTCOMES

After studying this chapter you should be able to:

- explain the contingency approach to leadership and describe the following contingency theories: Fiedler's LPC model, path–goal theory, the Vroom–Yetton–Jago model, the Hersey and Blanchard model and the substitutes for leadership model

- discuss recent approaches to leadership theory, including the difference between transactional and transformational leadership and the attributional approach

- appreciate the potential effects of national cultures on the appropriateness of different leadership styles

INTRODUCTION

This chapter follows on from Chapter 12 and starts with an exploration of 'contingency theory', a major group of leadership theories that deal with the circumstances that are likely to make one leadership style more appropriate than another. The chapter then examines some of the more recent developments in ideas about leadership. Since many theories covered in this chapter emphasise the importance of the context in which leadership is exercised, a brief consideration of the implications of national cultures is given, addressing the issue of whether culture has an impact on the appropriateness of different leadership styles. Finally, the different approaches in this and the previous chapter are compared and contrasted, and some general conclusions are drawn.

CONTINGENCY THEORIES OF LEADERSHIP

As noted at the end of Chapter 12, the realisation that there is probably no such thing as a 'one best style' of leadership appropriate in all circumstances prompted a new direction in leadership research. While this continued to use the concept of leadership style, the aim was not to identify a single style that is appropriate everywhere, but to pinpoint key situational variables that make one style more appropriate than others in certain specific circumstances, the underlying assumption being that effective leadership requires a person to use a style of behaviour that matches the conditions in which leadership is to be exercised.

Fiedler's Contingency Theory

This was the first true contingency theory of leadership. It first appeared some 30 years ago (Fiedler 1967) and is sometimes referred to as the LPC model. In Fiedler's view, the most appropriate style of leader behaviour is that which results in high task performance by a group, and this is said to be an outcome of two important factors: the preferred behavioural style of the leader and the contextual circumstances in which the group operates. The way that these variables interact is shown in Figure 13.1.

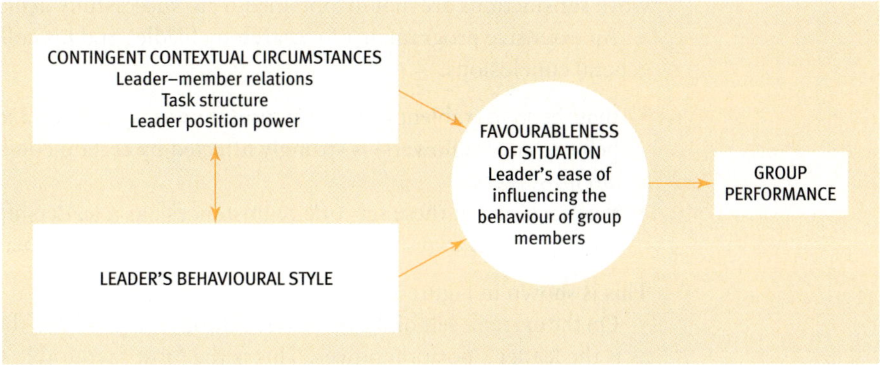

Figure 13.1
Interaction of variables in Fiedler's contingency theory

Table 13.1 Sample dimensions of the LPC scale

	8	7	6	5	4	3	2	1	
Cooperative									Uncooperative
Friendly									Unfriendly
Supportive									Hostile

The three key contextual variables that affect the appropriateness of a particular style are said to be:

- **Leader–member relations:** the quality of the relationship between leader and followers. This is good where leader and followers have confidence, liking, trust and respect for each other, which gives a situation that is favourable to the leader, favourable being defined as 'ease of influencing subordinate behaviour'.

- **Task structure:** the nature of the group's task. Where this is clear, unambiguous and routine, task structure is said to be high and the leader will find it comparatively unnecessary to guide, direct and supervise the group's work. This is also a situation which works in his or her favour.

- **Leader position power:** the formal organisational authority vested in the supervisor's role. Where power is high, the person has the authority to assign tasks directly to subordinates and to reward and punish them for good or bad performance. Again, this is a situation which is favourable to the leader.

Least preferred co-worker (LPC): the subordinate that a supervisor was least able to work with successfully on a prior occasion

A supervisor's preferred leadership style is normally assessed by using a scale that taps orientations towards the person's *least preferred co-worker (LPC)*, that is, the individual or subordinate that the supervisor was least able to work with successfully in the past. The supervisor is then asked to rate this person's characteristics on sixteen bipolar scales, three examples of which are shown in Table 13.1. Responses to all scales are added up and an average is obtained, which gives the supervisor's LPC score.

The idea here is that a supervisor with positive orientation towards a subordinate who is liked least (high LPC score) will be someone who is sensitive to other people and gets satisfaction from interacting with them at work, that is, a 'relationship-orientated' supervisor. Conversely, low LPC supervisors (those with negative orientations towards their least preferred colleague) are basically 'task-orientated', and their work satisfactions are mainly obtained from successfully achieving output goals.

An extensive programme of research by Fiedler and his colleagues resulted in two general conclusions:

- that the favourableness of a situation (how easy it is for a leader to influence the behaviour of followers) is strongly affected by certain combinations of external circumstances;
- that each one of these sets of circumstances has a leadership style that is most appropriate in terms of obtaining effective group performance.

This is shown in Figure 13.2.

On the extreme left of the diagram relations are good and the task structure is high, as is the leader's position power. This is the most favourable situation for the leader

Figure 13.2 Fiedler's contingency theory – circumstances and leadership styles

CONTEXTUAL CIRCUMSTANCES								
Leader–member Relations	Good	Good	Good	Good	Bad	Bad	Bad	Bad
Task Structure	High	High	Low	Low	High	High	Low	Low
Leader Position Power	Strong	Weak	Strong	Weak	Strong	Weak	Strong	Weak
FAVOURABLENESS OF SITUATION	HIGH				MEDIUM		LOW	
MOST APPROPRIATE BEHAVIOURAL STYLE	Low LPC Task-orientated				High LPC Relationship-orientated		Low LPC Task-orientated	

because the task does not require the person to become greatly involved in direct supervision; leader and followers are tolerant towards each other; the supervisor's power position allows rewards to be given to subordinates for good performance. Therefore, the most appropriate style involves a primary focus on the task. At the opposite (right-hand) extreme relations are not so good, the supervisor has little position power and, importantly, the task is more ambiguous. Task ambiguity requires that the leader becomes more involved in directing subordinates, but this has to be done without the benefit of being able to use rewards or punishments as inducements. Therefore, to spur people on to give maximum effort, the most appropriate style is also one which is strongly focused on the task. In the fourth column from the left there is a also a degree of task ambiguity and, once again, this requires that the supervisor gives more direction. However, while position power is weak, and rewards and punishments cannot be used, relations are good, which means that subordinates would not resent a high degree of supervisor involvement, and may even welcome it. Thus the most appropriate style for effective group performance is that of helpful, relationship-orientated behaviour.

Fiedler considers that since a leader's style (as measured by LPC score) is a function of the individual's personality it is relatively fixed and unchanging. Therefore, if a person's style does not fit the circumstances, there are two alternatives: either the leader can be removed and a new one appointed, or the circumstances must be changed. In his view the latter is by far the most appropriate step and (to use his own words) he advocates 'engineering the job to fit the manager' (Fiedler 1965). This might sound a difficult, or even impossible, task. However, in more recent work (Fiedler and Garcia 1987), a range of actions is suggested that can be used to bring about changes in the three contextual variables. These form the basis of a scheme for developing managers in leadership, the leader match programme, which has a somewhat unusual approach to leadership training. In most cases training of this type attempts to change a person's style of behaviour, but in Fiedler's method the aim is to teach the manager ways of changing the situation. An outline of his suggested ways of doing this is given in Table 13.2.

Although Fiedler's model is a huge advance on style theories, there are criticisms. Studies to test the validity of the theory have yielded mixed evidence about its accuracy (Graen *et al*. 1971). There are also arguments that variables other than the three suggested by Fiedler could influence leader effectiveness. For example:

Table 13.2 Leader actions to change the state of contingency variables

Contingency variable		
Leader–member relations	**To improve leader–member relations:** • spend more time with group members on an informal basis • ask for specific people to be allocated to the group • offer help or direction to difficult group members • transfer particular people in or out of the group • raise feelings of satisfaction by obtaining positive outcomes for group members	
Task structure	**To increase task structure:** • obtain structured and straightforward tasks for the group, together with detailed criteria for completion • break down the jobs and tasks into more tightly structured parts	**To lower task structure:** • obtain novel and unstructured problems or tasks to be solved by the group and/or • involve subordinates in working jointly with leader to solve problems
Leader position power	**To enhance position power:** • exercise in full those powers granted by the organisation to reinforce the appearance of being in charge • become the sole channel for information coming into the group	**To decrease position power:** • share decisions with group members • allow more autonomy to group members

Source: Fiedler and Garcia 1987, pp 49–93.

- there are strong criticisms of the use of LPC scores to evaluate a leader's normal behaviour, because while LPC probably gives an indication of a person's attitudes or even personality, these are often poor guides to actual behaviour;
- Fiedler's sole criterion for evaluating supervisor effectiveness is task performance, which neglects the equally important factor of follower satisfaction;
- perhaps most damning of all, it has been argued that Fiedler's model can take in virtually any set of research findings and show that they support his ideas, which ultimately means that it can be little more than a self-fulfilling prophecy.

For all these criticisms, Fiedler's work is a significant contribution to leadership theory and, in recognising that contextual circumstances can have a strong impact on the appropriateness of a leader's behaviour, the theory broke the strait-jacket of a 'one best style' approach. Perhaps more importantly, his work prompted an ongoing search for other potentially influential variables, and so subsequent developments owe a great deal to his ideas.

The Path–goal Theory of Leadership

This model of leadership was originally proposed by House (1971) and has its roots in the expectancy theory of motivation (see Chapter 8) which argues that the motivation to perform a task is a function of two connected factors:

CASE STUDY 13.1: Supervisor Behaviour at Gordon Engineering

Terry Peters and Bill Cook are supervisors at Gordon Engineering, a medium-sized manufacturing company. Both are in their early 40s and have similar backgrounds. They both joined the firm direct from school to serve their apprenticeships as toolmakers and both were promoted to supervisory positions about three years ago. Terry runs a small department of eighteen men which makes unique, purpose-designed precision products to customers' own specifications and Bill is in charge of a production line of twenty semi-skilled operators who assemble components into one of the firm's best-selling products, an industrial vacuum cleaner.

Terry and Bill's jobs each have their own inherent problems. In Terry's department, planning and organising the work is a major headache. Each job is very different and tends to require its own set of operations, which means there is a daily need to move men from one job to another to keep pace with promised delivery dates. Although most of the men enjoy the wide variety in the work, there are sometimes mild complaints that they never know from one day to the next what they will be doing. Therefore, Terry spends a great deal of time talking with his people to monitor the progress of work and is highly attentive to their preferences for certain types of job. Since the work is highly profitable (but erratic in nature), higher management allocate the department a monthly bonus pool, and Terry distributes this among his men on the basis of their performance. He is extremely well liked and respected by his subordinates and they frequently enjoy a social evening once a month to celebrate the bonus.

In Bill's department the major problem is keeping the line running at full pace. Each person has his or her allotted job to do and, unless someone is sick, there are few problems of moving people between jobs. However, the work can be somewhat monotonous and Bill occasionally finds that he needs to be fairly firm with the operators to ensure that they keep their minds on the job. For this reason, his relations with the workforce are sometimes rather strained. As Bill sees the situation, because they are all paid exactly the same rate, one problem with maintaining discipline is that he has virtually no power to reward good workers and penalise those who are less willing. As sometimes happens in a working environment like this, the work itself results in a distance between operators and their supervisor. Despite this, however, he tries hard to reduce the barriers by interacting with the people as much as possible and paying attention to their problems and needs.

Question

Using Fiedler's contingency theory, evaluate the appropriateness of the styles of the two supervisors, Terry Peters and Bill Cook.

- expectancy – whether a person believes that good performance will lead to certain identifiable outcomes;
- valence – the extent to which an individual values those outcomes.

In House's view effective leadership consists of selecting the most appropriate style of behaviour for a given situation, but unlike Fiedler he believes that leaders can change their styles to meet the prevailing circumstances. Path–goal theory defines an appropriate style as one which achieves two important outcomes:

Figure 13.3
The basics of the
path–goal process

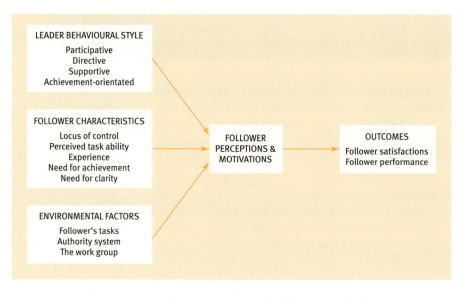

- tasks are successfully completed;
- followers achieve outcomes that they value for completing the task.

To achieve this state of affairs, House argues that a leader should structure the situation to have three important effects on a group:

- subordinates should only be able to achieve the valued outcomes if the task itself is completed effectively;
- reducing barriers to task completion;
- providing the necessary guidance and support.

From this it follows that House views effective leadership as behaving in a way that creates motivating circumstances for followers. However, since no two groups are exactly alike and the conditions can vary considerably, whether the outcomes are achieved depends on how followers perceive the leader and react to his or her behaviour. This is said to be affected by the three groups of variables shown in Figure 13.3.

Leader Behavioural Style

House distinguishes between four characteristic styles:

- **Participative:** a consultative style that involves seeking suggestions and ideas from subordinates, and involving them in decisions.

- **Directive:** a style in which subordinates are told clearly what is expected of them and are given specific guidance, and standards of performance to achieve.

- **Supportive:** a style that falls between the previous two and is characterised by the creation of a warm, friendly atmosphere in the group and consideration for the needs and well-being of subordinates.

- **Achievement-orientated:** a style that uses non-directive ways to set challenging goals for subordinates and seeks improvements in performance, usually by holding up excellent standards as a model to be achieved and by showing that there is confidence that they can achieve these standards.

Follower characteristics: the attributes and skill of followers that influence how they react to a particular leadership style

Follower Characteristics

These largely determine how subordinates will react to a supervisor's behaviour and are one of the two contingency factors that determine the need for variations in style.

- **Locus of control:** (discussed in Chapter 3) is a reflection of whether a person believes that outcomes are under his or her control, or whether they are determined by external factors that cannot be controlled. People with a strong internal locus are likely to find a participative leadership style more acceptable, whereas those with an external locus would probably be quite happy with a directive style (Mitchell 1973).
- **Perceived task ability:** reflects followers' own views of their abilities. Those who evaluate themselves highly and feel confident about performing tasks are unlikely to feel a need for directive leadership, while those with less confidence might prefer a directive leader.
- **Experience:** an important variable in this group that is likely to affect followers' confidence in their task ability.
- **Need for Achievement (N.Ach.):** (discussed in Chapter 7) influences whether a person welcomes the opportunity to overcome a challenge. Because participative or achievement-orientated leadership styles require people to solve problems independently, subordinates high in N.Ach. are likely to find these styles acceptable.
- **Need for clarity:** reflects subordinates' lack of tolerance to ambiguity. Those who have strong needs of this type are likely to feel at ease with a directive leadership style, while those with greater tolerance to ambiguity will be more at home with a participative or achievement-orientated style.

Environmental factors: features of a work context that make a leadership style more or less appropriate

Environmental Factors

This is the second contingency factor which affects the appropriateness of a particular style and it embraces features of the work context in which subordinates and supervisor interact.

- **Employee task:** refers to the characteristics of the work subordinates undertake. In a routine, predictable task subordinates need little direction and would probably welcome the concern for their welfare that goes with a supportive leadership style (Schriesheim and DeNisi 1981).
- **The authority system:** expresses the normal patterns of authority and power in the work environment, for instance whether directive styles of supervisor behaviour are the norm. Established behaviourial norms set up expectations about what is the usual way for a supervisor to behave, and if this suddenly changes it can create insecurity in subordinates.
- **The work group:** embraces characteristics such as whether it is cohesive and whether members support each other without the leader having to perform this function.

In terms of supporting evidence for the model, House's original aim was not to offer prescriptive recommendations, but to stimulate discussion and research. In this respect the model has largely been successful and research has resulted in some support for its basic ideas (Schriesheim and DeNisi 1981). Nevertheless, there are problems, for example, House argues that if a leader changes his or her behaviour to a style that is most appropriate to the circumstances, this will lead to subordinate satisfactions. However, Green (1979) suggests that the link between behaviour and satisfaction probably operates in the reverse direction, because leaders tend to change their behaviour when they perceive that subordinates are dissatisfied. In spite of this, House's use of subordinate satisfaction as a criterion of leader effectiveness overcomes a major omission in Fiedler's ideas and is a significant step forward in contingency theory.

The Vroom–Yetton–Jago Model

This model is much narrower in focus than many contingency theories; it deals only with the decision making aspect of leadership and is a revision by Vroom and Jago (1988) of an earlier model. The theory focuses on the characteristics of a situation in which it is more or less desirable for a leader to involve subordinates in the decision making process.

According to the authors, there are two criteria for evaluating the effectiveness of a decision:

- *decision acceptance*   broadly the extent that subordinates embrace a decision and commit themselves to its implementation;
- *decision quality*   expresses whether the decision results in effective task performance.

Like House, Vroom *et al.* argue that most leaders can change their patterns of behaviour and five styles of decision making are identified and placed on a continuum stretching from autocratic to highly participative, as shown in Figure 13.4.

The theory addresses the question of how a manager should identify which of these styles is the most appropriate. To do this, two criteria are suggested: (i) whether the decision issue affects the whole group or just a single individual; and (ii) whether the leader places a high priority on speed in decision making. This gives four basic situations:

1. Decision affects individual: fast decision required.
2. Decision affects individual: slower decision permissible.
3. Decision affects group: fast decision required.
4. Decision affects group: slower decision permissible.

Decision acceptance: whether subordinates embrace a decision and commit themselves to its implementation

Decision quality: whether a decision results in effective task performance

---

Figure 13.4
Vroom–Yetton–Jago decision styles (after Vroom and Yetton 1973)

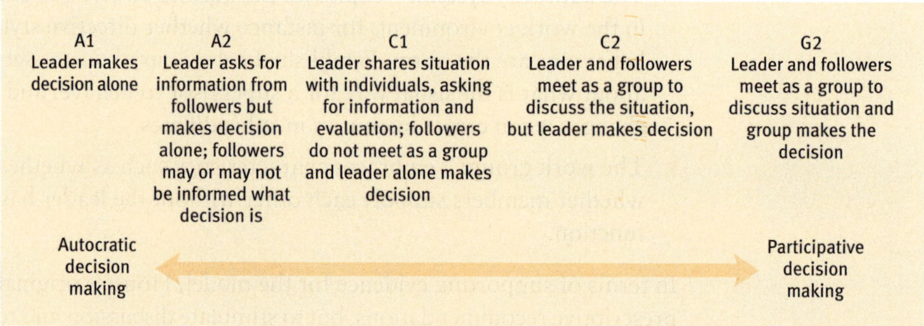

A1	A2	C1	C2	G2
Leader makes decision alone	Leader asks for information from followers but makes decision alone; followers may or may not be informed what decision is	Leader shares situation with individuals, asking for information and evaluation; followers do not meet as a group and leader alone makes decision	Leader and followers meet as a group to discuss the situation, but leader makes decision	Leader and followers meet as a group to discuss situation and group makes the decision
Autocratic decision making				Participative decision making

Figure 13.5 Vroom–Yetton–Jago decision tree (after Vroom 1977)

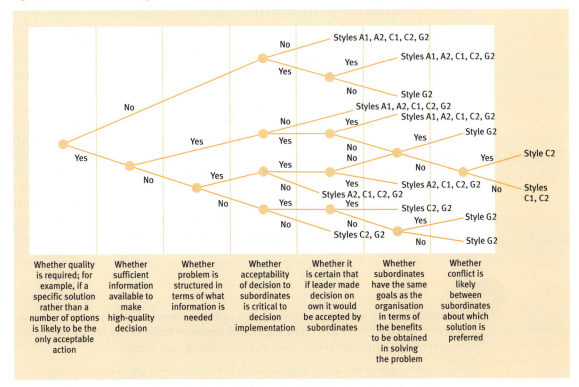

| Whether quality is required; for example, if a specific solution rather than a number of options is likely to be the only acceptable action | Whether sufficient information available to make high-quality decision | Whether problem is structured in terms of what information is needed | Whether acceptability of decision to subordinates is critical to decision implementation | Whether it is certain that if leader made decision on own it would be accepted by subordinates | Whether subordinates have the same goals as the organisation in terms of the benefits to be obtained in solving the problem | Whether conflict is likely between subordinates about which solution is preferred |

To enable the appropriate style to be selected, each of these combinations is covered by a separate decision tree. An example of one of these is shown in Figure 13.5, where the problem attributes are posed as questions and are shown below the tree. The most appropriate style to use is derived by following these through the legs of the tree.

By way of explanation, assume that a firm's engineering manager and his design team are faced with a situation in which a competitor has just introduced a new product that is superior in some crucial respect to the one currently sold by the firm. Time is of the essence, and the problem is how to counter the competitor's move by modifying the firm's existing design to give features that are the same or better than those of the competitor. Clearly the technical quality of the decision is highly important, and a single solution rather than a range of options is required. Therefore, in the first column the bottom leg of the decision tree is selected. Since it is a technical problem and the features of the competitor's design are clear, there is little ambiguity in what must be accomplished and so in column two the answer is 'Yes' and the upper leg is followed through to column four. The next question is whether the commitment of the rest of the team is important. Because the nature of the problem is very clear, there is a very good chance that if the manager went ahead and made the decision alone it could be explained quickly to the team who would then accept it without question. Therefore, the answer in column four is 'No' and any of the decision styles shown (A1, A2, C1, C2, G2) could be used. However, because time is an important constraint, A1 would probably be most appropriate.

The model clearly gives good insights into how the features of a problem and some aspects of manager style interact, and this is made all the more useful because it stands up well to the rigours of empirical testing. For instance, the authors give quite strong evidence that decisions made according to styles prescribed by the model tend to be more effective that those that are not (Vroom and Jago 1978). However, this is not to say that it is universally accepted as faultless and one criticism is that it is far too complex to be useful (House and Baetz 1979).

The model has also been strongly criticised for focusing exclusively on just one aspect of the leader–follower relationship. Moreover, like many leadership theories it classifies leader behaviour as falling somewhere between participative and autocratic, which reinforces the idea reflected in many other American theories of leadership, that the words 'manager' and 'leader' can be taken to mean the same thing. Indeed, there is something rather patronising about a philosophy which effectively regards a participative manager as a leader simply because he or she chooses not to rely on the formal authority vested in the manager role. What emerges, therefore, is more a model of managerial behaviour than a theory of leadership in a wider sense.

TIME OUT

Carefully reflect on a group to which you belong or of which you have been a member in the past. Now focus on its leader and aspects of his or her style that were either acceptable or unacceptable to both you and other group members.

1. Now examine the acceptability (or not) of the leader's behaviour in the light of the path–goal model of leader behaviour. What does this tell you about the appropriateness of the leader's style in your own case?
2. Now do the same thing using the Vroom–Yetton–Jago model. What does this tell you?

Situational leadership model: a situational theory of leadership which suggests that leader style should be varied according to the readiness of followers to direct their own actions

Task-related readiness: subordinate skills and abilities that enable subordinates to do a job without leader guidance

Psychological readiness: subordinate characteristics that make subordinates willing to accept the responsibility of working without leader guidance

The Hersey and Blanchard Contingency Approach

In leadership training a well-used approach is the situational theory of Hersey and Blanchard (1988), which is sometimes known as the *situational leadership* model. Hersey and Blanchard argue that a manager's style should be adjusted according to the readiness of followers to take responsibility for directing their own actions. Although the word readiness is used in an all-embracing way, it actually embraces two facets of subordinate behaviour:

- *task-related readiness*, which reflects whether subordinates have the necessary skills, knowledge and abilities to undertake a job without the leader having to plan, structure and direct their efforts;
- *psychological readiness*, which corresponds to subordinates' characteristics such as self-motivation and pride in work, which could make them willing to accept responsibility.

Using this basic framework Hersey and Blanchard define four basic categories of overall readiness:

R1 (Low)   people who are unable and unwilling because they have low task-related readiness and low psychological readiness.

R2 (Low/Moderate)   the willing but unable, who have low task-related readiness but some psychological readiness.

R3 (Moderate/High)   those who are able but unwilling and have high task-related readiness but low psychological readiness.

R4 (High)   the willing and able who are high in both task-related and psychological readiness.

Using dimensions similar to those developed in the Ohio State leadership studies to characterise manager behaviour, Hersey and Blanchard then define four basic leadership styles:

S1 – Telling   High on task behaviour and low on relationship behaviour, which involves a high degree of guidance but comparatively little in the way of supportive social behaviour.

S2 – Selling   High on both task-orientated and relationship-orientated behaviour.

S3 – Participating   A low degree of task orientation so that followers decide for themselves how to do things, but a high degree of relationship-orientated behaviour so that they receive encouragement to do so.

S4 – Delegating   A low task orientation and low relationship orientation so that followers are relatively autonomous.

These styles of manager behaviour and the way that they are said to match subordinate degrees of readiness can be expressed by the model shown in Figure 13.6.

The only contingent factor dealt with by Hersey and Blanchard is that of subordinate readiness. However, this enables three major implications of the model to be identified:

- in order to be able to select an appropriate style Hersey and Blanchard

Figure 13.6 The Hersey and Blanchard situational leadership model (*Source*: Hersey and Blanchard 1988)

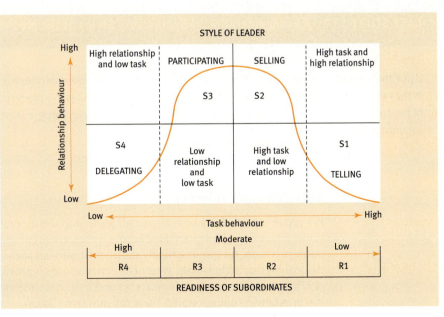

explicitly state that a manager needs to be able to evaluate the readiness of followers;

- managers must be able to vary their styles according to the prevailing degree of subordinate readiness;

- the authors also assume that as subordinates gain more competence, skills and self-confidence, their readiness rises and, since it can be argued that it is part of a manager's job to cultivate these attributes in subordinates, people are assumed to go through a cycle of development in which readiness rises, which in turn requires that the manager makes a corresponding adjustment in style.

While the model is a popular basis for leadership training, and equally popular with managers, there are a number of attendant problems. The strongest advocates of the theory are often management consultants or trainers, rather than researchers who have empirically tested the ideas, and while there is a small amount of evidence that gives it some support (Vecchio 1987), there are a number of disturbing concerns about its validity, for example:

- everything hinges on the need to accurately diagnose subordinate readiness, but it is by no means certain that all managers have the diagnostic skills or perceptive abilities to do this;

- the theory also asserts that managers are adaptable enough to change their styles, and there are powerful arguments to refute this idea, for example Fiedler, whose theory was described earlier;

- although the model incorporates the important variable of follower capability, it ignores all other contingencies, and some of these, such as the nature of the task, are shown by other work to be highly influential.

CASE STUDY 13.2: A Reconsideration of Supervisory Styles at the Medway Bank

Using the material given in Case Study 12.2 in the previous chapter, reconsider your answer to question 2 in the light of Hersey and Blanchard's situational model. In what way does this model provide an explanation of the appropriateness of the leadership styles of Jane Lewin and Allison Black in terms of the prevailing circumstances?

Substitutes for Leadership

If a group is to perform well almost all leadership theories take it for granted that a leader is necessary. However, there are many examples of people performing well without supervision, for instance highly skilled professionals such as barristers or doctors. An analysis that addresses the issue of leaderless groups is provided by Kerr and Jermier (1978) who point out that there are a number of circumstances in which leadership can be relatively unimportant. These fall into two classes:

Leadership substitutes: situational factors that enable subordinates to function well without leader guidance

Leadership neutralisers: workplace factors that remove the capability of a leader to influence subordinate behaviour

- where there are *leadership substitutes* situational factors that give subordinates the necessary guidance and/or provide them with some degree of work satisfaction and thus enable them to perform well;
- where there are *leadership neutralisers* where something in the work milieu that would normally make leadership theories important is absent, and this removes the capability of a leader to influence the behaviour of subordinates.

Kerr and Jermier argue that substitutes and neutralisers emanate from three possible sources:

- the characteristics of the followers;
- the characteristics of the task;
- the characteristics of the organisation.

However, not all of them completely remove the need for either or both aspects of leadership. Some, for example, only reduce the need for task-orientated aspects, others make relationship-orientated behaviour unimportant, and some negate both. These effects are shown in Table 13.3.

There are three ways to look at the Kerr and Jermier theory. It can be viewed simply as a theory of non-leadership, as another set of contingency factors, or even the ultimate in contingency theory. Whichever perspective is adopted, it should be noted that there is fairly strong empirical support for the idea that a leader is redundant in certain situations (Howell *et al.* 1990). As such, the ideas of Kerr and Jermier are very important, particularly in today's conditions where a number of popular initiatives such as downsizing and empowerment place a very strong emphasis on employees working without direct supervision.

Table 13.3 Substitutes for leadership

Characteristics	Neutralises relationship-orientated leadership	Neutralises task-orientated leadership
Of the Subordinate		
Ability, experience, training, knowledge	No	Yes
Need for independence	Yes	Yes
Professional orientation	Yes	Yes
Indifference towards organisational rewards	Yes	Yes
Of the Task		
Unambiguous and routine	No	Yes
No variation in method	No	Yes
Provides its own feedback on accomplishment	No	Yes
Intrinsically satisfying	Yes	No
Of the Organisation		
Formalisation (explicit objectives, plans and job specifications)	No	Yes
Inflexibility (fixed rules and procedures)	No	Yes
Active advisory staff roles with clear areas of responsibility	No	Yes
Close-knit, cohesive work groups	Yes	Yes
Organisational rewards that are not within the leader's control	Yes	Yes
Physical distance between superior and subordinates	Yes	Yes

Source: Kerr and Jermier 1978, p 378.

TIME OUT

Think carefully about the classes you attend at university or college as part of your programme of studies. While your lecturers cannot really be considered to be leaders, or even heads, they are still responsible for achieving what could loosely be described as a task-related output, that is, a class that successfully passes the course or module. However, achieving this is something that relies on student endeavours as well. Examine Table 13.3 and try to answer the questions below.

1. To what extent does achieving the task-related output rely on leadership substitutes or leadership neutralisers?
2. Do these reduce the need for relationship-orientated behaviour, or task-orientated behaviour?
3. Do these substitutes or neutralisers exist because of characteristics of the students, of the task or of the organisation?

AN OVERVIEW OF CONTINGENCY THEORIES

Like style theories, contingency models all focus on leader behaviour, and leader styles are invariably categorised as somewhere between relationship-orientated and task-orientated. What is different about these ideas is that the situation itself is deemed to make one style more appropriate than another, and no style is appropriate for all situations. Beyond this, the various contingency theories differ in two important respects: first, the situational factors that are taken to be the most important; and, second, whether the leaders are assumed to be able to vary their style to meet the needs of the situation. These similarities and differences are summarised in Table 13.4.

Perhaps the most important point to note from Table 13.4 is that while none of the theories are identical in terms of the contingencies covered, most of them assume that leaders can change their behaviourial style at will. In this respect, Fiedler's theory is unique because he believes that style is relatively permanent and reflects deep-rooted psychological characteristics.

REPLAY

- Unlike style theories, which assume that there is a single leadership style suitable for all situations, contingency theories assume that the situation itself makes a certain style more appropriate than others.
- There are a number of theories of this type and they tend to deal with different sets of circumstances that make particular styles of leader behaviour more or less appropriate.
- Because none of the theories deal with all possible circumstances that can influence the appropriateness of a leader's style, they should be regarded as complementary rather than in opposition.

Table 13.4 Summary comparison of contingency theories

	Fiedler's contingency theory	Path–goal theory	Vroom–Yetton–Jago decision theory	Hersey and Blanchard situational theory	Kerr and Jermier substitutes for leadership
How leader styles are classified	task- or relationship-orientated	participative, directive, supportive or achievement-orientated	autocratic to participative	tell, sell, participative, delegate	task- or relationship-orientated
Assumptions about leader's style	fixed and cannot be varied	can be varied at will	can be varied at will	can be varied at will	none
Implications of assumptions about style	choose the leader to fit the situation	motivations and needs of subordinates can be met if leader style is varied appropriately	leader can influence the effectiveness of decision process by varying style	leader style needs to be varied according to readiness of subordinates	leadership not necessary in certain circumstances
Major aspect of leadership addressed by theory	which style is most appropriate to the circumstances	effect on subordinates' motivations	involvement of subordinates in decision making	style most appropriate to subordinates' readiness	none
Contingency variables assumed to influence appropriate style	nature of task, leader position power, leader–subordinate relations	task needs, subordinate needs	subordinates and time constraints	readiness of subordinates	subordinates, task and organisation
Measures of leader effectiveness	task completion	task completion, subordinate satisfaction	task completion, subordinate satisfaction	task completion, subordinate satisfaction	task completion, subordinate satisfaction

Since the theories all deal with slightly different combinations of circumstances, they are complementary rather than contradictory but, once again, it is important to draw attention to a common feature which places limits on the application of the models. In every case a leader is regarded as someone who has been selected by people higher up in an organisation to be 'in charge' and this fails to distinguish between 'headship' and 'leadership'. To apply the word 'leader' to situations such as these is misleading because, if all else fails, the person can resort to the use of formal authority to influence the actions of subordinates. Subordinates are likely to be aware that this 'reserve' basis of authority exists, and this casts doubt on whether the theories describe leadership, rather than variations in styles of 'headship'.

RECENT PERSPECTIVES ON LEADERSHIP

It was noted earlier that it is commonly assumed that a leader exerts influence on the behaviour of followers and most of the theories covered so far are built on this assumption. However, they are silent about how the processes of influence work. The dilemma here is that unless we understand how people are able to exert influence without using

Influence perspective:
an approach to
leadership theory
which explicitly
addresses the issue
of 'how' leaders
influence follower
behaviour

power or coercion, leadership remains an abstract 'black box'. To some extent the functional approach (see Chapter 12) gives some hint about the processes at work. In addition, more recent theories purposely address this issue. Most of them adopt what has come to be known as the *influence perspective*, an approach that explores how leaders are able to influence the perceptions, behaviour and attitudes of followers. Compared to other theoretical approaches, this is still very much in its infancy, and because work so far has tended to focus strongly on the personal behaviour and characteristics of leaders, it looks very much like a re-emergence of trait ideas, in a more sophisticated form.

OB IN ACTION: Charismatic Leaders or Charismatic Actors?

What is a charismatic leader? Is the charismatic person more effective as a leader (or manager)? Is charisma innate or can it be developed? These are some of the issues addressed in a recent article by Professor Jay Conger, formerly of the University of Southern California. Conger, who has long been an enthusiast of charismatic leadership, falls short of answering the first of these questions and uses the words 'leader' and 'manager' interchangeably. However, he lists what he takes to be some of the important characteristics of charismatic managers, who are said to be:

* masters at motivating people;
* highly entrepreneurial;
* agents of change;
* superb communicators.

Conger argues that some elements of charisma can be developed, for instance by learning to think critically about the present in order to evaluate opportunities for the future, and by taking courses to improve public speaking and presentational skills. By far the most intriguing suggestion he makes is that would-be charismatic managers can enhance their capabilities to send more powerful messages by learning to stage-manage events. Doubtless this may help someone to 'create an effect', but it begs the question of whether Conger advocates development of proficiency in leadership or simply amateur dramatics. It is well known, for example, that skilled actors can convey the impression of being almost anything. Indeed, serious and well-designed research into the effects of different leadership styles sometimes uses professional actors, who have amply demonstrated their abilities to convey the signs of being task-orientated, people-orientated or charismatic at will. Conger argues that just about the only attribute of the charismatic leader that cannot be developed is how to be passionate about what he or she does. In the light of other things that he says, this inevitably prompts the question of whether it is really necessary to be passionate; perhaps, for example, it is simply enough to be able to convey the outward signs of being passionate as other actors do. As such, it is just as well that the one attribute that Conger does not list as essential for the charismatic manager is integrity.

Source:

Conger J (1999) Charisma and how to grow it, *Management Today*, December: 78–81.

Transactional versus Transformational (Charismatic) Leadership

The distinction between transactional and transformational leadership was originally made by Burns (1978), who contrasted successful leadership in a stable situation with that in changing circumstances. The ideas are perhaps most clearly articulated by Bass (1985), who points out that in *transactional leadership* the exchange between leader and subordinates depends heavily on a stable situation, in which a leader can identify the needs, wants and expectations of subordinates, and structure the context so that these needs can be met. In return for satisfaction of their needs, subordinates will then enter into a transaction with the leader in which they exert effort to achieve the aims the leader specifies. Here the crucial skills required by the leader are the ability to diagnose subordinate needs and adopt an appropriate behavioural style.

Where organisational change is required, perhaps because the environment is subject to rapid fluctuation, a leader's task is somewhat different from just keeping things ticking over. Here Bass believes that another pattern of leader behaviour, *transformational leadership*, is called for. This requires the leader to have a vision of what needs to be done to cope with the situation, the ability to communicate this vision to followers and the capability to energise or inspire them to change their current way of doing things. Bass then sets out what he believes to be the four key characteristics of the transformational leader: charisma, vision, intellectual stimulation of followers and an ability to take their emotional needs into account.

Charisma

The idea that someone with charisma is endowed with a natural authority is an old one – Max Weber (1947), for example, viewed charisma as one of the three primary bases of authority, an idea that re-emerged in the late 1970s as a theory of charismatic leadership which has more recently been incorporated into views on the necessary attributes of transformational leaders. However, while most people would acknowledge that charisma can exist, it is much harder to be precise about what makes someone charismatic and, as the OB in Action box above indicates, some of the practices associated with the so-called charismatic leader can be questioned on ethical grounds.

Attempts have been made to address the issue of what makes someone charismatic, and the main attributes that have been identified are expertise, articulateness, perceived trustworthiness, and perception and sensitivity to surrounding circumstances (Conger and Kanugo 1987). Unfortunately, these attribute names are plagued with the same problem that bedevilled the attribute lists in trait theory: what do the words mean? Having any one of these attributes is more a question of perception than objective reality, and what one person perceives as articulate can just as easily be seen by another as garrulous.

Vision

This is also extremely difficult to define. For instance, how much vision is required and vision about what? The word is well used by management gurus such as Wesley and Mintzberg (1989), but all too often it is used in a very loose and imprecise way. However, Selznick gives a precise description:

> sensitivity to changes in an organisation's environment, together with an accurate perception of the direction in which the organisation must move if it is to take advantage of environmental changes.
>
> (Selznick 1984)

Transactional leadership: the leadership style that is said to be the most appropriate to stable conditions

Transformational leadership: the approach to leadership which is said to be most appropriate in times of significant organisational change

Although this looks fine at first sight, it still leaves a feeling of unease. It implies, for example, that those with vision are special because they are able to foretell the future.

Intellectual Stimulation

This attribute is said to reflect an ability to energise followers to do something, usually by showing them that problems can be viewed in an alternative way and convincing them that the leader's way of solving the problems is a sound, rational path to follow. Once again this poses problems of definition.

Consideration and Sensitivity to Followers

This means that transformational leaders pay close attention to followers and their differences. Since this is a pattern of behaviour rather than a vaguely defined attribute, it is less controversial than the others. Usually a person of this type will be good at spotting where a skill or ability needs to be imported into a group and at selecting the appropriate person to meet this need. He or she will often spend a great deal of time with group members, and perhaps devote time and energy to such activities as coaching and mentoring to develop their talents. In return, group members are likely to obtain satisfaction of higher order psychological needs, such as achievement and recognition (Kotter 1990).

To summarise, although the contrast between transactional and transformational leadership is a useful one, it almost inevitably results in a feeling that leadership theory has come full circle. It adds little to the body of knowledge and only tells us what most people already know: that the prevailing circumstances surrounding a group dictate what type of leader is required. The main problem is that most of the attributes of the transformational leader are extremely difficult to define, let alone identify. By far the most problematic of these is charisma, and while advocates of the theory usually acknowledge that charisma on its own is not enough to make someone a transformational leader (Bass 1985), it still tends to be viewed as a vital prerequisite, and is often described in terms that verge on 'hero worship' (see Kets de Vries 1998). This is not to deny that there is such a thing as charisma, or that charismatic people are able to influence others. However, protagonists of these ideas somehow manage to convey the impression that transformational leadership is greatly superior to the transactional style, and in their enthusiasm to glorify the transformational type the transactional style almost inevitably gets denigrated. Moreover, there are potential contradictions in this idea. Maccoby (2000) argues that many charismatic leaders are likely to be narcissists, who have an overpowering self-image that leads them to believe that whatever they suggest is right. Furthermore, they often lack empathy and are more than willing to impose their visions on dissenters. This, it can be noted, is the typical behaviour of fanatics or the type of leaders encountered in 'cults' (Tourish and Pinnington 2002), which can all too easily lead to what has become known as 'the Hitler problem' in leadership. In all probability transactional and transformational types are complementary rather than mutually exclusive, and both are needed in organisations.

Notwithstanding these points, theories of transformational leadership have attracted a great deal of attention and the idea of charisma is extremely popular in management circles, perhaps because the word has a certain cachet that gives it an almost heroic ring. It implies that the person with charisma is both exceptional and exemplary, and the idea might well be popular because being charismatic is how many managers like to think of themselves.

The Attributional Approach

Attribution theory, which was introduced in Chapter 4, holds that humans are seldom content to take the behaviour of another person at face value: they also try to attribute a cause to a person's actions. This idea can be applied to the leadership situation by asking whether what happens is the result of leadership.

Most leadership theories unswervingly accept that outcomes such as performance or employee satisfaction are the result of a leader's actions, and this is particularly true of ideas about transformational leaders, where it would be near heresy to even question that leadership is a crucial determinant of an organisation's success. The important feature of attribution theory is that it alerts us to the possibility that leadership can be an illusion, or just an act of faith.

People in organisations have just as much need to explain events and happenings as those elsewhere. Since the words 'leader' and 'leadership' are endowed with almost mystic connotations, 'the effect of the leader' is a highly convenient factor that can be used to attribute a reason for success or failure (Meindl *et al.* 1987). Leadership can therefore be a matter of image building or myth making, and Pfeffer (1977) has developed a cogent argument to support this idea by giving three reasons why leaders are unlikely to have the effects on organisational performance that are usually attributed to them:

- If success or failure arises because an organisation has changed its way of doing things, the change is very unlikely to have been prompted by a change in leadership behaviour. People usually get selected for positions of authority in organisations because they 'fit in' and have certain acceptable attributes and styles of behaviour, and so they have every encouragement to stick to these behaviourial patterns.
- Flowing from the first point, even if a person with a different style should gain admittance to an organisation, the individual is usually socialised very rapidly into conforming to accepted patterns of behaviour.
- The success or failure of an organisation is often largely determined by environmental factors, over which even very senior managers have no control.

Pfeffer's arguments are very powerful and are quite strongly supported by empirical evidence. For example, Reich (1985) analysed the performance of a number of organisations in which success had been attributed to the dynamic leadership of a person in control. In almost every case success turned out to be more directly attributable to economic boom conditions than anything else. In more general terms, the way that success almost inevitably gets attributed to the leader of a group has been demonstrated in a tightly controlled experiment by Staw (1975). Groups were placed in a competitive situation, in which their success in a task was beyond the group's control and completely in the hands of the experimenters. Irrespective of whether the group had actually succeeded in the task, when groups were told they had succeeded, group members almost always attributed success to the effects of the leader.

Flowing from evidence such as this it is possible to identify three important implications of tendencies to attribute success or failure to leaders. The first and most obvious concerns the assumption that a leader has a direct effect on subordinates and that this necessarily produces desired outcomes. This can be a completely false assumption. While leaders undoubtedly have some effect on followers, the effect might not be a direct one. That is, the leader might have an effect on some other factor, and this in turn influences the behaviour and emotions of subordinates, for example by bringing about a change in the contextual circumstances in which they operate which makes it much easier for them to succeed in their task.

Second, it is possible that simply calling someone a leader unleashes very powerful forces. People seem to be most at ease in situations where they belong to a group that has a head, and so if someone is called 'the leader', it can allow the person to take on the mantle of leadership and from then on the situation becomes a self-fulfilling prophecy.

The third point, which follows from the second, has very direct implications for the rather romanticised and hyped-up ideas about the charismatic nature of so-called transformational leaders. These people may just have an intuitive grasp of how to act in a way that makes them appear as a leader to others. They can be sensitive to situations where people feel more comfortable if there is a leader and, in addition, they may have a good intuitive grasp of what these people believe are the characteristics of a leader and also the ability to convey the impression that they have these characteristics. Put this way, leadership may turn out to be simply a matter of impression management, in which psychological manipulation encourages people to put themselves in the role of follower and the would-be leader into a position of authority. There is a growing body of evidence that effects such as these actually take place (Weierter 1997). Although this paints a somewhat less romantic picture of leadership than the one that is normally encountered, impression management is a technique that almost everybody practises to some extent – some more successfully than others. It is also a technique that can be taught. Witness the long-lasting success of Dale Carnegie's book, *How to Win Friends and Influence People*, which for the last 50 years has been one of the consistent bestsellers in management literature. Even a cursory examination of Carnegie's book shows that some of its interactive principles are remarkably similar to the behaviours which are said to characterise transformational leaders.

LEADERSHIP AND NATIONAL CULTURES

The manager–subordinate relationship does not exist in a vacuum and, sometimes, managers lack the freedom to use a certain style of behaviour because it would be at odds with the way that things are normally handled in a particular organisation. Normal patterns of behaviour are often a function of an organisation's culture. Therefore culture, which is loosely defined here as 'the customary and traditional way of thinking and doing things, which is shared to a greater or lesser degree by all organisational members' (Jaques 1952), can be viewed as another factor that influences the appropriateness of certain behavioural styles.

Organisational culture is a topic in its own right, which will be covered in greater depth in Chapter 19. Here it is sufficient to note that an organisation's culture is powerfully influenced by the national culture of the country in which it is located. National cultures contain deep-rooted ideologies, values and beliefs, and these give a tendency for people to view things in the same way, which results in a degree of similarity in behaviour. This gives rise to the issue of whether these cultural differences can have an impact on the appropriateness of certain leadership styles, and what will be examined here is the idea that national cultures can influence patterns of leadership behaviour within organisations.

All contingency theories suggest that there are crucial factors that determine the appropriateness of a particular style. Since culture results in expectations about the way that people will behave, the effects of a culture might be strong enough to result in some leadership styles being considered highly inappropriate. To put matters more simply, this can be framed as the question 'Is culture a contingency factor in its own right?'

One way of exploring this is through a cultural classification system devised by the Dutch social psychologist Geert Hofstede (1980). Since this will be described in detail in Chapter 22, it is only necessary to draw attention to the more important points here. In the **United Kingdom** and **America** most employees would find autocratic, distant management styles unwelcome. In addition, people are fairly comfortable with a degree of ambiguity, they are usually willing to take some responsibility for their own actions and in these cultures individuality and achievement are highly prized. Therefore, it is fairly easy to see why employees in the United Kingdom and America strongly prefer participative leaders who involve their subordinates in decision making.

In some Latin countries, such as **France**, however, people have a much stronger acceptance of hierarchical structures in which those lower down are not expected to shoulder the responsibility for making decisions, and there is also less tolerance to ambiguity. Thus, managers are not likely to delegate to a large extent and, in any event, subordinates probably expect to be told what to do and would not adapt easily to the self-monitoring that goes hand in hand with autonomy. Thus, the less democratic or less participative styles are likely to fit well with the culture.

In **Japan**, being part of a team is fundamental to the Japanese way of life and it verges on bad manners to stand out too much as an individual. This militates very

REPLAY

- A comparatively recent development hinges on the distinction between transactional and transformational leadership, in which the former is portrayed as more appropriate to stable circumstances while the latter is needed for change situations.

- Another recent development is the attributional approach, in which people are accorded the quality of leadership as a way of explaining the success of a group.

- Differences in national cultures are likely to mean that certain styles of leadership are more appropriate in some countries than in others. Thus, culture can be regarded as another set of contingent circumstances that make some styles more appropriate than others in specific contexts.

strongly in favour of a shared ownership of decisions, and an ideal decision is one where everybody is fully committed to its implementation. Usually this means that everyone has been involved in reaching the decision and so participative leadership styles fit best with the cultural characteristics.

To summarise, even a brief contrast such as this shows that culture can have a strong impact on whether employees are likely to feel comfortable with certain management styles. For this reason, it is probably sensible to treat culture as an important contingency variable in its own right.

OVERVIEW AND CONCLUSIONS

In its comparatively short history leadership theory has come a long way. While the topic now contains a rich diversity of different approaches, this can give rise to some problems. The word leadership is used in different ways by different theorists and this makes it difficult to be sure what the word means. The trait approach, which is the simplest and oldest of all leadership theories, conspicuously failed to isolate characteristics that are common to all effective leaders, and turned out to be a sterile line of enquiry.

The next development, style theory, sought to identify the way in which effective leaders behave, 'effectiveness' usually being defined by the twin criteria of goal attainment and follower satisfaction. This approach resulted in many different theories, and the two dimensions of leader behaviour – concern for task and concern for people – are still very much alive in the leadership vocabulary.

The next stream of theoretical development, contingency theory, also accepts that the most valid way to describe leadership style is along the two dimensions of concern for task and concern for people. However, rather than specifying a 'one best' universal style, these theories try to identify which of the two dimensions should receive the most emphasis according to the circumstances in which leadership takes place. While this escapes the trap of assuming that there is a best way to lead, it gives rise to the problem of identifying the important factors that should influence style. A number of different contingency theories have emerged and these deal with different contingent circumstances but, as yet, there is no single contingency model that incorporates them all. One of the most interesting developments in this area is the 'substitutes for leadership' approach, which identifies certain circumstances in which leadership may well be redundant and unnecessary. Another promising but as yet comparatively underdeveloped approach is the idea that culture, either national or organisational, could be one of the more important contingency variables.

In recent approaches to theorising there is a sense in which ideas about leadership have come full circle. This is particularly noticeable in the distinction between transactional and transformational leadership, where the emphasis on charisma as a vital attribute of the transformational leader is something of a return to earlier trait ideas.

With such a rich diversity of ideas it can be difficult to draw generalised conclusions about leadership, but six major points are worth noting.

- Almost every book that discusses leadership stresses the point that leadership and management are not necessarily the same thing, but then ignores the point. Indeed, there is currently a deplorable tendency to equate the word leader with positions at the very top of an organisation, which creates the myth of the chief executive as a 'superhero'. Even where this is not the case, most leadership theories focus exclusively on the supervisory or management role, and it is not uncommon to find that the words 'leader' and 'manager' are used interchangeably, as are the words 'follower' and 'subordinate'. This tends to ignore the point that supervisors and managers invariably have a degree of position power that, in the final analysis, can be used to influence or control subordinate behaviour. Thus, much of what is called leadership theory actually deals with headship and, at best, only gives guidance on how headship can most effectively be exercised.

- The distinction between headship and leadership is an important one which concerns the source of authority in the role. In headship authority is conferred from above and headship exists because a manager is given the right to command the actions of subordinates, whereas leadership occurs where followers confer authority on someone (upwards) to command their actions. Because most theories deal with headship, they sidestep the important issue of how and why some people come to be seen as leaders and have this power conferred upon them. Nevertheless, there are theories which address this issue by treating leadership as a two-way process, for instance, the vertical dyadic linkage model, action-centred leadership theory and, to some extent, the attributional approach.

- As it has developed, leadership theory has become increasingly complex and so, while recent theories are regarded as more valid in academic circles, they have probably lost a degree of utility with managers. This probably accounts for the continued popularity of simpler, universal models and there is a strong parallel with motivation theory, an area that has also become more rigorous and complex but now tends to be beyond the comprehension of many managers (see Chapters 7 and 8).

- The leadership theories described in this chapter are all products of Western thought and, for this reason, they usually extol the virtues of the participative or democratic styles of behaviour. While this behaviour fits well with the cultural values of America and the United Kingdom it should be noted that other countries have cultures that can make this style of behaviour somewhat less appropriate.

- It is important to stress that leadership is not a discrete activity in organisations, nor is it a discrete topic in Organisational Behaviour. It therefore has strong connections with other topics in this book; for example, motivation is also concerned with influencing people's behaviour and, to the extent that someone is able to provide stimulating and motivating conditions for others, they are more likely to see the person as a leader. Similarly, whatever style of behaviour a leader adopts, he or she will need to be able to communicate ideas to others and so communication skills can be a vital part of being a leader.

- Although leadership and headship are different in terms of the source of authority, in practice both processes involve the use of power. Power is a complex topic in its own right and is important enough to deserve the next chapter to itself.

FURTHER READING

Adair, J (2003) (1998) *The Inspirational Leader*, London: Kogan Page. A useful book that is partly a reflection of the author's action-centred approach, with a strong emphasis on the need for leaders to connect strongly with those that they lead.

Bass, B M and R M Stogdill (1990) *Bass and Stogdill's Handbook of Leadership: Theory, Research and Managerial Applications*, New York: Free Press. Almost certainly the most comprehensive text yet written on leadership theories and their application.

Bryman, A (1992) *Charisma and Leadership in Organisations*, London: Sage. The book gives an extensive and constructively critical analysis of current approaches to leadership.

Hickman, G R (1998) (ed) *Leading Organisations: Perspectives for a New Era*, Thousand Oaks CA: Sage. A book of readings that has a strong American bias and is lacking in critical perspectives. However, it is comprehensive and up to date.

Northouse, P G (1997) *Leadership: Theory and Practice*, London: Sage. A very readable book that gives a brief but sound coverage of a wide variety of theoretical approaches to leadership and their practical applications.

Parry R (2003) *Enterprise – the Leadership Role*, London: Profile Press. While containing lots of useful advice the book is very much an anthem to the CEO as the 'all action superhero' school of thought. That is, it equates management (particularly top management) and leadership as being the same thing.

White, R P, P Hodgson and S Crainer (1996) *The Future of Leadership: A White Water Revolution*, London: Pitman. Rather a prescriptive text, but interesting because it speculates about the nature of leadership in the future.

Wright, P (1995) *Managerial Leadership*, London: Thomson. A very practical approach to leadership that will mainly be of interest to the manager (actual or would be).

REVIEW AND DISCUSSION QUESTIONS

1. Explain the underlying assumptions of the contingency approach to leadership and compare and contrast the Fiedler, House and Vroom–Yetton–Jago models in terms of their practical utility.

2. Explain Kerr and Jermier's argument that there are circumstances in which leadership can be relatively unimportant.

3. Explain the difference between 'transactional' and 'transformational' leadership and assess the practical utility of the transformational concept for devising programmes of leadership training.

4. Evaluate the assertion that 'most so-called theories of leadership tell us very little about the nature of leadership'.

| Chapter 14 | # Power, Politics and Conflict |

LEARNING OUTCOMES

After studying this chapter you should be able to:

- define power, describe the interpersonal and contextual bases of power in organisations and explain some of the ways in which power is used

- define organisational politics, describe the factors that give rise to behaviour of this type and describe the tactics of its use

- define organisational conflict, distinguish conflict from competition and explain traditional and current perspectives on conflict in organisations

- describe the factors that give rise to conflict in organisations and explain the stages of a conflict episode

- explain what is meant by functional and dysfunctional conflict and describe methods that can be used to resolve or stimulate conflict in organisations

INTRODUCTION

This chapter covers what are, to many people, three of the most uncomfortable aspects of organisational life: power, politics and conflict. While the first of these is an attribute or characteristic of a person or group, and the other two are processes, it is important to realise that they are closely related.

The first to be considered is power, and this section of the chapter defines 'power' and explains the sources (bases) from which individuals and groups derive their power. Discussion then turns to the use of power and the most frequently used power tactics.

The next section deals with organisational politics. It defines the phenomenon and describes the organisational circumstances which tend to give rise to political activity. The pervasive nature of political activity is then considered, together with the ethics of this type of behaviour. This section closes with a description of some of the political tactics used in organisations.

The final topic is that of organisational conflict. A definition is given and conflict is distinguished from competition. Traditional and contemporary perspectives on conflict are examined and, following this, the nature of organisational conflict is examined, together with an explanation of the factors that give rise to conflictual behaviour. Although it can exist beneath the surface for some time, conflict only tends to become visible when a conflict episode occurs. A model of a typical episode is given, followed by an explanation of methods of conflict management. The chapter closes with a conclusion and overview that highlights the interconnected nature of power, politics and conflict and some of the more significant implications for people in organisations.

POWER

Until fairly recently there was considerable debate about whether the use of power in organisations is widespread, but because there is a potential imbalance of power in all social relationships, any attempt to describe human behaviour in organisations would be incomplete without a consideration of power. Since power is an extremely complex topic, this chapter only gives an introduction to the subject. Historically, there have been numerous definitions of power, many of which imply that it is essentially an individual attribute, but since this chapter also deals with power as something that can be wielded collectively, it is defined here as:

> **the capacity of an individual or group to modify the conduct of other individuals or groups in a manner which they desire and without having to modify their own conduct in a manner which they do not desire.** **(Tawney 1931, p 229)**

A number of important implications flow from this definition and the reader is asked to keep them firmly in mind when reading the chapter. These are:

- that power does not exist in isolation, but is a characteristic of a relationship between two or more individuals or groups;
- for power to exist there must at least be a possibility that it can be exercised, otherwise it is only latent power;

- power is situational; a person or group seldom has the same amount of power in all circumstances and, sometimes, it is the situation itself that confers power on someone who is otherwise relatively powerless;
- few people have no power whatsoever; some might only have a small degree of power in a limited range of circumstances, and others have not yet mobilised their power so that it remains latent;
- in using power, what often matters most is not the absolute amount that a person or group has, but the relative amount compared to the other party.

Since power is a very abstract concept, different people use the word in different ways. For instance, although some texts use the words 'power' and 'authority' interchangeably, strictly speaking they are not the same thing. Authority is a special type of power that exists when a specific position or role is endowed with the right to make decisions or command the actions of other people. Unlike some other types of power, it is not a property or characteristic of a person, but is delegated from above (Weber 1947). It comes with the job, outlives the individual's occupancy of a role, and its use is usually regarded as legitimate by those over whom it is exercised (Katz and Kahn 1978). However, since it confers the rights to make decisions only about certain matters, authority is bounded and if someone exceeds these rights, it can sometimes be challenged. It is, of course, the most visible type of power in organisations.

Some writers also distinguish between power and influence, by stating that power involves a stronger element of force or coercion, while influence is more persuasive in nature. This, however, poses a huge conceptual problem. All forms of power, including coercion, are used to influence the behaviour of other people, and so it makes little sense to distinguish between influence and power (Mintzberg 1983).

TIME OUT

1. Think of someone whom you either know well or come into contact with regularly, whom you perceive to be a person who has power over other people, perhaps even over yourself. Try to identify why it is the person has this power over others, that is, where does his or her power come from?

2. Now consider yourself and your own situation. Do you have power over other people in any way (if you examine matters deeply you may be surprised to find that you have)? Where does your power over these other people come from, that is, what gives you this power?

THE ORIGINS (SOURCES OR BASES) OF POWER

In order to understand more about power and its use the first step is to identify why some individuals or groups have more power than others. Power often comes from several sources at the same time, some of which are located within an individual or group, some arise from the nature of an organisation and others may be more a reflection of specific contexts or situations. These all tend to have a cumulative effect and so they are all brought together in the comprehensive model shown in Figure 14.1.

Figure 14.1
Interpersonal and
contextual bases of
power

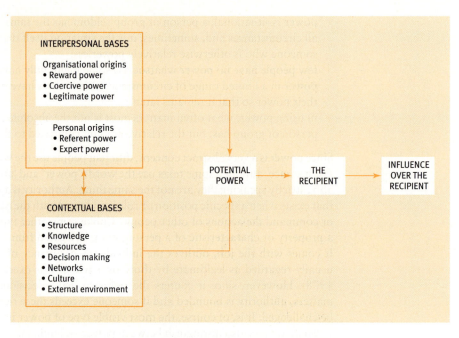

The Interpersonal Bases of Power

At this level power is exercised personally by one individual over others. Several different schemes have been suggested to categorise the sources of power of this type, the best known of which is probably French and Raven's (1959) 'five bases of power'. The original scheme simply describes these bases, but since some are derived from the power holder's position, while others are more a function of personal characteristics, they are split into two groups.

Organisational Origins

Reward Power

Providing that they value the rewards, someone who controls the distribution of rewards to other people has a degree of power over them. The more formally structured an organisation, the more likely it is that this type of power will be limited by rules, for instance supervisors might only be able to make recommendations about increased rewards for subordinates, but the actual decision is the prerogative of a higher-level manager. To some extent the use of *reward power* is also influenced by informal 'custom and practice' arrangements. Although a supervisor can have the official right to award paid overtime, it may be the normal practice to share it out between subordinates, and woe betide the supervisor who ignores this custom.

Reward power: the capability to confer rewards on others

Coercive Power

Coercive power is the opposite of reward power. It reflects a person's capability to compel someone else to behave in a particular way, usually because a sanction can be

Coercive power: the capability to compel others to behave in a certain way

imposed or a reward withheld in the event of non-compliance. Usually this is also a matter of delegated authority, and in most organisations the use of coercive power tends to be very strictly controlled. For instance, while supervisors commonly deal with all minor rule transgressions, the sanctions that they are allowed to impose are usually strictly limited and more severe sanctions are normally the prerogatives of higher levels of management. Indeed, punishment of any sort is a very touchy subject in most organisations because it is sometimes used to settle an old score. Therefore, if only to avoid wider employee relations problems, its use tends to be very strictly controlled.

This is not to say that coercive power is never used. Indeed, certain structural features of an organisation seem to make its use more likely and, importantly, these are often typical of current organisations that have been delayered or downsized. For example, the use of discipline is far more prevalent where supervisors and managers have very large spans of control, perhaps because time is short, relationships with subordinates are less personal and informal methods of handling are less convenient (Stahelski *et al.* 1989).

Legitimate Power

Legitimate power: the authority to command the actions of other people that goes with a particular role

Legitimate power exists where someone occupies an organisational role that carries the authority to make decisions or command the actions of others. Once again, the more formal and elaborate the structure of an organisation the more likely it is that boundaries will be placed on a person's legitimate power. For instance, while supervisors can instruct subordinates to undertake certain activities it is often the case that these can only be from within a strictly specified range. Subordinates also play a role in the exercise of legitimate power. For example, a supervisor might have the power to allocate a number of duties to subordinates, some of which are considered to be more unpleasant than others. Where it is the custom for everyone to take their turn at doing the dirty jobs, and the supervisor shields certain people from this work, he or she can easily find that the others take steps to demonstrate that power is being used unwisely, perhaps by refusing to cooperate over other matters.

Personal Origins

These are associated with the personal characteristics of a power holder. Unlike the three bases discussed above, which can be removed or reduced by a person's superior, whether or not personal bases remain intact is largely in the hands of the power holder.

Referent Power

Referent power: the capability to influence others that comes from having attributes or characteristics that make someone a source of reference or role model for other people

Someone with strong personal attributes that make the person a source of reference or a role model to others is said to have *referent power*. Usually this means that other people who come into close contact with the individual recognise these attributes, and so power of this type is not necessarily associated with position in the organisational hierarchy. One of the more tangible signs that someone has this type of power is that others imitate his/her characteristics, which can result in the person being perceived as a leader. However, as will be recalled from Chapter 13, leadership tends to be situational, and someone who is seen as the most appropriate person to lead in one set of circumstances may not be viewed in this way when the circumstances change. Thus referent power can sometimes be highly transient.

Expert Power

In all organisations there are people who occupy specialist positions and, in situations where their expertise is required, this gives them a degree of power. Because pockets of expertise often reside low down in an organisation, this type of power is not necessarily associated with rank. People higher up can sometimes be strongly dependent on those below, which means that *expert power* can be deployed upwards.

Expert power: the ability to influence others that exists because a person is seen to possess a particular expertise

Contextual Bases of Power

Lukes (1974) draws attention to an important distinction between *power over* (others) and the *power to* achieve something. Influencing the actions of others is often a means to an end rather than an end in itself. The 'power to' is often derived from the contextual circumstances that surround an individual or group, and these sources tend to complement and reinforce interpersonal bases. At least seven contextual sources can be identified, and these are explained below.

Organisational Structure

An individual's formal authority in an organisation is primarily determined by its structural design, which establishes certain patterns of communication and the authority to make certain decisions (Pfeffer 1981). Therefore, structure largely determines the extent of a person's reward, coercive and legitimate power, and an organisation chart is little more than a map of power and authority.

Knowledge and Information

There is a great deal of truth in the adage that 'information is power'. Information is required for most decisions, and if someone controls its flow, he or she has power over other groups to whom the information is vital. People in a position to do so often acquire this power base by becoming 'information gatekeepers'. An example of this is given in Pettigrew's (1973) study of a large retail firm that was one of the first in Great Britain to computerise its operations. Pettigrew describes how a single individual managed to manoeuvre himself into a position where he controlled the flow of information from the computer manufacturers who were able to supply a new machine. In this way, although the directors of the firm formally made the choice of which one to purchase, he was able to shape their decision in a way that was highly beneficial to himself.

Resources

Access to appropriate resources often gives an organisational sub-unit the ability to achieve its goals. However, in most organisations, resources are often rationed or shared out between sub-units, which makes subordinate units dependent on higher-level managers, and helps ensure their compliance. Therefore, access to a plentiful supply of resources not only gives a degree of independence from the power of those above, but also gives a better likelihood of achieving goals.

One of the most subtle uses of resource power occurs when one sub-unit becomes a vital resource for most other sub-units. In his description of the relationship between production and maintenance departments in a French tobacco factory, Crozier (1964) gives a penetrating insight into this situation. Since the key to the profitability of the factory lay in a smooth and uninterrupted flow of production, production departments had a great deal of formal power. However, real power was in the hands of maintenance workers, because they determined whether production machinery was kept in continuous operation. Thus, to achieve output goals, production departments were acutely dependent on the goodwill of maintenance.

Strategic contingencies: events or activities that are crucial in achieving organisational goals

Using Crozier's ideas, Hickson *et al.* (1971) developed a theory of sub-unit power based upon the concept of *strategic contingencies*. This was subsequently verified by Hinings *et al.* (1974), who examined power relations in seven manufacturing firms in America and Canada. In each firm, four departments (engineering, marketing, production and accounting) were examined to assess their power along the following dimensions:

- **Substitutability:** whether the service provided by a department could be obtained elsewhere.
- **Work flow pervasiveness:** whether the flow of work in a department affected work flow in one of the others.
- **Uncertainty:** ambiguity about the future.
- **Work flow immediacy:** the extent to which the work flow of a department had a rapid and noticeable effect on the output of the whole organisation.

Departments were then ranked in terms of overall power, according to the number of dimensions on which they had achieved high scores. If a department had a high score on just one of the power dimensions, it was found to have a low degree of power relative to the others. From this, Hinings and his co-workers concluded that relative power lay in the ability to cope with the three key contingency factors shown in Figure 14.2.

Figure 14.2 A strategic contingency model of sub-unit power (after Hickson *et al.* 1971; Hinings *et al.* 1974)

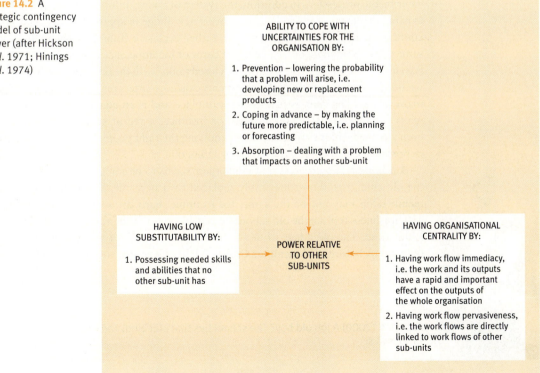

Decision Making

The ability to affect how decisions are made considerably enhances power, and sometimes it is possible to do this without actually taking part in the decision making process. For instance, a team that is charged with studying a range of options for marketing a new product may examine a very limited range of options, which leaves decision makers little to do but rubber-stamp the option that makes the team more influential in the future. Indeed, since some decisions are made sequentially in organisations, the individual or group that makes its decisions early can limit the range of options open to those who make their decisions later on.

OB IN ACTION: 'The Club' Still Reigns Supreme

There is a fairly extensive raft of legislation that tries to ensure equality of opportunity and, in addition, many organisations have policies that proclaim their commitment to this aim, all of which gives an impression that organisations are meritocracies. Nevertheless, being 'one of the chaps', or 'networking' as current jargon politely calls it, still seems to have tremendous advantages for those admitted to 'the club'. For instance, there are certain occupations, such as the law, where the 'old boy' discrimination network is highly effective in creating a barrier for those entering the profession. In addition, the system of taking 'informal soundings' from existing members of the judiciary before a new judge is appointed only serves to confirm the idea that the judiciary is a rather exclusive club. To some extent the same can be said in medicine; in recent cases of incompetence and/or malpractice, it seems likely that members of the club 'closed ranks' with the result that even though well-documented complaints from patients existed, matters remained concealed for many years. 'The club' is just as commonplace and is an equally potent force in many large business organisations. For instance, a recent survey revealed that even younger senior executives rated 'knowing the right people' as one of the most important factors influencing career progression.

A new twist, however, is that while there seems to be some tendency to unseat the old elite, it is almost inevitably replaced by a new one. While the criteria of membership may not be the same, for example, hard drinking, competitiveness and brashness replace the old school tie and an Oxbridge education, the end result is the same. The old adage of 'it's not what you know, but who you know' still operates as before, and members of the club are given preference over those who are not.

Source:

Palmer, C (2000) A job old boy? The school ties that still bind, *The Observer*, 11 June: 18.

Networks

Structure establishes formal patterns of interaction and, as the OB in Action box above indicates, those who interact often create informal links that are useful for enhancing their power. These links enable people to stay 'in the know' and trade favours so that power can be exercised in the future. Pfeffer and Salancik (1978) argue that these networks are often more influential than formal mechanisms because people are liable to increase their power by forming coalitions, or power blocs, that enable them to draw on each other's power when necessary.

Organisational Culture

Culture can often be a silent and highly unobtrusive source of power. It reflects implicit understandings and assumptions about the way that certain matters should be dealt with, and these become embedded in codes of behaviour that often confer a great deal of power on certain individuals and groups. These norms are often so taken for granted that they become what Lukes (1974) has called the third dimension of power. They determine whose viewpoint dominates, whether an issue can be brought out into the open or is regarded as non-discussable, and they often result in an acceptance of power holding by one group as the natural order of things.

The External Environment

Because a firm has little control over its environment, it is usually regarded as something that reduces organisational power. However, as will be seen in Chapter 17, most firms try to buffer their technical cores from the effects of environment so that they can operate under steady, stable conditions (Thompson 1967). Where environmental effects are particularly crucial, organisations often have sub-units to deal with segments of the environment that are subject to a high degree of change. Because these sub-units shield others in the organisation from the effects of change, they can come to occupy positions of great power, an example of which was given earlier when describing the work of Hinings *et al.* (1974).

THE BASIS OF POWER

To close this description of the bases of power and link it to the next section, a number of important points can be made. First, the distinction between interpersonal and contextual bases of power is an artificial one. In practice, the bases are strongly connected and some of the contextual sources, for example structure, culture, knowledge and resources, reinforce the coercive, reward and legitimate powers of individuals. Similarly, some of the interpersonal bases, notably expert and referent power, enable people to manipulate circumstances to acquire contextual power.

Second, the bases of power are additive, which is why interpersonal and contextual bases converge in Figure 14.1. Thus, someone who can draw on all the interpersonal bases has much more power than someone who can draw on only one, and individuals or groups that have access to both contextual and interpersonal bases will usually be much more powerful than those who can only draw on one source.

Third, as can be seen from Figure 14.1, the bases only give someone 'potential power'. In some situations power has to be used to demonstrate that it exists so that it can be used to exert influence in the future.

THE USE OF POWER

To use power to influence the behaviour of others, two conditions have to be met:

- the power holder has to recognise that he or she has this capacity and, unless this is the case, all that exists is latent power;
- the power holder has to identify and select tactics to use his or her power.

The second of these requirements will be dealt with here, but before doing so two common misconceptions about the use of power need to be examined: its assumed direction of flow and its assumed visibility.

Misconceptions about the Use of Power

The Direction of Power Flows

The most common misconception about power in organisations is that it is assumed to be synonymous with formal authority, which gives the impression that power is always exercised downwards, through the hierarchy. However, some of the interpersonal bases of power result in conditions where it can just as easily be exercised upwards. For example, expert power often makes a manager dependent on subordinates, and a subordinate who has referent power can emerge as an informal leader, whose co-operation can be vital to a manager. Some of the contextual bases also allow upwards influence, for instance by low-level personnel who control the flow of crucial information and other resources (Mintzberg 1985). It is also important to bear in mind at the current time that the workforce in many organisations has been cut back to the bare minimum and achieving objectives means that many managers are dependent on the active cooperation of employees. Whereas compliance can be enforced, this is not the case with cooperation, which needs to be given willingly, and it is this need for cooperation that enables employees to exert power upwards.

Hidden Power

Another common misconception is that power is a visible phenomenon, whereas hidden power is often the most potent form. People who keep their power hidden can often be one step ahead of the opposition and act before an opponent becomes aware. A simple explanation will perhaps demonstrate the point.

People in high positions can use their position power to control the agendas of committees where certain issues are discussed but, because most of us have some awareness of this practice, it is only a semi-hidden use of power. However, other people, notably those with expert or referent power, can have access to these individuals, and this enables them to exert a degree of hidden influence that prevents some items ever being discussed. Tactics such as these are part of organisational politics and will be discussed later in the chapter. For the present, the matter can perhaps be summarised most succinctly by drawing on a penetrating analysis by Paton (1983), who suggests that there are three primary domains in which hidden power can be exercised:

1. By shaping the terms on which matters will be discussed, typically by controlling information and agendas.

2. By developing or changing working practices in a way that suits the person or persons involved. This is often a reflection of managerial dependence on subordinates who, in return for this concession, give their cooperation about other matters.

3. By having some scope to prevent the emergence of conflicts which might result in a trial of strength. This is by far the most difficult way to use hidden power and it usually involves one of four tactics:
   - **latent intimidation** in which issues are suppressed by subtly inducing someone to believe that coercion or worse will follow if the issue is raised;
   - **promotion of values or beliefs to legitimise arrangements that can otherwise be contested**, an example of which are the behaviours and practices inherent in an organisational culture that acts as an unrecognised control mechanism;
   - **structuring work relationships** to 'divide and rule';
   - **by setting up institutional biases** so that people are relatively satisfied when only some of their concerns are met.

Power Tactics

There are many ways of using power. Some were briefly mentioned when describing the bases of power and others in contrasting the use of invisible and visible power. Here the discussion will mainly focus on power tactics that are used at individual and intragroup levels, where people, including managers and supervisors, use power in their immediate surroundings. To do this some of the research evidence will be described; this will be brought together at the end to draw conclusions.

The Kipnis Study

Kipnis *et al.* (1984) give a comprehensive picture of the tactics that are used by supervisors and managers to influence each other and their subordinates. Seven main tactics were identified and these are shown in Table 14.1, together with the behaviour associated with each one.

Table 14.1 Power tactics (after Kipnis *et al.* 1984)

Tactic	How tactic operates	Typical associated behaviours
Assertiveness	Direct use of authority	• issue direct instruction to comply • set deadline dates for completion • emphasise importance of compliance • remind other person(s) of obligation to comply
Friendliness or integration	Induce favourable disposition in other person(s) to comply	• praise prior to requesting compliance • exaggerate importance of compliance • act humbly to obtain cooperation and wait until other person is in receptive mood before making request
Rationality	Use the force of logical argument	• present information in a way that makes non-compliance seem illogical • develop well-argued case to show that other person is highly competent if he or she complies • explain exactly what is required
Sanctions	Compel compliance – the argument of force	• use or threaten to use the coercive power of organisational rewards and punishments, e.g. future performance appraisal, salary increases, privileges
Higher authority	Obtain support and backing from above	• support obtained and shown to be obtained before requesting others to comply
Bargaining	Obtain support from other power holders	• exchange favours to obtain compliance • call in debts for giving favours on prior occasions
Coalitions	Enlist the support of other people	• build up alliances with others (subordinates and co-workers) • network to identify where favours can be done for others and asked in return

The range of tactics identified by Kipnis and his co-workers is quite extensive and they were found to be used upwards, downwards and laterally. Some, however, are clearly more usable in one direction than another. For example, trying to use coercion upwards is likely to provoke unresistable coercion in return. Thus the order of popularity of a particular tactic tends to vary according to the direction in which it is used (see Figure 14.3).

The Yukl Analysis

Using French and Raven's five bases of interpersonal power, Yukl (1994) gives an analytical framework and set of guidelines that portray the different ways that power can be used in a downward direction. This relates the particular power base to the type of subordinate(s) on whom it is used and forecasts the likely outcome in terms of the subordinate's compliance with the power holder's wishes. The three types of subordinates used in Yukl's framework are:

- **the committed subordinate**   tends to identify with and accept the power holder; he or she is prepared to put additional effort into the task where it is seen as important to the power holder;
- **the compliant subordinate**   will normally work at a reasonable pace, so long as the power holder's wishes do not involve additional effort;

Figure 14.3
Preferred power tactics for using upwards or downwards influence (after Kipnis *et al.* 1984)

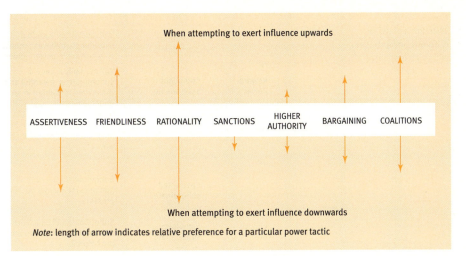

- **the resistant subordinate** is someone in conflict with the power holder and, in order to thwart the power holder's wishes, he or she will look for an opportunity to neglect the task.

Using these subordinate types, and applying them to the different bases of power, Yukl forecasts what the outcomes, in terms of subordinate responses to a power holder's request, will be (see Figures 14.4(A)–(E)).

AN OVERVIEW OF POWER AND ITS USE

By bringing together the results of Kipnis *et al.* (1984) and the ideas of Yukl with other points made in the chapter, some general conclusions can be drawn about power and its use. First, the tactic used must be appropriate to the circumstances. To some extent, successfully using a particular base of power depends on the type of person on whom it is used. For instance, aggressive or assertive managers, who are perhaps most likely to use sanctions or face-to-face confrontations to extract obedience, are often those who get the least compliance from their subordinates.

Second, power is used within a context, and all contexts have their own rules about how power should be exercised and in most cases an attempt to use coercion upwards would be a breach of the rules. Power bases can also be very fragile and have their own limitations in certain contexts. Managers who are legitimate experts in particular areas can seriously undermine perceptions of their expertise if they try to create an illusion that they are experts on everything. Similarly, people who have genuine referent power because they are seen by others to have high ethics and ideals can lose all credibility in a momentary lapse in which they use less reputable tactics.

Third, there are sometimes occupational or professional biases for or against the use of certain power bases. Technical experts and professionals (for example, engineers, scientists, lawyers or accountants) are probably more amenable to the tactics of rationality and friendliness from an expert in another field than they would be to other types of power. Thus it is unwise to rely too much on one power base, and a variety of sources may be needed as the circumstances dictate.

Figure 14.4
Outcomes of using
different power bases
with different types of
subordinate (after Yukl
1994)

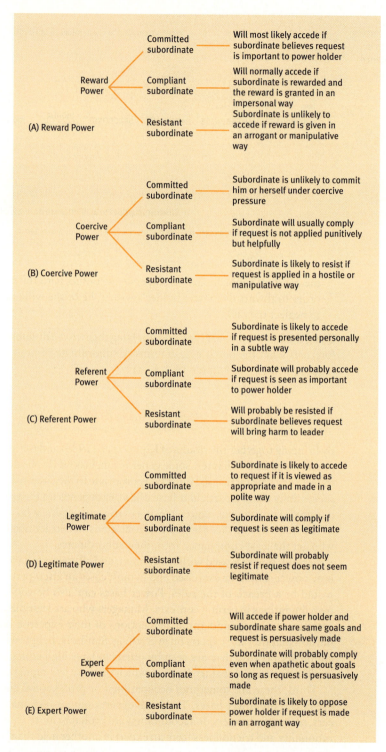

CASE STUDY 14.1: Mr Preston

Mr Preston manages a small department in a busy service organisation and, because of the nature of the work, he often has to ask his service engineers to put themselves out by making calls on customers during unsocial hours. Two of his subordinates are completely different in temperament. Bill Townsend is keen and committed towards his work, whereas Harry Left is disenchanted, disgruntled and, sometimes, downright obstructive. Therefore, when asking them to accept an inconvenient job, Mr Preston approaches them in different ways. With Bill he tends to emphasise that Bill will be doing him (Mr Preston) a personal favour, for which he will be paid overtime, but with Harry he just says here's an opportunity to earn a bit more money. Sometimes he persuades Bill by emphasising that they both have the customer's interests at heart, whereas with Harry he avoids this and often says that the customer is an acquaintance of the Managing Director, who has asked for the job to receive priority. However, Mr Preston is careful with both of them not be authoritarian; with Bill because he feels it would be unnecessary and with Harry because it would be inviting the answer no.

Question

Using the Yukl (1994) analysis of the use of power tactics, how appropriate is Mr Preston's difference in approach to Bill and Harry?

Fourth, the effectiveness of certain power bases and tactics can depend on the circumstances of the moment. In a crisis situation legitimate or expert power and, in some circumstances, coercion can often be considered appropriate. For instance, if your house was burning down and the fire brigade arrived, would you be happy to see the chief firefighter get the others in a circle and painstakingly persuade them what to do with a long-winded process of rational argument? However, the same power tactics can be highly ineffective in non-crisis circumstances, even if they are used by the same people.

Fifth, the sources of power do not appear overnight. While people acquire legitimate power and the reward and coercive bases that go with it when they are promoted to a position of authority, to be sustained even these bases have to be nurtured.

REPLAY

- Although power is most visible when it is used downwards, it can also be exercised upwards and laterally.
- Power is not always used in a visible way and often invisible power is the most potent form.
- A wide range of tactics of power use can be identified, some of which are more commonly used in different directions and in specific contextual circumstances.

Sixth, because the effect of different bases of power is additive, it is sensible to cultivate as many interpersonal and contextual bases as possible. To do this often means that a versatile range of tactics for acquiring, maintaining and using power has to be developed. This is the next topic.

ORGANISATIONAL POLITICS

To quote what by now is the most widely accepted definition, organisational politics:

> **involves those activities taken within organisations to acquire, develop and use power and other resources to obtain one's preferred outcome in a situation where there is uncertainty or descensus about choices.**   **(Pfeffer 1981, p 7)**

To many people this smacks of unsavoury manipulation, chicanery and devious underhand behaviour, and three implications can be drawn from the definition:

- although political behaviour is clearly related to the concept of power, conceptually, politics and power are two different things; organisational politics is more sharply focused on what people do to acquire and maintain power, and this includes the study of tactics used to achieve an end that could perhaps have been achieved in a different way;

- politics refers to situations of uncertainty, which means that political behaviour tends to come into play where it is unclear what a goal should be, or how to achieve it, and it tends to be used to turn a situation like this to the advantage of an individual or group;

- the definition refers to descensus about choices, which means that if there is disagreement about whose preferences should dominate, or whose interests should be served, the political process can be activated to resolve the issue.

With respect to the second point, because matters dealt with by top managers are usually more uncertain and ambiguous than those dealt with by people lower down, it can be expected that political behaviour is more prevalent at these levels. Indeed, Gandz and Murray (1980) comment that while most managers declare behaviour of this type to be unfair, bad and unhealthy, they also feel that being a good politician is a prerequisite for advancement to high levels.

In terms of the third point it should be noted that if a single individual has a firm hold on the reins of authority, there is probably less likelihood that political activity will occur, which explains why political behaviour tends to be viewed as aberrant. It usually goes well beyond the behaviour strictly associated with a person's role and is often outside the recognised system of organisational authority. Moreover, it is often intentionally used to pursue the interests of an individual or group, sometimes at the expense of the organisation as a whole (Madison *et al.* 1980).

FACTORS GIVING RISE TO POLITICAL BEHAVIOUR

Individual Factors

Individual factors can play a part in prompting political activity, and people with certain personality characteristics seem to have a far higher tendency to play politics.

For example, Machiavellians (see Chapter 3) like to exercise subtle control over others, are adept at manipulating them and are more strongly disposed to use politics (Gemmil and Heiser 1972). People with an authoritarian personality often like high-risk situations and are sometimes willing politicians who are quite reckless in their use of political tactics (Ferris *et al.* 1996).

Organisational Factors

While personal characteristics tell us which people are the more willing users of politics, this says nothing about the situations that provide an opportunity to bring political tactics into play. These situations are well documented in the works of Miles (1980) and Robbins (1998), and are given in what follows.

Ambiguous Goals

In most organisations there is usually some ambiguity about goals and while goals such as 'increase the market share', or 'enter new markets' are commonplace, they do not specify exactly what should be achieved. This vagueness can be used to justify almost any course of action that can be used for personal gain simply by saying that it will help achieve the goal.

Scarce Resources

When resources are distributed in an organisation few people get everything that they desire, especially when cutbacks are in progress. This creates a situation of winners and losers and the losers can engage in all sorts of tactics to try to acquire what they perceive to be their rightful share, for example by presenting misleading information, lobbying etc.

Technology and Environment

Changes in external circumstances, or in the technology used by an organisation, increase the uncertainty of organisational life. This often gives a tremendous opportunity to engage in manoeuvres that are designed to enlarge or preserve the power bases of individuals and groups.

Non-programmed Decisions

Where a decision is required on how to deal with a completely novel situation there are seldom any precedents to guide decision making. This gives huge scope for an individual to manoeuvre to get his or her definition of the situation adopted. If this is successful, it virtually guarantees that the person will be regarded as knowledgeable, which brings expert power.

Organisational Change

Since any situation involving change contains a degree of uncertainty, the circumstances are ripe for someone to redefine the situation and how it should be handled to his or her own advantage. In addition, uncertainty and ambiguity have been shown to result in heightened perceptions that political activity is commonplace in others (Ferris *et al.* 1994), which in turn prompts the perceivers to engage in political actions themselves.

Role Ambiguity

If someone occupies a role in which the required behaviour is unclear or ambiguous, the person has a golden opportunity to redefine the role in a way that best suits him or herself.

Unclear Criteria for Evaluating Performance

Those who appraise the performance of others often rely on very subjective evaluation criteria. Sometimes only a single measure of performance is used, and there are long intervals between the time that performance occurs and the point at which it is evaluated. In the interim period the appraisee clearly has a great deal of scope to redefine his or her role in an advantageous way.

Organisational Culture and Structure

The more that a culture contains values that encourage people to view situations in win–lose terms, the greater is the incentive never to be a loser. Thus, any type of behaviour that facilitates winning can come to be considered as justifiable. In addition, where a structure centralises decision making in the hands of a small number of people, others can feel starved of information and influence, which prompts them to engage in politicking.

Low Trust

Where people do not trust each other their tendency to use covert manoeuvrings in their dealings is greater. This is particularly the case when they percieve that others regularly engage in politicking, because in this situation they can come to believe that they have no alternative to behaving the same way themselves (Valle and Perrewe 2000).

TIME OUT

Imagine that you are an official of the student union at your university or college. Also imagine that the government announces that in the interests of saving money, as from the start of the next academic year, it will reduce its subsidy to each university by an amount equivalent to last year's expenditure on the student union. Most student unions run a number of services for students, and there are a large number of societies and activities that are subsidised in this way.

1. Would this situation be likely to result in an increase in the use of political tactics within the student union?
2. Of the factors discussed above, which ones in particular are likely to prompt increased political activity within the union?
3. What form do you feel this political activity would take?

THE PERVASIVENESS OF ORGANISATIONAL POLITICS

Although many people condemn organisational politics there is little doubt that it is extremely widespread. For instance, the survey of 428 managers by Gandz and Murray (1980) revealed that, while 55 per cent felt that behaviour of this type was unfair and unhealthy, over 75 per cent believed that successful executives need to be good politicians. More recent work by Lenway and Rehbein (1991) affirms this picture and indicates that most managers see political behaviour as an undesirable but inevitable part of organisational life. Why, then, is it likely to be so prevalent? To some extent, the prevalence of politics is connected with the circumstances outlined above, which are very common in organisations. However, there are almost certainly more basic reasons.

Organisations are made up of people, who have their own ambitions and interests to pursue and there is also a possibility that these personal ambitions will be thwarted in some way. Political manoeuvring is one way of overcoming the situation and Mintzberg (1985) argues that the incentives to use political behaviour are so strong that it can never be eradicated.

This gives rise to another interesting question. If political behaviour is so widespread, why is its use so heavily condemned? Pfeffer (1981) argues that this occurs because influential groups in society have a vested interest in deceiving themselves about the real nature of organisations and give voice to a highly inaccurate picture of organisational life. In this, organisations are portrayed as entities that behave rationally, logically and dispassionately, and exist for the greater good of society. Thus they have no need for internal politics. Since this is far from being the truth, it is perhaps more appropriate to accept that organisational politics is here to stay. This still leaves unanswered important questions about whether political activity has a positive or negative effect on an organisation, and whether political behaviour is ethical. Since these are important considerations in their own right they will be dealt with separately.

Political Behaviour: Positive or Negative Functions?

Political behaviour probably has both positive and negative organisational functions. For example, in his earlier work, Pfeffer (1981), while not actually condemning political behaviour, is far from endorsing its use. In more recent work, however, he argues that it is often the only way to overcome the inertia that is commonplace in hierarchically structured organisations, and may well be the only way to make things happen (Pfeffer 1992). Thus, like power, politics is *Janus-faced* and, depending on how it is used, it can be a force for good or a force for evil. The twin faces of politics have been cogently analysed by Mintzberg (1985), who draws a similar conclusion: it is not political behaviour itself that is dysfunctional, but how politics are used and the ends to which they are directed. A summary of Mintzberg's ideas is given in Table 14.2.

Janus-faced: having two (good and evil) aspects

The Ethics of Political Behaviour

Flowing from Mintzberg's ideas, this matter can perhaps be most conveniently addressed by asking, 'Are there circumstances in which political tactics are ethically justified?' This question is addressed by Cavanagh *et al.* (1981), who suggest three sets of criteria, which, if satisfied, justify political tactics on ethical grounds. These are:

Table 14.2 Positive and negative functions of organisational politics (after Mintzberg 1985)

Positive functions		Negative functions	
Organisational flexibility	The use of politics can correct the slowness of more formal methods of influence and add flexibility to these methods	Inequality, discrimination and unfairness	Political activity tends to result in 'in-groups' and 'out-groups', in which the interests of minority groups, which have little formal influence, can be ignored
Meritocracy	Political usage acts to ensure that the fittest and strongest in organisations are brought into positions of influence and leadership	Distorted decision making	Political activity tends to be used by individuals and groups to promote only their own interests which means that decision criteria can be narrow and parochial
Promotion of multiple perspectives	Politics can help ensure that all sides of an issue are aired and debated, while more conventional forms of influence can result in only one side being heard	Ignores interests of stakeholders	Because some individuals or groups are able to exercise the real power within an organisation other stakeholders simply have their interests ignored
Facilitates change	Politics can be used to promote changes that are otherwise blocked by normal systems of influence	Inefficiency and time wasting	Political behaviour, which often involves extensive lobbying, alliance building and subversion of the formal influence processes, uses up inordinate amounts of energy that could be put to better use
Decision implementation	Political activity can help ensure that decisions get implemented	Unequal power distribution results	Power corrupts and once tasted is an addictive drug. Thus the use of political behaviour develops a taste for power, which can all too easily gyrate in one direction. Power difference in organisations should desirably be minimised rather than allowed to become greater

1. **Utilitarian criteria**   Does the use of political tactics result in the optimal satisfaction of stakeholders both inside and outside the organisation (the greatest good for the greatest number of people)? Or, are there overwhelming reasons that justify one or more of these stakeholders having sub-optimal goal satisfactions?

2. **Individual rights criteria**   Will the use of political tactics still result in the individual rights of the affected parties being respected, e.g. free consent, free speech, conscience, privacy? Or, are there overwhelming reasons why individual rights should be ignored for one or more of the affected parties?

3. **Distributive justice criteria**   Will the use of political tactics respect the rules of natural justice by treating people equitably and fairly, rather than in an arbitrary fashion? Or, are there overwhelming reasons for ignoring the violation of justice?

While these criteria are helpful in highlighting ethical pitfalls, they still leave a feeling of unease. Every set of criteria has an opt-out clause, which provides a convenient reason to justify why it can be ignored. This leaves a feeling that if the matter is not examined in public, all sorts of rationalisations can be made, which poses a huge potential problem. The effectiveness of political behaviour essentially depends on covert activity and it can be rendered totally ineffective if matters become too open. Therefore, while Cavanagh *et al.* spell out the criteria that need to be satisfied, in practice it is unlikely that they can all be applied.

POLITICAL BEHAVIOUR

Having considered organisational politics at a theoretical level it is now time to examine some of the more practical considerations. Although a wide range of behaviour is possible, Schein (1977) notes that what is used tends to depend on three factors:

* goals – what a person hopes to achieve;
* personal characteristics – some people are more comfortable with using certain tactics than others;
* the situation – which places limits on the behaviour that can be used, for example, some behaviour is easier to defend and so it can be used in a visible way, while other tactics have to be concealed.

Political Tactics

Several authors have attempted to catalogue political tactics, an exacting task because it is very difficult to observe politics at work. Nevertheless, using the writings of Pfeffer (1981) and Mintzberg (1983), a list of tactics can be brought together and these are described in what follows. Since the purpose of these tactics is to acquire or maintain power, it should be noted that some of them have a connection with the bases of power described earlier in the chapter.

Control of Information

Where certain information is crucial, the smaller the number of people having access to it, the greater the influence of those who have the total picture. Thus, an extremely potent political tactic is to become the sole conduit for certain information.

Dominate Information Flows

Where it is not possible to be the sole source of information, people who are able to become the 'gatekeepers' and control access to it acquire a great deal of power. For instance, they can divulge only certain parts of the information so that only they have the complete picture.

Use of Outside Experts

Outside experts such as consultants have an air of impartiality and neutrality, and the people who sponsor their entry into an organisation are often able to frame the consultants' terms of reference in a way that enables only one set of conclusions to be drawn. In this way it is possible to obtain the support of an outside expert for proposals that might otherwise attract internal opposition.

Control of Agendas

Rather than get into an argument when alternative proposals are debated, it can be more effective to control the agenda and limit the number of proposals that appear. Under the guise of saving the valuable time of the main committee, a sub-committee can be set up to vet the alternatives. Where control over the whole agenda cannot be exercised, choosing the order in which items appear can be nearly as useful. This way it is sometimes possible to arrange for opponents to be absent, or at least ensure that supporters are in the majority.

Image Building

If people are seen as experts on a particular matter, or have the backing of people in power, their judgement is less likely to be questioned. Thus, a useful tactic is to create an image that conveys this impression.

Coalition Building

There is a saying that 'It's not what you know, it's who you know'. Thus, a viable tactic is to build up a network of alliances, perhaps by doing favours for others, so that support can be called on in return when it is needed.

Control of Decision Parameters

Astute politicians often ensure that the outcome of a decision most benefits themselves by establishing the criteria against which the acceptability of a solution to a problem is evaluated. Suppose, for example, that a manager favours a particular location for a new warehouse. If he or she is able to persuade the decision making body that certain criteria (such as location, ease of access, room for eventual expansion etc.) are the ones to use, information can be presented which makes the manager's preferred option the automatic choice.

Game Playing

In one sense game playing can be regarded as just another political tactic. However, Mintzberg (1983) views all tactics as 'games that are played within a political arena' and this perspective has the advantage of illustrating that tactics can be used in several directions depending upon those one is trying to influence. This is portrayed in Figure 14.5.

Authority Games

Authority games: political tactics to resist authority from above or counter resistance to authority from below

These are used either to resist authority from above or counter resistance to authority from below. The former are what Mintzberg calls **insurgency games**, which range from outright mutiny to mild resistance or, to avoid taking action, the use of delayed

Figure 14.5 The political arena (after Mintzberg 1983)

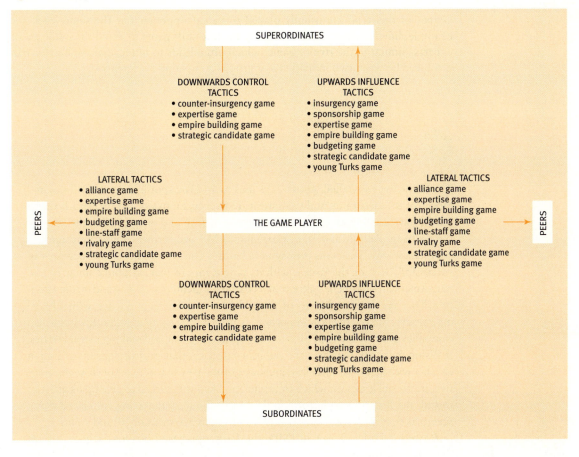

messages. These tactics can be used by individuals, groups or even a whole workforce if it has been collectively organised. As the name implies, **counter-insurgency games** are played by people in authority to regain compliance, often by making threats or introducing a stricter regime of control.

Power base games:
political tactics to
build or maintain a
power base

Power Base Games

Tactics of this type can be used in all directions to build or maintain bases of power. The **sponsorship game** is used to obtain resources, backing or prestige by convincing a senior, powerful figure of one's loyalty. A **budgeting game** simply involves making exaggerated bids to acquire resources. **Alliance games** are used laterally, to gain the support of colleagues, often by giving a pledge of support in return, while **expertise games** can be played in any direction and involve creating the impression of unquestioned expertise. Because it involves taking away the territory of someone else to enlarge one's own, the **empire building game** is one of the most risky of all. It must often be played in a very covert way, perhaps by taking on someone's tasks and responsibilities at a time of crisis, with the aim of holding on to the territory afterwards.

**Rivalry games:
political tactics to
defeat an opponent
at the same level**

Rivalry Games

Games of this type are usually played to defeat opponents at the same level, for example, line managers sometimes play the **line-staff game** to avoid the influence of experts. Similarly, the **rivalry game**, which often leads to bitter, divisive battles, can be played between two individuals or groups competing for territory.

👁 OB IN ACTION: Environmental Groups – Political Tactics

The battle over so-called 'ghost ships' has turned the spotlight on the politics and tactics of the environmental movement. However, lobbyists, led by Friends of the Earth, have come under attack for scaremongering and exaggerating the scale of the problem. Peter Mandelson, Hartlepool's MP and former cabinet minister, has complained of a 'ferocious propaganda battle'. The group's detractors accuse it of successfully hyping the issue – with its potent mix of fear, symbolic imagery and anti-American sentiment – as part of its battle for members, money and media attention. They say there is a history of 'green' lobbyists distorting evidence, while choosing emotive, but relatively unimportant, issues for their campaigns. Long-established campaign groups, such as FoE and Greenpeace, try to avoid making factual errors, realising that they reinforce the public's suspicion that pressure groups are often cavalier with facts. Nevertheless, pressure groups are often accused of choosing emotive, irrational issues on which to campaign. Shell was forced to give up its attempt to sink the Brent Spar platform in the North Sea despite having convinced many scientists that deep sea disposal was the most environmentally sound solution.

Professor Ulrich Steger of IMD, the Lausanne-based business school, argues that one reason why FoE chose to campaign on the ghost ships was its collective memory of a series of incidents in the mid to late 1990s when the UK accepted hazardous waste from other European countries, creating fears that it was being used as a waste dump. He notes that the largest campaigning groups have, in effect, divided the agenda between them, rarely speaking on the same issues. They also tackle issues in different ways: at one extreme are groups bent upon confrontation with business, while at the other are those striking alliances with businesses. Prof Steger says companies are often taken off guard when attacked by a pressure group and, with the exception of a few battle-hardened companies such as those in the oil or tobacco industries, most businesses are ill-prepared for an onslaught of this type. The costs can be devastating, as Monsanto discovered in its battle against UK non-governmental organisations over genetically modified food. Even in less extreme cases, a tarnished reputation can cost customers and staff dearly, says Prof Steger. 'You only realise what your reputation is worth when you have lost it.'

Source:

Holder, V (2003) Campaigning to win war of words, *The Financial Times*, 13 November.

Change games: political tactics to bring about or block change

Change Games

These games come to the forefront when someone wants to bring about change, or to block it. To alter unethical organisational practices the **whistle-blowing game** is used, which involves quietly informing people outside the organisation to attract bad publicity. At a time of organisational flux, when many things are up for grabs, people can play the **strategic candidate game,** by suggesting an apparent way out of the dilemma that promotes their own preferred alternatives. Finally, what Mintzberg calls the **young Turks game** is played for the highest stakes of all. Its aim is to depose the existing power holders, or bring about a complete change of direction in the organisation, and is usually played by a very dedicated set of rebels, who covertly build up alliances.

POLITICAL BEHAVIOUR: AN OVERVIEW

Clearly the range of political tactics is almost limitless. Some are more risky than others, for instance, violating the chain of command, losing personal control, or saying no to the ultimate power holder. Because they are visible, other tactics tend to be viewed as deviate and are difficult to defend, for example, divide and rule, excluding rivals from decision making fora and settling old scores. For this reason milder tactics, such as controlling information, image building and deflecting attention from oneself when something goes wrong, tend to be the ones that are most favoured (Madison *et al.* 1980).

Whatever the tactics, it is doubtful whether political behaviour can ever be eliminated. The rewards for using it successfully are highly cherished, and so the forces promoting its use are extremely strong. Nevertheless, it might be possible to remove some of the dysfunctional effects, and Moorhead and Griffin (1995) argue that three simple steps can be taken to head off the opportunities for people to play politics, or reduce the necessity for them to do so.

- **Open up communication**   so that everyone knows how and why scarce resources are allocated, which also prevents monopolies on information and its distribution.
- **Reduce uncertainty**   so that people have less opportunity to manipulate others with promises to remove their uncertainties and less reason to play politics to resolve their own ambiguities.
- **Be aware**   that there is an ever-present tendency for political behaviour to occur, and of the factors that give rise to its use.

REPLAY

- Political tactics are used to acquire, develop or maintain power and other resources or to bring about personally desired outcomes, and they are widely used in organisations.
- A number of personal and organisational factors are likely to give rise to political behaviour.
- A wide range of political tactics can be identified, and a useful way to view them is as games that people play to pursue desired outcomes.

TIME OUT

Using the scenario given in the previous Time Out exercise, which concerns the mythical situation where student union funding is withdrawn, answer the questions below.

1. Which political tactics do you feel would be most likely to come into play? Develop an example for each one that you feel would be used.
2. Which people do you feel would be most likely to use these tactics?
3. What do you feel that these people have to gain by the use of political tactics?
4. Is it possible that these ends could be pursued in some other way?

ORGANISATIONAL CONFLICT

The word 'conflict' is often used in an imprecise way and is defined here as:

the behaviour of an individual or group which purposely sets out to block or inhibit another group (or individual) from achieving its goals.

Note that conflict involves one party purposely standing in the way of another achieving its goals, and this distinguishes it from competition, a word with which it is sometimes used interchangeably. However, as Schmidt and Kochan (1972) point out, there is an important difference. In a competitive situation, although the parties can have incompatible goals, people can usually pursue their aims without impeding each other, but in conflict, it is impossible for one party to achieve its aims without blocking the other.

Perhaps the easiest way to appreciate this distinction is to examine sports activities which are often called competitive, but are inherently conflictual. For instance, in football, cricket and squash, each party sets out to prevent the other from achieving its aim. However, in sports such as gymnastics or mountaineering, each person or group tries to do its very best, with no attempt to thwart the other's goal attainment. There are many parallels to this in organisations. For example, individual sales people might all try to be the top one but, as long as they stick to their own geographical territories, they do not block each other, they simply compete. However, if some start poaching customers from other territories, goal-blocking activity has started and conflict is likely to ensue. This illustrates a point that is often overlooked: the dividing line between competition and conflict is sometimes very blurred. In many organisations competition is encouraged because it is assumed that it improves performance, but sometimes things go too far and conflict is triggered. Some degree of conflict is probably inevitable in most organisations, and so the critical issue is not whether it should be allowed to exist, but whether it can be handled in a way that removes its potentially detrimental effects on organisational functioning.

CONFLICT: TRADITIONAL AND CONTEMPORARY VIEWS

Because it is seen as something harmful and unpleasant conflict is often viewed with distaste, usually because people have very traditional views on the matter (Pinkley 1990). But there is an alternative viewpoint, which holds that conflict is a normal state of affairs and, in controlled amounts, can even be beneficial (Edwards 1986). Thus it is important to examine these alternative philosophies.

Alternative philosophies of conflict

The Unitarist Perspective

Unitarist perspective: a management frame of reference in which an organisation is seen as one large family, all on the same side and pulling in the same direction, and in which conflict is seen as deviant behaviour

This is very much the traditional view. It sees harmony and cooperation as the natural state of human affairs, from which it follows that conflict is at best an undesirable interruption to smooth-flowing normality – it usually has negative or destructive effects and is to be avoided at all costs. In organisations this results in an assumption that everyone is really on the same side, united behind one leader and in pursuit of the same goals, but that they sometimes fail to recognise this, either because of faulty communication, poor leadership, or simply because they have been led astray by wilful troublemakers. While there are cooperative elements in most organisations, this perspective grossly oversimplifies matters and fails to acknowledge that there could be in-built differences of interests that make conflict a perfectly normal occurrence. Nevertheless, it is a remarkably resilient view: Drucker (1984), for example, writes about organisations as places where everyone works (or should work) towards a common goal. Moreover, the unitarist ideology is commonplace with British managers (Poole and Mansfield 1993), who often make appeals for all employees to pull together in a team spirit. Indeed, the team idea is probably popular with managers because it is a unitarist concept – an appeal to pull together as a team is a way of discrediting anyone who questions the manager's wisdom.

The Pluralist Perspective

Pluralist perspective: a management frame of reference in which an organisation is seen as a collection of different groups, all with their own legitimate aims to pursue, and so a degree of conflict is a normal state of affairs

Although this perspective acknowledges that cooperation or harmony can exist in organisations, neither is viewed as a natural state of affairs. Rather, an organisation is regarded as a collection of groups which can have some goals in common, but others that are different and potentially opposed. Thus, conflict is seen as perfectly natural, and pluralists advance the idea that specific channels for handling conflict should be set up so that it can occur in a relatively ordered way that does not disrupt the whole organisation. At a theoretical level this viewpoint is widely accepted as more realistic than the unitarist perspective, but because it tends to sidestep the issue of wider social factors as a source of conflict, it has its critics.

The Radical Perspective

Radical perspective: organisational conflicts reflect conflict in wider society between capital and labour

The basic tenet of this view is derived from the Marxist idea that organisational conflict reflects inherent conflicts in society as a whole, that is, between the interests of those who own an enterprise and those who simply work in it. Although it takes a somewhat broader set of social forces into account, it views all organisational conflict as part of the struggle between capital and labour. Indeed, managers are seen as merely the agents of the owners, which assumes that all conflict is vertical and fails to recognise that managers can have interests that are different from those of owners, subordinate employees, or even other managers. As will be seen, not all organisational conflict takes place vertically, and much occurs between people at the same level.

Figure 14.6
Relationship between
levels of conflict and
organisational
performance

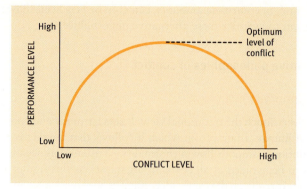

The Interactionist Perspective

**Interactionist
perspective:
organisational
conflict is seen as
neither bad nor good,
but simply inevitable**

Current views on conflict correspond to what is often called the *interactionist perspective*, which in many respects is a more refined version of pluralism. Conflict is seen as neither inherently bad nor good, just inevitable. It recognises that too much conflict will hamper an organisation's welfare and absorb a great deal of energy that could be devoted to doing other things. However, it also accepts that where no conflict exists, ideas are never challenged, and this stilts any impetus to change things for the better. Thus, an important difference between this and pluralism is the idea of an optimum level of conflict (see Figure 14.6).

There are two important implications of this idea. First, a great deal of conflict is concerned with challenging the *status quo*, which can have a positive outcome in dealing with complacency and lack of innovation. This idea has a strong intuitive appeal and, from what we know of organisations, is highly plausible. However, the main problem lies in identifying an optimal level of conflict, something that is often conveniently sidestepped by theorists in the area. The second implication is more practical and indicates that, rather than suppressing conflict, it is more important to learn how to manage it effectively. Since this is the view that currently holds sway, we will return to the important topic of conflict management later in the chapter.

TIME OUT

Carefully reflect on the organisation in which you work. If you are not in employment, consider your own university or college. Which perspective on conflict – the unitarist, pluralist, radical or interactionist – seems to you to most accurately reflect the nature of the organisation? Try to address this by answering the questions below.

1. Do people in the organisation express the view that everyone is on the same side and pulling in the same direction?
2. If your answer to question 1 is no, what are the different groups, what aims do they have in common and what aims do they have which could come into conflict?
3. Does any conflict in the organisation reflect divisions within wider society?
4. Is there an optimal level of conflict for the organisation, and how would you characterise the state of affairs when this exists?

THE NATURE OF ORGANISATIONAL CONFLICT

Two general points need to be made about the nature of conflict in organisations:

- that the roots of a conflict can go very deep, so deep that the people involved do not even realise what prompts their disagreement;
- while conflict is extremely widespread, it is rare to find that people engage in continuous hostilities; rather, these occur spasmodically, and while they are in progress people stop doing other things to pursue the conflict.

In practice it is often hard to divorce the roots of a conflict from how it is pursued, but since both are important in their own right they will be explored separately.

The Causal Factors in Conflict

Figure 14.7 gives a simplified model of a large number of factors that can prompt organisational conflict. For convenience, they have been broken down into four main groups.

Organisational Structure and Design Factors

The two most visible features of an organisation's structure are **horizontal differentiation** and **vertical differentiation**. The first divides an organisation into specialised activities and, although this gives the advantage of efficiency, it has a number of potential drawbacks. The more separate the activities, the more they are likely to develop their own particular viewpoints and have a tendency to pursue their own goals at the expense of others, which can all too quickly lead to conflict.

Figure 14.7
Causal factors in organisational conflict

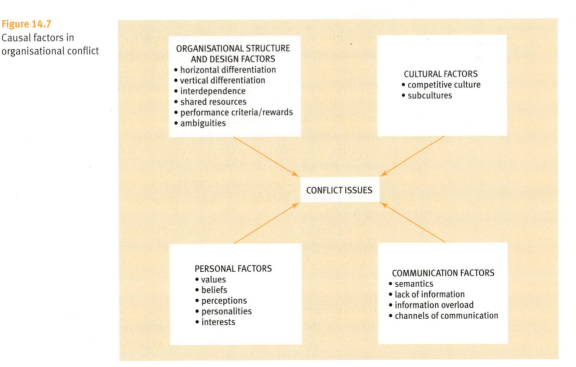

Vertical differentiation has a somewhat different effect. It establishes a hierarchy of authority which in theory should coordinate the activities of different departments and thus avoid horizontal conflicts. However, it gives rise to another source of conflict. Differences in authority result in decisions affecting people below and, while limits are normally placed on a person's authority, when a person is perceived to have exceeded his/her legitimate powers, those down below sometimes challenge the decision. A fairly obvious example of this is industrial relations conflict.

Departmental or functional interdependence is another feature of structure that can give rise to conflict. To achieve successful outcomes it is often necessary for two or more functions to coordinate their activities. This can mean that the performance of each one depends on the performance of the other(s), and they have to run their activities partly for the benefit of the other party. In this situation there is always a temptation for one function to put its own goals first.

Interdepartmental dependence and shared resources can have similar effects to interdependence. When resources are limited or rationed, departments do not always get all that they need, and if they are required to share resources, severe conflicts can occur about whether the distribution of resources is fair.

Performance criteria and rewards add to these problems. Like resources, rewards are usually rationed and one unit can be rewarded at the expense of another, which can lead to very bitter conflicts.

Ambiguities reduce the clarity about who is responsible for performing a certain activity and increase the likelihood that people will conveniently perceive that it is someone else's job. Ambiguities of this type are often the result of a badly thought-out structure and can lead to *post hoc* recriminations and conflicts when a job does not get done.

Personal Factors

Values are the positive and negative feelings that people have about the world, for example, whether something is inherently right or wrong, or good or bad. Because they shape whole patterns of behaviour and outlook, and give rise to ethical differences about the underlying purpose of an organisation, they can be potent sources of conflict.

Differences in **beliefs** sometimes result in conflicts about the means to an end rather than the end itself. For instance, there are strongly contrasting beliefs about what the expression 'organisational effectiveness' means. Some people hold that it simply means making a large profit, while others stress that effectiveness involves being responsible to a much wider constituency of stakeholders.

We do not see reality, but infer it from our **perceptions**, and since people's perceptions vary this sometimes results in genuine differences of opinion about what has been implied or said (see Chapter 4).

As explained in Chapter 3, people have unique **personalities**, and these can result in them finding it hard to get on together – the so-called 'personality clash'. People are usually able to get over these conflicts, but sometimes the incident affects their willingness to see things from the other party's point of view, which not only gives rise to further conflict but also makes the conflict harder to resolve.

People also have different **interests** in terms of what they want from work. To some, prestige and status are the most important rewards, while to others it is autonomy, job satisfaction and remuneration. These days many organisations are in an almost constant state of change, which upsets traditional patterns of reward, and since it is natural that people should want to hold on to what they already have, conflicts can arise when they try to do so.

Cultural Factors

An organisation's culture gives its members a guide to how they should conduct themselves. However, different parts of an organisation often have their own subcultures and, where these result in an issue being viewed in different ways, subcultures can give rise to conflicts.

Another way in which culture can establish a predisposition towards conflict is in those organisations where the culture emphasises competition. If top managers believe that it is good for sub-units to compete, they often establish structures and processes that encourage such behaviour, and matters can get out of hand and turn into conflict.

Communication Factors

As will be seen in Chapter 20, misunderstandings can all too easily arise in communication. There can be **semantic problems**, in which people attribute different meanings to the same information and **lack of information** creates ambiguity, which provides an opportunity for the use of political tactics that can eventually lead to conflict. Too much information leads to **information overload** and in this situation people tend to take in only that which is important to them. The use of **inappropriate channels** of communication can also give rise to conflict. Finally, it is important to recognise that even perfect communication will not ensure an absence of conflict. Differences in interests are inevitable in organisations and, in some cases, good communication only serves to highlight them (Pondy 1967).

CONFLICT EPISODES

One of the things that probably encourages the view that conflict is abnormal is that organisations tend to be characterised by long periods of apparent calm, interrupted by outbreaks of visible conflict, sometimes known as conflict 'episodes'. This does not mean, however, that prior to an episode there was no conflict. Indeed, conflict may well have been in progress in a less visible way for some time before an episode occurs. Thus, the main value of the concept of a conflict episode is to highlight the idea that conflict often follows a predictable pattern of stages. Figure 14.8 shows a simplified version of a more complex model derived by Kelly and Nicholson (1980), which deals with industrial relations conflicts. This has been adapted to embrace a wider range of organisational situations and by reading the model from left to right, a chain of conditions and events can be traced.

Pre-episode Factors

All conflicts involve an **issue** and, as is explained in the above, a large number of factors can be **sources of issues**. However, the presence of an issue does not guarantee

Figure 14.8 A simplified model of conflict causation and process (after Kelly and Nicholson 1980)

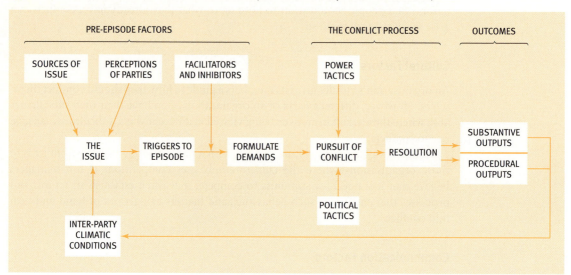

that a conflict episode will occur – merely that a set of circumstances exists in which one party might block the goal attainment of another. For instance, at an individual level two people in the same department might see themselves as the logical choice for a promotion vacancy.

The **perceptions** that the parties have of each other can also strongly influence what happens. In the example above, if either person has started to perceive the other as a potential threat, he/she is likely to become more willing to put up a fight.

Inter-party climatic conditions consist of a cluster of attitudes and frames of reference that influence the way the parties view each other. In the case of the two individuals, although both wish to get the job they may also be good friends, which establishes a climate where neither one desires to harm the other. Conversely, they may be relative strangers, which gives a climate more conducive to conflict.

None of these factors on its own is enough to give rise to open conflict. A **trigger** of some sort is required and this is usually something that brings it home to one or both of the parties that goal blocking is likely to occur. In the case of the two individuals, this might happen if one of them is offered the opportunity to attend an external course that marks him or her out as a stronger contender for the promotion. However, even this does not ensure open conflict will occur.

In most situations a number of **facilitators** and/or **inhibitors** to conflict exist. Facilitators are push factors that make conflict more likely and inhibitors have the reverse effect. One such factor is the behavioural predispositions of the parties. Are they, for example, people who have a distaste of overt conflict? Another factor is a past record of success in conflict episodes. People who have engaged in conflict before and have emerged as the winner can often be more willing to use the same tactics again. In the case of the two individuals, one of them might get a 'buzz' out of conflict and might have used it in the past to get his or her own way.

All these pre-episode factors are at work together, and the final step before conflict actually occurs is usually that the parties will **formulate their demands**. One or both of them will become much clearer about what he/she wishes to achieve, and acutely aware that aims could be blocked by the other party. This is usually accompanied by some indication to the other party that an impasse has been reached and that, if the matter is not resolved, the next phase could be entered. In the individual conflict above, the person not selected to go on the course might insult the other in some way and accuse him or her of taking unfair advantage.

The Conflict Process

When entering this phase both parties tend to have a clear aim of emerging as the winner, and many different tactics can be used to try to achieve this goal. In general terms these can be categorised as either **power tactics**, where the aim is to force the other party into compliance, or **political tactics**, which are used to undermine the opponent's power or acquire sufficient power to enable power tactics to be used. Since previous sections of this chapter have dealt with the topics of power and politics, the ground will not be covered here. However, it is worth noting that many people have characteristic ways of handling conflict situations and this will be discussed in the next section.

Most conflicts are capable of being **resolved** in one way or another. How this is done depends on handling styles and some of the factors leading up to the conflict, for instance, the importance of the issue to the parties, their perceptions of each other, the inter-party climate and whether there are facilitators or inhibitors to continuing the conflict. It is also important to note that how the conflict is resolved has a huge impact on the phase which is considered next.

Outcomes

In general terms, there are two types of output from most conflicts: substantive outputs and procedural outputs. Also note that in Figure 14.8 a feedback loop runs from the outputs of the conflict process to inter-party climatic conditions at the left-hand side. This reflects the idea that the terms on which the matter is resolved have a huge impact on what happens in the future.

Substantive outcomes are the terms of settlement that result in the parties abandoning the conflict. In the example of the two individuals in conflict over promotion, this could be a decision to promote one and not the other, or even to award the promotion to an outsider. Although this resolves the matter for the immediate future, it is important to recognise that substantive outcomes can have a strong impact on the other type of output.

Procedural outcomes are in part a result of the substantive terms of settlement, but since they can also be affected by how the conflict has been handled, they can have longer-term climatic effects. If the settlement has produced a clear winner and loser, the result can often be disastrous. In the euphoria of victory, winners can become very complacent and, in certain cases, assume an air of moral superiority, while losers can become tense and demoralised. More importantly, the situation can result in the inter-party climate becoming much worse. Nobody likes losing, and so losers sometimes try to save face and recover their morale by convincing themselves that the other party has only won the battle, not the war. From this it is but a short step to them actively looking for opportunities to engage in combat again. For this reason conflict management and resolution are all important, and it is worthwhile remembering a common saying among experienced industrial relations negotiators: 'Never force matters to the point where your opponent has to retreat without dignity; otherwise, the next time around he will go for the jugular.'

CONFLICT MANAGEMENT

Functional and Dysfunctional Conflict

Current ideas imply that the level of conflict in an organisation needs to be carefully managed – if there is too much, conflict needs to be reduced, and if there is too little, the level may need to be increased in a controlled way. In practical terms this means that a decision has to be made about whether to stimulate conflict or to resolve any conflicts that exist. This is difficult because there are no hard-and-fast guidelines to judge an appropriate level of conflict. However, in his comparison of functional versus dysfunctional conflict, Robbins (1974) suggests guideline criteria for distinguishing between situations where conflict can have positive effects and where it is more likely to be harmful. These criteria are shown in Figure 14.9.

Figure 14.9
Alternative approaches to organisational conflict (after Robbins 1974)

APPROACH OR TECHNIQUE	CONFLICT RESOLUTION	CONFLICT STIMULATION
CONDITIONS WHERE USED	WHERE: • conflict is disruptive to the organisation • excessive time and effort is devoted to pursuit of conflicts rather than devoted to productive activity • conflicts pursued to advance the goals of groups and sub-units rather than those of the organisation	WHERE: • people are complacent or stagnant and there is a shortage of new ideas • change is needed to revitalise the organisation and there is strong resistance to change • there is too much consensus between groups and sub-units coupled with a belief that cooperation is more important than performance

Since the conditions under which conflict will need to be resolved are probably more prevalent in organisations, and this has a strong connection with the previous section of the chapter, the matter of conflict resolution will be discussed first.

Assertiveness: a person's desire to satisfy only his or her concerns in a conflict situation

Cooperation: the willingness to look for a solution to a conflict that satisfies the other party's concerns

Conflict Resolution

One of the things that can make conflicts hard to resolve is the way that the parties behave towards each other. This is sometimes quite relentless and the key to a resolution is often found in a fuller understanding of their styles of behaviour. A useful analytical framework for doing this is given by Thomas (1976), who categorises conflict handling along two dimensions:

- *assertiveness* – a person's desire to satisfy only his or her own concerns
- *cooperation* – the willingness to satisfy the other party's concerns

These can be used to identify the five distinct styles (shown in Figure 14.10).

Figure 14.10
Alternative
approaches to
handling conflict
(after Thomas 1976)

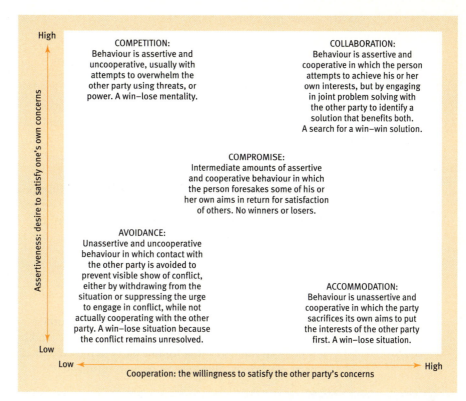

While it is probably true that the collaborative style is the most preferable, 'it takes two to tango' and for a conflict to be resolved in a collaborative fashion both parties need to approach the matter in this way. If either or both has already become locked into a win–lose approach, it can take a considerable time before a search for collaboration even starts. Moreover, some conflicts (for example those about pay) are essentially win–lose in nature and others need to be resolved very quickly, perhaps because they have become highly disruptive to everyone else in the vicinity. Here it often falls to a higher-level manager to resolve the situation and in a later paper Thomas (1977) gives guidelines for selecting the style that is most appropriate to the circumstances. Indeed, Thomas suggests that these can also be used by protagonists to adjust their own styles. However, this is a controversial point. From what we know of personality differences, people may well have a predisposition to approach episodes in a relatively fixed way and it will often be necessary for a third party to intervene. In this situation, the guidelines given below can be useful in deciding what style to use.

Use competition when:

- quick, decisive action is necessary;
- the future popularity of the decision is unimportant;
- the matter is essential to organisational success;
- one or both of the parties would take advantage of the other's less competitive behaviour.

Use avoidance when:

- the issue is trivial;
- neither party has a chance of satisfying its concerns;
- disruption cannot be allowed to continue;
- people need time to cool down;
- more information is needed to bring about a resolution;
- there are hidden agendas and the apparent issue could mask something more fundamental.

Use compromise when:

- the parties' goals are important but not worth the disruption that could arise from using more assertive approaches;
- the parties have equal power and stalemate is likely;
- temporary settlements are needed;
- time is short.

Use accommodation when:

- one party is patently in the wrong;
- the issue is much more vital to one party than the other;
- a trade-off for an issue that comes later needs to be established;
- it is necessary to find a way for one party to retreat with dignity;
- a party needs to be able to learn from its mistakes.

CASE STUDY 14.2: Negotiating Styles

Two shop stewards (union representatives) Phil and David have totally different approaches to representing their members' interests when negotiating workplace changes with their respective managers. In the opening stages of negotiation, David's style is to try to get the manager to show his hand about what he wants and how much ground he is prepared to give, but without revealing anything to the manager. When things have progressed a little, he also tends to be quite pushy. For example, to get his point over, he attempts to shout the manager down, and doggedly refuses to give ground until it is clear that an impasse has been reached.

Phil also tends to stand his ground, but in a different way. He always knows clearly what he wants to achieve before negotiation starts, but is prepared to be quite open about this in return for the manager being equally open. By doing this he is often able to get the manager to be clear about the overall result the manager wants to achieve. Using this as a criterion, Phil is then able to say, 'Look – in overall terms, you have told me what you want to achieve, and so if I can show you another way to achieve the same outcome in a way that also enables my members to get what they want, are you prepared to explore ways in which we can both get what we want?'

Question

How would you characterise the conflict-handling styles of Phil and David using Thomas's (1976) scheme?

Use collaboration when:

- time is relatively plentiful;
- it is vital that both parties learn from the experience;
- gaining commitment of both parties to implementation is vital;
- it is necessary to work through feelings that might give rise to future conflicts.

Someone who has to intervene to try to get the parties to adopt an appropriate style can use a number of strategies. One way to induce collaboration is to set a **super-ordinate goal**, which can only be achieved if both parties collaborate. Another way, which unfortunately is often not possible in practice, is to **expand resources**. This can be used to attack the root of the conflict by allowing both parties to have what they want. Finally, if all else fails, it may be necessary to **impose a solution**, but this has to be done with great care. While it often works in the short term, if the solution suits neither party, it seldom solves the problem itself. Indeed, there is always a danger that the apparent resolution has been achieved at the price of both parties uniting against the arbiter, who is now seen as a common enemy.

Conflict Stimulation

As noted earlier, the current view is that in certain circumstances there can be benefits in stimulating a degree of conflict within an organisation (Van de Vliert and De Dreu 1994). In situations such as this, the matter needs to be handled in a very careful and controlled way so that matters do not go too far and result in something that is highly dysfunctional. A great deal seems to depend on the type of conflict that results, and here it can be useful to distinguish between *relational conflict* (conflict in inter-personal relations) and *task-focused conflict* (conflict within a group about how it should complete its task). The research evidence suggests that people find relational conflict highly stressful, and so it often evokes strong emotional responses that lower productive effort and employee satisfaction. Conversely, mild task-focused conflict tends to result in a more rigorous examination of the way things are done, which can lead to innovation, productivity and satisfaction (Jehn 1997). For this reason, ways that can be used to stimulate conflict will be described in ascending order of the risk of something going wrong.

Relational conflict: conflict in inter-personal relations

Task-focused conflict: conflict within a group about how it should complete its task

Stimulating Competition

This is probably the least risky strategy of all and many organisations may have measures of this type in place. A fairly common one is the use of incentives, such as awards and bonuses for outstanding performance.

Communication

Because it often marks the point where political tactics can come into play, this is a more risky way of stimulating conflict and if not used with great care it can result in emotional conflicts. One tactic that can be deployed is to carefully use information to create ambiguity, or even an element of apprehension or fear. An example is the judicious use of a rumour that a major reorganisation is being considered. While this sometimes stimulates ideas and creates competition among sub-units, it can have unforeseen results, including a 'rush to the door', in which the organisation loses the very people it most needs to retain.

Altering Organisational Structure

This is another measure that contains pronounced risks. While structure can be used to make conflict less likely, it can also be a major source of conflict. A carefully selected structure can give a healthy degree of competition between sub-units and encourage innovation and improved performance but, like other things, matters can go too far: it is all too easy to pit units against each other in a way that produces something akin to outright war.

Bringing in Outside Individuals

This is often the most risky strategy of all. It is usually underpinned by the belief that if someone with different background values and attitudes is imported, he or she will be a source of inspiration to current employees and jerk them out of their complacency. However, it can also go sadly astray and result in a high degree of relational conflict because the people come to see the newcomer as a threat, and they all unite against the person.

REPLAY

- Organisational conflict can be an emotive subject and there are four main perspectives on its inevitability and legitimacy: unitarist, pluralist, radical and interactionist.
- The sources of conflict can usually be located in one or more groups of factors: organisational, personal, communication and cultural.
- Conflict can lie beneath the surface for some time before becoming visible as a conflict episode, which usually takes the form of a sequence of identifiable stages.
- Since some degree of conflict is probably inevitable, it can be vital to resolve conflicts in an appropriate way.

OVERVIEW AND CONCLUSIONS

To many people, power, politics and conflict are three of the least pleasant aspects of organisational life. There is a saying that 'power corrupts', which perhaps explains why those who seek power are viewed with suspicion. Because politics is mostly concerned with the pursuit and maintenance of power, the word probably has an even stronger effect. Conflict also gives rise to feelings of unease, not only because it can be disruptive, but because many of us are brought up to believe that harmony and cooperation are part of the natural order of things.

However, power, politics and conflict are all part of organisational life, and people have enjoyed wielding power since time immemorial. Since all organisations are hierarchically structured, it is possible that organisational life appeals to some people because it gives them the opportunity to pursue and use power. Political activity is often a way of doing this and so, where power exists, politics is never far behind. Since it can also be used to wrest power and territory away from someone else, it has a strong potential to generate conflict.

What, then, are the implications of power, politics and conflict in an organisation? There are four that are highly significant. First, it is important to shed our preconceptions about whether these features of organisational life are inherently right or wrong. Rather than condemn any of them, or work for their eradication, it is more practical to accept that they are inevitable.

Second, it is worth remembering that there are many bases of power, not all of which are immediately obvious. Thus, it can sometimes come as a surprise when we realise how much power other people have. Because of the formal authority vested in their positions, managers often think that they are the only people who have power, and it can come as an unpleasant shock when they discover how much dependence they have on those below them.

Third, using politics is a tricky business. It is never without risk and it also has a strong ethical dimension. The problem is, if one person refrains from playing politics, he or she can never be entirely sure that others will behave similarly. However, two wrongs do not make a right. Therefore, when faced with a choice about whether to use political tactics it is important to think matters through carefully and examine whether political behaviour is defensible, not only to oneself but also in the eyes of others.

Finally, in contemporary organisations some degree of conflict is probably unavoidable, and it is unlikely that anybody will escape becoming embroiled at some stage. For this reason it is important to avoid taking matters too personally. Thus, provided conflict occurs for constructive purposes and takes place in an orderly way, it probably does no harm and, in the long run, it may well do a considerable amount of good. One note of caution: conflict can be extremely stimulating in its own right and, like the people who fought duels in the eighteenth century, an increase in appetite can be caused by what it feeds on. This is to be avoided at all costs.

FURTHER READING

Ackroyd, S and P Thompson (1999) *Organisational Misbehaviour,* London: Sage. The authors adopt a radical perspective on conflict and use this to examine employee resistance and conflict.

Clegg, S R (1989) *Frameworks of Power*, London: Sage. A text that is full of useful insights and which has become a classic in the area.

De Dreu, C and E Van de Vliert (eds) (1997) *Using Conflict in Organisations*, London: Sage. A book of readings which contains a wide variety of perspectives on the functional and dysfunctional aspects of organisational conflict, and how it can be constructively used.

Fox, A (1973) 'Industrial Relations: a social critique of pluralist ideology', in J Child (ed) *Man and Organisation*, New York: Halstead. The author was the first person to distinguish between unitarist, pluralist and radical perspectives on conflict. Despite its age a very readable analysis that is full of useful insights.

Hardy, C (ed) (1995) *Power and Politics in Organisations*, Aldershot: Dartmouth Publishing. A book of readings that presents a diverse range of views on power and political activity in organisations.

Lee, R and P Lawrence (1985) *Organisational Behaviour: Politics at Work*, London: Hutchinson. A useful text which gives a political perspective on many topics in Organisational Behaviour.

Mintzberg, H (1983) *Power In and Around Organisations*, Englewood Cliffs N J: Prentice Hall. An easy-to-read book that makes a major contribution to thinking about power in organisations.

Pfeffer, J (1981) *Power in Organizations*, Marshfield, MA: Pitman. One of the most authoritative books yet written on the use of power and political tactics to acquire and maintain power. A classic in its field.

Pfeffer, J (1992) *Managing with Power: Politics and Influence in Organisations*, Boston, MA: Harvard Business School Press. An immensely practical guide to using power and politics in organisations.

REVIEW AND DISCUSSION QUESTIONS

1. Identify the main interpersonal and contextual bases of power in organisations and describe how and in what circumstances these sources of power can complement each other.

2. Distinguish between the tactics identified by Kipnis *et al.* (1984) that are used more frequently in a downward direction and those that tend to be used upwards. Explain why these differences are likely to exist.

3. Organisational decisions are often said to be political. What are the advantages and disadvantages of reaching decisions in this way?

4. Critically evaluate the decision tree derived by Cavanagh *et al.* (1981) for justifying the use of political behaviour.

5. Identify the characteristics of unitarist, pluralist, radical and interactionist perspectives on organisational conflict and explain how each one can influence how conflict is handled in an organisation.

6. Describe the three main stages in a conflict episode and the important factors and processes in each one.

Integrating Group Characteristics and Processes and the Links between Individuals and Groups

Although a group is made up of individuals, what emerges is an entity with its own characteristics and these have an impact on how the group functions. This, however, is not simply a matter of one-way cause and effect, but of reciprocal influences in which characteristics influence processes and in return new or modified processes have an impact on characteristics. To a large extent this is also true of the links between a group and its individual members and to explain these matters it is convenient to consider groups first, and then to explain some of the links between groups and their members.

LINKS BETWEEN CHARACTERISTICS AND PROCESSES AT GROUP LEVEL

In terms of a group's patterns of behaviour, one of its most important characteristics is the cohesiveness of the group. To a large extent cohesiveness depends on a group's degree of maturity; that is, whether the group has successfully negotiated its processes of formation (Tuckman 1965).

Cohesive groups usually devote more energy to their tasks (Shaw 1981), have higher morale (Seashore 1954) and generally have a lower incidence of problem behaviour such as absenteeism and turnover (Hodgetts 1991). However, there are also problems associated with cohesiveness, and one of these can be the impaired decision making that can result from risky shift and groupthink effects, which seem to be far more prevalent in cohesive groups (Janis 1972; Stoner 1961). Since cohesive groups have their own norms and values they also have an in-built potential for conflict with other groups (Ashtorth and Mael 1989). When this happens a cohesive group can come to view another group in a stereotyped way and as an enemy, which has huge implications for the use of political tactics.

In organisations groups tend to have formally appointed heads, for example managers or supervisors. Whether or not these people also occupy the position of leader is, however, a moot point. Leadership, as opposed to headship, is conferred from below and arises out of tacit negotiation, the result of which is that leader and followers accept complementary roles, and both of them get some of their important needs satisfied (Adair 1984; Danserau *et al.* 1975; Dunegan *et al.* 1992). Thus, followers affect the behaviour of the leader just as much as the leader affects follower behaviour (Green 1975), and this has strong implications for processes within groups.

Formally appointed heads of groups usually have certain bases of delegated power (reward, coercive and legitimate) that they can use to try to influence the behaviour of group members (French and Raven 1959). However, this is not necessarily the same thing as exercising leadership, where referent power and expert power can be more important. Thus, the style of behaviour adopted by a group's formally appointed head can have a huge impact on the behaviour of a group. In Chapter 13 a number of contingency theories were described, all of which point to the idea that, according to the prevailing circumstances, some styles of behaviour on the part of the head are more appropriate than others. One of the most important of these circumstances is the psychological maturity of group members (Hersey and Blanchard 1988), which has a strong impact on whether the use of formal organisational power is appropriate.

LINKS BETWEEN INDIVIDUAL AND GROUP LEVELS

As with many things, there are reciprocal influences between individuals and groups. In a group's formative stages individual characteristics and processes are likely to dominate matters. However, the successful formation process is one in which each individual eventually retains enough of him or herself to feel that self-identity is not threatened, but the person also gives up a certain amount of self-determination in order to accommodate other group members. When it has successfully formed, a group tends to satisfy those individual needs that can only be satisfied in a social situation, and also allows individuals to occupy roles in which they feel comfortable (Schein 1980). For this reason the group that results is, in part, a function of the characteristics of its individual members (Homans 1950). However, it is much more than simply the sum of all of its members' characteristics. Groups develop norms of behaviour that become a code of conduct for their members. They also develop systems of roles, each of which has its own expected behaviours. In addition, groups police the actions of their individual members, and in an extraordinarily successful way they enforce the patterns of behaviour that are expected (Asch 1951), even where this means that individual members have to adjust their perceptions (Sherif 1936) and this can have effects on individuals. Since occupying a role means that the individual has to conform to the behavioural expectations of others, this sometimes means that he or she encounters ambiguities in the role and, in addition, performing the role can result in role conflicts. These can be stressful to the individual concerned and result in adverse attitudes and impaired performance (Fisher and Gitelson 1983).

One of the roles that emerges is that of leader. The word leader is used here in a generic way, to embrace someone who occupies an appointed headship role, as well as a person who is acknowledged by followers as someone who provides leadership. As was noted above, followers can affect the behaviour of leaders just as much as leaders affect followers. Nevertheless, the personal characteristics of the person occupying the leader or head role can have an impact on group behaviour. People with a Machiavellian tendency, for example, are inclined to be manipulative with group members and are somewhat more inclined to drag the group into using political tactics in conflicts with other groups (Gemmil and Heiser 1972), as are authoritarians. Strangely enough, where authoritarians are group members rather than heads they tend to be the most slavish followers of orders (Szegedy-Maszak 1989), and this provides another example of how individual personalities can shape the nature of a group.

As noted in Chapter 13, the design of jobs can make leadership of any type superfluous in certain circumstances (Kerr and Jermier 1978) and, where this is the case, trying to exercise either a headship or leadership role may well have adverse effects on individual motivation and attitudes. Moreover, as was also pointed out in Chapter 13, some of the personal characteristics of both leaders and followers, for example their values, personalities and beliefs, can be potent sources of intragroup and intergroup conflict.

In summary, there is an ongoing interaction between individual-level characteristics and processes and those at the group level. Thus Figure I2 given at the end of Integrative Section 2 of the book can now be expanded to include group-level interactions, as shown in Figure I3.

Figure I3 Interactions between group and individual factors

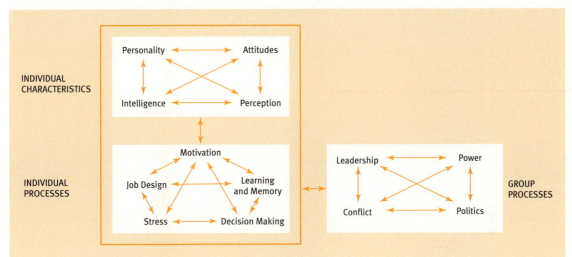

Organisational-Level Characteristics and Processes

This section consists of eight chapters dealing with matters at the level of the whole organisation and here the distinction between characteristics and processes is nowhere near as clear-cut as at lower levels. Because an overriding theme of this book is that understanding behaviour in organisations requires that account be taken of both macro and micro levels, two integrative sub-sections are included. Integration 4 brings the macro level processes together and Integration 5 traces links between macro and micro levels. Today many large organisations have expanded abroad, and some are so dispersed around the world that they can only be described as globalised organisations. Since they face a wide diversity of conditions and often need to cope with significant differences in their human resources, this has become an important issue in OB & A, an introduction to which is given in Chapter 22.

Section 5: The Organisational Level
Chapter 15: Goals and Effectiveness

Section 4: The Interpersonal Level
Chapter 11: Groups
Chapter 12: Leadership – Basic Theories
Chapter 13: Leadership – Advanced Theories
Chapter 14: Power Politics and Conflict

Integration 3

Section 3: The Intrapersonal Level
Chapter 6: Memory and Learning
Chapter 7: Motivation – The Foundations
Chapter 8: Motivation – Advanced Theories
Chapter 9: Decision Making
Chapter 10: Stress

Integration 2

Section 2: Individual Characteristics
Chapter 3: Personality and Intelligence
Chapter 4: Perception
Chapter 5: Attitudes

Integration 1

Section 1: Introductory Concepts
Chapter 1: Introduction to OB and OA
Chapter 2: Contemporary Challenges

Chapter 16: Organisational Structure

Chapter 17: Organisational Design

Chapter 18: Control

Chapter 19: Culture and Climate

Chapter 20: Communication

Chapter 21: Change and Development

Chapter 22: Globalisation and the Organisation Across Cultures

Integration 4
Integration 5

Organisational Goals and Effectiveness

Chapter 15

LEARNING OUTCOMES

After studying this chapter you should be able to:

- define organisational goals, distinguish between goals and related concepts, describe the five generic types of goal adopted by all organisations and distinguish between the official and operative goals of an organisation

- state the key results areas for which an organisation needs to formulate goals, explain the concept of the means–ends hierarchy for organisational goals, describe the goal-setting process in theory and in practice and the processes of goal adaptation and goal displacement

- explain the significance of organisational effectiveness and distinguish between efficiency and effectiveness

- describe the three major approaches to evaluating organisational effectiveness (goal approach, system resource approach and multiple constituency approach) and explain their strengths and weaknesses

INTRODUCTION

This chapter deals with two allied topics: organisational goals and organisational effectiveness. The first to be considered is that of organisational goals and the discussion commences with a section that defines goals and distinguishes between the term goal and other related concepts. This is followed by an exploration of the types of goal normally held by organisations, after which an explanation is given of the benefits that accrue to an organisation that has a system of clear and explicit goals. Goal formulation is covered next. This is considered in theory and practice and is followed by a brief exploration of goal adaptation and change.

The section on organisational effectiveness starts with an explanation of why effectiveness is an important attribute for organisations. Effectiveness is distinguished from efficiency and the remainder of the chapter deals with the three main approaches that can be used to evaluate effectiveness, each of which focuses on a different aspect of organisational functioning and has its own perspective on what being an effective organisation means. The chapter closes with a short section that overviews effectiveness and traces connections between this concept and that of organisational goals.

ORGANISATIONAL GOALS

Why Study Organisational Goals?

Chapter 1 of this book drew attention to the idea that organisations do not exist in nature, but are brought into existence by humans to serve a purpose. Without goals to achieve, there would be no purpose in the existence of an organisation. For this reason, if we want to understand behaviour of an organisation, we cannot hope to do so unless we know something about its goals.

Essential Definitions

A perennial problem when discussing goals is the use of a bewildering array of different terms, for example, goals, objectives, aims, targets, policy and strategy. Since some authors use these interchangeably, it is necessary to start by being explicit about the way that the words are used here.

Goals

Goal: a desired state of affairs which an organisation attempts to realise

Perhaps the most explicit definition of a *goal* is given by Etzioni (1964), who defines it as:

> **a desired state of affairs which an organisation attempts to realise.**
>
> **(Etzioni 1964, p 6)**

Since this definition is widely endorsed by many authors, such as Rouillard (1994), it is adopted here because it captures the three essential characteristics of a goal:

- it is an expectation that a future state will be achieved;
- the desired future state is specified in advance;
- (by implication) there will be activity directed at achieving the future state.

Objectives

As used here, *objective* describes a specific, short-term statement of results that should be achieved, which means that there are three important differences between goals and objectives:

- objectives specify desired outcomes over a shorter time horizon than goals;
- they are normally subordinate to goals and can be thought of as concrete steps necessary to achieve a goal;
- for each goal there may well be a number of corresponding objectives.

Mission

The *mission* is normally taken to be a somewhat global (and vaguer) statement of an organisation's goals, which expresses the fundamental reason for its existence (Barney and Griffin 1992). Almost inevitably this means that there can be confusion about whether an organisation's mission statement is also a statement of its goals and this point will be clarified presently when discussing types of goal.

Associated Terms

One term that is frequently encountered is the word 'aim'. Strictly speaking, this simply means a purpose or intention. As such, aims can sometimes be nothing more than vague statements of the direction in which an organisation intends to move. However, because the word is frequently used in conjunction with the term 'target', it is more convenient to think of aims and targets as another way of expressing objectives.

The Issue of Strategy and Policy

The words 'goal' and 'objective' are inescapable in the subjects of business policy and corporate strategy. Johnson and Scholes (1999) define strategy as:

> **the direction and scope of an organisation over the long term, which achieves advantages for the organisation through its configuration of resources within a changing environment to meet the needs of markets and fulfil stakeholder expectations.** **(Johnson and Scholes 1999, p 10)**

Put simply, and after Ansoff (1965), *strategy* is essentially a plan or design to achieve aims, goals or objectives. *Policies* can be described as guides to action that indicate how the tasks of an organisation might be accomplished, or as rules to guide future decision making, if and when certain contingencies arise (after Ansoff 1965). The important points to note about strategies and policies are:

- strategies are the chosen ways of achieving the desired end states and their formulation can sometimes occur after goals have been set;
- while goals and strategy are both strongly influenced by an organisation's environment, they also include considerations about things internal to the organisation and involve choices about structure, technology and a host of other matters;
- policies, on the other hand, are more closely connected with constraints that an organisation tries to observe in attempting to achieve goals and objectives, which means that policy often tends to exist before strategy is formulated and policies can put a limit on the strategies adopted.

Figure 15.1
The relation of goals,
objectives, policy
and strategy

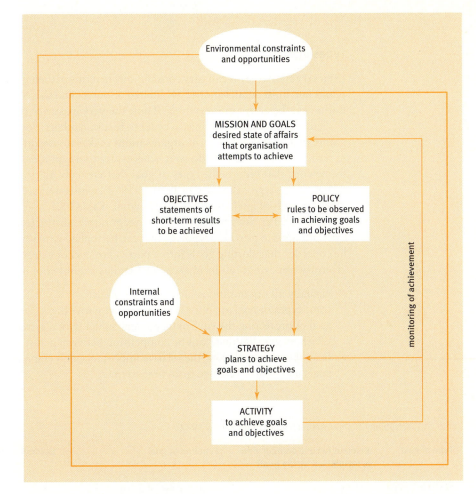

Bringing all the above terms together, matters can be expressed in the simplified form shown in Figure 15.1.

REPLAY

- The words 'goal' and 'objective', together with associated terms such as 'target' and 'mission' can be a source of some confusion.
- Goals are desired future states that an organisation wishes to achieve.
- Objectives are more specific short-term statements concerning results that should be obtained in order to achieve goals.
- There are strong connections between goals, strategy and policy. Strategy is the chosen way of achieving goals and policy is a set of decision guidelines that limit the strategies that can be used.

THE NATURE OF GOALS

Types of Goal

Even very similar firms can vary considerably in terms of their goals. As Perrow (1972) points out, most organisations have limited resources and so it is unlikely that an organisation can be active in everything. Thus, the very existence of a goal implies that it has had to forego certain things in order to focus on others. For this reason the diverse nature of activities in different organisations makes it very difficult to compare them in terms of their goals. To do so it is necessary to adopt a more abstract conceptual framework that reflects the types of goal that virtually all organisations embrace. A scheme of this type is provided by Perrow (1972), who distinguishes between five generic types or levels of goal and these are shown in Table 15.1.

Although Perrow's framework may seem rather abstract, it has to be, because it explicitly aims to provide a typology that can be applied virtually everywhere. Although he concedes that slotting goals into a particular level or category can be a somewhat arbitrary step, what results is a scheme that has a number of important implications:

- virtually all organisations have multiple goals;
- some types of goal are not easily reconciled with others, for example a derived goal of protecting the environment can conflict with a system goal of profit, which means that there can be competition between goals;
- from the previous point, the relative importance and emphasis placed on certain goals may need to change from time to time;

Table 15.1 A typology of organisational goals (after Perrow 1972)

Type of goal	Referent (whose point of view is recognised by the goal)	Function of goal	Examples
Societal Goals	society in general	distinguishes what the organisation is *vis-à-vis* the environment	whether it produces goods or services, whether it generates or maintains the core cultural values of society
Output Goals	the public in contact with the organisation	defines types of output in terms of consumer functions	whether outputs are consumer goods, business services, healthcare, education etc.
System Goals	the organisation itself	specifies the state or manner of organisational functioning, irrespective of the goods or services it produces	relative emphasis on growth, stability or profits modes of functioning such as loose or tight control
Product Goals	the goods/services produced	specifies characteristics of the goods or services produced	relative emphasis on quality, quantity, variety, styling, uniqueness, innovation
Derived Goals	top management	specifies what top management chooses to do with the power and resources accumulated in pursuing other goals	political aims, community service, employee development, environmental protection

- there can also be competing views about the category to which a goal belongs, for instance, is equal opportunities a societal, system or derived goal?

Most organisations have a multitude of different stakeholders and, as Chapter 1 points out, some attention should desirably be directed at catering for the interests of all of them. Since it is virtually impossible to derive a single goal that would do this, formulating organisational goals is typically a political process concerned with reconciling the potential conflicts between the interests of different stakeholders.

TIME OUT

Carefully consider the organisation for which you work (or that part of it in which you are located). If you have no experience of employment, use the university or college at which you are a student. Try to uncover its main goals and classify them into the types shown in Table 15.1.

Official versus Operative Goals

Despite its apparent simplicity, the concept of organisational goals can be one of the most slippery and treacherous concepts employed by those who analyse organisations, because organisations are not always what they seem (or pretend) to be, and this is as true of their goals as other aspects of their behaviour. Perrow (1961) draws attention to this when he distinguishes between two classes of goals: official and operative.

Official goals:
ideal states that an organisation would wish to achieve

Espoused theory:
the theory of action officially espoused by an organisation

Operative goals: the actual goals pursued by an organisation

Theory in use: the theory of action actually implemented by an organisation

Official goals are the general aims of an organisation expressed in its charter, mission statement, annual reports and other items intended for public consumption. Inevitably these are very broad, general statements of purpose, and while there are examples where these goals are reflected in concrete behaviour, these are all too rare, and official goals often reflect what Argyris and Schön (1978) call the organisation's *espoused theory* of action. Indeed, in recent research by Murphy and Davey (2002) there is evidence that employees tend to regard the values expressed in company mission statements as little more than 'corporate claptrap'. *Operative goals*, however, are the real intentions of an organisation, as revealed by how it actually operates. They reflect what Argyris and Schön call its *theory in use*, that is, the real theory of action, which means that these goals may not correspond with the organisation's professed aims.

An example which can be used to illustrate the difference is that of a prison. Officially, prisons have the aim of rehabilitating criminals and eventually returning them to society as reformed characters. In reality, perhaps because of overcrowding or shortage of appropriate staff and other resources, many prisons are unable to devote sufficient time or effort to rehabilitation and, instead, primarily focus on keeping inmates away from society by holding them in custody.

This is not to say that official goals have no utility. Even where they differ significantly from operative goals they still perform a number of useful functions. For example, they:

- can give an organisation a favourable public image that legitimises its existence and activities;

- send a signal to existing and potential employees about what the organisation stands for;
- describe something of the organisation's value system and what it would prefer to be.

Nevertheless, there are often significant differences between official and operative goals, which begs the question of how these differences come about. Here Bedeian and Zammuto (1991) suggest four potential reasons.

Disagreements about Goals

There can be considerable differences between people in an organisation about what its goals should be. While these can sometimes be resolved with a compromise goal, people often say nothing, but quietly go about 'doing their own thing'.

Different Perceptions of how to Achieve Official Goals

Even when people agree about what the goals should be, they can have very different ideas about how they are best achieved. For example, in a manufacturing organisation marketing people might argue that a good return for shareholders is best achieved by having a wide product range, whereas production staff argue that a narrow product range with long production runs minimises costs. Again, both functions can quietly go about pursuing what they believe is the most appropriate operative goal.

Unrealistic Official Goals

Official goals can be unrealistic and to avoid failure people adopt more realistic alternatives. For instance, an organisation that uses timber for its products might have an official goal of protecting the natural environment, which can result in it trying to avoid the use of hardwoods from the fast-depleting tropical rainforests. However, if customer tastes are such that it finds it difficult to sell its products unless this type of wood is used, it might well ignore its official goal.

Bargained Goals

As will be seen later, operative goals are typically compromise affairs that result from bargaining between groups or coalitions of organisational stakeholders. As such, operative goals tend to reflect the shifting balance of power between groups and, as Quinn (1977) argues, this often results in organisations purposely setting very vague official goals so that competition between groups is avoided.

In summary, it can be almost impossible to identify an organisation's actual goals from what it says in public pronouncements and its real goals can be identified more accurately from what it does, rather than what it says it does.

OB IN ACTION: Performance Improvement through Interlinked Goals and Objectives

While Great Britain has a sound economy in terms of growth, employment and inflation, paradoxically it languishes near the bottom of the international league in terms of productivity. Indeed, many companies recognise that they need to raise their game, but how to do so eludes them.

If companies are to improve their performance, they must take coordinated action in many areas at once and this has been borne out by the government-instituted and business-led panel of inquiry into work and enterprise – comprising Tesco, Lloyds-TSB, Astra-Zeneca, Microsoft UK, Eversheds and Manpower, together with Unison and the Work Foundation. The panel's research, covering more than 1,000 companies, identifies high performers as companies that grow more rapidly, create more shareholder value and adapt to changing market conditions more aggressively than their counterparts. What these companies have in common is that their managers focus on managing five goals interdependently. While they care about shareholder value, they also strive to maximise employee engagement, to meet customer needs, to promote creativity and innovation and keep their stakeholder networks in good order. Managing these tasks in isolation actually impairs performance and the most effective firms manage them in a coordinated way.

The panel's findings are startling: companies that run themselves in this multi-focused way are more than 40 per cent more productive than companies that do not and there are measurable increases in profits, revenue and growth that can be attributed to this approach. Thus, the message for corporate leadership is never to allow one objective to overwhelm the others, whether it is shareholder value or employee engagement.

Source:

Hutton, W (2003) Five ways for British companies to raise their game, *The Financial Times*, 12 November.

The Benefits of Goals

Those at the very top of an organisation usually spend considerable time in formulating, refining and clarifying goals because if an organisation is not clear about *what* it wishes to achieve, it is difficult to decide *how* it should be achieved, to say nothing of whether the organisation has succeeded in doing so. Thus, there are likely to be a number of advantages in having clear and explicit operative goals and these are summarised in Table 15.2.

Table 15.2 The benefits obtained from having clear and explicit goals

Benefit obtained	Rationale
Signalling Action Guidelines	Goals tell employees the future results that are required and where they should focus their efforts
Constraints on Action	By signalling what should occur, goals indicate priorities and (by implication) things that should not occur
Sources of Legitimacy	Goals justify an organisation's existence and activities to external stakeholders and, providing stakeholders consider the goals legitimate, this helps with the acquisition of necessary resources
Standards of Performance	By indicating what should be achieved, standards are set against which future performance can be evaluated, for example, how close the organisation has come to achieving the goal
Evaluation and Control	The existence of a goal implies that performance should be monitored and allows provision to be made for remedial action to be taken to correct performance deficiencies
Sources of Motivation	Fair, but explicit statements of what should be achieved can be a source of challenge to employees, which has a motivational effect
A Basis for Organising	Clear goals not only indicate what should be achieved, they prompt consideration of factors such as structure, technology and the human resources that are necessary for goal achievement
Facilitation of Planning	Clear and explicit goals not only specify what should be achieved, but also time horizons, which enables activities to be coordinated and resources to be available when they are needed

REPLAY

- Although goals are always unique to a particular organisation, Perrow's (1972) framework gives a scheme that describes the five generic types of goal adopted by all organisations.
- An important distinction can be drawn between the official and operative goals of an organisation: official goals are broad statements of organisational aims and purpose, whereas operative goals reflect an organisation's actual and more immediate intentions.
- There are often significant differences between official and operative goals, the reasons for which are well understood and documented.
- Although workable goals can be hard to formulate, there are definite benefits for an organisation in having clear, well understood and specific goals.

GOAL FORMULATION

Having discussed goals and their benefits, it is now time to turn to the matter of how goals are selected. Here it is important to stress that while organisations are goal-directed systems, this does not mean that an organisation itself has goals. As Cyert and March (1963) point out, it is people who have goals, not an organisation. Therefore, the so-called goals **of an organisation** are really the goals **for the organisation** and probably those selected by its dominant power holders. This leaves two main issues to be considered: what goals should an organisation have and how are they derived? Each of these will be considered in turn.

The Goals Required

Key results areas: areas of activity vital to an organisation's existence

Most writers in the area, for example Rouillard (1994), assert that an organisation should establish goals for all *key results areas*, that is, the areas or activities vital for its survival and continued existence. While these areas are bound to be specific for each organisation, there is some evidence that the goals need to be interrelated (see OB in Action box above) and a widely accepted scheme that specifies the necessary areas is proposed by Drucker (1984). Although this is highly prescriptive and is primarily designed for profit-seeking firms, with thought it is also applicable to public sector and not-for-profit organisations and is shown in Table 15.3.

THE MECHANICS OF GOAL SETTING

Goal Setting in Theory

In theory there are three main ways in which goals can be set, each of which envisages a different direction for the flow of influence and power in an organisation. These are shown in Figures 15.2(a), 15.2(b) and 15.2(c).

Top-down goal setting: goals for a particular organisational level can be imposed from above

In *top-down goal setting* (Figure 15.2(a)), which is by far the most common method, the goals for any level in an organisation are set by the level immediately above. If necessary, this is done by imposing the goals, but these days it is widely accepted that the process of goal setting should include a degree of prior consultation. The advantages of this method are said to be:

- it ensures that goals and objectives at a given level support those of the level above;
- it usually results in ambitious but achievable goals.

However, there are also three pronounced disadvantages:

- those who set the goals for a particular level can be remote from the reality of having to achieve them, which can result in goals being unrealistic and demotivating;
- senior managers can be out of touch with the realities of organisational life at lower levels, which means that goals can become outmoded;
- because people lower down are not involved in formulating them, goals can come to be seen as the property of top management, which can result in a lack of commitment to achieving them lower down.

Bottom-up goal setting: people set their own goals which are then agreed with their immediate superiors

In *bottom-up goal setting* (Figure 15.2(b)), power flows in the opposite direction. The process starts at the bottom of an organisational hierarchy, with people suggesting their own goals and individuals then have to agree the goals with their immediate superior. According to a number of writers, including Latham and Steele (1983), this has the following advantages:

Table 15.3 Key areas for organisational goals (after Drucker 1984)

Goal	Purpose	Example: profit-orientated organisation	Example: not-for-profit organisation
Market Share	Signals the organisation's intended position *vis-à-vis* competitors	increase market share from 10 to 15 per cent over five-year time period	A charity: increase the organisation's share of charitable donations by the public from 5 to 8 per cent over three years
Innovation	To stay apace with, or ahead of, competitors	at least 20 per cent of sales revenue to be derived from products less than five years old	shift the percentage of revenue acquired from public collections, as opposed to long-term covenanted donations, from 90 to 70 per cent over five years
Productivity	To promote internal efficiency	reduce production and distribution costs per unit of output by 5 per cent over the coming year	Local authority: provide specified additional services to ratepayers over the next year at no additional cost
Physical and Financial Resources	Ensure adequate finance and other resources for the business	A supermarket chain: increase number of retail outlets by 10 per cent over three years	Local authority: increase size of land bank available for building public housing by 200 acres over two years
Profitability	To ensure adequate return to financial stakeholders	increase earnings per share by 10 per cent each year for the next five years	Local authority: maintain present level of services over the next three years, with no increase in council tax (adjusted for the rate of inflation)
Manager Performance and Development	Manager quality is assumed by Drucker (1984) to be the most important factor in organisational success	increase the number of graduate trainees taken on each year; introduce annual performance and development reviews in the coming year	as for profit-orientated organisation
Employee Performance	If an organisation develops, its managers should also develop other employees	decrease absenteeism to a level of no more than 3 per cent per annum; reduce accident rate by 30 per cent over the next year	as for profit-orientated organisation
Social Responsibility	To ensure that the firm responds appropriately to wider society	sponsor five university scholarships each year for children of disadvantaged parents	introduce collection points for recyclable waste materials such as bottles

- goals are more likely to be realistic;
- they are more likely to reflect current conditions and what can be achieved in practice;
- because people play a part in setting their own goals, they are more committed to achieving them.

Nevertheless, Latham and Steele also note the following disadvantages:

- goals tend to be unambitious;
- because goals at a particular level are set in isolation, it is only by accident rather than design that they support goals at other levels;

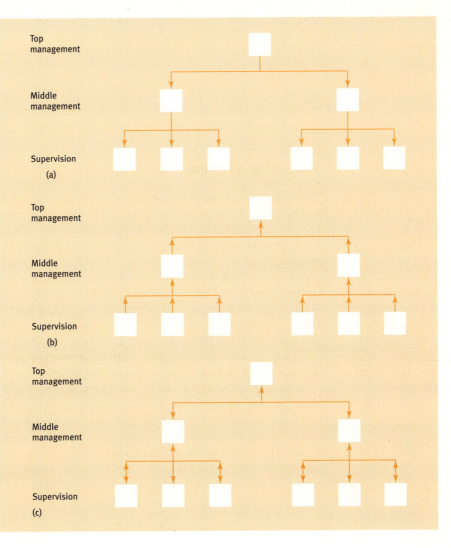

Figure 15.2 (a) Top-down goal setting; (b) Bottom-up goal setting; (c) Interactive goal setting (arrows indicate the direction of the flow of influence)

- the goals that result seldom provide clear direction and purpose for the whole organisation.

Interactive goal setting (Figure 15.2(c)) starts with people at each level stating their views about what the goals should be. However, superiors cannot impose goals on those below, but have to negotiate with subordinates to reach a consensus. This is said to have all the advantages of bottom-up goal setting, but few of its disadvantages. That is:

- goals are realistic and up to date;
- people are more committed to achieving the goals;
- goals can be coordinated to support each other at a particular level and at different levels.

Interactive goal setting: goals are initially set for a particular organisational level by its head, but are then negotiated to a consensus with subordinates at that level

Nevertheless, there is one disadvantage of this method:

- negotiating to reach a consensus is usually a complicated, time-consuming process.

Several authors, for example Pascale and Athos (1981), recommend the interactive process as the best all-round method, noting that it is a feature of Japanese companies and is associated with the success of these organisations.

Goal Setting in Practice

The work of Cyert and March (1963) points to the idea that goal setting is a political process in which the (sometimes covert) influence of a number of parties is at work. As such, the organisational goals that get adopted are often the outcome of covert negotiations between an array of internal and external interest groups, all of whom make competing claims on an organisation. Cyert and March reason that individuals or groups seldom have sufficient power to force an organisation to adopt goals that completely satisfy their interests. Therefore, stakeholders form *coalitions*, that is, temporary alliances of individuals and/or groups who perceive that something that they value can be obtained if they collaborate. The members of these coalitions can come from inside or outside the organisation but the important point is that while members of a coalition probably have divergent interests, their interests are not actually opposed, which means that they can exert pressure in a collaborative way.

According to Cyert and March, while organisational goals appear to be set by a select group of top managers, they are actually determined by a process of continual bargaining among coalitions. Thus, goals are compromise solutions which reflect the relative power of different stakeholders and stakeholder coalitions at a certain point in time. Here it is important to recognise that bargaining does not necessarily mean that all stakeholder groups sit around a table to thrash out goals, because bargaining can be a much more subtle and covert process than this.

Coalition: an alliance of groups and/or individuals who perceive that something they value can be obtained by collaboration

How Stakeholders Exert Influence

Because different stakeholders have different amounts of potential power to influence an organisation, a range of influence strategies can be expected. A general scheme for mapping the dynamics of influence, which also gives some clues about where coalition formation could be expected to occur, is provided by Frooman (1999), who addresses two basic questions:

- What are the different types of influence strategy available to stakeholders?
- What determines the choice of a particular influence strategy?

Frooman then uses resource dependency theory to answer these questions. The theory will be examined later in the chapter when exploring organisational effectiveness and for the present it is sufficient to note that it hinges on the idea that a firm's need for resources provides an opportunity for other organisations or groups to exert influence on its actions. There are two basic strategies for doing this:

Figure 15.3
Firm–stakeholder
relationships,
influence strategies
and exertion of
influence (after
Frooman 1999)

		Whether the stakeholder is dependent on the firm	
		No	**Yes**
Whether the firm is dependent on the stakeholder	**No**	**Relationship:** Low interdependence / **Influence Strategy:** Withholding / **Strategy Exerted:** Indirectly	**Relationship:** Firm power / **Influence Strategy:** Usage / **Strategy Exerted:** Indirectly
	Yes	**Relationship:** Stakeholder power / **Influence Strategy:** Withholding / **Strategy Exerted:** Directly	**Relationship:** High interdependence / **Influence Strategy:** Usage / **Strategy Exerted:** Directly

- a **withholding strategy**, where a stakeholder discontinues or rations the supply of a resource to make the firm change its behaviour (or exerts a credible threat to do so);
- a **usage strategy**, where the stakeholder continues to supply the resource but attaches conditions to its supply.

Clearly the withholding strategy is the most potent. Theoretically, however, either of these strategies can be exercised in two different ways:

- directly, in which case the stakeholder itself takes the action;
- indirectly, where the stakeholder induces someone else, who has a direct relationship with the firm, to exert the influence.

However, much depends on whether, and to what extent, the firm is dependent on the stakeholder, or whether the stakeholder is dependent on the firm. Thus there are four types of influence relationship, which are shown in Figure 15.3 and are discussed in what follows.

The 'Stakeholder Power' Relationship

Here it is possible for the stakeholder to exert influence directly by using a withholding strategy. This can occur if the stakeholder is a monopoly supplier of a certain product. An example here is Microsoft, which is the sole owner and producer of the 'Windows' computer operating system which is virtually a 'must have' for any manufacturer of personal computers.

The 'Firm Power' Relationship

Here it is the stakeholder who is dependent on the firm. The stakeholder cannot risk exerting direct influence for fear of retaliation, and for the same reason the possibility of using a withholding strategy is very low. Thus the stakeholder's only option is to set conditions on its supply of resources to the firm, and to do this indirectly. For example, if the stakeholder is a supplier to firm A and is also a customer of firm B, which in turn is a monopoly supplier to A, it could seek a coalition with B, which could then exert direct pressure on A.

The 'Low Interdependence' Relationship

Here, neither the firm nor the stakeholder is dependent on each other. Once again the stakeholder would need to seek a coalition arrangement with another stakeholder who could exert influence directly.

The 'High Interdependence' Relationship

This is by far the most interesting situation because neither the firm nor the stakeholder can do without each other. The classic example of this relationship is labour relations, where an employer needs the services of employees just as much as they need the pay from their jobs. Assuming that the stakeholder is employees who are adamant about obtaining a certain level of wage increase, they would need to induce top management to meet their requirements. To do this it can sometimes be sufficient for employees to demonstrate their willingness to forego the pay for a period of time, for example by holding a ballot on strike action.

Side Payments

Side payments: inducements that are paid for cooperation or collaboration

As can be seen from the examples given above, in some cases the only way that influence can be exercised is through a coalition of stakeholders in which one party gives its support to another(s). This support seldom comes free; it has to be bought in one way or another. Cyert and March (1963) refer to this as making *side payments*, and they are commonplace in goal setting. These inducements can take many forms, such as the promise of future cooperation, or foregoing something now in order to receive something in the future. For instance, in return for wages employees agree to expend effort, and in return for the promise of future dividends shareholders agree to invest. Therefore, in order to satisfy their goal of obtaining a good rate of return on money invested, shareholders make a side payment (usable finance) to the organisation. In doing this they may well attach conditions about the minimum rate of return expected. It is important to recognise that side payments to one group normally have to be found from contributions made by other groups. For example, when customers place orders, there is an implicit promise to pay for the goods, which allows the firm to borrow money from the bank to pay for labour and other resources to produce the goods. When this finance is acquired, the money then enables the organisation to honour its implied promise to manufacture and deliver the goods to customers. With some validity, Cyert and March argue that an organisation can only survive and prosper if it is able to maintain this reciprocal flow of inducements and contributions and this applies to contributions and inducements from all stakeholders.

Organisational Slack

Organisational slack: the difference between the total resources available to an organisation and those necessary to make side payments to ensure contributions from stakeholders

Under favourable conditions an organisation is sometimes able to accumulate excess resources, over and above those necessary to make current side payments. Cyert and March call this surplus *organisational slack*. Essentially, it is a cushion of excess resources that enables a firm to adjust to unforeseen internal and external pressures. The most obvious form of slack is liquid financial assets or unused fixed assets such as property. The important point about slack is that if it is available, it allows an organisation to weather temporary storms such as downturns in the market, or to acquire resources in order to make significant changes without interrupting the current pattern of reciprocal flows of inducements and contributions. Where slack exists, it is also much easier to satisfy the competing demands of different groups, because slack enables an organisation to avoid the situation where an increased level of demands by one group can only be met by offering a reduced level of inducements to another one.

In summary, while the above is a very simplified picture of a very complex theory, it illustrates a number of important points about goal setting in organisations:

- organisational goal formulation is essentially a political process;
- goals are the outcome of reciprocal relations between groups with diverse interests;
- any group that accumulates enough power to force other groups to pay attention to its preferences is likely to have an impact on the goals that are adopted;
- goals are more accurately viewed as complex statements that reflect the multiple (or compromise) requirements of many groups, rather than the prerogatives of one group (top management);
- in organisations that accumulate slack, the goal formulation process and the process of change are likely to be far easier than in organisations with no reserves of slack.

TIME OUT

Carefully reconsider the organisation you identified in the previous Time Out exercise and answer the questions below.

1. Who are the stakeholder groups that could influence the goals of the organisation?
2. What are the side payments that are likely to be made to stakeholders to obtain their support?
3. Does the organisation accumulate slack and to what use is it put?

The Goals and Objectives Hierarchy

Means–ends hierarchy: goals at one level in an organisation are the means of achieving the goals of the level immediately above

Since virtually all organisations have multiple goals, it is important that goals at a particular level in an organisation do not conflict with each other. It is also important there should be no conflict between goals at different levels in an organisation. For this reason goals and objectives are usually set out in a hierarchical way. This is sometimes referred to as the *means–ends hierarchy* and the principle used is that goals for any particular level are the means of achieving the goals of the level immediately above. The exception to this is the organisation's mission, which exists at the very top of the hierarchy and, as can be seen from the example that follows, consists of very broad, all-encompassing goals which are ends in their own right. Goals at other levels can conveniently be classified into one of three types, each of which is associated with a particular level in the organisation: the strategic level, the tactical level and the operational level.

Figure 15.4
The goals and
objective hierarchy for
a British university

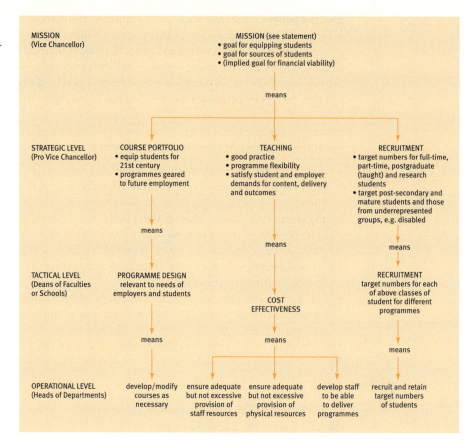

Using the example of a university this will be illustrated shortly, but first it is appropriate to set out the mission statement of the university in full. This is:

> **The university's prime objective is to enable students to reach their full potential by equipping them with the knowledge, attitudes and skills they need to meet with confidence the requirements of work and society in the twenty-first century. It will draw its students from those seeking learning opportunities throughout their lives as well as those from suitably qualified school leavers and postgraduates, from both the United Kingdom and overseas.**

Like most mission statements, this one consists of goals that are expressed in very general terms that can be interpreted in a number of ways. These are the official goals of the organisation and, although mission statements are commonplace, they can sometimes be misleading documents; note that the one above makes no mention of the financial viability of the institution because at this level a goal of this nature tends to be assumed to exist. Everything that follows is likely to be in more specific terms. Assuming there is no clash between official and operative goals, the goals at each level are shown in outline in Figure 15.4, where it can be noted that because it is important to goals lower down, for completeness, a goal for financial viability has been inserted at the mission level.

GOAL ADAPTATION AND CHANGE

Goal succession: the goal(s) of an organisation is deliberately replaced with another one because the original goal(s) has been achieved or has become seriously outdated

Goal displacement: an organisation or one of its sub-units substitutes a goal for which the organisation was not created, or for which resources were not allocated, for its legitimate goal(s)

Means–ends inversion: the method of doing something becomes a goal in its own right, which displaces the end state (goal) that the method was supposed to achieve

Number magic: the tendency to replace an important and necessary goal with another one that can be measured, simply because it can be measured

Sub-optimisation: sub-unit goals are accorded greater importance (by people in sub-units) than the goals of the organisation as a whole

Adaptation and change of goals tends to occur in a continuous way, sometimes as a response to changes in an organisation's environment and sometimes because there have been (or will be) internal changes. In general terms there are two ways in which this happens: goal succession and goal displacement, both of which will be considered separately.

Goal Succession

Goal succession occurs when the primary goal of an organisation has been achieved (or has become seriously outdated) and it is deliberately replaced with a new one. This can be particularly important when it becomes clear that there has been a shift in the requirements of an important element in an organisation's environment and that staying with the existing goal threatens its very survival.

Goal Displacement

This occurs when an organisation or one of its sub-units abandons an existing legitimate goal and substitutes one for which the organisation was not created, or for which resources were not allocated (Etzioni 1964). This is said to be particularly prevalent when intangible or ambiguous goals exist, for instance if:

- goals are incapable of being expressed in a precise way;
- the goals are not clearly identifiable;
- it is hard to operationalise goals in a way that permits achievement (or failure) to be observed and measured.

It is widely accepted that the main causes of goal displacement are threefold. By far the most frequent reason given is called *means–ends inversion*. Here the method of doing something becomes a goal in its own right and this displaces the end state (goal) that the method was supposed to achieve. This is often said to characterise the behaviour of people in highly bureaucratic organisations, where following procedures becomes more important than achieving the ends that the procedures were supposed to accomplish.

The second cause is what Gross (1968) has called *number magic*. When this happens a goal that is easily measured is elevated in importance (or substituted for) an important goal where achievement is harder to ascertain or measure.

Finally, goal displacement can occur because many large, complex organisations have a strong tendency to engage in *sub-optimisation*, in which people tend to have a limited focus that only extends to the boundary of their own department or function. As such, they can sometimes come to regard the goals or objectives of the sub-unit as more important than those of the whole organisation. This is an extremely common phenomenon that occurs in many, if not all, large organisations (Mintzberg 1979), the underlying reasons for which can often be found in an organisation's structural design, a point that will be covered in Chapters 16 and 17.

REPLAY

- Although the phrase 'the organisation's goals' is commonplace, organisations do not have goals, only people do, and so it is more accurate to speak of the 'goals for the organisation'.

- Theoretically goals can be formulated in three ways, each of which reflects a different pattern of the flow of power and authority in an organisation: top-down goal setting in which managers at each level set and, if necessary, impose goals on their immediate subordinates; bottom-up goal setting where subordinates set their own goals and agree them with an immediate superior; interactive goal setting where the manager and the subordinate negotiate to reach a consensus on the goals to be achieved.

- In practice goal setting is a political process that reflects the shifting balance of power between various coalitions of stakeholders, each of whom attempts to ensure that its interests are recognised in the goals adopted for the organisation.

- The goals of an organisation should desirably be capable of being arranged into a means–end hierarchy, so that the goals or objectives at any level are designed to be the means of achieving the goals of the level immediately above.

- From time to time the goals of an organisation change, either by a process of goal succession, in which new goals are formally selected to replace a prior set, or by goal displacement, which is a more informal process in which goals that are still officially active are displaced by others that are more acceptable to organisational actors.

ORGANISATIONAL EFFECTIVENESS

The Significance of Effectiveness

'Effectiveness' is one of the most frequently used (and misused) words in discussing organisations. There is no universally accepted theory of organisational effectiveness. Neither is there a universally accepted definition and set of criteria that allows the effectiveness of an organisation to be evaluated. Since organisations are brought into existence to achieve some purpose, early theorists such as Barnard (1938) argued that an effective organisation is one that achieves its goals. As will be seen later, this still remains an influential approach.

One problem that besets the use of the word 'effectiveness' is that it can be applied at all levels of an organisation and at each level it is likely to mean something different and be influenced by a different set of factors. Important as it is, effectiveness at individual and group levels will largely be ignored in this chapter, because these matters are considered in earlier chapters of the book. As such, the main consideration is effectiveness at an organisational level, the first step being to clarify some of the terms used.

CASE STUDY 15.1: Van Brecht and Associates

Van Brecht and Associates is a human resources consultancy which was formed approximately ten years ago by occupational psychologist Geert van Brecht, who took Peter Maesten, another psychologist, into partnership some two years later. In its sales brochure and articles of association it describes its primary aims as the provision of: '(i) a full and comprehensive range of services to enable employers to locate and recruit the most appropriate applicants to fill employment vacancies in their organisations, (ii) training and development services that enable human resources in organisations to reach their full potential, thus bringing about a relationship which better meets the needs and expectations of both organisations and their employees, (iii) services that facilitate the development of organisations and their employees to meet new challenges and the changing needs of the business environment.'

In addition to Geert and Peter, the Van Brecht organisation employs two full-time consultants and two secretarial staff, but in periods when the volume of work is too great to be handled by the partners and full-time employees, freelance consultants are hired on a daily basis for specific assignments. Over 90 per cent of the firm's turnover is derived from providing specialist psychological testing services for clients, and there are two main reasons for this state of affairs. First, when the organisation first came into existence, psychometric testing was fast becoming a more widely accepted and highly fashionable activity with clients, many of whom lacked the experience and expertise to undertake the activity themselves. It was this that first prompted Geert, who was an expert in this field, to branch out on his own and take Peter into partnership with him two years later, after the firm was firmly established. Second, although there are signs that the market for psychometric testing has reached its full potential, the work is still relatively easy to obtain and this results in a steady stream of income that keeps the organisation viable in financial terms. Nevertheless, both partners would dearly like (and have always intended) to expand the range of services offered by the firm into other areas, such as executive search (headhunting), career counselling, management development and organisational change and development. To date, however, nothing has come of this. To start with, the partners and other staff are fully occupied in coping with the volume of psychological testing work. In addition, the firm's reputation lies in this area and so clients who want other services tend to look elsewhere. Another reason is that although the partners have a theoretical knowledge of the expertise necessary for these additional activities, the last ten years have kept them so busy that they have had little opportunity to acquire practical knowledge in the areas. Finally, to employ an additional member of staff who could either devote his or her time to expanding into other areas, or free up one of the partners to do so, would severely stretch the financial resources of the firm.

Questions

1. What, if any, are the differences between the official and operative goals of Van Brecht and Associates and how can you account for these differences?

2. What are the 'key results areas' for which Van Brecht should establish goals?

3. Using your answer to question 2 construct a goals and objectives (means–ends) hierarchy for Van Brecht and Associates.

Table 15.4 Effectiveness and efficiency compared using goal achievement as the criterion of effectiveness (after Bedeian and Zammuto 1991)

	Efficiency without effectiveness	Effectiveness without efficiency
Goal	1 million units to be produced at a maximum cost of £2 each	
Outcome	750,000 units produced at a cost of £2 each	1 million units produced at a cost of £2.30 each, due to wastage of labour and materials
Effectiveness	not effective: output goal not achieved	effective: output goal achieved
Efficiency	highly efficient	inefficient

Effectiveness and Efficiency

How 'effectiveness' is defined rather depends on the perspective adopted. Thus, definitions will be considered when the different approaches to evaluating effectiveness are presented. However, a common error that occurs is to use the words 'effectiveness' and 'efficiency' interchangeably, which is incorrect because they refer to two different attributes of an organisation.

Efficiency: a measure of resource usage, usually expressed as a ratio of inputs used to produce a given level of outputs

Efficiency is a measure of resource usage, usually expressed as a ratio of the inputs used to produce a given level of outputs. Effectiveness is a much more ambiguous concept and it can be defined in a number of ways according to the approach used in evaluating the attribute. At a conceptual level, however, what all these methods have in common is that they judge effectiveness on the basis of whether the organisation as a whole behaves in an appropriate way. Where they differ is in terms of the particular aspect of behaviour that they consider to be the most important. For this reason, Bedeian and Zammuto (1991) crisply distinguish between the two concepts by noting that efficiency is 'doing things right', whereas effectiveness is 'doing the right thing'. It is therefore possible to be efficient without being effective and vice versa (see Table 15.4).

APPROACHES TO EFFECTIVENESS

As noted earlier, effectiveness can be defined in several ways, each of which has its own distinctive approach. To avoid dealing with theories that have had very little impact on the topic, only the three most influential approaches will be considered here. These are: the goal approach, the system resource approach and the multiple constituency approach, each of which will be considered separately.

Goal approach: evaluation of organisational effectiveness against the criterion of the extent to which an organisation achieves its goals

The Goal Approach

This is by far the oldest and best-known approach and mention of it can be found in the work of early theorists such as Barnard (1938). It defines effectiveness as 'the extent to which an organisation achieves its goals', which means that its main focus is on the outputs of an organisation. The approach is underpinned by two major assumptions:

- that the goals of an organisation can be clearly established;
- that all the necessary resources to achieve the goals are available.

In theory, so long as the evaluation includes multiple goals, both official and operative goals can be considered (Etzioni 1964). However, because official goals are often vague and abstract, a number of writers argue that only operative goals should be used (Strasser *et al.* 1981). The advantages of the approach and the rationale for its use can be simply stated as:

- it is easily understood;
- organisations unquestionably have goals and achieving them is what an organisation is supposed to do;
- it is the way that most firms evaluate themselves;
- it fits well with many other methods of evaluating effectiveness that are used at lower organisational levels, for example management by objectives and budgetary control.

Nevertheless, since it is beset with a host of problems, in academic circles the model has been much criticised because:

- it is immensely difficult to use the approach with an organisation that does not produce tangible outputs, which makes it unsuitable for many not-for-profit organisations;
- most organisations have multiple goals and achieving one of them often precludes achieving another; for example, since safety costs money, maximising profits can sometimes be incompatible with providing a safe working environment;
- the idea that an organisation has a set of goals, to which all of its members are committed, is highly questionable;
- goals are essentially 'ideal' (target) states and since some discrepancy between goals and performance is virtually inevitable, using only goals to evaluate effectiveness is to invite an assumption of failure (Etzioni 1964);
- if goals are set too low and are achieved too easily the organisation can look effective when it is not;
- some goals are so inherently ambiguous that achievement can be virtually impossible to ascertain, for example, employee satisfaction or human resource development.

Notwithstanding these criticisms, the goal model is still the most widely used approach to evaluating organisational effectiveness, probably because all organisations set goals of some sort and attempt to determine whether they have been achieved.

The System Resource Approach

System resource (or resource dependency) approach: evaluation of organisational effectiveness against the criterion of whether the organisation maximises its bargaining position *vis-à-vis* the environment in order to acquire an optimal level of scarce and valued resources

This approach was first suggested by Georgopolous and Tannenbaum (1957), largely as a way of overcoming some of the shortcomings of the goal approach. It purposely adopts an open systems view of an organisation, an important feature of which is that it regards an organisation as something that is in continuous interaction with its environment. As was pointed out when discussing goals earlier, an organisation that is able to acquire more inputs than those necessary to produce its outputs accumulates slack, which gives it tremendous advantages. In this approach, therefore, effectiveness is evaluated against the criterion of whether an organisation maximises its bargaining position *vis-à-vis* the environment, in order to acquire an optimal level of scarce and necessary resources.

Here it should be noted that the model takes a somewhat broader view of resources than the one that is normally adopted. As well as the conventional resources that most immediately spring to mind (money, raw materials, physical facilities and labour), in appropriate circumstances it would view such things as knowledge, ideas and reputation as scarce and valued resources. In general terms, however, the evaluation of effectiveness is set against criteria that are less precise than for the goal model, four of which are suggested by Cunningham (1978):

- the ability of an organisation to exploit its environment in acquiring scarce and valued resources;
- the ability of organisational decision makers to interpret correctly the true properties of the environment, for example, the constraints and opportunities it presents;
- whether day-to-day activities run smoothly in the organisation;
- whether the organisation responds appropriately to changes in its environment.

Note that the model is focused almost exclusively on input relationships, which means that it is underpinned by an assumption that all will be well if sufficient resources are acquired. As such, little or no attention is focused on what is done with the resources. Nevertheless, the system resource model has the great advantage of being able to deal with situations where achieving output goals can be hard to evaluate. For instance, in the case of not-for-profit organisations, output goals are often ambiguous or difficult to measure and so it is sometimes hard to evaluate whether they have been achieved. For organisations of this type input goals sometimes have to be used as surrogate measures. Using the example of a university again, the vague output goal of providing a good education for the widest number of students tends to be evaluated in terms of the institution's ability to attract sufficient students from a wide range of backgrounds. Here the assumption is made that students will not be attracted to the university unless it achieves its output goal. However, while the system resource model directs attention to the organisation's relationship with its environment, and this gives an important alternative to the goal model, it has a number of widely recognised limitations, of which the three given below are the most important:

- Although the model emphasises optimal exploitation of resources, no indication is given of what is an optimal state of exploitation, which makes it difficult to evaluate effectiveness. If, for example, a firm draws too heavily on resources from the environment, it can deplete them and jeopardise its own long-term survival. Is this being effective?

- No guidance is given about determining what the scarce and valued resources are, without which effectiveness can hardly be determined.

- Because the approach focuses totally on resource acquisition, it ignores the equally important issue of the uses to which resources are put, which can be crucial to both effectiveness and efficiency.

TIME OUT

Carefully consider the organisation for which you work (or that part of it in which you are located). If you have no experience of employment, use the university or college at which you are a student. Try to identify the scarce and valued resources that it needs to obtain from its environment to operate in a satisfactory way and to safeguard its longer-term survival. Now answer the questions below.

1. What are these resources?
2. How good is the organisation at obtaining the resources you have identified?
3. Are the resources it obtains primarily used to pursue short-term operating efficiency or longer-term survival?

Multiple constituency approach: an evaluation of effectiveness against the criterion of the extent to which an organisation satisfies the interests of its internal and external stakeholders

The Multiple Constituency Approach

Figure 15.5 summarises the approaches covered so far.

Clearly both goal and system resource approaches have something to offer and they both provide valid, if somewhat restricted, views of effectiveness. The problem is that neither tells a full story, and using either one in isolation has inherent dangers.

The current approach to effectiveness, which first appeared in the late 1970s (Pfeffer and Salancik 1978), has a more comprehensive and integrative view. This is the multiple constituency (sometimes called the stakeholder) approach. In common with the system resource model, it addresses the matter of an organisation's relationship with its environment and, like the goal model, it directs attention to the outcomes of an organisation's performance.

The basic premise of the approach is surprisingly simple; that all stakeholders who enter into a relationship with an organisation do so in the anticipation that there will be some gain for themselves. Therefore, each group (constituency) of stakeholders has preferences for the way in which an organisation will behave, that is, to satisfy a constituency's particular interests. Thus, each constituency has its own criteria against which it judges the effectiveness of an organisation, some examples of which are shown in Table 15.5.

Figure 15.5 Systems resource and goal approaches to effectiveness compared

Model of Effectiveness	System Resource	Goal Model
Criterion of Effectiveness	Ability to acquire scarce and valued resources	Achievement of output goals

Resource Inputs → Organisational Process → Organisational Outputs: products and/or services

Table 15.5 Stakeholder constituencies and their effectiveness criteria

Stakeholder constituency	Stakeholder effectiveness criteria
Shareholders	dividends, share value
Employees	pay, working conditions, work satisfaction, security
Customers	price of goods or services, quality, delivery, after sales service
Suppliers	prompt payment, creditworthiness, future sales
Government	tax revenues, observation of laws
Immediate community	community support
Wider society	provision of employment opportunities, social responsibility, care for the environment

Because an organisation cannot exist, function and prosper without the support of all these groups, the multiple constituency approach defines effectiveness as 'the extent to which the organisation satisfies the interests of its internal and external stakeholders', which, in general terms, is widely acknowledged to have a number of advantages over the goal and system resource approaches:

- it gives a much richer picture of effectiveness than other approaches;
- it considers factors inside and outside the organisation;
- it considers inputs and outputs to be important criteria of effectiveness;
- it acknowledges that effectiveness is a complex, multidimensional phenomenon, for which there is no single measure;
- it can, if used appropriately, be applied in a way that reconciles both the goal and system resource views (Tsui 1989);
- it is compatible with goal-setting theory and, in particular, with the political nature of the goal-setting process.

Nevertheless, the approach has three fundamental problems:

- organisational performance is likely to be viewed by stakeholders in a self-interested way;
- almost any aspect of the performance of an organisation is likely to benefit some stakeholders more than others;
- since resources in all organisations are likely to be limited, increased satisfaction for one stakeholder group can mean decreased satisfaction for another group.

The burning question therefore tends to be 'whose interests should the organisation attempt to satisfy?' One way out of this dilemma is suggested by Connolly *et al.* (1980), who advocate assuming that all stakeholder interests are equally valid. An alternative and more pragmatic stance is suggested by writers who approach the question from a perspective of 'relative stakeholder power'. For example, Pfeffer and Salancik (1978) argue that while every stakeholder constituency has control of resources that are valued by an organisation, at any point in time some resources are more important than others. For this reason, being effective comes down to satisfying the interests of the stakeholder group that controls access to the most important resources at that particular time. A third suggestion (Keeley 1984) advocates taking a 'social justice perspective', that is, a strong focus on satisfying the needs and expectations of the organisation's most disadvantaged stakeholders.

In summary, therefore, although there is no shortage of suggestions about how to resolve the dilemma, unfortunately there is little consensus about which one is the most appropriate way forward. This inevitably detracts from the practical utility of the multiple constituency approach and for this reason it is time to direct attention to a theory that goes some way towards explaining what organisations do in practice.

TIME OUT

In an earlier Time Out exercise in this chapter you identified the stakeholders of an organisation and their potential effect on its goal-setting process. For the same stakeholders, identify the interests that you feel they expect the organisation to satisfy. Now rank the stakeholder groups in terms of what you perceive to be the organisation's order of priority in satisfying their interests. Rank those that you feel are given the highest priority as 1, those who are next in priority 2, and so on.

What conclusions can be drawn from your analysis?

Competing values model: an explanation of how manager values influence the criteria used to evaluate an organisation's effectiveness

The Competing Values Model

This theory has its origins in the work of Robert Quinn and his co-workers (Quinn 1988; Quinn and Rohrbaugh 1983). It is not so much a theory of organisational effectiveness, but more an account of where managers put their major emphasis in conducting the affairs of an organisation, which, by implication, tells us something about how they evaluate its effectiveness.

Quinn and his colleagues start from the proposition that all judgements about effectiveness are value judgements. For this reason, they argue that if we want to understand what organisational managers believe to be the best indicators of effectiveness, we need to know something of their value systems. Quinn and his colleagues conducted extensive research from which the conclusion was drawn that managers are virtually forced to choose between value systems that can vary along two dimensions:

- **structure**   whether tight control or flexibility is emphasised;
- **focus**   whether the manager primarily directs his or her attention to the interior of an organisation or outwards towards its environment.

According to the combination of choices made, a matrix of four main styles can be derived (see Figure 15.6). The implied criteria of effectiveness that would be used by managers are also given in the figure.

Quinn points out that there is always a certain amount of pressure on managers to try to satisfy everybody. However, managers have their own value systems and these will be reflected in where they choose to put their emphasis, which in turn will influence the criteria that they use to evaluate organisational effectiveness. By implication, this also gives some indication of the stakeholder interests that managers consider to be the most important. For instance, an internal focus combined with a flexible structure implies a strong emphasis on employees as important stakeholders, whereas an internal focus with an emphasis on control through structure places satisfaction of shareholder interests high in the order of priority.

Figure 15.6
The competing values
matrix (after Quinn
and Rohrbaugh 1983)

	FOCUS	
	Internal	**External**
Control	**Values:** primary focus is internal to the organisation and top-down control is preferred **Implied Effectiveness Criteria:** productive efficiency and profit	**Values:** primary focus is external to the organisation and top-down control is preferred **Implied Effectiveness Criteria:** whether organisational goals are achieved
Flexible	**Values:** primary focus is internal to the organisation and flexible structure is preferred **Implied Effectiveness Criteria:** employee satisfaction and employee development	**Values:** primary focus is external to the organisation and flexible structure is preferred **Implied Effectiveness Criteria:** competitiveness and the organisation's ability to develop and renew itself

(STRUCTURE label on vertical axis)

REPLAY

- The words 'effectiveness' and 'efficiency' are sometimes wrongly taken to mean the same thing; efficiency is the ratio of inputs to outputs used in a process or activity, whereas effectiveness can be defined in a number of ways, all of which are concerned with whether an organisation as a whole behaves appropriately.

- The goal approach evaluates effectiveness according to the extent that an organisation achieves its goals.

- The system resource approach evaluates effectiveness according to the extent to which an organisation maximises its bargaining power *vis-à-vis* its environment in order to acquire scarce and valued resources.

- The multiple constituency (stakeholder) approach evaluates effectiveness in terms of the extent to which an organisation satisfies the interests of its internal and external stakeholders.

- The competing values model of effectiveness points out that, according to their particular value systems, managers direct their attention to certain aspects of organisational functioning, success in which becomes the criteria against which they evaluate organisational effectiveness.

CASE STUDY 15.2: Van Brecht and Associates – Further Analysis

Re-examine the details provided in Case Study 15.1 and answer the questions below.

1. Using the goals and objectives hierarchy you established for Van Brecht and Associates as your answer to question 3 in Case Study 15.1, how would you evaluate the organisation in terms of the 'goal' approach to organisational effectiveness?

2. What would be your evaluation of the effectiveness of Van Brecht and Associates according to the criteria established by the system resource approach?

OVERVIEW AND CONCLUSIONS

Since organisations are brought into existence to serve a purpose, they all have goals of some sort. Although the concept of a goal is clear enough in theory, considering goals in a practical way is sometimes made more confusing by the imprecise and interchangeable use of different terms such as 'goal', 'objective', 'mission' and 'aims'. With respect to the goals of a particular organisation, an important distinction can be made between its official goals and its operative goals. The former are broad general statements of aims and purpose that are designed for public consumption, whereas operative goals reflect the actual intentions of the organisation, which may or may not correspond to its professed aims. Where differences between official and operative goals exist this is usually because a combination of well understood forces are at work.

There are distinct benefits for an organisation in having a system of clear, explicit goals that are arranged hierarchically, so that goals at one level are the means of achieving goals at the level immediately above. Formulating, refining and clarifying goals can be a time-consuming business which, in theory, can be accomplished in one of three ways: top-down, bottom-up, or interactively. In practice, however, goal formulation is more likely to be the outcome of political processes which reflect the shifting balance of power between alliances and coalitions of different stakeholders.

'Effectiveness' and 'efficiency' are much used words when discussing organisations and there seems little doubt that they are prized attributes. While the words are often used interchangeably, they are not the same thing.

While all approaches to evaluating effectiveness judge an organisation against the criterion of whether its behaviour has been appropriate, there are considerable differences in terms of the behaviour used as the basis of evaluation. The goal model focuses on outputs, the system resource model focuses on inputs and the multiple constituency perspective evaluates effectiveness in terms of whether the interests of internal and external stakeholders are satisfied – effectively a mixture of inputs and outputs. However, different stakeholders are likely to have divergent interests and since most organisations do not have a superfluity of resources, satisfying the interests of one stakeholder group can mean that other groups will not have their interests satisfied. This gives rise to the main difficulty with the model, which is encapsulated in the question of whose interests should take priority. This is illustrated by the competing values model of effectiveness, which clearly shows that managers select their own criteria of effectiveness according to the aspects of organisational functioning that they consider to be the most important, a conclusion that is supported in recent research by Walton and Dawson (2001).

FURTHER READING

Barney, J B and R W Griffin (1992) *The Management of Organisations: Strategy, Structure and Behaviour,* Boston, Mass: Houghton Mifflin. The book has an excellent, if rather managerialist, chapter on the subject of organisational goals.

Bedeian, A and R F Zammuto (1991) *Organizations: Theory and Design,* Orlando, FL: Dryden. An excellent, comprehensive text that gives a thorough consideration of goals and organisational effectiveness.

Cyert, R M and J C March (1963) *A Behavioural Theory of the Firm,* Englewood Cliffs, NJ: Prentice Hall. A classic text that explores the political processes involved in goal setting. Some readers might find the econometric/mathematic approach heavy going though.

Daft, R L (1996) *Organizational Theory and Design*, 3rd edn, St Paul, MN: West Publishing. Gives a useful, if brief, coverage of organisational goals and effectiveness.

Etzioni, A (1964) *Modern Organizations*, London: Prentice Hall. A classic text that gives a detailed consideration of organisational goals.

Rouillard, L A (1994) *Goals and Goal Setting,* London: Kogan Page. A very comprehensive text that gives an extensive, if somewhat managerialist, coverage of the problems and issues involved in setting organisational goals.

Simon, H A (1964) 'On the concept of Organisational Goals', *Administrative Science Quarterly*, 10(1), 1–22. A classic paper, which gives a penetrating exploration of the whole concept of organisational goals.

REVIEW AND DISCUSSION QUESTIONS

1. Distinguish between official goals and operative goals and explain why the official goals of an organisation can differ from its operative goals.

2. Describe three theoretical ways in which the goals of an organisation can be determined and explain how goals tend to be derived in practice.

3. Define the terms 'coalition', 'side payments' and 'organisational slack' and describe their roles in the goal formulation process.

4. Explain the difference between efficiency and effectiveness and the circumstances in which it is possible for an organisation to be efficient without being effective and effective without being efficient.

5. Contrast the goal approach and system resource approach to evaluating organisational effectiveness in terms of their strengths and weaknesses, and explain why the goal approach tends to be seen by many people as the most appropriate one to use.

6. Describe the multiple constituency approach to evaluating organisational effectiveness and why this has strong connections with what we know of the ways in which organisational goals are derived in practice.

Chapter 16

Organisational Structure:

Basic Concepts

LEARNING OUTCOMES

After studying this chapter you should be able to:

- define organisational structure

- discuss the purpose of structure and identify some of the consequences of structural deficiencies

- describe the structure of an organisation using the dimensions of configuration, centralisation, specialisation, formalisation and standardisation

- describe recent developments in the structural features of organisations

INTRODUCTION

The preceding chapter took an 'outside looking in' perspective in order to examine certain facets of organisations. Although this chapter still focuses on an organisation as a whole, it delves into its interior to consider structure – the way that an organisation's parts are related to each other to make up the whole.

It starts by exploring the meaning of the expression organisational structure and examining its importance in terms of effectiveness and performance. This is followed by an examination of the nuts and bolts of structure, which includes an explanation of the dimensions that are commonly used to categorise and describe the structural features of an organisation. The next section of the chapter explores evolving trends in organisational structure, which is followed by a description of some of the more recent structural initiatives adopted by organisations.

ORGANISATIONAL STRUCTURE

The Meaning of Structure

If someone is asked to describe the structure of a familiar organisation, the person usually sketches some sort of organisational chart, perhaps something like the one shown in Figure 16.1.

Assuming the chart is accurate, it tells us something about structure, but in other ways it is an incomplete description, because all that it portrays is two features of structure: how the organisation is split up horizontally and its hierarchy of authority. Although these are important, there are many other equally important aspects of structure not shown; for instance, the flow of work through the organisation, or how orders are transformed into finished products and then delivered to customers. In addition, an organisation chart only gives a very restricted idea of the flow of communication and information in the organisation, which might be crucially necessary for it to achieve something, or to run smoothly.

Figure 16.1 An organisational chart

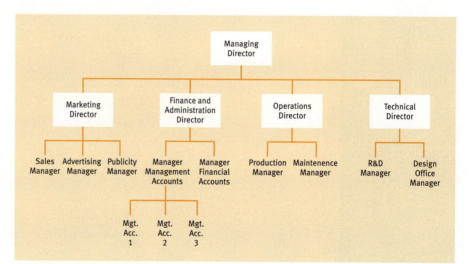

Thus, although organisation charts have their uses, they can be a rather impoverished way of expressing the complexities of structure. Indeed, structure can be a rather abstract concept. It is unlikely that anybody has actually seen an organisational structure in totality and, at best, all that can be seen is some evidence that a structure exists (Gibson *et al.* 1994). With this in mind, it is as well to define how the expression will be used in this chapter:

Organisation structure is taken to be the fundamental and relatively unchanging features of an organisation which are officially sanctioned by those who control it and consist of the way activities and component parts are grouped, controlled and coordinated in order to achieve specific aims and outcomes.

A number of important points arise from this definition which the reader should try to keep in mind when reading this chapter and the one that follows:

- although an organisation's structure is relatively permanent and is intended to facilitate achieving something, this does not mean that it never changes; what has to be achieved can change, or changes in structure might come about because top management alters its views about the most appropriate structural form to achieve certain outcomes;

- the formal structure of an organisation is chosen by its top management and, by inference, this is a matter of considered choice;

- since structure divides up the organisation into component parts and specifies what roles these will play in achieving specific aims and outcomes for the whole organisation, it also provides for control and coordination of the parts to achieve these goals.

THE IMPORTANCE OF STRUCTURE

To survive, all organisations have to achieve something and this requires completing certain tasks. Structure divides the task of the whole organisation into manageable sub-tasks and allocates them to organisational units that are held responsible for their completion. It also ensures that all the different sub-tasks are coordinated and controlled in a way that results in the organisation achieving what it has to achieve. While this is only a very general statement of the purpose of structure, it is clear that, as a minimum, an appropriate structure should ensure:

- that tasks occur in the correct sequence;
- that activities are monitored so that coordination and control can occur;
- that decisions can be and are taken at appropriate points to ensure that adjustments which may be necessary to achieve goals and objectives are made;
- that responsibility and authority for completing certain tasks is assigned to individuals and groups, and also that they accept accountability for task completion;
- that resources are used effectively and efficiently so that the level of resource utilisation matches the level of activity and resources are only deployed on what needs to be done.

Figure 16.2 Aspects of structure (after Child 1984)

ASPECT	PURPOSE	HOW PURPOSE IS ACHIEVED	ASSOCIATED ACTIVITIES	EXAMPLES
BASIC STRUCTURE	To indicate in a general way what behaviours are expected of the organisation's members	By specifying how the work of the organisation is divided up and assigned to individuals, groups and departments	Specify and define what tasks need to be undertaken Allocate tasks and responsibilities to individuals and specify their decision making freedoms	Organisational chart Job descriptions Membership of boards, committees, working parties etc
		By specifying how different tasks will be coordinated	Define how tasks shall be brought together and what formal reporting relationships for task completion shall exist	
OPERATING MECHANISMS	To indicate in greater detail what is expected of individuals	Attempts to ensure that individuals accomplish objectives that contribute to organisational goals and motivate them to do so	Division of main activities into sub-activities and delegation of authority Provide methods of setting objectives and monitoring activities and motivating members of the organisation	Control procedures (e.g. budgets and budgetary control) Operating procedures Staff appraisal Training & development Planning procedures

Therefore, structure is concerned not only with what is in place to facilitate achieving goals and objectives, but also with the mechanisms or processes for doing so. For this reason it is helpful to look upon structure as having two aspects: the **what** and the **how**. These are known respectively as *basic structure* and *operating mechanisms* (Child 1984) and, as can be seen in Figure 16.2, together they make provision for two inter-related facets of operations.

An important feature that distinguishes these two aspects of structure is the human element. Basic structure attempts to ensure that the necessary parts of an organisation exist, and a parallel can be drawn with the human anatomy. With no stomach or an ineffective digestive tract the food that fuels the body cannot be converted into energy. Similarly, if an organisation is to survive and achieve its goals it needs an appropriate set of parts. However, basic structure only provides a facility for the organisation to operate effectively and it can never guarantee that this will happen. As Drucker (1984) points out, while a poor (basic) structure makes high performance impossible, the best structure in the world will not ensure good performance, and so the second aspect of structure is needed. This is much more deeply concerned with the human element and specifies in greater detail how things are to be done.

Whatever it is that organisations do, it is ultimately done by humans. People are not just passive recipients of their experiences – they are affected by their surroundings and, in turn, they react to what they encounter. For instance, the way that their work is organised affects how they relate to their tasks and influences their attitudes,

Basic structure: expresses the general form of structure and what is expected of organisational members

Operating mechanisms: indicates in greater detail what is expected of individuals in a structure behaviour, morale and productivity. Therefore, it is important that operating mechanisms specify how things are done in a way that makes the most of human resources. If a structure is too rigid people can feel that there are very few opportunities for personal growth and self-fulfilment (Argyris 1964) and if it is too loose, or lacks clarity, it can be equally damaging because it tends to give rise to feelings of role ambiguity, anxiety and stress. For this reason, it is worthwhile examining in more detail the potential outcomes of structural deficiencies, which are considered next.

The Consequences of Structural Deficiencies

Structural deficiencies not only stand in the way of goals being achieved, but they can also result in a whole host of human problems. Five of these are cogently articulated by Child (1984) and are outlined below.

Motivation and morale can be adversely affected because, in the absence of standardised rules, decisions appear to be inconsistent and arbitrary. Narrow spans of control, together with insufficient delegation, can result in people feeling that there is little recognition of their worth or that they have little responsibility or opportunity for achievement. Poorly defined roles can also result in people being unclear about what is expected of them and how their performance is assessed, and unclear priorities or work schedules can mean that people are subjected to competing pressures from different parts of the organisation.

Decision making can be slow and of poor quality where there are no adequate procedures for evaluating the results and learning from similar decisions made in the past. This can also occur where the hierarchy has too many levels or where key decision makers are cut off from each other in separate units. It also tends to be common where there is inadequate provision to coordinate the activities of decision takers, or where they are overloaded because they fail to delegate.

Conflict and lack of coordination can occur if goals have not been structured into a single set of objectives and priorities because people can come under pressure to follow departmental priorities at the expense of product or project goals. Where people are not brought together into teams, or where liaison mechanisms have not been laid down, they can also work out of step with each other. Conflicts between planning and operations can happen when those who are aware of changing contingencies are divorced from those who carry out operations.

Failure to respond innovatively to changing circumstances tends to be commonplace where the structure does not include specialised jobs concerned with forecasting and scanning the environment. It also tends to occur where innovation and planning of change are not mainstream activities that receive the support of top management and adequate resources. In addition, lack of innovation and capability to change is frequently encountered where there is a lack of coordination between those parts of an organisation that identify changing market needs and those who are responsible for producing technological solutions.

Rising costs can be particularly prevalent in administrative areas where there are tall, extended hierarchies with a high ratio of 'chiefs' to 'indians'. It also tends to occur where there is an excess of procedure and paperwork that distracts attention away from productive work and leads to administrative overstaffing.

TIME OUT

Reflect on the structure of an organisation with which you are familiar. If you have no experience of working for an organisation use your university or college for this exercise. Now answer the questions below.

1. What do you perceive the major goals of the organisation to be?
2. How is the whole organisation split up into its major parts and what roles do you think these play in achieving its goals?
3. Can you conceive of ways in which these parts can be or are coordinated and controlled so that they contribute towards the organisation as a whole achieving its goals?
4. Can you identify any of the problems that arise from structural deficiencies in the organisation and what do you feel causes these problems?

REPLAY

- One purpose of structure is to divide up the overall task of an organisation into manageable tasks and allocate responsibility for their completion.
- The second purpose of structure is to provide for coordination and control of those tasks so that the organisation achieves its goals.
- There are two main aspects of structure: basic structure and operating mechanisms.
- Structural deficiencies can result in a number of organisational problems, some of which are not just concerned with goal achievement, but can also affect human motivations and morale.

DIMENSIONS OF STRUCTURE

To describe organisational structures it is useful to be able to highlight important features in a way that allows the similarities or differences of organisations to be compared. One way of doing this is with an organisation chart, but since this only gives a very crude representation of basic structure, a multidimensional scheme, in which each dimension consists of a specific structural characteristic is required. Many such schemes exist, all of which have some degree of overlap. Therefore, a compromise scheme which describes the five most prominent structural dimensions (configuration or grouping, centralisation, specialisation, formalisation and standardisation) is used here. Although these are all described separately, it is important to recognise that some are strongly connected.

Dimension 1: Configuration or Grouping

To achieve its aims and objectives, an organisation has to accomplish an overall task, and to do this usually requires that many different activities are undertaken. A sound

CASE STUDY 16.1: The University of South East England

The University of South East England is a medium-sized university with a clearly defined structure. At its head is a Vice Chancellor to whom two Pro Vice Chancellors report directly. The first is responsible for planning and resources, which broadly encompasses all long-term forward planning and control of support services such as computing, library, estates and premises. The second is responsible for academic affairs, which constitutes the seven schools into which the university is divided (Humanities, Science, Computing and Mathematics, Education, Physical Sciences, Business and Management, Engineering).

For each school, all money acquired from student fees, the per capita grant from central government and any income a school can acquire from other activities is divided into two parts. The larger proportion (about 65 per cent) is allocated directly to the school that has the students, and the remainder is retained by the institution to finance support services, accommodation etc. Within certain limits, schools may spend this money how they wish – a decision that is usually taken by the Dean of School together with Heads of Department. As a result, some schools spend heavily on additional teaching staff and other resources. In others the money is spent on the pet projects of the Dean, and in some schools nothing is spent and the money seems to be hoarded. Schools also arrange their own rooming for teaching and this leads to some of them having surplus teaching accommodation while others have to cram students into what space they have available. Although there are rules and regulations governing student assessment and examinations, schools mostly make their own examination arrangements. As such, there are sometimes clashes, with students being scheduled to take an examination in their own school and one in another school at the same time. This leads to problems with reassessment.

Activities in schools tend to be strongly 'course driven'. All lecturers report directly to Heads of Departments, who have to timetable the activities of up to 40 lecturers. Thus it is often the case that people who specialise in a particular subject end up teaching in unfamiliar areas. While most schools primarily deliver teaching to their own courses, a certain amount is provided by other schools. However, there is little cooperation between schools in this matter and most seem to pursue a policy of allocating resources to their own courses first, only providing service teaching to other schools if they have any teaching hours that remain unused. The university would like to gain a reputation for high-quality research, but despite frequent exhortations to schools to become more active in this respect, little is produced.

Questions

1. Produce an outline organisational chart for the University of South East England.

2. Based on the evidence provided above, to what extent do you feel that the University of South East England has a coherent and appropriate structural design?

3. Other than the problems identified in the case study, what other problems do you feel may exist and to what extent can these be identified with structure?

structure will allocate these activities to groups of people and/or individuals according to a basic criterion or organising principle and also establish a coherent link between the activities to provide a basis for their coordination and control. This is referred to as the organisation's structural *configuration* and can be described in terms of two features: **horizontal differentiation**, which is concerned with the **division of labour** and is sometimes referred to as the basis of departmentalisation; and **vertical differentiation**, which is more concerned with integration and coordination of the parts.

Configuration: the basic arrangements for differentiation and integration in a structure

Horizontal Differentiation

Horizontal differentiation: the division of an organisation's overall task into different activities according to a set, organising principle

This can take a number of forms; theoretically each one is underpinned by a different organising principle that is intended to cope with a particular set of circumstances. **Functional grouping** is by far the most common basis and is shown in Figure 16.3(a). This groups activities together according to the major functional specialisms of the organisation and is widely used in both manufacturing and service organisations. Its major advantages are:

- all the experts in a particular field are brought together, which encourages efficient use of resources and discourages duplication;
- because specialists understand each other, coordination within these groups is made easier;
- the structure is easily understood by those involved.

Nevertheless, there are some potential drawbacks:

- very parochial viewpoints can arise;
- functional goals can be pursued at the expense of those of the whole organisation, which can result in sub-optimal performance.

A variant of this is **process grouping,** in which work activities are more specifically grouped according to a narrower range of specialist skills. It is most often found in manufacturing when a functionally grouped firm gets very large and complex. Figure 16.3(b) illustrates the principle at work for a car manufacturer. To a large extent the advantages and disadvantages are the same as for functional grouping, but because the degree of specialist differentiation is greater, these can be somewhat amplified.

Product or **service grouping** is shown in Figure 16.3(c) and is most often found where an organisation has a number of distinct product lines, which happens when a firm diversifies, or when it is taken over or merged. Usually each product or service group is managed separately, and this has a number of advantages:

Figure 16.3(a)
Functional grouping

(a)

Figure 16.3(b)
Process grouping

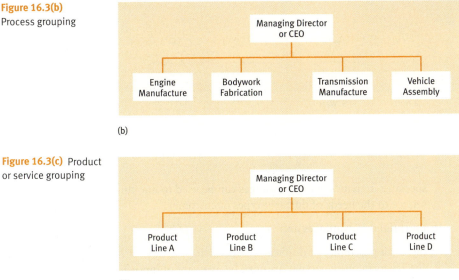

(b)

Figure 16.3(c) Product
or service grouping

(c)

- everything connected with a particular product line is brought together, making coordination and specialisation easier;
- each product line is identifiable as a cost or profit centre which facilitates financial control;
- rather than coordinating day-to-day activities, top management can spend its time focusing on longer-term strategic issues.

Like all structural forms, however, it also has disadvantages:

- people can become too focused on their own product or service and lose sight of advances made in other product groups;
- because all divisions want to control everything that affects their own product area, some overresourcing and duplication of effort can be almost inevitable.

Market or **customer grouping** brings together all the jobs or activities that serve the specialist needs of particular groups of customers. However, it is more commonly used where the same basic product or service is provided for distinct groups of customers, albeit with slightly different needs. Figure 16.3(d) gives an example which illustrates how a road transport company might have different units to deal with long-haul, local and international goods transport. The main advantage is that:

Figure 16.3(d) Market
or customer grouping

(d)

Figure 16.3(e)
Geographic grouping

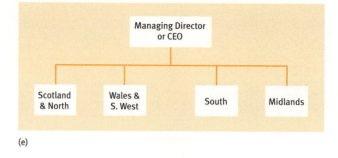

(e)

- specialist activities and/or resources can be used to fine-tune the product or service to the needs of different types of customer.

Its potential disadvantages are:

- there is a possibility of duplication of effort;
- specialists in one customer area can be unaware of innovations in other areas.

Geographic grouping is shown in Figure 16.3(e) and is really a form of market grouping that is used where localised populations need to be served, for example bakeries. The advantages are:

- reduction in transport costs;
- an ability to cater for different local tastes;
- for international operations units can adapt to different legal, political and economic constraints.

Its potential disadvantages are:

- coordination and control of the whole organisation is made much more difficult;
- there is some danger that regional loyalties will take precedence over those of the whole organisation.

A **matrix grouping** attempts to gain the advantages of both functional and product grouping, but minimise the potential drawbacks of each one. The basic principle is to superimpose a horizontal, product-based structure on to a conventional functional arrangement, and this is shown in Figure 16.3(f).

The aim is to provide the different products or projects with the specialised functional expertise they require, but without incurring the duplication of resources that is often found in a conventional product-grouped organisation. In Figure 16.3(f), for example, there are three project managers who oversee projects X, Y and Z respectively. Each project manager needs the services of one-third of a manufacturing engineer, a marketing specialist and a designer. By locating the specialists A, B and C respectively in manufacturing, marketing and design departments the firm has the same range of expertise as in a conventional functional structure, and these people are the subordinates of functional managers. However, each person from each function divides up his or her time equally between the three projects, and for the time spent working on each one acts as a subordinate of its project manager.

This structure originated in the American aerospace industry, in which highly complex products are designed, developed and brought into production with their own

Figure 16.3(f) Matrix grouping

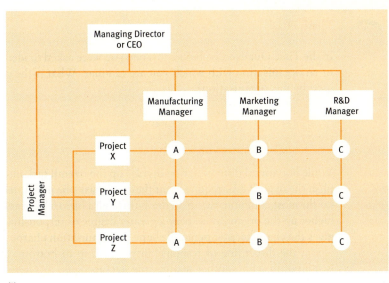

(f)

dedicated teams, and where obtaining the most efficient use of resources is a constant problem. The matrix organisation is said to be the most appropriate structure for these circumstances (Davis and Lawrence 1977). Its potential advantages are:

* improved coordination of diverse activities which does not rely on cooperation between separate functional heads but is undertaken by the project manager;
* the multiple perspectives of different functions are brought to bear on problems and this tends to give fast and highly innovative solutions;
* efficient utilisation of scarce resources and improved lateral communications.

A structure like this can be a difficult place to work, and commentators such as Davis and Lawrence (1977) have highlighted a number of potential problems:

* people never have fewer than two bosses, which can give rise to dual loyalty issues;
* power struggles often occur about use of resources and decision making prerogatives;
* because decisions are made by teams rather than individuals, decision making can be very time-consuming;
* cooperation between specialists with different viewpoints is not always easy to achieve;
* in highly complex matrix structures with many specialisms it can sometimes be difficult to determine who really has authority about certain aspects of a task.

Most of these structural configurations have one thing in common: with the exception of the matrix organisation all are 'pure' types that represent different ideas about the best way to handle the division of labour. In practice it is quite common to find mixed structures in organisations.

TIME OUT

In the Time Out exercise before this one you were asked to identify the basic structure of an organisation with which you are familiar. What is the configuration principle used by this organisation?

Vertical Differentiation

Vertical differentiation: the establishment of a hierarchy of authority in the organisation

Scalar chain: a direct line of authority from the top to the bottom of an organisation

Span of control: the number of subordinates reporting to someone

Flat organisation: a relatively small number of levels in the management hierarchy

Tall organisation: a relatively large number of different levels in the management hierarchy

While horizontal differentiation divides up the overall task into sub-tasks, to accomplish the overall task requires that these sub-tasks be integrated and coordinated. By far the most common way to do this is through a hierarchy of authority, in which those higher up the organisation bear a greater degree of responsibility for outcomes. This gives the characteristic pyramid shape of organisation charts, and produces a *scalar chain*, the direct line of responsibility from top to bottom. In practical terms this is bound up with another feature, the average *span of control*, which refers to the number of subordinates reporting to each level in the hierarchy. Where the average span of control is wide it is normally the case that there are fewer levels in the hierarchy, which gives the *flat organisational* configuration shown in Figure 16.4(a). Conversely, narrow spans of control usually result in a large number of levels and give the so-called *tall organisation* shown in Figure 16.4(b).

Classical management theory, which is discussed at the beginning of Chapter 17, assumed an ideal span of control equally applicable in all circumstances, and narrow spans were assumed to be better because supervising a relatively small number of people means that each one receives more of the supervisor's attention. However, a wide span of control results in more autonomy for subordinates, which later research associated with increased job satisfaction and employee performance (Ivancevich and Donnelly 1975). The current trend is for so-called **delayered** designs, which gives very wide spans of control lower down, often accompanied by the use of **empowerment** techniques, which are described in Chapter 2. Because they are assumed to result in employees having more satisfying and interesting jobs, these are often portrayed in glowing terms (Pickard 1993). However, it is likely that the main reason for their use is the desire to cut costs and to increase effort by employees, rather than to make a

Figure 16.4(a)
Flat organisation

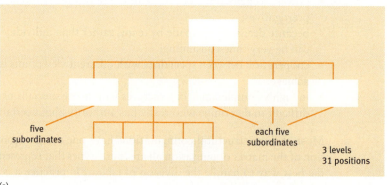

five subordinates

each five subordinates

3 levels
31 positions

(a)

Figure 16.4(b)
Tall organisation

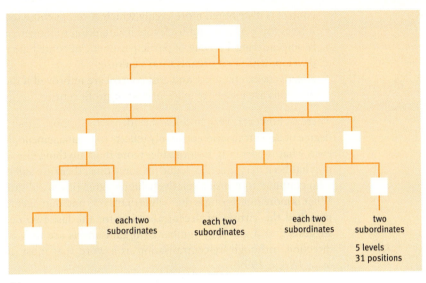

each two subordinates

each two subordinates

each two subordinates

two subordinates

5 levels
31 positions

(b)

concerted attempt to improve the quality of their working lives. A return will be made to these recent initiatives towards the end of the chapter.

Dimension 2: Centralisation

Centralisation: the locus of decision making in an organisation

Responsibility: the obligation to achieve something

Authority: the legitimate power to make decisions in a given area of activity

This expresses the locus of decision making in an organisation and thus reflects patterns of responsibility and authority in a structure. Put simply, *responsibility* places an obligation on someone to achieve something. The other side of the coin is that a degree of *authority*, which is the legitimate power to take decisions, should be delegated as well, so that a person can meet his or her delegated responsibilities.

In **centralised** structures decision making tends to be retained in the hands of a small number of people at the top of the organisation, while in those that are **decentralised**, decision making authority is delegated. As will be explained later, certain basic structures lend themselves to decentralisation more than others, and so there is a strong connection between this dimension and configuration. The arguments for centralisation are said to be:

- those at the top can coordinate the whole organisation more effectively;
- different parts of an organisation are prevented from duplicating resources, which results in more efficient resource utilisation and economies of scale;
- common policies are easier to adopt throughout the organisation because sub-units are prevented from 'doing their own thing' and becoming too independent;
- decision making tends to be faster because of the smaller number of people involved.

On the other hand, there are a number of arguments in favour of decentralisation:

- the organisation is more flexible and special circumstances can be taken into account if decisions are made at a point closer to operational levels;

- control is distributed more evenly which develops those lower down;
- it frees top management to devote its attention to longer-run strategic issues;
- by engendering a feeling of participation it can contribute positively to the development of an organisation's culture;
- effectiveness, efficiency and cost control are improved if the levels at which decisions are taken are made at cost or profit centres.

There is, however, very little hard evidence to support either point of view, and the degree of decentralisation probably reflects top management philosophies (or possibly even what is currently fashionable) more than anything else. Although decentralisation has been very much in vogue for some time, there are still many influential writers who continue to praise a relatively high degree of centralisation (e.g. Jaques 1990). What is more interesting is that while managers and management gurus have strongly preached the virtues of decentralisation for the last two decades, recent evidence suggests that a growing number of organisations are now moving in the opposite direction, although 're-centralisation' is a word that most of them seem fearful of using (Arkin 1999).

Dimension 3: Specialisation

Specialisation: the degree of division of labour and patterns of work organisation at lower organisational levels

This dimension, which expresses the division of labour and general patterns of work organisation at lower levels, has some relationship to configuration. However, it is much more strongly focused on the micro elements of structure and reflects management philosophies about whether it is advantageous to have narrow, specialised jobs rather than those which are broad and multi-skilled. In theory, a high degree of specialisation has the following advantages:

- economic efficiency – a narrow, specialised task only requires a small range of skills, which makes it easier for a person to pick up speed; the person does not have to regularly interrupt one operation to do another and, because the job is usually simplified and operators can be trained quickly, people are easily replaced;
- because a specialised structure is easily understood, people tend to feel comfortable with it, particularly if the degree of specialisation reflects past ways of doing things and the way a firm has evolved.

Set against these advantages, there are also some potential drawbacks:

- boredom, tedium, lack of interest and a shortage of intrinsic satisfactions often occur and, as a result, absenteeism, labour turnover and (in some cases) antagonisms between the workforce and management can arise;
- specialisation can sometimes result in duplication of effort, overmanning and rigid job demarcation; for example, even where they are capable of doing so, craftsmen will often refuse to handle the smallest task which is regarded as part of the job of another trade.

In a competitive world where economic efficiency is vital, it is seldom possible to abandon job specialisation altogether. However, its potential for demotivating employees is well recognised and, while there are strong economic advantages, potential disadvantages can negate some of the economic gains. Attempts to mitigate some of the demotivating effects of high specialisation are sometimes made by using techniques such as job rotation, enlargement, enrichment and empowerment, which are discussed in more detail in Chapter 7. Once established, any pattern of specialisation can also be very difficult to change and is often only possible if specialisation is 'bought out' with increased pay rates (Ingram 1991).

Dimension 4: Formalisation

Formalisation: the number of formal rules and procedures governing organisational activities

This reflects the extent to which formal rules and procedures govern activities in an organisation and, in particular, whether the nature of work is prescribed in rules that specify what shall be done and, often, how it will be done. Rules and procedures can be implicit as well as explicit, and can be used either to prescribe what should be done or to proscribe what is forbidden. Explicit rules are usually set down in writing, for example in job descriptions, policy documents and standard operating procedures. However, these cannot cover all the day-to-day adjustments that are necessary to adapt to changing conditions. Implicit or informal rules are often constructed in an *ad hoc* way (Brief and Downey 1983) but, unless they are eventually formalised, these tend not to become part of an organisation's formal structural arrangements.

To some extent increased formalisation is a function of organisational size. Once an organisation grows beyond a certain point it becomes almost impossible to rely on the personal and informal interactions that are commonly used to control and coordinate activities in a small firm. As an organisation gets larger it also tends to employ more specialists, the number of levels in the hierarchy increases and top management may need to divorce itself from day-to-day activities to concentrate on strategic issues. Thus procedures and rules become the main way of controlling activities and introducing a degree of predictability into the organisation.

Dimension 5: Standardisation

Standardisation: the extent to which formal rules and procedures are applied in all circumstances

In practice, although this dimension has a strong practical connection with formalisation, in theory they are different dimensions of structure. Formalisation simply reflects the number of rules and procedures, whereas standardisation expresses whether they are applied in all circumstances. For instance, in a firm with low standardisation there may be a large number of rules and procedures, but some are only applied in certain parts of the organisation. Conversely, a highly standardised organisation can have comparatively few rules, but apply them strictly throughout.

Like formalisation, standardisation is essentially a method of coordinating activities and Mintzberg (1979) distinguishes between three forms that it can take.

- **standardisation of work process**, where coordination is achieved by designing the flow of work to link different activities together as, for example, on an assembly line, where one operation leads naturally to the next;

- **standardisation of work output**, where task elements are coordinated by relating them all to an end result, for example in stock levels, where the aim is to avoid the high costs of large inventories but also to avoid a 'no stock' situation;

- **standardisation of worker skills,** which tends to be used only where the other two forms of standardisation cannot be applied and specifies what knowledge and skills are needed for a particular task; for example, although nurses in a hospital are responsible for day-to-day patient welfare, the diagnosis and prescription of a patient's treatment is strictly in the hands of medical doctors.

Mintzberg also points out that the size and complexity of an organisation normally governs how strongly standardisation and formalisation go together. In small firms, where employees adjust to each other using informal communication methods, standardisation is seldom needed to achieve coordination and control; but as firms get larger it becomes more difficult to rely on these methods and so supervisors coordinate the activities of people. In very large organisations the scale and wider scope of activities are much more complex and so standardised procedures are used to reduce the coordination burden on supervisors.

The Relationship between Dimensions of Structure

For the purposes of this discussion it is convenient to simplify matters by viewing configuration and specialisation as dimensions that are primarily concerned with differentiation, while centralisation, formalisation and standardisation are those that integrate the parts. All structures are a compromise between the competing demands of different pressures. For instance, although specialisation gives efficiency and economy, it can result in people losing sight of the goals for the whole organisation. Therefore, where it is used, it gives rise to the need to integrate and coordinate activities using some combination of formalising activities through rules and procedures, standardising the activities that take place and centralising the authority to take decisions. This in turn gives rise to another problem. The more these integrating methods are used, the more the organisation lacks flexibility and, to some extent, personal initiative is stifled as well. This makes it clear that there are no easy answers in the matter of structural design, but it is possible to draw two general conclusions about what tends to happen in practice:

- where a functional configuration with a high degree of specialisation is used there seems to be a strong tendency for formalisation, centralisation and standardisation to be adopted together as coordinating mechanisms (Grinyear and Yasai-Ardekani 1980);
- as organisations grow, some delegation of authority to specialists becomes virtually inevitable and this brings about a decrease in centralisation that is counteracted to some extent by strong tendencies to increase formalisation and standardisation (Pugh and Hickson 1976).

However, there are limits to the extent that these two conclusions can be applied in a general way. Above a certain size, firms tend to have much more diverse product lines, and this makes it much harder to use a pure functional grouping. Thus product-based, market-based and geographic configurations become more common. With these configurations it is often necessary to decentralise authority to divisions and, within a division, the structural form used tends to depend on the nature of its markets or the technology. Thus, to make sense of structure, beyond a certain point it is probably necessary to view a division as a separate organisation (Mintzberg 1979).

REPLAY

- The most significant dimensions of structure are: *configuration*, which describes the basic pattern of differentiation and integration; *centralisation*, which reflects the extent to which decision making is centralised; *specialisation*, which reflects the extent of lower-level division of labour and patterns of work organisation; *formalisation*, which indicates the number of formal rules and procedures governing organisation activities; and *standardisation*, which indicates the extent to which rules and procedures are applied in all circumstances.

- The dimensions are not independent and there tend to be characteristic patterns of combinations of those described.

CASE STUDY 16.2: The University of South Wales

In terms of its senior management and structure of schools, this institution is virtually identical to the University of South East England described in Case Study 16.1. However, it differs significantly in terms of other aspects of structure. Schools operate on a strict system of budgets, which are agreed annually with the senior management of the institution. These are based on target numbers of students to be recruited each year (set by the centre) and staffing in the schools is set by senior management of the institution and is determined by student numbers. Teaching accommodation is also allocated from the centre, and there is a strict system of rules and regulations governing such matters as student enrolment, student assessment, conduct of examinations etc. These are applied universally and firmly to all schools, as are procedures for authorising expenditure.

Internally, most schools have a matrix structure, in which courses are managed by course leaders and teaching resources (lecturers) are managed by divisional heads, each of which is in charge of all lecturers in a specialist subject area (nine on average). Most schools also have their own internal budgetary systems in which sub-budgets are devolved to divisional heads. As in most institutions, while schools primarily deliver teaching to their own courses, a certain amount of teaching is provided by other schools. This is handled by a system of 'servicing requests' that must be lodged with the service provider before the end of the previous academic year so that teaching resources can be allocated well in advance. The university has a strong emphasis on research and being active in this area is a responsibility that is devolved to schools, most of which have staff that publish regularly in learned journals.

Questions

1. Produce an outline organisational chart for the University of South Wales.

2. Based on the evidence given above, to what extent do you feel that the University of South Wales has a coherent and appropriate structural design?

3. Would you expect the structure to give rise to any particular problems?

RECENT DEVELOPMENTS IN ORGANISATIONAL STRUCTURE

The dimensions described so far can be found in virtually all organisations and, as explained above, to some extent the positioning along different dimensions of structure go hand in hand. For many years there has been a tendency for organisations to adopt more flexible structures and a number of the more recent developments in this direction will be described presently. To put these in context, however, it can be useful to examine a scheme given by Morgan (1989), which portrays what he considers to be an almost inevitable move from the rigid structures of the past to the highly flexible structures that are now beginning to emerge. This is given in outline in Table 16.1.

As can be seen, what prompts the evolution of increasingly more flexible forms of structure is the nature of an organisation's environment. The more this becomes variable and diffuse, the more the organisation needs to remove the rigidities from its structure in order to speed up its responses to the demands of the environment. All of the first three types are variants on the classical bureaucratic structure that will be

Table 16.1 The changing nature of organisational form (after Morgan 1989)

Organisational type	Environment	Characteristics
1. Rigidly organised bureaucracy	Highly stable	Similar to classical Weberian bureaucracy (see Chapter 17). Under strict control of head of organisation. Functional configuration, with high degree of centralisation, specialisation, formalisation and standardisation. Integration by hierarchical authority.
2. Bureaucracy run by a senior executive team	Slightly more variable with some novel problems arising	Similar to type 1.
3. Bureaucracy with cross-departmental teams and task forces	More variable with novel problems arising even more frequently	Similar to type 1 but with a greater degree of integration and coordination at operational level by permanent cross-departmental teams. Bigger problems are referred upwards to be resolved by senior managers.
4. Matrix organisation	Diverse and diffuse with higher rate of change, giving rise to an even greater number of unique problems	A product-based structure is superimposed on a conventional functional structure to give a matrix in which equal emphasis is given to traditional functions and to different business or product areas. Dual focus allows operating teams to combine functional skills with an orientation to particular problems in their respective product areas.
5. Project-based organisation	Similar to type 4 but more volatile	Nominally a functional structure may exist but it only plays a supporting (servicing) role to project teams (usually based on product areas) who run the core activities of the organisation. Frequent exchange of ideas and information between teams.
6. Loosely coupled network organisation	Similar to type 5 but even more volatile	The organisation becomes a loosely coupled network of small (usually product-based) teams which are semi-autonomous mini firms that operate under a common identity. Teams handle strategy and operations in their respective product areas, but virtually all operational work is subcontracted to outside the organisation.

described in more detail in Chapter 17. Organisations of this type are still very common because as they grow (and some of them are very large indeed) they tend to acquire a capability to exert a degree of influence over their environments, which is a force for stability. However, not all organisations are this big and powerful and for those that are not some degree of progression to types 4 and 5 could become necessary. Type 6, however, is still comparatively rare and a move from type 5 to type 6 is a step of quantum proportions. For this reason, many organisations prefer to adopt minor incremental adjustments to structure, and some that have emerged across the last two decades are described presently.

Many of them appeared in response to recessionary conditions, more volatile markets and a perceived need to cut back on the number of people employed – often as 'off-the-shelf' solutions or prescriptions to obtain increased efficiency and profits. They tend to have an intuitive appeal to managers, and fashionable names that trip easily off the tongue have now become part of the acceptable vocabulary of 'management speak'. While the names differ, virtually all of them involve reducing the size and altering the shape of an organisation (at least below the level of the board room). In addition, they all have remarkably similar prescriptions for the desirable characteristics of a structural design. They assert that a sound structure should provide for:

- a closer relationship with customers;
- a rapid response to environmental changes;
- where necessary, the use of advanced technologies;
- the effective and efficient use of human resources.

Before describing these techniques, it is worth examining the origins of the ideas and arguments that underpin them.

Customer Relations and Adaptability

The argument that structure must allow for a closer relationship with customers and a rapid response to their needs and wants first appeared in the early 1980s and can be traced to Piore and Sabel's (1984) *flexible specialisation* thesis. This argues that most large firms have hitherto been based on a Fordist production paradigm, in which the aim was to cater for a large market for standardised goods. This virtually dictates the use of mass production techniques, with a high degree of task specialisation in order to obtain the economies of scale that enable a firm to compete on the basis of price. Piore and Sabel argue that a radical change in customers' tastes has resulted in the disappearance of mass markets for standardised goods. Thus firms are faced with fragmented markets, composed of discerning customers who have diverse tastes and requirements, which means that survival depends upon the ability to cater for a high degree of change and customisation of outputs. This does not mean that customers are automatically willing to pay the price of custom-made goods. Rather, the dominant theme has changed from 'everything the same' to 'variations on a standard product', and to be successful firms have to find ways of being specialist and flexible at the same time.

Whether flexible specialisation is just a catchy phrase or represents a new order in manufacturing is a contentious issue. Nevertheless, there are signs that firms are willing to cater to more diverse consumer tastes.

Flexible specialisation: the argument that organisational survival now depends on gaining the economic advantages of specialisation, but being flexible at the same time

Advanced Technology

There is much stronger evidence about the widespread adoption of new technologies and, in terms of structure, two particular developments are worth noting. The first is **computer-integrated manufacture,** in which different operations are controlled and coordinated electronically. This enables inputs of raw materials and components, various operations and the output of finished goods to be synchronised. In addition, machines are often computer controlled and sometimes robotically operated, so that when a machine is switched from one operation to another it does not have to be reset by hand. Instead, resetting instructions are fed into the computer that controls the machine, which saves considerable time and adds flexibility to the production system. Before the availability of this technology large economies of scale were only obtainable using mass production techniques, in which machines were dedicated to specialist operations. While this works if there is a mass market for the same product, where product life cycles are shorter and a more varied range of products is required, the technique is inherently inflexible and restrictive (Buitendam 1987). Thus computer-integrated manufacture gives the flexibility of multipurpose machinery together with unit costs that are nearly as low as in mass production.

Another development is **advanced information technologies** which are deployed in data networks that greatly increase efficiency and streamline coordination and control. Perhaps the easiest way to illustrate the point is with the example of 'Electronic Point of Sale' (EPOS) technology, now widespread in large supermarket chains. When an item passes through the checkout an electronic scanning device reads the bar code, and records the item and its sale price. Because the cashier does not have to punch the price into a cash register this clearly saves time. If the information is also sent to the stock room, shelves in the sales area can be replenished as necessary. Moreover, if the same data is supplied to the central warehouse of a supermarket chain, it can be used to decide what should be included in the next delivery to a particular store.

Human Resources

Productivity through people has been a much emphasised theme since the mid-1980s, and the idea has been strongly linked with arguments about the performance of so-called 'excellent' companies (Peters and Waterman 1982). Moreover, the drive for cost savings, coupled with a desire to cultivate customer loyalty, has introduced an emphasis on 'quality' of output as much as quantity. Thus, new production methods and their associated technologies often go hand in hand with methods such as **total quality management** and **just in time**. However, because there are fewer routine or specialised jobs, and the different activities are often coordinated by the machinery or its associated control software, other demands are placed on employees. The pace of work can be faster and workers are often required to maintain the machinery and solve minor problems. These features not only require new skills, such as judgement and literacy, but also increased levels of willingness, flexibility and commitment (Walton 1985). Thus, most of the new structural initiatives emphasise methods such as teamworking, empowerment and employee involvement.

In what follows, while the suggestions for redesign will be described in the approximate order in which they appeared, this is only approximate because there is a considerable degree of overlap in their introduction and some of the older ones are only just being introduced into some organisations.

Figure 16.5
The flexible firm

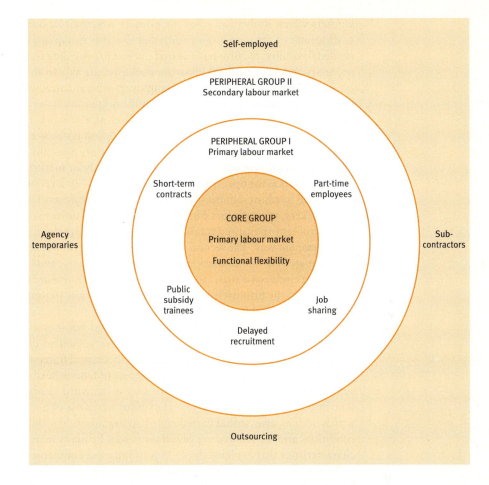

The Flexible (Core–periphery) Firm

Across the last two decades the environments of many organisations have become increasingly volatile and this has resulted in two significant problems. The first is the problem of changing products and production methods to cater for changes in customer tastes and to take advantage of new technologies. The second is to be able to respond rapidly to changes (either upwards or downwards) in the level of demand for products. To address these two problems, the organisation needs to be flexible in two different ways. Rapid adjustment of products and processes requires *functional flexibility*, that is, being flexible in what is done. Coping with changes in the level of output, however, requires *numeric flexibility*, usually in the number of people employed. A structural remedy for both of these problems is suggested in what has become known as the 'flexible firm or core–periphery' model (Atkinson and Meager 1986), which is shown in Figure 16.5.

The flexible firm concept is most applicable to large manufacturing organisations, and the key idea is that the firm becomes much more responsive to changes in its product markets if the workforce is structured into two main groups. The first consists of a relatively small but permanent core workforce of highly competent, multi-skilled

Functional flexibility: an organisation's capability to vary what is done and how it is done

Numeric flexibility: an organisation's capability to vary its number of employees and, in so doing, its level of activity

workers which is obtained from the primary (internal) labour market and is shown at the centre of the model. To ensure that this core group has the skills to deliver the needed flexibility, the firm has a vested interest in providing training and retraining as necessary and, because the skills of the workforce are akin to an investment, the organisation seeks to retain this group of employees with an attractive package of rewards.

To obtain numerical flexibility so that the organisation can adjust its levels of output, the firm has up to three peripheral sub-groups of workers. The first consists of employees with skills that are important to the firm but which are general skills that are relatively easy to import at short notice. These are normally permanent employees but are people who tend to exit and re-enter the labour market – for example, typists and word-processor operators – and gives a fairly high level of natural turnover that can be used to adjust numbers. This sub-group also consists of employees such as part-time workers, whose hours can quickly be adjusted upwards if need be, and people on government-sponsored training schemes who are employed by the firm in an even less permanent way. The second sub-group of peripheral workers are drawn from secondary (external) labour markets as and when necessary, and these people are shown in the next circle outwards. Finally, beyond the outer circle are workers who are never employed by the firm itself, but who enter it from time to time to give an additional degree of numerical flexibility.

The model is essentially a conceptual one and was never designed to present a picture of what is taking place in a wholesale way. Neither does it offer a universal prescription for success. Rather, it is simply a theoretical framework that explains steps taken by some firms to achieve higher degrees of labour flexibility. Having said this, since flexibility has become something of a watchword in organisations, the model is an important one. For some years flexibility in the use of human resources has been widely seen as an essential ingredient of an organisation's ability to weather market conditions and the flexible use of labour is seen by many managers as one of the key characteristics that explains the success of Japanese companies.

So far as adoption of this structural form is concerned, there is a small amount of historic case study research that supports the real-world utility of the core–periphery model (Kallenberg 2001). Nevertheless, the evidence suggests that, until recently, a full core–periphery design is rare and confined to about 10 per cent of organisations, with most firms tending to use only selected elements from the core–periphery menu (Hakim 1990).

Downsizing, Rightsizing and Delayering

These measures are not really structural designs so much as strategies for reducing the headcount. All are predictable extensions of the trend that started in the 1980s, when vast numbers of employees at the lowest organisational levels were declared redundant in response to a tightening of market conditions, and those remaining were required to work differently and much harder.

Kozlowski *et al.* (1993) define downsizing and rightsizing as a choice made to reduce the workforce, which is intended to improve organisational performance. They distinguish between two main approaches to this matter:

- **proactive**   a planned approach which is part of a business strategy to re-orientate the organisation to its environment and which usually involves reductions in targeted business areas;

OB IN ACTION: Restructuring of Cadbury Schweppes

Cadbury Schweppes, the world's biggest confectionery company, is to shed 10 per cent of its 55,000 workforce and close or sell a fifth of its 133 factories. The UK group – which makes Dr Pepper and 7 Up carbonated drinks, as well as chocolates, sweets and gum – has unveiled a cost-cutting programme named Fuel for Growth, noting that recent acquisitions had left it with a complex organisational structure for a business of its size together with a disproportionate cost base.

The initiative seeks to cut Cadbury's annual costs by £400m by 2007. However, it will have to spend an estimated £900m to achieve these savings and Cadbury said it would reinvest up to a third of the £400m savings in a new programme called Smart Variety that would seek to increase product innovation and overall marketing spend. Todd Stitzer, the new Cadbury chief executive, said it was time to exploit the potential of the product portfolio that Cadbury had been building through acquisitions such as the $4.2bn (£2.5bn) purchase of Adams, the US gum and sweet maker. Mr Stitzer said Cadbury's history of buying businesses and allowing them to exercise local autonomy had created a group that was not efficient enough and on the back of the forthcoming job losses and factory closures, Cadbury announced new financial targets for the 2004–07 period. It is targeting annual net sales growth of 3 to 5 per cent, compared with a recent trend for increases of about 3 per cent. The group wants to boost underlying operating profit margins by 0.5 to 0.75 percentage points each year. It is also aiming for free cash flow totalling £1.5bn over the 2004–07 period.

Cadbury's goals are superficially similar to the targets set by Unilever, the maker of Lipton tea and Dove soap, under its Path to Growth restructuring, which is due to finish in 2004. However, Unilever has recently been struggling against its sales growth target. Mr Stitzer shrugged off any comparisons with the Unilever plan, saying, 'We have crafted goals that are unique to Cadbury Schweppes'.

Cadbury confirmed that trading for the current year would be in line with its already announced first half and has dismissed 2003 as a transitional year.

Source:

Jones, A (2003) Cadbury cuts 10% of jobs in restructuring, *The Financial Times*, 28 October.

- **reactive** an approach in which the organisation makes a 'knee-jerk' reaction to conditions in its environment, usually aimed at cost-cutting using across-the-board reductions in headcount.

Most evidence (see Kinnie *et al.* 1998) strongly suggests that the majority of downsizing initiatives adopt the second of these approaches and that far from making an organisation more successful, performance often declines severely (Morris *et al.* 1999).

Although the reasons for this are very complicated, Evans *et al.* (1996) draw two general conclusions about why downsizing that adopts the reactive approach fails to deliver its expected benefits:

● because headcount reductions tend to occur across the board, removing organisational fat only occurs by accident and, quite frequently, the very people who will be needed to ensure future organisational success disappear as well;

● there is a huge impact on the survivors, many of whom become demoralised, dispirited, insecure, demotivated and highly stressed to the extent that they are unable to deliver the commitment and performance required to rescue the organisation.

Empowerment

So far as delayering is concerned, the introduction of new information technologies has resulted in organisations dispensing with the services of whole layers of supervision and middle management. As a result, hierarchies are flatter, day-to-day decision making is devolved to the operational level, and lateral rather than vertical communication is much more common. Almost inevitably this has been accompanied by some of the human resource measures outlined above and a buzzword in organisations where this has happened is 'empowerment'. The aim is usually to mobilise the skills, energies and commitment of employees to enhance operational effectiveness and efficiency, and its use is underpinned by an assumption that if certain aspects of control and responsibility are devolved from senior levels to lower down, this confers benefits on everybody. Employees are more satisfied because they have more interesting and responsible jobs, which raises their keenness and commitment. In return managers get a more efficient, effective and flexible workforce.

This, however, is empowerment in theory. In reality there would seem to be a great deal of ambiguity about what managers mean when they speak of an 'empowered' workforce (Cunningham *et al.* 1996). In addition, a number of rigorous empirical studies have shown that many empowerment initiatives fail to deliver their expected advantages and that employees can end up less committed than before (see, for example, Cunningham and Hyman 1999).

Business Process Re-engineering

In theoretical terms this can be most easily conceptualised as the 'scrap it and start again' approach to organisational structure. Its originators (Davenport 1992; Hammer and Champey 1993) argue that the aim is to force an organisation to think itself through from first principles. This starts with attempting to discover what it is that customers really want, followed by a strategy and design to cater for customer needs. The fundamental principle that is supposed to guide these considerations is 'do only that which is necessary'. Thus, nothing, be it organisational processes, existing procedures and rules, or structural form, is immune from consideration. The aim is ruthlessly to dispense with anything that is not vital to obtain cost savings. In theory, although it is not usually envisaged by the advocates of re-engineering, this can just as easily result in an organisation deciding to do something extra, and so there are no clear-cut structural implications. However, there are a number of practical lessons that can be learned.

Since the publication of Davenport's and Hammer and Champey's books a wave of re-engineering mania seems to have swept America and, to a lesser extent, Great Britain. When the books first appeared the management perception of the business and economic environment seems to have prompted a belief that re-engineering had only one aim: cost cutting. Thus many such initiatives quickly became nothing more than an exercise in downsizing and/or delayering. Indeed, it seems that most re-engineering has been so badly applied that one of its originators has criticised what tends to occur as 'a fad that forgets that there are people in organisations' (Mumford and Hendricks 1996). Moreover, as two recent and penetrating analyses (see Blair *et al.* 1998; Grey and Mitev 1995) reveal, there are huge contradictions in business process re-engineering. To deliver the advantages it promises, re-engineering is heavily dependent on engendering high levels of employee commitment but since it has become so strongly associated with headcount reductions and redundancy this is analogous to asking turkeys to vote for Christmas, and has the same predictable consequences.

OVERVIEW AND CONCLUSIONS

This chapter has been strongly focused on explaining the elementary principles of structure, for example, defining what structure is, its importance, how it can be portrayed in an accurate way and describing some of the recent trends in structural design. To do this it has been necessary to adopt a very descriptive approach, and this has its drawbacks. It can, for example, convey the impression that structure is a relatively straightforward topic and that the subject extends no further than simply being able to describe a structure. In reality there is much more to structure than this, but like many things in Organisational Behaviour and Organisational Analysis, it is necessary to understand the basics before trying to master more advanced concepts. While the dimensions of structure described in this chapter will be found in virtually every organisation, no attempt has been made to explain why different organisations adopt different patterns of structure. This is covered in the following chapter, which deals with the matter of organisational design, that is, the main factors that impinge on an organisation and limit its choice of where it should position itself along each of the five dimensions of structure.

FURTHER READING

Atkinson J and N Meager (1986) *Changing Work Practices: How Companies Achieve Flexibility to Meet New Needs*, London: National Economic Development Office. A comprehensive, but easy-to-read explanation of the 'flexible firm' concept.

Bedeian, A G and R F Zammuto (1991) *Organizations: Theory and Design*, Orlando, FL: Dryden. A readable and thorough exploration of organisation theory and organisational design.

Blair, H, S G Taylor and K Randle (1998) 'A pernicious panacea – a critical appraisal of business re-engineering', *New Technology, Work and Employment*, 13(2), 116–28. A penetrating analysis of the pitfalls of re-engineering.

Child, J (1984) *Organization: A Guide to Problems and Practice*, 2nd edn, London: Harper and Row. Perhaps the most thorough and penetrating consideration of structure yet written, but one that is very easy to read and understand.

Hammer, M and J Champey (1993) *Re-engineering the Corporation: A Manifesto for Business Transformation*, New York: Brearley. A highly influential book, widely read by managers, because it gives a detailed recipe for the practice of re-engineering.

Mintzberg, H (1977) *The Structuring of Organisations*, New York: Prentice Hall. A classic of its type which gives an easy-to-read account of how organisations are structured.

Piore, M J and C F Sabel (1984) *The Second Industrial Divide: Possibilities for Prosperity*, New York: Basic Books. By now, a classic book. It explains its authors' 'flexible specialisation' thesis, to which can be traced many of the current trends in organisational structuring.

REVIEW AND DISCUSSION QUESTIONS

1. Define the term organisational structure and describe the five primary purposes fulfilled by an appropriate structure.

2. What characteristics of an organisation are described by the structural dimension of configuration (grouping)? Describe six common configurations that can be used by organisations.

3. In what ways are the structural dimensions of configuration, centralisation, specialisation, formalisation and standardisation connected?

4. In what ways can measures such as downsizing, rightsizing and delayering be said to be structural responses to the four principles that recent thinking suggests should be reflected in a sound structural design?

5. In what ways does business process re-engineering represent a new theory of structure?

Chapter 17

Organisational Design

LEARNING OUTCOMES

After studying this chapter you should be able to:

- contrast classical and contingency approaches to organisational design

- understand the ways in which the characteristics of an organisation's environment influence the appropriateness of its structural design

- understand the ways in which the contingency variable of size influences the appropriateness of an organisation's structural design

- understand the ways in which the contingency variable of technology influences the appropriateness of an organisation's structural design

- understand the ways in which the culture of an organisation and the culture of its top management group can be a contingency variable that influences its structural design

INTRODUCTION

While the previous chapter was largely confined to explaining dimensions that can be used to describe organisational structures, this one has a rather different aim: to give the reader an understanding of important factors that restrict an organisation's choice of its structural design. It commences by contrasting two perspectives on organisational design. The first is derived from classical organisation theory and gives universal principles that are said to be applicable in all organisations. The second is what is now known as the 'contingency approach'. This rejects the idea of a set of universally applicable design principles and reflects the argument that the most appropriate design for an organisation is the one that best suits its circumstances in terms of the presence of certain contingency factors. The most important of these are usually taken to be its environmental circumstances, organisational size and its technology. Each of these is considered in turn, together with some of the research evidence that indicates that each factor has a significant effect on structural design. The chapter then examines the idea that organisational culture is also an important contingency factor and this is followed by a description of the theory of strategic choice, which gives insights into how, in practice, top managers make decisions about structural design. The chapter closes with an overview section which reviews matters covered in this and the previous chapter.

ORGANISATIONAL DESIGN: CLASSICAL VERSUS CONTINGENCY APPROACHES

The Classical Approach

Charismatic authority: that acquired when a person becomes the focus of a particular set of ideals and principles, e.g. Christ

Traditional authority: that which rests on the established sanctity of a traditional position, e.g. a king

Rational–legal authority: that which rests on the assumption that rational rules should guide the conduct of society and hence people in high office should command the actions of those below

Max Weber and Bureaucracy

Weber's (1948) contribution to organisation theory is one of the most misunderstood and misquoted pieces of work to find its way into textbooks on Organisational Behaviour. His description of the bureaucratic organisation is part of a much more extensive examination of power and authority in society as a whole, in which he distinguishes between three basic forms of authority: *charismatic*, *traditional* and *rational–legal*, and it is the latter in which his study of bureaucracy is grounded.

Above all, Weber was a social scientist who observed and documented the world of his day. In the nineteenth century scientific rationality was considered to be the essential vehicle of social progress and the bureaucratic form of organisation, which is based on highly rational principles, was seen as having a number of characteristics that made it the most suitable for emerging institutions. Through patient observation, Weber documented the characteristics of the 'ideal type' bureaucracy, the most significant of which are given below:

- **Specialisation**   in the bureaucracy each office has a clearly defined sphere of influence or set of tasks.
- **Hierarchy**   there is a clear chain of command from the top to the bottom of the organisation and a lower office is under the control and supervision of the one above.
- **Rules**   clearly defined rational rules prescribe the functions of an office and these provide uniformity, coordination of effort, continuity and stability.

- **Impersonality**   the conduct of officials is dominated by cool professionalism. Those with whom an official deals, whether they be above, below or from inside or outside the organisation, are treated equitably.
- **Appointment**   officials are appointed on the basis of technical competence rather than family connection or favouritism.
- **Progression**   upwards movement through the bureaucracy is based on merit and/or seniority so that it offers a career for life.
- **Exclusivity**   holding an office is the individual's sole or primary occupation.
- **Segregation**   official activity (and resources) are regarded as distinct from those outside the organisation.
- **Accurate written records**   these are regarded as the lifeblood of the organisation. They ensure impartial treatment of office holders and clients, and give rules, procedures and information to guide future conduct.

The bureaucratic model has been severely criticised and the word 'bureaucracy' is often used in a derogatory way to refer to all that is bad. Crozier (1964), for example, criticises bureaucratic theory as an unreal account of how people behave in organisations, and is particularly scathing about the idea that impersonal, conflict-free behaviour characterises the bureaucracy. Other writers are equally critical and some point out that Weber was incorrect in assuming that rules always promote uniformity, order and rationality. A case in point is Gouldner's (1954) classic study of an American gypsum company, which clearly demonstrated that workers and managers quietly went about bending and ignoring rules as part of a pattern of indulging each other. In addition, Selznick (1966) points out that a surfeit of rules results in disadvantages, such as **goal displacement**, in which slavishly obeying a rule becomes a goal in itself. Finally, there are a number of influential writers who draw attention to the potentially adverse effects of the bureaucracy on its members. Merton (1957) writes of the narrow and restricted experience it provides, which ill-equips people to operate elsewhere and results in the trained incapacity of the bureaucrat. Perhaps the severest critic in these terms is Argyris (1964), who considers that high degrees of specialisation, rule-regulated behaviour, impersonality and emphasis on hierarchical decision making restrict the psychological growth of individuals and result in feelings of frustration, which damp down creativity and innovation.

Although some of these criticisms are probably valid, Weber's work is seriously misinterpreted by many writers. His description of the main characteristics of bureaucracy is an 'ideal type', which does not mean 'highly recommended', but is simply a situation where all the characteristics exist together at the same time. Weber's model is essentially a **descriptive tool**, and he acknowledges that relatively few organisations conform to it in every respect. Nevertheless, his work is frequently misquoted in many American textbooks as 'Weber's ideal bureaucracy', where he is also unfairly criticised for offering a prescriptive design that has a number of inescapable drawbacks. In reality, Weber merely argued that a bureaucracy was superior in a technical sense to other systems of authority prevalent in his time and far from advocating bureaucracy, in many respects he was highly sceptical about its effects. For instance, he notes that rationality can stifle the scope for individuality, and so office holders tend to become specialists without spirit, trapped in the bureaucratic iron cage of bondage (Weber 1948). Moreover, for all that they criticise bureaucracy, many of the so-called management gurus of today, such as Peters (1987), give universal prescriptions that are just as unworkable and more recent thinking points out that the rules and routines that characterise bureaucratic organisations can be a source of flexibility and adaptability (Feldman and Rafaeli 2002; Feldman and Pentland 2003). Perhaps more importantly, it is virtually inconceivable that the bureaucratic hierarchy will ever be abandoned completely. Many of the currently fashionable initiatives, for instance 'delayering' or 're-engineering', always seem to leave the top two layers in an organisation untouched, and what remains is still a bureaucratic hierarchy, albeit a flatter one. The opposite of the bureaucratic hierarchy is the so-called *adhocracy*, or networked organisation, which has been advocated by a number of writers such as Morgan (1989). This would consist of a loose, very flexible and constantly evolving set of structural features that dispense with traditional hierarchies, job titles and rules. However, power holding is usually very high in the management value system and because bureaucratic structures centre power in the hands of a small number of top managers, it seems unlikely that they will ever be fully eclipsed by anything else. In any event, more recent work argues that it is not bureaucracy as a set of organising principles that results in the dysfunctional effects. Rather, it is misapplication of the principles that has these effects, which occur because of highly inappropriate organisational designs (Adler and Borys 1996).

> **Adhocracy:** a loose, very flexible and constantly evolving set of structural features that dispenses with traditional hierarchies, job titles and rules

Classical Organisation Theory

This is not so much a unified theory as a set of remarkably similar ideas put forward by a diverse group of writers, who set out what they believed to be the guiding principles for designing an appropriate structure. Although these ideas differ in detail, they are remarkably similar in terms of basic approach and, for the most part, they were based on the work experience or personal opinions of the authors. Collectively, the approach is usually referred to as the 'classical management school', which stresses that productive efficiency is most easily obtained by:

- adherence to the bureaucratic organisational form;
- narrow spans of control;
- tightly prescribed roles;
- clear and explicit formal procedures;
- a high degree of task specialisation;
- a clear and explicit hierarchical system of management.

Perhaps the best-known example which typifies the approach is Henri Fayol's (1916) fourteen principles, an outline description of which is given in what follows.

- **Division of work** the object of an organisation is to produce more and better work for the same effort, which means there are advantages to be derived from specialisation of labour.

- **Authority and responsibility** these must be matched and, in particular, managers should have the right to give orders and expect obedience, which goes hand in hand with the responsibility to reward people for good performance and to punish them if it is not forthcoming.

- **Discipline** this is essential for the efficient running of the organisation; it is a sign that employees respect the organisation and so it is management's duty to decide on and apply appropriate sanctions where discipline is not forthcoming.

- **Unity of command**   an employee should receive orders from one and only one superior.
- **Unity of direction**   this supports unity of command and dictates that there should only be one plan for activities that are designed to achieve an objective.
- **Subordination of interests**   the well-being of the organisation should come before that of groups and individuals.
- **Remuneration**   this should be fair and satisfy both employer and employee; it should encourage keenness and performance but avoid overpayment.
- **Centralisation of authority**   this is necessary and will always be present to some extent.
- **A scalar chain**   there should be a direct line of authority from the top to the bottom of the organisation.
- **Order**   both material and social order should exist; the former avoids loss and the latter ensures that everyone knows his or her place.
- **Equity**   the desire for equality of treatment should guide the vertical division of authority in the scalar chain.
- **Stability of tenure**   this should be encouraged, particularly in managerial personnel.
- **Initiative**   this should be fostered, the best vehicle for which is said to be the unity of command principle.
- **Esprit de corps**   the team spirit should be promoted because this builds loyalty to the organisation.

Guidelines such as these give a highly prescriptive recipe for organisational design which has been much criticised. For example, it takes no account of interactions between people and, because it underestimates their mental capacities, it has a very naive view of the way they think. In addition, it understates the potential for conflict in organisations (March and Simon 1958). Indeed, so prescriptive and mechanical is the approach that it has been called a description of 'organisations without people' (Bennis 1959). Nevertheless, it gives a clear and unambiguous set of guidelines that are easy to understand and apply. It is remarkably resilient in management circles and, dressed up in different words, it is still common to find the ideas espoused in current management textbooks. In academic circles, however, the strongest criticism centres on the idea that there is a valid set of principles which is applicable everywhere. Current thinking on organisational design purposely avoids this assumption, and it is this approach which is considered next.

REPLAY

- The classical approach to organisational design establishes principles of structure that are said to be universally applicable in all organisations.
- Modern approaches take a contingency perspective which holds that the most appropriate structural design for an organisation is the one that best suits its particular circumstances.

The Contingency Approach

The great problem with classical management theory is that it ignores the possibility that there are influential factors that make some structures more appropriate than others. In the late 1950s a number of theorists began to seriously question the 'one size fits all' assumptions of the classical approach, and took as their guiding principle the simple but elegant idea that the most appropriate structure for an organisation is the one that best suits its particular circumstances. Although the term was not coined until some time later, this subsequently came to be known as *contingency theory*.

Contingency theory of structure: that the most appropriate structure for an organisation is the one that matches its particular circumstances

CONTINGENCY FACTORS IN ORGANISATIONAL DESIGN

The three variables that have received most research attention in organisational design are an **organisation's environment, organisational size** and **organisational technology**, and these will be considered shortly. However, more recent thinking on the subject, for example the strategic choice model, reveals that the **preferences and values of top management** can also have a huge impact on what structures are selected. Since it can be argued that these are a powerful contingency factor they will also be considered. The following discussion starts at the outside of the organisation and works inwards.

Environment

An organisation's environment often contains elements over which it has no direct control, but which can strongly influence its performance. Thus organisations have little choice but to adapt to their environments, and this has been a concern of organisation theory for a number of years.

Burns and Stalker: Mechanistic and Organic Structures

Burns and Stalker (1994) set out to explore whether differences in the technological and market elements of environment affected the structure and management processes in firms. They investigated twenty manufacturing firms in depth and classified environments between 'stable and predictable' and 'unstable and unpredictable'. Because the organisations studied were drawn from several different industries, they identified diverse structural arrangements, but also found that firms could be grouped into one of two main types, with management practices and structures that Burns and Stalker considered to be logical responses to environmental conditions. Neither type is inherently right or wrong. Rather, the firm's environment is a contingency factor that prompts a structural response. The two contrasting forms, the names used by Burns and Stalker to identify them and the general structural and management style which characterises each one are given in what follows.

Mechanistic organisation: roughly corresponds to a more bureaucratic firm and is best suited to stable environmental conditions

The Mechanistic Organisation
This has a more rigid structure, is typically found where the environment is stable and predictable and is an appropriate response to these conditions. Its characteristics are:

- tasks facing the concern as a whole are broken down into **specialised, functionally differentiated** duties and individual tasks are **pursued in an abstract way**, that is more or less distinct from the concern as a whole;

- the **precise definition** of rights, obligations and technical methods is attached to roles, and these are **translated** into the responsibilities of a functional position so that there is a **hierarchic structure** of control, authority and communication, in which performance requirements for each level in the hierarchy are reconciled by **immediate superiors**;
- the hierarchic structure is reinforced by locating **knowledge** of the whole organisation exclusively at the top of the hierarchy, with greater importance and prestige being attached to **internal and local** knowledge, experience and skill rather than that which is general to the whole organisation, which gives a tendency for interactions between members of the concern to be **vertical**, that is, between superior and subordinate;
- a tendency for operations and working behaviour to be **governed by superiors** with **insistence on loyalty** to the concern and obedience to superiors as a condition of membership.

The Organic Organisation

Organic organisation: an organisation that has more fluid structural arrangements and is better suited to variable and dynamic environments

This has a much more fluid set of arrangements and is an appropriate response to an environment that is turbulent and which requires new and innovative responses to changing conditions. Its characteristics are:

- special knowledge and experience is valued for its **contributive nature** to the common task of the concern and the **nature of individual tasks** is seen to be set by the total situation faced by the organisation;
- a **continual redefinition** of individual tasks through interaction with others, with little **shedding of individual responsibility** upwards, downwards or sideways;
- the **spread of commitment** to the concern beyond any technical definition, and a **network structure** of control, authority and communication that has a **lateral** rather than a vertical direction of communication through the organisation;
- omniscience is not imputed to the head of the concern and **knowledge** may be located anywhere in the network, with this location becoming the centre of authority;
- communication consists of **information and advice** rather than instructions and decisions, with **commitment** to the concern's tasks and to the 'technological ethos' of material progress and expansion being more highly valued than loyalty;
- importance and prestige are attached to those **affiliations and expertise** that are valid in the industrial and technical and commercial milieux external to the firm.

Although mechanistic and organic types are quite different they are only the extremes of a continuum and, in some firms, a mixture of both types could be expected. Nevertheless, the broad structural characteristics that are likely to be associated with each of the two types follow fairly naturally from the descriptions given above.

Mechanistic organisations are likely to have tall structures, a high degree of specialisation, centralisation of authority and standardised rules and procedures. Employees are likely to be 'procedure-orientated' and most interactions and communications, including resolution of conflict, will take place through the chain of command. Conversely, organic organisations will have much flatter structures and lower degrees of specialisation, centralisation of authority and standardisation. People are likely to be much more 'goal-orientated' and there will be more lateral interaction between them.

Management will tend to give advice rather than orders, and prestige and status will come from expertise rather than position.

When first published the Burns and Stalker results were something of a milestone. They not only demonstrated a clear link between environment and structure but also showed that the successful use of different structures requires people in the organisation to have appropriate patterns of values and attitudes. This means that structural arrangements need to be matched by appropriate organisational cultures, and we will return to this point later in the chapter.

Lawrence and Lorsch

The work of Lawrence and Lorsch (1969) is regarded as the classic study linking the effects of environment to structure. The authors set out to identify the most appropriate structural characteristics for dealing with different environmental conditions and addressed four important issues of whether:

- the different demands placed on organisations by their environments relate to structural designs;
- organisations with stable environments make greater use of centralised patterns of authority to achieve coordination and control and, if so, whether this is because fewer integrating decisions are required or because decisions can be made more effectively by a small number of people at a high level;
- organisations in different environments have the same degrees of specialisation of functions;
- firms in different environments have greater degrees of functional specialisation, giving rise to differences in the extent to which organisational functions are coordinated, or use different ways of integrating functional activities.

To address these issues the authors coined three terms which have subsequently become an important part of the vocabulary used in organisational design. **Differentiation**, as used by Lawrence and Lorsch, goes beyond the normal meaning of specialised functional activities. They point out that different organisational functions usually deal with distinct segments of the environment, which can mean that people in different functions develop unique perspectives and emotional orientations. For instance, marketing people can be far more focused on the pressures exerted by customers; this can give them a very different perspective from production people, who tend to be more sensitive to the views of trade unions and suppliers. Therefore, the Lawrence and Lorsch view of differentiation took cognisance of whether some functions:

- focused more on their own goals and objectives, rather than those of the whole organisation;
- had longer time horizons because of differences in the time taken for the results of their decisions to become apparent with respect to that part of the environment with which they dealt;
- were managed differently in terms of being task-orientated or person-orientated;
- tended to be more bureaucratically managed than others.

Integration reflects the ways in which functional activities are coordinated and controlled to achieve the goals for the organisation. Lawrence and Lorsch acknowledged that different functions are likely to have different orientations, but they avoided the assumption that integration is just a matter of minimising differences to produce a common outlook. Rather, their aim was to determine whether ways had been found to allow the differences in orientation to exist, while getting the functions to focus on achieving organisational goals. Thus, attention was directed on two alternative methods of coordination: 'vertical coordination', using rules and procedures through the hierarchy to control functional behaviour; and 'horizontal coordination', using lateral processes designed to encourage functions to make mutual adjustments to each other.

Environment is not conceptualised as 'everything out there' but as three specific sub-environments, normally dealt with by three major specialist functions in firms:

- The **market sub-environment**   dealt with by the marketing function.
- The **technical-economic sub-environment**   dealt with by the production function.
- The **scientific sub-environment**   dealt with by research and development.

They reasoned that each sub-environment can differ in an number of important ways:

- its rate of change;
- the certainty about prevailing conditions at any particular time;
- the time span of feedback before the results of a decision with respect to the environment become known.

These differences are reasoned to result in the three functions having to deal with different degrees of ambiguity or uncertainty, which can result in them evolving their own functional sub-structures and processes. This gives rise to three testable predictions about the functions, that:

1. **Production** will have a short time horizon focused on the demands of the here and now, such as meeting quality and output targets. It will operate in a fairly stable internal environment of known methods and rely mostly on rules and procedures.
2. **Research and development** will operate on a much longer time horizon and deal with an unstable, moving situation concerned with innovation. As such it will have a fluid, organic type of structure.
3. **Marketing** will tend to lie somewhere between these two extremes.

Several studies were conducted, but the one giving the most definitive findings was a comparative study of firms in three different industries, chosen on the basis of their environmental characteristics.

- The *plastics industry* had a very dynamic, highly uncertain environment characterised by rapid changes in customer requirements and a high rate of scientific and technological development.
- The *containers (canning) industry* had a stable, certain environment with predictable customer requirements and an established, unchanging technology.
- The *consumer foods industry* had an intermediate environment and a moderate rate of change in customer requirements and technology.

In each industry high-performance firms (high profits and many new product innovations) were compared with low performers and two general sets of findings and associated conclusions emerged:

- the more uncertain the environment, the greater the degree of differentiation within firms; that is, plastics (high), consumer foods (medium), containers (low), giving the conclusion that the more dynamic and uncertain the environment the more that specialist sub-units are needed, each dealing with the dynamics of its own sub-environment;

- within each industry, the more successful firms were those that also had the highest degrees of integration, giving the conclusion that success (in the terms measured) is associated with mechanisms that are concerned with ensuring that all sub-units contribute towards achieving a common goal.

However, the most interesting finding is related to the methods of integration used. Successful firms all had high degrees of integration, but the mechanisms used in each industry were quite different and depended on the amount of differentiation present. Firms in the canning industry, which had a very stable environment, had the lowest degrees of differentiation and tended to integrate activities by using rules, procedures and centralised decision making. In consumer foods, where the environment was intermediate in uncertainty, these integrating devices were also used but, in addition, lateral integrating mechanisms, such as cross-functional task groups or special coordinating roles, were sometimes found. The plastics industry, with the most dynamic and uncertain environment of all, invariably had permanent, lateral integrating mechanisms, for instance, cross-functional coordinating teams at several levels and sometimes permanent departments whose role was to integrate functional activities.

To some extent the work of Lawrence and Lorsch can be viewed as an extension of the ideas of Burns and Stalker. However, Burns and Stalker treat an organisation as an undifferentiated whole that is either organic or mechanistic, whereas the Lawrence and Lorsch dimensions of differentiation and integration go to the very heart of organisational design and enable matters to be considered in a more sophisticated way. For instance, they acknowledge that mechanistic and organic structures can exist side by side in different parts of an organisation.

Nevertheless, there are criticisms of the theory, the most important of which is that it treats organisations as passive recipients of environmental influence and postulates a one-way chain of causality, such as that shown in Figure 17.1.

In Figure 17.1 environment is shown as the independent variable and performance as the dependent variable, which means that structure is a mediating factor that must be adjusted to ensure excellent performance. This neglects the important idea that, rather than slavishly responding to environmental changes with disruptive structural reorganisations, most organisations try to exert some influence on their environments.

Organisational Size

Size is normally taken to refer to the number of employees in an organisation and a simple example of its effects can be given by considering a small corner shop which

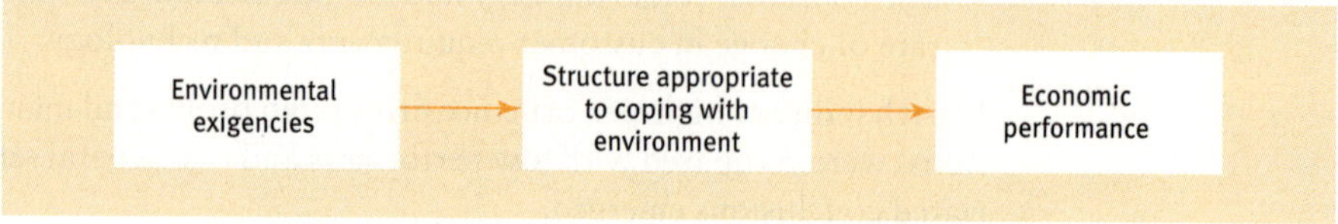

Figure 17.1 Causal chain implied by Lawrence and Lorsch

develops over time into a large successful business. Initially the owner will also be the manager and do everything – selling, buying, ordering and keeping the accounts. If the business is successful, it may well expand, perhaps by acquiring additional outlets and eventually by having a large store in the city centre. Later on it might even become a national chain. In the first stage of expansion the owner will require managers in each outlet and, to take advantage of bulk-buying discounts, he or she might make purchasing and accounting separate activities, with warehousing and publicity added shortly afterwards. Eventually, if the firm becomes a national chain, it might be decided to group stores into geographical areas, each with its own manager.

Even from a simple story such as this a general principle emerges which has been shown to be applicable, even with multinational corporations (Malnight 2001). As organisations grow their structures become much more elaborate, internal activities become more specialised and the structure becomes more vertically and horizontally differentiated, which in general terms has two opposing consequences. First, clear economic advantages accrue from specialisation and formalisation, and there is extremely strong evidence that larger firms that adopt these principles outperform those that are more loosely structured (Child 1984). However, this can result in people finding the organisation a less satisfying place in which to work; job satisfaction can be lower and different forms of conflict and protest behaviour can sometimes increase with size.

TIME OUT

Carefully consider your own university or college. Like most of the higher education institutions it has probably grown significantly across the last ten or fifteen years. Make enquiries to determine what its structure was about fifteen years ago and compare it with the structure now, then answer the questions below.

1. In what ways has the structure become more elaborate and complex?
2. Have the problems of coordination and control of the different parts become more difficult?
3. How has the institution tried to resolve the issues?

Technology

Technology is often thought of in terms of machines and hardware but, in the words of Rousseau (1979), it can be more simply described as the application of knowledge to perform work, which has the advantage of embracing both what is done and how it is done. To some extent technology is dictated by the tasks that must be performed and, once selected, it often completely determines the order in which tasks are undertaken. Thus there can clearly be a relationship between technology and structure, which can be examined at a number of levels. In this section the perspectives of two influential theorists will be examined.

Thompson and Organisational Interdependencies

Thompson (1967) deals with the technology of a whole organisation and distinguishes between the three basic technologies portrayed in Figure 17.2. Each one is associated

Figure 17.2
Thompson's technological types and associated interdependencies
(a) The mediating technology (pooled interdependence);
(b) The long-linked technology (sequential interdependence);
(c) The intensive technology (reciprocal interdependence)

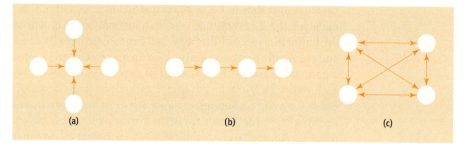

(a)　　　　　　　(b)　　　　　　　(c)

Mediating techno-logy: the parts of an organisation are linked through its centre

Pooled interdepend-ence: organisational sub-units safeguard each other by con-tributing discretely to the whole, which safeguards them all

Long-linked tech-nology: all activities have to be performed in a set sequence

Sequential inter-dependence: each stage is interdepend-ent with the one before and the one after

Intensive technology: all parts contribute together to perform the task

Reciprocal inter-dependence: the parts are dependent on each other to perform their respective tasks

with a particular flow of work, which means that an organisation's parts are inter-dependent in a characteristic way. In addition, each technology is characterised by the amount of discretion or problem solving that is needed for its operation. This gives rise to differences in the degree of complexity inherent in coordinating the activities of the interdependent parts, together with characteristic remedies to shield the organ-isation's operating core from the uncertainties of the environment.

In the *mediating technology* the parts of an organisation are linked together through its centre. Each renders its own contribution to the whole and in return receives sup-port from the centre. This is a situation of *pooled interdependence*. There is little direct interaction between sub-units, but they are interdependent in the sense that unless each one makes a contribution to the whole, others are placed in jeopardy. Examples of organisations using mediating technologies are banks, building societies, retail chains and insurance companies. Providing each sub-unit follows procedures and makes the same contribution in the same way, this technology is the least complex in terms of coordination, which is done by **centralising authority** and by **formalising** and **stand-ardising operations**.

The *long-linked technology* is exemplified by the mass production line, where task A must be performed before B, B before C and so on. This is *sequential interdependence* and because everything else has to be adjusted if one of the operations in the chain does not perform as required, it is rather more difficult to coordinate. An organisa-tion using this technology tends to devote a great deal of time and effort to planning and scheduling to coordinate activities. Dealing with environmental fluctuations is also more of a problem, and this is typically addressed by vertical integration, either back-wards or forwards. For example, a car manufacturer could integrate backwards by acquiring a component supplier, or forwards by owning car dealerships.

In terms of coordination the *intensive technology* is the most complex of all. Each sub-unit is interdependent with all the others, which results in *reciprocal interdependence*. Organisations of this type, for example, hospitals or travel agents, offer a custom opera-tion where the tasks undertaken, the skills used, the mix of techniques deployed and the order in which they occur are determined by feedback from the client or customer. Sub-units need to be highly responsive to one another and there can be an ongoing need for mutual adjustment. Because it is always hard to predict what is required in advance, coping with environmental uncertainty is extremely difficult, and sometimes this can only be done by acquiring surplus resources that are held in reserve, just in case they are needed.

Thompson points out that the effectiveness of an organisation's 'technical core' (the operational units that transform inputs into outputs) depends on it being able to get on with its tasks in a smooth, uninterrupted way. This requires shielding the core from environmental fluctuations, which is done by incorporating appropriate sub-units into the structure to deal with the problematic parts of the environment. For example, the core of the mediating technology is particularly vulnerable to fluctuations on the output side, and so stability is sought by having a very active marketing function. The long-linked technology is vulnerable to fluctuations on both input and output sides, and so it devotes a great deal of effort to forecasting demand and usually has specialist departments that plan activities and ensure continuity of supplies. In the intensive technology, fluctuations on the input side are the greatest problem, and the only way the core can be shielded is to have a surplus of resources. However, it is not just a matter of the different technologies having different structures. The progression from mediating, through long-linked to intensive technology results in an exponential increase in the difficulties associated with coordination, which in turn gives a corresponding increase in structural complexity. This is because if sequential interdependence exists, there is also a degree of pooled interdependence. Similarly, the existence of reciprocal interdependence means that sequential and pooled interdependence are present as well.

Thompson's ideas stand up well to empirical examination, for example, Mahoney and Frost (1974) tested the relative importance of the different coordinating mechanisms in firms conforming to the technological types and the results obtained strongly support Thompson's predictions.

TIME OUT

Review the Thompson scheme of classifying organisational technologies and carefully examine the structure of the organisation in which you work or study.

1. Which of the three technologies do you feel is used by the organisation or institution?
2. Identify the component parts that are interdependent in some way and show what type of interdependence exists between them.
3. What would you identify as the organisation's technical core?
4. In what activities does the organisation or institution engage to shield its technical core from environmental uncertainties?

The Woodward Studies: Technology, Structure and Performance

The original aim of Woodward's (1965) work was to determine whether an association exists between business success and the structural prescriptions given by classical organisation theory. Data was collected from over 100 manufacturing firms, all of which were larger than 100 employees. Business success was measured in the usual financial terms. In addition, data was collected on a number of structural variables, such as the number of levels in the management hierarchy, span of control and what is now referred to as administrative intensity (the ratio of managers and supervisors to direct production workers). Firms were classified in terms of performance as below average, average and above average. Initially, no consistent relationship was identified between structural variables and performance, but subsequent re-analysis revealed that if technology was held constant, there was a connection between structure and performance. To explain this it is necessary to describe Woodward's scheme for classifying manufacturing technology. This used three broad technology types and represents what Woodward and her colleagues called a scale of increasing *technical complexity*, in which coordination and control become more difficult as the scale is ascended. The types are:

Technical complexity: a measure of the ease of coordination and control of a manufacturing technology

- **Low technical complexity: unit and small batch production,** for example unique products made to a customer's specification, prototypes and small batches made to customer order.
- **Medium technical complexity: large batch and mass production,** which usually involves large batches made on multipurpose machinery or on assembly lines using purpose-designed machinery.
- **High technical complexity: process production,** for instance production of chemicals, liquids and gases under continuous flow (24 hours per day, seven days per week) conditions.

This classification needs to be interpreted with some caution. While it classifies process technology as the most technically complex, unit and small batch production is also full of unpredictability and it is equally valid to argue that this is the most difficult to coordinate and control. Nevertheless, Woodward found that in each technology type the most successful firms had structures which were the average of all firms in the type: the most successful unit and small batch production firms were those where supervisors had the average span of control etc. for firms using this technology. Moreover, when the structural characteristics of the successful firms were plotted against the type of production technology used, distinct relationships were revealed, some of which are shown in Figure 17.3.

The important conclusion that Woodward draws is that different production technologies require their own structural arrangements, and replication studies provide strong support for this idea (Collins and Hull 1986). Nevertheless, there are criticisms of her findings, one of which is noted above and concerns the way that technical complexity is evaluated. In addition, the work is exclusively focused on manufacturing industry. Since there are no direct equivalents of the technological types in service industries it is hard to generalise the findings beyond manufacturing. Another important point is not really a criticism of Woodward, but of the way that her results are sometimes taken too much at face value and it is rather simplistically inferred that technology alone determines structure. As firms grow or acquire more stable markets the volume of work can result in a move from small batch methods into mass production.

Figure 17.3
Woodward studies – selected relationships between structure and technology type

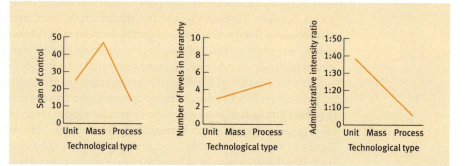

This means that there is an increase in size (or at least in scale) of the organisation, as well as a change in production technology, and any structural changes are almost certainly the result of both variables being at work together.

Culture as a Contingency Variable

Organisational culture is considered in greater detail in Chapter 19 and for the purposes of this discussion it will be defined more simply as:

> **the basic values, ideologies and assumptions which guide and fashion individual and business behaviour.** **(Wilson and Rosenfeld 1990, p 229)**

Although organisational design is concerned solely with structure, there are strong connections between culture and structure, and two important issues arise. First, a culture prompts people to behave in characteristic ways and since structure also requires people to behave in a certain way, the behaviour required by one needs to be compatible with that required by the other. Second, the values of the top management group in an organisation can have a huge impact on the decisions it makes. Since values are an important part of culture, the culture of top management can influence its decisions about structure. In practice there are two issues – for convenience these are called the **limiting factor on design** and the **limiting factor on top management decisions**.

Issue 1: Culture as a Limiting Factor on Design

Until comparatively recently technology was thought to have the major determining effect on structure. However, there is an alternative argument that culture and structure are so interconnected that they go hand in hand. A simple way to illustrate this is to use the basic four-part classification scheme of cultures set out by Harrison (1972), which is given below.

The **role culture** typifies the bureaucracy or mechanistic organisation in which the duties, responsibilities and the authority attached to roles are tightly specified, with activities controlled and coordinated by senior managers. In organisations of this type, power resides in a person's position and the activities of individuals are regulated by rules and procedures.

The **task culture** roughly corresponds to the organic organisational form and is the complete opposite. There are few rules and procedures and getting things done tends to be far more important than how things are done. Status comes from expertise and adaptability in achieving results and this is facilitated by giving individuals a considerable degree of autonomy.

The **power culture** is also lacking in formal rules but tends to be one in which a powerful individual or small group is the source of all authority. This elite controls and coordinates everything and often changes the rules as it goes along. The essential qualities required of those employees who are not part of the power structure are personal loyalty to power holders, working extremely hard and doing what they are told without question. Again this promotes a set of values and sentiments which enable people to work and survive within this structure.

The **person culture** is seldom found outside small voluntary groups and is only described for completeness. This type of organisation exists to serve its members and is often brought into existence by those who staff it. To some extent it allows its

OB IN ACTION: Reorganisation at Nokia

Nokia, the world's leading maker of mobile phones, recently announced a sweeping reorganisation of its operations involving the biggest reshuffle of senior management for two years. The moves will see Olli-Pekka Kallasvuo, chief financial officer, become head of the group's mobile phones business, which accounts for 80 per cent of group sales. Matti Alahuhta, the current head of Nokia Mobile Phones, will become chief strategy officer, and Rick Simonson, a 45-year-old US citizen who has been head of customer finance since 2001, will become chief financial officer.

Jorma Ollila, who remains chairman and chief executive of the group, has said in the past that moving senior management around from time to time is a good way to stop them entering 'comfort zones'. The last major reshuffle took place in 1998 and the current reorganisation will increase speculation as to who will eventually take over from Mr Ollila. He has led Nokia since January 1992, overseeing its transformation from unfocused conglomerate to European technology leader, and his current contract runs until 2006.

Nokia is also implementing a new organisational structure, saying the change is designed to 'strengthen its focus on convergence, new mobility markets and growth'. Alongside its traditional mobile phone and network divisions, there will be two new divisions – Multimedia and Enterprise Solutions. Multimedia, which will focus on games, imaging and music, will be headed by Anssi Vanjoki, currently the number two in Nokia Mobile Phones. A new head for Enterprise Solutions, which was announced in July 2003, has still to be appointed. The changes will be implemented from 1 January 2004. Sari Baldauf will remain head of Nokia's networks division and Pekka Ala-Pietila will remain president. Mr Ollila said the reorganisation reflected the tremendous changes in the mobile phone world over the last ten years. 'The industry and corporate structures that were established a decade ago at the dawn of mobile communications were very different from what is needed going ahead.'

Source:

Brown-Hulmes, C (2003) *The Financial Times*, 26 September.

members to collectively pursue aims that would not be possible as individuals, and is often no more than a loose alliance of people who share some common facilities. Other than behaving with mutual respect to each other, there will probably be no coordination and control. Nevertheless, structure, or rather the lack of it, goes hand in hand with the sentiments and values.

Two important conclusions can be drawn from this typology. In each case, a set of values and sentiments that promotes characteristic patterns of behaviour is interwoven with a set of structural features. In the role culture, for example, people perform their own roles and do not trespass on the territory of others. They channel communications through the hierarchy and avoid making decisions which are beyond their formally designated level of authority. Conversely, in the task culture, roles are extremely flexible and people are expected to be versatile and act on their own initiative. Thus, these structural arrangements can effectively become a mental programme that indicates the reality of 'how the organisation should operate', which suggests that an organisation's culture should be an important consideration in the design of its structure.

Issue 2: Culture as a Limiting Factor on Management Decisions

In organisational design the dictum that 'structure follows strategy' (Chandler 1962) is often accepted without question, but from what has been said earlier, decisions about the structural design of an organisation are not this straightforward. They usually require a balance to be struck between the sometimes competing demands of size, technology and environment. Since an inappropriate design is likely to jeopardise achievement of business strategies, a more sophisticated view of the strategy formulation process is needed. This is provided by the strategic choice model (Child 1997), which reflects the idea that when constructing strategies top managers can purposely incorporate measures that leave existing structures and processes relatively unaltered. Child argues that top managers are like other people: they have their own foibles, preferences and personalised performance criteria and do not always pursue high profitability and growth. Sometimes these are sacrificed for an organisational structure with which managers feel comfortable, because it reflects their philosophies about control and coordination. Thus, top management's values and culture, both of which are neglected in the conventional contingency approach, can be important contingency variables in their own right.

There is a considerable body of evidence to show that the personal preferences of top managers, particularly those about methods of monitoring performance, can have a strong influence on decisions about structure (Hinings *et al.* 1996) and this alone makes the strategic choice model an important one. In addition, there is a body of knowledge that suggests that the prior experience, preferences and ideologies and values (cultures) of key decision makers actually influence the way that they perceive the environment (Finklestein and Hambrick 1996; Winter 2003). For instance, Weick (1979) observes that managers 'perceive' environments, rather than actually see the totality of what is there – they tend to focus their attention on only specific parts of the whole environment and other parts are excluded from consideration. Weick calls this the *enacted environment*, and it is this to which top managers respond in terms of structural arrangements. To illustrate how organisations define and modify their environments, by selecting strategies that have an impact on structural design, these ideas have been developed further by Miles and Snow (1978), who examined the extent to which enacted environments produce predictable patterns in structural design. They give three distinct patterns of strategy–structure linkage used by successful organisations.

Enacted environment: management's mental construction of what the environment is, which arises from its selective perceptions of environment

Defender strategies involve having a relatively restricted field of activity in terms of product lines and markets served. The firm's aim is to have a secure, stable niche in the market and it tries to protect this by offering outputs of a higher quality or lower price than competitors. An organisation of this type is not usually an innovator in terms of products or services, but concentrates on internal efficiencies so that it can focus its efforts on doing a job well in a limited field, and this has distinct structural implications. Internal efficiency is typically obtained by a high degree of specialisation and centralisation of authority and a reliance on rules and procedures for coordination and control.

The **prospector strategy** aims to obtain market advantage by being the first organisation with a new product or service. To do this it usually has to serve a very broad environment, watch closely for changes and respond to them very quickly, which also has structural implications. Responding quickly to opportunities that arise usually requires decentralised decision making, together with lateral communication. Thus project and product teams are often used for coordination and control.

The **analyser strategy** falls between the above two types. Here the aim is to have a stable but limited product line and this is used to finance fairly quick moves into carefully selected new developments. This strategy seldom involves the organisation being the first into a developing area. Rather, it monitors what other firms do and can often enter a market in its early stages of development with a product or service that is more cost-efficient. This tends to produce a mixed structural form. Those parts of the organisation operating in the stable part of the environment will have structures similar to the defender, and those dealing with the emerging part will tend to have market-based, fluid structural characteristics.

Miles and Snow also identify a fourth strategy type: **the reactor**. Because this tends to result in inconsistent strategy–structure arrangements, often because an inappropriate structure is used to pursue a particular strategy, firms are seldom successful and the type is not considered further here.

The Miles and Snow strategic choice perspective has received a great deal of support and currently receives much attention in organisation theory. Since empirical studies are highly supportive of the original work (Boschken 1990) a number of important conclusions may be drawn:

- managers seldom react to all of the environmental factors that can affect an organisation, but tend to focus on specific parts and thus 'enact' an environment;
- different organisations operating in the same environment can perceive it in different ways, which results in diverse strategies for dealing with the same environment;
- because strategies not only involve choices about the markets that are served, but also the ways of serving markets, this results in different structural designs (see OB in Action box above);
- once a strategy and structural design are put in place it is likely to result in what Miles (1982) has called a **strategic disposition**, which establishes a 'mind set' about what is seen to be an appropriate strategy for the organisation.

This final conclusion is tremendously important. Put another way, it means that the structural choices that have already been made can inhibit the adoption of other strategies, and even affect views on whether future strategies are viable (Hinings *et al.* 1996).

An Integration of Contingency Factors

Depending on the particular factor on which a contingency theory is focused, it gives valuable insights into the way that the factor influences structure. However, most theories usually focus on a single contingency factor, and this conveys the impression that this factor has the major influence on an organisation's structural characteristics. The exception here is the strategic choice model, which is much more behavioural in its approach. It incorporates the idea that managers who exercise choice can try to influence organisational environments, or even serve them selectively, which gives them greater degree of freedom about structural options.

Figure 17.4 Structure and strategic choice

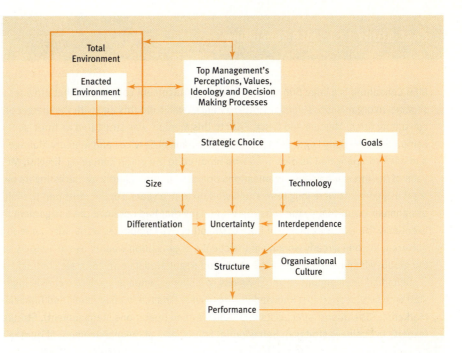

However, the strategic choice perspective does not contradict more conventional contingency theories. By introducing values and ideologies of senior decision makers as another contingency factor, it results in something that is complementary rather than contradictory. Nevertheless, it gives a somewhat more complex view of the determinants of structure and, in order to bring all these influences together, Figure 17.4 reflects the inferences about the major forces at work that can be drawn from all the contingency theories covered in this chapter.

REPLAY

- The classical approach to organisational design establishes principles of structure that are said to be universally applicable in all organisations.

- Modern approaches take a contingency perspective, which holds that the most appropriate structural design for an organisation is one that best suits its particular circumstances.

- Contingency theorists have attempted to identify how structural design needs to vary to accommodate particular organisational circumstances, and three factors which have received most attention are organisation size, the technology an organisation uses and an organisation's environment.

- In addition, because an organisation's culture needs to match its structure, there are grounds for arguing that culture is also an important contingency variable.

- The cultural values of top management are also likely to exert an influence on the structural designs chosen for an organisation.

CASE STUDY 17.1: MEB Consulting

MEB Consulting is a large firm of international management consultants that provides a wide range of services to organisations. It came into existence twelve months ago with the merger of two separate consulting firms, Mercury and Delta. Prior to this Mercury was structured as three separate, specialist companies – Mercury Legal Services, Mercury Financial Services and Mercury Management Consulting – and each company had its own head who reported to the group managing director, Mr Donald Irons. Each of the three subsidiary organisations operated independently by marketing its own services and most assignments were long term and lasted up to two years. For the most part the initial stages of an assignment involved only the consulting company that had obtained the assignment from the client, but eventually the expertise of one or both of the other two companies would also be required. When this occurred, the one already working in the client's organisation would pass an enquiry to another firm in the group, which then contacted the client and negotiated its own separate contract.

Delta had been organised into divisions of a single company, each one consisting of a group of staff with similar specialist knowledge. These were Finance (management and financial accountants), Marketing, Operations (specialists in production and operations management), Strategy and Economics (experts in business strategy), Behaviourial (all aspects of the management of human resources). Delta's assignments also tended to be long term and usually involved staff from all five divisions, who were assembled into a multidisciplinary team under a senior consultant. This enabled the services of specialists from each division to be used as and when they were required, and enabled the disciplinary bias of the team to change in focus across the duration of the assignment.

As most often happens, there was a dominant party in the merger, in this case Mercury, whose managing director, Mr Donald Irons, became the MD of MEB Consulting. His first step was to order a complete restructuring into five separate organisations: MEB Legal Services; MEB Financial Services; MEB Marketing Services; MEB Business Services; MEB Management Services. In his written message to staff announcing the new arrangements he stated that it was his belief that clients strongly associated their needs with a particular area of expertise. For this reason he felt that the most promising future for the new firm lay in providing a range of sharply differentiated services, which would be delivered by the practices formerly adopted by Mercury.

Questions

1. What do you feel has been the guiding logic underpinning Mr Irons' selection of MEB Consulting's structure?

2. Do you envisage the structure to be more advantageous or disadvantageous than either of those of the two previous organisations?

3. What problems, if any, do you feel might arise from the new structure?

OVERVIEW AND CONCLUSIONS

Organisational structure can have a significant influence on effectiveness and efficiency. Its basic purpose is twofold: to divide up organisational activities and allocate them to sub-units, and to provide mechanisms for coordination and control of these activities so that the organisation as a whole achieves its aims. The most common way of portraying structure is the organisational chart, which tends to mask the true complexity of matters, but an oversimplified view can be avoided if a multidimensional perspective is adopted. However, since dimensions are related, they should not be treated as discrete features.

Early ideas on structural design, for example those of the classical management theorists, attempted to identify universal principles that would give a structural design suitable for all organisations. These ideas reflected the belief that high degrees of specialisation, centralisation of authority and the formal specification of activities are all necessary in organisations. Thus any dysfunctions of these features tended to get ignored.

In the last four decades new ideas have emerged that reject universal principles and take a contingency approach, in which the most appropriate structural design for an organisation is the one that best copes with its particular circumstances. Contingency theory has extensively considered the effects of organisational size, the technology it uses and the demands of its environment and, in the light of more recent work, it can also be argued that organisational culture is a factor of some importance.

Most theories in organisational design tend to accept that structure is, or should be, an outcome that flows logically from the goals and strategy of a firm. However, the theory of strategic choice points out that matters are not quite this simple. Because managers are likely to be more at ease with some structural arrangements than with others, the values and ideologies of top management are also influential factors in the choice of a structural design. Thus, structure does not always flow logically and inevitably from a set of organisational goals and strategies. Strategies and goals can sometimes be subject to a degree of revision in order to accommodate structural arrangements that are more comfortable to managers.

FURTHER READING

Bedeian, A G and R F Zammuto (1991) *Organizations: Theory and Design*, Orlando, FL: Dryden. A readable and thorough exploration of organisation theory and organisational design.

Burns, T and G M Stalker (1994) *The Management of Innovation*, Oxford: Oxford University Press. This is a reprint of the original (1961) book, which is by now a classic in organisation theory.

Child, J (1984) *Organisation: A Guide to Problems and Practice*, 2nd edn, London: Harper and Row. Perhaps the most thorough and penetrating consideration of structure yet written, but one that is very easy to read and understand.

Child, J (1997) 'Strategic Choice in the Analysis of Action, Structure, Organisations and Environments: Retrospect and Prospect', *Organisational Studies*, 18(1), 43–76. The paper restates its author's theory of strategic choice and reviews the evidence on this matter.

DuGuy, P (2000) *In Praise of Bureacracy*, London: Routledge. In the light of the very bad press which bureaucratic organisations have received across the last four decades, a timely book. It explores many of the positive aspects of bureaucracy as well as dealing with its criticisms.

Hinings, C R, L Thibault, J Slack and L M Kikulis (1996) Values and organisational structure, *Human Relations*, 49(7), 885–916. An interesting paper that provides support for the idea of a strong connection between organisational structure and culture.

Lawrence, R and J W Lorsch (1969) *Organisation and Environment: Managing Differentiation and Integration*, Homewood, IL: Irwin Dorsey. Despite its age the book is still a classic in the literature on organisational design.

REVIEW AND DISCUSSION QUESTIONS

1. State nine prominent characteristics of Weber's 'ideal type' bureaucracy and explain what each one describes.

2. Define what is meant by a contingency approach to organisational design and explain how this differs from classical organisation theory.

3. Distinguish between mechanistic and organic organisations and the type of environmental circumstances to which each is most suited.

4. State the four research questions addressed by Lawrence and Lorsch (1969) in their studies of the relationship between environment and structure, and describe the three prominent conclusions that emerged from their work.

5. Name the three types of technology that Thompson (1967) uses to distinguish between organisations and explain the distinguishing features of these technologies.

6. What is the major conclusion of Woodward's study of the effects of technology on structure in manufacturing organisations?

7. Describe the way in which the culture of an organisation can place limits on its freedom to adopt a new structural design and the ways in which the culture of the top management group in an organisation can be a limiting factor on decisions about a structural design.

Chapter 18

Control

LEARNING OUTCOMES

After studying this chapter you should be able to:

- define control, explain its purpose and the connection between planning and control in organisations

- explain three alternative perspectives on control in organisations: managerialist, open systems and political

- distinguish between open-loop (feedforward) and closed-loop (feedback) control and use the control model to diagnose elementary faults in systems of control

- in outline, describe the main features of eight traditional methods of behavioural control used by organisations: recruitment, selection and socialisation; appraisal, training and development; direct control; technology and job design; rewards and punishments; structure (bureaucratic control); output control; culture

- explain why employees sometimes resist control

- describe recent developments in behavioural control

INTRODUCTION

To ensure that goals and objectives are achieved it is necessary to coordinate an organisation's activities, and this makes control an important process in any organisation. However, because this involves controlling the behaviour of people, which smacks of coercion, manipulation, or even exploitation, control can be a controversial matter. To explore these issues the chapter starts by defining control and tracing its purpose in organisations, which is followed by a description of the relationship between planning and control. The next section explores three different perspectives on control, after which the control model, a device for analysing control systems, is presented. The remainder of the chapter focuses on behavioural control, which commences with a description of some of the traditional ways of controlling human behaviour in organisations. Resistance to control is then explored, and this is followed by an examination of current developments in behavioural control. The chapter closes with a short overview section.

THE PURPOSE OF ORGANISATIONAL CONTROL

There are many definitions of control, but in this chapter, the definition adopted is a broad one:

> **the regulation of organisational activities so that some targeted element of performance remains within acceptable limits.** **(Barney and Griffin 1992, p 329)**

As was noted in Chapter 1, organisations are brought into existence to achieve something and this involves structuring human activity in an enterprise. Thus, the primary purpose of control is to coordinate different organisational activities in order to achieve the goals for the whole organisation. For this reason, control is normally applied at all organisational levels: the organisation as a whole has to be controlled in order to ensure that it adopts an appropriate stance *vis-à-vis* its environment and, at lower levels, control is applied to synchronise the activities of groups and individuals to ensure that they play their respective parts in the process. This means that control is not a 'one-off' activity, but an ongoing process that:

- monitors what is achieved;
- compares what is achieved with what should be achieved;
- makes provision for remedial action to be taken where a discrepancy appears.

Goals, Planning and Control

From the above, goals or objectives are a crucial part of control and, as was pointed out in Chapter 15, goals are normally arranged as a means–ends hierarchy, with goals at one level being the means of achieving the goals at the level immediately above (see Figure 15.5). Ideally, therefore, it is desirable that a control mechanism should exist for every goal that is set. Using a simplified example that considers only a single item from an organisation's mission statement, this principle is reflected in Figure 18.1.

Figure 18.1
Simplified outline of hierarchical goal-setting and control

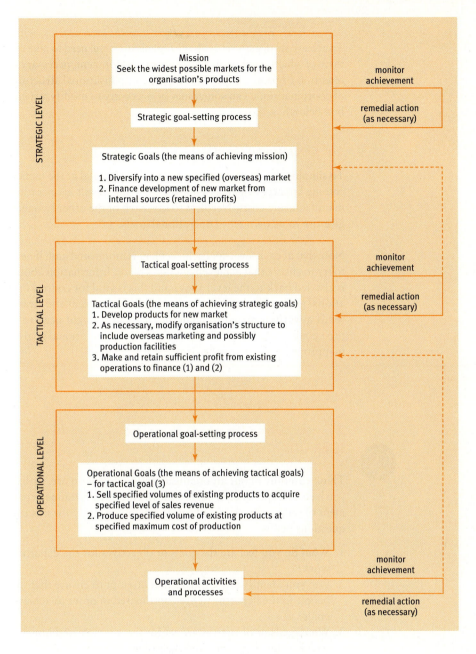

The Strategic Level

Mission statements are usually worded in very vague terms and in Figure 18.1 this goes no further than seeking the widest possible markets for the organisation's products. Nevertheless, this gives rise to more specific goals for its relationship with the environment: here, goals for the particular markets that will be entered and how this expansion will be financed.

The Tactical Level

To achieve strategic level goals the organisation will need to take certain definable actions, three of which are shown: new product development, necessary structural changes and retention of profits. Note that because organisational structure is a powerful means of coordination, it can sometimes be necessary to modify structures (see OB in Action box below).

The Operational Level

To simplify the discussion the only goal considered at the tactical level is the one concerning finance, which, as a minimum, would result in operational goals for sales and manufacturing costs. Needless to say, each of the other two tactical goals would also give rise to its own set of operational goals.

Note that at each level goal achievement is monitored and, if necessary, action is taken to try to ensure that achievement takes place. Information about achievement (or not) is also fed back to the level above and this is vital for control in a wider sense. If operational goals and objectives are achieved, but tactical and strategic goals are not, this sends a warning signal to higher levels, which might need to take action to modify their goals. For example, it can mean that the operational goals are too modest, or are inappropriate in some other way.

TIME OUT

Think carefully about an organisation in which you are, or have been, employed. If you have no experience of paid employment, either full-time or part-time, use the department of the university or college at which you study for this exercise and answer the questions below.

1. What do you feel are the goals or objectives for the department in which you work?
2. Can you identify any controls that attempt to ensure that the activities of the people in the department are coordinated in order to achieve the departmental goals?
3. What goals or objectives are set for these people and how is it determined whether they have achieved their objectives?
4. If everyone in the department achieved his or her objectives, would this result in the goals for the department as a whole being achieved?

- Control systems do not exist in a vacuum, but are intended to make it more likely that formal goals are achieved.
- Any future desired state that is important enough to warrant a goal being set should have its own associated control mechanism; establishing control systems and methods should, therefore, be part of the planning process.
- Different organisational levels (strategic, tactical and operational) have their own sets of goals that get progressively more specific and quantifiable at lower levels.
- Since goals are arranged hierarchically, with those at one level being the means of achieving the goals for the level above, strategic and tactical goals are only achieved if goals are achieved at the operational level.

OB IN ACTION: Attending to Work

In some British organisations, a new phenomenon has appeared whereby employers lavish hitherto unheard of levels of benefits and perks on employees, for example, free hairdressing, car servicing and other personal services. According to Richard Reeves, Futures Director at the Industrial Society, while this may be no more than an attempt to be a caring employer who tries to make the work environment more enjoyable, it can be far more insidious than it appears at first sight. For instance, it could be a rather subtle control mechanism designed to induce people to be in attendance for extremely long hours. Organisations that attempt to achieve this end are what Reeves calls 'the absorbers'; their ultimate aim is for employees to live their lives for the organisation. Firms of this type first appeared in America, which is perhaps not surprising since America has the reputation of being the home of the 'workaholic'. Prominent examples are the pharmaceutical giant Merc and computer software companies such as Sun Microsystems and Netscape. In these organisations it would almost be possible for employees to live their lives 'on site', with everything catered for, including leisure activities – presupposing, of course, that employees actually get leisure time – and it is probably no coincidence that working hours in America now exceed those in Japan.

Reeves notes that firms of this type are now becoming more commonplace in Great Britain, a notable example being British Airways. What is surprising is that the phenomenon has appeared at a time when there is increasing concern in some companies to stamp out a culture of 'presenteeism', and to encourage employees to develop a more appropriate work–life balance. It seems, therefore, that in some organisations the phrase 'appropriate work–life balance' is used in a very one-sided way.

Source:

Reeves, R (2000) Have you been absorbed? *The Guardian*, 12 April: 9.

ALTERNATIVE VIEWS ON CONTROL IN ORGANISATIONS

While few people would deny that complex organisations need to be controlled, this gives an impression that control is a harmless, neutral activity. However, control can exist for a number of reasons, and it can be exercised for a wide variety of motives and in an equally wide variety of ways. There are a number of different schools of thought on the use of control in organisations but, for simplicity, three contrasting perspectives will be discussed: the managerialist perspective, the open systems perspective and the political perspective. These are shown in Table 18.1.

The Managerialist Perspective on Control

This reflects the view that controlling others is a legitimate prerogative of managers – the so-called 'right to manage'. Its origins can be traced to the writings of classical management theorists and, in particular, Henri Fayol (1916), who defined the five major functions of management as: planning, organising, command, coordination and control. Many managers would argue that control is the most important of these because it goes to the very heart of the management process of achieving goals and objectives.

While it is not surprising that most managers feel this way, the view is also reflected in a number of academic texts, such as Barney and Griffin (1992) who write about control as something akin to a management right. Mullins (2002) goes even further by suggesting that when an employee asks his or her manager 'how well am I doing?' the person is asking to be controlled, which comes close to portraying the control activity as a piece of managerial social work. Many managers, it can be noted, argue that what differentiates them from other employees is that they are allocated resources and are made responsible for their efficient and effective utilisation. From this it is but a short step to laying claim to a right to command employee actions.

Table 18.1 Three perspectives on control

	Managerialist perspective	Open systems perspective	Political perspective
Underlying assumptions	Control of resources (including human resources) is a legitimate management activity. Therefore, managers have the right to exercise control over the behaviour of subordinates	Control mediates processes that transform inputs into outputs, for instance budgetary control attempts to regulate financial resources used in the transformation process and performance appraisal to achieve the most appropriate use of human resources While control itself is neutral, it can have adverse consequences for humans	Control is synonymous with the exploitation of human resources
Major focus	How managers can best maintain control	Modelling control systems for design and analysis purposes	Understanding the internal dynamics of control, e.g. how control is exercised and whether it gives rise to resistance or counter-control

The Open Systems Perspective

This perspective neither condemns nor endorses control, but takes the view that large complex organisations have no alternative but to install and operate control mechanisms, the major benefits of which are:

- improved economic efficiency and the best use of scarce resources;
- predictability, stability, order and reliability;
- people know what they have to do, which avoids the ambiguity that many people find distressing.

Notwithstanding these advantages, the perspective also acknowledges that control can be applied inappropriately or for suspect reasons, which can have a number of dysfunctional effects:

- coercion, manipulation or exploitation;
- people lose their individuality and innovation can be stifled;
- people have little or no say in matters that affect them and can become dependent on being controlled.

The Political Perspective

Social control: achieving compliance, conformity or obedience through interpersonal or intergroup processes

This perspective has become highly influential over the last two decades and a number of authors, such as Willmott (1997), have argued that control in organisations often goes well beyond the search for economic efficiency. It contains strong elements of domination and exploitation. This is made much easier because managers control the distribution of rewards, which allows them to obtain compliant behaviour and facilitates the strong in manipulating and exploiting the weak. For this reason, the political perspective on control has a strong focus on *social control*, in which compliance, conformity and obedience are achieved through processes that occur between groups and individuals.

REPLAY

- Because organisations need to perform a host of different activities to achieve their goals and objectives, control is necessary to try to ensure that these activities are coordinated.

- In theory, control is a neutral activity solely concerned with coordinating organisational activities, but because organisations are structured hierarchically, control tends to reside in the hands of a relatively small number of people, which gives a potential for control to be abused or used for exploitative, rather than neutral, purposes.

- The managerialist perspective on control views it as something that managers exercise by right.

- The open systems perspective views control as something that is necessary in organisations, but which can have a number of adverse consequences.

- The political perspective focuses on the internal dynamics of the control of people in organisations and assumes that control can lead to exploitation, which in turn leads to resistance to control.

It has been observed that managers' activities tend to be more concerned with controlling employees than coordinating them, which results in ever-increasing inequalities in the distribution of rewards, and an inbuilt tendency for workers to resist control. Thus, the main focus of this perspective is the attempted subordination of labour and employee attempts at counter-control.

THE CYBERNETIC MODEL OF CONTROL

What makes control such a controversial matter in organisations is its application to humans as well as machines. To understand the processes involved, it can be useful to approach the matter in a detached way, leaving ethical considerations temporarily on one side. For this reason a concept will be borrowed from *cybernetics*: the theoretical study of control processes in electrical, mechanical and biological systems. While cybernetics can be highly mathematical, one of its basic tools – the *control model* – gives a symbolic representation of the components necessary for a system of control, their functions and how they relate to each other. This model has two main uses: as a checklist for designing control systems and as a diagnostic tool to pinpoint faults if a control system is not functioning correctly. It will be used for both of these purposes at various points in the remainder of the chapter. First, however, it is necessary to explain the model.

Control: the Basic Requirements

The starting point of the control model is that a process or activity exists which needs to be controlled. This is shown in its simplest form in Figure 18.2. Note that the process has inputs and outputs and in almost all cases it is the outputs that people wish to control. The first requirement for control is to know something about the relationship between the inputs and the outputs. Thus, in an organisational process that produces goods or services, we would need to be sure that the required quantity of labour with the appropriate skills, together with tools, machines, raw materials etc., are present. From here onwards it is necessary to distinguish between two basic control options: open-loop (feedforward) control and closed-loop (feedback) control. These are shown in Figures 18.3 and 18.4 respectively.

As can be seen, the only difference between the two options is that in closed-loop control there is a sensor on the output side of the process, together with a feedback loop to a comparator, the functions of which will be considered presently.

Open-loop Control

Open-loop control is underpinned by an assumption that the workings of the process or activity are so perfectly understood that the required outputs will be obtained so long as the required inputs are fed into the process. There are plenty of examples in

Cybernetics: the theoretical study of control processes in electrical, mechanical and biological systems

Control model: a symbolic representation of the components necessary for a system of control, how they relate to each other and their functions

Open-loop (feedforward) control: a method in which the inputs to a process or activity are carefully determined, but with no monitoring of outputs

Figure 18.2
The process or activity to be controlled

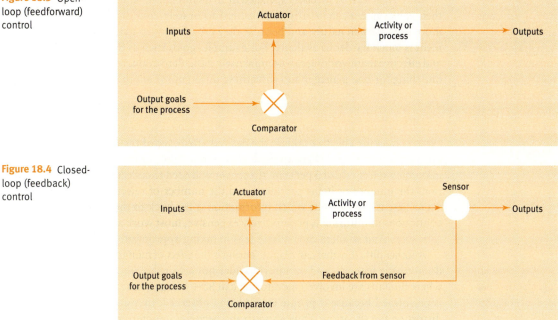

Figure 18.3 Open-loop (feedforward) control

Figure 18.4 Closed-loop (feedback) control

everyday life where open-loop methods are encountered. For instance, in convenience foods such as cake mixes and TV dinners, the ingredients all come pre-packaged and if the instructions are closely followed with respect to mixing, cooking times, temperatures etc. a usable finished product is obtained. In many organisational activities, particularly those with human inputs, the workings of the process are not precisely known so it is not considered safe to rely on open-loop control. This does not mean that it is never used and we will return to this point later when current developments in control are discussed.

Closed-loop Control

Here the basic sequence of activities is:

* the outputs of the process or activity are evaluated by a sensor;
* information is fed back from the sensor to a comparator which compares the output goals for the process to those actually achieved;
* if there is a discrepancy between desired and actual outputs, information is fed to an actuator which adjusts the inputs to the process or activity accordingly.

This sounds very simple in principle but to work effectively it requires that the components of the control system must all be able to perform certain functions and, for this reason, it is necessary to consider each one in more detail.

Goals and Comparator

A first requirement is to be able to specify the output goals for the process, and this is true whether closed-loop or open-loop methods are used. Here it is useful to distinguish between two types of goal: hard and soft.

Closed-loop (feedback) control: a method in which the outputs of a process or activity are monitored and, if necessary, inputs are adjusted to achieve the desired outputs

Comparator: something (or someone) that compares the desired attributes of the outputs of a process or activity with those actually achieved

Hard goals can be precisely specified in an unambiguous and quantifiable way. Thus their achievement can usually be measured accurately. *Soft goals*, however, are much more subjective in nature and because they are often open to interpretation, achievement is much harder to evaluate. For example, goals such as high workgroup morale and effective teamworking can be immensely difficult to evaluate because they can mean one thing for one manager and something different for another.

Sensors and Feedback

Sensors must be able to evaluate the desired attributes of the outputs of the process. For instance, if the workgroup used as an example so far has a quality goal of say a maximum reject rate of 3 per cent, the sensor will need to collect two pieces of information: the number of items produced and the number of rejects. A problem that can occur here is the speed at which information is fed back to the comparator. Because continuous monitoring is prohibitively expensive, most work activity is monitored by *sampling*. And so there can be time lags in taking appropriate remedial action.

Another difficulty that can plague sensing is the effect of monitoring outputs. Machines do not have feelings, and monitoring does not affect the process or the activity, but where humans are involved monitoring can have a huge impact on the way an activity is performed because if people resent being observed, they can usually find ways of distorting the situation. Thus, monitoring becomes counter-productive.

The Actuator

Since many processes or activities have multiple inputs, separate *actuators* are required to regulate the supply of each one. Indeed, separate actuators are often needed to regulate different attributes of an input. For instance, in the case of the workgroup described above, the actuator that adjusts the quantity of labour (number of people or hours worked) would need to be very different from the one that adjusts the skills of the workforce.

While it is usually fairly easy to determine whether an acutator works properly in a mechanical system, this is not always the case with humans. For instance, if jobs are designed by using scientific management principles (see Chapter 7) payment is usually made contingent on effort, which assumes that the main (if not only) thing that motivates people is money. Since we know that people also require a degree of intrinsic motivation, this is a half-truth, and it is now widely acknowledged that a host of *normative inputs*, such as values, attitudes, beliefs and motivations, are important inputs to any process that involves human effort. These all come from within the person and although managers might like to think that they can directly control them, this is nothing more than wishful thinking.

The Control Model: An Evaluation

As was pointed out earlier, the control model has two main uses: as a device to design control systems and as a tool to diagnose problems with existing systems of control. While it can be a powerful instrument for either purpose, it is important to recognise that a number of criticisms of the model have been voiced, the most important of which are:

- it results in a mechanical approach which tends to treat control as an engineering exercise in which the properties of everything are unvarying and well known, whereas some of the greatest difficulties arise in the use of highly variable human factors;

- because the model has an exclusive focus on achieving goals that have already been decided, it takes these for granted, which ignores the possibility that the goals themselves could be inappropriate;

- it regards goals and goal setting as unproblematic, whereas in Chapter 15 it is pointed out that goals are often compromises rather than statements of unassailable logic;

- it tends to assume that links between cause and effect are perfectly understood, and in many cases this not a safe assumption;

- it tends to assume that all the resources for a process or activity are readily available in sufficient quantities and qualities;

- it implicitly ignores the points made in Chapters 11 and 14 which indicate that there are often multiple systems of goals in an organisation;

- it assumes that control is neutral and is not used for purposes of dominance or exploitation.

Although these criticisms are perfectly valid, it should be remembered that the model is simply an analytical tool and so everything depends on how it is used. If suitable allowances are made for these points, it is too valuable a model to discard and, for this reason, it will be used at various points throughout the chapter to illustrate some of the problems that arise in control systems.

TIME OUT

Reflect carefully on the study activities that you undertake as a student at the university or college that you attend. Focus on a particular module or subject that you study and answer the questions below.

1. What standards of performance are set for you and who sets these standards?
2. What are the inputs to the process in which you learn the subject material?
3. Assuming that an important output of the learning process is that you understand (and can apply) the subject material, is this output monitored in any way and, if so, how is this done?
4. Is there any provision to compare this output (learning) with the standard of performance you identified in question 1? If so, who or what makes this comparison?
5. If a discrepancy was identified between your actual output and the targeted output you identified in question 1, what provision is there to adjust the inputs to the learning process? Who or what makes this adjustment?
6. Map your answers to questions 1–5 on an appropriate control model. In your view is the learning process controlled by open-loop or closed-loop methods?
7. In your view how effective is this control?

REPLAY

- The control model, which originated in the field of cybernetics, gives a symbolic representation of the components in a system of control, their functions and how they relate to each other.
- Open-loop (feedforward) control assumes that the workings of the process or activity to be controlled are perfectly understood and that the required outputs are obtained by using inputs of the required quantities and qualities.
- Closed-loop (feedback) control contains a stage in which the outputs of a process or activity are monitored in order to detect discrepancies between actual and desired outputs so that remedial action can be taken if necessary.
- Either model can be used as a tool to design control systems or diagnose faults in those that exist.

CASE STUDY 18.1: The Control of Customer Enquiries Staff

A number of external factors have put pressure on the organisation's profits and, as a result, the number of teams in the department is to be reduced from 30 to 24. Therefore, each remaining team will experience a 25 per cent increase in workload. However, the organisation is still very sensitive about its image and is concerned that there shall be no reduction in standards of service. As a result, the Customer Enquiries Manager has set the following objectives for team leaders:

- to answer all enquiries in a courteous and efficient way;
- in order to avoid long telephone queues of customers waiting to have their queries answered, the time for each call must be kept down to an absolute minimum;
- if a query cannot be answered on the spot by one of the advisers, to transfer the customer to a technical specialist immediately.

Questions

1. Produce a closed-loop control diagram that makes provision for the performance of a team to be monitored.

2. Identify and place on the model: performance goals for the team; all the inputs to the customer enquiries activity; and the outputs of the activity.

3. In the case where a team underperforms suggest what action might need to be taken to remedy the situation, together with who or what would take this action.

NOTE: This case concerns the group of five customer enquiries advisers described in Case Study 11.3 in the Instructors' Manual and Student Website. You will need to read through Case Study 11.3 in order to understand fully the group's tasks and functions.

BEHAVIOURAL CONTROL

Power and Control

Manager-directed control: managers specify exactly how and what should be done and closely monitor employee behaviour

Bureaucratic control: the use of tight job specifications and standard operating procedures to specify employee behaviour, which become the accepted ways of doing things to which employees conform

Employee-centred control: a 'hearts and minds' strategy that involves influencing the way that employees think about themselves and what they do so that they willingly subscribe to management's aims

Managers and supervisors are usually granted a degree of authority by an organisation and so control cannot be divorced from the use of power. Because they are likely to assume that they have the right to control the behaviour of others, this can have a strong impact on the relationship between an organisation and its employees. Stewart (1991) points out that one of the dilemmas created by the desire to be 'in control' is that managers feel a need to obtain two different patterns of employee behaviour that are not easily reconciled. They want order and predictability in employees, which implies tightly specifying required behaviour, but, on the other hand, they also seem to want employees to be flexible and innovative, which implies giving them a high degree of discretion. Unfortunately these twin requirements are so different that it is all too easy for an emphasis on one to lead to a near absence of the other. Thus, controlling employee behaviour always involves a trade-off between order and flexibility. Stewart illustrates this by contrasting three control strategies which can be placed along the continuum shown in Figure 18.5.

Manager-directed control has a strong emphasis on the predictability of employee behaviour and, in control model terms, this corresponds to a strict application of closed-loop control techniques. At the middle position on the continuum is *bureaucratic control*, in which limits are placed on employee discretion by clearly defining roles using tight job specifications and by using standard operating procedures to specify how things should be done. While there would still be some surveillance of employees, overall there would be a somewhat looser application of closed-loop methods.

Employee-centred control has a strong emphasis on obtaining a high degree of flexibility, creativity and motivation in employees. In theory this means that employees exercise a high degree of self-control and the task of management is to get employees to control themselves in a way that delivers the behaviour that managers want. In theory this reduces the need for monitoring employee behaviour, which means that it is much nearer to open-loop control.

Figure 18.5
Management control strategies (after Stewart 1991)

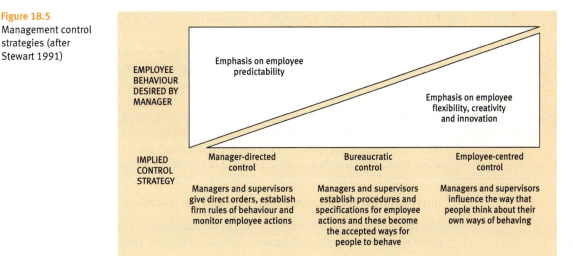

A move from left to right on this continuum represents what Friedman (1977) calls a shift from 'direct control' to 'responsible autonomy', which uses what Walton (1985) calls a commitment strategy. Note, however, that both are equally control orientated. For instance, over 40 years ago Tannenbaum (1962) argued that by using participation to create an impression of shared decision making, managers can lower employee resentment at being controlled and retain the better part of control to themselves. Thus, management control strategies always involve the use of power and it is not so much a question of whether power is used, but how it is used.

REPLAY

- Behavioural control is mainly exercised by supervisors and managers who are given a degree of formal authority by an organisation to direct the activities of subordinates and so control cannot be divorced from the use of power.
- Supervisors and managers have control strategies, which can be thought of as ways of using their formal authority to exercise control and one way of classifying control strategies is along a continuum, the extremes of which are manager-directed control and emloyee-centred control.

TIME OUT

Carefully reflect on the organisation/institution for which you work or study, either full-time or part-time, and answer the question below.

All organisations require their members (whether employees or volunteers) to comply with rules that constrain their behaviour within certain limits. What type of control (manager-directed, bureaucratic or employee-centred) is used by the organisation to obtain compliance from you and other organisational members?

TRADITIONAL METHODS OF BEHAVIOURAL CONTROL

Portfolio approach to control: the use of different strategies for controlling human behaviour according to which one is seen to be most applicable at the time

Because there are other, more subtle ways that managers can use to influence employee behaviour, an exclusive focus on the overt use of power gives a misleading picture of control strategies. Child (1984) argues that managers use a *portfolio approach to control*, that is, different methods are applied to different groups of employees (or at different times) according to what managers hope to achieve. Thus, rather than attempting to classify traditional methods of control according to an overarching scheme that fits in with other writers, a number of the most commonly used methods will be described and we will return to how they are related at the end of the section.

Input Control: Recruitment, Selection and Socialisation

Organisations usually try to employ people who can be relied on to behave as required; those who are seen to 'fit in'. In order to make decisions about this management has a wide range of techniques at its disposal to attract, recruit and select employees. While selection is far from being a precise art, the process enables a line to be drawn between those allowed to become organisational members and those who are not, and a recent study by Callaghan and Thompson (2002) illustrates the length to which some employers go to achieve these aims.

Once admitted to an organisation people come under a variety of pressures from peers and superiors to conform to established ways of doing things (see Chapter 19). Like selection, this process of socialisation is a method of behavioural control that can be used to try to ensure that those admitted to organisational membership are amenable or susceptible to other methods of control. In control model terms, both these processes (selection and socialisation) attempt to regulate the quantity and/or quality of human resources as inputs to organisational processes. While managers seem to have great faith in their abilities to select appropriate entrants to an organisation, there is strong evidence that the selection process is not very effective in predicting the performance of prospective entrants. For this reason, it is often socialisation that plays a far bigger part in the process of control.

TIME OUT

Using the same organisation as in the previous Time Out exercise, try to remember the time when you were selected to enter the organisation and answer the questions below.

1. In what ways do you feel that the selection process was a conscious attempt by the organisation to exercise control over the quality of human resource inputs to organisational processes and activities? What evidence do you use to support this idea?

2. To what extent do you feel that any induction process you received when first joining the organisation (including interaction with your peers and immediate superior) was concerned with exercising control over your future behaviour in the organisation? What evidence do you use to support this idea?

Rewards and Punishments

There are many ways in which rewards and punishments are used to try to bring employee behaviour under control. Although there is an assumption that employees will expend effort in return for any type of reward, the link between reward and effort is very much more direct in some cases and this gives rise to significant differences in the basis on which rewards are allocated. With lower-level employees, many managers have a sublime belief that incentive payments place them firmly in control of the effort that people put into their work and so reward power (see Chapter 14) is used to obtain their compliance. Conversely, incentives for salaried workers are usually vague and indeterminate, and consist of such things as merit payments, fringe benefits, security or the prospects of promotion. Moreover, most salary earners look upon themselves as distinctly different from those who earn wages, and it is often assumed that higher-level salaried workers have a degree of moral involvement with the organisation. Thus, normative power is used to obtain their compliance.

To some extent punishment – the reverse of reward – is also used to obtain compliance (see Chapter 14). However, trade unions and the law often put limits on management's freedom of action in this matter.

Appraisal, Training and Development

Just as selection can be likened to a filter that admits only some of those who apply to join an organisation, appraisal, training and development are processes that can be used to reinforce the desired characteristics of those who are admitted. In most appraisal schemes superiors evaluate their subordinates and decisions about whether some form of training or development will be provided are usually made by the immediate superior. Thus, the processes are strongly linked and both present opportunities to control the behaviour of employees.

Since an explicit link between performance and rewards is usually made in appraisal, the process can become little more than a very crude form of psychological conditioning, in which employees learn to shape their behaviour into something that is personally acceptable to their superiors (Salaman 1978).

Direct Control

Personal surveillance by supervisors and managers is the oldest method of behavioural control and to some extent everybody is subject to it. Nevertheless, the ways in which this occurs can vary considerably, as can the intensity with which control is applied. For instance, mild control might consist of giving instructions on what should be done, with periodic checks to see that the instructions are observed. At the other extreme, very explicit instructions can be given about what is to be done and how it must be done, with almost continuous surveillance of the subordinate's actions and results.

Because other systems of control are now beginning to appear, it is often assumed that direct control has largely disappeared (Thompson and Ackroyd 1995). However, detailed research in organisations that have adopted modern control methods has clearly revealed that supervisors still have important control functions – either to make these newer methods work, or to exercise control where the newer methods fail to work as intended (Mulholland 2002). Thus, the redundancy of direct control is almost certainly exaggerated.

Technology and Job Design

Technology generally denotes the means by which tasks are accomplished. This is usually a management choice, and can have a huge effect on the ability to exercise control. A fairly obvious example of this is the machine-paced nature of work on a mass production assembly line, where the speed at which the line moves dictates how much effort employees have to expend.

Another way in which management can attempt to control the efficiency and effectiveness of employees is to design jobs with an eye to their motivational content. How to get the most willing work performance from subordinates has long been a concern of management, and across the years there have been a whole string of theories about what motivates employees, all of which imply that human behaviour can be made more controllable (see Chapters 6 and 7).

CASE STUDY 18.2: Control by Motivation and Job Design

An example of an experiment in the use of job enrichment techniques to control employee behaviour is given by changes that took place in a large British manufacturer of chemicals. The exercise involved sales representatives who, although having a high degree of job satisfaction, were given very little discretion over the way they operated.

The company had already embarked on a number of job enrichment studies and, despite the fact that its products were fully competitive, there was no improvement in sales levels over those for the previous year. Thus, sales representatives were seen as a suitable group for investigating the effects of changes which, it was reasoned, could have positive effects on performance. The changes were generated by managers senior to the direct supervisors of the sales representatives, and were introduced gradually, by the methods normally used for introducing change.

In the changed situation representatives were allowed to pass on or request information at their own discretion instead of writing a report on every customer call. They were also allowed to determine calling frequencies, how to deal with defective or surplus stock, request calls from the technical service department and, if they were satisfied it would not prejudice the company's position, to settle customer complaints by authorising small payments to reimburse customers. They were also given 10 per cent discretion on the prices of most of the products sold.

As a matter of deliberate policy, representatives whose jobs were enriched were not informed that they were part of an experiment. This was to avoid any artificial effect of simply knowing they were under observation. For comparison, a control group, which was not subject to the changes and was unaware of the experiment, was used.

Question

What do you feel would be the likely results of these changes?

Control through Structure

Organisational structure and design, which are covered respectively in Chapters 16 and 17, result in some degree of specialisation of activities, together with a hierarchy of authority. A characteristic way of achieving control is through this hierarchy, for example, by specifying roles and rules that lay down the activities undertaken by role occupants. These details are often included in job descriptions, works rules and operational procedures, and are incorporated into the contract of employment, which gives a large measure of control over employee behaviour.

These features also shape behaviour in other, more subtle ways. Differences in authority not only map out the formal power of managers to reward some behaviour and punish that which is prohibited; differences in power also have psychological effects. They establish embedded rules of conduct that are taken for granted and which legitimise management power so that those down below cooperate in their own subjugation. Thus, pursuing management's will becomes organisational common sense (Weick 1979).

Output Control

Bureaucratic control focuses on two main aspects of a process or activity: what is done and how things are done. A variant of this approach, which introduces an element of open-loop methods is *output control*, which consists of:

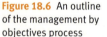

Output control: results to be achieved are specified in terms of outputs, a degree of discretion is permitted in how they are achieved, and outputs are subsequently monitored

- specifying the desired results (outputs) that should be obtained, perhaps by setting targets and time scales;
- holding the person concerned responsible for achieving these ends, but also granting a degree of discretion about how this is done;
- reviewing achievement at a later date.

This is fundamental to most schemes of performance appraisal and it is widely used at middle management levels in systems of budgetary control, in which managers are set output and resource usage targets. For managers and other employees who have responsibilities that are not so easily translated into financial results, a popular way of using output control methods is the use of a scheme of management by objectives (MBO). In theory this consists of a number of steps, which are shown in outline in Figure 18.6.

Because it is concerned with achieving goals, monitoring feedback and, if necessary, some regulation of inputs, in control model terms MBO conforms to closed-loop principles and the following advantages are usually claimed for it:

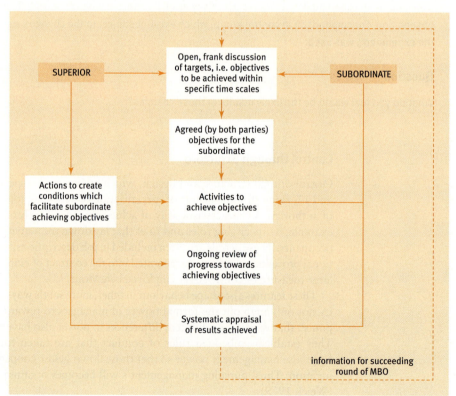

Figure 18.6 An outline of the management by objectives process

- because the subordinate is involved in selecting targets and defining his or her own job, the person is said to be more highly motivated to perform well;
- the joint setting of targets also means that the superior gains a better understanding of the subordinate's problems and is able to assess what changes are needed to remove impediments to objectives being achieved;
- information from the goal-setting and appraisal stages can be valuable in identifying training needs, education and personal development programmes;
- information from the MBO process can provide a thorough and systematic method of deciding whether individuals are ready for promotion;
- the criteria (performance achievements) are applied to everybody, which in the case of promotion decisions demonstrates that decisions are fair.

Notwithstanding these points, it is important to stress that what is shown in Figure 18.6 is MBO in theory, and in practice things can be somewhat different because:

- power is unequally distributed in all organisational hierarchies and this results in an ever-present danger that goals are imposed, rather than agreed;
- unless jobs can be redesigned before using MBO so that a subordinate becomes responsible for a complete unit of output, the running of which is completely under his or her control, it is hard to see how meaningful goals can be derived and it can even result in resistance to the control (Covaleski *et al.* 1998);
- goals preferably need to be set in quantitative terms but for some jobs the most important outputs are qualitative.

Despite these reservations, in one form or another MBO is widely used and in the guise of performance appraisal it is applied at almost all organisational levels.

Control by Culture

Because culture is an important topic in its own right and is covered in the next chapter, an extended discussion would be out of place here, and it is sufficient to highlight its control implications.

A culture is a system of shared beliefs and values, which tells people about the behaviour that is accepted as normal by other people in a particular context. This means that people within that context are likely to bring pressure to bear on each other to behave in certain ways. For this reason, in America cultural control is sometimes referred to as 'clan control' (Ouchi 1979). The interest of managers in culture is essentially as a mechanism of control, because if they are able to control the culture of an organisation, they can exert the ultimate degree of control over employees: control of their hearts and minds. Thus, attempts to manipulate culture are an essential element in recent developments in control that will be described presently. In the meantime, a summary of matters relating to traditional methods of behavioural control are brought together in Table 18.2.

RESISTANCE TO CONTROL

As noted earlier, the political perspective on control argues that in order to avoid being exploited, resistance on the part of workers can occur in the face of attempted

Table 18.2 Comparison of traditional methods of behavioural control

Method	Aims	Control model components and type of control	Most frequently used in conjunction with	Comments
A Recruitment, selection and socialisation	Control quality of inputs of human resources	Actuator in open- or closed-loop control	All other methods	Fundamental step in all methods of control
B Appraisal, training and development	Set goals for individuals and monitor performance Identify what is necessary to maintain/improve performance	Goals, monitoring, comparator and actuator in closed loop	ditto	
C Direct control	ditto	ditto	ditto	
D Technology and job design	Place constraints on employee behaviour by regulating what is done, how it is done and how much is done	Actuator, monitor and comparator in closed-loop control	E and F	
E Rewards and punishment	Provide inducements to behave as required and disincentives to unwanted behaviour	ditto	B, C and G	
F Structure (bureaucratic control)	Establish rules and procedures to limit discretion and make behaviour more consistent and predictable	ditto	B and D	Used as substitute for C
G Culture	Control hearts and minds to induce employees to think in the way managers want them to think, i.e. to endorse management goals	Actuator in open- or closed-loop control		

control by management. Almost inevitably, however, resistance is seen as a matter of economics, which ignores the possibility that resistance can be an emotional reaction because:

- exercising valued skills can be an important part of a person's self-identity and tight control can remove this opportunity;
- changed patterns of control can upset social relationships and the structure of an established workgroup;
- people may not want others to know the exact way in which they obtain good results because this makes them more replaceable, and so control contains an implied threat to security;
- people who have a modicum of power and/or prestige can feel threatened by controls that might transfer this power into other hands.

In these circumstances control can easily result in adverse emotional reactions, which prompt resistance or attempted counter-control, and Barney and Griffin (1992) argue that this type of resistance can be traced to one or more of four general conditions, which are described in what follows.

Over-control

Too much control can result in people feeling that they are not trusted, or are being treated like irresponsible children. Over-control can also occur when employees feel that there is an attempt to extend control into an area which is beyond the boundaries of the normal working relationship. For example, a demand that subordinates supply their home telephone numbers so that they can be contacted in the evenings, at weekends or when on holiday.

Inappropriate focus of control

Resistance can occur where control is too narrow or specific in scope, perhaps because it is totally centred on quantifiable aspects of performance while ignoring the importance of qualitative aspects. For instance, where there is a strong emphasis on how much work is done without considering the quality of the work.

Inequities

A control system that penalises people who are efficient and rewards those who are inefficient is almost bound to give rise to resentment. For example, suppose that there are two departments 'A' and 'B' and at the end of the financial year the manager of 'A' discovers that he has a large amount of money remaining unspent, while in department 'B' there is an overspend of the same amount. In many organisations this could easily result in 'A' having his budget reduced for the next financial year, and in 'B' getting an increased budget. The moral of this becomes all too clear to the manager of 'A':

- make sure that the budget is always spent;
- if possible, artificially inflate requirements when bidding for next year's budget.

Accountability avoidance

If people feel that control exerts a pressure to work too hard, they can start to view the bargain between themselves and the organisation as being rather one-sided. In this situation they predictably look for ways of resisting or circumventing the controls by banding together, either by making covert alliances or even by joining a trade union to negotiate an acceptable solution.

There are morals to draw from the above four reasons for resistance. The first is to realise that the presence of a control system does not guarantee that control exists. Most workers have their own ideas about reasonable boundaries for management authority and where these differ from management's ideas, resistance to control is almost inevitable. It is also important to realise that where resistance occurs, there are no panaceas or recipes for removing it. Each case of resistance needs to be treated as unique and an attempt made to understand why employees perceive that control has gone beyond the bounds of what is reasonable.

TIME OUT

Carefully reflect on the organisation for which you work, either full-time or part-time. If you have no experience of paid employment use another organisation of which you are, or have been, a member. Now answer the questions below.

1. Are there any signs of resistance to control by the organisation on your part or that of your colleagues?
2. Why do you feel that this resistance occurs? Is it for economic reasons, or an emotional reaction to:
   Over-control?
   An inappropriate form of control?
   Inequities revealed by the control actions?
   Accountability avoidance?
3. What form does this resistance take?

REPLAY

- Traditional methods of behavioural control rely on a combination of: input control (recruitment, selection and socialisation); rewards and punishments; appraisal, training and development; direct control (personal supervision); technology and job design; control through structure; output control; and cultural control.
- Employees often have some degree of resistance to control, partly for economic reasons and partly because control actions can result in emotional reactions.

OB IN ACTION: A Change in Control Structure at Boots

Richard Baker, the new Boots chief executive, recently moved to stamp his authority on the health and beauty retailer with a shake-up of its top management. The move, coming six weeks after he joined Boots from supermarket chain Asda, underlined Mr Baker's determination to rejuvenate the group's flagging stores and signalled the likelihood of radical changes to the property portfolio. The changes include the departure of two leading directors – Andy Smith, the board director with responsibility for human resources, and Ann Francke, the marketing director who joined the group in February.

Mr Baker said it had been important to move quickly and create a leaner management structure. 'This is a clear signal to the organisation about the pace and decisiveness and clarity needed,' he said. 'When you are new you cannot afford to take ages over a decision like this.' Boots insiders highlighted two changes: the news that Mr Baker intends to appoint a new trading director, probably from outside the group, and the fact that he has handed responsibility for the property portfolio to Howard Dodd, the group's ambitious finance director.

Earlier it was revealed that Mr Baker's first strategic move at Boots had been to devolve power to store managers – breaking the group's traditional model of command and control from the Nottingham headquarters. He said the management changes were designed to support that move, especially the creation of a retail director – with Mr Baker convinced that Boots does not have enough top retail talent at head office. While some at Boots felt Mr Baker was bound to recruit from Asda or Tesco – with supermarkets presenting the biggest competition challenge – he refused to say where he would be looking: 'But I know we could attract somebody into a big role like this who is a very strong retail player.' The director will work alongside David Kneale, chief operating offer, who will take the new role of chief commercial officer with responsibility for trading, marketing and formats. Paul Bateman, operations director in change of factories and logistics, adds human resources to his job. Howard Dodd will take responsibility for Boots' 1,420 stores and its massive head office infrastructure, a substantial increase in power for a man whose reforms have annoyed some long-time staff.

Source:

Voyle, S (2003) Leading directors exit in shake-up at Boots, *The Financial Times*, 29 October.

CURRENT DEVELOPMENTS IN BEHAVIOURAL CONTROL

Over twenty years ago Edwards (1979), in reviewing the historic sequence of changes in control methods, predicted that some form of post-bureaucratic control was likely to emerge. He also forecast that this would most likely be based on more sophisticated monitoring techniques, utilising advanced information technology.

Managers have long desired self-disciplined employees who do what managers want of them in a willing, productive and conscientious way, without the need for their efforts to be directly supervised. Electronic surveillance offers the tantalising prospect of ensuring workplace discipline by open-loop control. This is infinitely cheaper and more flexible than closed-loop methods because it potentially gives a 'self-correcting' work system. As was noted earlier, however, open-loop control can only be used where two conditions are satisfied: inputs are accurately regulated and there is a perfect knowledge of cause–effect relationships in the process or activity. So far as work systems are concerned, in practice this means that:

- it is known for certain that all the required inputs are fed into the work system in the correct quantities;
- the qualitative characteristics of these inputs are exactly known;
- there is certain knowledge of the effects that these different inputs have on each other.

With physical inputs these things are not usually problematic, but humans are highly variable. They have feelings, emotions and minds of their own and react to situations according to how the situation is perceived. Therefore, open-loop methods can only be used if control can be exercised over hearts and minds, so that people think in the way that managers want them to. This is a lot easier said than done.

Because thoughts are invisible, we have no idea of what people think until the results of their thoughts appear as visible action. Nevertheless, this does not stop managers yearning for self-regulating work systems and so the current trend is to try to get as near as possible to open-loop conditions. To do this some organisations are beginning to make use of control techniques that were relatively unknown in a prior era. However, although there is a school of thought which argues this is a radical break with the past, the perspective adopted here is that recent systems of control use additional techniques that have been superimposed on older methods to give new and more intense control regimes (Casey 1999). As yet no definitive model that describes these regimes has yet emerged, but Gabriel (1999) points out that they have some or all of the following features:

- the use of symbolic manipulation of meanings in a concerted attempt by managers to change employee cultures so that workers internalise the importance of service, quality, excellence, teamwork and loyalty;
- changes to structures and, in particular, the use of flatter hierarchies, flexible working practices, continuous benchmarking and performance measurement;
- changes in manufacturing techniques to introduce lean production, total quality management and just-in-time methods;
- changed methods of surveillance, including widespread use of electronic cameras, performance monitoring technologies, electronic tagging and methods that enable identification of individuals who are the source of operational problems.

An important thing about these features is that they are mutually reinforcing. This is shown in Figure 18.7 and the ways in which they combine is explained in what follows.

Cultural Control

The potential advantages of cultural control were briefly discussed earlier, and in the new systems of control the cultural element is designed with three ends in mind:

- to make more acceptable the surveillance practices that are described later;
- to lead to greater effort on the part of employees;
- to reduce levels of dissent or discontent (Casey 1999; Purcell 1993) including any form of resistance or protest via trade unions.

Figure 18.7 Current developments in behavioural control: the key elements

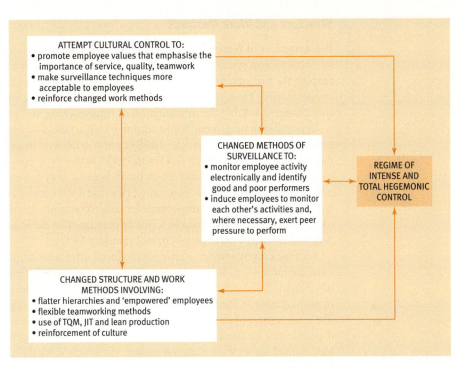

Figure 18.7 Current developments in behavioural control: the key elements

The objective is a total 'hearts and minds' approach, which results in employees embracing a highly personalised relationship with the organisation, with an individual's self-identity being derived from being part of the enterprise (Jermier *et al*. 1994). Effectively the firm becomes a family to which the employee has strong emotional and psychological ties and comes to accept that unswerving loyalty, intense effort and unquestioning obedience must be given to remain part of the family. In short, a system of totalised control in which any allegiances to other bodies, such as unions or occupational or professional bodies, is abandoned.

Cultural change is not easily accomplished and the ways of trying to do this are outlined in Chapter 19. It is important to stress again that the aim of cultural control is to control hearts and minds and, as Sewell (1998) notes, this is greatly

Hegemonic control:
control exercised by
an elite body whose
power is accepted as
supreme

facilitated by replacing earlier forms of bureaucratic control with *hegemonic control* (Rosen and Baroundi 1992). While bureaucratic control is really a rudimentary form of hegemonic control, which extracts compliance in a very unobtrusive way by using apparently neutral rules that are considered to be legitimate by employees, true hegemonic control is much more personal. It exists when people come to believe that a source of authority is near infallible. Thus, employees adopt a set of values that leads them to believe that managers and workers are both on the same side, pulling in the same direction and towards the same common goals. For this reason managers come to be seen as leaders whose instructions also represent the interests of the workforce. This removes the need for a set of behavioural rules because employees can deduce rules to fit any situation by simply asking themselves 'What is it that the manager wants?'

Structure and Work Methods

For a number of reasons that are largely economic, total quality management, just-in-time and lean production often feature strongly in current work systems. However, reaping the full advantages of these methods is acutely dependent on people working cooperatively. Thus, they are usually accompanied by structural and work organisation changes, notably the introduction of teamworking and empowerment.

In popular management books teamworking tends to be presented as a humanistic act that frees workers from the drudgery of job designs based on scientific management principles (Katzenbach and Smith 1993). In theory, employees become more committed, highly motivated and trustworthy because they have feelings of self-control, personal effectiveness and autonomy (Tjosvold 1991) and its main advantage is that it makes people personally responsible for task accomplishment. However, teamworking often conceals the restrictions of scientific management behind a rhetoric of emancipation and enhances managerial control (Sinclair 1992).

Because empowerment is often introduced after a workforce has been cut to the bare minimum, it is less of an opportunity for self-development than an imperative or obligation for people continually to improve their performance in order to stay in employment (Claydon and Doyle 1996). At first sight, therefore, while it looks like a relaxation of control, at a psychological level the reverse is true. Nevertheless, if people can be persuaded that they have really been empowered, and accept this idea within the culture outlined earlier, the result is likely to be highly significant. Employees will achieve goals set by managers by making the decisions management want them to make, and will believe that they have made the decisions of their own free will. Thus, a high degree of behavioural control is achieved in a nearly invisible way (Willmott 1993).

Monitoring (Surveillance)

Direct monitoring of employees is very expensive and is a contradiction of the rhetoric of empowerment. Nevertheless, managers have a tendency to feel that they are not 'in control' unless employee behaviour is monitored in some way (Felstead *et al.* 2003), which poses the problem identified by Sewell (1998) – 'How do you achieve control without appearing to control?' The answer lies in new surveillance technologies.

Vertical surveillance: a person's actions are monitored by someone above him or her in the organisational hierarchy

Horizontal surveillance: a person's actions are monitored by someone at the same level, who is part of the same workgroup

Poster (1990) argues that technology has enabled highly sophisticated surveillance methods to emerge that are so unobtrusive that they tend to go unnoticed. Moreover, the facility for electronic monitoring of employee activities is advancing by leaps and bounds and management's interest in remaining 'in control' is so strong that some of the latest advances are highly dubious in ethical terms. For instance, there is the reported case of a lecturer in cybernetics at Reading University who was approached by an American company to design a microchip that could be implanted under the skin of employees, to track their movements throughout the working day (Welch 1999).

Sewell (1998) points out that many of the emerging work systems that make use of teamworking by employees contain two certain principal forms of surveillance:

- *vertical surveillance*, by people above the employee in the hierarchy using electronic monitoring of individual performance;
- *horizontal surveillance*, by other people in a workgroup, who observe each other and exert peer pressure on individuals to perform.

Horizontal surveillance is the most significant feature of the new control methods. Instead of monitoring the outputs of a work system, monitoring is shifted to within the system itself. In effect, people oversee the efforts of each other, which is relatively cheap. It enables closed-loop control at all the stages within a work system, and so the system as a whole is much nearer to being controlled by open-loop methods.

A number of authors have commented on the effects that this has on people who work under these conditions. Far from being the emancipated, empowered and self-actualising experience that is claimed for it, teamworking often turns out to be a highly stressful set of conditions that sets worker against worker (Parker and Slaughter 1988; Taylor *et al.* 2003). The whole process is made possible by attempting to manipulate cultures to promote the values and attitudes outlined above. If this is successful, it is seen as the natural order of things and workers are induced to police each other's actions, which means they are subject to an immensely tighter control regime.

Resistance in the New Control Regimes

As noted earlier, the cultural component of new methods of control is designed to remove employee resistance and one school of thought argues that managers have been highly successful in doing this (see Casey 1999). Conversely, there is an argument that when managers introduce new methods of control, employees find new forms of resistance that remain hidden from managers for some time. The middle view, which for the time being appears to be the most pragmatic, is that while it is too soon to tell whether resistance has withered away (Thompson and Ackroyd 1995), there is an emerging body of evidence to show that it may have taken on a new form. Collinson (1994), for example, points out that workplace resistance can manifest itself in two ways:

Resistance through persistence: an aggressive or assertive and overt way of resisting control

Resistance through distance: a defensive way of resisting control by psychologically opting out

- *Resistance through persistence*, in which employees go on the offensive.
- *Resistance through distance*, which is a defensive form in which people create their own physical and emotional space to opt out psychologically.

For the present it seems to be true that the first of these is largely absent. Nevertheless, a number of authors point out that in place of the overt resistance of earlier times, employees seem to have found ways of undermining the new control regimes that are equally as subtle as management's new ways of trying to exercise control (see Bain and Taylor 2000; Geary and Dobbins 2001; Knights and McCabe 2000; Timmons 2003). In particular, Jermier *et al.* (1994) identify the following as employee actions that can have this effect:

- sabotage, pilfering and whistle-blowing;
- bloody mindedness (being obstructive), legal retaliation and output restriction;
- developing counter-cultures, rumour mongering and refusal to accept autonomy and discretion.

With the exception of the first line, it can be noted that none of these are overt acts of defiance that would justify dismissal. The others are all what used to be called 'dumb insolence' and, as many managers have found out to their cost, there is no answer to this.

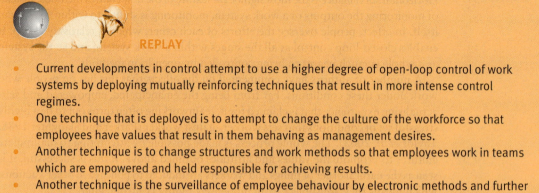

REPLAY

- Current developments in control attempt to use a higher degree of open-loop control of work systems by deploying mutually reinforcing techniques that result in more intense control regimes.
- One technique that is deployed is to attempt to change the culture of the workforce so that employees have values that result in them behaving as management desires.
- Another technique is to change structures and work methods so that employees work in teams which are empowered and held responsible for achieving results.
- Another technique is the surveillance of employee behaviour by electronic methods and further surveillance by group members who exert peer pressure on individuals to behave in ways desired by managers.
- These steps tend to result in more stressful working environments and there are suggestions that employees resist these controls in covert ways.

OVERVIEW AND CONCLUSIONS

If large complex organisations are to achieve their goals and objectives, it is necessary to coordinate activities, which means that control of some sort is vital. Humans react to attempts to bring their behaviour under control and have their own interpretations about why this control is applied. Thus, even though control is often portrayed as a neutral activity, those who are controlled do not necessarily interpret matters in this way.

The control activity can be viewed from a number of different perspectives. Managers tend to believe that controlling the activities of others is a prerogative that comes with the job, while political theorists point out that control cannot be divorced from the use of power and is often used for exploitative purposes. Between these two extremes lies the open systems perspective, which views control as necessary, but also acknowledges that it can have unforeseen consequences and is capable of being used for exploitation. Since control can be viewed as something that is intended to aid an organisation in achieving its goals, it is strongly connected with the process of goal setting. Thus, each item of organisational performance which is important enough to have goals should ideally have an associated control system.

Many of the control activities in organisations attempt to regulate human behaviour and, since control is normally exercised by supervisors and managers, it cannot sensibly be divorced from the use of power.

A wide range of methods have been developed to try to bring human behaviour under control in organisations. For example, recruitment, selection and socialisation seek to regulate the quality of human resource inputs. Appraisal and other output control methods are deployed to review performance and, where necessary, training and development are used to modify the qualitative attributes of people. Direct supervision, technology and job design, rewards and punishments, certain aspects of structure and, more recently, manipulation of organisational culture are also methods of controlling human behaviour. However, people often have emotional reactions to attempted control and there are arguments that a degree of resistance is commonplace.

Current developments in organisational control tend to result in more intensive control regimes. These use a number of mutually reinforcing elements which seek to obtain the ultimate degree of behavioural control – control of hearts and minds. It is not surprising, therefore, that some scholars argue that these can result in new forms of resistance that might ultimately turn out to be extremely difficult, if not impossible, to handle.

FURTHER READING

Berry, A J, J Broadbent and D Otley (1995) *Management Control: Themes, Issues and Practices*, London: Macmillan. A wide-ranging book written from what is basically a managerialist perspective, but which nevertheless gives good coverage of the topic.

Collinson, D L (1994) 'Strategies of resistance: power, knowledge and subjectivity in the workplace', in J M Jermier, D Knights and W R Mond (eds) *Resistance and Power in Organisations*, London: Routledge. A penetrating chapter which deals with employee resistance to control in organisations.

Etzioni, A (1975) *A Comparative Analysis of Complex Organisations: On Power, Involvement and their Correlates*, New York: Free Press. A revision by the author of his earlier (1964) text, in which he further develops the idea that an organisation's relationship with its employees is strongly influenced by the way power is used and the way that this engenders characteristic patterns of attachment by organisational members. A useful basic text that explains the underpinnings of control and resistance.

Johnson, P and J Gill (1993) *Management Control and Organisational Behaviour*, London: Sage. The book has a focus on organisational structure, culture and power. It uses these to explore the use of formal control systems and behavioural control.

Mitchell, D (1979) *Control without Bureaucracy*, London: McGraw-Hill. A useful text on industrial organisation that takes a humanistic stance on the matter of control.

Purcell, J and R Smith (eds) (1979) *The Control of Work*, London: Macmillan. A penetrating analysis of control from an industrial relations perspective.

Rosen, M and J Baroundi (1992) 'Computer based technology and the emergence of new forms of control', in A Sturdy, D Knights and H Willmott (eds) *Skill and Consent: Contemporary Studies in the Labour Process*, London: Routledge. A penetrating chapter that fully explores emerging systems of behavioural control.

Thompson, P and D McHugh (1995) *Work Organisation: A Critical Introduction*, 2nd edn, London: Macmillan. A book that has an excellent chapter on power and control.

REVIEW AND DISCUSSION QUESTIONS

1. Define what is meant by the word 'control' in an organisational context. What are the purposes of control in an organisation?

2. Describe the connection between planning and control.

3. Compare and contrast the managerialist, open systems and political perspectives on control in organisations.

4. Explain the difference between open-loop and closed-loop control. What are the respective functions of the following components in closed-loop control: actuator, sensor, feedback path and comparator?

5. Explain the connection between power and organisational control. Why is it impossible to divorce power from control in an organisational context?

6. Describe eight methods that have traditionally been used to try to bring human behaviour under control in organisations. Which of these methods are most frequently used in combination?

7. Describe recent developments in behavioural control in organisations and explain why the use of these is likely to result in more intense control regimes.

Chapter 19

Organisational Cultures and Climates

LEARNING OUTCOMES

After studying this chapter you should be able to:

- define and understand the nature of organisational culture, its historical roots, how it is maintained and replicated and how it affects the behaviour of organisational members

- describe a traditional (Peters and Waterman) perspective on organisational culture and contrast this with the more recent (Goffe and Jones) contingency framework

- describe the methodology and techniques that can be deployed in culture change initiatives

- define the nature of organisational climate, describe its antecedents and consequences and its effect on the behaviour of organisational members

- compare and contrast the concepts of organisational culture and organisational climate

INTRODUCTION

The visible characteristics of an organisation can reveal a great deal about how it operates in a physical way, but this tells us little of how people experience organisational life. Nevertheless, if we ask people to describe what it is like to work for a firm they often reply in terms of their feelings or emotions, for example, by saying that it's a very dynamic firm or perhaps that it is chaotic. These people would be telling us something about their perceptions of the atmosphere in the firm, which is one of the less tangible facets of organisational life and is encompassed by the two concepts covered in this chapter: culture and climate.

The first to be considered is culture, a topic that came to the fore in the early 1980s, largely as a result of the appearance of a number of books and articles that linked organisational culture with commercial success. Since culture is rather intangible and difficult to define, the discussion commences with an explanation of the emerging consensus on what the term means which is followed by an exploration of its nature. Since organisational culture first came into prominence because of its assumed link with commercial success, the next matter to be examined is the evidence for this link. This is followed by an outline of some of the more influential theories and perspectives on culture and, since these mostly imply that some cultures are more beneficial than others, the topics of culture management and cultural change are examined. To round off the discussion a brief consideration of the effects of national cultures on organisations is given.

The second topic of the chapter is that of organisational climate. This is a more mature and well-developed concept, which deals with dynamic and changeable organisational features. Climate is defined and distinguished from culture and is then explored in greater depth by examining the nature, origins and outcomes of organisational climates. The chapter concludes by comparing and contrasting the concepts of culture and climate, together with an examination of the organisational implications of both.

ORGANISATIONAL CULTURE

The word 'culture' has been used by many different people to explain a variety of phenomena, and because each one tends to adopt a slightly different perspective there is no universally accepted definition. For example, in a survey of 58 published sources Ott (1989) identified over 70 different words or phrases used to define organisational culture. As such, the most appropriate way forward is to define how the word will be used in this chapter, which is:

> **a pattern of basic assumptions – invented, discovered or developed by a given group as it learns to cope with its problems of external adaption and internal integration – that has worked well enough to be considered valuable and, therefore, to be taught to new members as the correct way to perceive, think and feel in relation to those problems.**
> **(Schein 1992, p 9)**

Culture has been, and still is studied by several different disciplines, all of which have their own distinct approach. The main disciplines include **anthropology**, which can be defined as the study of human cultures and how they influence the structure and functioning of a society. **Sociology** adopts a somewhat different perspective, linking particular sets of values and beliefs to patterns of social action. **Social psychology** explains the internal dynamics of a social situation, focusing especially on how culture produces observable patterns of behaviour and the ways in which people communicate their expectations to each other. For example, the work of Martin and Power (1983) shows that stories and anecdotes are powerful vehicles for communicating the cultural values of an organisation.

THE NATURE OF ORGANISATIONAL CULTURE

The details of an organisation's culture are carried in people's minds and, even though they may not be aware of doing so, they use this information to interpret what surrounds them, and to judge whether it is right or wrong, appropriate or inappropriate. If these meanings are shared by all or most of the people in an organisation, it has definitive culture, but the details from which the meanings are constructed can exist at different levels of visibility – some are directly observable while others are nearly invisible. In this respect Schein (1990) conceptualises culture as a 'layered' phenomenon which has three interrelated levels of meanings: basic assumptions; values and beliefs; and artefacts and creations. This is shown diagrammatically in Figure 19.1.

Figure 19.1
Schein's layered conceptualisation of culture

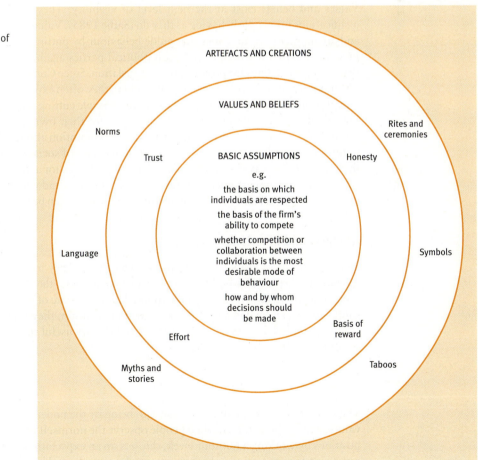

Basic Assumptions

These lie at the innermost core of a culture. In Schein's view they are fundamental beliefs that are so taken for granted that most people in a cultural unit subscribe to them but not in a conscious way. If we dig deep enough, it is not difficult to identify the basic assumptions in the cultures of different organisations. For instance, they are quite different in the major political parties in Great Britain. The Labour Party has an assumption that society is or should be a collective body, in which individuals should display a high degree of social responsibility towards each other. Conversely, Conservatives believe that the individual is paramount and their prime responsibility is their own welfare, an idea succinctly expressed in Margaret Thatcher's famous (or infamous, according to one's views) statement 'there is no such thing as society – only individuals'. Business organisations also tend to differ in the basic assumptions contained in their cultures, for example, about whether people deserve respect because of the position they hold or because of their skills and abilities; what lies at the root of the firm's ability to compete; or whether competition between individuals is a good thing or should be suppressed.

Values and Beliefs

Values and beliefs exist at the next level of visibility. They consist of reasons or justifications for people behaving as they do (Sathe 1985). Values are consciously held, and are moral or ethical codes that guide behaviour by putting the assumptions into practice. To use the example of British political parties again, values can be seen in their policy guidelines for programmes of legislation. Since Conservatives have a basic assumption about the primacy of the individual, they often express values that dictate how this should be reflected in legislation, for example cutting taxes and encouraging individuals to use the money to make provision for their own health insurance and retirement. Conversely, the Labour Party's basic assumption about collective responsibility strongly advocates the funding of state schemes of social security. Once again there are parallel ways in which values serve as guidelines for action in organisations, such as whether the customer's interests should come first, and whether conflict should be suppressed or is best brought out into the open where it can be handled and resolved.

Artefacts and Creations

These are the most visible manifestations of a culture. They include everything from the physical layout of a building to the way people dress, the way they talk to each other and, often, the things they talk about. Although some of these features are very subtle and it can be dangerous to view them in isolation, they often give vital clues about the underlying values and beliefs. It is therefore useful to distinguish between the different signs that can be used.

Norms

These are a code of behaviour brought into being by the underlying assumptions and values, and are perpetuated when people observe the norms. If people only reach high positions by working a 60-hour week, this sets up an expectation that these hours are a criterion for promotion, which permeates downwards and becomes accepted as the normal behaviour for ambitious people.

Language

The language people use can be a valuable indication of culture. For example, how managers talk to subordinates and vice versa can reveal much about the status values at work, and jargon and current 'buzzwords' are often used to signal who is accepted and who is not.

Symbols

Status symbols communicate social position and pecking order in the hierarchy, and their grandness gives a good indication about how much importance is attached to hierarchy as an organising principle.

Rites and Ceremonies

Formal and informal ceremonies abound in most organisations, and these often have important meanings for those involved. Retirement or farewell parties can be used to signal the idea of a happy family or a caring organisation. The ritual of taking a newcomer around and introducing the person to new colleagues is often a way of speeding up the integration process.

Myths and Stories

These are often a way of communicating core values and assumptions to people. Anecdotes are useful for this purpose because they often have an element of drama and are interesting to hear. Myths are stories that are partly fictional and are of questionable accuracy (Ott 1989) but, nevertheless, convey a central message in a more dramatic form and increase its salience.

Taboos

These signal what should not be done and an example is the story about the junior employee who addressed a director by his first name. This can be used to provide a humorous illustration for a newcomer that respect for someone higher up is a fundamental part of the culture.

TIME OUT

Carefully reflect on the organisation in which you work, either full-time or part-time. If you have no experience of being an employee use another organisation of which you are, or have been, a member. Using Schein's layered concept of culture, and starting with the most visible level, try to answer the questions below.

1. What artefacts and creations are there? For example, are there any identifiable norms of behaviour, particular language or mannerisms that are encouraged, or symbols, rites and ceremonies, myths, stories or taboos?
2. What basic values are indicated by the things you identified in question 1?
3. What are the basic assumptions underpinning the values you identified in question 2?

Although it has been convenient to describe all these signs separately, it is important to recognise that they complement each other and are often used in combination as reminders of what the culture is and what is expected. For instance, basic assumptions are often expressed in values and, in turn, artefacts, creations and visible behaviour are practical ways of expressing the values.

CHARACTERISTICS OF CULTURES

Pervasiveness or Homogeneity

In some respects the expression organisational culture is misleading. It conveys the impression that everyone in an organisation has common and uniform perceptions that guide their actions.

Martin (1992) distinguishes between three distinct perspectives on the nature of organisational cultures. The *integrationist perspective*, which is the way matters have been discussed in this chapter so far, sees culture as an organisation-wide set of values and beliefs that makes life less ambiguous for organisational members. This is the view that probably appeals most to managers, because it holds out the prospect of being a potent force to help deliver superior organisational performance. At the other extreme Martin identifies what she calls a *fragmentationist perspective*, in which organisations are so full of ambiguities and inconsistencies that they cannot be said to have a culture in the sense that has been used so far in this chapter. Rather, people respond in an *ad hoc* way to constantly changing conditions. Martin also identifies a middle-ground position, which she calls the *differentiationist perspective*. This acknowledges the possibility that within an organisation's overall culture there can be variations in which different groups of people have slightly different cultures. Here Sackman (1992) shows that there are often distinctly different subcultures within firms.

An interesting insight on Martin's ideas is given by Harris and Ogbonna (1998), who show that all three perspectives commonly exist side by side in different parts of the same organisation. Perhaps because they like to view the organisation as one big family, top managers tend to adopt an integrationist view, whereas middle managers, who are more sharply focused on their own functional roles or specialisms, have differentiationist perspectives. At the very bottom of an organisation, where people often have to keep their heads down and focus on their immediate tasks with no sight of a bigger picture, shopfloor workers are prone to take a fragmentationist view.

The evidence for the existence of subcultures in anything other than very small firms is overwhelming, and the larger the firm, the more likely it is that distinct subcultures will emerge. For example, in a study of a large Danish insurance company, Hofstede (1998) identified three highly distinctive subcultures (production, administrative and professional) that embraced virtually everyone in the organisation. In the light of this and other evidence, the currently prevailing view is that the differentiationist perspective presents the most realistic view of culture in organisations.

It can also be argued that the advantages accruing from having different subcultures outweigh any disadvantages. Subcultures give different perspectives, which makes

Integrationist perspective on culture: culture is an organisation-wide phenomenon which consists of shared values to which all or most employees subscribe

Fragmentationist perspective on culture: organisations are so full of ambiguities and inconsistencies that frames of reference are individual and constantly changing so culture is inherently unstable

Differentiationist perspective on culture: organisations are made up of different groups with their own subcultures

the 'groupthink' phenomenon described in Chapter 11 less likely. In addition, since subcultures are associated with the professional expertise and specialist perspectives of different groups, the resulting differences are of great organisational value. For instance, in a marketing department that deals with a very uncertain environment, a dynamic, thrusting subculture of risk taking can be just what is needed. However, to ensure that matters do not get out of hand, it is probably desirable to counterbalance this with the cautious, risk-averting subculture that is often found among accountants. After all, this is why specialists are employed – do we really expect accountants to have the same values as marketeers?

Strength of Culture

A recurring theme in popular texts is that strong cultures are associated with superior organisational performance (Deal and Kennedy 1982; Peters and Waterman 1982). Luthans (1995) argues that cultural strength is a function of two factors:

- **sharedness**, which corresponds to what has been described above as homogeneity and expresses the extent to which all organisational members have the same core values;
- **intensity**, which corresponds to the degree of commitment of all the people in the organisation to these values.

Taken together these imply that the strength of a culture needs to be assessed in a multidimensional way, which is probably a very sound point. However, Luthans' ideas about the factors that influence these dimensions are open to severe criticism. He states that both are a function of the way that an organisation rewards its members. This implies that they are under management's control and are easily manipulated by the judicious use of rewards and punishments, which grossly overestimates the extent to which deeply held values and beliefs can be controlled by external stimuli. In addition, Luthans somewhat uncritically accepts that a high degree of sharedness is desirable and, as was pointed out earlier, there are inherent dangers in having an organisational culture that is too homogeneous.

The most controversial point, however (and Luthans is by no means unique in this respect), is the way he accepts that a strong culture leads to organisational success. This point will be addressed in detail later, but for the present two brief points can be made. First, a strong culture may only be a good predictor of performance in the short term (Gordon and DiTomaso 1992). Second, it is only safe to assume that a strong culture is an aid to success if it is also an appropriate one, that is, one that is suitable for coping with the conditions faced by an organisation.

Cultural Evolution and Replication

Although it is important to be able to describe an organisation's culture accurately, two questions of equal significance are: how did the culture come to exist? and what forces are at work to enable it to persist in this state? The first of these is a matter of origins and evolution, where it should be noted that organisational members bring certain preconceived basic assumptions and values with them into work each day, many of which are part and parcel of the culture, customs and social values of the wider society within which the firm exists. Therefore national and, to some extent, regional cultures play a part in shaping organisational cultures, and there is a need for the culture of an organisation to be compatible with the national culture within which it exists.

Cultural Evolution

Schein (1983) argues that the history of an organisation inevitably has a huge impact on its culture and that some cultural elements can be traced back to the values and ideologies of a firm's founder. Those who bring organisations into existence often have a strong entrepreneurial disposition. They can be highly dynamic people who communicate their vision to others and, in the early days of a firm, they tend to attract and recruit a core of like-minded people. What emerges is a key group that has shared assumptions and values and, as the firm grows, these people become role models for new entrants.

Cultural patterns such as these can last a long time and may well persist for generations. For instance, certain British firms founded in the nineteenth century were set up by prominent Quaker industrialists who, because of their religious convictions, felt a sense of obligation and duty to their employees and attempted to mitigate many of the harsh industrial conditions of the day by devoting considerable financial resources and effort into improving the lot of the workforce. In these organisations welfare schemes, medical attention and, in one famous case, the building of a whole model village that took employees out of the slum conditions of the industrial revolution were put in place and, to some extent, this tradition of welfare paternalism carries on today. An imprint of the founder is still often encountered in firms, even if it only extends to a portrait in the entrance lobby. What remains, however, is seldom identical to the culture that existed in the early years – as firms grow they face new challenges and have to cope with these by adopting new structural forms and methods (Beekun and Glick 2001). They seem to go through what Schein calls a succession of 'hybridisation of culture' phases, in which there is always some link with the previous phase but additional elements of culture are adopted to cope with changed conditions. Clearly this is a slow and continuous process but, in one sense, the problems are the same at every stage. In Schein's view these are concerned with two generic problems: that of **ensuring external adaptation and survival** and that of **ensuring internal integration**. These in turn give rise to more specific problems which are summarised in Table 19.1. What emerges from this ongoing process is the core element of culture, the basic assumptions that consist of shared views on the solutions to these problems. Once adopted, these are held at a subconscious level and are so taken for granted that they are taught to new entrants to the organisation as the appropriate way to view things.

Cultural Replication

In the short run, cultures are maintained and replicated by the socialisation processes shown in Figure 19.2.

To a large extent, when new organisational members are selected, those who are allowed to enter are the ones who are perceived to fit in with what is already there. Later on, if some of them are viewed as deviating from what is required, they might well be deselected (removed). In cultural terms new entrants are seldom a perfect match and, almost immediately, another set of processes come into play. These are concerned with inducing these people to adopt the required feelings and behaviours and this occurs in a variety of ways.

Table 19.1 External and internal problems which, when resolved, partially determine organisational culture (adapted from Schein 1983)

Problem orientation	Potential problem
External problems to be resolved: those concerning adaption and survival	1 Developing consensus on the primary task, core mission and latent functions of the group, i.e. strategy 2 Consensus on goals, with goals being a reflection of core mission 3 Developing consensus on the means to be used to achieve goals, e.g. division of labour, organisation structure, reward systems etc. 4 Developing consensus on the criteria to measure how well the group is performing against its goals and targets, e.g. information and control systems 5 Developing consensus on remedial strategies that may be needed when the group is not achieving its goals
Internal problems to be resolved: those concerning internal integration	6 Common language and conceptual categories need to be derived so that group members can communicate with each other, without which group functioning is impossible 7 Consensus on group boundaries and criteria for inclusion and exclusion needed in order that one of the most important areas of culture (consensus on who is or is not part of the group and what criteria determine membership) are clear 8 Consensus on criteria for the allocation of power and status needed so that the organisation's pecking order, its rules for obtaining and retaining power, are understood in order that members can manage their own feelings of aggression 9 Consensus on criteria for intimacy, friendship and love so that rules for the way that peers relate to each other and relationships between the sexes are handled and the degrees of openness and intimacy that will be used in working on organisational tasks are clearly understood 10 Consensus on criteria for the allocation of rewards and punishments so that people in the group know what behaviours are lauded and what are deprecated, what rewards are available, what behaviours are punished by withdrawing rewards, up to and including exclusion from the group 11 Consensus on ideology and religion because, like societies, groups must have ways of giving meaning to 'unexplainable' events so that people are able to respond to them without feeling anxious in the face of the 'unexplainable'

Figure 19.2
Organisational socialisation

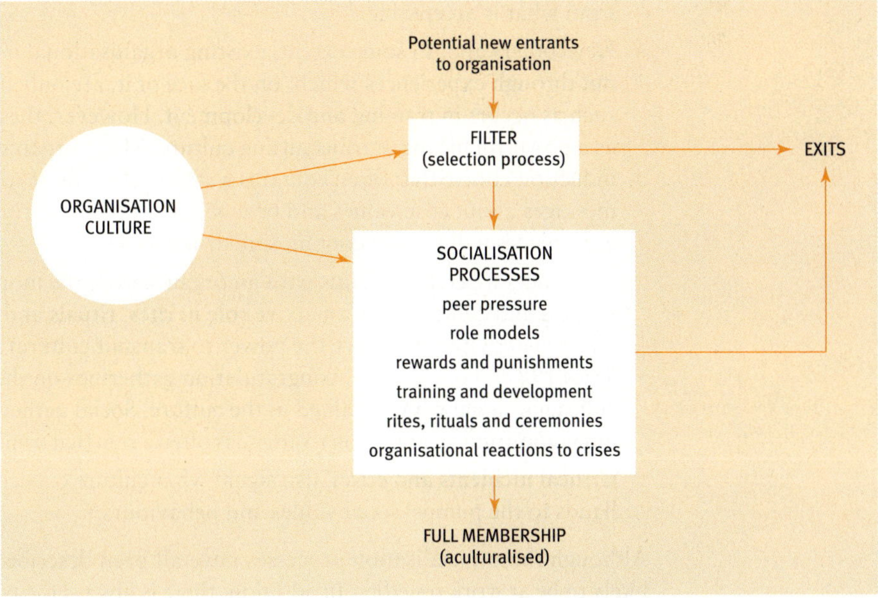

- As an immediate measure, those who are already members and have absorbed the organisation's culture pass on their knowledge so that newcomers 'learn the ropes'. Most newcomers view this in a positive way and inducting a new starter does a great deal to help the person settle in and come to know what is expected, which helps reduce any anxieties associated with starting a new job in unfamiliar surroundings (Reichers 1987).

- Most new entrants are likely to experience a certain amount of **peer pressure,** which can take the form of enquiries about how things were done at the previous place of employment which, if necessary, are followed up with pointed comments about how the new situation differs.

- Where cultures are very strong and existing members know that the newcomer will find things very different, a new recruit can purposely be put through experiences that seem designed to induce a degree of humility. For instance, the person might be given particularly onerous jobs to do, or perhaps have an extremely high workload. This tends to have the effect of making people question their own prior assumptions, which in turn makes them more open to accepting new norms and values (Pascale 1985).

- It is also common for a new entrant to pick up **role models** early on. For example, newcomers tend to be placed under the wing of a senior, trusted person for a while and it is natural for the newcomer to see him or her as someone who fits in well. This can lead to a feeling that arguments or potentially embarrassing incidents can be avoided by taking cues on how to behave from people such as this.

- As the newcomer becomes more familiar with the surroundings, the person also picks up clues about the **criteria for rewards and punishments,** which are salient reminders about what the culture requires. Rewards provide clear indications of the criteria that are used to evaluate performance and, by absorbing this knowledge, the routes to promotion, higher status and prestige can be learned. Conversely, punishment is an indication of behaviour that is viewed as deviating from what is acceptable.

- Newcomers and, to some extent, existing organisational members may well be put through experiences which, on the face of it, are only designed to teach skills, such as occurs in **training and development.** However, these processes also act as a powerful means of transmitting culture. Many organisations use a formal induction course that often contains a strong element of company history and messages about core values and beliefs. Later on, mentoring or specific training experiences will usually contain similar messages.

- The longer a person remains with an organisation, the more he or she is likely to witness and come to play an active role in **rites, rituals and ceremonies.** Rites are planned activities that have the power to transmit cultural norms (Beyer and Trice 1987). For example, congratulation gatherings on the promotion of a colleague signal what is valued in the culture. Social gatherings emphasise integration and an invitation to attend is often a sign that someone has been accepted.

- **Critical incidents and crises** also signal what culture expects, for instance, an 'all hands to the pumps' set of values and behaviours.

Although these socialisation processes have all been described separately, many are likely to be at work together. In addition, there is always the possibility that someone cannot adapt to the new culture and either exits voluntarily, or is asked to leave. It is also important to recognise that when someone does absorb the culture it does not mean that the person has become some sort of a clone. In most organisations there is a degree of tolerance and a degree of individual deviation, so long as core values and beliefs are not violated.

TIME OUT

In an earlier Time Out exercise you examined the culture of an organisation in which you work or, alternatively, the student body at your university or college. Take your analysis one stage further and answer the questions below.

1. How homogeneous is the culture? For example, does everybody seem to be part of the same culture, or are there different groups of people that have their own subculture? If so, how different are the subcultures?
2. How strong is the culture (and, if they exist, subcultures)?

The Effects of Culture on Organisational Performance

Although it is known that culture has a strong effect on people's behaviour, management's interest is less likely to be prompted by curiosity about why this happens than by its possible bottom-line effects on the commercial or financial performance of an organisation. To a large extent this interest was kindled by the writings of popular authors such as Peters and Waterman (1982), who view culture as a key component in the performance of successful companies. These ideas resulted in an increased awareness among managers of the potential effects of culture but, as is often the case (because these writings conveyed the impression that there is a 'one best culture'), a more dangerous turn of events was set in motion.

Unfortunately, managers have a tendency to look for 'off the shelf' solutions to organisational problems. Therefore, when the cultural characteristics of successful companies were set out in these books in a catchy, marketable and easily grasped way, there was an understandable tendency for some managers to believe that, at last, social science had come up with something of immense practical use – a sure-fire recipe for success.

However, other than in the writings of these popular authors, there is little evidence of a strong association between culture and organisational performance, and none whatsoever for a set of cultural characteristics that are likely to be appropriate in all circumstances. Indeed, when the firms held up as shining examples in the popular works were examined a few years later, no coherent link between culture and performance could be established (Hitt and Ireland 1987), and several of the firms were in serious financial difficulties.

There could be sound reasons why this is the case and these have been investigated by Miller (1994), who notes that after a successful period certain patterns of behaviour can appear in these firms, all of which have an impact on future success:

- **inertia**, in which they cling strongly to the past recipe for success, which may no longer be viable;
- **immoderation**, where very bold gambles are made, perhaps because previous success gives a feeling of invulnerability;

- **inattention**, which is similar to a form of institutional 'groupthink', where top managers only pay attention to a very restricted range of signals about what occurs in the environment;
- **insularity**, where there is a failure to adapt to the environment, even where the signs that this is necessary are readily available.

It is similarly important to recognise that the idea of a 'one best culture' is oversimplistic and is misleading enough to be potentially dangerous. To this end Kilmann *et al*. (1985) reason that the following three features of a culture can affect performance:

Cultural direction: the extent to which an organisation's culture helps it achieve its goals

- *Cultural direction*, which expresses the extent to which a culture actually helps an organisation achieve its goals and here Kilmann *et al*. note that cultures can be either positive and facilitate goal achievement, or negative and inhibit it. For instance, where markets have become highly volatile, it can be argued that cultural norms and values of flexibility and shared responsibility are needed.

Cultural pervasiveness: the homogeneity of an organisation's culture

- *Cultural pervasiveness*, which denotes the extent to which an organisational culture is homogeneous. To some extent subcultures are probably inevitable, which has some potential benefits. However, if the subcultures are very different and this leads to intergroup conflicts, people can spend more time in internecine warfare than in pulling in the same direction.

Cultural strength: the influence of a culture on the behaviour of organisational members

- *Cultural strength*, which expresses the influence it has on the behaviour of people. A culture that is positive and strong will clearly have a most beneficial impact, while one that is strong and negative is likely to have adverse consequences.

Because it takes time to socialise people into an organisation, one factor that can rapidly dilute cultural strength is staff turnover. Unfortunately, many firms have a regrettable tendency to shed staff when the organisation hits a bad patch and to hire fresh employees when an upturn arrives. Thus, they can deprive themselves of the strong culture that

REPLAY

- Culture is one of the less tangible features of an organisation and is carried in the minds of organisational members.
- It can be thought of as a layered phenomenon with largely invisible basic assumptions at its core, values that arise out of the basic assumptions as the next level outwards, and visible artefacts and creations that express the culture on the surface.
- Different perspectives exist on whether organisational culture is pervasive throughout a whole organisation or whether subcultures exist, but strong cultures (provided that they are appropriate to an organisation's circumstances) are usually acknowledged to be beneficial in terms of organisational performance.
- The roots of a culture can often be located in an organisation's history, but culture is usually sustained and replicated by socialisation of new organisational members and resocialisation of people as culture adjusts to changing circumstances.

they need to take advantage of an upturn, to say nothing of the demoralising effects redundancies have on the culture of those who remain.

PERSPECTIVES ON CULTURE

Smircich (1983) distinguishes five different streams of research that link the concepts of culture and organisation. Although these all have their own underlying assumptions, she also points out that they can be divided into two strongly contrasting schools of thought. The first is what will be called here the *key variable or application school*. This makes use of open systems ideas and views an organisation as something that has to acquire the right properties to remain in balance with its environment. Viewed this way, culture is a property in the same way that structure and size are properties that enable an organisation to cope with environmental demands; that is, culture is something an organisation 'has'. A key assumption of this school is that culture is a crucial ingredient of organisational success. It allows the firm to marshal the commitment of its members to achieving the firm's goals and so it is similar to Martin's (1992) integrationist perspective. Since this offers the prospect of using culture to influence organisational performance, it is the perspective that has the strongest appeal to managers and has given rise to a considerable volume of work in the area, the vast majority of which has attempted to identify cultures that promote success, and how to obtain these cultural characteristics (Kanter 1995). In non-academic circles this is by far the most influential school and it spawned a growth industry for organisational development practitioners who have long sought to manipulate cultures to serve the interests of management (see Chapter 21).

The second approach is what Smircich calls the culture as a *root metaphor school*. This views culture as something that an organisation 'is'. It is less concerned with trying to link culture with organisational performance than with trying to understand how cultures are experienced by organisational members, and how this affects the way they behave. While research in this area has great appeal to academics, it finds far less favour with managers, probably because the accounts are difficult to understand and are far too deep and complex for their tastes. Therefore, the better-known perspectives are firmly located in the application school, one of which will be described in what follows. Before giving this description however, it is important to point out that the ideas appeared nearly twenty years ago, and are what could be described as the views of the 'founding fathers' of the cultural movement. In academic circles these are widely acknowledged to be incomplete, if not downright simplistic. Nevertheless, many managers still cling tenaciously to them and it is necessary for the reader to have some appreciation of the origins of these ideas.

Peters and Waterman: The Characteristics of 'Excellent' Companies

The management interest in organisational culture was greatly stimulated by the publication of Peters and Waterman's (1982) best-seller, *In Search of Excellence*. The two authors, who were management consultants, set out to document management practices that they felt accounted for the superior performance of a number of highly successful American companies. One of their major conclusions was that these organisations all had similar cultures, the eight chief characteristics of which are shown in Table 19.2.

Key variable (application) school: culture is viewed as an organisational property (something an organisation has) that can be changed at will

Root metaphor school: culture is assumed to reflect the essence of what an organisation 'is'

Table 19.2 Peters and Waterman – the attributes of excellent companies

Attributes or characteristics	Example
Bias for action	Decisions get made, even in the absence of complete information
Staying close to the customer	The customer is regarded as the source of most of the valuable information the company needs to guide its actions
Autonomy and entrepreneurship	The company is often divided into smaller, more manageable business units to foster innovation and initiative
Productivity through people	People should be treated with dignity and respect and be given opportunities
Hands-on management	Senior managers maintain close contact with operational levels, often by 'walking the floor'
Sticking to the knitting	The company refrains from entering areas of business outside its competence and expertise
Simple form: lean staff	Flat structures with few levels of management and relatively small numbers of headquarters personnel
Simultaneous loose–tight organisation	Tightly knit in terms of common values held by people and at the same time loosely organised in terms of absence of rules and regulations

Bias for Action

Peters and Waterman noted that successful firms have a strong bias for action and outperformed firms where this is absent, for example, managers are expected to make decisions, even in the absence of full information.

Staying Close to the Customer

The authors argue that firms where the customer is valued above all else outperform firms without this frame of reference. Where this viewpoint is held the customer is seen as a source of information about the quality of current products and a source of ideas about products for the future. Thus meeting and, where necessary, pandering to customers' needs is argued to be an action that leads inevitably to superior performance.

Autonomy and Entrepreneurship

Peters and Waterman argue that while successful firms are often very large they actively fight tendencies towards bureaucracy and lack of innovation. This is accomplished by dividing the firm into small, manageable units which are encouraged to be independent and creative within their respective areas.

Productivity through People

The authors note that successful firms have a genuine recognition that their most important assets are people at all levels, and this gets translated into committed action.

Hands-on Management

In many large companies senior managers tend to lose touch with the fundamentals of the firm, but Peters and Waterman note that successful firms purposely try to counter this tendency by encouraging the view that the best way to manage is to stay in contact with what goes on by 'walking the floor' rather than exercising control from behind closed doors.

Stick to the Knitting

Another value that is said to characterise excellent firms is a reluctance to become involved in business outside their spheres of expertise. There is a strong emphasis on relying on the firm's core competencies and doing well what it does best.

Simple Form, Lean Staff

Unlike many organisations where managers measure their status, prestige and importance by the number of their subordinates, Peters and Waterman noted that successful firms have fewer layers of administrative staff and relatively small groups of headquarters personnel. In what the authors call 'excellent' companies, a person's importance is measured by his or her impact on the organisation's performance rather than the size of his or her empire.

Simultaneously Loose and Tight Organisation

The final attribute identified by Peters and Waterman looks like a contradiction at first sight – how can something be loosely and tightly organised at the same time? What is meant by a loose and tight organisation is connected to the core values. In one sense they are tightly organised because everyone understands and believes in the firm's values, and these provide the glue that holds the firm together. However, in a physical sense they have fewer staff and fewer rules and regulations, which means they are loosely organised. Peters and Waterman argue that the loose physical structure is only possible because of the strong common value system. Thus the tight structure of common cultural values facilitates the loose control structure which is said to encourage innovation and risk taking.

Comments on the Peters and Waterman Contribution

Peters and Waterman's work has attracted strong criticism for its lack of rigour in terms of research methodology, and it has been forcefully argued that the link between cultures, excellence and performance is tenuous and highly fragile. Some of the so-called excellent companies subsequently encountered huge performance difficulties and, in addition, there are severe criticisms of some of the cultural characteristics used by Peters and Waterman. For instance Silver (1987) is particularly scathing about the reality of the 'people orientation' in some of the firms, and in a descriptive parody entitled 'McFactory' cites McDonald's as an example of one of the companies identified as 'excellent'. He notes that McFactory relies heavily on cheap, minimum-wage, non-unionised labour, which is usually made up of teenage workers in part-time employment. Behind the façade of what is portrayed as a stimulating work environment there is a reality of dull monotony, where the emphasis is on deskilling the work by using the principle of scientific management so that the last ounce of effort can be extracted from employees (Silver 1987).

Notwithstanding these criticisms, the Peters and Waterman research played an important part in stimulating interest in organisational culture and this was accompanied by other work in the same style, which, for interest, is given in the further readings at the end of this chapter. However, things have moved on since then and it is to more recent developments that attention must now be directed.

A Recent Perspective: The Goffee and Jones Contingency Framework

The Peters and Waterman (1982) perspective was firmly part of what is now known as the 'excellence movement', which holds that culture is a key ingredient in the commercial success of an organisation. Because the authors list cultural characteristics that are said to lead to this outcome, it is easy to see why the ideas have an instant appeal to managers. The problem, however, is that this perspective and others like it imply a 'one best culture' suitable for all organisations. This is a rather simplistic idea and although culture almost certainly has a part to play in organisational performance, it is only likely to have this effect if it helps in coping with the circumstances that confront an organisation. Since different organisations face different circumstances, the most useful approach to the culture–performance relationship is likely to be a contingency perspective, a matter that is addressed in a more recent development by Goffee and Jones (1998), who start with an assumption there is no such thing as a 'right' or 'best' culture for all organisations. Rather, the most appropriate culture for an organisation is the one that best helps it cope with the exigencies of its business environment.

Goffee and Jones commence their analysis by giving a framework for classifying the characteristics of different organisational cultures. To do this they return to a stream of sociological work by Durkheim (1966), from which they extract two basic dimensions that reflect the way that humans relate to each other: sociability and solidarity.

Sociability: the degree of friendliness between members of a community or group

Sociability

This expresses the degree of friendliness between members of a community or group and where sociability is high, people help each other because they want to, with no thought of favours in return. This dimension of the relationship between people is essentially based on feelings and emotions and where it exists, people tend to value the relationship for its own sake. While those immersed in a relationship of this type sometimes take it for granted, it is usually recognised by a newcomer to an organisation as something special. For instance, if one person has a reason to celebrate, they all celebrate; if someone has a reason to feel low, everyone tends to rally round; when people go into hospital they are visited by colleagues, and the people often socialise away from work.

The advantages to an organisation of a high degree of sociability in its culture are said to be:

- high morale, because most people working in these conditions find work a pleasure and work is viewed as fun;

- it fosters teamwork, creativity, openness and sharing of ideas and because they genuinely want to help each other rather than simply look good, people are likely to go beyond their formal job requirements;
- it promotes innovation and uninhibited cross-fertilisation of ideas;
- people seldom have a mentality of being there for the shortest possible time, but work until the job is done.

Nevertheless, high sociability can have its downside because:

- strong friendships can mean that poor performance is tolerated and people can be reluctant to disagree with or criticise friends;
- in extreme cases it can degenerate into cliques, cabals, in-groups and out-groups, which results in behind-the-scenes politicking;
- it can be an unpleasant situation for people who value their own personal space and privacy of thought.

Solidarity

Solidarity: the degree of collectiveness in the relationships between people

This dimension is not so much a reflection of people's feelings and emotions, but their thoughts. It expresses the degree of collectiveness (as opposed to individuality) in the relationships between people. Where solidarity is high people have a sense of common purpose because they have shared goals, tasks or mutual interests. Thus, even if people do not particularly like or admire their colleagues, they tend to make common cause and work together like a well-oiled machine. Its advantages are said to be:

- a ruthless commitment to getting done what (by consensus) needs to get done;
- many people find it stimulating to work towards and achieve mutually agreed goals and the behaviour of other people is a constant reminder of the behaviours that are considered acceptable;
- people are usually very clear about the rewards for good behaviour.

Again, however, solidarity can have its dark side:

- cultures that are high in solidarity can be ruthless in suppressing dissenters, even when they are also innovators;
- too strong a focus on group goals can oppress or hurt individuals.

Using high and low values for sociability and solidarity, the two dimensions can be brought together to give a matrix of four cultural types, which Goffee and Jones call the 'Double "S" Cube' (Figure 19.3). Notice that there is a third dimension (depth) to the matrix. This reflects the idea that sociability and solidarity can have positive and negative aspects, the latter being expressed in the far (shaded) end of the cube. The four cultural types and the environmental circumstances for which they are said to be most appropriate are described in what follows.

The Communal Culture

Communal culture: one that is high in sociability and solidarity

While this is most frequently found in thrusting, successful, small to medium-sized organisations, it is occasionally found in larger firms that have taken great care to retain a culture of this type since their early, formative years. Examples cited by the authors

Figure 19.3 'The Double "S" Cube' from Goffe, R and Jones, G (1998) *The Character of a Corporation*, copyright © by Rob Goffee and Gareth Jones. Reprinted by permission of HarperCollins Publishers Ltd and HarperCollins, Inc.

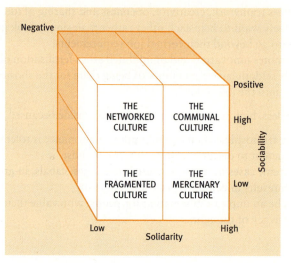

are Hewlett-Packard and the pharmaceutical company Johnson & Johnson. Strong sociability results in people working in a highly collaborative, flexible and mutually supportive way, and their high solidarity unites them in a common sense of purpose. Thus, there is a strong ethos of people being protective of the organisation and what it stands for or, as Goffee and Jones put it, 'the competition tends to be seen as an enemy that needs to be defeated' (1998, p 29). Since maintaining a communal culture in a large organisation is difficult, a great deal of emphasis is placed on careful selection of new entrants, with only those who are perceived to 'fit in' being admitted. In addition, extensive and somewhat intensive induction programmes are used to inculcate the core values of the organisation and appraisal is not only against performance targets, but also adherence to the desired organisational ethos.

The Networked Culture

Networked culture: one that is high in sociability and low in solidarity

This culture, which is high in sociability but low in solidarity, is said to be most appropriate for large organisations that face highly competitive environments. Typically the critical success factor in these industries is a free and open flow of information across functional, geographic or even national boundaries and examples cited by the authors are Unilever, Heineken and the international electrical giant Philips. The culture is often found in large, highly successful companies which perhaps had communal cultures at an earlier stage of development. Because it is hard to retain the right balance of sociability and solidarity to sustain a communal culture, there is a natural transformation to the networked type of organisation. Even so, there is often a strong legacy of sociability and people expect to be friendly with their colleagues.

The Mercenary Culture

Mercenary culture: one that is low on sociability and high on solidarity

Organisations of this type are low on sociability but high on solidarity, and this culture is said to be most beneficial in a fast-changing business environment where competitive pressures are extremely high. In these circumstances success and even survival can depend on establishing priorities, goals and strategies to beat off the competition, and an ability to move quickly, decisively and cohesively can be all important. Because solidarity is high the culture tends to promote an 'all hands to the pumps' mentality, but this is unencumbered by a compulsion to maintain friendly relations with everybody, which allows the relentless pursuit of effectiveness and efficiency to become the norm. Organisations of this type tend to be highly goal-orientated and goals are usually ambitious and specific – not just improve market share, but improve market share by 10 per cent each year. Here the examples identified by the authors are the confectionery giant Mars, PepsiCo and the financial conglomerate Citicorp. These organisations can be extremely demanding of their employees and the lack of sociability might mean that people only cooperate with each other when they can see a clear personal benefit in doing so. While people are probably well rewarded, the organisation can be merciless and intolerant of those who do not achieve and so people tend not to remain with the organisation for too long.

The Fragmented Culture

Fragmented culture: one that is low on both sociability and solidarity

This culture is low on sociability and solidarity. It applies to companies in which interdependence between the different activities is low and the critical success factor is having employees who are the star individuals in a particular field. In these circumstances sociability and solidarity are unlikely to have strong effects on performance and organisations of this type tend to be relatively small in terms of staffing levels, for instance, law firms, consultancies or merchant banks. However, this culture is sometimes found in much larger organisations that subcontract or outsource most of their activities, for example, the clothing manufacturer Benetton, or franchised operations such as fast-food chains.

An Appraisal of the Goffee and Jones Framework

The Goffee and Jones framework is an important advance in the study of organisational cultures. Because it is a true contingency theory, it does much to enhance the utility of the culture concept and since it fits well with other work in the area it is not a 're-invention of the wheel', but a genuine advance in the body of knowledge. This can perhaps be best illustrated by drawing attention to a number of important implications that arise from the work.

- Although the authors state that an organisation's dominant culture can usually be categorised as one of the four types described above, they also point out that subcultures are almost certain to exist in most organisations. Thus they avoid the pitfall of treating culture as an undifferentiated whole, and this is in line with other important work in the area.

- They point out that no culture is likely to last forever. Indeed, they put forward the idea that there seems to be a natural life cycle with three of the four cultural types and that this is connected to the changes that inevitably take place as an organisation grows and develops. Companies often start out with communal cultures, which fits well with Schein's (1983) ideas about the effect that the founder of an organisation has on its culture. As it grows, it meets new challenges and for this reason there is probably a natural progression to the networked type in many organisations. Later on, however, complacency can set in and the organisation can come under siege by its competitors. Thus, emergency measures may be needed, which prompts a move to the mercenary culture.

- Goffee and Jones explicitly point out that none of the cultures is inherently good or bad in itself. Sociability and solidarity can both result in human behaviour that is dysfunctional for an organisation in certain circumstances. Thus it is the blend of these two dimensions at a certain point in time that is important. For this reason, the cultural types are more (or less) appropriate at coping with the different environmental exigencies that can be encountered by organisations.

- Although Goffee and Jones do not specifically address the matter of difference in national cultures, they draw attention to the idea that these can have an impact on the cultural type with which an organisation is likely to feel most at ease. For example, in contrasting Procter and Gamble and Unilever, which are direct competitors facing almost identical competitive pressures, they note that the former has long had characteristics typical of the mercenary culture, whereas Unilever has only recently made moves in this direction. The important difference here is that Procter and Gamble is an American organisation, while Unilever is Anglo-Dutch. American organisations are much more likely to be at home with the centralisation of authority, a high task focus, ruthless internal competition and the 'all shoulders to the wheel' ethos of the mercenary culture. European organisations, however, have a much stronger focus on relationships and decentralised authority, both of which characterise the networked culture.

- Finally, although the authors deal with the matter of changing organisational cultures, they avoid the trap of understating the problems involved. Thus, while they view change as possible, which puts them firmly in what has been called earlier the 'application' school, they do not suggest, as do so many others in this school, that culture can be manipulated in an easy way. Indeed, they are at great pains to point out that cultural change is often prompted by a crisis, which itself brings about a degree of modification to culture.

TIME OUT

Before reading the next section, re-examine the culture you explored in the two previous Time Out exercises and answer the questions below.

1. Is the culture an appropriate one from the point of view of:
   (a) the employees (or students)?
   (b) the organisation or institution?
2. If your answer to questions 1(a) and 1(b) is yes, how can this culture be maintained?
3. If your answer to questions 1(a) or 1(b) is no, what changes in culture do you feel the organisation would like to see?
4. How can these changes be brought about?

CASE STUDY 19.1: StereoCo

StereoCo is a large manufacturer of personal computers and peripheral equipment. This is a fast-moving business where products rapidly become outdated. However, computer manufacture seldom involves more than assembly of bought-in components. Therefore the firm uses a matrix structure in which design, marketing and production staffs often work together under a product manager. To keep in touch with the market, managers from all functions are strongly encouraged to visit customers (usually large retailers and dealers) and so StereoCo is always fast off the mark in bringing out new and innovative products. These visits often result in ideas for new products, and staff are encouraged to pursue their ideas. While the composition of a product team tends to be constantly changing, managers and supervisors at all levels are expected to take a proactive stance in getting to know subordinates and to operate an 'open door' policy to deal with their concerns.

It is the organisation's policy to stay strictly within the 'personal computer' market, and so there is little temptation to become involved in areas such as mainframe computers. Indeed, an often quoted saying in the organisation is that 'We know what we do best, and our aim is to do it better than anyone else!' People are expected to be highly flexible in what they do and, if there is a problem to be solved, to put this before everything else, even family responsibilities. However, employees are extremely well paid and 15 per cent of the organisation's annual net profit is set aside to be shared among employees as a bonus.

Question

Using an appropriate published approach for evaluating culture, say whether StereoCo has a culture that is likely to lead to commercial success.

CULTURE CHANGE AND CULTURE MANAGEMENT

Culture change: modification of an existing culture

Culture management: maintaining or making slight modifications to fine-tune an existing culture

If it is accepted that culture has an important influence on the success of an organisation, managers clearly have a vested interest in being able to influence culture. This can be done in one of two ways: by modifying the existing culture through *culture change*, or using *culture management* to retain one that is felt to be appropriate. However, to regard either of these as a practical possibility it is necessary to assume that culture is something that can be changed at will. This idea still provokes heated debate, and nowhere is it more apparent than in the suggestion that all employees throughout an organisation can be induced to embrace a market-orientated culture; a very fashionable 'must have' in many organisations (Greenley and Foxall 1996). The assumption is that a culture of this type will result in superior organisational performance (Selnes *et al.* 1996). While this may just be a bid for increased power on the part of marketeers in organisations, it can be noted that inculcating a stronger customer focus in employees is also a fundamental part of the new control strategies described in Chapter 18. However, in an extremely penetrating analysis of these ideas, Harris and Ogbonna (1999) conclude that what is proposed is so conceptually and practically flawed that it is doomed to failure because it:

- rests on an integrationist perspective, which assumes that an organisation's culture is common to all its members, whereas the more realistic differentiationist view acknowledges the inevitability of subcultures;
- assumes that top managers can impose a culture on the rest of an organisation at will, but this is only possible in certain, rarely encountered circumstances;
- flies in the face of a substantial body of evidence that cultures perpetuate themselves until such time as culture holders decide that change is desirable.

Many theorists argue that because culture is so deep-rooted, it is highly resistant to manipulation. For example, Ogbonna (1993) points out that while some behavioural change results from a culture change initiative, it is very unlikely to change deeper values. Thus, all that occurs is a cosmetic impression of culture change. An even stronger position is taken by Ray (1986), who argues that one of the main functions of a culture may well be to enable people to resist changes of this type. For this reason it is not surprising to find that unanticipated consequences and backlash effects often occur in cultural change initiatives. For instance, a study of 530 American companies by Gilmore *et al.* (1997) found that while quality, service levels, competency and productivity often improve, climate, employee morale and work enthusiasm decline considerably. Indeed, Woodall (1996) argues that many attempts at cultural change are so badly conducted that they result in degradation of the workforce and raise questions about the ethics of these initiatives.

In the light of this evidence it is important to understand something of the theory of culture change as it is expressed in most of these change programmes. This will be explained in two stages: first, by giving an overview of the methodology itself and, second, by describing some of the techniques that have been advocated to bring about changes.

The Methodology

Almost all culture change models are derived from the four-step process suggested by Silverzweig and Allen (1976), which are summarised below.

Step 1: Analyse Existing Culture

This usually consists of an extensive survey of organisational members to establish specific objectives for cultural change.

Step 2: Experiencing the Culture

Here organisational members are given the opportunity to examine the existing culture, identify its dysfunctions (hopefully) and participate in identifying the culture that is required (again hopefully).

Step 3: System Installation

This is where the actual change process occurs, usually by making use of group discussion workshops. The active participation of organisational leaders is said to be vital in this stage, primarily to provide those lower down with something on which to model their own behaviour. It is usually recognised that if it is not completed effectively, all that is likely to result is superficial surface change, for instance people seeking to please those higher up by displaying signs of the behaviour they believe top people want to see.

Step 4: Ongoing Evaluation

Here the degree of actual change is assessed and, as necessary, other methods are used to bring about or reinforce the desired changes.

Techniques

Most of the techniques described here would probably be deployed in stages 3 and 4 of the above methodology. They are also said to be useful ways of reinforcing existing cultures where they are already considered appropriate.

Taking Advantage of Existing Culture

This is sometimes described as 'working around an existing culture', and requires that a comprehensive understanding of the organisational value system is obtained in stage 1 of the methodology. If this is achieved the picture can be compared with the cultural values that management would like to see in place and, where necessary, discussion and explanation can be used to correct any discrepancies.

When examined closely, some of the best publicised examples of so-called cultural change probably turn out to be little more than working around an existing culture. One example is given in Ackroyd and Crowdy's (1990) study of slaughtermen, which showed how managers hijacked a culture that was already in place and portrayed the results as something that occurred because of their endeavours.

Socialisation

This has been described earlier and consists of a set of processes that enable employees to learn about their firm's culture and pass on their knowledge and understanding to others. While socialisation seldom brings about a radical change in people's values, it can help them to become more aware of any differences between their own values and those of an organisation, and to develop ways of coping with the differences.

Managing Symbols

As noted earlier, a number of authors suggest that a powerful way to understand a culture is to take note of the values communicated in stories and through other symbolic events. This being the case, one way to promote cultural change is to introduce stories and myths that spread the new cultural values.

Change Reward Systems

Behavioural psychologists argue that the behavioural elements of a culture are learned and can just as easily be extinguished. Thus cultural change can be encouraged by changing the organisation's system of rewards and punishments. An example of how a behaviourist approach might bring about a stronger customer service orientation is given in Chapter 8, where Organisational Behaviour modification techniques are described.

Add New Members

New values can sometimes be a lot harder to develop than starting from scratch. Therefore, providing they actually have the desired new culture, adding new organisational members can be a powerful strategy. However, if it is to be effective, there must be enough new people to swamp the existing culture, otherwise they will simply be socialised into it.

Implement Culture Shock

Culture shock is something that causes an organisation to take a serious look at its own values and behaviour, for example the loss of a key customer, a scandal of some sort, an unsuccessful lawsuit, or something that threatens its existence. When events like these are attributed to something lacking in organisational culture it is often the case that drastic changes are made very quickly.

Change the Top People

As well as having a potential shock value, change at the top can have a major impact on an organisation's culture by sending reverberations throughout an organisation. The person at the top often sets the norms of behaviour and when he or she goes, the next level down soon seems to follow, perhaps because these people are key symbols of the old regime and will have difficulty in adapting to the new one.

Involve Organisational Members

Strictly speaking, changing a culture involves changing its underlying assumptions, values and beliefs. Therefore top-down culture change can be interpreted by people below as something that forces them to give up assumptions and values that are almost sacred. Therefore, because people are usually more willing to implement decisions they have helped to make, participative techniques can often be more successful.

What, then, are the general conclusions that can be drawn about the ease of cultural change? There are three in particular that are highly significant:

- cultures are the result of complex social processes that tend to take place over a long period of time, so a programme of cultural change which becomes a 'quick fix' solution to an organisational problem can do more harm than good;
- all cultures are different, and what can be an effective change strategy in one organisation may be far less effective elsewhere;
- the more deeply ingrained a culture, the more difficult it will be to change, and the more an organisation contains multiple subcultures, the more complex and time-consuming will be the change process.

Organisations therefore need to consider very carefully whether they should try to interfere with a culture or simply let other changes that have been put in place give rise to an appropriate culture that emerges at its own pace (Hope and Hendry 1995).

OB IN ACTION: One View of How to Succeed in Culture Change

Many managers have attempted to revamp their business culture, some by benchmarking themselves against their most admired competitors. This offers few insights for those attempting a business turnaround and the task is all the more daunting because culture is not just about 'how we do things', but also about 'what we do'. Thus, it is instructive to revisit the lessons learned in the banking sector in the 1990s and nine years later, when looking at the results, the scorecard looks dismal: only 7 per cent of the transformation programmes had succeeded. The rest were long on intentions and short on delivery. When one chief executive was asked, 'How would you describe the bank's culture pre-rationalisation?' he said, 'Then, it was dog eat dog' and when asked about now, he replied, 'It is the other way round'. Thus it was clear that the more things changed, the more they remained the same. However, five lessons were learnt.

First, focus on outputs, not inputs. Many of these programmes ended up putting undue emphasis on corporate values and mission statements, but not enough on actions and outcomes. In contrast, successful institutions reshaped behaviour by setting clear targets, providing the necessary support and rewarding success.

Second, recognise that corporate culture is like a giant jelly: unless one shakes it hard, it wobbles back into its original position. It is unwise to underestimate the magnetism of the past, or to assume that change is smooth and painless. If it ain't hurting, then it ain't working.

Third, mindset change is about engagement of the individual. It is vital for senior executives to be proactive and have convincing answers to the four most frequently asked questions by employees in any business transformation: **Direction**: what are our goals and why? **Deliverables**: do we have the leadership to deliver them? **Impacts**: how will the goals affect individual teams? **Motivation**: what is in it for me? Changing the employee mindset requires deep insight into human nature and the ability to respond convincingly to those frequently asked questions.

Fourth, promise only what you can deliver. The history of change programmes is littered with clever words that say a lot about nothing and promise far more than they can deliver. This only creates corrosive cynicism that frustrates sensible action.

Finally, remember that clarity of thinking leads to clarity of actions. That means all new ideas about business growth need to be put through a reality check.

The history of business transformation has shown many failures inside and outside the finance sector; not because there is anything inherently wrong with the concept, but because of the absence of common sense in its implementation.

Source:

Rajan A (2003) Culture Change: how it works *The Financial Times*, 1 September. Professor Amin Rajan is chief executive of Create, a research institute specialising in good practices in the workplace.

A NOTE ON NATIONAL CULTURES

At an intuitive level almost everyone is aware that customs, attitudes and values vary between countries. Indeed, the need to adjust our behaviour can sometimes become very obvious if we travel outside our native country. These days many organisations operate internationally, with branches or subsidiaries abroad, and there is an increasing realisation that people in organisations need to be aware of cultural differences and adjust their behaviour accordingly. For this reason an important area of study is now that of cross-cultural differences and how these can influence patterns of behaviour (Adler and Bartholomew 1992). Because this matter will be covered at some length in Chapter 22, it would be inappropriate to introduce an extended discussion here. Nevertheless, it is important to note that the culture of an organisation needs to be compatible with the culture of the country or region in which it is located. If this is not the case, people can find that expected patterns of behaviour in the enterprise clash with what they have been brought up to regard as normal and acceptable.

There is a great deal of evidence to show that national cultures vary considerably in terms of beliefs and values that are held sacred, and some of this evidence will be presented in Chapter 22. Until then the important point to note is that these cultural effects prompt people in different locations to behave in different ways. Thus, what has been presented in this chapter in terms of desirable cultural characteristics is only a point of view. It reflects values in North America and to some extent Europe and is by no means the last word on the matter.

REPLAY

- Culture is one of the less tangible features of organisational life and, while it is hard to define, there is a growing consensus that it consists of a deeply ingrained set of values that provide people in an organisation with a code of acceptable behaviour.

- A number of different perspectives on organisational culture exist, the most pronounced difference being that between integrationists, who view the phenomena as a relatively homogeneous set of values shared by all organisational members, and differentiationists, who hold that there are different subcultures in most organisations.

- While the evidence for a universal 'one best culture' is weak, this is the approach adopted by most popular writers in the area, whose descriptions are often taken as a prescription for an ideal culture. An exception to this, however, is the more recent contingency framework of Goffee and Jones (1998).

- Changing an organisation's culture is likely to be tremendously difficult and, if it can be accomplished, the process will probably take a considerable amount of time and effort.

- Organisational culture nearly always contains elements of the culture of the country in which an organisation is located, which means that a culture that is appropriate for a firm in one country may not be appropriate for a branch or division of the organisation elsewhere.

ORGANISATIONAL CLIMATE

Although the concept of organisational climate is closely allied to culture, it has existed in a developed form for considerably longer and can be traced back to the work of Kurt Lewin (1951). Like culture, it can be difficult to define precisely and, since some academic definitions can be rather obscure, in the interests of simplicity it is defined here as:

> **a characteristic ethos or atmosphere within an organisation at a given point in time which is reflected in the way its members perceive, experience and react to the organisational context.**

A number of important implications arise from this definition. First, note that climate is something that is 'felt' by people and it is an 'experienced' state of affairs rather than a set of hard, quantifiable attributes. One way to think of it is as the way that people subjectively describe relevant features of an organisation to themselves and interpret what they find (James and Jones 1974).

Second, climatic conditions can be short-lived and this is one of the features that distinguishes climate from culture. Therefore sub-climates are probably inevitable (Powell and Butterfield 1978).

Finally, since climate is experienced by people and affects their attitudes, it gives a basis for the way they will behave (Schneider 1983). The most significant outcome is usually taken to be whether people feel that their membership of an organisation is a psychologically rewarding experience, together with the effect this has on their levels of morale, motivation and the desire to remain as organisational members (Litwin and Stringer 1968).

TIME OUT

Carefully consider a group of up to 25 people to which you belong. Preferably this should be a formal group, for instance a section or department at your place of work or, if you choose a group at your university or college, it could be a class or even all the students in your year of the course. You have probably noticed that from time to time there are what seem to be attitude changes in the group. Try to identify some of these that have occurred fairly recently and answer the questions below.

1. What attitudes have you identified? For example, are they attitudes to the organisation as a whole or to a smaller part of it? If you chose an academic location, are the attitudes to a course as a whole, a particular subject or class, or towards the institution?

2. What was the nature of these attitude changes? For example, did attitudes become more positive or negative?

3. To what extent do you feel that these attitude changes represent a shift, albeit a temporary one, in climate?

THE NATURE AND ORIGINS OF CLIMATE

The Relation of Climate to Culture

Although there are certain similarities between climate and culture there are also differences. While both are phenomena that are felt or experienced by people, climate tends to be something of which they are more consciously aware. In addition, although both have effects on behaviour, this occurs in rather different ways. Culture provides a code of conduct that tells people the expected and appropriate ways to behave, whereas climate tends to result in a set of conditions to which they react. Culture is also more permanent and deeply ingrained, and in Smircich's (1983) words it can be regarded as 'something an organisation is', whereas climate is usually more short-term – a phase that an organisation passes through.

One way in which cultures and climates are similar is that both are linked to the value system of organisational members. Values are a fundamental part of a culture and, to some extent, culture itself gives people their values. However, climate is more often a reflection of whether current organisational conditions are in accord with the values that people hold. Therefore, culture is often a significant background factor to a particular set of climatic conditions.

Before closing this brief contrast between culture and climate it is important to note that this is very much the traditional view of the two concepts. There is another viewpoint that holds that the differences are really much smaller, and that culture and climate may well be the same phenomenon, but measured in different ways (Denison 1996). This is far too important an idea to be ignored or glossed over but, for the present, it is more convenient to use the conventional perspective. The alternative view will be discussed further at the end of the chapter.

Individual or Group Level Construct?

Although the very expression organisational climate implies that it is an organisation-wide phenomenon, it is something that arises in individual feelings and experiences, which means that it is strongly connected with individual mental processes (Kozlowski and Doherty 1989). For this reason it is necessary to draw a distinction between climate at the individual level and climate at the group level. The individual effect is normally referred to as *psychological climate* (Koys and DeCotis 1991), which reflects how a person experiences and reacts to his or her surroundings. In this book, however, the focus is primarily on *organisational climate* as a social phenomenon that affects the behaviour of groups, or even the whole organisation. Nevertheless, there is an important connection between the two levels. Organisational climates are not simply the sum of individual feelings and the Homans (1950) model of group formation discussed in Chapter 11 tells us that where a group of people is exposed to the same organisational surroundings, people share their interpretations of the circumstances. Thus, what often emerges is a degree of consensus among group members about climate.

Psychological climate: how the individual experiences and reacts to his or her surroundings

Organisational climate: how people collectively experience and react to their surroundings

Outcomes or Phenomena?

Climate can have pronounced effects on attitudes and behaviour, but there is sometimes a great deal of confusion about whether it is a phenomenon that results in something

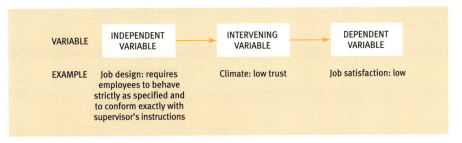

Figure 19.4
Connections between independent, intervening and dependent variables

happening or whether it is an outcome of something else. Its origins and outcomes will be covered in detail presently, but for now it is important to note that most definitions and measures treat climate as something that is both a phenomenon and an outcome, that is, as an intervening variable. This is shown in outline in Figure 19.4.

Note that the independent variable **job design** does not affect the dependent variable **job satisfaction** directly. Rather it influences the climatic dimension of **trust** which in turn affects **job satisfaction**. The reason for treating climate in this way is largely to provide conceptual clarity; for instance, although we might observe that job satisfaction alters if the design of a job is changed, it is difficult to explain how job design has a direct effect (causes) on job satisfaction. However, if an intervening variable is placed between the two variables, the causal link is broken down into two stages and the process can be made much clearer.

TIME OUT

Using the group and its attitude changes that you identified in the previous Time Out exercise, apply the model of cause and effect given in Figure 19.4 and answer the questions below for each attitude.

1. What particular factor (independent variable) prompted the attitude change?
2. What climatic condition (intervening variable) did this create?
3. What was the outcome in terms of attitude?

Hint: You may find it easier to consider matters in the reverse direction, that is, starting with the outcome.

CLIMATE: A MODEL OF ANTECEDENTS AND OUTCOMES

Since climate is usually treated as an intervening variable, it is important to distinguish between the factors that result in climatic conditions and those that are affected by climate. Using some of the results from a diverse range of studies, a model can be constructed which portrays these factors (see Figure 19.5).

Factors inside and outside an organisation can have an impact on climate. Inside the organisation influential variables are shown at three levels: the wider organisation, the immediate context and the individual. These can all affect perceptions of climate and, in turn, climate can result in attitudinal and behaviourial outcomes. Before describing the variables in detail it is necessary to emphasise two important points.

Figure 19.5 The origins and outcomes of organisational climate

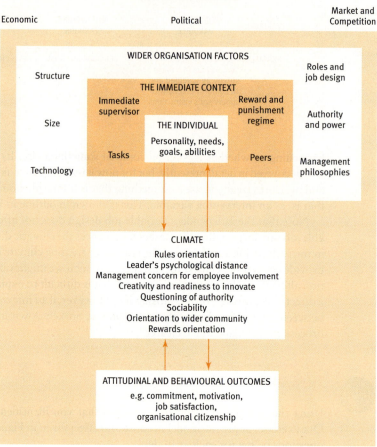

ENVIRONMENTAL FACTORS

Economic   Political   Market and Competition

WIDER ORGANISATION FACTORS

Structure   Roles and job design

THE IMMEDIATE CONTEXT

Immediate supervisor   Reward and punishment regime

Size   Authority and power

THE INDIVIDUAL

Personality, needs, goals, abilities

Tasks   Peers

Technology   Management philosophies

CLIMATE

Rules orientation
Leader's psychological distance
Management concern for employee involvement
Creativity and readiness to innovate
Questioning of authority
Sociability
Orientation to wider community
Rewards orientation

ATTITUDINAL AND BEHAVIOURAL OUTCOMES

e.g. commitment, motivation,
job satisfaction,
organisational citizenship

- There is an arrow on the model leading from climate to outcomes and another one in the opposite direction. This indicates that climates are often self-reinforcing; that is, poor climatic conditions can result in lowered commitment, motivation and job satisfaction and these feelings can result in people perceiving that the organisation has a poor climate.

- A similar pair of arrows is shown between climate and the individual. This reflects the idea that some of a person's individual characteristics will shape perceptions of climate, for example, needs, goals and personality characteristics. Thus, if there is a poor match between what a person needs or wants and what the organisation provides, there can often be an adverse effect on perceptions of climate. However, people are not totally inflexible and, over a period of time, the climatic conditions can sometimes result in them adjusting their aspirations downwards.

In what follows the different variables and some of their effects are all described separately, but in practice most of them are at work together and they can all affect perceptions of climate. For convenience, the explanation starts by describing the dimensions of climate and then its outcomes. Then the explanation proceeds by working from the environment inwards.

Organisational Climate

Since people are usually aware of several organisational characteristics or attributes, they experience life in several different ways at the same time. Thus, climate is a multi-dimensional phenomenon and the most robust measures evaluate it in this way. Although there are several different measurements that can be used to evaluate climates, what is given here is a description of the dimensions used in three of the most prominent scales: Litwin and Stringer (1968), Payne and Phesey (1971) and Dastmalchian (1986). Scales of this type are usually pencil-and-paper questionnaires that are completed by the employees of an organisation. They are used to tap perceptions of:

- **a rules orientation**   whether behaviour in the organisation is governed by formal rules and regulations;
- **leader psychological distance**   whether those in senior positions emphasise their greater authority and hold themselves apart from subordinates;
- **creativity and readiness to innovate**   whether the organisation and its management are seen as receptive to new ideas and ways of doing things;
- **questioning authority**   whether it is permissible to question the decision of a senior person;
- **sociability**   the extent to which a team spirit exists;
- **an orientation to wider community**   whether the organisation and its policies are seen to be sensitive to the needs of a wider community;
- **a rewards orientation**   whether the organisation and its management are seen to encourage effort with rewards, rather than using punishments for lack of effort.

These dimensions are used by people to describe the organisation to themselves and, according to what is perceived, they experience membership as being somewhere between psychologically stimulating and rewarding at one extreme to stultifying at the other. Predictably, the former is more likely to lead to positive attitudinal and behavioural outcomes.

Outcomes

Outcomes shown in the model are both attitudinal and behavioural. Although the list of outcomes is potentially endless, for simplicity only four examples are shown. These are commitment to organisation, motivation, job satisfaction and organisational citizenship.

It is now time to examine some of the factors that influence climate. The description starts from the outside and works inwards.

The Environmental Context

Environmental forces and events can limit an organisation's freedom of manoeuvre and prompt courses of action that can have climatic repercussions. Three groups of environmental factors can have a noticeable impact: economic, political and market factors.

Economic Factors

The buoyancy and general health of the surrounding economy can result in management feeling optimistic or pessimistic about the future. Where managers are pessimistic costs might be scrutinised or investment curtailed to hoard reserves for hard times ahead.

Employees can be remarkably sensitive about these signs, which have a habit of promoting a climate of insecurity. One way that the message is transmitted is by an increased formality in the structures and procedures used to cope with the uncertainty, which results in climates with less egalitarianism and greater psychological distance between managers and employees (Dastmalchian 1986).

Political Factors

In Great Britain central government policies have forced most public sector organisations to make internal adjustments to comply with legislation that requires them to put work that was hitherto performed by their own employees out to tender. Steps such as this can prompt structural changes that give rise to insecurity, which is quickly reflected in climate.

Market and Competitive Factors

The market for a firm's products can have a dramatic effect on its prosperity, and market conditions can sometimes threaten an organisation's very existence. Where this occurs the climate of insecurity can prompt a 'rush to the door' as people look for more secure jobs. However, these conditions can sometimes have surprisingly positive effects. Organisational members can perceive that they are all faced with a common threat, which prompts them to pull together to remedy the situation, and in turn promotes egalitarianism, open mindedness, sociability, creativity and a reduced psychological distance between managers and subordinates (Dastmalchian 1986).

The Organisational Context

Size, Structure and Authority Patterns

One of the important points made in Chapter 17 is that as organisations get larger they tend to become more formal and bureaucratic, which means that size, structure and authority patterns can conveniently be considered together. Bureaucratic organisations usually have a strong rules orientation and a high emphasis on following established procedures, and size often goes hand in hand with increased job specialisation, lowered interpersonal communication and a greater centralisation of decision making. All of these characteristics tend to result in climatic conditions in which people feel that there is a lack of freedom to use initiative and skills.

Roles and Job Design

This topic is covered in Chapters 7 and 11, where its effects on the way that people experience work are covered in more detail. The work of Hackman and Oldham (1975), for example, clearly demonstrates that certain aspects of job design have psychological effects in terms of whether people feel that work is a stimulating and meaningful experience.

Technology

Technology often has a strong impact on the way that jobs are designed, and there is some suggestion that using automation for repetitive and fragmented jobs can enrich work, enhance feelings of worker control and lower feelings of alienation from work (Crawley and Spurgeon 1979). Conversely, there is some evidence that computerised clerical work results in lowered feelings of personal control and responsibility. However, much seems to depend on the nature of computerisation and the jobs to which it is applied. In some cases it results in more varied, interesting and responsible work with a more positive impact on climate (Oborne 1994).

Management Philosophies

Philosophy is used here to describe the views that managers hold about the roles and functions of subordinates. This usually has a strong impact on the way they are treated and gives rise to climatic effects. One indication of these philosophies is the payment system used within an organisation – too strong an emphasis on incentive payments can create the impression that managers believe that the only thing which motivates subordinates is money (Dastmalchian and Mansfield 1980).

Authority and Power

The way that authority and power are used can also have climatic repercussions. An organisation that is run in a highly autocratic way by a small, powerful clique of executives can be expected to have a climate lacking in collaboration and high in fear.

The Immediate Context

The immediate context contains a number of factors that directly impinge on an individual, and these play an important part in shaping his or her perceptions of the work situation.

The Immediate Supervisor

A person's immediate supervisor can have a strong effect on climate. While some supervisors can mitigate the effects of frustrating organisational policies and practices, others tend to make these features of working life much worse. Therefore, to the extent that a supervisor shields subordinates from these things, there can be a positive effect on climate. In addition, the interpersonal relationships between a supervisor and subordinates can make the overall work experience more pleasant or unpleasant, and this also has an impact on climate.

Tasks

Some tasks are inherently more psychologically rewarding than others, and so the nature of the work that a person performs is virtually certain to colour his or her experience of an organisation.

Rewards and Punishments

In order to encourage certain behaviours and discourage those that are considered less desirable organisations usually have a system of rewards and punishments. Most organisational members are aware of this, if only at a subjective level, and this has an effect on how they experience organisational life.

Peers

While climate is an individually experienced phenomenon, people in the immediate context usually share their experiences and interpretation. This enables them to test their perceptions of reality on others and if these perceptions are confirmed as accurate, what has been perceived becomes the reality of the situation.

CASE STUDY 19.2: University Research Climate

In the early 1990s Birkwood College of Higher Education became the University of Birkwood. Until then, like most colleges, it was basically a teaching institution. However, to enhance the institution's standing, it had always encouraged its academic staff to engage in research, although the practical support it was able to provide in terms of funding and remission from teaching tended to be very limited. Nevertheless, many staff responded to the institution's wishes and did research, in their own time, and a number of them were successful in publishing their findings.

Upon its change of status, there was an increasing emphasis on research, an initiative which most of the staff suspected was an attempt to shed its prior image and make it appear more like a traditional university. Despite a significant rise in student numbers, the number of lecturing staff barely increased. However, a number of research professors and their support staff were recruited. The majority of these people came from traditional universities where teaching workloads were much lower and it had been part of their role to build up a research profile in the employer's time. The net result of their arrival, however, was that other staff had to cope with the ever-increasing number of students. In the eyes of these staff, this resulted in a situation where they had to work much harder in order to provide funds to pay for the upkeep of research staff. To make matters worse, it became clear that producing published work was fast becoming one of the most significant criteria for promotion. However, the vast majority of funding acquired by the institution for research was now being directed towards the research staff and comparatively little was available to provide assistance for other staff, even those who, until then, had been active researchers in their own time. Nevertheless, since the amount of public funding for research is dependent on an institution's overall output (largely determined by a count of published articles), and this could not be achieved by the small number of research staff alone, there was increasing pressure on all staff to engage in research. For almost all of them, however, this would have meant doing this work in their leisure hours.

Silently, but in a determined way, most staff resisted this pressure. Some ceased to use their own time for research and those who continued to do so were careful when publishing a paper to make sure that the article made it clear that they operated as an independent researcher. Thus, these staff could refuse to declare their research output and, in time, there were some signs that the overall research output of the institution had started to decline.

Questions

1. How would you describe the new research climate at the University of Birkwood?

2. Trace the antecedents of the changed climate and account for its outcomes.

REPLAY

- Because people in organisations take in information about their surroundings and construct personal realities from what they perceive, organisations always have climates of some sort.
- Thus, climate is an experienced phenomenon and, since people in the workplace share their experiences and interpretations, climate tends to emerge as a collectively experienced state of affairs.
- Climate is influenced by a number of organisational features and conditions and, since these can change, climates can also fluctuate.

The Individual

Chapters 3–10 all deal with individual differences, that is, the ways in which people are unique and have their own **personalities**, **abilities**, **needs** and **goals**. An organisation that provides a facility for individuals to satisfy their needs and achieve cherished goals is more likely to be one where membership is perceived as a rewarding experience, which in turn shapes perceptions of climate at the individual level. Nevertheless, as is pointed out above, group effects are also very powerful. Since groups have some capability to shape the views and perceptions of their members, the ensuing climate is more often manifest as a collective phenomenon.

OVERVIEW AND CONCLUSIONS

The concepts of organisational culture and organisational climate clearly have some similarities. Both deal with intangible aspects of the way that employees relate to and experience an organisation, and both acknowledge that this results in distinctive patterns of employee behaviour. Nevertheless, the traditional view is that culture and climate are different concepts and deal with different facets of organisational life. There are three ways in which they can be contrasted and these are discussed in what follows.

Culture and Climate as Theoretical Constructs

Culture and climate are both abstract constructs that are used to explain a state of affairs within an organisation. Of the two, culture describes a more ephemeral and intangible state of affairs – the values that are part of what it is, in much the same way that an individual's personality is fundamental to what he or she is. Climate, on the other hand, is much more explicit and precise. It has no pretence of explaining what an organisation is, but expresses the mental reactions of its members to what they perceive it to be.

Although it has long been recognised that organisations have cultures, serious application of the concept is a fairly recent development. The most penetrating work in the area uses an anthropological frame of reference, the output of which usually produces no more than a description of an organisation's culture, perhaps because many anthropologists see the main role of the discipline as describing and documenting. Climate, however, is largely the preserve of social psychologists, who set out to explain how particular sets of climatic conditions arise and how these have discernible effects on the behaviour of organisational members. Thus, the way the concepts are defined tends to reflect the views of two very different groups of social scientists about ways in which human behaviour in organisations can best be understood. Needless to say, instead of trying to find ways of reconciling their different points of view, researchers from one school are often dismissive of those from the other. Culturalists criticise climatologists for trying to be too precise about measurement, and those who study climate tend to criticise culturalists for adopting an approach which is too strongly focused on producing one-off descriptions that make it impossible to compare organisations. Commenting on this problem, Denison (1996) argues that it is far from clear that culture and climate are concerned with two distinctly different aspects of organisational life. Both, for example, have similar theoretical foundations and, ultimately, they both address the issue of 'How does this affect behaviour?' Indeed, in Denison's view, the apparent difference has resulted in something of a self-fulfilling prophecy. Since culturalist and climatologists come from different academic backgrounds, they tend to use different methods of investigation, the net result of which is that although they can be studying the same phenomenon the results they produce create the impression that the two phenomena are totally different.

Culture and Climate as Organisational Phenomena

The conventional view about culture and climate is that they exist at different levels. Culture is usually taken to be deeply embedded in subconsciously held values, and so many organisational members might not be aware that a culture exists, let alone how it affects their behaviour. Conversely, climate tends to be regarded as more of a surface phenomenon, with easily identifiable effects on behaviour. Although subcultures are usually found within organisations, until fairly recently there has been a strong tendency to view culture as a pervasive phenomenon, whereas micro climates tend to be regarded as more inevitable because many of the important factors directly influencing climatic conditions are located in a group's immediate context.

Because cultures are taken to be enduring and slow to change it can be difficult to correct a culture that is considered inappropriate. The antecedents of climates are better understood and it is usually assumed that climates change more quickly than cultures. Although this does not mean that climates are any easier to modify, at a theoretical level it probably means that poor climates are more avoidable.

The Utility of Culture and Climate Concepts to Managers

At the present time it is likely that most managers view culture as a more important topic than climate. The rather naive ideas set out in popular texts on the subject have resulted in something of a managerial love affair with the word, perhaps because managers have been encouraged to believe that a universal set of cultural characteristics can be selected as an off-the-shelf recipe for organisational success. These very simplistic ideas probably mean that the concept has less real utility than appears at first sight. This is not necessarily the fault of managers. They are busy people and if they are encouraged by self-styled gurus (many of whom should know better) to believe that culture is a 'quick-fix' solution, it is probably the self-appointed experts who should be blamed. Nevertheless, the idea that an appropriate culture can make a significant contribution to organisational success is an important one and, as research in the area progresses, it is likely that a definitive picture will eventually emerge on the cultures that are most appropriate for organisations in different circumstances. In addition, it seems likely that viable methods to move from one set of cultural characteristics to another can be evolved, and when both of these requirements have been satisfied, culture is likely to come into its own as a highly usable concept. Until then, however, its use can sometimes be nothing more than a blind act of faith.

While it has never caught management's imagination in quite the same way as culture, climate has always been important to organisations. There has long been a recognition that work-related attitudes and behaviour are important for organisational performance. In addition it has been known for some time that structure and immediate contextual factors, such as supervisor style and the influence of workgroups, all play a part in shaping attitudes and behaviour. Climate is also a concept that has been exposed to a more rigorous academic exploration and is less plagued with simplistic ideas than culture, so it is, or should be, a concept that has a great deal of practical utility to managers.

FURTHER READING

Cray, D and G R Mallory (1997) *Making Sense of Managing Culture*, Thomson: London. For those who subscribe to the idea that culture can be easily modified, this book is an interesting 'how to do it' guide.

Deal, T E and A A Kennedy (1982) *Corporate Culture: The Rites and Rituals of Corporate Life*, Reading, Mass: Addison Wesley. A book by two of the 'founding fathers' of the culture movement. Very firmly located in the application school and, in its time, highly influential in management circles.

Goffee, R and G Jones (1998) *The Character of a Corporation*, London: HarperCollins. The book gives a full description of the authors' more recent contingency application of the culture concept.

Kanter, R M (1995) *The Change Masters: Corporate Entrepreneurs at Work*, London: Allen and Unwin. A highly influential book, written by a management 'guru'. It is more about cultural change than anything else and, because it tends to portray culture change as something that is not too difficult to accomplish, it needs to be taken with a pinch of salt.

Martin, J (1992) *Cultures and Organisations: Three Perspectives*, Beverly Hills, CA: Sage. A penetrating analysis of the concept of culture as applied to organisations.

Moore, J D (1997) *Visions of Culture: An Introduction to Anthropological Theories and Theorists*, London: Sage. A book of readings by 21 major theorists on culture and an analysis of their impact on contemporary thought.

Ouchi, W G (1981) *Theory Z*, Reading, Mass: Addison-Wesley. The author, who was one of the 'founding fathers' of the excellence movement of the 1980s, compares and distinguishes between American and Japanese company cultures. He draws the conclusion that the superior performance of Japanese firms is attributable to their corporate culture.

Parker, M (2000) *Organisational Culture and Identity*, London: Sage. The book takes a critically symbolic perspective on culture by exploring how organisations shape the identities of their members. It also addresses the important questions of the ethics of this process.

Peters, T J and R H Waterman (1982) *In Search of Excellence: Lessons from America's Best Run Companies*, New York: Harper and Row. A book which is also by two of the 'founding fathers' of the 'excellence' movement. More than any other book, it established culture as a highly fashionable topic in management circles.

Sackmann, S A (ed) (1997) *Cultural Complexity in Organisations*, London: Sage. A book of readings in which different authors deal with culture, subcultures and national cultures.

Schein, E H (1992) *Organisational Culture and Leadership*, San Francisco, CA: Jossey-Bass. A thorough exploration of organisational culture from a social psychological perspective.

REVIEW AND DISCUSSION QUESTIONS

1. Using Schein's (1992) conceptualisation of culture as a layered phenomenon that exists at three levels, analyse the culture of an organisation of your own choice and state what you perceive to be its:

  basic assumptions

  values and beliefs that reflect these basic assumptions

  artefacts and creations that reflect its assumptions and value system.

2. Critically evaluate the idea that a strong culture results in commercial success for an organisation.

3. Describe the assumptions of the 'key variable' (application) and 'root metaphor' conceptualisations of organisational culture and distinguish between the ways in which these two schools view the role of culture in an organisation.

4. In outline describe a four-stage process that could be used to try to change the culture of an organisation and some of the associated techniques that might be used in these stages.

5. Define organisational climate and compare and contrast culture and climate as:

  theoretical constructs

  organisational phenomena

  constructs that have utility for managers in organisations.

Chapter 20

Communication

LEARNING OUTCOMES

After studying this chapter you should be able to:

- define communication and effective communication and understand the importance of effective communication in organisations

- using the communication model, explain the communication process in terms of its major component activities and understand the barriers to effective communication

- explain the main directions of information flow in organisations and distinguish between formal and informal communication

- explain the characteristics and the strengths and weaknesses of the two traditional methods of communication used in organisations: verbal (face-to-face) methods and written communication

- understand the significance of new information and communication technologies (ICTs) and whether these are likely to result in radically different organisational forms, i.e. the 'virtual organisation'

INTRODUCTION

This chapter, which deals with organisational communication, adopts a 'back to basics' approach to the topic. It starts by defining communication and then highlights its crucial importance to organisations.

Although communication is often viewed as a straightforward matter, it is a complex process in which many things can go wrong. Therefore, the next section of the chapter presents a model of communication that illustrates its complexity and this is applied in the following section, to consider the barriers to effective communication. The remainder of the chapter focuses more explicitly on communication in organisations, first, by considering the main flows of information and then by exploring in detail two important ways of communicating: by face-to-face methods and written communication.

Across the last two decades the emergence of advanced information and communication technologies (ICTs) has significantly changed the nature of communication and there are arguments that the use of these tools will result in a radically new type of organisation – the 'virtual organisation'. The next section of the chapter explores this matter in some depth and examines the evidence for the widespread emergence of organisations of this type. The chapter closes with a section that integrates and overviews its contents.

THE IMPORTANCE OF COMMUNICATION

Communication: a process in which information and its meaning is conveyed from a sender to receiver(s)

'*Communication*' is a widely used (and in some ways misused) word. It has been defined in many different ways, perhaps the simplest of which is 'the process of transmitting information from one person to another' (Weick and Browning 1986, p 244). This, however, is simplistic because it covers situations where information is transmitted but is only understood by the sender. More penetrating definitions usually point out that 'meaning' (rather that just 'information') must be conveyed, and some go much further by stating that communication must involve an exchange of information. Desirable as it may be for other reasons, feedback is not necessarily part of the communication process, and with these points in mind, communication is defined here as:

> **a process in which information and its meaning is conveyed by a sender to receiver(s).**

An elementary but important implication can be drawn from this definition, and the reader should keep it in mind for the remainder of the chapter. This is that whatever the message conveys, and whatever means are used to convey it, the sender and the receiver must have consensus about its meaning, otherwise communication has not taken place, merely the transmission of information.

Effective communication: the extent to which the sender and receiver of a message both attribute it with the same meaning

It is virtually impossible to identify an aspect of organisational functioning that is not affected by communication and serious problems can arise if communication is not effective. In accordance with the definition above, *effective communication* is defined here as:

the extent to which the sender and receiver of a message both attribute it with the same meaning.

In general terms, there are three aspects of organisational functioning in which effective communication can be particularly crucial, each of which will be considered in turn.

Coordination

Organisational structure establishes different functions and departments that make their own contributions to an organisation's overall task. Unless they inform each other about what is required, coordination of activities is pretty well impossible.

Control

Achievement of goals cannot be left to chance and so it is normal to set up a method of control that monitors goal achievement. Clearly control activities are acutely dependent on a flow of accurate information (see Chapter 18).

Human Factors

Inadequate or ineffective communication probably has its most visible effects in terms of the impact on employees. If employees do not know what is required of them, or how they are affected by changes, the effects on morale, motivation and the psychological contract can be disastrous (Guest and Conway 2002). In some organisations, employees do not get to hear about matters that impact on their working lives until they are overtaken by events. As a result, they impute sinister motives for being kept in the dark and if the situation persists for any length of time, those who are starved of information become only too ready to listen to rumours, which quickly become accepted as 'the truth'. With this in mind, the next section of the chapter explores the communication process in some depth to uncover what is necessary for it to be effective.

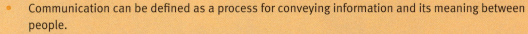

REPLAY

- Communication can be defined as a process for conveying information and its meaning between people.
- The effectiveness of the communication process can be evaluated in terms of the extent to which the sender and receiver both attribute the same meaning to a message.
- The effectiveness of communication in an organisation can have a strong impact on its performance and, in particular, on its ability to coordinate and control its component parts and to make effective use of its human resources.

CASE STUDY 20.1: The Luxor Company

The Luxor Company manufactures domestic and office furniture and employs approximately 750 people at its headquarters and manufacturing facility on the outskirts of Paris. Although the firm is over 50 years old, until the mid-1960s it was a relatively small, family-owned firm. In the mid-1980s, the founder retired and was succeeded as chairman by his eldest son, Charles Binochet. About eight years ago the company embarked on a serious programme of expansion and has doubled its size in the last five years. This involved a great deal of change and disruption for almost everybody in the organisation and things changed so fast that everyone from the chairman downwards seemed to have to work at a furious pace. At times, some of the senior executives came into conflict and this was particularly noticeable with the heads of production and marketing. For instance, the marketing director constantly complained that he never knew when customers' orders would be filled and, in return, the production director grumbled that salespeople seemed to be making promises to customers about delivery dates that were impossible to meet. At one point the firm also came dangerously close to being declared insolvent because, while it had a full order book, the financial control procedures failed to alert top management to a situation in which incoming cash flows were insufficient to service its borrowing requirements. Matters were even worse at the bottom of the organisation. Because change was rapid and continuous, supervisors and junior managers were run off their feet trying to cope with a constant flow of alterations to product lines and new arrangements for manufacturing, storage and delivery. There were inevitable teething troubles in anything new that was introduced and tempers quickly became frayed. Employees constantly complained about being kept in the dark, and at the time of the financial crisis, when word of the situation inevitably leaked out in the firm, a serious strike was narrowly averted. Try as he might, the chairman and his immediate colleagues could find no explanation why the organisation had reached this state of affairs. As Charles Binochet remarked at the time, 'When I was a boy and first came into the firm, everybody knew everyone else and if they had problems to be resolved or anything to say, they just knocked on the door of my father's office.'

Questions

1. How do you explain this state of affairs?

2. Identify any particular areas in which you feel communication has been ineffective.

3. In what ways does the organisation still need to improve its communications?

THE COMMUNICATION MODEL

Most of us tend to take communication for granted and when we find that communication is not effective, we blame the other person. The problem is that the process is much more complex than it appears at first sight and, to appreciate this, it is useful to start by exploring it from a theoretical standpoint. The approach which dominates

Figure 20.1
The communication model

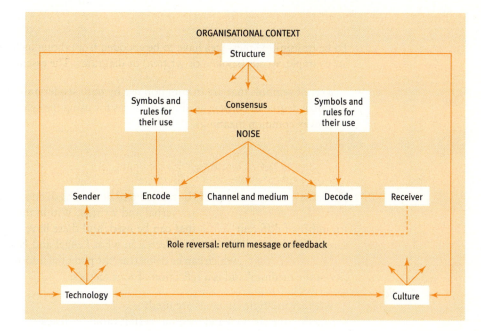

thinking and research in the area is the 'information processing' perspective, and a model derived from the works of Berlo (1960) and earlier workers is given in Figure 20.1. Despite it age, this model has stood the test of time and it is still the most widely used conceptualisation of the process.

Before exploring the model, however, it is necessary to make three important points:

- The model is not intended to be a faithful representation of communication in practice, but a specification for the components that should be present and the functions that they should perform.
- Strictly speaking the three elements (structure, technology and culture) shown as part of the organisational context are not part of the process itself and were not included in earlier information processing models. However, since they can have a huge impact on communication in organisations they have been included for completeness.
- As shown in Figure 20.1, the process portrays a one-way flow of information from sender to receiver. In practice, many messages evoke a response in which the receiver becomes the sender of a new message and the sender becomes the new receiver. This is reflected in the model by the dotted line labelled 'role reversal: return message or feedback'.

Components of the Model

The Source of the Message (sender)

Source of message: the person from whom a message originates

All messages originate in the brain of the sender, for whom they have a meaning.

Symbols and Encoding

Encoding: a process in which a message is transformed into a set of symbols that can be conveyed by a channel

To be transmitted messages have to be encoded from thoughts into a set of symbols, for example, words (spoken or written) or diagrams. The essentials for this are:

- a set of symbols that are in common use by both sender and receiver;
- a high degree of consensus about the rules for using the symbols so that they convey common meanings.

The Channel and Medium

Channels of communication: the carriers of the message

Media: specific ways of conveying a message along a channel

Information richness: the potential information-carrying capacity of a communication medium

The same message can usually be transmitted in more than one way, but the two basic *channels of communication* are verbal and written. Within these channels there are a number of different *media* that can be used, and these have different capacities to carry information. This idea is reflected in what Lengel and Daft (1988) refer to as *information richness*, which can be defined as 'the potential information-carrying capacity of the medium' and is a reflection of four factors:

- whether multiple channels are used;
- whether the channel and medium permit rapid feedback to the message sender;
- the type of communication – personal (person-to-person) communication that occurs in the here and now, or impersonal communication that is not addressed to anyone in particular;
- the language sources used, together with the variety of information cues available for establishing meaning.

These ideas are summarised in Table 20.1.

The work of Daft and Lengel permits a number of generalisations to be made about selecting an appropriate channel and medium in order to achieve effectiveness in communication:

- spoken channels are best for some messages and written ones for others, and for some messages a mixture of both is more appropriate;
- certain messages can be notoriously difficult to encode in written form, notably sincerity, integrity and trustworthiness, which are all much more difficult to detect on paper than they are in the face-to-face situation;
- certain types of message can seriously overload a channel; it is hard to avoid confusion if an attempt is made to give a purely oral description of something very complex, such as details of new organisational structures or methods of work organisation, which can often be done more effectively with the aid of diagrams;
- face-to-face communication is usually much richer than the written form because it has a more personal focus and there are many additional clues to help the receiver understand what is said;
- face-to-face communication also allows instantaneous feedback from the receiver, which in turn allows the sender to check whether the receiver has correctly interpreted the message.

Table 20.1 The information richness of selected communication media (after Lengel and Daft 1988)

Medium	Channel(s)	Potential for feedback	Type of communication	Sources of language (symbols)	Information richness
Face to face	Verbal and visual	Immediate	Personal	Words, intonation, gestures, eye contact	Very high
Telephone	Verbal	Fast	Personal	Words, intonation, phraseology	High
Personal written: memos, letters and e-mail	Written	Slow	Personal	Words	Medium
Formal written: bulletins, notices etc.	Written	Very slow	Impersonal	Words	Low
Formal numeric: budgetary reports	Written and encrypted	Very slow	Impersonal	Numerals	Very low

Decoding

Decoding: a process in which the receiver of a message uses the symbols in which it is conveyed to attribute it with a meaning

The receiver must decode the symbols into thoughts in order to be able to understand the message. Thus, if the receiver is to be able to attribute the same meaning to the message as its sender, both parties need to have a high degree of consensus about the meaning of symbols and the rules for their use.

The Receiver

Receiver (of the message): the person to whom a message is directed

Assuming that we are not dealing with a case of eavesdropping, this is the person to whom the message is directed. The person not only has to take in the message using his or her sensory processes, but also process the information mentally to attribute it with a meaning.

Noise

Noise: any extraneous signal that interferes with or masks a message

Noise can be defined as any extraneous signal that interferes with, or masks, the message. Since this is something that acts as a barrier to effective communication, it is more appropriate to consider it later in the chapter, where barriers are dealt with in more detail.

Feedback

Feedback: a process in which sender and receiver exchange roles, so that the receiver responds to a message

In many situations sender and receiver exchange roles, and this is acknowledged in the model by a feedback loop. However, since some communication is purposely designed to be one-way, this does not always take place.

Where it is available, feedback has great value to the sender because it enables the person to gauge the receiver's reaction to the message (Ashford 1986). However, unless sender and receiver intentionally exchange roles, or the receiver reacts in a way that makes the sender pause, this exchange tends not to happen (Windahl *et al.* 1992).

Feedback can be of two types. **Direct feedback** occurs if there is an almost instantaneous exchange, as described above. The verbal channel gives far greater opportunity for this to take place, particularly if it is in a face-to-face situation where non-verbal cues such as facial expression and body language can be used. Nevertheless, direct feedback is also possible with written channels, for example, where a message evokes or calls for a response. Because this is delayed feedback, however, it is less helpful in adding to the immediate effectiveness of the process.

Indirect feedback occurs when the sender does not obtain an explicit signal from the receiver about whether the message has been attributed with its intended meaning. Thus it tends to be less useful in maintaining the ongoing effectiveness of the process. For example, a receiver might interpret a message in a different way from that desired by the sender and in good faith do exactly the opposite to that which the sender requires. While this is still feedback, the message has already given rise to a problem.

Although very simple, this basic model alerts us to the complexity of communication and some of its inherent problems:

- it is a discontinuous process, containing several breaks;
- the sender of a message has to translate his or her thoughts into a message *before* it can be sent and the receiver has to translate the message back into thoughts *before* he or she can attribute it with a meaning;
- the channel needs to be capable of conveying the intended meaning and some messages can be notoriously difficult to transmit via certain channels.

Contextual Factors

Like any other aspect of human behaviour, communication can be strongly influenced by contextual factors and there are three that can have a particularly strong impact on effectiveness.

Organisational Structure

As pointed out in Chapter 16, structure not only reflects a hierarchy of power, but it also determines the flow of work through an organisation and gives rise to a number of necessary information flows. Moreover, it not only influences who talks to whom about what, it also tends to shape styles of communication. Very tall structures are characterised by a large number of levels in the management hierarchy and are associated with centralisation of authority at the top. Where this type of structure exists, top-down, one-way communication methods dominate, and this tends to give communication a very authoritarian flavour (Luthans 1995). In addition, tall structures have more levels through which a message has to pass in travelling downwards, which delays its journey and makes it less likely to reach its destination with the same meaning that the sender intended.

Organisational Culture

Culture gives organisational members strong guidelines about acceptable patterns of behaviour and can influence all manner of organisational practices, including communication. If deference to authority is a characteristic of the culture, this can influence the way that managers communicate with subordinates and also has a bearing on whether people feel free to be the originators of messages, or feel they have to content themselves with being passive recipients. Since information is power (see Chapter 14), if power holding and the exercise of power are high in the organisational value system, this can influence how much information people withhold in the interests of protecting their power bases.

Most large organisations, particularly those with a high degree of specialisation, are likely to have a number of subcultures. To some extent, subcultures develop their own identities and this can result in them developing their own repertoires of 'buzzwords', which make communication with other parts of the organisation more difficult.

There is usually a high degree of correspondence between the structure of an organisation and its culture. In a formal bureaucratic structure anything other than communicating through formal lines of authority is likely discouraged. Perhaps more importantly, if the structure is one in which a free flow of information through formal channels is difficult, a compensatory mechanism of relying on informal channels (the grapevine) can spring into existence, a matter that will be considered in more detail later.

Finally, since there is an ongoing trend for organisations to become more culturally diverse, these organisations have their own inbuilt difficulties with communication. People are likely to speak different languages and can also have different norms and values, which sometimes results in a whole host of different meanings being attributed to verbal, non-verbal and written messages (Lewis *et al.* 1995).

Technology

Communication does not depend on technology, but on the people who communicate. Over the last decade, however, there have been significant developments in the technology of communicating, and such things as fax, e-mail, voicemail, Intranet and Internet are now commonplace. Where it is available, and providing it is used in an appropriate way, technology has a tremendous part to play in effective communication. Note, however, that there is a caveat of 'providing it is used in an appropriate way' and there are different schools of thought on whether the widespread and unrestrained adoption of new information and communication technologies has produced a desirable state of affairs in organisations.

Nevertheless, so widespread is the use of these technologies that they warrant consideration in their own right, and a return to this matter will be made later in the chapter.

TIME OUT

Carefully consider a particular class that you attend at your university or college and use the communication model to identify the following components in the instruction process:

1. Who or what is the source of the message(s)?
2. What is the main channel used to convey the message(s)?
3. What media are used in the channel(s)?
4. Who or what is the receiver?

REPLAY

- The basic components in the communication process are the sender or source of a message (who has to encode his or her thoughts into symbols that can convey the message via the channel), the channel that carries the message and the receiver of the message (who must then decode the symbols into a message that has a meaning).
- Each channel uses one or more media to carry its messages.
- In order for meaning to be conveyed, it is vital that both sender and receiver have a high degree of consensus about the meaning of the symbols used and the rules for their use.
- Noise (extraneous signals that obscure or distort the message) can enter the process via the sender, channel or the receiver.
- All communication takes place within a context and factors within the context can have an impact on the way that messages are sent and interpreted on receipt.

BARRIERS TO EFFECTIVE COMMUNICATION

Many things can impair the effectiveness of the communication process. Some are associated with the source of a message, some with the receiver, some are common to both, while others are associated with the channel of communication.

Barriers Associated with the Sender

Message Formulation

While the originator of a message can have a clear idea of the meaning he or she wishes to convey, people differ considerably in their capabilities to express their thoughts and where skills of this type are poor, there can be considerable barriers to communication.

Perceptions

Our perceptions of other people are not necessarily true but are our own versions of reality. This can sometimes lead to problems in the way that messages are formulated. For instance:

- if a sender perceives that a message is unlikely to be well received, it can be toned down to the extent that its real meaning is obscured;
- a sender can underrate the receiver's capability to cope with a complex message, which can prompt the person to 'talk down' to the recipient, who can then feel that he or she is being patronised, with all the annoyance and resentment that this causes;
- if the sender perceives that the intended recipient is a 'difficult' person to deal with, there can be a tendency to tell the receiver what he or she wants to hear, which can give rise to huge distortions.

Table 20.2 Communication barriers associated with the sender of a message

Type of barrier	Associated problems
Message formulation	Inability to transform thoughts into appropriate symbols for the channel selected
Perceptions	Inaccurate perceptions of receiver's ability to understand the message or reactions to the message
Encoding	Semantics (word meanings), jargon and use of media are unable to convey the complexity of the message

Encoding

Even when the sender can clearly express thoughts and has accurate perceptions of the receiver, there can still be problems. Most communication in organisations uses words as symbols and while these can be expressed in written or verbal form, people differ in the meanings they attribute to the same words. A common problem here is the use of jargon, which can be a distinct barrier when people hold different conventions about the meaning of jargon words.

These problems are not confined to words alone. Although diagrams and models can sometimes be a considerable aid in communicating an idea, a diagram or model is just a simplified representation of reality. Thus, while one person can take an organisation chart to be a reflection of the distribution of power in an organisation, someone else can regard it as a way of portraying the degree of specialisation. Errors of this type often result from the sender failing to put him or herself in the position of the receiver and to do this is to expect the receiver to be a mind reader.

In summary, the major barriers associated with the sender are shown in Table 20.2.

Barriers Associated with Media and Channel

Noise

This is the most readily identifiable barrier associated with these components of the model and noise can be of two types:

- **Physical noise** involves an extraneous signal masking or drowning out a message; for example, the din in a factory workshop, or bright sunlight that shines on a screen and makes a projected image almost invisible.

- **Psychological noise** has an impact when something concerned with either the message itself or the setting in which communication takes place interferes with its transmission or attributed meaning.

In face-to-face communication, a significant source of psychological noise can be an unintended clash between what is said and the speaker's non-verbal signals. These have a huge impact on verbal messages and in a face-to-face situation evidence suggests that only about 7 per cent of the impact of a message comes from the words used, 39 per cent from the way the words are uttered (inflection, tone and content) and 55 per cent from non-verbal cues such as a facial expression, eye contact and body language (Mehrabian 1971). More importantly, where a clash between verbal and a non-verbal cues occurs, it is the non-verbal message that is taken to be the factual one (Eckman and Friesen 1975).

The setting in which communication takes place can also be a potential source of psychological noise and if, for example, a manager berates someone in front of other subordinates, the chastised person can sometimes focus more on the reactions of his or her colleagues than on the message itself.

Space proxemics, the use of interpersonal space when communicating with others, can also be a source of noise. Hall (1966) shows that there are four zones of proximity for communicating with others. For most Americans these were identified as:

- an intimate zone – from actual contact to about 18 inches;
- the personal zone – from 18 inches to 4 feet;
- the social zone – from 4 to 12 feet;
- and the public zone – over 12 feet.

An individual's intimate and personal zones are private space reserved for very close and intimate encounters. To enter these without invitation can often make the receiver feel so uncomfortable that barriers are erected which interfere with the message.

Finally, the timing of a message can often erect huge perceptual barriers to its reception and accurate interpretation. For instance, announcing a drop in profits can be interpreted in different ways according to when the message appears. If it is said at one time it could be taken by employees to mean that productivity needs to be improved, but if it is said in the middle of wage negotiations, it can be interpreted as an underhand trick by management to pave the way for a meagre offer.

Inappropriateness of Media and/or Channel

Written and oral channels tend to be more appropriate for certain types of message. Because written material gives the recipient the facility to go over the information at his or her own pace, it can be highly effective for lengthy, detailed messages. It also provides a permanent record and so it tends to make the sender more precise about what is said. Because it can be difficult for a receiver to hold and integrate different parts of a long, complex verbal message in his or her memory, the latter parts of the message can interfere with understanding of what has been said earlier. Written communication can overcome this obstacle.

The verbal channel, however, is much richer than the written form, particularly if it is used in a face-to-face situation where it has a more personal focus and gives the receiver an opportunity to use additional, non-verbal signals that can aid understanding. It is also faster than many written channels, both in transmission and feedback. Perhaps most important of all, feelings and emotions are much more easily communicated in this way, and so where a message is controversial and its sender needs to convey honesty, integrity and trustworthiness as part of the message, it has tremendous advantages.

These days, the facility to use multi-media methods for a message is much greater. Video conferencing can use both written and verbal channels simultaneously, and even a face-to-face presentation supplemented by visual aids gives this facility. The great advantage of using multiple channels is that these methods are able to make use of **redundancy** – the repetition of the same message in different ways – which vastly increases the likelihood that the message will be received with its meaning intact (Hsia 1977).

Table 20.3 Communication barriers associated with media or the channel

Type of barrier	Associated problems
Noise: physical	Swamping or covering of message
Noise: psychological	Conflicting symbols (e.g. verbal and non-verbal) result in contradictory message
	Setting conveys its own (sometimes contradictory or intimidating) message
	Space proxemics: the invasion of the receiver's personal space
Inappropriate media and/or channel	Meaning of message cannot be fully conveyed by the channel or medium

As such, these methods can be particularly appropriate where complex ideas need to be communicated in an emotionally charged atmosphere, for example, in employee relations.

These potential barriers associated with media and channel of communication are summarised in Table 20.3.

Barriers Associated with the Receiver

Decoding

Perception and selectivity can be huge barriers to the accurate receipt of messages. Recipients can have preconceived ideas about what they 'expect' to see or hear which can distort their perceptions and interfere with the sender's intended meaning. A great deal can depend on whether the receiver has faith in the honesty and integrity of the sender, which tends to be influenced by prior experience. If someone has been less than honest on a prior occasion, people can suspect an ulterior motive for the current message and assign a meaning before all of it is received. As such, the receiver attends only to those parts of the message that confirm existing beliefs and the remainder is blocked out.

Information Overload

This is becoming a significant problem in many organisations and to some extent it is associated with the increased use of information technology. When information overload occurs, the receiver is swamped with a surfeit of messages and is unable to cope with them all. The sheer difficulty of trying to assimilate everything forces the person to ration his or her attention (Finholt and Sproull 1990) with the attendant risk of something important being overlooked or messages receiving no attention at all.

These potential barriers are summarised in Table 20.4.

A Short Note on Cross-national Influences

Any of the barriers to effective communication identified above can be considerably magnified when we try to convey meaning to people whose culture and language is different from our own. To start with there is the obvious problem of the absence

Table 20.4 Communication barriers associated with the receiver

Type of barrier	Associated problems
Decoding	Selectivity: attention is paid to only part of message
	Perceptions and value judgements about sender or meaning of message
Information overload	Receiver has too many messages to which he or she must attend

of common symbols and consensus about rules for their use. Even where a common language is used, however, there can be huge differences in the meanings attributed to non-verbal signals and, as was noted earlier, where there is a clash between the spoken message and the one conveyed non-verbally, it is the latter that tends to be believed.

As Varey (1999) points out, while the acquisition of linguistic skill is necessary for establishing a cross-cultural dialogue, this on its own may not be enough to convey meaning. Competence in communication also involves the ability to appreciate the differences between our own culture and the culture of those with whom we try to communicate, because culture gives rise to different world views, which can sometimes erect barriers to effective communication.

TIME OUT

In the previous Time Out exercise, you considered a class that you attend at your university or college and identified the main components in the communication process. For the same class, now try to identify any barriers to communication. Are there:

noise barriers?
barriers associated with the source of the message?
barriers associated with the media and/or channel?
barriers associated with the receiver?

REPLAY

- The main barriers to effective communication associated with the sender are poor message formulation, perception and encoding difficulties.
- The main barriers associated with the channel and media are physical and psychological noise and inappropriate channel selection.
- The main barriers associated with the receiver of a message are perceptions, decoding difficulties and information overload.
- The effects of barriers can be amplified when people from different countries or cultural backgrounds attempt to communicate.

CASE STUDY 20.2: The Luxor Company – Further Developments

In one of his frequent reflections on the firm Charles Binochet realised that it had grown significantly in a short period of time and that this had not always been handled smoothly. He also realised that future changes planned for the next wave of expansion could make things even more difficult to handle. However, by bringing in consultants to sort out matters the firm had successfully tackled two of its major problems: the lack of liaison between production and marketing and its practically non-existent system of financial control. As a result, new procedures and methods had been introduced and things seemed to be working well. However, this still left the matter of relations with the workforce, and he felt that a significant attempt to improve employee relations in the firm was needed. Accordingly, Charles Binochet formed a 'Human Resource Committee' and one of its first considerations was to find ways of improving communication with employees.

After some discussion it was decided that there should be an ongoing attempt to keep employees informed about the company and its operations. It was concluded that a relatively simple way to do this would be to display a number of large charts in a prominent place. Initially it was intended that there should be four of these, but at the insistence of the production director, who was extremely safety conscious, a fifth one showing accident rates was added. The first batch of charts giving the company's position with respect to the previous twelve months are shown in Figure 20.2.

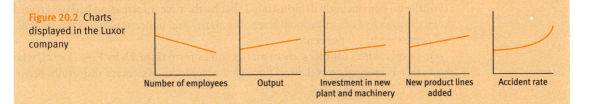

Figure 20.2 Charts displayed in the Luxor company

| Number of employees | Output | Investment in new plant and machinery | New product lines added | Accident rate |

Shortly afterwards it was brought to the attention of the Human Resource Committee that there were a substantial number of vacancies in the firm and that employee turnover was on the increase. It was also noted that trade union representatives in the company were taking an increasingly tough line with supervisors and managers about the payment of allowances for 'waiting time' when machinery was halted to make adjustments to change from one product to another. Representatives had also become particularly obstructive about the allocation of work duties and were threatening that if the time allowance for some jobs was not improved there could be a strike. The production director stated that one representative had told him that rumours about an impending shakeout were rife on the shopfloor, and that the general mood among employees was that they should grab what they could while they still had a job. To cap it all, the managing director reported that at the meeting of the Joint Negotiating Committee on the very same morning, the trade union side had tabled a claim for the biggest pay rise ever, well over twice the current inflation rate.

Question

How do you account for these reactions?

COMMUNICATION IN ORGANISATIONS

Although many organisations are awash with information, not all of these communications are intended or sanctioned by an organisation. For this reason, it is more convenient to distinguish between formal and informal communication and consider these separately.

Formal Communication

Formal communication normally occurs in three directions: vertically (upward and downward), laterally and diagonally (see Figure 20.3).

Vertical (Downward) Communication

This is the dominant form of formal communication in organisations and it normally follows the hierarchical lines established by an organisation's structure. A great deal of what is communicated originates at the highest level and while there is evidence that employees who receive the information they need from above usually perform better as individuals and in groups (O'Reilly 1977), there is also evidence that this state of affairs is not as commonplace as it should be (Callan 1993). Unfortunately there is often a significant information loss as messages are conveyed downward. This was uncovered over 40 years ago in a classic survey of 100 firms undertaken by Nichols (1962), who convincingly demonstrated that by the time information had progressed down through five organisational levels, the clarity and understanding of the message had decreased by 80 per cent.

One explanation for this state of affairs comes form research by Erez (1992), who shows that as messages travel down through the hierarchy, systematic distortions occur.

Figure 20.3 Formal and semi-formal information flows in organisations

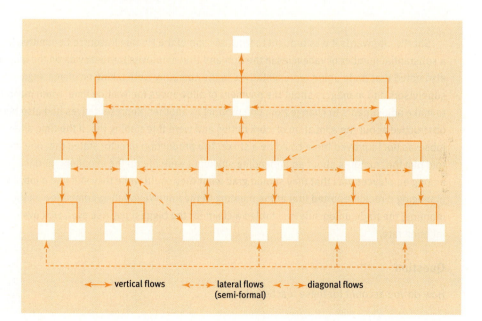

These are of two main types:

- *sharpening of messages*, in which selective retention on the part of receivers at each level prompts them to exaggerate certain parts of a message;
- *levelling of messages*, which is the selective omission of other details.

These distortions seldom come about by conscious intent, but occur for a number of predictable psychological reasons:

- people attach meaning to information according to their **expectations** (what they expect a message to convey) and pass on the information in this form;
- an **association** is made between the current message and prior messages that had certain outcomes, and where a message of a similar type heralded certain outcomes in the past, it is assumed that the likely meaning of the current one is the same;

- at each link in the communication chain, a recipient who has to pass on a message engages in *condensation*, in which he or she extracts what are perceived to be the important points, and what gets passed on is typically shorter and less detailed;
- people who have to relay ambiguous messages have a tendency to try to absorb the uncertainty by engaging in *closure* (March and Simon 1958), that is, they fill in the gaps and amplify certain points in the message to turn it into one that seems more plausible and understandable.

Vertical (Upward) Communication

Although downwards communication is the dominant form, many organisations try to make some provision for information to flow in the opposite direction. It can often be beneficial for managers to receive open, honest and accurate information for control purposes, and an effective upward flow of communication is said to be a key element in the success of Japanese organisations (Erez 1992). One way for this to occur is through the use of employee opinion surveys, which are discussed in Chapter 5, or perhaps a suggestion scheme. In addition in today's fast-moving conditions, where employee commitment and enthusiasm are strongly desired attributes, some knowledge of how people react to top management's decisions can be vital. The problem is that many employees can be wary of raising their concerns without invitation, and to some extent this can be because employees feel that those above pay little attention to what they say and develop an attitude of 'why bother'. Thus, if upwards communication is to occur, it usually needs to be actively encouraged, which requires a distinctly participative approach by management.

Diagonal Communication

Because it cuts across the hierarchy of an organisation and tends to be disliked by many managers, this type of formal communication has traditionally been the least used. Nevertheless, some degree of diagonal flow of information is probably inevitable and Bedeian (1984) notes that most communication of this type occurs between line managers and staff specialists, such as personnel officers and industrial engineers. This is hardly surprising since the primary role of many staff specialists is to gather information and disseminate it throughout the organisation.

Lateral Communication (Networks)

Most of the lateral communication that occurs in organisations happens through networks, and while these are not always part of an organisation's structure, they are sometimes acknowledged to exist. Indeed, some of them, such as cross-functional liaison teams and project groups, eventually become a formal part of the structure, and in a matrix structure (see Chapter 16) lateral communication would be the main method of coordinating functional activities. As such, formal networks do not exist in a random way, and a number of distinct network structures are identifiable, for instance, 'circle', 'chain', 'wheel', 'Y' and 'all-channel' (Bavelas 1950; Leavitt 1951), which are described in Chapter 10.

Informal Communication

The Grapevine

Grapevine: an informal channel of communication

In most organisations informal communication channels usually exist alongside formal mechanisms. This is often referred to as the *grapevine*, and while its existence is not officially recognised, almost everyone acknowledges that it operates and it is found almost everywhere.

It is a powerful means of communication that does not depend on formal organisational channels and, for the most part, it supplements any formal system that exists. Its prime function is to disseminate information that is of interest to people – usually information that is not available through formal channels. Thus it is an important, if not the most important, part of the communication network for any social group in an organisation (Noon and Delbridge 1993) and there are a number of reasons why it exists and flourishes:

- because there is a lack of information available through formal channels;
- because people feel insecure, which prompts them to communicate with each other to seek comfort in the face of perceived threats;
- because there are conflicts between a superior and his or her subordinates, in which the latter feel the need to share information;
- because people engage in political tactics, in which protagonists circulate negative information about each other;
- because there is a need to spread new information quickly.

The last point illustrates a distinctive feature of the grapevine. It is often much faster at carrying a message than formal channels and research evidence tells us that it is somewhere between 75 and 95 per cent as accurate (Watson 1982). Indeed, most employees regard it as a more reliable source of information than that handed out by management (Robbins 1998), mainly because the message gets to almost everybody, even though only about 10 per cent of employees are active message carriers.

For the most part, managers deprecate the very existence of these informal channels, although they sometimes deliberately make use of them when it is convenient. Thus formal methods are often introduced with the aim of eliminating the grapevine. One of these – team briefing – will be described presently. The problem is that informal channels are so useful to employees that it is unlikely that they can ever be completely eliminated. For this reason, it has been argued that managers are foolish to try to do so and instead they should take greater pains to ensure that official channels match the informal ones, so that both reinforce the same message (Foy 1983).

Rumour and Informal Communication

A much criticised feature of the grapevine is its ability to circulate (and sometimes originate) rumours. Although a *rumour* is unverified information of uncertain origin, this does not mean that a rumour is untrue. Mishra (1990) gives four general types of rumour that commonly occur in organisations, all of which are likely to arise in conditions of ambiguity and uncertainty about the future:

* **pipe dreams/wishful thinking,** which express the wishes or desires of the people who spread the rumour, perhaps with the hope that if a rumour is started, it will come true;
* **bogeys,** which express fears and anxieties, often because there is speculation about the future;
* **wedge drivers,** which spread aggressive, damaging and sometimes downright untruthful information about someone, often because political manoeuvring is in progress;
* **home-stretchers,** which are items of information that anticipate the future in a prophetic way.

The Effects of the Grapevine

As noted above, the grapevine is often faster and more efficient than many formal means of communication and assertions that it has a detrimental impact on organisational effectiveness are probably grossly exaggerated. For instance, Zaremba (1988) draws attention to a number of its highly beneficial features:

* it can act as a safety valve that enables people to release their frustrations and anger about those in authority;
* because it gives people a sense of being 'in the know', the grapevine can also give groups and their members higher morale, feelings of security and belonging;
* the grapevine can be a reminder to managers that they may need to be more effective in their own communications;
* if taken in the right spirit, it can become a valuable source of feedback to management about how subordinates actually perceive managers and their decisions.

TIME OUT

Reflect carefully on communication at your university or college and try to identify the following:

1. Any formal provisions that are made for the institution to communicate with its students.
2. Any formal provisions that exist for students to be able to communicate upwards to lecturers, more senior academics and the management of the institution.
3. Any formal provisions that exist for students in one school or department to communicate with students in other schools and departments.
4. Any informal communication networks of which you may be aware.

DIFFERENT FORMS OF ORGANISATIONAL COMMUNICATION

The two main channels of communication in organisations are verbal and written and since each has its own strengths and weaknesses, it is convenient to consider them separately.

Verbal Communication

Verbal methods are widely used in organisations and evidence suggests that over three-quarters of managerial communication occurs in this way (Luthans and Larson 1986). Because most verbal communication occurs in a face-to-face situation, this will be the main focus of discussion.

OB IN ACTION: Improving Dialoguing

Senior managers in most organisations would seem to agree that communication is a vital competency for even the most junior of managers and many of them also admit that their organisations can be beset with communication problems that have a serious effect on organisational performance. In an attempt to make communication easier, many firms have invested heavily in technology, for instance, e-mail facilities. However, while this is useful in providing an easy-to-use vehicle for communicating, e-mails lack the richness of face-to-face methods, a richness that can be vital in ensuring understanding and building working relationships.

One company that has recognised this and is making a determined attempt to improve the quantity and quality of dialogue at workplace level is the British supermarket chain Asda. For instance, Asda has created opportunities for people to talk freely and informally about their work and the organisation at the start or finish of the working day and has also arranged more formal sessions in which managers listen to their staff. This is said to have resulted in noticeable improvements, not only in communication, but also in staff satisfaction, motivation and performance. Along with other large organisations such as British Gas, Comet and the Royal Bank of Scotland, Asda is also involved in a longer-term research project conducted by the Item group, which aims to improve the quality of face-to-face communication. Although this research is still in progress, useful findings have already emerged in terms of identifiable core skills that are necessary for an effective dialogue. The Item group is now in the process of using these to develop training sessions (known as the 'communication gymnasium') which enable people to explore ways of improving their dialoguing abilities.

Source:

Hirst, S (1999) Verbal remedy, *People Management*, 11 March: 50–1.

Theoretical Considerations: Communication Styles

Many of the problems that influence the effectiveness of face-to-face communication can be traced to perceptual differences on the part of sender and receiver. People interpret the world according to their own backgrounds and prior experiences, and this has a strong impact on how they behave when communicating. One approach to understanding the effect that this has on the process is to use the concept of *interpersonal communication style*, which can broadly be described as the way that people prefer to relate to other people in the communication situation.

In a conversation between two people, it is seldom (if ever) the case that either of them knows everything that the other person knows. This unknown information not only concerns the substantive topic of conversation, but also includes knowledge about personal feelings and potential reactions. For instance, if I talk to someone about food, I may be unaware of the other person's tastes, or whether he or she has some religious or ethical objection to certain foods. Similarly, he or she may not know this about me, and so we can both have a degree of wariness about what we say. Thus, communication situations can be classified according to how much each person knows at the outset about three matters:

- substantive knowledge of the issue;
- the person's own stance on the matter;
- the other person's stance.

For a dyadic (two-person) interaction, this can be classified along two dimensions: the amount of information possessed by self and the amount of information possessed by the other person. The usual way of expressing this is by using what is known as the 'Johari window' (Hall 1973), which can be used to portray the four communication situations shown in Figure 20.4.

Interpersonal communication style: the way a person prefers to relate to other people in a communication situation

Figure 20.4
The Johari window

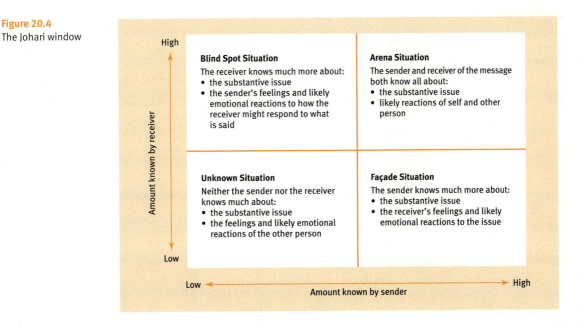

In the **blind spot** situation, the receiver has an advantage over the sender because he or she knows more about the substantive issue, his or her own likely reactions to what might be said and the likely feelings and emotional reactions of the sender. Thus the sender is at a disadvantage and communication can be impaired.

The **unknown situation** is one where neither party knows anything about the substantive issue or the other person. Here there is a danger of the blind leading the blind, and since any meaningful dialogue only occurs by chance, interpersonal communication will be poor.

In the **façade situation**, the sender of the message knows much more than the recipient. Therefore, the receiver may try to convey the impression that he or she understands or, for fear of offending the receiver, the sender can withhold information. Either of these is merely a façade of effective communication in terms of transferring understanding.

The **arena situation** is said to be the one that is most likely to result in effective interpersonal communication because sender and receiver both know all that needs to be known about the issue and each other. However, for this situation to occur the parties must first gain a clear understanding of each other's feelings, together with the meaning of the information that is to be exchanged.

Three of the situations shown in the Johari window result in communication that is only partially effective. Polsky (1971) points out that effectiveness comes down to a willingness to engage in self-disclosure (revealing ourselves to others) and a willingness to give and receive feedback. People vary considerably in these respects and this gives rise to characteristic patterns of behaviour (interpersonal styles) that impair effectiveness. This is shown in Figure 20.5.

Where the sender of the message has a **self-exposing** style of behaviour, he or she encourages the receiver to focus on the sender, probably by constantly asking for feedback. However, because the person is essentially self-centred, little attention is given

Figure 20.5
Interpersonal communication styles (after Polsky 1971)

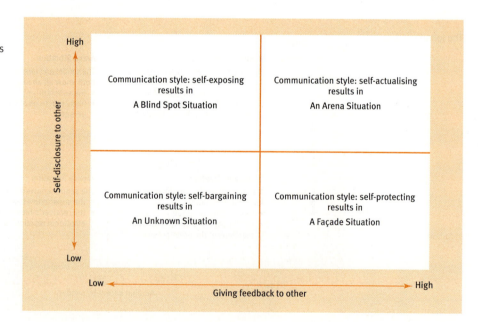

to any feedback the receiver provides, and there is little feedback given to the receiver. Thus a 'blind spot' situation is created.

If people in the role of sender have a **self-bargaining** style, they are willing to open up to the receiver and also give a measure of feedback. This, however, is something like a game of 'tit-for-tat'. Because the sender is only willing to engage in these behaviours to the extent that he or she perceives that the receiver does the same, an 'unknown situation' is created.

People with a **self-protective** style are unwilling to be open with the receiver about their own feelings and views, but tend to probe the other person's meaning and give a great deal of feedback. In effect, therefore, a 'façade situation' results.

Finally, those who have a **self-actualising** style are willing to provide a great deal of information about themselves, and give and receive feedback, all of which tends to bring about an 'arena situation'.

Polsky's scheme suggests that the self-actualising style is universally the best and that something is wrong if it is not used everywhere. While this is far too sweeping an assertion to be plausible, the idea that using a self-actualising style encourages effective communication is a useful one. However, because this depends acutely on a person's ability to adopt a self-disclosing approach and to give feedback, it is worthwhile considering these aspects of behaviour.

Self-disclosure

Self-disclosure: information that people consciously communicate about themselves to others

This can be defined as information that people consciously communicate about themselves to others. This can take place non-verbally as well as through the spoken word and to some extent many people do it unconsciously. Nevertheless, because people can be wary of revealing too much, lest the other person take advantage of them, this is different from intentionally disclosing personal details. Moreover, the willingness to self-disclose can be affected by the context and circumstances in which communication takes place. For instance, people who have formal power over others can be reluctant to self-disclose because they see it as part of the job to conceal their personal likes and dislikes in the interests of not putting pressure on their subordinates.

Feedback

Team briefing: a cascade system of communication starting at the top of an organisation, in which managers at each level brief their direct subordinates about matters relevant to the subordinates

Nobody can give accurate feedback unless he or she is fully cognisant with what the other person has said. Thus, the key to being able to give (and receive) feedback is usually understanding a message. This means listening, and listening in an active way, which involves a conscious effort to search for the speaker's meaning, suspending judgement until he or she has finished and, if matters are still not clear, asking questions to obtain clarification (Brownell 1986).

Face-to-Face Communication in Practice

What is given above mostly relates to dyadic communication, but in organisations it is often more convenient to disseminate information in a situation where there is one sender and several receivers. One method of doing this that has been in vogue for several years is *team briefing*. This is essentially a cascade system which commences at the top, with managers at each level briefing the next level below, and continues downwards through the whole organisation. It is important to note that while briefings include some information about company-wide matters, the main emphasis is on issues specific to the workgroup being briefed. The operational guide to the process (produced by the Industrial Society (Middleton 1983)) lays down the six cardinal principles on which it is based.

1. **It is face-to-face**   although time is left for questions at the end, this is primarily to check that the message has been understood and general discussion is discouraged.
2. **Small briefing teams**   usually not less than four and no more than fifteen people.
3. **Leaders**   briefing is by the line manager or supervisor responsible for the team.
4. **Regularity**   it should occur regularly, preferably at fixed intervals of about one month, and briefing itself should last no more than 30 minutes, including questions.
5. **Relevance**   it primarily concentrates on local information that is considered to be most relevant to the team. The 'core brief', which comes from higher levels of management, should occupy no more than one-third of the session.
6. **Monitoring**   leaders need to be trained on how to brief others and it is usually considered important for higher levels of management to monitor the effectiveness of a supervisor's briefings.

As can be seen, although there is a built-in check that those who are briefed understand what is said, team briefing focuses heavily on top-down, one-way communication. The benefits claimed for it are:

- it reinforces the role of line managers and supervisors because, as providers of information, it differentiates them from their subordinates;
- by giving work a purpose and relating people to the organisation as a whole, it increases the commitment of subordinates;
- it reduces misunderstandings by avoiding the assumption that people know what is going on, and instead explicitly sets out to ensure that all employees receive a common message;
- because the early provision of information can assist in people's understanding of why changes are necessary, it helps with the acceptance of change;
- because employees receive a common official message, it helps control the grapevine;
- it should not be used for consultative or decision making purposes, but because people are better informed, this can promote feedback to management via other channels and thus improve the flow of upward communication.

Having noted these points, whether the stated advantages are obtained in practice is a contentious point. While most employees would rather be better informed than kept in the dark, the ideas underpinning team briefing are aimed at reinforcing managerial prerogatives, and it can be expected that in certain circumstances employees may well be suspicious that the information being conveyed is rather one-sided and selective. Indeed, what evidence there is on the outcomes of communication schemes such as these tends to show that the expected benefits of improved employee attitudes are largely unrealised.

TIME OUT

Carefully reflect on a recent face-to-face communication that you experienced with a single individual. This could be a colleague at work, a fellow student, a friend or parent, or a lecturer at your university or college. Try to identify the following:

1. What was the communication style that you used in this encounter: self-denying, self-exposing, self-protective, self-bargaining or self-actualising?
2. Is this your normal style with most people or was there something special about this encounter that prompted you to adopt the style? If so, what?
3. What was the communication style that the other person used in this encounter: self-denying, self-exposing, self-protective, self-bargaining or self-actualising?
4. Do you feel that this is the other person's normal style with most people, or was there something special about this encounter that prompted him or her to adopt the style? If so, what?
5. Having identified the styles that you and the other person used, to what extent do you feel that these made it easier to communicate, or inhibited effective communication in the encounter?

Written Communication

Evidence suggests that written channels are still the major method used by organisations for communicating with their employees. For instance, a survey of over 900 organisations of all sizes in all industrial sectors by the Industrial Society reveals interesting insights on this matter, a summary of which is given in Table 20.5.

As can be seen, written methods are heavily used within organisations, which is hardly surprising because they are relatively cheap and convenient and, if used well, are highly effective in certain circumstances, for example, where:

Table 20.5 Frequency of use of different methods of workplace communication and effectiveness of methods

Method	Frequency of use for communicating about workplace matters (%)	Effectiveness of method (%)
Bulletins and noticeboards	97	6
Team briefing	82	57
Newsletters	78	7
House journals	65	6
Roadshow meetings	53	11
E-mail or other electronic	38	4
Videos	29	1
Other	23	5

Source: Industrial Society 1994.

- accuracy or precise wording is vital;
- a detailed explanation is desirable;
- there are a large number of employees dispersed over several locations;
- there is a need for employees to have a permanent record.

While this does not mean that the written channel is always the most effective, there are several ways in which it can be used to good effect. Some firms develop *employee handbooks*, which can be particularly useful for new entrants, or as a source of reference for information that is relatively unchanging. Many companies also provide summary annual reports to inform employees about the activities and performance of the enterprise. As the Industrial Society survey shows, bulletins and noticeboards are probably the most widely used methods, and in the case of the latter, these are sometimes the only form of written communication. The great problem here is that not everybody stops to read noticeboards and so it can never be guaranteed that the message has been received. For more regular dissemination of information, many large organisations also produce in-house journals and newsletters, which often contain social as well as organisational items.

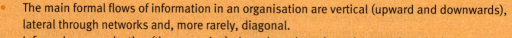

REPLAY

- The main formal flows of information in an organisation are vertical (upward and downwards), lateral through networks and, more rarely, diagonal.
- Informal communication (the grapevine) also takes place through networks, which are sustained by employees because they serve a useful purpose.
- The main ways of communicating in organisations are interpersonally, using face-to-face methods and different forms of written communication.
- All channels of communication have their own strengths and weaknesses and each one is more suitable for some types of message than others.
- Face-to-face communication is potentially the richest form in information, but taking advantage of this richness requires people to adopt appropriate communication styles.

Electronic Communication

Across the last decade huge advances have been made in methods of electronic data transmission. Voice messaging facilities now allow desktop computers to act as sophisticated answering machines that can reply to a message and relay it onwards to interested parties. Electronic bulletin boards, which are similar to noticeboards but operate through computers, can communicate routine information to large numbers of people, thus reducing paperwork and filing. The Internet allows literally millions of people to obtain information on nearly everything, and potentially makes it possible for anyone who has a computer to communicate with others who are also equipped in this way. Finally, the Intranet, which is really only an internal form of the Internet, allows people inside the organisation to send written messages to each other with tremendous ease. All of these can be of great benefit to organisations, but because in many cases these methods have been the subject of a great deal of 'hype', there are a number of issues that require examination in greater detail and each will be explored separately.

E-commerce

One of the greatest boons of electronic communications seems to be its potential for so-called e-business. By using the Internet organisations can potentially reach customers in markets that they have not yet tapped. It can also bring convenience to customers, who can now order even mundane articles such as the weekly groceries via the Internet. However, while services such as this attract a great deal of publicity, so far it is the business-to-business sector in which the most significant level of activity lies. Firms availing themselves of this facility are reputedly able to achieve savings equivalent to 15 per cent of turnover by eliminating paperwork and unnecessary warehouse stocks. In America, for example, the three largest car manufacturers – Ford, General Motors and Chrysler – have announced plans to create a single automotive parts service run via the Internet, and other groups of manufacturers are forming similar partnerships. In the light of these developments, traditional companies are said to be finding it increasingly difficult to market their goods and services.

Nevertheless, not everything in e-business is plain sailing. While Internet banking seems to have found favour with some customers, a number of embarrassing fiascos have occurred, notably at Barclays and the Halifax, where it was possible for complete strangers to access people's bank account details, creating a temporary crisis of confidence (Jones 2000). In addition, the comparatively low cost of setting up a website to take orders for goods seems to have encouraged a degree of unscrupulous trading practices. Taking orders is easy, but being able to fulfil an order and get the goods to the customer is much more difficult and expensive. A number of firms selling via the Internet seem to have forgotten (or conveniently ignored) that warehousing and delivery facilities are required to do this. This has also resulted in a degree of wariness on the part of consumers (Naughton 2000).

Finally, the more that individuals and organisations make use of the Internet, the more susceptible they become to a complete breakdown because their computer system has been sabotaged by the unwitting importation of a virus (Davidson 2003) – see OB in Action box overleaf.

Electronic Communication within Organisations

Like most things, while there are huge potential benefits in using electronic methods to communicate, the benefits are not always realised, and some of the disadvantages are now beginning to show. With voicemail, for example, while it was supposed to be an aid to efficiency and cutting costs, many organisations now consider it to be useless and about half of all new voicemail systems are abandoned within one year (Gwyther 1999). Quite simply, callers do not like being treated as an anonymous entity and a National Opinion Poll survey conducted in 1999 revealed that among customers voicemail is the third most detested feature of business organisations.

While e-mail can be a great boon in some circumstances, a number of drawbacks are also starting to appear. Not everyone has the skills to encode their thoughts into the written word and it seems likely that the ability to communicate in writing has

OB IN ACTION: The Hunt for Virus Writers

In November 2003 Microsoft put $250,000 (£150,000) in bounties on the heads of two computer virus writers as it stepped up its fight against the tide of malicious code aimed at desktop PCs. The software giant and law enforcement officials in the US also sought to turn public sentiment against virus writers, who are often depicted as underground heroes in technology circles and popular culture. The bounty follows a spate of attacks by viruses and worms, many aimed at weaknesses in the Windows computer operating system. Steve Ballmer, Microsoft's chief executive officer, said the company had been 'humbled'. The onslaught also brought an attempt by class action lawyers in the US to hold Microsoft responsible for losses suffered by computer users. However, while software companies are excluded from product liability claims by contract, this has not been tested in the courts.

Microsoft said it would pay rewards of $250,000 for information leading to the arrest and prosecution of the people behind two viruses this year. One, known as Blaster or MSBlast, spread through an estimated 1.2 million computers. Three people face prosecution in connection with variants of the virus, including an 18-year-old in Minneapolis and a man in Romania. Microsoft said the reward was tied to 'variant A' of the virus, designed to attack the website the company uses to distribute fixes for security flaws. The other reward covers the SoBig virus, designed to turn infected computers into machines that outsiders could use to send spam e-mail.

Source:

Waters R (2003) Microsoft offers reward to catch virus writers, *The Financial Times*, 6 November.

declined considerably in the population over the last 30 years. So serious is this problem that several large companies, for example Marks & Spencer, Tesco and Unilever, are having to spend significant sums of money in teaching staff how to write simple written communications (Arlidge 2000).

Second, because information can be sent and received with great ease, there is a distinct possibility of information overload and 'spam' (unsolicited messages) (Clegg 2003). This can all too easily lead to messages not being read and, in the case of e-mail, there is a danger that something that was intended to be a means of sending messages cheaply and more effectively has actually become a distinct barrier to communication (Gleick 2003).

Third, there are other, less visible effects. While e-mail is a convenient way of sending messages, it is very impersonal compared to face-to-face methods and it can all too easily become a substitute for face-to-face communication, which tends to deprive people of one of the things that they value most about work – the social experience.

Finally, more insidious features of e-mail are beginning to appear. There is no such thing as a 'confidential' e-mail and so it can become a control tool that intrudes into a person's private life and innermost thoughts. Even worse is the recently recognised

Flamemail: the use of e-mail to abuse others in the workplace

and growing phenomenon of a *flamemail*: the use of e-mail to abuse others in the work-place. In essence, this is a form of bullying that can all too easily lead to higher levels of stress for individuals.

THE DIGITAL AGE AND THE VIRTUAL ORGANISATION

The expression 'digital (or information) age' is now widely used to convey the idea of a society in which information and communication technologies (ICTs) will result in a new wave of economic development. Predictions on this matter first came to promin-ence in the 1980s in the writings of a number of self-styled prophets of the new age (for example, Drucker 1988). These arguments have a strong element of *technological determinism*, in which the new ICTs are seen as an irresistible driving force for change, the key to which is said to be the so-called 'information superhighway' (Internet), which will create boundless opportunities for the revitalisation of industry.

Technological determinism: the belief that technological advances drive changes, e.g. to organisational structures

To some extent the efficacy of the new ICTs has probably been 'talked up' as an off-the-shelf solution to reverse the decline of Western economies, because it is argued that failure to modernise in this way is a sure recipe for further deterioration (Birchall and Lyons 1995). For this reason governments everywhere have exhorted organisa-tions to become involved before it is too late (Bangemann 1994).

Off-the-shelf recipes for success seem to have an irresistible appeal to managers. One of the things that makes this one so acceptable is the argument that the new tech-nology will inevitably result in a radically different form of organisation, and this is considered next.

New Organisational Forms

The new organisations that are said to result from embracing ICTs are known by a number of names, for example 'networked organisations' (Miles and Snow 1986) or the 'virtual organisation' (Davidow and Malone 1992). In some cases ICTs are merely seen as the enabler of this type of organisation while others argue that the technology forces an organisation to adopt new ways of working. Nevertheless, it is argued that in the information age economic advantage accrues to organisations which turn information into usable knowledge, rather than those which turn physical inputs into outputs. Thus, the resulting organisational form is an extremely loose network of relatively high-status knowledge workers. Unlike conventional firms, these organisa-tions do not exist in a physical sense, but only in cyberspace, as what have been described as 'organisationless organisations' (Nohria and Berkley 1994), which have fluid bound-aries that expand or contract as required, and with capital and other inputs assembled as they are needed for a particular endeavour. By those who advocate these arrange-ments, these organisations are said to deliver the ultimate in economic efficiency and flexibility. Their main characteristics are:

- lean, flat and stripped down to the bare necessities;
- an absence of hierarchy;
- support functions, such as accounting and personnel, are outsourced, as are manufacturing and delivery;
- most tasks are accomplished by project teams which vary in size according to the task in hand;

- the organisation does not need to exist at any particular location but is an *ad hoc* assembly of skills required for a particular project;
- people are connected by ICTs and work collaboratively.

The advantages of these arrangements are said to be:

- a strong competitive advantage because knowledge can be exploited almost immediately;
- the organisation is in continuous interaction with its environment, from which it learns almost instantaneously, with very rapid reaction to environmental changes;
- economy in the use of resources;
- people work in an empowered, autonomous and therefore enthusiastic and committed way.

Teleworker: someone who works at a place other than the one where the results of the work are needed, by using information and communication technology

Virtual organisations are assumed to be staffed by some form of *teleworkers*, that is, people who work at a place other than the one where the results of the work are needed, using ICTs (Bertin and Denbigh 1996). Some advocates of the virtual organisation, such as Negroponte (1995), argue that many of these people will be portfolio workers who work for a whole range of organisations on a freelance basis. Since it is argued that routine work will largely disappear in the information age (EC 1996), it is also assumed that people who work in virtual organisations will be technical, managerial or professional staff who can be trusted to work enthusiastically without supervision (Handy 1995), and these enterprises are portrayed as exciting, stimulating places in which to work. All this sounds a near perfect situation for both organisations and those who work in them. For this reason it is important to examine the evidence on virtual organisations.

The Virtual Organisation

The technology enabling the creation of virtual organisations already exists. The Internet is up and running and software that enables people to work collaboratively in teams also exists (Nunamaker 1997). However, while other developments, such as video-telephony, that might also facilitate the virtual organisation have been developed, to date they are reported to be commercially unsuccessful (Kraut and Fish 1997).

So far as the existence of virtual organisations is concerned the most significant thing is that, except for a small number of isolated cases, they do not actually exist (Furnham 2000). The notable exceptions are sportswear manufacturers Reebok, Nike and Puma, in the field of computing Dell Computers and Gateway and in furniture retailing IKEA (Stanworth 1998). These are all high-profile organisations, which only serves to fuel the unfounded assumption that a mass transformation to the virtual organisation is in progress. Nevertheless, there are a fairly large number of companies that call themselves virtual organisations, probably because the expression has a catchy, up-to-the-minute ring that appeals to managers who wish to convey the impression that their organisations are at the cutting edge of innovation. Thus, there seems to be a tendency for any firm with a flat structure and an emphasis on teamworking to identify itself as a virtual organisation. However, most of these firms are really traditional organisations that have restructured themselves with downsizing and delayering initiatives and, where it is used, teamworking is not necessarily of the empowered and autonomous variety because workers are still controlled through traditional hierarchical arrangements (Stanworth 1998). Thus, while information and communication technology is widely used in these firms this is merely to speed up communication or to perform traditional coordination and control activities in a more economical way.

Accounting for the Lack of Virtual Organisations

One reason for the dearth of organisations of this type may be that the arguments for their existence are based upon a false premise, that is that the very existence of the technology results in the formation of virtual organisations. However, because the evidence that structures are not solely determined by technology is so overwhelming, this idea must be discarded (see the theory of strategic choice (Child 1997) in Chapter 17).

In addition, Symon (2000) gives a penetrating analysis of the supposed link between ICTs and the predicted organisational form, which reveals other reasons why the virtual organisation is unlikely to exist. She argues that there are five major assumptions that underpin the existence of this link, all of which are contradicted to some extent by the prior research evidence and this is explained in what follows.

Assumption 1: That All the Required Information can be Transmitted Electronically

While this is theoretically possible, it is also likely that too much information would be made available, so that information overload occurs. Here Symon points out that several studies, such as the work of Finholt and Sproull (1990), show that people develop strategies to cope with this situation, the most favoured of which is simply to ignore many of the messages. More important perhaps is the point that media such as e-mail are devoid of many of the social cues that support interpersonal relations, for example, non-verbal signals such as eye contact and facial expression that convey meaning and intention are all absent (Garton and Wellman 1995). Since interactions between geographically dispersed strangers who make up project teams would be acutely dependent on quickly establishing meaning and intent, one of the main advantages of this type of organisation – rapid decision making – would be lost. For these reasons Symon argues that there are grave doubts about whether ICTs can transmit all the required information.

Assumption 2: That Most Employees are Willing to Use Electronic Forms of Communication

Here Symon points out that people usually act in accordance with previous group norms about the appropriate way of communicating certain types of message (Zack and McKenney 1995). If these norms dictate face-to-face methods for certain messages, people will find ways of using this method and ignore electronic methods.

Assumption 3: That an Increase in Electronic Communication Links Overcomes Barriers to Communication and Participation

A participative, collaborative and non-hierarchical work environment is said to be essential to reap the full advantages of the virtual organisation. However, as Symon points out, ICTs in themselves do not create these conditions (Ciborra and Patriotta 1996).

While the anonymity afforded by electronic messaging can lead to increased openness, participation and democracy are much more dependent on prior organisational contexts and cultures (Zack and McKenney 1995). Thus, if the organisation is already riddled with notions of status and hierarchy, introducing electronic methods is unlikely to remove the effects of these features.

Assumption 4: That Electronic Networking Enables More Autonomous and Flexible Working

In order to encourage workers to give of their best in terms of knowledge and creativity, autonomy and flexibility are said to be essential features of the virtual organisation. While ICTs may help by providing communication links, so far as employees are concerned there can be distinct drawbacks about flexibility. It usually results in people becoming more dispensable and job losses, particularly among lower-status clerical workers, are commonplace (Boddy and Gunson 1995). Moreover, a combination of teleworking and globalisation has raised the spectre of jobs being exported to developing countries where labour costs are lower. It is no coincidence, for example, that India is now the preferred location for call centres, because of lower labour costs. For this reason there is also a possibility of insecurity for higher-status workers.

Employees are usually well aware of these matters and so it is by no means certain that they willingly accept autonomy or give flexibility, no matter how much is provided in the way of electronic communications technology. As if this were not enough, Symon also points out that teleworking is not necessarily a liberating experience. For instance, call centres demonstrate how little autonomy and flexibility can be allowed to people who work in this way and so there are grave doubts about whether ICTs always result in more autonomous and flexible working conditions.

Assumption 5: That Work Using Communication Technologies Supports Achievement of Management Goals

According to Symon, while the use of ICTs can lead to much more efficiency and effectiveness in the way people work, a number of studies have shown that there are also counter-tendencies. For instance, e-mail can result in time wasting on social chatter and it can also be used for politicking or even to support personal aims that are counter to those of the organisation (Romm and Pilskin 1998). Thus, it is far from certain that ICTs always result in an easier achievement of management's aims.

Overall, therefore, Symon's analysis provides a number of convincing reasons that explain the rarity of virtual organisations. At present there is no widespread transformation from prior organisational forms, and ICTs have merely been introduced in a piecemeal way to support management's traditional methods of controlling the workforce (Murray and Willmott 1997).

Teleworking

While teleworking can be used in many other contexts than the virtual organisation, it is envisaged that teleworkers will staff organisations of this type, and so it is relevant to examine trends in work of this nature. An extensive examination is provided by Stanworth (1998), who notes that while there has been some growth in teleworking in Great Britain, and that this is forecast to continue, there are several types of teleworker and the forecasts are different for each one.

Employed Teleworkers

There are a significant number of these workers in Great Britain (Brewster *et al.* 1993), which is associated with the growth of the call centre industry and the increased number of remote offices set up by banks to deal with clerical work formerly undertaken in high street branches (Cressey and Scott 1992). This is usually routine, semi-skilled work, often undertaken by part-time employees, and the volume is expected to grow in the future.

Self-employed Teleworkers

Although there has been a small amount of research to examine these working arrangements, it tends to have been undertaken for specific occupations such as publishing or language translation. This makes it impossible to extrapolate the results of the whole working population and no future trends can be determined. However, little future expansion is envisaged.

Home-based Teleworkers

Here there are three discernable sub-groups. Those based at home for part of the week are usually high status, regular employees who periodically work at home, sometimes because an employee's services can only be retained if he or she can achieve a better balance between work and home life. With the exception of possible crisis periods, such as a complete breakdown of transport services, a major growth in this area is not expected.

People who are home-based for all of their working time are usually women doing low-skilled clerical work for low pay, and are similar in employment status to 'out-workers' that were once commonplace in some manufacturing industries. They often have unpredictable workloads and work unsocial hours. However, in terms of the economic advantages that accrue to organisations from using them, a modest increase in numbers can be expected.

Finally, freelance teleworkers are usually reluctant recruits to this type of work. They are rarely people who are attracted to the idea of self-employment as is predicted by the virtual organisation model. Rather, they tend to be former full-time employees made redundant by a downsizing or other cost-cutting initiative, to whom the job has now been outsourced as a self-employed person.

As can be seen, any forecast growth in teleworking is likely to be in low-skill occupations. Thus, the vision of a new generation of highly skilled technical and professional teleworkers who staff virtual organisations is no more than a figment of the imaginations of those who prophesied the rise of this type of enterprise. When taken together with Symon's (2000) arguments, this means that the virtual organisation may be the way that things move in the future, but any movement will be at a very slow pace.

OVERVIEW AND CONCLUSIONS

As the definition given at the start of the chapter points out, communication is much more than simply transmitting and receiving information. It consists of conveying meaning and, for this reason, the effectiveness of communication can be gauged by the extent to which the sender and the receiver of a message are in agreement about its meaning. From this it follows that if agreement is absent, communication has not taken place, only the output of information from the source of a message. As such, an abiding theme in the chapter has been to focus on the effectiveness of the process.

Despite its apparently straightforward nature, communication is a complex process. It involves the interaction of many components, all of which need to function in the correct sequence and in an appropriate way for meaning to be conveyed. Two of these, the sender and the receiver, are human and for both of them human sensory and cognitive processes are involved. Since these processes are unique to individuals, people can attribute different meanings to the symbols used to communicate an idea, which means that there is no certainty that a sender will produce a message that is interpreted in the same way by its recipient. Moreover, because the channel selected for a message may be inappropriate for conveying its meaning, other problems can arise.

Like all human activities, communication occurs within a context, and this can also have an impact on the way that messages are interpreted. Therefore, the effectiveness of communication is not something that can be taken for granted. It is an activity that requires thought before any attempt at communication takes place, and it is almost certainly one in which the amount of mental activity that precedes the activity is directly proportional to its effectiveness.

In terms of the cues they provide to convey meaning, certain methods of communication are much richer than others. Verbal methods, particularly if they take place in a face-to-face situation, provide a host of non-verbal cues as well as the words that are spoken. This method is also more likely to result in the provision of a degree of feedback to the sender, which can be used to check whether meaning has been conveyed. However, for face-to-face methods to work effectively, the parties need to adopt appropriate interpersonal communication styles by being open to each other and providing feedback.

Many organisations now place emphasis on face-to-face verbal communication with employees. Nevertheless, written channels are still the dominant method used for this purpose and the effectiveness of the process is almost certainly impaired by the oft-quoted decline in effective writing skills. This problem is compounded by the increasing use of methods made available by cheap and reliable electronic technology, for instance, e-mail. Because people may have little experience in exercising written communication skills, many of them are ill-equipped to use these methods, and so other problems that impede effectiveness in communication are starting to appear, for example, information overload.

FURTHER READING

Beck, C E (1999) *Managerial Communication: Bridging Theory and Practice*, London: Prentice Hall. A useful book which, as its title implies, covers organisational communication in theory and practice.

Carysforth, C (1998) *Communication for Work*, Oxford: Butterworth-Heinemann. For those who like the 'how to do it' approach, a useful volume that contains many practical tips that can be used to improve personal communication skills.

Hargie, O and D Tourish (eds) (2000) *Handbook of Communication Audits for Organisations*, London: Routledge. A book of readings presenting a number of methodologies to evaluate the effectiveness of communications with a view to making improvements.

Lewis, P S, S N Goodman and P M Fondt (1995) *Management Challenges in the 21st Century*, St Paul: West Publishing. An interesting book which, among other things, deals with the implications of communication in organisations that in the future are likely to be more culturally diverse.

McNeill, D (2000) *The Face*, London: Penguin. A penetrating analysis of the extremely rich variety of signals that we communicate (non-verbally) in our facial expressions.

Pease, A (1997) *Body Language: How to Read Others' Thoughts by Their Gestures 3rd edn*, London: Shaldon press. An interesting guide to decoding non-verbal communication.

Rosenfeld, P, R A Giacalone and C A Riordan (1995) *Impression Management in Organisations: Theory, Measurement and Practice*, London: Routledge. An impressive book that draws widely on the research evidence in the area.

Windahl, S, B Signitzer and T J Olson (1992) *Using Communication Theory: An Introduction to Planned Communication*, London: Sage. A Very useful introduction to communication theory and its application.

REVIEW AND DISCUSSION QUESTIONS

1. Define communication, state the criterion against which its effectiveness can be evaluated and explain why effective communication is vital to organisations.

2. In outline, describe a model of the communication process and explain the respective roles of the key components in the process.

3. Describe the major barriers to effective communication that are associated with:
- the sender of a message
- the channel and media used to convey the message
- the receiver of a message.

4. Explain the advantages and disadvantages of face-to-face verbal communication and written communication and the types of message best suited to each channel.

5. What is the informal communication network in an organisation called? Explain why it exists and critically comment on its effectiveness, speed and accuracy.

Chapter 21

Organisational Change and Development

LEARNING OUTCOMES

After studying this chapter you should be able to:

- understand the significance of change for organisations, distinguish between different types of change, and identify external and internal triggers for change

- understand reasons for resistance to change in organisations, describe the tactics that can be used for overcoming it and distinguish between planned and emergent approaches to introducing change

- describe different approaches to bringing about change (systems approach, Lewin approach and Action Research approach)

- define organisational development (OD), describe its distinctive characteristics, its underlying philosophies, the role of the change agent and describe an outline model of the OD process, together with techniques that can be used in OD interventions

- explain the concept of the 'learning organisation' and its implications for change in organisations

INTRODUCTION

While there is nothing new about organisational change, it is fair to note that organisations now have to change more often, and some face changes of considerable magnitude. These changes are not always easy to accomplish and to consider these matters the chapter starts by explaining why organisational change can be virtually inevitable. This is followed by a description of the main external and internal factors that can trigger changes and the next part of the chapter explores in more detail the types of changes that organisations undertake.

When an organisation changes, its members are also required to adapt and it is widely assumed that people have a degree of resistance to change. Therefore, the next part of the chapter explores the reasons for resistance and the strategies that can be used to overcome it.

The remainder of the chapter deals with the two main approaches to organisational change: planned change and the emergent approach. The first of these is typified by organisational development (OD). This is defined and its distinctive characteristics explained, together with the values and assumptions underpinning this approach. An outline model of the OD process is given and this is used to trace its different stages. A description is then given of some of the methods used in OD to try to bring about changes in the values, attitudes and behaviour of people in organisations. Following this the practical utility of OD is examined by considering three issues: whether it delivers what its promises, its relevance for contemporary organisations and whether it is an ethical process. The next matter to be considered is the emergent approach to organisational change, which also includes a consideration of the so-called 'learning organisation', which theoretically equips an organisation for continuous change. The chapter concludes with an overview section.

THE SIGNIFICANCE OF ORGANISATIONAL CHANGE

Organisational change: a move from being in one organisational state to being in another state

The expression 'change' means that an organisation shifts from one state to another (Ford and Ford 1995). In the past, change was often a matter of gradual adaptation but, for a variety of reasons that will be considered presently, the past is no longer a good guide to the future and a number of authors (e.g. Kanter 1995) now consider that the very ability of an organisation to survive will depend on its ability to master the process of change.

Organisations have no control over what happens in their environments and Peters (1987) argues that in order to be able to cope with this they will have to adopt radically new ways of functioning. The general direction of the changes that they will need to make is summarised in Table 21.1.

If only a part of what Peters suggests comes true, it is clear that many organisations will need to change considerably. This will inevitably mean a move away from bureaucratic structures that are best suited to coping with the stable, relatively unchanging conditions, towards organisational forms that are better able to adapt to rapid environmental change (Kanter *et al.* 1992).

Table 21.1 Forecast changes in core business functions (after Peters 1987)

Function	Traditional emphasis	New emphasis
Production	Capital (to automate) more important than people; low-cost efficiency emphasised more than responsiveness and quality	Short production runs; fast change-over of products; people, quality and responsiveness the most important attributes
Marketing	Mass markets; extensive advertising, market research and market testing	Fragmented markets; emphasis on market creation; small-scale, short-lived markets
Financial control	Centralised control; specialised staff to vet investment proposals and set investment policy	Decentralised control with financial specialists becoming part of business teams; spending authority devolved to local levels
Management information systems	Centralised information control and data processing	Decentralised data processing and information control to suit the needs of local units
Research and Development	Centralised; emphasis on large projects; innovation limited to new products and services; technical sophistication more important than reliability and quality	Innovation not limited to new products and services; speed of development more important; increased emphasis on wide portfolio of small projects; innovation in the way that the organisation operates is more important

TYPES OF ORGANISATIONAL CHANGE

Adaptation: an incremental change that occurs as an organisational reaction to a change in its environment

Fine-tuning: an incremental change that occurs as a result of an organisation's anticipation of changes in its environment

Re-creation: a transformational change that occurs as a result of drastic changes in an organisation's environment

Re-orientation: a transformational change that occurs in anticipation of drastic changes in an organisation's environment

Change comes in many shapes and sizes. It can vary in scope, sometimes only affecting parts of an organisation, while in other changes the whole organisation is affected. It can also vary in depth and involve only small, incremental modifications, while other changes consist of abandoning existing ways of doing things. One way to conceptualise these differences is by using a framework provided by Nadler and Tushman (1986), which identifies two dimensions along which change can be categorised:

- the scope of change, which can be either incremental or strategic;
- the timing of changes, that is, whether change is a reaction to something that has already happened or is in anticipation of what is expected to happen.

This gives the four-part typology of changes that is shown in Figure 21.1.

Adaptation is an incremental change that is a reaction to environmental changes. *Fine-tuning*, while still incremental, occurs when an organisation can foresee a change in its environment.

The right-hand quadrants in Figure 21.1 are classified by Nadler and Tushman (1986) as 'organisational transformations' and both involve moving an organisation to a completely new state. However, they are transformations of a different type. *Re-creation* is a reaction to drastic changes in the environment. It involves a complete re-think of the organisation's strategy and can involve changes throughout the whole enterprise. *Re-orientation* is somewhat different and involves similarly dramatic steps but these are usually in anticipation of external changes.

In view of today's turbulent environmental conditions, there is an increasing emphasis on strategic change that can involve a major refocus of the organisation.

Figure 21.1
A typology of
organisational change
(after Nadler and
Tushman 1986)

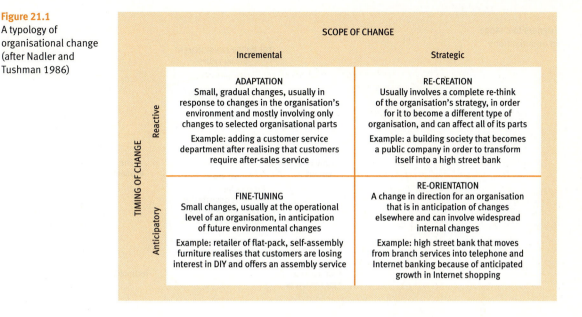

It can sometimes result in a complete redesign of the firm to do something new, or at least do what it does in a radically new way. For this reason it is important to consider factors that can trigger changes in an organisation in more depth, and this matter is addressed next.

THE TRIGGERS TO ORGANISATIONAL CHANGE

Most organisations have learned to make minor, day-by-day changes to adjust to unplanned or unanticipated events and it is changes of some magnitude, particularly where they are undertaken quickly, that tend to be the most problematic. Changes of this nature are not undertaken lightly and usually occur because something prompts the firm to re-evaluate its situation, and respond to pressures from elsewhere. These triggers for change can come from outside or inside an organisation and are summarised in Figure 21.2.

EXTERNAL TRIGGERS TO CHANGE

Before describing these factors it is important to stress that environment is not just 'everything out there'. To distinguish between those parts that are usually considered more important by organisations and those that are not, the terms 'task environment' and 'wider environment' are borrowed from a classic study by Dill (1958). Wider environment is one step removed from the organisation, whereas task environment is that part of the total environment that is most relevant (or potentially relevant) to an organisation in terms of achieving its goals or objectives. Because its impact is experienced as direct and pressing, this is where firms tend to concentrate most of their attention.

Figure 21.2
Triggers to change
in organisations

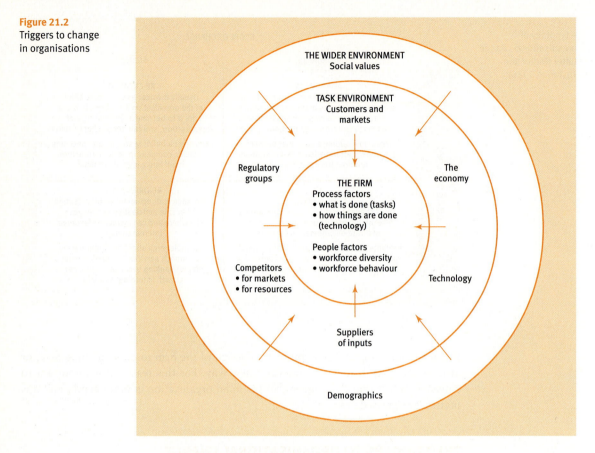

Wider Environmental Triggers

While changes in this part of the environment occur relatively slowly, they can eventually have an impact on one or more of the factors in the task environment, and can evoke anticipatory change.

Demographics

These can ultimately have a significant impact on customers and markets. For instance, young people today have very different lifestyles and purchasing patterns from previous generations. At the opposite end of the age spectrum people now live longer, are healthier into old age and also expect a lifestyle of their own. Thus, both ends of the age spectrum tend to have become separate market segments that require their own products.

Wider Social Values

People now get married later, relationships are probably less permanent, there are many more single households and a far higher proportion of women work than at any time since the Second World War. Clearly, these trends affect the tastes of consumers and they can alter the characteristics of markets.

Task Environment Triggers

Customers and Markets

Because they have a direct impact on profit, markets are often the strongest triggers to change. These days firms not only face threats from domestic competitors, but many markets have become globalised. Thus, organisations often have to adapt to market and competitive changes merely to survive and, to do so, they often look to changes that will make them more flexible and adaptable in the future.

The Economy

Certain changes in wider economic conditions can be very powerful triggers for change. While the industrialised world has slowly pulled itself out of recession since 1995, in 1998 a renewed fear of worldwide recession was prompted by what looked like economic meltdown conditions in Japan and South America. Events such as these tend to prompt firms to look for new internal economies to remain competitive.

Technology

Since technology is often seen as a way of keeping pace with, or getting ahead of, the competition, it is strongly related to market triggers. Failure to keep abreast of new technological developments can mean that costs rise relative to those of competitors, and this can have severe consequences. Because technology advances rapidly, it can result in a never-ending series of changes.

Suppliers of Inputs

On the input side of an organisation there are a number of factors that can be equally important as triggers to change. **Suppliers of capital** such as shareholders and banks usually have expectations about a firm's level of profits and managers can come to feel that the only way to meet these expectations is to reduce costs through greater internal efficiency, which can result in radical alterations to working arrangements and the use of new technologies.

Suppliers of materials are also important and the reliability or stability of suppliers can prompt internal changes, particularly in firms that have a heavy reliance on bought-in components. **Suppliers of labour**, which traditionally means the firm's employees, are also a vital consideration. To serve their markets firms have to acquire the appropriate quantity of human resources of the right quality, and at the right time, which often requires complex, long-term strategies.

Suppliers of equipment are another important group on the input side. The past decade has been one of fairly rapid technological change. Therefore, in a developed economy, a vital item of equipment is knowledge and acquiring new equipment and techniques, together with the knowledge of how to use them, has become a vital weapon in the battle for survival.

Competitors

Very few goods and services have no substitutes, and the fact that there are competitors for markets puts severe limitations on a firm's room for manoeuvre. Nothing quite makes a firm sit up and take notice as much as competitor activity, particularly where it affects profitability. Similarly, competition for resources such as capital, equipment, materials and labour can have knock-on effects that prompt internal changes.

Regulatory Groups

Although not involved in the input–output chain in a direct way, this part of task environment contains sources of disturbance which can affect inputs, outputs or internal processes and thus prompt change within the firm.

Consumer groups come in a variety of forms. For example, utilities such as transport, telecommunications, gas, electricity and water are all subject to scrutiny and regulation of prices. Somewhat less powerful in formal terms, but highly influential in terms of media publicity, are bodies such as the Consumers' Association. Almost every industrialised country has an increasingly influential environmental lobby, and anti-pollution legislation can force radical changes in production methods and processes. Thus, all of these groups can exert powerful pressures on a firm's markets or internal processes.

In certain industries **trade and employer associations** can have a huge impact on a firm's conduct, and in some instances they can be a trigger to change. For example, associations that negotiate with trade unions on behalf of employers influence wage rates. Some associations can also play a part in regulating competition between their members, which clearly has market-related effects.

So far as employee behaviour is concerned, **trade unions** are a prominent regulatory group. Their basic purpose is to limit management's freedom of action *vis-à-vis* employees, and this can also prompt changes, for example, to reduce or marginalise the influence of trade unions.

Finally, **government** can influence the firm in many ways. Some of its activities have an effect on commercial matters, such as exporting, which influences the size of a firm's markets. Others, such as employment legislation, can have a more direct impact on employee relations and can be a strong trigger to internal change. A prime example here is the increased amount of legislation that is starting to appear in Great Britain to ensure that the country complies with European social legislation.

INTERNAL TRIGGERS FOR CHANGE

Process Factors

Changes to process factors often occur because of the impact of triggers in the task environment. Some, however, can arise internally and act as a spur for change in their own right. Examples of those that can require internal change are innovations that improve the way that something is manufactured, or allow a service to be delivered at a lower cost, or the development of new products that enable the firm to diversify. When a change to the top management of a firm occurs, there inevitably seems to be an element of 'the new broom sweeping clean', which can often result in structural changes or changes in reporting responsibilities. In a period of expansion, firms sometimes embark on radical structural changes to expand geographically and this can also mean internal change.

People Factors

Although changes to people factors are often prompted by external triggers, there are some that mainly originate inside an organisation. One that has affected many organisations in the last two decades is an increasingly diverse workforce. Large numbers of employees now come from ethnic groups with cultures and norms that are different from those in the traditional British workforce, and to comply with equal opportunities legislation firms have found it necessary to make changes. Many organisations also have workforces that are largely composed of women, and changes can be needed to facilities and patterns of work to allow women to reconcile home and work responsibilities. In addition, some employees only wish to work on a part-time basis, and this can also bring changes in working arrangements.

TIME OUT

Carefully consider the situation of the organisation in which you work. If you have no direct experience of being an employee, use the university or college at which you study. Develop a list of the major changes that the organisation and others in the same industry have undergone over the last three years. Try to discover what prompted these changes and answer the questions below. If necessary, use other people who have been part of the organisation for some time as the source of your information.

1. Were there any forces in the environment of the organisation (and others in the same industry) that triggered the changes and what were these forces?
2. Were there any forces within the organisation that could have triggered some of the changes and what were these forces?

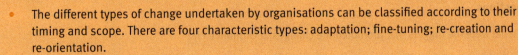

REPLAY

- The different types of change undertaken by organisations can be classified according to their timing and scope. There are four characteristic types: adaptation; fine-tuning; re-creation and re-orientation.
- Organisational change consists of moving an organisation, or one or more of its parts, from one state to another state.
- The triggers for organisational change can be either external (located in an organisation's wider environment or task environment) or internal (process factors or people factors).

RESISTANCE TO CHANGE

Because change can be rewarding for some people and an unpleasant experience for others, people perceive it differently. Those who propose change are most likely to view it in positive terms, but in most cases these are people at the top of an organisation, who are likely to remain untouched by the change. Those lower down can see matters in a different light, particularly if they perceive that those who advocate the change will not be affected. For these reasons there is a widespread assumption that resistance to change is inevitable, and this has led to a strong interest in studying this phenomenon in the change process. However, there are reservations in some quarters about whether this assumption is valid and a return will be made to this point presently. In the meantime, it is more convenient to consider the potential sources of resistance and, to structure the discussion, the phenomenon will be considered at two levels: the organisational level and the individual level.

CASE STUDY 21.1: Ordnance Plc

Ordnance Plc, a government defence contractor, is a wholly owned subsidiary of a large conglomerate. Its business is solely concerned with the design and manufacture of armaments, with over 90 per cent of its output being supplied to the armed services of the country in which it is located. Until the late 1980s it was a highly profitable concern. However, with the end of the Cold War the government's requirements for its outputs severely declined, markets became highly competitive and by the early 1990s the company was in a loss-making situation and found itself with a huge inventory of unsold products and work in progress.

In 1990 the board of the parent company met to review the future of Ordnance Plc and reached two main conclusions. The first was that while the market was much smaller, there was still a potentially profitable future for the firm. Indeed, there were exciting new products under development and since the firm had a first-class reputation, the decision was taken that it should be retained by the group and stay in its present industry. The second decision was that Ordnance Plc could not be allowed to stay as it was. Somehow the firm had to be returned to profitability, which meant that there had to be a severe cutback in the scale of its operations, together with radical changes within the company. At that time, Ordnance Plc employed in excess of 2,500 people and a large proportion would have to go. In addition, armament products were becoming increasingly more sophisticated and so continued development and rapid assimilation of technological advances into new products would be vital. Thus the firm would need to become far more flexible in its design and manufacturing methods.

Questions

1. What were the triggers that prompted the changes at Ordnance Plc?

2. Using the Nadler and Tushman (1986) model, identify the type of change to be undertaken by Ordnance Plc.

3. What particular changes do you feel that Ordnance will need to make?

4. What impact are these changes likely to have on the people who work for the organisation?

Figure 21.3
Organisational
sources of resistance
to change

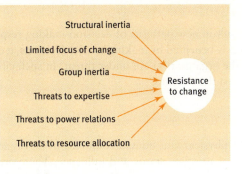

Organisational Sources of Resistance

By their very nature organisations have an in-built streak of conservatism (Hall 1987) and so it is hardly surprising that resistance can occur at the organisational level. Katz and Kahn (1978) give six potential reasons for this and these are shown in Figure 21.3.

Structural Inertia

The structure of an organisation gives it a strong element of stability that establishes regular patterns of behaviour that go unquestioned in the minds of organisational members. These become 'the way that things should be done' (Stephenson 1985). They give people a feeling that things are predictable and create a strong force to maintain matters as they are.

A Limited Focus of Change

It can be difficult to change one part of an organisation in isolation because most of them are interdependent. However, many change initiatives try to do this and the people in the part that is changed find themselves out of step with people in other parts. As a result people in these parts can find it hard to complete their tasks, which results in a degree of hostility to the changed part and this in turn leads to resistance to change.

Group Inertia

Since groups develop their own norms that are used to regulate the behaviour of their members, the *status quo* is usually very comfortable and if a proposed change upsets its rules and norms, this can result in the group developing a degree of resistance to change.

Perceived Threats to Expertise

One of the most potent sources of a group's power is its expertise. Any change that threatens to reduce the responsibility of a group or individual for exercising this expertise affects its potential influence, and in these circumstances resistance is only to be expected.

Perceived Threats to Power Relations

Changes often result in new patterns of decision-making responsibility and where a group has previously benefited by making crucial decisions, it can feel that its prestige and standing in the organisation are under threat. In such circumstances, the group will invariably resist the changes.

Perceived Threats to Resource Allocation

The allocation of physical and human resources in an organisation is often taken to be a reflection of prestige, status and influence. Therefore, those who are most satisfied with the current allocation can be highly resistant to a change that upsets the situation.

Individual Sources of Resistance

In addition to organisational sources of resistance there are a number of personal reasons why people resist change. Drawing on the work of Kotter and Schlesinger (1979), Bedeian and Zammuto (1991) gives four generic reasons for resistance, and these are shown in Figure 21.4.

Parochial Self-interest

Almost everybody has something that he or she values about work, for instance income or its substitutes, power over others, prestige, status, security or convenience. People often acquire these things by personal expenditure of time, energy and commitment and unless things carry on as they are, this is a 'sunk cost' that cannot be recovered. This creates a force for maintaining the *status quo*, and engenders a degree of resistance.

Misunderstandings and Lack of Trust

The less a person knows about the reasons for a change and its impact on him or herself, the more likely it is that the individual will resist the change. This is greatly amplified where there is lack of trust in the proposer of the change because this tends to result in selective perceptions about what the proposer says.

Figure 21.4 Individual sources of resistance to change

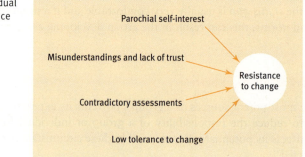

Contradictory Assessments of the Change

People differ in their assessments of the personal costs and benefits of a change. Proposers tend to focus only on what they see as the positive outcomes and they sometimes forget that what they see as a benefit can be perceived by others as a threat. Where this happens there is a wealth of evidence to suggest that people become resistant to changes long after they have been put in place (Savery *et al.* 1998).

Low Tolerance to Change

People also vary in their capabilities to absorb change. To some extent, this depends on their tolerance of ambiguity and to someone with a low tolerance, a change with unknown consequences can be highly threatening.

Dealing with Resistance to Change

It is so widely assumed that resistance is inevitable that the benchmark of successful change is often taken to be 'overcoming resistance'. However, because resistance can occur for such a wide range of reasons, it is doubtful if there is a single method that can deal with them all. Thus, a contingency approach, in which the method used is centred on the reason for resistance, is likely to be more appropriate. This matter it is addressed by Kotter *et al.* (1986) who set out seven ways of overcoming resistance. These can be used singly or in combination and Kotter *et al.* stress the need to choose a tactic that is most appropriate to the circumstances. Their advice on this matter, together with the strengths and weaknesses of the tactics, is summarised in Table 21.2.

Is Resistance Inevitable?

The idea that resistance to change is virtually inevitable is found in almost all textbooks on management and Organisational Behaviour and usually the assumption is made that resistance will be an individual-level phenomenon. It is important to recognise, however, that people are seldom resistant to change *per se*. Rather, they tend to resist changes that have an adverse impact on themselves.

Perhaps more significantly, there is a wealth of evidence to show that individual resistance is comparatively rare. For instance, Kotter (1995) shows that the design for a change initiative may well have an influence on whether resistance is encountered. In addition, Spreitzer and Quinn (1996) point to the idea that it is people higher up who cling to the *status quo*, which means that resistance can be more of an organisational-level phenomenon than one that exists in lower-level employees.

Some indications as to why this might be the case are provided in a penetrating article by Dent and Goldberg (1999), who note that the idea of individual resistance has been the received wisdom for over 50 years. As such, it has become part of the standard vocabulary adopted by each successive generation of managers in an unthinking way, the net result of which is three important outcomes that perpetuate the myth:

- since managers are likely to assume that there will be resistance, they can be tempted to use devious strategies such as manipulation or concealment to head off resistance, which then occurs when these strategies are discovered – a self-fulfilling prophecy effect;

Table 21.2 Tactics for dealing with resistance to change (after Kotter *et al.* 1986)

Tactic	Most appropriately used where	Advantages	Disadvantages
Education and/or communication	Resistance is based on a lack of information or inaccurate information and analysis	Once persuaded, people will often help with the implementation of the change	Can be very time-consuming if large numbers of people are involved
Participation	Initiators do not have all the information needed to design the change and where others have considerable power to resist	People who participate are usually more committed to implementing change. Any relevant information that participants have will be integrated into the change plan	Can be very time-consuming Participants can design an inappropriate change
Facilitation and support	People resist because of adjustment problems that are involved	No other tactic works as well where there are adjustment problems	Can be time-consuming, expensive and still fail
Negotiation	Someone or some group will clearly lose out in a change and where they have considerable power to resist	Sometimes a relatively easy way to avoid major resistance	Can be too expensive in many cases Can trigger other groups to negotiate
Co-optation	There is a specific situation in which other tactics are too expensive or infeasible	Can help generate support for implementing a change, but less so than participation	Can create problems if people recognise the co-optation
Manipulation	Other tactics will not work, or are too expensive	Can be a relatively quick and inexpensive solution to resistance	Initiators are likely to lose some of their credibility and this can lead to future problems
Coercion	Speed is essential and change initiators possess considerable power	Speed can sometimes overcome a great deal of resistance	Risky: can leave people angry with the initiators

- because resistance is seen as something that only occurs in subordinates, and is then overcome by successful managers, managers have every incentive to maintain the myth because it allows them to present themselves in a favourable light;
- as a final resort, the widespread assumption that resistance occurs in subordinates allows managers to absolve themselves from blame for the failure of a badly designed change initiative (Krantz 1999).

TIME OUT

Carefully consider any significant changes that have occurred in the last few years that have had an impact on you or on other students at your university or college. These could be changes in grant or fee arrangements, changes to the way your course is delivered or assessed, or even changes in the way your college or university is run. Now answer the questions below.

1. Name these changes, and state who they affect and why.
2. Which of these changes encountered resistance and what form did the resistance take?
3. How was the resistance overcome by the initiator of the change, or was the resistance successful in getting the changes abandoned or modified?

REPLAY

- Resistance can arise at two levels: organisational and individual.
- Seven tactics can be used (singly or in combination) to try to overcome resistance: education and communication; participation; facilitation and support; negotiation; co-optation; manipulation; and coercion.
- While it is widely assumed that resistance to change on the part of individuals is inevitable, there is a stream of research evidence that suggests that this is not the case.

CASE STUDY 21.2: Ordnance Plc: The Outline Change Initiative

When the board of the parent company reached the conclusions outlined in Case Study 21.1, it also decided that there had to be a radical break with the past. Therefore, a new top management team was installed and the chief executive was given the brief of producing a long-term corporate plan for the company. The top management team gave its immediate attention to this matter and quickly came to the conclusion that a 'clean sweep' exercise was needed to equip the organisation to service the more demanding market in the most profitable way. A business process re-engineering (BPR) exercise was chosen as the vehicle to tackle this matter. In practical terms this involved importing management consultants to devise and structure the BPR programme. After an initial study, the consultants recommended a staged plan to re-engineer the firm. Information technology would be the driving force of a system of computer integrated design and manufacture (CIDM) to give tight coordination of design, engineering and production. This would involve considerable changes to the way that work was organised in the firm. Hitherto Ordnance had been structured in a very rigid, functional way, with sales, development, design, engineering and manufacturing as separate functions with strict boundaries. Manufacturing was the largest function and its activities were of two main types: assembly of components, which was largely done by semi-skilled workers, and manufacture of precision products, which was undertaken by highly skilled craftsmen in a large number of different trades.

The new organisational design recommended by the consultants involved a number of highly significant changes. To give a more flexible and modern approach, it was decided to abandon the strict functional structure and replace it with a product structure that was considered to be 'closer to the customer'. All

(Box continued)

(Box continued)

activities from sales to production for a particular group of products would be located in self-contained product cells consisting of semi-autonomous teams. People in each cell would be required to be multi-skilled and would no longer work in a specific department or for a single boss. It was realised that this would require a completely new factory layout and so the decision was taken to build a new plant adjacent to the current facility. As an interim step, a number of alterations were made to the existing factory to allow new methods to be piloted there. The aim of this was to reduce the shock to workers of having to move to a new site and embrace new methods in one step. In addition, a considerable amount of retraining for skilled workers was undertaken to enable them to become multi-skilled.

Finally, it was decided that all assembly work would be put out to subcontractors, which meant that semi-skilled workers would no longer be required. Clearly the new design required significant staffing cuts, not only among semi-skilled workers, but throughout the whole company and over a three-year period it was planned to reduce the total workforce from 2,500 to approximately 750.

Questions

1. To what extent do you feel that the changes proposed for Ordnance Plc would be resisted?

2. At what levels in the organisation do you feel that this resistance would be likely to appear?

3. What do you feel would prompt any resistance to appear?

4. What would be the most appropriate ways for the management of Ordnance Plc to handle any resistance that appeared?

APPROACHES TO IMPLEMENTING ORGANISATIONAL CHANGE

Planned organisational change approach: a set of internal actions designed to produce specific outcomes

There are two main approaches to implementing change. The *planned organisational change approach*, which is closely associated with organisational development, is by far the most developed and easily understood. Porras and Silvers (1991) describe it as 'a set of internal actions designed to produce specific outcomes'. It is underpinned by a belief that change is best accomplished through a predetermined sequence of steps. This implies that there is a universal formula for success and the whole area is resplendent with what Huczynski and Buchanan (2001) call 'recipe' models for success (see Kotter 1995 for an example). While convenient, the reader should be aware that there are very serious criticisms of these models. They give an impression that if a preordained sequence of steps is followed, change can be tackled in a straightforward, linear way, which tends to underestimate the complexity of the process. Buchanan and Storey (1997), for example, argue that these models are far from what is actually involved, because change is a very messy business that often triggers intense political activity as people strive to be the ones that profit by a change or remain with their empires untouched. For this reason, writers such as Burnes (2000) argue for what he calls the *emergent approach*, which rejects the idea that there is any such thing as a universally valid recipe

Emergent approach: a contingency perspective that rejects the idea of a universally applicable recipe for organisational change

for successful change. Rather, change is assumed to be an unfolding and continuously developing process in which the issues that arise cannot be predicted but have to be tackled as and when they occur.

THE PLANNED CHANGE APPROACH

The Systems Model of Change

Many planned change initiatives use a systemic approach in which an organisation is treated as a set of interacting variables, all of which are likely to need to change together. This idea is shown in Figure 21.5.

The important point about this perspective is its recognition of interdependencies, which has two main implications:

- if arrangements in the pre-change situation work well, all of the five variables are in balance, so that structure is compatible with strategy, technology and so on;
- if a change is made to one of the variables, this is almost bound to require some degree of modification in the others to restore the balance of compatibility.

Here it is worth noting that some of the major difficulties encountered in change initiatives occur because these interconnections are ignored (see Redman and Grieves 1999; Oxman and Smith 2003), and the most neglected variable is often the people. For this reason, much of the effort in planned change is devoted to bringing about change in human behaviour and there are two basic models that underpin these activities: the Lewin model and the Action Research model.

Figure 21.5
The systems model of change

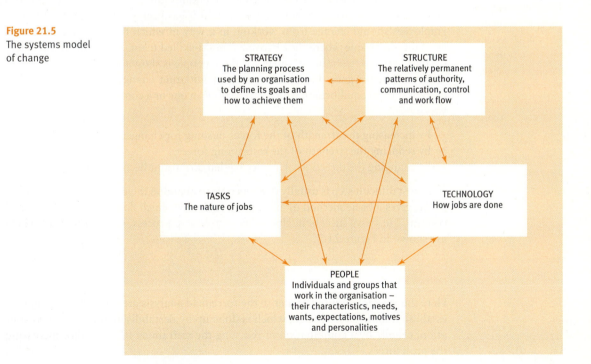

Figure 21.6
An example of Lewin's force field analysis

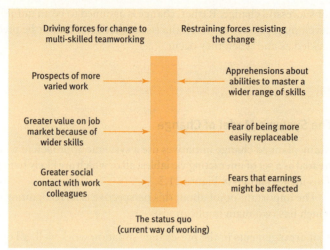

The Lewin Model

Lewin model: a three-stage (unfreeze–move–refreeze) method of bringing about change in human behaviour

Force field analysis: a way of conceptualising a stable situation as forces pushing (in favour of) change, balanced by those restraining change

Force Field Analysis

Lewin (1951) views change as a dynamic process which takes the form of an ongoing struggle between two sets of forces: one pushing in the direction of change and the other pulling in the opposite direction. This is normally portrayed as a 'force field', where a stable situation consists of a state of equilibrium (balance) between the two sets of forces. To give an example, assume that it has been proposed that a group of employees should change from working in a way in which they all have their own special tasks to one where they become a multi-skilled team. A simplified force field of 'pushing' and 'restraining' forces for these people is shown in Figure 21.6.

Lewin then argues that the first step in initiating change is to destabilise the current state of equilibrium, which can be done in one or a combination of three basic ways:

- by increasing the strength of the forces pushing for change;
- by reducing the strength of the restraining forces;
- by changing the direction of a force so that a restraint becomes a push factor.

The most difficult step is usually to get people to abandon their old ways, and Lewin's model gives a basic method of attempting to do this which flows from his force field concept. He views successful change as a three-step process, the essentials of which are shown in Figure 21.7.

Unfreeze

Here the principles set out earlier in the force field analysis are applied. The aim is to establish a motive for change, which is done up by destabilising the *status quo* situation, usually by a combination of reducing the restraining forces and/or increasing the push forces.

Figure 21.7 Lewin's three-step change process

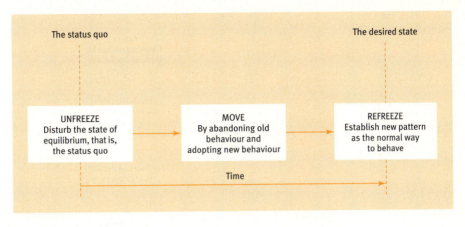

Move (to the new situation)

This is often easier said than done. When people already have a familiar way of behaving, it can be hard for them to abandon it. However, people have a greater incentive to change if they can see others around them doing the same thing and so some of the organisational development (OD) techniques described presently would normally be used.

Refreeze

The aim here is to fix the new pattern of behaviour as 'normal', often by conditioning people, i.e. by rewarding the new, desired behaviour and discouraging them from regressing to the prior behaviours. Again, because behaviour seems much more normal if it fits in with what others do, peer pressure can be a potent source of reinforcement.

The Action Research Model

The Lewin model implies that there is a very clear specification for the required, new pattern of behaviour. However, there may only be a vague idea of the ways in which behaviour needs to change. In this situation an incremental approach is required, desirably one that draws on employee ideas about what is needed so that they become the joint authors of the change. This is the province of *Action Research* and an outline five-step method is shown in Figure 21.8.

Action Research: a participative method of bringing about change in human behaviour that involves stages of data collection, problem diagnosis, action planning, action and re-evaluation

Problem Identification

The cycle commences when the proposer of change identifies that existing patterns of employee behaviour are incompatible with a changed situation. As an example, assume that a customer service department handles queries and complaints by directing them to specialists, according to the nature of an enquiry. This sometimes leads to customers experiencing delay and frustration in getting an answer, which can probably be avoided if all queries are answered promptly in a single call.

Figure 21.8 The
Action Research cycle

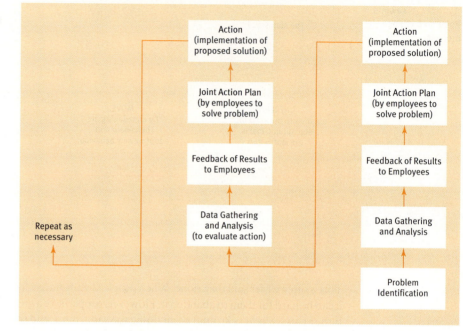

Data Gathering and Diagnosis

In Action Research, this is sometimes done by an outside consultant and can be likened to a doctor diagnosing the cause of a patient's illness. Starting with the suspected symptoms (potential customer frustration), data is gathered to reveal its cause, which involves gathering information from customers and also from employees to obtain their version of matters.

Feedback

A fundamental part of the Action Research method is to involve the target of a change (employees) in identifying the extent of a problem and suggesting potential solutions. This is done by a joint exploration of the data that has been gathered by employees and the consultant.

Action Plan

Working together, consultant and employees develop a potential solution to the problem. Since it is hoped that a discussion of this type will lead to a degree of unfreezing of the *status quo*, there is a clear connection with Lewin's three-step model.

Action

The proposed solution is put into practice by employees, who adopt the new patterns of behaviour.

Re-evaluation

Data is gathered to determine whether there is an improvement, how much of an improvement has been made, and how workable the solution is. The cycle is then repeated as necessary.

Clearly the Action Research method has a number of advantages:

- the people who have to implement any changes are involved at an early stage, which can help reduce resistance to change;
- change is objective-centred and goes far enough to solve the problem but not so far that it creates new, unforeseen problems;
- because change is introduced in increments, knock-on effects that may become problems in their own right can be identified; for instance, in the example above it might be necessary to retrain employees so that they can answer a wider range of queries.

TIME OUT

Carefully consider the change(s) you identified in the previous Time Out exercise and answer the questions below.

1. What strategy was used to try to introduce the change(s) you identified?
2. Do you feel the strategy was an appropriate way of introducing the change? If not, why not?
3. Identify any other strategies that could have been used and state whether you feel these would have been more or less effective than those used.

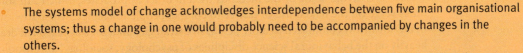

REPLAY

- The systems model of change acknowledges interdependence between five main organisational systems; thus a change in one would probably need to be accompanied by changes in the others.
- Lewin's model of change, which is a natural development of his force field analysis, gives a basic, three-step method of unfreeze–move–refreeze, to bring about changes in human behaviour.
- The Action Research model of change gives an incremental approach, in which people who are the target of change become involved in planning and implementing the changes.

ORGANISATIONAL DEVELOPMENT

Organisational development (OD), which is firmly located within the area of planned change, uses the models given in the previous section to underpin its approach. It can be defined as:

a planned, systematic process in which applied behavioural science principles and practices are introduced into organisations, towards the goal of increasing individual and organisational effectiveness. (French and Bell 1999, p 1)

It is concerned with equipping the management of an organisation with a method of bringing about organisational change and has a distinctive approach that lays claim to being much more than just another recipe for change management.

The Distinguishing Characteristics of OD

While OD has some things in common with other approaches, in theory it has a number of unique characteristics, and these are given in what follows.

A Planned, Medium to Long-term Strategy

OD is not a quick fix solution to problems. Indeed, it condemns *ad hoc* approaches and, because it deals with fundamental and/or transformational changes, the process can be one that takes years to complete.

A Systematic and Systemic Focus

The basic perspective adopted in OD is that of the organisation as a system of subsystems (see Figure 21.5). Therefore, it is strongly concerned with identifying the multitude of simultaneous changes that may need to be made.

Process-orientated focus

Although OD sets out to achieve a better functioning organisation, it is strongly focused on the process of change itself and assumes that how change takes place has a huge impact on whether the objective of a more effective organisation is likely to be realised.

A Normative Re-educative Orientation

OD tends to avoid some of the methods used in other approaches, which can sometimes verge on the naked use of power to compel people to change. Most advocates of OD are firmly committed to more persuasive strategies and, for this reason, it draws heavily on the behavioural science disciplines of psychology, sociology, anthropology and political science for its techniques.

Change agent: an expert from either inside or outside an organisation who facilitates and guides an OD intervention

The Use of a Change Agent

This role is central to the OD process and is discussed in its own right presently. The change agent is an expert who champions, facilitates and guides the change process.

While this person can come from inside the organisation, he or she is increasingly imported as a consultant.

An Orientation to Organisational Self-help

Although OD often involves the use of an outside expert (the change agent), OD practitioners like to think of themselves as somewhat different from other types of management consultant. Many of them would argue that their role is not simply to provide expertise to solve organisational problems, but to improve the organisation's long-term abilities to diagnose and solve its own problems.

In theory, these points mean that OD is a very distinctive way of approaching the matter of change and so it is not surprising that it lays claim to a unique set of philosophies and assumptions. Above all, it adopts a very humanistic approach which contains fundamental assumptions about people in organisations (Porras and Robertson 1992). These are that:

- effective organisations will de-emphasise hierarchical authority and control by involving people in decisions about matters that affect them, which means that OD has anti-bureaucratic values;
- the effectiveness and efficiency of an organisation will increase if work is organised in a way that meets people's needs for responsibility and challenge (Pasmore and Fagans 1992);
- most people want and need opportunities for personal growth and achievement and, if these needs are met, they will respond positively to opportunities that the organisation offers for increased responsibility and challenge;
- it is possible to identify ways in which the design of individual jobs, the tasks of groups and the structure of the organisation can all be modified to meet the needs of the organisation and its human resources;
- while conflict often stands in the way of people accomplishing organisational goals, it is counter-productive to smooth over conflicts; it is better to bring them out into the open where they can be resolved because this results in a more trusting, supportive climate.

So strongly are these values emphasised by writers on OD that it takes on something of a messianic, evangelical flavour. Indeed, the humanistic agenda is so paramount in the OD literature that it leaves an uneasy feeling that the pursuit of this is the main aim, and any talk of organisational effectiveness is just attractive packaging. Therefore, 'effectiveness', as OD practitioners define it, can be very different from the meaning that managers and other people attribute to the word. For this reason there are a number of important criticisms of OD. These, however, are more appropriately left until later in the chapter.

The Change Agent in OD

Because this person acts as the catalyst for change and assumes the responsibility for steering it through to completion, the change agent occupies a focal role in OD. Broadly speaking, there are three approaches that can be used in this role. The first is what can be called the 'engineering model'. This is similar to the role of a conventional management consultant in which the person plays little part in diagnosing what is needed, probably because the management of an organisation has already decided what it wants. Rather, the main function is to install a new system, for example, Total Quality Management, and to leave when the new system is up and running.

At the other extreme is what is sometimes called 'the medical model', where the function is to help diagnose an organisation's problems, but not necessarily to play an extensive part in implementing change.

The most widely used approach, however, tends to fall between these two extremes and this is known as the 'process model'. It uses the technique of process consultation in which the change agent works in a highly collaborative way with organisational managers, but with a strong emphasis on helping them to decide what changes are necessary, how they can be brought about, and then guiding managers in the early stages of implementation.

Although a change agent often comes from outside an organisation, the person can also be an insider. External change agents are usually employed on a consultancy basis and tend to be people trained in behavioural science techniques. The disadvantages and advantage of employing an outsider are said to be:

- the person can be viewed by employees as someone who has no understanding of how the firm operates;
- he or she can be strongly mistrusted and branded as management's lapdog;
- on the other hand, outsiders usually have the advantage of a fresh and unbiased pair of eyes.

Appointing a change agent from inside also has its inherent advantages and disadvantages:

- because the person comes from the inside, he or she can be seen as a more plausible advocate of change;

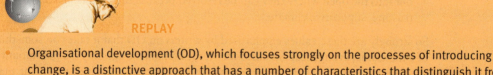

REPLAY

- Organisational development (OD), which focuses strongly on the processes of introducing change, is a distinctive approach that has a number of characteristics that distinguish it from other approaches to change: a medium to long-term focus; a systematic and systemic focus; a focus on processes; a normative re-educative orientation; the use of a change agent; and an organisational self-help orientation.

- OD is underpinned by a humanistic philosophy and a set of assumptions about people in organisations.

- The change agent's role in OD is to act as a catalyst for change and to steer a change initiative through to completion.

- The three main models for the way in which a change agent fulfils this role are: the engineering model, the medical model and the process model.

- set against this, because of his or her prior organisational background, there can be suspicions that the individual will give special favours to his or her own unit, or find ways of exempting it from change.

For these reasons, and irrespective of whether the person is appointed from inside or outside the organisation, the change agent role can be a difficult one and there are strong suggestions that the person needs to have special aptitudes and competencies. Burke (1987) defines these as:

- a tolerance of ambiguity;
- the ability to influence people;
- a capability to confront difficult issues;
- to be supportive and nurturing with other people;
- awareness of his or her own feelings and intuitions;
- an ability to teach and coach others;
- a sense of humour;
- a strong belief in the OD method;
- self-confidence;
- good conceptual skills;
- energy and self-direction.

Organisational Development Interventions

OD intervention: a programme to bring about change in an organisation, or one or more of its parts

An *OD intervention* is a programme used to bring about change in an organisation, or one or more of its parts. It can be focused on problems at one or more of four organisational levels: the whole organisation; the intergroup level; the intragroup level; and the level of the individual. There are many models of the process in the OD literature and these usually divide an intervention into distinct stages. While there are criticisms of this approach, a model that is capable of capturing some of the complexity of what might be involved is provided by Gibson *et al.* (1994). For the purposes of discussion, this is shown in a slightly modified form in Figure 21.9.

Forces for Change

These have already been discussed earlier in the chapter. Note, however, that there is a connection with the box entitled 'Organisational mission and goals', which conveys the idea that there is an interaction between the forces for change and an organisation's goals.

Problem Diagnosis

It is here that problems in the organisation start to be revealed, together with possible remedies and ways of achieving them. This means that diagnosis is one of the most important steps in the OD cycle, which in many cases will be undertaken by an external consultant.

Goals for Change

While these might seem to flow from the previous stage, note that the model contains a box entitled 'Limiting conditions' with arrows going to the 'Goals' box and the 'Select

Figure 21.9 An outline of the organisational development process

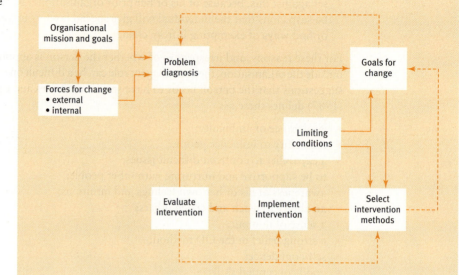

intervention methods' box. This reflects the idea that the current state of an organisation puts limits on what can feasibly be achieved, and in this respect a factor that puts limits on what can be done is 'current management styles'. For instance, Total Quality Management (TQM) only works well if managers have supportive, open styles and if they cannot accept this way of working, severe problems are likely to be encountered (Redman and Grieves 1999). Another limiting factor can be the formal organisation. Structures, policies and systems of control all tend to reflect top management's philosophies about how organisations should be run and if this is not compatible with the changes envisaged lower down, it can be a recipe for disaster (Ziera and Avedisian 1989). Finally, some proposed changes run counter to the expectations and attitudes in workgroups, and so the organisation's culture can put strong limits on what is feasible (Harris and Ogbonna 2002).

Intervention Methods

These are the selected ways of delivering the objectives of the intervention, particularly those concerned with bringing about change in people and they will be described in more detail in the next section of the chapter.

Implementation and Evaluation

Depending on the methods employed, this can be a lengthy process. However, in order to determine whether it has achieved its objectives, and if not, to identify further problems that need to be resolved, it is vital to monitor the success of the implementation stage.

Feedback

It is important to note that all the boxes in the model are connected by feedback loops. This reflects the idea that OD is not a precise science, but one in which the choice of appropriate goals and intervention methods depends on the quality of problem diagnosis. Thus, a number of iterations may be required to ensure that something important has not been overlooked.

Methods of Intervention

Organisational development has evolved an extremely wide-ranging tool-kit of techniques to bring about change in people. Space precludes giving anything other than a brief description of some of them and to structure the discussion, it is convenient to describe the techniques according to the level at which they are normally applied.

Organisational-Level Interventions

Organisational Structure

Most interventions at this level involve an element of structural redesign, for example, installing Total Quality Management (TQM). An even more radical step is business process re-engineering (BPR), which could involve completely restructuring the organisation. Almost inevitably this creates a need to address lower-level aspects of structure.

Although structural interventions chosen by top management can look fairly straightforward, it is people lower down who actually determine whether a structure works. Changes of this type can be extremely disruptive for those involved and they are often the ones that engender a high degree of resistance. Thus, when structural redesign is involved, interventions at intergroup, intragroup and individual levels can also be necessary to try to bring about attitude changes. One way of starting this process is described next.

Survey Feedback

It is sometimes important to identify existing patterns of values and attitudes at the diagnosis and planning stage of an intervention, by conducting a survey of people across the whole organisation. This would normally attempt to tap opinions on such matters as management's behavioural style, communication, levels of motivation, job satisfaction, satisfaction with supervision, or the organisation's culture and climate in a more general way. The results of the survey are then fed back to organisational decision makers and sometimes to employees as well. The information can then be used to identify problems and the techniques to address them.

Intergroup Interventions

Because conflict between groups is fairly common in organisations, interventions at this level usually try to change perceptions and attitudes that groups hold about each other.

Intergroup Confrontation

In this method two groups that have a conflictual relationship work with the change agent to resolve the problem. The first step is usually for the groups to meet separately, with the people in each group being asked to come to conclusions about:

- how they view the other group;
- what they expect of the other group;
- what they believe the other group expects of them.

In the second step, the groups exchange their conclusions, which is followed by a meeting of the two groups to explore perceptions. This meeting is often designed to be confrontational, but in an objective, fact-finding way. Therefore, the change agent needs to keep a firm control on the process, to ensure that the groups move towards collaborative working by exploring similarities and differences, rather than simply exchanging 'blame stories'.

Intragroup Interventions

At this level the aim is to help a group to work more effectively in terms of its internal processes.

Process Consultation

This is one of the main techniques used in OD and Schein (1969), who is perhaps its foremost advocate, argues that many groups are riven with dysfunctional behaviour, much of which originates in distortions of reality by group members. In process consultation, the change agent acts as a facilitator or catalyst to help the group diagnose its own problems and generate action plans to remedy the situation, and he/she purposely avoids prescribing a remedy for the group, but helps it explore its own processes so that group members become the authors of any changes that are made.

Team Building

OD places a very high value on collaborative behaviour, which is underpinned by a belief that participative working results in a willingness to embrace change (Woodman and Sherwood 1980). The aim is to develop more effective groups by helping them to explore potential shortcomings in their own internal processes. Thus group members work with a change agent to diagnose how well the group works, and to plan changes to improve its functioning, usually by persuading the group to focus on one or more of a number of key activities, such as:

- how it sets its goals and priorities;
- how work is allocated within the group;
- how it works together;
- interpersonal relations within the group.

The group then draws up an action plan of what needs to be done, often by calling on each member to do something specific to improve matters. According to French and Bell (1999) this is the single most important and fastest-growing technique in the OD repertoire. It is said to be particularly useful in global organisations, where groups can have members from very different cultural backgrounds and also with new groups that have come into existence as a result of a reorganisation or a merger.

Sensitivity Training

This is one of the most highly publicised and controversial techniques used in OD (Bramlette and Tucker 1981) and it goes by a number of names, such as 'T' (training) groups or encounter groups. It is based on the assumption that poor group performance can be caused by people's emotional problems, and has the aim of sensitising people to their own behaviour and how this influences relations with others.

T-groups typically work with (but not under) a facilitator and the process often starts with the people seated in a circle facing inwards, with no agenda, no leader and no directions about what to do. Therefore, all the problems encountered in a new group emerge fairly quickly, for example, thrusts for leadership and disagreement about what to do, and how to do it. This tends to result in emotions and personal remarks quickly surfacing, and it is this that gives rise to the controversial nature of T-groups. People have to expose themselves to a fairly high degree of criticism and take emotional and psychological risks to participate and not everybody is well equipped to do this. Indeed, many people are unable to cope with the psychological strains. Thus, there are very mixed reports about the usefulness of the process, although the evidence suggests that participants learn to take a more realistic view of themselves, develop a clearer understanding of how they view others, and develop enhanced levels of interpersonal sensitivity.

Individual-level Interventions

Because of its main focus on people working together OD has evolved relatively few techniques that are specifically targeted on individuals. Those that are used tend to be what would normally be considered part of the repertoire of a line manager, or possibly of a human resource specialist, for example, career planning or, where stress is encountered, some of the methods described in Chapter 10.

An Evaluation of Organisational Development

Since Organisational Development can be an expensive and time-consuming process it is important to examine its utility. From an organisational perspective two questions can be asked: does OD deliver the benefits that it promises? And is OD relevant in today's conditions? In addition, it is also important to address a third question: is OD ethical?

Does OD Deliver What it Promises?

The definition of OD given earlier makes it clear that its implicit promise is to deliver two things:

- a more effective organisation;
- a happier, more satisfied and more committed workforce.

Unfortunately, it is near impossible to tell whether these aims are achieved. The vast majority of research conducted to assess the success of OD tends to be of dubious methodological soundness (Beer and Walton 1987) and a penetrating study by Porras and Berg (1978) was only able to identify 35 out of 160 published reports that had methodologies sufficiently sound to enable them to be included in a meta-analysis. Of these, only nine attempted to evaluate the effects of OD on economic performance, and only half of these reported an improvement. While most of the 35 studies commented on employee variables such as satisfaction and motivation, only 30 per cent of these studies reported improvements. Clearly, this gives little support for OD's claim to improve performance and human process variables.

The problem is that studies which report improvements tend to reflect what the word 'improvement' means in the eyes of OD practitioners, for instance, greater creativity, more openness and enhanced opportunities for personal development. It is virtually impossible to devise foolproof measures for these things and so improvement is little more than a subjective judgement on the part of the researcher. This gives rise to another problem. French and Bell (1999) note that most OD practitioners have a blind faith in its utility and so they see little need to produce evidence that it actually works. Therefore, much of the so-called evaluation research comes from reports by consultants who undertake interventions, and this gives a clear risk of 'positive results' bias and self-fulfilling prophecies.

As if these things were not enough, there is some evidence that OD can result in highly dysfunctional outcomes. To start with, change initiatives that aim to develop a strong performance orientation in employees have a habit of upsetting the psychological contract and this can result in feelings of unfairness and/or a lack of trust (Stiles *et al.* 1997). In addition, culture change initiatives, which are often the pivotal selling feature of an OD intervention, can result in rather unpleasant organisational climates, in which blame stories and a decline in employee commitment and morale can occur (Gilmore *et al.* 1997; Harris and Ogbonna 2002). Moreover, some of the techniques used can have a boomerang effect, for example sensitivity training, which for some people can be such a painful and harrowing process that it results in a great deal of resentment at being forced to undergo the experience for no apparent reason. In summary, therefore, there are grave reservations about whether OD delivers what it promises.

The Current Relevance of OD

While OD has a strong focus on matters such as respect for people, trust, egalitarian relationships and participative management, these days, managers' eyes are usually fixed on bottom-line performance. Thus, most organisational changes are primarily directed at lowering costs or increasing profits (Van Eynde and Bledsoe 1990) and many initiatives such as Total Quality Management are seen by managers as 'quick-fix, off-the-shelf' solutions, rather than long-term development initiatives (Worren *et al.* 1999). In the last two decades managers have found it all too easy to bring about change without using a persuasive approach. Thus, it may well be asked whether OD has any relevance to managers, most of whom prefer to concern themselves with hard, tangible features of the organisation such as productivity, quality, continuous improvement and costs, rather than intangibles such as attitudes, openness and trust.

The Ethics of OD

The great paradox of OD is that while it has a humanistic rationale, it conveniently ignores power differences in organisations (Greenwood *et al.* 1993). Whether this is because it has its origins in America, where academics are far less reluctant to serve the interests of management, or whether it is simply naive, is a moot point. However, there is a strong thread in the OD literature that accepts management's goals as sacrosanct, and in practice this means that OD can become little more than finding a way of manipulating employees into a seemingly willing adoption of management's definition of what is needed, all of which raises questions about the ethics of OD.

Nowhere is this more apparent than in the aim of changing an organisation's culture. Woodall (1996), for example, notes that those who advocate the importance of cultural change usually base their argument on four assumptions:

- that successful organisations have strong cultures;
- that only management is far-sighted enough to recognise the culture required, and that the rest of the workforce is blind;
- that employee values need to be aligned with management's vision;
- that these values can be easily changed.

Setting aside the last of these, which is highly questionable, Woodall also notes that most culture change initiatives implicitly follow Lewin's unfreeze–move–refreeze methodology and this leads to some highly unethical practices. In unfreezing, for example, there are obvious questions about who defines what is wrong with the existing culture and why a new culture is needed. In practice this often amounts to telling employees not only what to think, but how to come up with the right conclusions. This tends to be done by bombarding people with an endless stream of criticism of the existing culture, which is almost bound to induce a sense of psychological insecurity. From then on, because a culture can be highly resistant to change, most of the remainder of the process is devoted to overcoming any resistance. This is not necessarily done in a supportive way, but by trying to induce degradation and shame for holding the values inherent in the old culture. Thus, far from being humanistic, the whole process rests on a set of practices of questionable ethical content.

REPLAY

- An Organisational Development intervention (which can be focused on one or more of four organisational levels) is a programme of steps that is used to bring about changes in an organisation, or one or more of its parts. However, an intervention can be highly iterative and the steps should not be thought of as a sequence that is necessarily completed in a single pass.

- Methods of intervention are normally keyed to the level at which the intervention takes place: whole organisation; intergroup; intragroup; individual.

- OD is open to some criticism on three grounds: for not delivering what it promises; for not being particularly relevant to current organisational circumstances; and for the questionable ethics of some of its practices.

THE EMERGENT APPROACH TO ORGANISATIONAL CHANGE

Unlike planned change, which is a highly developed approach with its own well-understood conventions, the emergent approach is not yet as cohesive, well-integrated body of knowledge. Rather, it consists of developments by a disparate group of theorists who only have one thing in common – their opposition to the tenets of planned change (Burnes 1998). The approach is emergent in two ways: first, because it is still emerging as a school of thought and, second, because change is viewed as an emergent process of experimentation and adaptation, in which there is a search for ways of coping with the exigencies of a very uncertain environment that is itself in a constant state of flux.

For this reason proponents of the approach reject the idea that change can follow a set of pre-planned steps that occur in a neat, fixed way to a set timetable (Senior 1997a). After all, if the environment itself is constantly changing, how can a valid and fixed plan be drawn up in advance? Therefore, it is argued that change should be viewed as an ongoing, virtually continuous and open-ended process of transition, usually achieved by a host of small, incremental changes that can eventually add up to a major organisational transformation. However, while the approach rejects the idea of a universally applicable strategy that can be specified in advance, a number of workers in the area have developed what can be described as guideline recipes; see, for example, Pettigrew and Whipp (1993) and Kanter *et al.* (1992). These, however, are not linear sets of stages, but more things to be achieved along the way. Nevertheless, as Burnes (2000) notes, while most advocates of the emergent approach avoid prescriptive rules, they all draw attention to five organisational features that need to be taken into account in the change process. These are not necessarily targets for change, but are interacting factors that can either facilitate or inhibit proposed changes, and are:

- organisational structures;
- organisational culture;
- management behaviour;
- patterns of power and politics;
- organisational learning.

Since the last of these has strong connections with what proponents of the emergent approach would probably regard as an ideal organisational situation for change, it is considered next.

CONTINUOUS CHANGE: THE LEARNING ORGANISATION

Most current ideas about organisational learning argue that continuous change is required to survive and prosper in a fast-moving, globalised environment, which makes the learning organisation an important concept. In organisations of this type, change is said to be a way of life, which means that many of the traditional problems associated with organisational change would largely be absent. This can be seen from the five characteristics of the learning organisation set out by Senge (1991):

- all organisational members have a shared, mutually agreed vision;
- people readily disregard old ways of thinking, together with the standard routines that they have used to solve problems and do their jobs in the past;

OB IN ACTION: And Finally, The Living Company

Arie de Geus, who is best known for his role in the development of the concept of the 'learning organisation', has recently produced a series of works that takes a holistic view of companies and their environment. He argues that in the future, a company's only sustainable advantage may be its ability to learn and, in his view, learning and knowledge-gathering are not peripheral management activities, but go to the very heart of management and so the company that learns how to do them well can not only compete, but win. His article Planning as Learning, published in the *Harvard Business Review* in 1988, made the 'learning organisation' into one of the most talked-about management concepts of our time and his new work, *The Living Company*, goes further in understanding how the learning organisation functions. He compares it to a living organism, and links its ability to learn with the extent to which it is integrated into its environment. Living organisms scour their environment for sustenance: the 'living company' uses its environment to acquire knowledge, which is equally important to its survival.

Mr de Geus believes that companies should develop strong bonds with their customers and shareholders and develop a 'harmony of values' with them. These strong relationships enable a greater depth of learning, which then becomes built-in, enabling companies to grow organically and even become self-aware. He argues that companies cannot exist in isolation and so the 'learning organisation' and the 'living company' are simultaneous concepts. However, there are no hard and fast rules for creating a living company. Companies evolve and their systems for learning will change over time. Learning should always happen, though, as a natural part of business activity. Learning organisations learn as entities; effective learning is shared, not locked up in individuals. If shared effectively, the sum total of an organisation's knowledge is much greater than the pooled knowledge of individuals can ever be. The strength of the 'living company' model is not its stress on learning, but its ability to integrate key concepts: knowledge management, communication, culture, systems and ethics. This has been called 'the most original and innovative model of business to emerge in the latter half of the 20th century' and it is said to offer a route to sustainable success in the new millennium.

Source:

Witzel M (2003) Birth of the Living Company, *The Financial Times*, 21 August.

- they are able to conceive of all the organisation's processes, activities, functions and interactions with the environment as part of a system of interrelationships;
- people openly communicate with each other across vertical and horizontal boundaries without fear of criticism or redress;
- they subordinate their own personal interests and fragmented departmental interests to work together towards the organisation's shared vision.

So far as can be determined, examples of the fully fledged learning organisation are extremely rare, and it presents a picture of 'what could be' rather than 'what is' (Pedler *et al.* 1997). Indeed, McGill and Slocum (1993) point out that to become a learning organisation, a conventional firm probably has to go through a number of intermediate stages. To this end, Koffman and Senge (1993) identify the three main barriers that must be overcome to become a learning organisation.

The Barrier of Fragmentation

The fundamental building block of most organisations is specialisation. Unfortunately this tends to go hand in hand with territorial boundaries that divide different functions into warring kingdoms. Therefore, people lose sight of the interconnected nature of the organisation, which often results in solutions that create a problem for someone else.

The Barrier of Competition rather than Collaboration

In most conventional organisations competition between sub-units is the dominant mode of behaviour. While there is nothing inherently wrong in this, it tends to result in people competing with those with whom they should collaborate. It also results in a regrettable overemphasis on looking good, which not only reduces collaboration, but also inhibits learning because people have a tendency to conceal what they do not know or do not understand.

The Barrier of Reactiveness

Life is less stressful for people if they only change as and when it is absolutely necessary. This results in a firefighting approach in which a great deal of attention is devoted to problems, but only when they are known to exist. This in turn promotes risk-avoidance strategies, which are the main enemy of innovation and creativity.

All this begs the question of how a conventional firm can overcome the above barriers. To some authors, such as Kreitner and Kinicki (1995), the answer is 'effective leadership' and this prescription can be little more than American 'management speak' for 'put yourself in the hands of the top person and somehow, his or her god-like presence will make itself felt, and all will be well'. Others, for example Robbins (1998), advocate something that looks remarkably like OD, and from what has been said earlier, there must be some doubt about whether a glib prescription such as this will actually work. In addition, there is another issue of importance which, as yet, nobody seems to have addressed.

The learning organisation is a highly managerialist concept that is intended to benefit the top management of an organisation rather than anyone else. While an organisation of this type probably has a strong capacity to survive and prosper, its top managers are the people who reap the rewards without having to undergo change themselves. As in most prescriptions for change, they will probably be left untouched, and those lower down will have to cope with the radically different patterns of organisational life that are probably more hectic, stressful and insecure. The important question, therefore, is whether anybody has bothered to ask the people lower down whether this is the sort of life that they want.

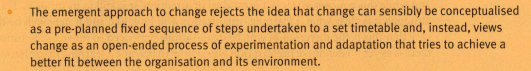

- The emergent approach to change rejects the idea that change can sensibly be conceptualised as a pre-planned fixed sequence of steps undertaken to a set timetable and, instead, views change as an open-ended process of experimentation and adaptation that tries to achieve a better fit between the organisation and its environment.

- Because it deals with organisations that are equipped for continuous change, a great deal of current attention is focused on the concept of the learning organisation.

- Transforming a conventional organisation into a learning organisation means that a number of important barriers need to be overcome and, as yet, no prescription for doing this has emerged.

OVERVIEW AND CONCLUSIONS

Although organisations have always had to change and adapt, the need to do so is now greater than ever. This need is often prompted by changes in an organisation's task environment and, at the present time, there is a greater tendency for change to occur for strategic reasons, often because top management feels the need to reposition the organisation with respect to its environment. Moreover, while some of the changes that take place are adaptations to environmental conditions that have already changed, there is a growing tendency for them to be in anticipation of how the environment is expected to develop in the future.

Although change of some sort can be an inevitability, this does not mean that it is wholeheartedly welcomed by everyone. For those required to change, it can be extremely disruptive and can result in the loss of some facet of organisational life that people have come to value and can be even more unpalatable when they realise that the strongest advocates of change are those who will remain relatively untouched by the changes. For this reason, it is possible that many changes go hand in hand with a measure of resistance and any strategy for dealing with resistance needs to be carefully selected according to the reasons why resistance has appeared.

There are two basic approaches to implementing organisational change: the planned approach and the emergent approach. The first of these is exemplified by organisational development (OD), which is strongly focused on changing the human element. It is underpinned by a set of philosophies and assumptions about the nature of human behaviour in organisations, uses a systems perspective and assumes that change in human values and attitudes are necessary if people are to accommodate themselves to a changed situation. However, arguments still rage about whether OD delivers what it promises in terms of a more effective organisation and more satisfied and committed employees. In addition, there are questions about the relevance of OD to contemporary organisations, and about the ethics of the approach.

The emergent approach rejects the major tenets of planned change, and in particular the idea that change can be introduced by a universally applicable set of sequenced steps. Instead, change is regarded as an open-ended process in which issues are dealt with as they arise, often by way of a number of small, incremental initiatives which can eventually add up to a major transformation.

A recent concept that is compatible with the emergent approach is that of the learning organisation. This envisages organisations that are continuously ready for change and while this concept attracts a great deal of attention, it is still in its infancy. Thus, although it is clear what a learning organisation will look like and it may well be the case that this is the direction in which organisations may need to move in the future, there is as yet no definitive prescription about how to become a learning organisation.

FURTHER READING

Argyris, C (1999) *On Organisational Learning*, 2nd edn, Oxford: Blackwell. A classic text, which gives a penetrating exploration of organisational learning and some coverage of organisational development and change.

Burnes, B (2004) *Managing Change: A Strategic Approach to Organisational Dynamics*, 4th edn, Harlow: Financial Times/Prentice Hall. A comprehensive text that covers a great many approaches to change.

Collins, D (1998) *Organisational Change: Sociological Perspectives*, London: Routledge. A penetrating examination of organisational change that critically discusses many of the myths and populist quick-fix approaches.

Cummings, T G and C Worley (1997) *Organisational Development and Change*, 7th edn, St Paul, MN: West Publishing. A comprehensive text containing many practical examples and case studies.

French, W L and C H Bell (1999) *Organisational Development: Behavioural Science Interventions for Organisational Improvement*, 6th edn, Englewood Cliffs, NJ: Prentice Hall. A classic text that gives comprehensive, if somewhat uncritical, coverage of OD.

Kotter, J P (1995) Leading change: why transformation efforts fail, *Harvard Business Review*, March/April, 59–67. An American article illustrating the recipe approach in which the author describes his eight-step process for successful change.

Senior, B (1997) *Organisational Change*, London: Pitman. A well-written text which explores different approaches to managing organisational change.

REVIEW AND DISCUSSION QUESTIONS

1. Describe the main triggers to organisational change that are located in:
the wider environment
an organisation's task environment
the organisation.

2. Distinguish between and describe the four types of change identified by Nadler and Tushman (1986).

3. Why do people resist change? Is resistance inevitable and, if so, how can it most appropriately be handled?

4. Describe the systems model of change and trace its implications for the design of an organisational change initiative.

5. Describe Lewin's method for bringing about change in human behaviour.

6. What is organisational development (OD)? What distinguishes OD from other approaches to organisational change?

7. Critically evaluate OD in terms of:
its likelihood to deliver what it promises
its relevance to managers in present-day conditions
its ethics.

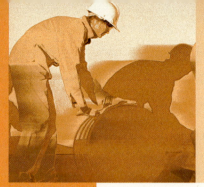

Integrating Macro Level Characteristics and Processes

The task of this integrative section is to trace the links between the topics covered in the seven preceding chapters. Some of these aspects of organisation (for example, Goals and Effectiveness, and Structure) are clearly characteristics, while others, such as Communication and Change and Development, are processes. Others, however, notably Control and Culture, can be viewed as either. To sidestep this dilemma and enable the section to be broken down into easy stages, Goals and Effectiveness and Structural Design and Control, which are covered in Chapters 15–18, will (arbitrarily) be treated as characteristics and the first part of the section will trace links between them. The second part will then trace some of the links between these characteristics and the processes of Culture, Communication, and Change and Development, which are covered in Chapters 19–21.

LINKS BETWEEN ORGANISATIONAL CHARACTERISTICS

By far the most popular and obvious way of evaluating the effectiveness of an organisation is to use the criterion of whether it achieves its goals. This gives a clear conceptual link between goals and effectiveness and, in theory at least, the connection between goals and structure is equally clear. Goals are part of an organisation's strategy and its structural design is, or should be, chosen to make it possible to implement the strategy (Chandler 1962). Whether structure actually flows from strategy in this neat linear way is, however, a matter of some debate and the theory of strategic choice (Child 1997) argues that managers can become so attached to a certain set of structural arrangements that they modify strategies to suit structures. However, this in no way negates the strong link between the two.

In addition, there is an equally strong link between structure and effectiveness. Basic structure (Child 1984) makes provision for an appropriate set of organisational parts to enable an organisation to do what it has to do and, for this reason, a poor basic structure is a barrier to organisational performance and effectiveness (Drucker 1984). A second aspect of structure, the organisation's operating mechanisms (Child 1984), specifies in more detail how things get done and how they are coordinated and controlled.

Thus the two essential features of any structure – differentiation and integration – have clear links with goals and effectiveness. Differentiation establishes the necessary parts of an organisation to allow it to achieve its goals, and integration provides for coordination and control of these parts to ensure achieving the goals.

Another characteristic that has links with structure is culture. For example, Harrison's (1972) scheme, given in Chapter 17, shows how certain structural features go hand in hand with patterns of sentiments and values, which points very strongly to a link between culture and structure. It is also likely that there is some connection between culture and effectiveness. For instance, prescriptive writers on organisational culture such as Peters and Waterman (1982) argue that strong cultures are a vital element in organisational success. This idea has been criticised as highly simplistic and it is now recognised that if it is to be an important factor in success culture must be appropriate as well as strong, this only serves to reinforce the idea that culture and effectiveness are linked.

LINKS BETWEEN ORGANISATIONAL CHARACTERISTICS AND PROCESSES

Goals and goal achievement have some connection with patterns of communication in organisations. Coordination and control would be impossible without a flow of information, and there is some evidence that different strategies may need different methods of communication. For instance, Kanter (1995) argues that an innovation strategy requires a free flow of information, which implies a greater reliance on informal channels, while cost reduction strategies require more formal arrangements. This tells us that structure can have a huge impact on the process of communication. For example, the long chain of command prevalent in tall structures often results in information exchange being shaped and controlled by those above. Conversely, flat structures, in which power and authority are decentralised, tend to result in less distortion of information because the communication chain is shorter and the decision making process is nearer to the operational level.

Communication also has links with culture. Strong cultures often contain powerful ways of communicating the core values to new organisational members, and most cultures have their own methods of communication. This is often what is colloquially referred to as 'the grapevine', which is the organisation's quickest and most effective communication system. Culture also has strong links with the process of change. Cultures and structures can be sources of comfort and predictability to those who have lived with them for some time, and to some extent this means that they contain inbuilt forces to resist change (Ray 1986). Thus, where managers are able to bring about cultural change, they exercise the ultimate degree of control over people in an organisation. However, whether an organisation's culture can be easily changed is a highly contentious issue. Cultural pragmatists assume that it is possible, while cultural purists such as Ogbonna (1993) assert that culture is too deeply rooted to be easily modified. A more pragmatic, middle-ground proposition is that advanced by advocates of the so-called learning organisation (McGill and Slocum 1993), described in Chapters 2 and 21. This explicitly acknowledges a link between culture, change and effectiveness, and seeks to establish cultures that are receptive to continuous change.

Finally, there are also strong connections between goals, effectiveness and change, if only because a strong trigger to change is a perceived reduction in organisational effectiveness, or its failure to achieve certain goals.

In summary, therefore, there are very strong links between organisational-level characteristics and processes and this is shown in Figure I4.

Figure I4 Interaction between factors at macro level of organisation

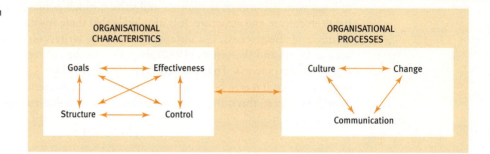

Integrating Macro and Micro Levels of Organisation

INTRODUCTION

Throughout the book integrative sections have drawn attention to connections between topics covered in a number of preceding chapters, and these have progressively traced links between groups of chapters. As was pointed out in Chapter 1, it is impossible to understand the complexity of human behaviour in organisations without taking account of two organisational levels: the micro level that has been covered in Chapters 3–14 and the macro level that has been covered in Chapters 15–21. The task of this section is to trace links between these two levels. To do this the discussion is split into two main sections. The first describes some of the effects that the macro level can have on the micro level, and the second deals with the effects that micro level factors have on the macro level.

As with every other integrative section in the book, space precludes identifying every possible effect, so the discussion is restricted to some of the more prominent and easily identifiable influences. Nevertheless, since this brings together the important points (but not the detail) from all prior chapters in the book, of necessity this is the largest integrative section of all. For this reason, and unlike prior integrative sections, this one provides short, bulleted lists of 'Replay' points at intervals throughout the text in order to summarise its main conclusions.

THE EFFECTS OF THE MACRO ON THE MICRO LEVEL

Organisational Structure

Structure has a huge effect on individual and group processes, and it is usually intended that this be the case. However, structure does not directly determine behaviour in the same way as an individual's mental processes; rather, it establishes a set of contextual circumstances that encourage certain behaviours and inhibit others. There are two fundamental features of an organisation's structure: differentiation, which divides the organisation up into component parts; and integration, which makes provision to control and coordinate the parts to achieve goals. In practice these go hand in hand, but here it is simpler to concentrate on the first and defer discussion of integration until control is considered.

The more an organisation is split up into highly specialised units (the extreme of which is the highly bureaucratised structure), the more likely it is that units come to see themselves as different, which means that people lower down can lose sight of the overall goals for the organisation. To try to overcome these effects, bureaucracies often put limits on the behaviour of individuals by making extensive use of standardised and formalised procedures that specify exactly what should be done. This, however, can have attitudinal and motivational effects, and a number of writers have commented on the way that a highly bureaucratised structure can result in people just following the rules, even if the rules are inappropriate (Merton 1957; Selznick 1966). This is bureaucracy in the extreme, and a more typical example is given in Chapter 17, in Burns and Stalker's (1961) description of the mechanistic organisation. Nevertheless, this still illustrates that structure is likely to affect patterns of behaviour and can also give rise to distinctive attitudes.

The principle of specialisation in the broader structure is often repeated lower down, and this influences the way that jobs are designed. Highly differentiated structures often have jobs with small, restricted task elements, which can result in boredom, low intrinsic satisfaction, and a stifling of personal initiative for individuals with few opportunities for personal growth (Argyris 1964). In highly specialised structures there is sometimes an attempt to alleviate some of these problems with slight modifications to job design, for instance the job rotation, enlargement or even enrichment steps described in Chapter 7.

All structural forms have their own strengths and weaknesses, and the current trend towards flatter structures can have its own associated difficulties, albeit of a different type. Decentralised authority can result in more autonomy and increased job satisfaction, but the structure that results can sometimes be so loose that it gives rise to ambiguity, anxiety and stress. In addition, all structural forms, whether they are mechanistic or organic, establish bases of power, notably the power to reward and/or coerce subordinates that is described in Chapter 14. While the effects of these will be put on one side until control is discussed, there is another phenomenon that must be highlighted. Since sub-units can sometimes come to see themselves as different from others, it is often but a short step from this for sub-units to pursue their own aims at the expense of other groups. Thus structure can establish a tendency for competition between groups, and in some cases this can develop into outright conflict. This is the case even in loose structures and it has been noted, for example, that matrix structures are usually riven with conflict (Davis and Lawrence 1977). Thus, although the effects of structure are not always as adverse as the picture painted here, it can be asserted with some confidence that the differentiation aspect of structure can have effects on work-related attitudes of organisational members, and also on their motivations and tendencies towards intergroup conflict.

Organisational Control

As was explained in Chapter 18, organisational control systems are essentially put in place to monitor progress towards achieving goals or objectives and, where necessary, to set corrective action in motion. This is a process that starts at the macro level, extends downwards, and represents the integrative aspect of structure. For this reason, when an organisation is divided up into departments or functions, an important element in the design is to include a facility to coordinate and control the parts. Since control also extends downwards to individuals and groups, the type of control used at this level is often a reflection of the general structural characteristics of an organisation. While a high degree of specialisation usually gives economic efficiency and people know where they stand, if this is reflected too heavily in job design, the associated tedium and monotony sometimes result in higher absenteeism or turnover and a degree of antagonism between the workforce and managers.

Structure also tends to reflect management philosophies about how much control is needed. In general terms, the more an organisation is differentiated, the greater the need for coordination of the parts. Thus structures of this type are often associated with a high degree of standardisation, for example, the use of standard operating procedures and tight job specifications, to set out what individuals can or cannot do.

There is little doubt that the nature of control in an organisation can affect attitudes, perceptions and motivations of employees. Therefore, while tight coordination and control might help to head off propensities for intergroup conflict, it has its own pitfalls and Walton (1985) argues that managers have to choose between imposed control and attempting to elicit commitment. In theory, a high degree of employee commitment makes control at the individual level less necessary, and even some degree of commitment probably enables control systems to operate in a way that engenders less hostility. Nevertheless, the desire to obtain employee commitment should be recognised for what it is: an attempt to obtain control by other means.

Culture and Climate

Because people carry a culture in their minds it has a direct and highly pervasive effect on behaviour. Whichever way it is defined, culture provides people with a set of normative rules to regulate certain aspects of their behaviour, and this becomes an invisible force that prompts many of their actions. Therefore, if an organisation has a strong culture and everybody subscribes to the same set of core values, this may well give rise to attitudes, motivations and a sense of shared identity that contributes to its effectiveness, providing, of course, that the culture is appropriate for the goals the organisation seeks to achieve (Luthans 1995). However, it must also be remembered that culture and structure tend to go hand in hand. Harrison's (1972) four-part scheme for classifying cultures shows how structures are associated with value systems that probably result in the existing structure being seen as the most appropriate way for organising and controlling activities. New employees are likely to be socialised into these values and attitudes by those already in the organisation, which in the highly differentiated functional structure is likely to mean that subcultures are virtually inevitable (Sackman 1992). Since these represent different value systems, they may well play a part in promoting intergroup conflict, and possibly a level of political activity to pursue conflicts that arise.

Climate tends to have similar, but perhaps more easily identifiable, behavioural effects. While culture provides a code of behaviour that tells people what is appropriate and expected, climate is what they perceive the organisation to be, and is a set of conditions to which they react. Therefore, while both are linked to people's value systems, culture is what the values are and climate is more a reflection of whether current organisational conditions are concordant with the values that people hold. Where these conditions conflict too heavily with cultural values a poor climate can arise. For this reason climatic conditions are almost bound to have a huge impact on attitudes, perceptions, motivations and the level of conflict in an organisation.

Returning now to a point that arose when discussing control, as Ray (1986) points out, managers have tried almost every way of controlling employees, only to find that whatever controls they use have limited effect. As such, there is now a tendency to try to exercise control in a more subtle way by eliciting commitment or, to put matters differently, by controlling hearts and minds. To some extent this probably occurs of its own accord where culture and structure are compatible, but cultures are extremely slow to change, and if there is an attempt to introduce a radically different and incompatible structure, all sorts of adverse motivational and attitudinal effects can be encountered. There is some evidence that this has happened in recent structural changes made by many organisations, for example in the delayering, re-engineering and empowerment initiatives described in Chapter 2. To work well these changes require attitudes that make cooperation and commitment more likely (Macduffie 1995), but many of these changes have been introduced in organisations that previously had conventional structures and in all likelihood they had developed cultures to match. Thus empowerment often fails to work because managers and supervisors find it hard to let go of the previous way of doing things (Cunningham *et al.* 1996) and people in these organisations often report feelings of demoralisation, demotivation and frustration.

Organisational Change

Many of the points that can be made about change are implicit in what has already been said. As Chapter 21 points out, change can occur at all organisational levels and can be extremely varied in its scope. People come to work for a variety of motives, all of which are usually connected with their self-interests. If someone has learned to play a useful role in an organisation, he or she has almost certainly invested time, energy and brain power into trying to make things work a little better. Thus, the person has 'sunk costs' in the organisation that cannot easily be recouped (Patti 1974). For this reason change can be highly threatening to many people and it is not surprising that it can engender emotive feelings, stress, adverse attitudes, lowered motivations and highly selective perceptions.

Almost any change has different effects on different people – to some it gives more of what they seek to obtain from work, while to others it can take away what they most value. Thus there can be winners and losers. Predictably, those who perceive themselves to be the winners can experience the prospective change as stimulating and motivating and develop more positive attitudes towards the organisation, even to the extent of ignoring any potential drawbacks. For those who see themselves as the losers, however, the change can have the reverse effect.

As well as these effects at the individual level, change can have an impact on group and intergroup processes. It sometimes results in a degree of uncertainty in which goals become more ambiguous, the ground-rules for making decisions are less clear and people become unsure of how resources will be distributed in the future. This is a tremendous spur to political activity as people manoeuvre to retain what power they have, or acquire the levels of power that they desire.

Organisational Communication

Communication has an impact on the downward effects of all the organisational characteristics and processes so far discussed. To some extent, culture is a silent system of communication in its own right, and since this was discussed earlier it needs no further explanation. Moreover, no structure will serve its purpose without effective communication. Control and coordination are crucially dependent on a good flow of accurate information; for instance, people are not really empowered unless information flows freely to them so that they can make appropriate decisions. In addition, change is made much harder without effective communication and people can hardly be expected to welcome a change unless its details and the reasons for the change are clear in their minds. Thus communication affects attitudes, perceptions, motivations and levels of conflict.

These downward effects from the macro level can now be used to commence linking the two levels. This is shown in Figure I5, which embraces Figure I4 from integrative section 4 of the book and Figure I3 from the third integrative section.

REPLAY

- The differentiation and integration aspects of structure can have implications for patterns of attitudes, motivation and tendencies towards intergroup conflict at lower organisational levels.
- Culture and climate can also have an impact on attitudes and behaviour at lower levels.
- Organisational change is often experienced as disruptive or threatening by people at lower levels, and this can also give rise to attitudinal and motivational effects.
- Communication influences the effectiveness of organisational control mechanisms and has a strong impact on attitudes and motivations lower down, particularly in situations of change.

THE EFFECTS OF THE MICRO ON THE MACRO LEVEL

As was explained in an earlier integrative section, there are strong links between many of the micro level factors. However, in the interests of clarity it is more convenient to consider the influence of three clusters: individual characteristics, individual processes and group processes and characteristics.

Individual Characteristics

Certain individual characteristics are relatively fixed and others are subject to a degree of variation in the light of prevailing organisational circumstances. Thus there are two sets of influences and these will be considered in turn.

Dealing first with the relatively permanent characteristics of personality, intelligence and aptitude, their most obvious impact is on the suitability of individuals to occupy specific organisational roles. Since individual performance dovetails into the performance of a group and this feeds into the performance of a whole organisation, individual characteristics can have an impact on goal achievement and hence organisational effectiveness. **Personality** also has an upward impact on employee reactions to change and some change can be so radical that it conflicts with what an individual has come to accept as the reality of how an organisation should function, which gives one reason why change can encounter resistance.

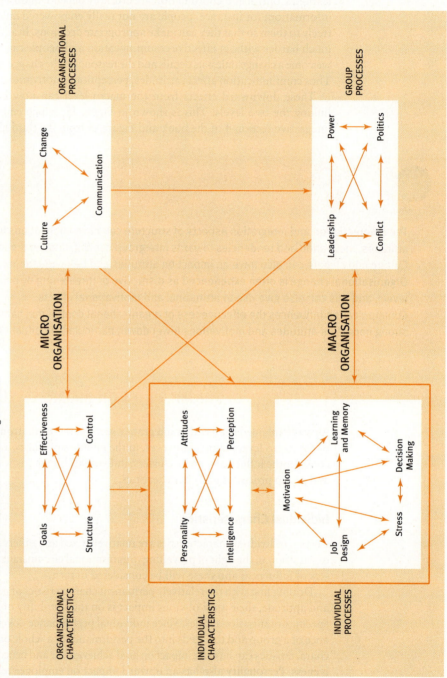

Figure I5 Influence of the macro on the micro level of organisation

Turning now to the characteristics that can change with organisational circumstances, **perceptions** can have a strong influence on the way that downward communications are interpreted. This is particularly the case when a communication contains an unwelcome message about impending change. Perceptions also have an impact on how methods of control are interpreted. Moreover, perceptions have a profound influence on the way that individuals react to the organisation that surrounds them. For example, in a situation of change, if the organisation fails to show people that the change poses no threat, adverse perceptions can become the first stage in the self-fulfilling prophecy that ultimately leads to resistance.

Attitudes are also subject to a degree of modification in the light of circumstances, and they can have a huge impact in reactions to change. The more central an attitude to a person's concept of self, the harder it is to change. Festinger's (1957) theory of cognitive dissonance tells us that unless behaviour and attitude are compatible, the individual experiences some degree of psychological discomfort, tension or even stress. Thus, when a change requires patterns of behaviour that are incompatible with an individual's attitudes, the change tends to be perceived as threatening, the predictable consequence of which is that attitudes harden and the change is resisted. In these circumstances attitudes can also help to erect perceptual barriers. If an impending change is felt adversely to affect personal freedom, the attitudes this engenders can result in any communication about the change being perceived as one-sided or lacking in credibility (Brehm 1972), and what happens then can depend on how the organisation reacts to this situation. If attitudes have hardened and strong pressure is applied from above, it is likely that pressure will be exerted in return, to give the so-called boomerang effect (Heller *et al.* 1973) in which people do the exact opposite of what they are asked. Finally, work-related attitudes such as job satisfaction and organisational commitment can have a strong impact on the way individuals perform their roles, and clearly this ultimately has implications for organisational goal achievement and effectiveness.

Individual Processes

Motivation gives a person the impetus to engage in a course of action that he or she perceives to be rewarding. Therefore, to the extent that an organisation provides conditions that people experience as motivating, there are implications for individual performance which can ultimately have effects on goal achievement and organisational effectiveness. However, motivation is an inner mental state that is not directly under management's control and, because of this, it is difficult to find a set of conditions that are equally motivating for all people. Process theories of motivation, such as expectancy theory (Porter and Lawler 1968; Vroom 1964), tell us that motivation is influenced by expectations about the actual receipt of rewards. Thus, if someone was informed in the past that valued rewards were obtainable and this subsequently turned out to be untrue, it is unlikely that a similar promise will have a motivating effect a second time, which has clear implications for the process of communication. Equity theory (Adams 1963) also draws attention to the idea that motivation can be strongly influenced by people's evaluations of the fairness of their rewards compared to those obtained by other people and this has implications for the effectiveness of structures and reward systems throughout an organisation.

Job design, which is often a micro level reflection of the structural design and control system of an organisation, cannot sensibly be considered in isolation from motivation. The design of a job can either make it a stimulating experience or one that is boring, monotonous and full of drudgery. For this reason a design that seeks only economic efficiency, and ignores the necessity for satisfaction of intrinsic needs, can actually become a barrier to motivation.

Individual decision making also has important upward effects. Integrating mechanisms embedded in an organisation's structure are unlikely to be effective unless appropriate decisions are made at appropriate times – something that can have a clear effect on achievement of goals and organisational effectiveness. Moreover, in certain circumstances individual decision making can result in interactions between the macro and micro levels of organisation. If decision making criteria are ambiguous, or decisions have to be taken in conditions of high uncertainty, low quality decisions can be made and this can result in goals or objectives not being achieved, which in turn creates even more ambiguity down below.

Individual learning processes also have a fairly clear implication for two macro level aspects of organisational functioning. Change almost always involves an element of unlearning the old and learning something new, and the process of adaptation can be dependent on the speed at which this takes place. Thus successful organisational change is strongly influenced by individual learning processes. People seldom restrict themselves to learning only what the organisation wants them to learn and ignore everything else. They also learn to behave in a way that is calculated to maximise their pleasant experiences and minimise unpleasant situations and this has a huge impact on organisational systems of control.

Finally, there is another individual process that has strong implications for organisational functioning. Because it can result in low morale, lowered motivation, decreased performance and lack of job satisfaction, all of which have identifiable economic effects, individual **stress** costs money. Importantly, stress can also have some highly recursive effects. The absenteeism, lowered output and lack of individual effectiveness that result from stress sometimes sound the wrong alarm bells in organisational control systems. Instead of examining whether prevailing stressful conditions have made the organisation the author of its own lack of effectiveness, the result is increased pressure on those lower down to make up the shortfall, the net result of which is even more widespread stress.

Group Processes and Characteristics

Many of the upward individual influences described above are exerted through individuals. However, there are some that are predominantly group-level phenomena and occur only because a group exists. The Homans (1950) model in Chapter 11 shows that important organisational outcomes such as economic efficiency, goal achievement and organisational effectiveness can be strongly influenced by the members of a group. Therefore, unless a clash between the objectives that an organisation has for a group and those that the group has for itself is avoided, the likelihood of achieving these objectives can be poor (Keller 1986).

Groups have a huge influence on their members that can sometimes extend to the shaping of their perceptions. Thus information can be subject to a high degree of distortion as it is reinterpreted through a group's communication structure, and this can have a strong impact on an organisation's capability to bring about change.

A group is unlikely to perform its role well unless it has achieved a degree of maturity (Tuckman 1965) and, if it is a temporary one (as is quite common these days), its composition in terms of the complementary skills and abilities of members can be vital (Belbin 1993). While cohesive groups tend to have higher levels of performance, cohesiveness can have its drawbacks, one of which is decision making. What is perhaps more important from an organisation's point of view is that coordination and control through the structure of the organisation can be seriously impaired if groups are too cohesive. Indeed, the more that control is exerted downwards on a highly cohesive group, the greater will be the group's resistance to the control (Buller and Bell 1986).

If an organisation is to function well, groups have to interact with each other, which means that organisational effectiveness can be highly dependent on smooth relations between groups. However, cohesive groups have a higher propensity to view themselves as perfect and others as having nothing but faults, which can result in a situation ripe for intergroup conflict. This not only wastes time and energy, but it can also have some highly recursive effects. For instance, conflict can result in winners and losers, with the winners often becoming more self-righteous and complacent, while the losers become tense or demoralised and look for opportunities to regain their honour.

The **headship** role is the most visible one in most groups, and whether this is also a role of leadership is a matter of some importance. Leaders are usually able to exert a degree of influence over followers without recourse to formal authority, which can have implications for willing and committed performance of tasks and ultimately have a bearing on goal achievement and organisational effectiveness. Thus, whether the person in charge is a leader or simply a head, this person's behavioural style has implications for the outcomes of a group's endeavours. Contingency theories of leadership all indicate that high group performance is more easily achieved if the head's behavioural style matches certain contingent circumstances. However, a leader's style is a function of his or her personality and since this is likely to be relatively unchanging (Fiedler 1965, 1967), there are implications for successful adaptation to change. Moreover, in situations of radical change, it seems likely that very different styles of leader behaviour are required. Bass (1985) points out that the transactional style of behaviour required under steady stable conditions is quite different from the one needed in a dynamic changing situation, where a transformational style is more appropriate.

With respect to **power** in organisations, Chapter 14 points out that a common misconception about power is that it is only exercised in a downward direction. However, two of French and Raven's (1959) bases of power are often capable of being exerted upwards. Referent power can establish informal leaders in groups on whom formal heads can become dependent, and the formal head of a group can also be highly dependent on the expert power of subordinates. This is often the case in today's downsized and delayered conditions, where organisations have been so slimmed down that goals can be difficult to achieve without the commitment of the workforce. To achieve this state of affairs employees may well require that managers put limits on the use of formal authority.

As was noted earlier, **political tactics** tend to be used to acquire, maintain or enhance power. Chapter 14 points out that political activity is commonplace in many organisations, and it is probably even more prevalent in today's fast-changing conditions, which are full of ambiguity. This can call into question the reality of formal structures and their associated control mechanisms, and also has an impact on the change process. For example, if people use the change situation to manoeuvre for

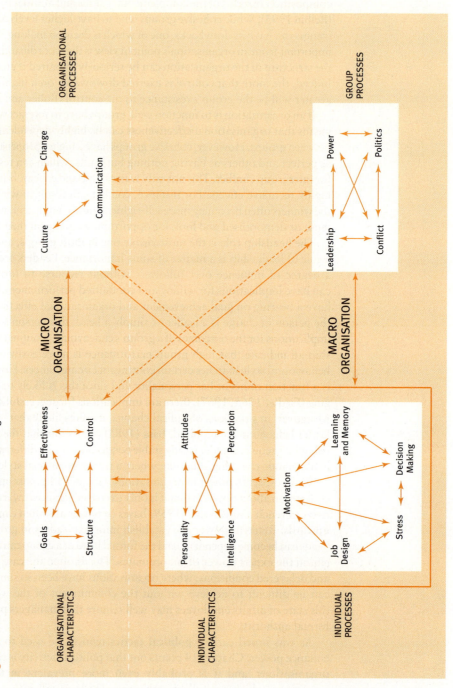

Figure I6 Interaction of the macro and micro levels of organisation

REPLAY

- The relatively unchanging characteristics of individuals can affect their suitability for roles and also their reactions to prospects of change, and characteristics that are more changeable in the light of prevailing organisational circumstances also have a strong impact on reactions to change, while work-related attitudes have an impact on certain aspects of employee performance.

- Individual processes such as motivation, decision making, learning and stress all have upward influences and these in turn are affected by the downward effects of structure and control systems.

- Many of the upward influences are expressed through groups and, in addition, group characteristics and processes have their own impact on the whole organisation.

personal advantage, change will probably take much longer and may even be found to have taken a form that was never intended.

Finally, all organisations seem to have a degree of conflict, either between individuals or groups. The interactionist perspective argues that there is an optimal level of conflict for an organisation and if there is too much, it absorbs energy that could be devoted to other things, which has implications for macro level matters such as goal achievement, effectiveness and change. However, if there is insufficient conflict, it is argued that the *status quo* is likely to remain unchallenged. Thus, the organisation can become characterised by inertia, stagnation and lack of innovation, all of which are likely to have an impact on goal achievement, effectiveness and the willingness to change when necessary. With these points in mind, Figure I5 can be supplemented with the influences identified above, to give Figure I6.

OVERVIEW AND CONCLUSIONS

Since individuals and groups are all influenced by the context in which they exist, macro level features such as structure, control, goals, culture and communication all have some influence on the behaviour of individuals and groups lower down. In many cases, while these features are largely put in place to try to influence micro level behaviour, people are not just passive recipients of this influence. They experience it with varying degrees of favourability and react to what they experience. Thus, there are micro level phenomena that affect those at the macro level, and often in a way that has a bearing on the effectiveness of an organisation's structure, its control mechanisms, its processes of communication and change and the effectiveness of the organisation itself.

For these reasons there are dangers in viewing either the macro or micro levels of organisation in isolation. To obtain a more accurate perspective it is desirable to view a process or characteristic as part of a system of interconnected parts. In this way it is often possible to gain a better understanding of why a phenomenon exists, why it is what it is, how it is affected by other phenomena and how, in turn, it affects them.

Globalisation and the Organisation Across Cultures

LEARNING OUTCOMES

After studying this chapter you should be able to:

- explain the increasing significance of cross-national business organisations and the pressures prompting an increased level of international business

- describe different types of cross-national organisation, distinguish between them in terms of their strategic focus and how this influences the structural form typically found in each type

- explain the impact of wider social cultures on behaviour in organisations

- describe Hofstede's four-dimensional scheme for distinguishing between national cultures and the implications that this has for explaining behaviour in organisations

- describe the ways in which differences in wider social cultures can create a need for cross-national organisations to vary their practices for the management of human resources in different cultural contexts

INTRODUCTION

Until recently this chapter would not have appeared in a book on Organisational Behaviour, but these days firms cannot insulate themselves from the effects of foreign competition and many of them now seek new opportunities abroad. Because Organisational Behaviour and Organisational Analysis originated in America and northern Europe, most topics covered in this book have a particularly Western flavour. However, since there are important differences in the way that people think and behave in other countries, the conclusions you have probably drawn from reading earlier chapters should not be taken to be the last word and a cross-cultural perspective is fast becoming a necessity.

To address these matters, the chapter commences with a section that traces the increase in cross-national business activity and the pressures that have resulted in a globalised economy. Although the volume of international trade is now greater than it has ever been, there are different types of cross-national organisation that represent a continuum of development that stretches from the domestic (country of origin alone) organisation to one that is global or transnational in its scope. Therefore, the next section of the chapter distinguishes between these different types of organisation in terms of their strategic aims and the way that they pursue them. One of the main tools used by a firm to pursue its strategic aims is organisational structure and so the next section of the chapter describes the major features of the structural designs adopted by the different types of cross-national organisation.

The remainder of the chapter is more sharply focused on the factors that affect human behaviour on a cross-national basis. The first matter to be considered is national cultures, the ways in which they can differ, and how this can affect the behaviour of people in organisations. This is followed by an explanation of a scheme for classifying cultures in different countries and the final section of the chapter considers the matter of managing human resources in overseas locations. To do this, material given earlier in the chapter is used to consider seven different aspects of human behaviour in organisations and for each one an explanation is given of why allowances may need to be made for overseas cultures in terms of the way that an organisation manages its human resources.

THE GROWTH OF INTERNATIONAL BUSINESS

Large business organisations increasingly see their markets as international rather than purely domestic. This represents a new way of thinking in which the world is perceived as a smaller place, and new business strategies are required (Bartlett and Ghoshal 1991). This did not come about overnight but as things now stand, there are three very large trading regions: the so-called golden triangle of North America, which embraces the USA, Canada and Mexico; the Pacific Rim countries of Japan, South Korea, Taiwan, Singapore, Hong Kong and Australasia; and the European Union, which at present embraces 25 European nations. However, the position is fluid and other countries are likely to join these regions in the near future. Countries such as China, Malaysia, Indonesia and Thailand are industrialising rapidly and are likely to become part of the Pacific Rim group. Some of the Latin American countries are also making great strides in industrialisation and, in addition, the former Soviet command economies have all more or less embraced a free market system.

Factors Facilitating the Growth of International Business

Except for a few rare cases, there were no really large cross-national organisations prior to the Second World War, and global organisations only started to appear in the 1970s. Although this was helped along by the gradual appearance of the three major trading regions identified above, Bedeian and Zammuto (1991) argue that there have been four main developments that prompted the increase in international trade, and these made the emergence of globalisation virtually inevitable.

Industrialisation

With the exception of Japan, prior to the Second World War the major industrialised countries were all located in the northern hemisphere, and after the War most of them quickly sought to re-establish their export trades. Although an exporting country largely keeps its expertise at home and merely sells its goods abroad, its prosperity and power are visible to the rest of the world. This provides an imperative for every non-industrialised country to industrialise and so lesser countries, many of which had previously been colonial outposts of a European nation, pursued conscious policies of industrialisation with the aim of becoming just as prosperous and powerful.

Rising Living Standards

In the two decades following the end of the Second World War, living standards rose tremendously in Western countries, but more rapidly in the industrialising nations of the Far East. In the West, national markets were fairly mature and Western firms tended to see countries in the East as extremely attractive export markets because they had higher rates of economic growth. Since these countries were rapidly developing an industrial base, they also had an incentive to export, sometimes to the less developed countries of South East Asia, but increasingly to the northern hemisphere.

Rapid Technological Change

Rising living standards bring changes in consumer tastes and these days tastes change quite rapidly. This shortens product life cycles and increases the proportion of profits that need to be ploughed back into development. It also means that the length of time in which development costs can be recouped is shorter, and for this reason firms every-where seek to sell their outputs in the widest possible range of markets.

Improvements in Global Transport and Communication

Since the 1960s, the declining cost of foreign travel has enabled people to experience other countries first hand. In addition, mass communication brings increased famil-iarity with lifestyles and customs in other parts of the world, and to some extent this also prompts a convergence in consumer tastes which, although not identical every-where, are often similar enough to enable a basic product to be adapted in minor ways to cater for local tastes. Rapid developments in communications technology have also removed many of the barriers to operating internationally; satellite telephone gives easy access to remote locations and fax machines and e-mail enable complicated documents to be transmitted in seconds.

Pressures to Engage in Cross-national Activity

Although the facilitating factors given above greatly ease the problems of international trade, there are more specific motives that apply to individual organisations and prompt them to look abroad.

Access to Resources

For reasons of cost and security of supply, many organisations, particularly those in manufacturing industry, tend to feel a need to be close to their sources of supply of vital raw materials (Mendenhall *et al*. 1995). While this usually results in small subsidiaries that deal only with the supply of resources, if organisations also see market opportunities close to these sources, they may also engage in manufacturing abroad.

Economic and Political Changes

In the three very large trading regions mentioned earlier countries are bound together by political treaties that influence cross-border trade. For instance, while the European Union permits free movement of goods and labour between its member states, it has tariff barriers to the rest of the world and, to some extent, the same is true with most major trading blocs. To do business in these areas can sometimes mean becoming more deeply integrated with the area in question. A case in point is the European Union (EU), which has a requirement that goods are only free of import duties if a minimum percentage of the product is manufactured within the EU. Japanese and American manufacturers cannot afford to ignore the potential for sales in the EU, which has prompted them to set up manufacturing facilities in Europe (notably in Great Britain) to ensure access to European markets.

Product Markets

The most important single factor prompting an organisation to internationalise is the quest for new markets. An outstanding example of this is Nestlé, the confectionery manufacturer, whose country of origin (Switzerland) has far too small a population to sustain the growth that Nestlé has been able to achieve through international trading.

Lower Costs of Production and Distribution

Capital tends to migrate to the cheapest centre of production. Since the European Union consists of some nations where wage rates are high and others where they are very low, it had a fear that there would be a tendency for this to happen within its member states. This led to the construction of the Social Chapter, which seeks to harmonise employment legislation for all its members, so that the differences between countries would eventually disappear (Marginson *et al*. 1995). Nevertheless, large organisations always seem to be on the lookout for cheaper centres of production and this is a strong motivation for engaging in overseas activities.

Figure 22.1
Facilitators of, and
pressures to engage
in, cross-national
business activity

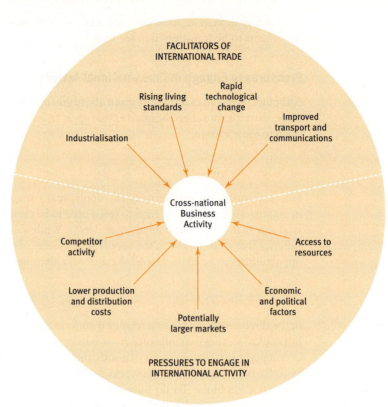

**FACILITATORS OF
INTERNATIONAL TRADE**

Rising living
standards

Rapid
technological
change

Improved
transport and
communications

Industrialisation

Cross-national
Business
Activity

Competitor
activity

Access to
resources

Lower production
and distribution
costs

Economic
and political
factors

Potentially
larger markets

**PRESSURES TO ENGAGE IN
INTERNATIONAL ACTIVITY**

Competitor Activity

As more and more organisations enter the international marketplace, it becomes increasingly difficult for other companies to insulate themselves from foreign competition. Indeed, a company can wake up one morning and find that a competitor in an overseas country is now a competitor on its own doorstep. A study by Martin *et al.* (1998) shows just how sensitive firms are to the activities of their competitors. For example, if a firm is a major supplier to another firm in its home country and this customer sets up an overseas facility, there is strong impetus to do likewise for fear that an overseas competitor will acquire the business.

The facilitators and pressures for cross-national business activity are summarised in Figure 22.1.

TYPES OF CROSS-NATIONAL ORGANISATION

The difference between an organisation whose markets are in a single country and one that operates on a worldwide basis is a leap of quantum proportions. When the first wave of international expansion started in the 1960s, many firms attempted to do so through international joint venture arrangements (IJVs) with foreign partners (Park and Ungson 1997). However, the IJV situation is particularly fertile ground for coordination and communication problems arising from cultural differences and so many

IJVs were unsuccessful. Although joint ventures are still fairly common, many firms now try to make the transition to cross-national activity alone. Becoming a globalised organisation, however, is seldom accomplished in a single step, as is graphically illustrated by Barney and Griffin (1992), who describe the transitional stages in the following way:

Stage 1 – From national to international, in which domestic organisations that derive their revenues within a single country seek to become international organisations, still based in the country of origin but with additional operations elsewhere.

Stage 2 – From international to multinational, where some of the firms go on to become even more dispersed, with subsidiaries and facilities spread across the globe, for example, the Ford Motor Company.

Stage 3 – From multinational to globalised, which is a much more recent phenomenon and consists of a tendency to transcend national borders. The firm not only operates on a global scale, but thinks of itself as one that is no longer primarily located in its country of origin.

These intermediate stages give rise to different types of cross-national organisation, each of which has its own strategic focus. This enables organisations to be located along a continuum, the extremes of which are the large domestic organisation and the global or transnational organisation. Drawing on the work of Bartlett and Ghoshal (1991) and others, the differences between these types of organisation are summarised in Table 22.1. However, caution needs to be exercised in drawing conclusions from Table 22.1. The table simply reflects the idea that there are five different types of organisation, and it should not be inferred that a progression from left to right indicates superiority. Whether an organisation can move from one extreme to the other is greatly dependent on the markets for its products and Beamish *et al.* (1991) provide convincing reasons why some product markets push an organisation into serving only local markets, whereas for others the nature of the product market means that failure to compete on a worldwide basis can be commercial suicide.

Domestic Organisations

Domestic organisation: one that mainly trades within the borders of its country of origin

Although these can be very large, for the most part they do not trade outside their country of origin, although they might well engage in exporting. Their dominant focus is on home markets and they try to find a strategy that captures the largest possible market share, often by becoming multi-product companies that are controlled from the centre.

International Organisations

International organisation: one that is primarily located and managed in its country of origin, but also either exports to or produces identical or similar goods and services in overseas subsidiaries

These companies tend to have some overseas operations, the scope of which can vary considerably. However, even in its most advanced form, the organisation simply attempts to expand its markets overseas, using the same or very similar products as those sold at home. This is done by exporting its technology and knowledge to a number of host countries, with operating subsidiaries to handle production and marketing. This arrangement is fairly commonplace in manufacturing industries that produce standardised products that are very similar the world over, for example, car tyres and chemicals.

Table 22.1 Major strategic characteristics of different types of cross-national organisation (Bartlett and Ghoshal 1991)

	Domestic organisation	International organisation	Multinational organisation	Global organisation	Transnational organisation
Markets served	Home market in country of origin	Home and overseas	Home and overseas	Worldwide	Worldwide
Strategic assumptions	There is one best way of serving the market	There are several best ways to satisfy different markets	There is a single least-cost way to satisfy different markets	There are many good ways to satisfy different markets, all of which can be used simultaneously	As global organisation
Strategic focus and competitive strategy	On home markets alone	Transfer of knowledge and technology from country of origin to produce at home and abroad	Products or services developed and made to suit different markets at home and abroad	Develop standardised products that can be produced for a wide variety of markets, but customise to meet specific requirements of each market	Develop skills, products and technology in all units and transfer wherever needed
Responsibility for strategy formulation	Headquarters in country of origin	Centralised at headquarters in country of origin	Decentralised to overseas subsidiaries	Shared between all divisions around the world	Shared between all divisions
Structure and control	Functional with divisions	Functional with an international division. Centralised with strong hierarchical control from home country	Several different lines of business Decentralised semi-autonomous overseas divisions	Independent overseas divisions whose activities are coordinated by headquarters	Interdependent units operating nationally and worldwide
Degree of adaptation to host countries	None necessary	High in legal terms, but managers usually from home country	High degree of social and cultural diversity	High: very diverse culturally and socially	As global organisation

Overseas divisions are usually responsible to, and controlled by, the organisational headquarters in the country of origin.

Multinational Organisations

Multinational organisation: one that is primarily located and managed from the country of its origin, but produces goods or services in relatively autonomous overseas subsidiaries to meet the needs of local markets

Here the aim is to expand even further, but doing so requires servicing more diverse markets. Because new products can be required to satisfy different overseas markets, overseas subsidiaries often need a higher degree of operating autonomy, for example, to be able to design, develop and market their own products. Examples of this type of organisation can be found in industries that produce branded goods that have some degree of similarity worldwide but also need to be varied to meet the requirements of particular overseas markets, for example, food and clothing (Beamish *et al.* 1991).

Global organisation:
one that is not tied to
a single nation, but
operates wordwide
as an independent
set of subsidiaries
coordinated by a
headquarters

Global Organisations

This type of organisation aims to produce standardised products that can be easily adapted to suit the requirements of a wide range of different markets. The product can be designed or developed anywhere so long as it is adaptable to other markets. In this type of organisation strategy is a shared responsibility of all divisions and although control is centralised in the hands of corporate headquarters, this is less concerned with detailed regulation of the activities of subsidiaries than with getting them to work with each other. Thus the organisation has a strong emphasis on the interdependence of its parts in order to be able to service worldwide markets.

CASE STUDY 22.1: Quatrostar

Quatrostar is a worldwide electronics company that manufactures a wide portfolio of products, ranging from computers, peripherals and other office machinery to telecommunications equipment. It has subsidiaries in 37 different countries and these are grouped into five geographic regions: North America, South America, Europe, the Middle East and the Far East, which embraces Australia. In some countries subsidiaries are only engaged in marketing and distribution, but each geographic region has a number of manufacturing plants. The company has its headquarters in West Germany and commenced its process of international expansion in the early 1980s, first by exporting its products, and eventually by acquiring overseas subsidiaries to replicate the manufacture of products made for home markets. This pattern has been followed up to the present time. However, while most goods made abroad are still designed and developed in Germany, many of them are subject to some degree of customising to meet local market requirements.

Company headquarters assumes responsibility for formulating corporate strategy, which is then relayed to the regions. Each region is headed by its own managing director and team of functional directors. However, there is little collaboration or trade between regions. Without exception, senior personnel and, until recently, most middle managers in overseas subsidiaries were appointed by headquarters, traditionally from people who have made their long-term career with the company. For the last five years, however, the organisation has gradually increased the proportion of local nationals who occupy certain middle management posts, for example in human resource management, accounts, marketing and production.

A number of problems have recently appeared. First, the organisation has seen a significant decline in profitability. Worldwide sales volumes have decreased and competitors seem to have no difficulty in undercutting Quatrostar's prices. Second, the organisation is slow to keep pace with the competition in terms of getting new and innovative product lines into the market. Third, communication between headquarters and subsidiaries is becoming increasingly difficult to handle and a large number of misunderstandings seem to occur. Finally, subsidiaries are slow to put the new policies of headquarters in place, particularly those concerning the management of human resources.

Question

How do you account for these problems?

Transnational organisation: one that operates simultaneously as an international, multinational and global organisation

Transnational Organisations

In terms of strategy, these organisations are by far the most complex and sophisticated type. They try to incorporate the productive efficiency found in the globalised organisation with the ability to transfer technology and know-how found in international organisations. Where necessary, they also try to be highly responsive to localised markets in the same way as a multinational (Harzing and Ruyssveldt 1995). If anything, therefore, the degree of interdependence between subsidiaries is even higher than in the globalised organisations.

Each of these different types of organisation has its own characteristic way of operating and this can be seen in the penultimate row of Table 22.1, which indicates that structures tend to be very different. The different types of organisation also have different degrees of cultural adaptation to their host countries. However, the first step is to examine structure and organisational design in the different types.

TIME OUT

Carefully examine the different types of cross-national organisation, the details of which are described above and summarised in Table 22.1. Imagine that you are just about to leave university or college, having completed your degree, and have been offered four different positions as a management trainee: one in a large domestic organisation, one in an international organisation, one in a multinational and one in a global organisation. Assuming that all four jobs have very similar remuneration conditions:

1. Which would you accept?
2. Why would you choose this job in preference to the others?

STRUCTURE AND THE CROSS-NATIONAL ORGANISATION

Structure: A Brief Review

In theory organisational structure (see Chapter 16) is intended to facilitate achieving organisational goals and its two main features are:

- differentiation, which divides the organisation into component parts and specifies what role each will play in achieving specific aims and outcomes for the organisation;
- integration, which provides for these parts to be controlled and coordinated so that their activities mesh together to achieve organisational goals.

As organisations grow, they tend to develop more elaborate and complex structures and in most cases the degree of specialisation increases with size, authority becomes more centralised, and procedures and practices become more formalised. If allowance is made for such factors as size and industry type, the general tendency for specialisation, formalisation and centralisation to increase as organisations grow holds good for many countries in the world (Hickson and McMillan 1981), but this does not mean that organisations are the same everywhere. Indeed, the evidence suggests that firms in different countries do things differently, which begs the question of whether a cross-national firm should vary the way it does things according to the country in which it operates. As will be seen later in the chapter, the answer to this question is broadly yes, and the explanation as to why lies in cultural differences. However, cultural differences establish a requirement for variation in the internal structures of different subsidiaries, and here the concern is with the structure of a cross-national organisation as a whole.

Structural Designs for Cross-national Operations

The functional, divisional and matrix designs given in Chapter 16 meet the needs of most domestic organisations, and many years ago Stinchcombe (1965) pointed out that new organisational designs only tend to appear when two conditions arise together:

- where existing designs cannot adequately cope with a new situation; and
- when social and technical conditions make it possible to adopt a new design.

To a large extent these conditions came together when each of the different cross-national designs emerged. The designs for international and multinational organisations evolved some time ago, and the latest one to emerge is that which is often used by global organisations. To make it easier to understand the differences, the designs that can be used for domestic, international and multinational companies will be described first.

Domestic Organisations

Strictly speaking these are not cross-national organisations, but the first step towards international activity is often exporting products made in the home country. At this stage organisations use what Porter (1986) calls an '*international trade strategy*', in which an international division is grafted on to an existing functional or product structure. This allows company headquarters in the country of origin to exercise tight control and coordination and a typical structure is shown in simplified form in Figure 22.2.

International trade strategy and structure: one that is primarily geared to serving a wider set of markets by exporting goods or services from the home country

International and Multinational Organisations

A simplified example of the structure used by these types of organisation is shown in Figure 22.3. Both international and multinational organisations can be regarded as a

Figure 22.2
Structural design for international trade

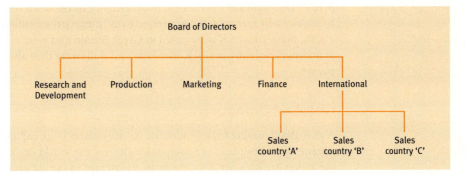

Figure 22.3 Country-focused structural design

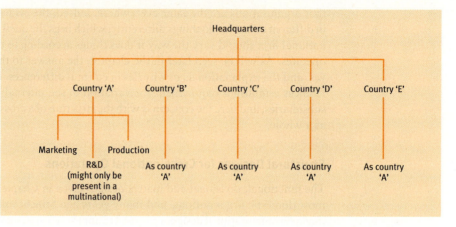

Country-focused strategy and structure: primarily geared to serving a wider set of markets by producing goods or services in overseas subsidiaries for sale in local markets

federation of divisionalised operating units that service different national or regional markets. In general terms both tend to use what can be described as a '*country-focused strategy*' (Porter 1986). As Table 22.1 illustrates, however, they differ in one important respect. In the international organisation, overseas subsidiaries produce the same or slightly modified products and services as they do for home markets. Therefore, activity in subsidiaries bears a strong resemblance to what occurs in the country of origin, which means that authority tends to be centralised at headquarters and subsidiaries are strongly controlled. Subsidiaries in multinationals tend to develop and manufacture different products and services which are specifically targeted at markets in host countries, and the products or services required for one country or region can be very different from those required elsewhere. Thus, subsidiaries need a much higher degree of autonomy and there is less direct control by headquarters.

To some extent there is a natural tendency for an organisation to export the structure it uses in its country of origin, particularly its control and coordination mechanisms (Harzing and Sorge 2003). The ability to do this, however, tends to be limited because competing in international markets often depends on knowing the rules of the game, which can sometimes be very different from those learned in the organisation's past. Learning these rules quickly can be vital for organisations that are behind others in entering international operations, a case in point being West German firms which, until comparatively recently, restricted themselves to export-orientated, international trade strategies. When organisations in West Germany eventually entered the field of international operations, in an attempt to make up for lost time they tended to acquire what are sometimes referred to as 'vanguard subsidiaries' (Ferner and Varul 2000), many of which were based in Great Britain and were already heavily involved in international operations. Know-how and skills were then absorbed into the German parent.

Globalised Organisations

A globalised market for a product or service creates huge expansion opportunities for organisations, but because companies all over the world can enter the same market, the stakes are high for all of them. In an attempt to outbid each other in markets, the rate of development and improvement of products tends to be very fast, which means that product life cycles are shorter. For this reason the research and development costs of staying in business rise, and profitability is acutely dependent on achieving:

- the economies of scale that can be derived from standardised products;
- a high sales volume over a short time span.

Except for a few products such as petroleum, it is virtually impossible to think of any good or service that is identical the whole world over. Thus, taking advantage of a globalised market requires a design than can successfully cater for two separate but diametrically opposed requirements:

- a high degree of sensitivity to local conditions, together with the flexibility to adapt products, marketing methods and distribution to local markets, which is a feature of the country-focus design;
- an ability to integrate activities into a global strategy for achieving economic efficiency in all countries where the organisation operates.

Globally integrated strategy and structure: a diffuse network of highly interdependent subsidiaries, each of which specialises in some degree, but none of which has the capability to operate as a totally independent and autonomous business unit

To reconcile these requirements, companies tend to adopt what Bedeian and Zammuto (1991) call a '*globally integrated strategy and structure*', a simplified example of which is shown in Figure 22.4.

The design gives a highly interdependent networks of geographically dispersed divisions, whose activities are coordinated through headquarters. Interdependence comes from divisions in each country having a degree of specialisation, which reduces duplication of effort and gives economies of scale. For example, in Figure 22.4, the division in country 'A' may handle research and development, the division in country 'B' production of components, while 'C' and 'D' may handle final assembly, with all divisions undertaking the marketing and distribution of finished goods. As an alternative, as well as marketing and distribution in their own host countries, divisions in countries 'A', 'B', 'C' and 'D' may also produce a distinct part of an overall product line that is exported to the others. The net result is that none of the divisions has the complete capability of a single autonomous organisation and they are all dependent on each other for products, resources, technology, information and exporting opportunities.

Figure 22.4 The globally integrated structural design

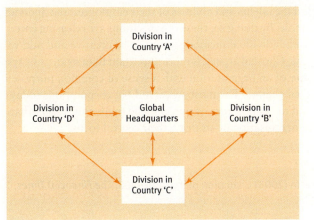

In the globalised design, top managers at headquarters have the vital task of coordinating strategic objectives, policies for the whole organisation, activities of divisions and the flow of information. Divisional managers tend to be responsible for adjusting their respective divisions to the overall global strategy, ensuring that headquarters get to know about opportunities in their own areas and servicing their local markets (Bartlett 1986). Note, however, that headquarters and divisions share in devising the global strategy, whereas in the international organisation the strategy of overseas divisions is imposed by headquarters and in a multinational there are different strategies for

OB IN ACTION: Beyond the Transnational Organisation

Sumantra Ghoshal first came to prominence through his work with Christopher Bartlett in the late 1980s. This set out the concept of the 'transnational' corporation and suggested that a new model of international business strategy and organisation was emerging. They argued that old-style multinational and global corporations were being forced to change by the simultaneous demands of global efficiency and local responsiveness and that rather than choosing between globalisation and localisation, corporations were forced to adopt both strategies at the same time. The result, they said, was the emergence of the 'transnational' corporation, which had the characteristics of both big and small companies and could operate globally and locally. Rather than centralised, hierarchical structures, transnational companies operated as networks, with increasingly specialised units worldwide that are integrated into a seamless whole and work in harmony. At the heart of their thinking was a mindset that requires managers to work across boundaries, pulling together far-flung teams and resources in order to achieve strategic goals.

Their most recent book, *The Individualised Corporation*, has a more far-reaching look at the changes in business. They argue that a revolution is happening, which is being led by pioneering companies such as ABB and General Electric, which are no longer forcing employees to conform to a rigid conception of what an employee should be and do, but are reconfiguring the organisation itself to fit around the talents and abilities of their employees: the 'individualised corporation' of the title. By doing so, these organisations are releasing entrepreneurial hostages, allowing individual members room to be creative and add value to the business. Purpose, Ghoshal argues, is more important than strategy or systems. Infusing every member of an organisation with a sense of common purpose is the key to organisational change. The most successful big corporations today are those that have realised the importance of purpose and made this, rather than preconceived ideas about organisation or strategy, their central focus.

Source:

Witzel M (2003) Champion of the Individual, *The Financial Times*, 7 August.

each country. Probably the most outstanding example of a globalised organisation is Coca-Cola. Some of its products are sold worldwide, while others that cater for local tastes are sold only in certain countries or geographical areas. To avoid cultural clashes in advertising, products are also marketed in slightly different ways in different parts of the world. Moreover, products are distributed via different channels in different places, according to local customs. For example, in some countries through supermarkets in large bottles, while in others nearly everything is sold ready-chilled in cans (Herbert 1988).

Transnational Organisations

As noted in Table 22.1, these organisations have some of the characteristics of all other types of cross-national organisation. Therefore, structure depends to a great extent on the mix of products and services that each organisation provides, and it is impossible to identify any general trends in structural design. Some will be remarkably similar to globalised organisations, while others will be more like multinationals.

Inter-organisational Designs

The preferred method for a company that chooses to become involved in cross-national activities, but not through the route of exporting or becoming an international organisation, is a cooperative arrangement with an overseas company (Aldrich and Whetten 1981). Sometimes this is done to share risks, and in other cases to gain economies of scale or to obtain complementary skills. The joint venture is probably the most popular form of collaborative arrangement between organisations and where this occurs, structural differentiation already exists. Thus, the main consideration is to integrate the activities of the partners. Here much depends on the closeness of the relationship. In some joint ventures the partners have equality and a very close relationship, while in others the relationship is fairly distant and limited in scope; for example, it can be confined to marketing and distribution arrangements, a research and development partnership, or a temporary consortium, which is common in very large civil engineering projects. Again, it is impossible to be specific about coordinating mechanisms used because so much depends on the nature of the contractual relationship.

TIME OUT

Carefully consider the structural characteristics of the international, multinational and globalised organisation, paying particular attention to how each of these types of organisation controls and coordinates the activities of its overseas subsidiaries.

Now consider the jobs of production manager, design and development manager and marketing manager in each of these types of organisation and try to identify what you think would be the likely characteristics of each of these jobs in terms of: degree of autonomy in the job; freedom to innovate; and career prospects within the organisation as a whole.

REPLAY

- A number of factors have facilitated the increase in international business activity, and these have created an impetus for firms to expand cross-nationally. The main motives for doing so being to gain access to resources, to achieve lower costs of production and distribution, to expand product markets and to keep pace with competitors.

- The move from being a purely domestic organisation to one that operates worldwide is a leap of quantum proportions which usually takes place in a number of stages and this results in four different types of cross-national organisation: international, multinational, globalised and transnational. Each type has a different strategic focus and different ways of pursuing its strategic aims.

- One of the major tools for pursuing these aims is organisational structure and so international, multinational and globalised organisations tend to have different structural designs.

CULTURE AND THE CROSS-NATIONAL ORGANISATION

Wider Social Cultures

In Chapter 19 it was noted that people who have absorbed a culture share deep-seated and taken-for-granted assumptions that have a subtle, but powerful, influence on their behaviour. This happens during their upbringing and what results is a set of values and assumptions shared by the vast majority of the inhabitants of a society. While we can all think of ways in which people in other countries seem to have cultural norms different from our own, it is simplistic to speak of national cultures because cultures do not confirm neatly to national boundaries. For this reason, the expression 'wider social culture' is used here.

Individuals in an organisation will expect to be able to conform to the wider social norms that they have absorbed, and if placed in a culture in which values and beliefs are different from their own, they can have great difficulty in adjusting (Feldman and Thompson 1992).

The culture of an organisation normally replicates many of the characteristics of the wider social culture in which it is located (Nelson and Gopalan 2003). For this reason it is important that cross-national organisations take account of how different cultures prompt different patterns of behaviour and Adler (1997) sets out four very important propositions with respect to this matter:

- because wider social cultures in different parts of the world result in different attitudes and values, patterns of behaviour in organisations are also likely to differ;

- although factors such as different standards of living can account for some of this variation in behaviour, wider social cultures are a major factor in their own right;

CASE STUDY 22.2: Quatrostar – Further Developments

In view of its declining profitability and competitive performance, nine months ago Quatrostar formed a task force of senior directors to examine its position and remedy the situation. To aid its deliberations, the task force commissioned a consultancy study from the business school of a prestigious American university and one month ago the consultant's report was presented to the board of Quatrostar. Its main conclusions were:

- The electronics industry is one that is characterised by a rapid rate of technical development, which results in very short product life cycles.

- For this reason, the key to success in the industry is a focus on standardised products that can be sold worldwide, but with (mainly cosmetic) modifications to customise them to local market conditions.

- Quatrostar's major competitors all operate as globalised organisations, which gives them significant advantages in terms of costs, flexibility, rapid response to market conditions and the ability to assimilate new technology and incorporate it into products.

- Unless Quatrostar effects a radical shift in the way it is organised (i.e. to become a globalised organisation) it faces a bleak future.

On receiving this news, the managing director was dumbfounded and said, 'What on earth does this mean? We operate in 37 different countries around the world, and if that is not being a globalised organisation, I really don't know what is.'

Questions

Using the information above, together with that given in Case Study 22.1, answer the questions below, giving reasons for your answers.

1. If Quatrostar is not a globalised organisation, what sort of an organisation is it?

2. What steps would Quatrostar need to take to transform itself into a globalised organisation?

3. How difficult do you think it would be to make this transformation and, in particular, what structural changes would be needed?

- thus, while organisations in different cultural settings have a tendency to become increasingly similar in terms of organisational design and technology, the people who work in them can still differ considerably in terms of culture and a person who moves from one cultural setting to another may need to change his or her behaviour to match the cultural norms of the new location;

- for the above reasons it is not safe to assume that the same motivational techniques, job designs and reward systems will be equally effective everywhere, and so cross-national firms need to develop global strategic approaches to managing a diverse workforce.

Figure 22.5 Some cultural characteristics that can give rise to differences in behaviour

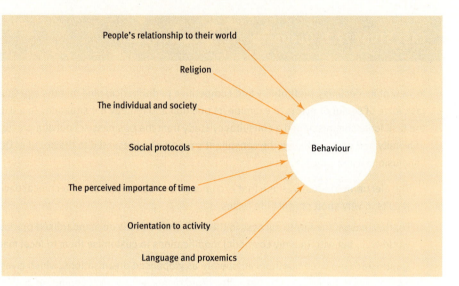

The Impact of Wider Social Culture on Behaviour

There are a number of ways in which the cultural norms of a society can give rise to tendencies for people to behave in different ways. Note, however, that these are tendencies and not absolute certainties. People everywhere have different personalities and these can moderate the effects of cultural beliefs and values. Nevertheless, there are seven significant factors that can affect behaviour (see Figure 22.5) and these are briefly explained in what follows.

People's Relationship to Their World

In some cultures, notably in the industrialised countries of the West, it is culturally acceptable to try to bring nature under control. For example, we store water for irrigation purposes, and deploy intensive farming techniques using artificial fertilisers and insecticides. Other cultures are far more fatalistic. A drought or a flood is regarded as an act of God. There is a belief that nature has to be accepted and these differences predispose people in organisations to view matters in different ways. For instance, in a fatalistic culture, while poor performance by an individual would not be condoned, there could be an acceptance that people differ in what they can do well. In a culture such as this, someone who is not a high performer might not be entrusted with certain tasks, whereas in one where attempts to control events are normal, poor performance could result in disciplinary measures.

Religion

This has a powerful effect on how people behave, which spills over into organisational life. In some countries the Sabbath is virtually ignored and in others it is strictly observed (Friday in Islamic countries, Saturday for Jewish people and Sunday for Christians). This has a bearing on the willingness of people to work certain days or certain hours. In addition, although strict Moslems accept that doing business for profit is normal, lending money for high interest rates is considered sinful, whereas in most Christian countries this is not the case. Finally, in certain countries the Western way of dressing would conflict with religious norms; for example, in strict Moslem countries, such as Iran, women are expected to wear veils and cover their faces.

The Individual and Society

Some cultures, such as those of Great Britain and America, extol the virtues of individual effort, which results in a strong emphasis on personal accomplishment and recognition. Thus, people are slotted into organisations according to job descriptions, which often explicitly hold individuals responsible for achieving certain outcomes (Adler 1997). In addition, rewards, promotion and recognition are all seen as things that people have to acquire by their own efforts and for this reason it is culturally acceptable for individuals to have a primary loyalty to themselves. In other cultures, however, notably in Germany and Japan, there is a much stronger norm of collective responsibility (Garten 1992), in which the individual is considered to be a part of something bigger, for example a group or organisation. Therefore, achievement tends to be interpreted as 'making a contribution to the larger unit achieving its goals'.

Social Protocols

In different parts of the world the social conventions that we commonly call etiquette or good manners differ considerably, and this spills over into how people conduct themselves in organisations. This can be quite different from the way that things are done in the West and a penetrating example is given by Muna's (1980) study of Arab business executives. In the Arab culture personal relationships are all important. For instance, when executives sit down to a business meeting, they commonly spend up to half an hour engaging in social conversation that is purposely kept away from business matters, and to do otherwise would be regarded as impolite. Similarly, the strong kinship structure in Arab countries means that people feel an obligation to hire relatives, something people in the West might label as nepotism (Parnell and Hatem 1999).

The Perceived Importance of Time

In North European and American cultures we are acutely aware of time; we are taught not to waste it, to be punctual for appointments, and regard it as a precious resource. In general, people in these cultures also prefer to do only one thing at a time (Hall and Hall 1990), whereas in other parts of the world time is a more elastic concept. In some of the Mediterranean and central American countries, for example, so long as things eventually get done, nobody is really bothered. People have a relaxed attitude about some of the things that we in the West would find infuriating, for instance, queuing, or being kept waiting by someone when a firm appointment has been made.

Orientation to Activity

Gibson *et al.* (1994) distinguish between what they call 'results-orientated' cultures and 'being' cultures. In the former, people who take action in a thrusting way to achieve results tend to be admired as 'go-getters'. Conversely, in a 'being' culture, such as some of the Mediterranean or South American countries, people are lauded for going with the flow of events, making the most of life and living for today. This facet of culture tells us a great deal about the relative importance that people attach to work and leisure time. For instance, in a results-orientated culture, work is more likely to be seen as a central part of people's lives, whereas in a 'being' culture it may be more of a means to an end.

Language and Proxemics

While language is a very different thing from culture, language and the way it is used can often reflect dominant cultural values. One of the most significant ways in which this happens is in terms of unspoken signs, or non-verbal communication. A significant example here is the matter of proxemics (see Chapter 20). In the West we tend to regard a distance of between 18 inches and 4 feet as the appropriate one to conduct a normal conversation. Anything above this is regarded as impersonal and lacking in intimacy, whereas anything less is an invasion of a person's personal space.

The important point to note here is that proxemics set standards about what is considered to be polite behaviour in different parts of the world. People from Northern Europe tend to feel very uncomfortable when someone comes too close, and in those cultures where closeness is the norm, to stand too far away tends to be regarded as aloofness.

TIME OUT

Carefully consider the impact that different national cultures can have on the behaviour of people within a country. Identify a foreign country that you have visited, perhaps on holiday. Based on your experience of that country, try to identify its culture and how it is different from the culture of your home country. If you have never visited a foreign country, compare the cultures of different parts of your home country with which you may be familiar, for example, North and South, rural and city dwelling. Now answer the questions below.

1. In what ways do the two cultures differ?
2. Do these differences result in different patterns of behaviour in the people in the two cultures?
3. Are there any ways in which you might need to change your own behaviour if you moved from one culture to the other and, if so, why would you need to do this?

DIMENSIONS OF CULTURAL DIFFERENCE

From the above, customs, attitudes and values can vary between countries and the need to adjust our behaviour can sometimes become very obvious if we travel abroad. For this reason, cross-cultural differences and how they can influence patterns of behaviour in organisations has become an important area of study (Adler and

Bartholomew 1992). However, a problem that plagues the area of international comparisons is the glib and imprecise way in which culture is used as an explanatory variable (Child 1981).

Although there is a long pedigree of trying to identify the way in which national cultures can affect the behaviour of people in organisations, until the late 1970s, the majority of work consisted of comparisons between two countries. More recently, however, attempts have been made to conduct wide-ranging international comparisons, the foremost example of which is the work of Geert Hofstede (1980).

Hofstede: The Hermes Study

Hofstede's original study was based on two surveys of employees in a large multinational corporation (IBM) that had branches in over 100 different countries. In total, over 116,000 completed questionnaires were obtained from subsidiaries in 40 countries and to allow strict comparisons to be made, Hofstede used only sales and service staff, all of whom were nationals of the country in which the subsidiary was based. Samples in each country were matched as closely as possible in terms of age and gender composition, and so the most significant difference between the samples was in terms of the nationality of the people. Therefore, any differences in attitudes and values could be mainly attributed to cultural rather than demographic or organisational factors.

Hofstede identified four basic dimensions along which the differences between national cultures could be expressed. However, before describing them, the reader should be aware that in later work (Hofstede 1991) a fifth dimension (time orientation) is added, which is said to be based on Confucian values. While this looks appealing, several scholars, such as Newman and Nollen (1996), argue that it is the least relevant and most difficult to understand of all the dimensions. Moreover, in a penetrating exploration of the theoretical roots of the dimension, Fang (1998) points out that it is a gross distortion of Confucian philosophy. Therefore, in the interests of keeping matters as simple as possible, Hofstede's original scheme is used here. This uses only four dimensions: power–distance, uncertainty avoidance, individualism–collectivism and masculinity–femininity, and these are considered next.

The Hofstede Dimensions

The Power–Distance Dimension

This portrays the extent to which a culture encourages superiors to exercise power, and for subordinates to accept that this is a legitimate way for superiors to behave. In a high power–distance culture, power inequalities between people are accepted and this is how the boss is expected to behave, but where power–distance is low, superiors and subordinates treat each other more as equals and there is a strong tendency to try to minimise social inequalities.

The Uncertainty Avoidance Dimension

Here the dimension reflects the cultural acceptance of risk taking. In a culture characterised by strong uncertainty avoidance people tend to feel threatened, uncomfortable, anxious and stressed by ambiguous situations and prefer highly stable conditions, where there are clear rules of behaviour. Conversely, where uncertainty avoidance values are weak, the ambiguities of life are more readily accepted, and rules are not sacrosanct and can be abandoned with ease.

The Individualism–Collectivism Dimension

This dimension reflects the extent to which people derive their sense of identity from being individuals rather than as part of a group. In an individualistic culture, a person's identity is derived from his or her sense of uniqueness, and individual initiative and achievement are highly prized. Thus, a person's loyalty is primarily to him or herself and privacy of thought and life are strongly respected. In contrast, collectivist cultures are characterised by much tighter social frameworks and the aim of most people is to be a good group member.

The Masculinity–Femininity Dimension

This dimension can perhaps most easily be described as the extent to which being 'macho' is what counts. In masculine cultures, performance counts above all. Money, material possessions and driving ambition epitomise what is seen to be good. Conversely, the so-called feminine cultures are characterised by a far stronger concern for the quality of life. People rather than possessions are considered important and a high value is placed on service to others.

Classifying Cultures with the Dimensions

Using the dimensions described above, Hofstede classified the 40 countries examined according to their scores on each one. From this he derived a set of eight 'cultural groups', each of which consists of countries that have similar cultural characteristics but which differ strongly from those in other groups. The names given to the groups are somewhat arbitrary. These were chosen on the basis of prominent countries located in each one. The clusters are shown in Figure 22.6.

As can be seen, with the possible exceptions of Italy, which is located in the Germanic group, and Yugoslavia, which is put with the less developed Latin cluster, the groupings fit well with the historical and linguistic development of the countries, and this gives a plausible feeling to the clusters. It is important to remember that because the values given for the different dimensions are the averages for respondents in a particular country, the scheme tends to present a somewhat stereotyped picture of national cultures, which are seldom as homogeneous as this. Thus, the values should not be taken to mean that everybody in a particular nation has the same cultural characteristics. For instance, in Japan there are many people who are risk takers and people with high power–distance attitudes are not uncommon in Israel. Therefore, the scales only portray what can be described as the commonly encountered core values of the culture.

A number of interesting comparisons can be made from Figure 22.6, for example:

- high power–distance scores characterise Latin, Asian and Near Eastern clusters, but low scores on this dimension are a feature of Germanic, Anglo and Nordic clusters;

Figure 22.6
Hofstede's country clusters and their characteristics

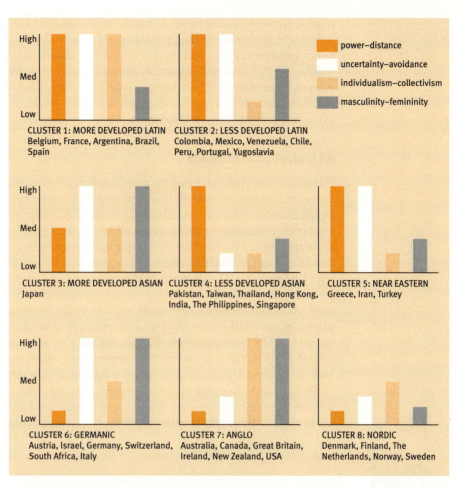

- high uncertainty avoidance has a different pattern and it is predominantly found in Latin, developed Asian, Germanic and Near Eastern clusters;
- high individualism only seems to be prevalent in certain developed countries, while those that are still developing tend to have more collective orientations;
- the Germanic, Anglo and more developed Asian groups are the only ones high in masculinity and these are markedly different from the Nordic group where femininity dominates;
- one group contains only a single country, Japan, which has a combination of characteristics that is quite different from all the others.

A feature that stands out clearly from the results is that there are clear and systematic differences in work-related attitudes in the different cultural groups. Hofstede therefore argues that since the cultural values in each one are likely to give rise to different conceptions of what is an appropriate way to behave, we should not expect leadership styles, management practices and organisational processes to be the same everywhere. For instance, we might expect that the combination of high power–distance, low uncertainty avoidance and low individualism in the less developed Asian group could result in an organisation functioning as something like a large family, in which the decisions of an all-powerful father figure dominate its actions. Interestingly, this is what tends to be found. In countries in the Germanic group, however, power–distance is low, uncertainty avoidance is high and there is a moderate degree of individualism. Here it is more likely that firms will operate as something akin to society in miniature, so that rules and procedures will be designed to specify the rights and obligations of organisational members and to regulate their actions, which means that the firm can operate as a community of interests. Once again, this is also what tends to be found in practice.

An Evaluation of Hofstede

Hofstede's system of classifying the general cultural characteristics of countries shows how cultures can impact on the functioning of organisations and this is clearly of some significance. Nevertheless, in academic circles it has its detractors and, almost inevitably, some of the criticisms concern his methodology. For example, Tyson and Jackson (1992) draw attention to the fact that the sample was drawn from a single company, which limits the extent to which the results can be generalised to other firms in the same country. Needless to say, Hofstede argues the reverse. Because matched samples were used for each country, the only thing that varies between them is the wider social environment, and so any differences genuinely reflect cultures. Hofstede has also been accused of treating national boundaries as synonymous with national cultures, which we know is not true. At a more abstract level, the work has also been criticised for producing a scheme which merely describes cultures, rather than explaining how and why different national cultures arise and how they are maintained (Furnham and Gunter 1993).

Set against these criticisms, there is a great deal of practical utility in the Hofstede scheme. With respect to the point made by Furnham and Gunter, Hofstede never set out to explain the origins of cultures, merely to document differences in work-related

REPLAY

- The culture of an organisation needs to be compatible with the wider social culture within which the firm operates.

- Wider social cultures give rise to distinctive patterns of attitudes, values, beliefs and behaviours on the part of people who have absorbed these cultures and this gives rise to differences in: people's relationship to their world; the effects of religion; the individual's place in society; social protocols; the perceived importance of time; orientations to action; language and proxemics.

- Hofstede's scheme distinguishes between national cultures by classifying them along four dimensions (the power–distance dimension, the uncertainty avoidance dimension, the individualism–collectivism dimension, the masculinity–femininity dimension) and, using this scheme, different countries can be located in one of eight clusters according to the characteristics of their cultures.

- Each cluster has its own cultural characteristics that have implications for the way in which people think and behave.

attitudes and values that probably have cultural foundations. As such, it is couched in terms that allow fairly obvious behavioural inferences to be drawn. More importantly, other research workers such as Grey and Thone (1990) adopt a similar approach to cultural clustering, which provides a degree of validity to his scheme. Perhaps the strongest evidence of the utility of Hofstede's scheme lies in the large number of respected researchers, such as Smulders *et al.* (1996), who continue to use it to investigate cross-cultural effects in organisations.

CROSS-NATIONAL DIFFERENCES IN ORGANISATIONAL BEHAVIOUR

While the initial focus of a company that expands into overseas operations is likely to be on tangible features such as structure, control mechanisms and procedures, it is becoming increasingly evident that the success of cross-national operations can depend on making allowance for the human factor (Adler 1997). For this reason, the aim in this section of the chapter is to draw attention to the ways that some of the matters covered in prior chapters in the book might need to be varied in different cultural settings.

Motivation

As noted in Chapter 5, nearly all theories of motivation have their origins in America and Adler (1997) draws attention to the idea that while these theories are assumed to be universally applicable, they consistently fail to provide useful explanations outside the country of origin. The vast majority of cross-cultural research in this area uses content theories (see Chapter 7) and there is evidence that these are not applicable in the same way everywhere. To use Maslow as an example, although it appears to be true that most people have a hierarchy of needs, the order of priority of these needs varies in different cultures. For instance, in Peru, India, Mexico, the Middle East and Canada, it is broadly the same as that set out by Maslow (Adler 1997). However, in countries such as Japan and Greece, safety needs tend to be more important and in Scandinavian countries social needs dominate (Adler *et al.* 1986). Similarly, while all cultures have hygiene factors and motivators as suggested by Herzberg, hygiene factors in one culture can be motivators in another and vice versa. What this means is that we cannot expect people to be motivated by the same things in different cultural contexts. Evidence on this comes from a study by Black (1999), who addressed the matter of whether 'high commitment management' (HCM) techniques are likely to work as well in other countries as they do in the USA, where the expression originated. High-commitment management is normally associated with the use of a number of key practices:

- employee involvement and participation using teamworking, team briefings and quality circles;
- employee autonomy achieved through jobs that are designed to give added responsibility and flexibility;
- job security, and opportunities for advancement;
- recruitment practices aimed at obtaining committed employees whose skills can be developed;
- good relations between employees and management.

Using Hofstede's (1980) classification of cultures, Black (1999) examined whether HCM is equally effective in motivational terms in different cultures and his major conclusion is that this varies considerably from country to country. In what Hofstede calls 'high individualism' cultures, these techniques have a reasonably high motivational effect because people are culturally acclimatised to value opportunities that enable them to stand out as individuals. Similarly, in 'low uncertainty avoidance' cultures they are likely to motivate individuals because people have been culturally conditioned to taking risks and being assertive. Where these values are not part of the wider social culture, however, HCM techniques will probably not have the same motivational effects and may even be demotivating. This conclusion is not really surprising in the light of a more recent study by Gibson and Zellmer-Bruhn (2001), which clearly shows that conceptions of what constitutes 'teamworking' can vary widely according to differences in national culture.

Orientations to Work

In broad terms, orientations to work reflect people's perceptions of the purpose and meaning of work, for example, whether it is seen simply as a means to an end or whether work is a dominant and significant part of their lives. These are important because they provide insights into what motivates people in different cultures. People the world over go to work to earn a living but, as Chapter 7 points out, there are a number of intrinsic and social rewards that people get from work which may (or may not) have the same relative importance everywhere. Ronen (1986) offers some insights into this by citing results from a wide-ranging international study on the meaning of work, a summary of which is given in graphic form in Figure 22.7.

As can be seen, while income is rated as the most important function of work in all countries, there are considerable differences in terms of the relative importance of other

Figure 22.7 Relative importance of different functions of work for selected countries (after Ronen 1986)

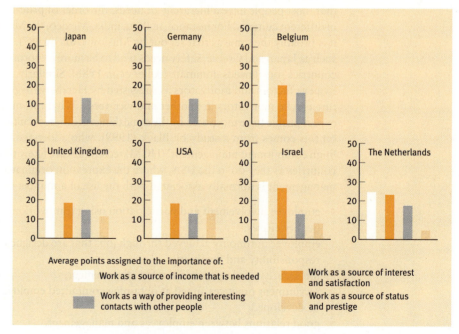

factors. In Japan, for example, income is much more important than in the UK, the USA, Israel and the Netherlands. However, in Israel and the Netherlands, interesting and satisfying work is almost equal in importance to money, which implies that in these two countries, it would be unwise to rely too heavily on financial incentives to motivate people.

Management Style (Leadership)

As is pointed out in Chapters 12 and 13, most so-called theories of leadership are simply explanations of why certain styles of management behaviour are more appropriate in some circumstances than in others, and for this reason, the expression 'management style' is used here. The manager–subordinate relationship does not exist in a vacuum and normal patterns of behaviour in an organisation are often a function of what is considered appropriate in its wider social culture. Hofstede (1991) points out that only in America is the manager regarded as a cultural hero. In Germany, for example, people expect their immediate superior (the person who assigns them tasks and evaluates their efforts) to be a person of proven technical competence in a particular field (a qualified engineer or its equivalent in other occupations). This is very different from someone who has simply been granted the power to determine the actions of subordinates. Moreover, as the term is normally used in America or Great Britain, the 'manager' is largely absent in Japan, where the core of the firm is not a management cadre but permanent workers who are answerable to their peers as much as to formal superiors. Finally, in China, people tend to have higher levels of personal loyalty and commitment to their immediate supervisor, rather than to the organisation as a whole (Chen *et al.* 2002).

In this matter it is more a case of doing what is appropriate within a particular context than anything else, which is borne out in an extensive study by Brodbeck *et al.* (2000) of over 6,000 middle managers in 22 different European countries. This used cultural clusters almost identical to those derived by Hofstede (1980) and the results provide strong support for the idea that people in different cultures hold different 'leadership prototypes', that is, mental models of the attributes or characteristics that distinguish leaders from non-leaders.

It can also be noted that contingency theories of leadership (see Chapter 13) suggest that there are crucial factors that determine the appropriateness of a particular style of management behaviour. Since a culture reflects the expectations of the way people should behave, it is more than possible that some contingency factors have less influence in certain countries than others. Some evidence of this comes from the work of Shaw (1990), who argues that in high power–distance cultures, people expect the boss to make most of the decisions and so participative management does not work well. Conversely, where power–distance is low, people expect a greater say in how jobs are done and if a manager is too directive, he or she is courting trouble. Another thread of evidence comes from studies of management attitudes in a wide number of countries by Ricks (1983). This shows that managers in France and Italy believe that the main purpose of hierarchy is to show who is the boss. Thus, it is not permissible to bypass the chain of command in the interest of getting things done and managers also believe that they should always have the knowledge at hand to answer a subordinate's job-related questions. In other countries, for example in Great Britain, Ricks found that these beliefs were much weaker.

Figure 22.8
Locations of France,
Japan, the UK and USA
on Hofstede's four
dimensions of culture

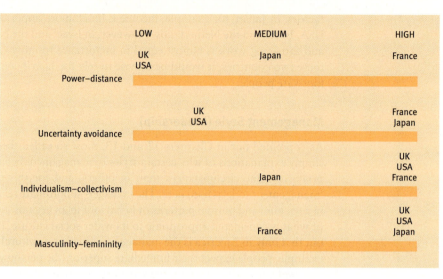

Perhaps the most straightforward way to illustrate that different management styles are needed in different cultural contexts is to apply the work of Hofstede (1980), who argues that different cultures have different work-related values which, in turn, produce implicit mental models of what is considered to be an appropriate way for a manager to behave. To illustrate the point, four of the countries studied by Hofstede – France, the UK, the USA and Japan – will be contrasted. Their positions on Hofstede's four dimensions are shown in Figure 22.8.

In the *United Kingdom* and the *USA* scores on the power–distance dimension are low, which means that most employees would find autocratic, distant management styles unwelcome. In addition, uncertainty avoidance scores are medium to low. Thus, people are fairly comfortable with a degree of ambiguity and are willing to take some responsibility for their own actions. These cultures also prize individuality and achievement and have high scores on the masculinity–femininity dimension. If all these features are brought together, it is fairly easy to see why employees in the UK and USA strongly prefer participative managers who involve their subordinates in decision making.

In *France*, however, power–distance is high and hierarchical structures in which people lower down are not expected to shoulder responsibility are accepted. Thus, employees are strongly encouraged to pass decision making upwards, which also suits the strong uncertainty avoidance characteristic of the culture. Individualism is also high and there is a medium level of masculinity. Therefore, managers are not likely to delegate to a large extent and, in any event, subordinates probably expect to be told what to do and would not adapt easily to the self-monitoring that goes hand in hand with autonomy, and so less participative styles are likely to fit well with the culture.

In *Japan* power–distance and individualism are only of medium strength, but uncertainty avoidance and masculinity are both high. Being part of a team is fundamental to the Japanese way of life and it verges on bad manners to stand out too much as an individual. Therefore, people avoid uncertainty by submerging their identities in a group, which militates strongly in favour of a shared ownership of decisions. This means that subordinates expect to shoulder some responsibility for solving the group's problems and, in return, managers tend to be less concerned with the decision itself than with whether it can be implemented without problems. Indeed, an ideal decision is one where everybody is fully committed to its implementation. Usually this means that everyone has been involved in reaching the decision and so participative leadership styles fit best with the cultural characteristics.

Even a brief contrast such as this shows that culture can have a strong impact on whether employees are likely to feel comfortable with certain management styles. Perhaps the most important point to note is that the UK and the USA have cultures in which the participative style is important, but so is employee autonomy. Therefore, participation needs to take a form in which the manager shares decision making with subordinates but also gives them some independence in action. In Japan, however, participation tends to be interpreted in a different way. It is generally taken to mean that manager and subordinates share decision making and also act collectively as a group to implement the decisions – a difference that is highly important. A style that is viewed as participative in the Western sense may well be interpreted altogether differently elsewhere.

Communication

In conceptual terms the communication problems encountered in a cross-national company are the same as those that exist within a single country. One of the most important requirements is that senders and receivers of messages agree about the meaning ascribed to the symbols that are used to communicate. In a cross-national organisation where people use different languages, the same word can mean different things to different people and the problem of consensus about meaning can be particularly problematic.

This is particularly the case with non-verbal signals, where the meanings attributed can vary significantly. In Greece, shaking one's head up and down means 'no' and wagging it from side to side means 'yes' (Bragganti and Deveine 1984) – the opposites to meanings normally attributed in the UK. If everyone freely acknowledged that these differences exist and made allowances accordingly, there would probably be few problems. Problematically, almost all cultures have a degree of *ethnocentricity*, the 'our culture is right' syndrome, which is probably inevitable because a culture promotes certain values over others. A spin-off from this is the phenomenon of stereotyping (see Chapter 4), and in cross-national situations this can result in people being attributed with a whole host of characteristics just because they come from another country (McAndrew *et al.* 2000). This creates strong perceptual barriers to communication, in which people develop preconceived notions about the meaning of messages.

> **Ethnocentricity:**
> a frame of reference in which members of a cultural group view their culture as superior to all others

Finally, Schneider and Barsoux (1997) argue that cultural preferences for organisational features such as hierarchy, formalisation or participation shape expectations about what is normal in terms of the information that should be circulated, how it should be circulated and to whom. For instance, French organisations are highly structured and there are clear hierarchical divisions between the different levels. Thus, the flow of information is very limited and French managers tend to see information as power, which is not something to be shared. For this reason French employees tend to rely much more on informal communication networks. Conversely, in the Swedish culture, where much less attention is paid to hierarchical position, there is a correspondingly greater willingness to share information with anyone who wants to know (Holden 1999).

Conflict and Conflict Handling

Conflict tends to be more acceptable in some cultures than others. If you examine Figure 22.8 again, you will see that the United Kingdom and the USA are located at the same positions on all four of Hofstede's dimensions and in both countries a certain amount of conflict is accepted as an everyday part of organisational life. Moreover, power–distance is low and people do not readily accept that someone should have power over them, which gives a tendency for disagreements to be expressed openly. In addition, individualism is high and people cherish their individuality. Both are masculine cultures in which people pursue their own views rather than allow them to be submerged in a false consensus. Finally, until conflict is resolved, there is a degree of uncertainty, and since the tendency to avoid uncertainty is low in both of these countries, people are less stressed by conflict than elsewhere.

In Japan, however, there is an intense dislike of conflict and the ideal state of affairs is one where everyone sees the firm as a harmonious family. Thus, the higher levels of conflict, confrontation and adversarial relationships that are found in the British and American organisations are largely absent, which can also be reasoned from the Hofstede dimensions. Although Japan is a masculine culture, individualism and power–distance are only of medium strength. Thus, people are far less likely to want to stand out from their fellows and there is a greater acceptance of power differentials. Moreover, uncertainty avoidance is very high and so people probably find conflict a stressful experience.

Unfortunately there is little definitive empirical evidence to indicate whether people handle conflict differently in different cultures. Here, Schneider and Barsoux (1997) suggest that some of Hofstede's cultural characteristics probably give rise to natural tendencies to use certain of the different handling styles given in Chapter 14, for instance:

- in France, where individualism, power–distance and uncertainty avoidance are all high, conflict is likely to be avoided by passing the problem upwards to be resolved;
- in Sweden, where power–distance and individualism–collectivism are both low, there is a concern for mutual gain and a collaborative conflict-handling style will be more prevalent;
- in countries where power–distance is high and individualism–collectivism low, there may be a pronounced tendency towards accommodation by the party that sees itself as the weakest.

Performance, Evaluation and Rewards

How goals are set, performance is evaluated and the way it is rewarded can vary considerably in different countries. In cultures where there is a strong sense of collectivism and group solidarity there is evidence that individual goals, performance evaluation and incentive schemes are probably far less acceptable than in the individualistic cultures such as the UK (Ramamoorthy and Carroll 1998). Moreover, a recent study in Russia, which also has these cultural characteristics, supports this idea (Tower *et al.* 1997).

One way to examine this is to compare the likely impact of management by objectives (MBO) – see Chapter 18. To function effectively, MBO requires:

- a culture of low power–distance, so that subordinates have sufficient independence to be able to negotiate objectives with their boss, rather than have the objectives imposed;
- employees who are willing to take the risk of accepting delegated responsibility for achieving goals and to be judged by the results they produce, that is, a culture of low uncertainty avoidance;
- a strongly individualistic culture, in which people are willing to try to make their mark by achieving as individuals;
- a masculine culture, in which both manager and subordinate are strongly results orientated.

If you look closely at the cultural characteristics shown in Figure 22.6 you can see that these conditions only exist in the Anglo cluster. Note that MBO is an American invention that is widely used in the USA and Great Britain, where, if it is operated correctly, it mostly works as intended.

Now look at the Germanic group of countries in Figure 22.6. While power–distance is low and masculinity is high, individualism is much lower than in Great Britain and uncertainty avoidance is much higher. Thus, the German version of MBO works in a very different way. It is usually called management by joint goal setting, which has a much stronger emphasis on developing participative procedures and achieving team objectives.

Finally, look at the more developed Latin cluster, which includes France. Power–distance is extremely high and so is uncertainty avoidance. French firms are probably the most hierarchically structured in Europe and so employees expect managers to give instructions and shoulder the lion's share of responsibility. While this removes a great deal of ambiguity from the lives of employees, it runs counter to the very idea of subordinates shouldering individual responsibility and monitoring their own progress. As such, although there have been some rather half-hearted attempts to introduce MBO in a few French companies, it has never been used in a widespread way.

With respect to rewarding performance, Adler (1997) gives two examples in which American managers on overseas assignments applied their prior experience in America with results that went sadly astray. In the first, salaries were increased for Mexican workers, who promptly began to work fewer hours. In Mexico, quality of life is important to people and since these employees now had more money to spend, they felt that they needed time to enjoy a better lifestyle. The second example involved a Japanese employee who, on being promoted by an American manager as a reward for high performance, became demoralised because the promotion made him feel that he was no longer part of his workgroup.

While amusing, stories such as these have a serious side. They indicate that cross-national organisations need to give careful thought to the way that standards of performance are set, how performance is evaluated and how it is rewarded. If it is intended that these things should provide a degree of motivation to perform well they must suit the cultural conditions in which they are used.

Decision Making

Chapter 9 deals with individual decision making and contains a number of models that give different explanations about the ways that decisions are made. One of these

Table 22.2 Culturally induced variations in the way that decisions are made (after Adler 1997)

Steps in decision making process		Extremes of culturally induced variations in step	
1. Recognition of problem	Great Britain and USA: tendency to see problems as situations that require solutions that will involve changing the *status quo*	⟷	Indonesia and Thailand: a tendency to adopt a more fatalistic view that some problems have to be lived with
2. Search for information	Cultures high in uncertainty avoidance: decisions require 'facts' to be gathered if the 'one best' solution is to be identified	⟷	Cultures low in uncertainty avoidance: information should be seen as something that opens up a range of possible alternatives
3. Developing alternative solutions	USA: an assumption that because people are easily able to adapt and change, solutions requiring radical change are acceptable	⟷	Great Britain: an assumption that because people find it hard to change, alternatives should preferably involve small, incremental changes
4. Choosing between alternatives	Individualistic and masculine cultures such as Great Britain and USA: decisions should be made quickly and only by those people who have decision making authority	⟷	Collectivist cultures such as Japan and Germany: decisions should be made in a careful, deliberate way, preferably by all those who have to implement the decision
5. Implementation	Great Britain and USA: managed top-down implementation by individuals with authority	⟷	Japan: a shared responsibility for implementation that involves a high degree of participation

is the 'rational choice' model. Using something very similar to the steps in this model, Adler (1997) draws attention to the idea that there are differences between cultures in the way people conduct themselves at each stage. These ideas are summarised in Table 22.2 which shows that in each step there can be variations because culture induces people to perceive matters in different ways.

REPLAY

- The different patterns of values, beliefs, attitudes and behaviours that are prompted by wider social cultures mean that human resource practices that work well in one context may not work as well in another.

- Organisations that operate cross-nationally may need to vary their human resource practices according to the characteristics of the wider social culture in which their subsidiaries are located.

- Aspects of human resource practice that may need to be varied according to location are: how people are motivated; management style; making allowances for different orientation to work; patterns and methods of internal communication; how conflicts are handled; how performance goals are set and performance is evaluated and rewarded; and how decisions are made.

OVERVIEW AND CONCLUSIONS

Organisations increasingly see their sphere of operations as being global rather than confined to their countries of origin, and a number of factors have prompted some organisations to engage in cross-national activities. The most prominent of these are: economic and political changes; changes in the characteristics of product markets; the need to gain access to or secure supplies of resource inputs; the tendency of firms to migrate to areas where the costs of production and distribution are lower; and the activities of competitors.

There are four major types of cross-national organisation: international, multinational, globalised and transnational, and in this order they are progressively further removed from being purely domestic organisations. The category into which an organisation falls tends to be a reflection of its strategic aims with respect to the markets it serves, and what it sees as the appropriate way to achieve these aims.

Just as the domestic organisation that grows over time tends to adopt new structures to achieve its strategic aims, the same is true of firms that engage in cross-national activities. From this it follows that since different types of cross-national organisation have different strategic aims, each type tends to have a characteristic approach to structure.

Organisations that operate cross-nationally also encounter a greater diversity in the people with whom they deal, that is, their customers, suppliers, governments and employees. Each country in which a firm operates can have its own cultural and social characteristics and these can be quite different from those encountered in the firm's country of origin. Some of the major ways in which these characteristics vary are: people's relationship to their world; religious norms and customs; individuals' attitudes towards society as a whole; social protocols and customs; perceptions of the importance of time; and orientations towards action. These factors all combine to result in wider social cultures and a useful way of classifying the cultures of different countries is provided by Hofstede's four-dimensional scheme.

Cultural variation results in conditions that mean that it is seldom possible for a cross-national organisation to run an overseas subsidiary in exactly the same way that its affairs are managed in the country of origin. As such, there is usually a need to recognise that different cultures require the firm to vary the way that it manages its human resources. There are seven aspects of organisational behaviour that can be strongly influenced by wider social cultures. These are: work motivation; communication; conflict and conflict handling; orientations to work; goal setting, performance evaluation and rewards; decision making; and management style.

FURTHER READING

Adler, N J (1997) *International Dimensions of Organisational Behaviour*, 3rd edn, London: Thomson. Although written from a rather managerialist perspective, the book presents a well-argued case supported by evidence for varying management approaches for dealing with people in different countries.

Bartlett, C A and S Ghoshal (1991) *Managing Across Borders*, Boston, Mass: Harvard Business School Press. A readable but informative book that sets out the strategic bases of different cross-national organisational structures and practices.

Bartlett, C A and S Ghoshal (1997) *The Individualised Corporation*, London: Random House. A recent development by these authors, which argues for a more individualised approach to the use of human resources.

Hall, E T and M R Hall (1990) *Understanding Cultural Differences*, Yarmouth, ME: Intercultural Press. A useful and informative book which gives a good overview of cultures in different countries and how they influence patterns of behaviour.

Harzing, A W and J W Ruyseveldt (1995) *International Human Resource Management*, London: Sage. Although rather managerialist in its approach, the book gives sound arguments for firms varying the way they manage human resources in different countries.

Hofstede, G (2001) *Culture's Consequences: Comparing Values, Behaviours, Institutions and Organisations Across Nations*, 2nd edn, Thousand Oaks, CA: Sage. A new and revised edition (with considerable re-analysis of the original data) of Hofstede's seminal study of cultures in different countries.

John, R, G I Gillies, H Cox and N Grimswade (1997) *Global Business Strategy: An Introduction*, London: Thomson. A readable introduction to international business.

Mendenhall, M E, B J Plunket and D Ricks (1995) *Global Management*, Cambridge, Mass: Blackwell. Although written with a strong managerialist slant, a useful guide to the problems of managing cross-national organisations.

Schneider, S C and J L Barsoux (1997) *Managing across Cultures*, London: Prentice Hall. A comprehensive and readable book that gives useful insights into the necessity for varying the approach to managing human resources according to the wider social culture in which an organisation is located.

REVIEW AND DISCUSSION QUESTIONS

1. Describe the factors that have facilitated the growth of international business and explain the effects of pressures that prompt organisations to engage in cross-national business activity.

2. Distinguish between domestic organisations, international organisations, multinational organisations, globalised organisations and transnational organisations in terms of their business strategies and structures.

3. Why is it important that the culture of an organisation is compatible with the wider social culture of the environment in which it operates?

4. Describe seven ways in which wider social cultures can differ and the effects of these differences on the behaviour of people.

5. Outline the four dimensions of wider social culture that Hofstede (1980) uses to distinguish between the cultures of different countries.

6. In terms of its management of human resources, in what ways might an organisation that has overseas subsidiaries need to take account of the effects of the wider social cultures in the countries in which it operates?

A

Achievement tests: tests that assess what a person can currently do

Action Research: a participative method of bringing about change in human behaviour that involves stages of data collection, problem diagnosis, action planning, action and re-evaluation

Actual self: the self as the person currently views him or herself

Actuator: something that adjusts the inputs to a process or activity

Adaptation: an incremental change that occurs as an organisational reaction to a change in its environment

Adaptive behaviour: that aimed at removing or circumventing a situation where goal blocking occurs

Adaptive learning: learning how to adapt to environmental change

Adhocracy: a loose, very flexible and constantly evolving set of structural features that dispenses with traditional hierarchies, job titles and rules

Adjourning: the group is disbanded

Adjustment function (of attitude): helps the person adjust to his or her world

Affective component (of attitude): emotional feelings (likes or dislike) about an attitude object

Altercasting: the process of tacit negotiation between a role occupant and senders about behaviour which is acceptable to both

Ambassadors: group members who represent a group with other groups

Analysis by synthesis: a self-adjusting cycle in which an estimate of the identity of an object is derived from incoming sensory data. This is compared with a schema for the object and if the initial inference is confirmed, a search for confirmatory information is made

Anchoring or judgement heuristic: a decision maker arrives at a final judgement by starting at an initial position and then making adjustments to reach the solution that is eventually chosen

Aptitude: the facility or potential to be able to do something (the latent ability)

Aptitude tests: tests that assess what a person will be able to do if given the required training

Artificial intelligence: a branch of cognitive psychology which uses computer models to try to simulate the activities of mental processes

Assertiveness: a person's desire to satisfy only his or her concerns in a conflict situation

Attention and selection (perception): the tendency to acknowledge some stimuli and ignore or mask out others

Attitude: a mental state of readiness, organised through experience to behave in a characteristic way towards the object of the attitude

Attribution: imputing a cause for an observed action

Authoritarian personality: people who place a high value on power and status differences, both in their behaviour downwards towards subordinates and upwards towards superiors

Authority: the legitimate power to make decisions in a given area of activity

Authority games: political tactics to resist authority from above or counter resistance to authority from below

Autocratic leaders: those who strongly control subordinates and make all major decisions

Availability heuristic: a rule-of-thumb used by a decision maker to assess the probability of the outcome of a decision

B

Basic structure: expresses the general form of structure and what is expected of organisational members

Behaviour: activity directed at achieving something

Behavioural component (of attitude): the tendency to act towards the attitude object in a consistent and characteristic way

Behavioural consensus: whether a person's behaviour in a particular situation is typical of other people in the same situation

Behavioural consistency: whether a piece of behaviour is typical of the way that the person normally behaves

Behavioural distinctiveness: whether a person behaves in the same way in several different circumstances

Behavioural outcomes (stress): the effects of stress on overt behaviour

Behaviourism: the branch of psychology which holds that all human behaviour is determined by factors outside the person

Belief: the assumption that something exists and that it has certain characteristics

Bottom-up goal setting: people set their own goals which are then agreed with their immediate superiors

Bottom-up processing (perception): perceptual processes driven by incoming data imported through sensor organs

Bounded problems: problems that can be more easily defined and treated as separate from the context in which they exist

Bounded rationality: the recoginition that a person's ability to take a position of perfect rationality in decision making is constrained by limited time, limited information or limited capacity to process information

Bureaucratic control: the use of tight job specifications and standard operating procedures to specify employee behaviour, which becomes the accepted ways of doing things to which employees conform

Burnout: a chronic outcome of stress characterised by a general feeling of complete exhaustion, depersonalisation, disinterest and lack of personal accomplishment

Business process re-engineering: a fundamental re-think and, if necessary, radical redesign of business processes, with the aim of making dramatic improvements to critical aspects of performance, such as cost, quality, service and speed

C

Centralisation: the locus of decision making in an organisation

Centrality (of attitude): the extent to which an attitude is part of a person's concept of self

Change agent: an expert from either inside or outside an organisation who facilitates and guides an OD (organisational development) intervention

Change games: political tactics to bring about or block change

Channels of communication: the carriers of the message

Charismatic authority: that acquired when a person becomes the focus of a particular set of ideals and principles, e.g. Christ

Classical organisation theory: a diverse group of theories which set out to derive universal rules and guidelines for the design and functioning of organisations

Closed-loop (feedback) control: a method in which the outputs of a process or activity are monitored and, if necessary, inputs are adjusted to achieve the desired outputs

Closure (of messages): the receiver fills in what he or she perceives to be gaps in a message before transmitting it onward

Closure principle (perception): gaps between stimuli are filled in so that discrete stimuli are perceived as connected

Coalition: an alliance of groups and/or individuals who perceive that something they value can be obtained by collaboration

Coercive power: the capability to compel others to behave in a certain way

Cognitive appraisal: a person's perception of a stressor, e.g. whether it is harmful, threatening or challenging

Cognitive complexity: the number of independent dimensions used by a person to evaluate objects and people

Cognitive component (of attitude): the perceptions and beliefs about an attitude object

Cognitive dissonance: the unpleasant mental feeling that arises when behaviour towards an object is not consistent with the attitude towards the object

Cognitive outcomes (stress): the effects of stress on thought processes

Collective bargaining: a process in which employees are represented collectively by a trade union in determining, jointly with management, the terms and conditions of the employment relationship

Command groups: permanent groups of people, all under a single manager, who perform like activities

Communal culture: one that is high in sociability and solidarity

Communication: a process in which information and its meaning is conveyed from a sender to receiver(s)

Comparator: something (or someone) that compares the desired attributes of the outputs of a process or activity with those actually achieved

Competing values model (of effectiveness): an explanation of how manager values influence criteria used to evaluate an organisation's effectiveness

Concept of self: a person's view of what he or she is

Condensation (of messages): the extraction of what the receiver of a message perceives to be its key points and transmitting only these onward

Conditioned response: a reflex behaviour elicited by pairing a neutral stimulus with an unconditioned response

Conditioned stimulus: a relatively artificial trigger to the production of a reflex response in an organism

Configuration: the basic arrangements for differentiation and integration in a structure

Consistency principle: that people attempt to maintain consistency between the three components of an attitude: cognitive, affective, behavioural

Constancy effect (perception): the perceiver is able to make adjustments for distance etc. so that the object is experienced as the same size irrespective of its distance

Content theories: focus on the needs of people as the prime impetus for motivated behaviour

Context effect (perception): the use of information from the context of the object to infer its identity

Contingency perspective: an approach to problem solving which assumes that there is no universally applicable solution to a particular type of problem and so remedies have to be tailored to the situation in which the problem exists

Contingency theory of structure: that the most appropriate structure for an organisation is the one that matches its particular circumstances

Continuity principle (perception): the existence of missing stimuli is inferred, resulting in a perception of links between unconnected stimuli

Continuous reinforcement: a reward is given each time the desired behaviour occurs

Control model: a symbolic representation of the components necessary for a system of control, how they relate to each other and their functions

Control strategy (stress): a problem-focused attempt to tackle the root cause of stress by changing the nature of the situation, to remove or reduce the impact of stressors

Cooperation (conflict): the willingness to look for a solution to a conflict that satisfies the other party's concerns

Country-focused strategy and structure: primarily geared to serving a wider set of markets by producing goods or services in overseas subsidiaries for sale in local markets

Cultural direction: the extent to which an organisation's culture helps it achieve its goals

Cultural factors: wider social beliefs, values and motives that are absorbed by an individual and guide behaviour towards that which is acceptable within a particular social context

Cultural pervasiveness: the homogeneity of an organisation's culture

Cultural strength: the influence of a culture on the behaviour of organisational members

Cultural systems metaphor: organisations regarded as analogous to cultural systems in which the members have common beliefs, values and shared assumptions

Culture change: modification of an existing culture

Culture management: maintaining or making slight modifications to fine-tune an existing culture

Cybernetics: the theoretical study of control processes in electrical, mechanical and biological systems

D

Decision acceptance: whether subordinates embrace a decision and commit themselves to its implementation

Decision making: the process of making a choice between alternatives

Decision quality: whether a decision results in effective task performance

Decoding: a process in which the receiver of a message uses the symbols in which it is conveyed to attribute it with a meaning

Deconstruction: a method used in postmodernist analysis to reveal underlying assumptions (in discourse) and challenge them with counter arguments or alternative explanations

Delayering: a reduction of the number of levels in an organisation's hierarchy, usually by removing one or more levels of supervision and/or middle management

Democratic leaders: those who involve followers in decisions

Descriptive approach to leadership: theories that describe leadership in terms of either what a person is or his or her distinctive style of behaviour

Differentiationist perspective on culture: organisations are made up of different groups with their own subcultures

Discourse: the idea that language is more than just a tool of communication, but that what is said can be used to convey something that can be made to seem the essential truth of how things are, which has the effect of disarming challenges to an argument, suppressing alternative meanings and supporting particular interpretations or conclusions

Diversity management: a systematic, proactive approach aimed at promoting the positive image of workforce diversity, which usually involves steps to affect the composition of a workforce so that it reflects the degree of diversity in wider society

Domestic organisation: one that mainly trades within the borders of its country of origin

Double-loop learning: a style of learning which goes beyond learning how to achieve existing goals and which involves questioning whether the assumptions that underpin the goals are appropriate for the organisation

Downsizing: a reduction in the size of an organisation or the scale of its activities, theoretically to attain the appropriate size for its volume of sales

E

Effective communication: the extent to which the sender and receiver of a message both attribute it with the same meaning

Efficiency: a measure of resource usage, usually expressed as a ratio of inputs used to produce a given level of outputs

Effort to reward probability: the perceived liklihood that a reward will follow successful task performance

Ego: a component of personality that grows out of the id and which strives to reconcile the demands of the id, superego and the realities of the outside world

Ego-defensive function (of attitude): helps the person to defend his or her self-image

Emergent approach (to change): a contingency perspective that rejects the idea of a universally applicable recipe for organisational change

Employee-centred control: a 'hearts and minds' strategy that involves influencing the way employees think about themselves and what they do so that they willingly subscribe to management's aims

Employee voice: a two-way dialogue, which enables employees to have a say in, or influence on, matters that affect them

Employment relations: the relationship between an organisation and its employees, which includes the full range of interactions and communications between the two parties and the processes through which they adjust to the needs and wants of each other

Empowerment: giving people the authority to make decisions in their own area of operations without the approval of someone above

Emotional intelligence: an ability or competence in managing one's own feelings and recognising (and dealing effectively with) other people's feelings

Enacted environment: management's mental construction of what the environment is, which arises from its selective perceptions of environment

Enacted role problems: inappropriate role behaviour

Encoding: a process in which a message is transformed into a set of symbols that can be conveyed by a channel

Environmental factors (groups): characteristics of a group's environment that influence its degree of cohesiveness

Environmental factors (leadership): features of a work context that make a leadership style more or less appropriate

Environmental stressors: forces external to the organisation that can be potential sources of stress for individuals

Episodic memory: a memory store containing information about episodes and past events in our lives

Epistemology: a branch of philosophy dealing with the nature and origins of knowledge

Equal opportunities: a systematic approach to ensuring there is no unjustifiable discrimination for appointment or promotion on the basis of gender, race, religion, ethnic origin and, more recently, disability

Equity: the fairness of treatment of a person compared to the way that another person is treated

Escalation of commitment to a failing course of action: a decision maker's tendency to persist with a failing course of action in the face of clear evidence that the decision taken is an inappropriate one

Escape strategy (stress): an emotion-focused attempt to lower the impact of stressors, but without trying to change the nature of the situation

Espoused theory: the theory of action officially espoused by an organisation

Ethics: an individual's moral beliefs about what is right and wrong, or good and bad that provides a guide to his/her behaviour

Ethnocentricity: a frame of reference in which members of a cultural group view their culture as superior to all others

Expectations: an anticipation that certain behaviours will result in achieving goals

Expected role problems: a clash between role sender and role occupant about the content of their respective roles

Expert power: the ability to influence others that exists because a person is seen to possess a particular expertise

Explicit knowledge: knowledge that is available to everybody and which is easy to codify, articulate or express

External attribution: the cause of a person's behaviour is assumed to be connected with a factor in his or her environment

External orientation (locus of control): individuals who believe that external events determine their actions

Extinction: a decrease in the occurrence of a behaviour arising from its non-reinforcement

Extroversion–introversion: one of the two fundamental dimensions of personality used in Eysenck's type theory

Extrinsic rewards: rewards conferred from outside the individual

F

Feedback: a process in which sender and receiver exchange roles, so that the receiver responds to a message

Figure-to-ground effect (perception): the tendency to organise data so that all figures are seen as existing against a background

Fine-tuning: an incremental change that occurs as a result of an organisation's anticipation of changes in its environment

First-level outcomes (motivation): the immediate results of behaviour

Fixed interval schedule: reinforcement delivered at fixed time intervals

Fixed ratio schedule: reinforcement delivered after a fixed number of desired responses

Flamemail: the use of e-mail to abuse others in the workplace

Flat organisation: a relatively small number of levels in the management hierarchy

Flexible specialisation: the argument that organisational survival now depends upon gaining the economic advantages of specialisation, but being flexible at the same time

Follower characteristics (leadership): the attributes and skill of followers that influence how they react to a particular leadership style

Force field analysis: a way of conceptualising a stable situation as forces pushing (in favour of) change balanced by those restraining change

Formal contract: the formally agreed terms of the employment relationship, i.e. the legal concept as reflected in the 'contract of employment'

Formal groups: groups brought into existence by the structure of an organisation

Formalisation: the number of formal rules and procedures governing organisational activities

Forming: the first stage of group development, in which it is essentially a collection of individuals

Fragmentationist perspective on culture: organisations are so full of ambiguities and inconsistencies that frames of reference are individual and constantly changing and so culture is inherently unstable

Fragmented culture: one that is low on both sociability and solidarity

Functional approach: the assumption that attitudes are held because they serve a useful purpose for the holder

Functional approach to leadership: theories that explain leadership in terms of the functions performed by the leader with respect to the followers

Functional flexibility: an organisation's capability to vary what is done and how it is done

Functional significance (perception): the dimensions of evaluation used by a person because they are useful in making sense of the world

Fundamental attribution error: the tendency automatically to attribute internal causes for behaviour

G

General Adaptive Syndrome: a three-stage physiological process that takes place when an organism is subject to a stressor

General intelligence (g): an individual's overall intelligence level as measured by a test

Generative learning: a constant re-evaluation of the environment, together with the creative adaption that enables anticipation of environmental changes and the development of appropriate responses

Genetic factors: inherited factors that influence physical and mental characteristics

Glass ceiling: a metaphor for the invisible barrier that seems to exist, which prevents women progressing beyond a certain level in organisations

Global organisation: one that is not tied to a single nation, but operates worldwide as an independent set of subsidiaries coordinated by a headquarters

Globalised economy: the 'one-world' economy, in which large firms compete for business on a worldwide scale

Globally integrated strategy and structure: a diffuse network of highly interdependent subsidiaries, each of which specialises in some degree, but none of which has the capability to operate as a totally independent and autonomous business unit

Goal: a desired state of affairs, which an organisation attempts to achieve

Goal (motivation): a milestone that is perceived to lead to satisfaction of needs

Goal approach (to effectiveness): evaluation of organisational effectiveness against the criterion of the extent to which an organisation achieves its goals

Goal blocking: a state where motivations are aroused but goal attainment is thwarted

Goal difficulty: how challenging and demanding a goal is

Goal displacement: an organisation or one of its sub-units substitutes a goal for which the organisation was not created, or for which resources were not allocated, for its legitimate goal(s)

Goal specificity: how clear and explicit a goal is

Goal succession: the goal(s) of an organisation is deliberately replaced with another one because the orginal goal(s) has been achieved or has become outdated

Grapevine: an informal channel of communication

Gravitational hypothesis: over the course of their time in the labour market people with certain mental characteristics sort themselves into jobs compatible with their interests, values and abilities, to achieve a good person–job fit

Group cohesiveness: the attractiveness of a group to its members and their desire to retain membership

Group factors: characteristics of the group and its members that affect its degree of cohesiveness

Group norms: the rules of behaviour adopted by the members of a group

Grouping effect (perception): the tendency to organise data into meaningful groups or patterns

Groupthink: impaired decision making by a group because the desire for unanimity overrides examining the consequences of a decision

Guardians: group members who shield the group from external pressure

H

Halo effect: the assumption that because a person has a certain trait, he or she automatically has other traits

Hard goals: those that can be precisely specified in an unambiguous and usually quantifiable way and whose achievement can be measured accurately

Hardiness: a psychological characteristic that helps a person withstand the effects of stressors

Headship: the formal authority over subordinates granted as part of a manager's position

Hegemonic control: control exercised by an elite body whose power is accepted as supreme

Heuristics: rules-of-thumb or simplifying strategies that help a decision maker cope with information overload in the search for solutions

Holistic: the belief that reality is made up of unified wholes that are greater than the simple sum of their parts

Horizontal differentiation: the division of an organisation's overall task into different activities according to a set, organising principle

Horizontal surveillance: a person's actions are monitored by someone at the same level, who is part of the same workgroup

Human capital approach: a recognition that the contribution made by human skills and knowledge to the production of goods and/or services is a vital ingredient of organisational success

Human relations movement: a view of the employment situation which holds that employees respond primarily to the social context of the workplace, an important part of which is interpersonal relations at work

Hygiene factors: features of the work environment which, if present, help avoid dissatisfaction with work

I

Id: the biologically driven component of personality that consists of inherited drives etc., and which demands immediate gratification of its pleasure-seeking drives

Ideal self: the self as the person would like it to be

Idiographic: theories which describe personality in terms that are unique to the person

Immediate social stressors: features of a person's immediate (social) work context that can be stressful

Individual stressors: features of a person's job that can give rise to stress

Information richness: the potential information-carrying capacity of a communication medium

Informal contract: a less formal expression of the employment relationship, which reflects a degree of 'give and take' between the parties

Influence perspective: an approach to leadership theory which explicitly addresses the issue of 'how' leaders influence follower behaviour

In-group members (leadership): those on whom the leader relies to go beyond the minimum level of performance required

Instrumentality (motivation): the perceived strength of the connection between first- and second-level outcomes

Integrationist perspective on culture: culture is an organisation-wide phenomenon which consists of shared values to which all or most employees subscribe

Intelligence quotient (IQ): mental age (as indicated by an intelligence test) divided by actual (chronological) age

Intensive technology: all parts contribute together to perform the task

Interactionist perspective (conflict): organisational conflict is seen as neither bad or good, but simply inevitable

Interactionist perspective (personality): that hereditary factors and environment interact to determine behaviour

Interactive goal setting: goals are initially set for a particular organisational level by its head, but are then negotiated to a consensus with subordinates at that level

Intermittent reinforcement: a reinforcer is not given every time the desired response occurs

Internal attribution: the cause of a person's behaviour is assumed to be connected with his or her psychological characteristics, e.g. attitudes, personality etc.

Internal orientation (locus of control): individuals who believe they can influence external events

International organisation: one that is primarily located and managed in its country of origin, but also either exports to or produces identical or similar goods and services in overseas subsidiaries

International trade strategy and structure: one that is primarily geared to serving a wider set of markets by exporting goods or services from the home country

Interpersonal communication style: the way a person prefers to relate to other people in a communication situation

Interrelatedness (of attitude): the extent to which an attitude is related to a person's other attitudes

Intrinsic rewards: psychological rewards that come from inside the person

J

Janus-faced: having two (good and evil) aspects

Job enlargement: horizontal expansion of a job to provide variety for the individual

Job enrichment: enlargement of a job both horizontally and vertically to give the employee more responsibility and control over how the job is performed

Job rotation: the systematic rotation of workers from one job to another to reduce boredom

Job satisfaction: a pleasurable or positive emotional state resulting from a person's appraisal of his or her job or job experience

Job simplification: the breaking down of a job into its simpler constituent elements

Job-related barriers (to motivation): features of the job that remove the likelihood that it can satisfy a person's needs

K

Key result areas: areas of activity vital to an organisation's existence

Key variable (application) school (of culture): culture is viewed as an organisational property (something an organisation has) that can be changed at will to achieve success

Kinaesthetic:motor intelligence (K:M): that part of an intelligence test which assesses practical, mechanical and spatial skills and abilities

Knowledge function (of attitude): helps the person mentally to structure and organise his or her world so that it is more understandable

Knowledge management: a process or practice of creating, acquiring, capturing, sharing or using knowledge (wherever it resides) to enhance learning and performance in an organisation

L

Laissez-faire leaders: those who abdicate from the leadership role

Leadership neutralisers: workplace factors that remove the capability of a leader to influence subordinate behaviour

Leadership substitutes: situational factors that enable subordinates to function well without leader guidance

Learning: a relatively permanent change in behaviour, or potential behaviour, that results from experience

Least preferred co-worker (LPC): the subordinate that a supervisor was least able to work with successfully on a prior occasion

Legitimate power: the authority to command the actions of other people that goes with a particular role

Level of stress management: whether dealing with stressors is focused at the level of the individual or the level of the organisation

Levelling of messages: omission of certain details of a message as it is transmitted onward

Lewin model: a three-stage (unfreeze–move–refreeze) method of bringing about change in human behaviour

Libido: the source of all psychological energy, including the sex drive

Locus of control: whether a person believes outcomes and events are under his or her control, or whether they are determined by external factors that cannot be controlled

Long-linked technology: all activities have to be performed in a set sequence

Long-term memory: the relatively permanent store in which information and knowledge is retained

M

Machiavellianism: a strategy of social conduct that involves manipulating others for personal gain, often against their self-interests

Machine metaphor: organisations regarded as analogous to a machine that is designed for a purpose

Manager-directed control: managers specify exactly how and what should be done and closely monitor employee behaviour

Managerial grid: an application of style theories of leadership used for training and development purposes

Means–ends hierarchy: goals at one level in an organisation are the means of achieving the goals of the level immediately above

Means–ends inversion: the method of doing something becomes a goal in its own right, which displaces the end state (goal) that the method was supposed to achieve

Mechanistic organisation: roughly corresponds to a more bureaucratic firm and is best suited to stable environmental conditions

Media: specific ways of conveying a message along a channel

Mediating technology: the parts of an organisation are linked through its centre

Memory: the ability of an organism to retain information internally and demonstrate this retention through behaviour

Mercenary culture: one that is low on sociability and high on solidarity

Metaphor: a figure of speech in which a term is transferred from an object it ordinarily designates to another object it can designate by implicit analogy

Mission: a statement of an organisation's fundamental reason for existence

Monitoring of outcomes: examining whether the behaviour used has resulted in needs satisfaction

Motivators: features of the job itself that people find enjoyable and which have a motivational effect

Motives and drives: subconscious processes that provide the energy to engage in the goal-directed behaviour

Multinational organisation: one that is primarily located and managed from the country of its origin, but produces goods or services in relatively autonomous overseas subsidiaries to meet the needs of local markets

Multiple constituency approach (to effectiveness): an evaluation of effectiveness against the criterion of the extent to which an organisation satisfies the interests of its internal and external stakeholders

N

Nature vs nurture debate: the question of whether hereditary factors or the environment have most effect on behaviour

Need for Achievement (N.Ach): the need to succeed or excel in areas of significance to the person

Need for Affiliation (N.Affil): the need to interact with, and be liked by, other people

Need for Power (N.Pow): the need to control the activities of other people

Needs: experienced deficiencies between what someone is or has and what he or she wants to be or have that result in a desire to remove the deficiency

Negative affectivity (NA): a tendency to focus strongly on the negative aspects of work and life

Negative reinforcement: the removal of an aversive stimulus as a result of an organism exhibiting a desired behaviour

Networked culture: one that is high in sociability and low in solidarity

Neuroticism–stability: the second fundamental dimensions of personality used in Eysenck's type theory

Neutral stimulus: a stimulus which does not evoke a reflex response on the part of an organism

Nihilism: a now discredited doctrine that nothing really exists and thus there can be no knowledge of anything and hence knowledge cannot be communicated

Noise: any extraneous signal that interferes with or masks a message

Nomothetic: theories which describe personality in terms of set dimensions that could be applied to all people

Non-adaptive behaviour: that which is directed at shutting out the realisation that goal attainment is blocked

Non-standard workers: those employed other than on a permanent basis or for less than what is normally regarded as 'full-time' working in a particular organisation or industry

Normative inputs: human values, attitudes, beliefs and motivations

Norming: the third stage of group development, in which ground rules for a group's ways of functioning begin to emerge

Number magic: the tendency to replace an important and necessary goal with another one that can be measured, simply because it can be measured

Numeric flexibility: an organisation's capability to vary its number of employees and, in so doing, its level of activity

O

Objective: specific, short-term statement of results that should be achieved

OD intervention: a programme to bring about change in an organisation, or one or more of its parts

Official goals: ideal states that an organisation would like to achieve

Open system: a system not sealed off from its environment and, therefore, subject to the intrusion of environmental influences

Open-loop (feedforward) control: a method in which the inputs to a process or activity are carefully determined, but with no monitoring of outputs

Operating mechanisms: indicates in greater detail what is expected of individuals in a structure

Operative goals: the actual goals pursued by an organisation

Optimise: to seek a solution or decision option that maximises expected utility

Organic organisation: an organisation that has more fluid structural arrangements and is better suited to variable and dynamic environments

Organisational change: a move from being in one organisational state to being in another state

Organisational climate: how people collectively experience and react to their surroundings

Organisational commitment: an attitude towards the organisation as a whole, reflecting the individual's acceptance of its goals and values, his or her willingness to expend effort on its behalf and an intention to remain with the organisation

Organisational factors (groups): organisational features that influence a group's cohesiveness

Organisational slack: the difference between the total resources available to an organisation and those necessary to make side payments to ensure contributions from stakeholders

Organisational stressors: characteristics of the whole organisation that can be potential sources of stress for individuals

Organism metaphor: organisations regarded as analogous to biological organisms

Out-group members: people who give only a basic level of performance

Output control: results to be achieved are specified in terms of outputs, a degree of discretion is permitted in how they are achieved, and outputs are subsequently monitored

P

Perceived role problems: a misinterpretation by a role occupant of a role sender's expectations

Perception: a mental process involving the selection, organisation, structuring and interpretation of information in order to make inferences and give meaning to the information

Perceptual defence: the resistance to acknowledging a stimulus because doing so would contradict a person's deeply held values or what he or she already believes

Perceptual inference: a conclusion about an object is reached on the basis of incomplete evidence

Performing: the final stage of group development, in which the group becomes capable of effective functioning

Phenomenal field: the perceptions and meanings people attach to external events which result in them experiencing the world in a particular way

Physiological outcomes (stress): the effects of stress on a person's bodily health

Planned organisational change approach: a set of internal actions designed to produce specific outcomes

Pluralist perspective: a management frame of reference in which an organisation is seen to be a collection of different groups, all with their own legitimate aims to pursue and so a degree of conflict is the normal state of affairs

Policy: rules to guide future decision making, if and when certain contingencies arise

Political systems metaphor: organisations regarded as analogous to a political system composed of diverse groups, all of which have their own objectives

Pooled interdependence: organisational sub-units safeguard each other by contributing discretely to the whole, which safeguards them all

Portfolio approach to control: the use of different strategies for controlling human behaviour according to which one is seen to be most applicable at the time

Positive reinforcement: any outcome occurring after a behaviour that tends to maintain the repetition of the behaviour

Postmodernist: either (i) a new era in which the fundamental nature of organisations will be different from hitherto, or (ii) a philosophical stance which questions current assumptions of the nature of reality

Potential harms and benefits approach: a way of identifying the relevant stakeholders of an organisation as those who potentially benefit or are potentially harmed by its actions

Power base games: political tactics to build or maintain a power base

Predictive validity: whether test scores are good predictors of behaviour or job performance

Primary factors: the factors which, in Cattell's personality theory, are the fundamental building blocks of personality

Proactive approach (stress): attempts to remove or lessen the influence of stressors before stress occurs

Proactive interference: recall of material learned earlier interferes with recall of material that has been learned later

Problem solving: the process of producing a solution to a recognised problem

Process theories: focus on mental processes which transform the motive force into particular patterns of behaviour

Productivity: a measure of efficiency consisting of the ratio of inputs to outputs

Prototypes: mental schemes which categorise people into types based on the assumption that each type has distinctive attributes

Proximity principle (perception): objects are perceived as related because of their closeness

Psychological climate: how the individual experiences and reacts to his or her surroundings

Psychological contract: an unvoiced set of expectations that the parties (to the employment relationship) have of each other and the obligations that they feel towards each other

Psychological outcomes (stress): the effects of stress on a person's mental health

Psychological readiness: subordinate characteristics that make subordinates willing to accept the responsibility of working without leader guidance

Punishment: the application of an aversive stimulus (or removal of positive reinforcement) after a response by an organism that reduces the probability of a repetition of the response

Punishment by application: an aversive stimulus is applied immediately following an act of behaviour that is to be eliminated

Punishment by removal: a positive reinforcement is removed after behaviour which is to be eliminated has occurred

R

Radical perspective: organisational conflicts reflect conflict in wider society between capital and labour

Rational choice: the assumption that decisions are taken with full knowledge of all the relevant facts and that the option chosen maximises expected utility

Rational–legal authority: that which rests on the assumption that rational rules should guide the conduct of society and hence people in high office should command the actions of those below

Reactive approach (stress): attempts to help people better cope with the effects of stress after it has occurred

Receiver (of a message): the person to whom a message is directed

Reciprocal causality (leadership): the idea that followers affect leader behaviour as well as the leader influencing followers

Reciprocal interdependence: the parts are dependent upon each other to perform their respective tasks

Re-creation: a transformational change that occurs as a result of drastic changes in an organisation's environment

Reductionist: the belief that complex systems can be understood completely by understanding their constituent parts

Referent power: the capability to influence others that comes from having attributes or characteristics that make someone a source of reference or role model for other people

Reification: to treat an abstract idea as something that actually exists

Relational conflict: conflict in interpersonal relations

Reliability: whether a test produces the same results when applied to the same person on two separate occasions

Re-orientation: a transformational change that occurs in anticipation of drastic changes in an organisation's environment

Representativeness heuristic: a rule-of-thumb used by a decision maker to judge the likelihood of the outcome of a current decision option by using a stereotyped similarity to something in the past

Resistance through distance: a defensive way of resisting control by psychologically opting out

Resistance through persistence: an aggressive or assertive and overt way of resisting control

Responsibility: the obligation to achieve something

Retrieval: the processes used to recall information or knowledge from the long- (or sometimes short-) term memory store

Retroactive interference: the most recent material learned interferes with recall of material that has been learned earlier

Reward power: the capability to confer rewards on others

Rightsizing: see downsizing

Risky shift: the tendency of groups to make riskier decisions than their members would as individuals

Rivalry games: political tactics to defeat an opponent at the same level

Role: a set of expectations and obligations to act in a specific way in certain contexts

Role ambiguity: the role occupant is unsure of the requirements of his or her role

Role conflict: a clash between the different sets of role expectations

Role expectations: the role occupant's expectations about what the role entails

Role senders: individuals who have behavioural expectations of a role occupant

Role set: the total of all role senders for a given role

Root metaphor school (of culture): culture is assumed to reflect the essence of what an organisation is

Rumour: unverified information of uncertain origin

S

Salience (of attitude): the degree of conscious awareness of holding an attitude

Sampling: the characteristics of the total output of a process or activity is estimated by examining only a proportion of the output

Satisfice: to seek a solution or decision option that is 'good enough' rather than perfect

Scalar chain: a direct line of authority from the top to the bottom of an organisation

Schema: a structured mental representation of what the world is like or what it contains

Scientific management: a set of techniques for organising work methods to give managers greater control over the labour process, i.e. the exchange of effort for rewards

Scouts: group members who maintain contact with their environment and import information

Second-level outcomes (motivation): those that flow in the longer term from first-level outcomes

Self-disclosure: information that people consciously communicate about themselves to others

Self-efficacy: a person's belief in his or her ability to act in a certain way

Self-fulfilling prophecy: a prophecy that comes true solely because it has been made

Self-monitoring: examining one's own behaviour to see whether it has had the desired result

Semantic memory: a memory store recording information of an abstract, conceptual nature

Semi-autonomous work groups: self-managed teams that have a high degree of responsibility for their own work activities

Sensor: something (or someone) that monitors the attributes of the output of a process or activity

Sensor organs: organs that detect information about stimuli in the environment, i.e. the eye for visual information

Sensory registration: the memory stage in which environmental stimuli are first registered for onward transmission into memory

Sequential interdependence: each stage is interdependent with the one before and the one after

Sexual harassment: unwelcome sexual advances, requests for sexual favours or other verbal or physical conduct of a sexual nature

Sharpening of messages: selective attention to only part of a message

Short-term (working) memory: the stage in which information from the sensory register enters a short-term memory store

Side payments: inducements that are paid for cooperation or collaboration

Similarity principle (perception): the tendency to infer that two objects alike in some respects are alike in other ways

Single-loop learning: learning how to improve performance in achieving goals and objectives when the goals and objectives remain fixed and unchanging

Situational factors: the effect of a specific experience or situation on a person's feelings and behaviour

Situational leadership model: a situational theory of leadership which suggests that leader style should be varied according to the readiness of followers to direct their own actions

Slack: unexploited opportunities or undiscovered economies such as surplus resources

Sociability: the degree of friendliness between members of a community or group

Social control: achieving compliance, conformity or obedience through interpersonal or intergroup processes

Social factors: factors that influence personality that arise from interactions with other people

(corporate) Social responsibility: an organisation's obligation to contribute to, or protect, the environment of which it is a part

Social rewards: psychological rewards obtained through interaction with other people

Social support (stress): emotional support received through interaction with other people

Socialisation: the process of being taught how to behave and how to feel by other (influential) people within a specific social setting

Socio-emotive (group maintenance) leader: the person who ensures that group members have their social needs catered for

Socio-technical systems: an approach to work design in which the people and the technical systems (and the relationships between them) are accorded equal importance

Soft goals: those that are more subjective and qualitative in nature, open to interpretation and whose achievement is much harder to evaluate

Soldiering: working at a much slower pace than the one of which a person is capable

Solidarity: the degree of collectiveness in the relationships between people

Source of message: the person from whom a message originates

Source traits: those that cannot be observed directly and whose existence can only be inferred

Span of control: the number of subordinates reporting to someone

Specialisation: the degree of division of labour and patterns of work organisation at lower organisational levels

Specificity (of attitude): the extent to which the attitude is specific to some attribute of the attitude object

Stability (of attitude): the attitude's resistance to change

Stakeholder: people or groups with an interest in the activities of an organisation and the outcomes of those activities, whether or not the organisation has an interest in them

Stakeholder economy: an economy which is theoretically run for the benefit of all participants who have an interest in the performance of the economy

Stakeholder management perspective: simultaneous attention to the legitimate interests of all the appropriate stakeholders of an organisation

Standardisation: the extent to which formal rules and procedures are applied in all circumstances

Stereotyping: attributing a person with qualities assumed to be typical of members of a particular category (e.g. age, sex etc.) because the person falls into that category

Stimulus organisation and recognition (perception): the organisation of stimulus information into meaningful patterns that form identifiable wholes

Storming: the second stage of group development, which is characterised by interpersonal conflict

Strategic contingencies: events or activities that are crucial in achieving organisational goals

Strategy: a plan or design to achieve aims, goals or objectives

Stress: an adaptive response to external stimuli that place excessive physical or psychological demands on a person

Stressors: external factors that impinge on a person and potentially result in stress

Strong situations: those where personality characteristics are good predictors of behaviour

Sub-optimisation: sub-unit goals are accorded greater importance (by people in sub-units) than the goals of the organisation as a whole

Superego: a component of personality that reflects the learned rules of society which are absorbed in upbringing

Surface traits: those that are directly observable in behaviour

Symptom-management-strategy (stress): an attempt to live with, but mitigate, the effects of stressors

Systems resource (or resource dependency) approach (to effectiveness): evaluation of organisational effectiveness against the criterion of whether the organisation maximises its bargaining position *vis-à-vis* the environment in order to acquire an optimal level of scarce and valued resources

T

Tacit knowledge: individualised personal knowledge and understanding which, although understood by the person, is difficult to describe, articulate and disseminate because it embraces the person's experiences and intuitions

Tall organisation: a relatively large number of different levels in the management hierarchy

Task-focused conflict: conflict within a group about how it should complete its task

Task groups: temporary formal groups formed for a specific short-term purpose

Task leader: the person who occupies the role concerned with ensuring that a group completes its task

Task-related readiness: subordinate skills and abilities that enable subordinates to do a job without leader guidance

Teams: strongly task-orientated formal group

Team briefing: a cascade system of communication starting at the top of an organisation, in which managers at each level brief their direct subordinates about matters relevant to the subordinates

Teamworking: the current name for use of semi-autonomous work groups

Technical complexity: a measure of the ease of coordination and control of a manufacturing technology

Technological determinism: the belief that technological advances drive changes, e.g. to organisational structures

Teleworker: someone who works at a place other than the one where the results of the work are needed, by using information and communication technology

Theory in use: the theory of action actually implemented by an organisation

Top-down goal setting: goals for a particular organisational level can be imposed from above

Top-down processing (perception): perceptual processes driven by the higher brain

Total Quality Management (TQM): an organisation-wide strategy that focuses on achieving or exceeding customer expectations

Traditional authority: that which rests on the established sanctity of a traditional position, e.g. a king

Trait theory (leadership): the assumption that certain people have inherent characteristics which enable them to be leaders

Traits: individual characteristics of thought or feeling that result in tendencies to behave in specific ways

Transactional leadership: the leadership style that is said to be the most appropriate to stable conditions

Transformational leadership: the approach to leadership which is said to be the most appropriate in times of significant organisational change

Transnational organisation: one that operates simultaneously as an international, multinational and global organisation

Two-factor theory of leadership: that there are two independent dimensions to leader behaviour, that is, initiating structure and consideration

U

Unbounded problems: ambiguous problems that are harder to define and which cannot easily be separated from the context in which they exist

Unconditioned response: a reflex response built into the nervous system of an organism

Unconditioned stimulus: a naturally occurring stimulus to which there is an inbuilt response in an organism's nervous system

Unitarist perspective: a management frame of reference in which an organisation is seen as one large family, all on the same side and pulling in the same direction, and in which conflict is seen as deviant behaviour

V

Valence: the strength of preference for a particular outcome

Valence (of attitude): the degree of positive or negative feelings about an attitude object

Value: what a person wants to be true

Value of reward: the extent that a person values a reward

Value-expressive function (of attitude): allows the person to derive satisfaction from expressing attitudes that reflect his or her central values

Variable interval (VI) schedule: reinforcement is delivered at non-uniform time intervals

Variable ratio (VR) schedule: reinforcements which are delivered after a random number of desired responses

Verbal:educational intelligence (V:Ed): that part of an intelligence test which assesses verbal, numeric and educational skills and abilities

Vertical differentiation: the establishment of a hierarchy of authority in the organisation

Vertical surveillance: a person's actions are monitored by someone above him or her in the organisational hierarchy

W

Weak situations: those where personality characteristics are poorer predictors of behaviour

Whistle-blowers: people (usually employed by an organisation) who make public unethical or questionable activities of an organisation

Workplace stress: stress that arises from an interaction between people and their jobs

A

Abramson, L Y and H A Sackheim (1977) A paradox in depression: uncontrollability and self-blame, *Psychological Bulletin* 84(6): 838–51

ACAS (2000) *ACAS Code of Practice on Disciplinary Practice and Grievance*, London: HMSO

Ackroyd, S and P A Crowdy (1990) Can culture be managed? Working with raw material: the case of English slaughtermen, *Personnel Review* 19(5): 3–13

Ackroyd, S and P Thompson (1999) *Organisational Misbehaviour*, London: Thompson

Adair, J (1984) *The Skills of Leadership*, Aldershot: Gower

Adair, J (1986) *Effective Team Building*, London: Pan

Adair, J (2003) *The Inspirational Leader*, London: Kogan Page

Adam, E C (1972) An analysis of changes in performance quality with operant conditioning procedures, *Journal of Applied Psychology* 56(6): 480–6

Adams, J S (1965) Inequity in social exchange. In L Berkowitz (ed.), *Advances in Experimental Social Psychology*, Vol. 2, New York: Academic Press

Adler, A (1928) *Understanding Human Nature*, London: Allen and Unwin

Adler, N J (1997) *International Dimensions of Organisational Behaviour*, 3rd edn, London: Thomson

Adler, N J and S Bartholomew (1992) Academic and professional communities of discourse: generating knowledge on transnational human resource management, *Journal of International Business Studies* 23(3): 551–70

Adler, N J and G H Ghadar (1990) Strategic human resource management: a global perspective. In R Pieper (ed.), *Human Resource Management: An International Comparison*, Berlin: De Gruyter

Adler, N J, R Doktor and G Redding (1986) From the Atlantic to the Pacific century, *Journal of Management* Summer: 295–318

Adler, P S and B Borys (1996) Two types of bureaucracy: enabling and coercive, *Administrative Science Quarterly* 41(1): 61–89

Adorno, T W, E Frenkel-Brunswick, D J Levinson and R N Sandford (1950) *The Authoritarian Personality*, New York: Harper and Row

Ajzen, I (1988) *Attitudes, Personality and Behaviour*, Milton Keynes: Open University Press

Alderfer, C (1972) *Existence, Relatedness and Growth: Human Needs in Organisational Settings*, New York: Free Press

Aldrich, H and D A Whetten (1981) Organisation-sets, action-sets and networks: making the most of simplicity. In P Nystrom and W H Starbuck (eds), *Handbook of Organisation Design*, Vol. 1, New York: Oxford University Press

Alford, H (1994) Cellular manufacturing: the development of an idea and its application, *New Technology, Work and Employment* 9(1): 3–18

Algera, J A (1983) Objective and perceived task characteristics as determinants of reactions by task performers, *Journal of Occupational Psychology* 56(2): 95–107

Allen, T D, D M Freeman, J E A Russell, R C Reizenstein and J O Rentz (2001) Survivor reactions to organisational downsizing: does time ease the pain? *Journal of Occupational and Organisational Psychology* 74(2): 145–64

Allinson, C W and J Hayes (1988) The learning styles questionnaire: an alternative to Kolb's inventory? *Journal of Management Studies* 25(3): 269–81

Allinson, S T, A M R Jordan and C E Yeatts (1992) Cluster-analytic approach toward identifying structure and content of human decision making, *Human Relations* 45(1): 49–72

Allport, G W (1954a) Attitudes in the history of social psychology. In G Lindzey and A Aronson (eds), *Handbook of Social Psychology*, Vol. 1, Reading, MA: Addison-Wesley

Allport, G W (1954b) *The Nature of Prejudice*, Reading, MA: Addison-Wesley

Allport, G W (1961) *Pattern and Growth in Personality*, New York: Holt, Rinehart and Winston

Alvesson, M (1995) The meaning and meaninglessness of postmodernism: some ironic remarks, *Organization Studies* 16(6): 1047–75

Amado, G (1995) Why psychoanalytical knowledge helps us to understand organisations: a discussion with Elliot Jaques, *Human Relations* 48(4): 351–7

Anderson, C, D Hellriegel and J Slocum (1977) Managerial response to environmentally induced stress, *Academy of Management Journal* 20(2): 260–72

Ansoff, I H (1965) *Corporate Strategy*, Harmondsworth: Penguin

Appignanesi, R and C Garratt (1995) *Postmodernism for Beginners*, Cambridge: Icon Books

Argyris, C (1964) *Integrating the Individual and Organization*, New York: Wiley

Argyris, C (1982) *Reasoned Learning and Action*, San Francisco: Jossey-Bass

Argyris, C (1999) *On Organisational Learning*, 2nd edn, Oxford: Blackwell

Argyris, C and D Schön (1978) *Organisational Learning*, Reading, MA: Addison-Wesley

Argyris, C and D Schön (1996) *Organisational Learning II: Theory, Method and Practice*, Reading, MA: Addison-Wesley

Arkin, A (1999) Return to the centre, *People Management* 6 May: 34–41

Arlidge, J (2000) Online Britain fails the English test, *The Observer* 16 July: 9

Armitage, C J and M Conner (1999) The theory of planned behaviour: assessment of predictive validity and perceived control, *British Journal of Social Psychology* 38(1): 35–54

Arnold, J, C L Cooper and I T Robertson (1998) *Work Psychology: Understanding Human Behaviour in the Workplace*, Harlow: Financial Times/Prentice Hall

Arnold, J, I T Robertson and C Cooper (1991) *Work Psychology: Understanding Human Behaviour in the Workplace*, London: Pitman

Arthur, A (2003) A utility theory of truth, *Organisation* 10(2): 205–21

Arvey, R D and J M Ivancevich (1980) Punishment in organizations: a review, propositions and research, *Academy of Management Review* 5(1): 123–32

Asch, S E (1946) Forming impressions of personalities, *Journal of Abnormal and Social Psychology* 50(3): 258–90

Asch, S E (1951) Effects of group pressure upon the modification and distortion of judgements. In H Guetzkow (ed.), *Groups, Leadership and Men*, New York: Carnegie Press

Ashford, S (1986) Feedback seeking in individual adaptation: a resource perspective, *Academy of Management Journal* 29(3): 465–87

Ashtorth, B E and F Mael (1989) Social identity theory and organization, *Academy of Management Review* 14(1): 20–39

Astley, W G and R A Braham (1989) Organisational designs for post-industrial strategies. In C Snow (ed.), *Strategy, Organizational Design and Human Resource Management*, Greenwich, CT: JAI Press

Atkinson, J and N Meager (1986) *Changing Work Practices: How Companies Achieve Flexibility to Meet New Needs*, London: National Economic Development Office

Atkinson, R L, R C Atkinson, E Smith and E R Hilgard (1987) *Introduction to Psychology*, 9th edn, Orlando, FL: Harcourt Brace Jovanovich

Austin, J T and P Bobko (1985) Goal-setting theory: unexplored areas and future research needs, *Journal of Occupational Psychology* 58(4): 289–308

B

Baddeley, A (1976) *The Psychology of Memory*, New York: Harper and Row

Baddon, L, L Hunter, J Hyman, J Leopold and H Ramsay (1989) *People's Capitalism? A Critical Analysis of Profit Sharing and Employee Share Ownership*, London: Routledge

Bailey, J (1983) *Job Design and Work Organisation*, London: Prentice Hall

Bain, P and P Taylor (2000) Entrapped by the electronic panoptican? Worker resistance in the call centre, *New Technology, Work and Employment* 15(1): 2–18

Bales, R F (1950) *Interaction Process Analysis: A Method for the Study of Small Groups*, Reading, MA: Addison-Wesley

Bammer, K and B H Newberry (eds) (1982) *Stress and Cancer*, Toronto: Hogrefe

Bandura, A (1982) Self-efficacy mechanism in human agency, *American Psychologist* 32(2): 122–47

Bandura, A (1997) *Self-efficacy in Changing Societies*, Cambridge: Cambridge University Press

Bandura, A and R H Walters (1963) *Social Learning and Personality Development*, London: Holt, Rinehart and Winston

Bandura, A, D Ross and S A Ross (1961) Transmission of aggression through imitation of aggressive models, *Journal of Abnormal and Social Psychology* 63(3): 575–82

Bangemann, M (1994) *Europe and the Global Information Society: Recommendations to the European Council*, Brussels: European Commission

Banker, R D, J M Field, R G Schroeder and K K Sinha (1996) The impact of work teams on manufacturing performance: a longitudinal field study, *Academy of Management Journal* 39(4): 867–90

Bannister, D (1970) *Perspectives in Personal Construct Theory*, New York: Academic Press

Barker, R A (2001) The nature of leadership, *Human Relations* 54(4) 469–94

Barnard, C I (1938) *The Functions of the Executive*, Cambridge, MA: Harvard University Press

Barney, J B and R W Griffin (1992) *The Management of Organisations: Strategy, Structure, Behaviour*, Boston, MA: Houghton Mifflin

Baron, R A (1994) The physical environment of work settings: effects on task performance, interpersonal relations and job satisfaction. In B M Staw and L L Cummings (eds), *Research in Organisational Behaviour*, Vol. 16, Greenwich, CT: JAI Press

Barrick, M R and M K Mount and R Gupta (2003) Meta-analysis of the relationship between the five-factor model of personality and Holland's occupational types, *Personnel Psychology* 56(1): 45–74

Barron, R A and J Greenberg (1990) *Behaviour in Organisations*, Needham Heights, MA: Allyn and Bacon

Bartlett, C A (1986) Building and managing the transnational: the new organisational challenge. In M E Porter (ed.), *Competition in Global Industries*, Boston, MA: Harvard Business School Press

Bartlett, C A and S Ghoshal (1991) *Managing across Borders*, Boston, MA: Harvard Business School Press

Bartlett, C A and S Ghoshal (1997) *The Individualised Corporation*, London: Random House

Bartlett, F C (1932) *Remembering*, Cambridge: Cambridge University Press

Bass, B M (1983) *Organisational Decision Making*, Homewood, IL: Irwin

Bass, B M (1985) *Leadership and Performance beyond Expectations*, New York: Macmillan

Bass, B M and R M Stogdill (1990) *Bass and Stogdill's Handbook of Leadership: Theory, Research and Managerial Application*, New York: Free Press

Bauman, Z (1992) *Intimations of Postmodernity*, London: Routledge

Bavelas, A (1950) Communication patterns in task-oriented groups, *Journal of Acoustical Society of America* 22(4): 725–30

Bazerman, M H (1994) *Judgement in Managerial Decision Making*, 3rd edn, New York: Wiley

Beach, L R (1997) *The Psychology of Decision Making*, London: Sage

Beamish, P W, J P Killing, D J LeCraw and H Crookell (1991) *International Management: Text and Cases*, Homewood, IL: Irwin

Beck, C E (1999) *Managerial Communication: Bridging Theory and Practice*, London: Prentice Hall

Beck, N and A Kieser (2003) The complexity of rule systems, experience and organisational learning, *Organisation Studies* 24(5): 471–81

Becker, T E, R S Billings, D M Eveleth and N L Gilbert (1996) Foci and bases of employee commitment: implications for job performance, *Academy of Management Journal* 39(2): 464–82

Bedeian A G (1984) *Organisations: Theory and Application*, New York: Holt-Saunders

Bedeian, A G and R F Zammuto (1991) *Organisations: Theory and Design*, Chicago, IL: Dryden

Beehr, T A (1995) *Psychological Stress in the Workplace*, London: Routledge

Beehr, T A and J E Newman (1978) Job stress, employee health and organisational effectiveness: a facet analysis, model and literature review, *Personnel Psychology* 31(4): 665–99

Beekun, R and W H Glick (2001) Development and test of a contingency framework of coupling: assessing the covariance between structure and culture, *Journal of Applied Behavioural Science* 37(4): 385–407

Beer, M and A L Walton (1987) Organisation change and development, *Annual Review of Psychology* 38: 339–67

Belanger, J, P K Edwards and M Wright (2003) Commitment at work and independence from management: a study of advanced teamwork, *Work and Occupations* 30(2): 234–52

Belbin, R M (1993) *Team Roles at Work*, Oxford: Butterworth-Heinemann

Bell, P A, J D Fisher, A Baum and T E Green (1990) *Environmental Psychology*, 3rd edn, New York: Holt, Rinehart and Winston

Bennis, W G (1959) Leadership theory and administrative behaviour: the problem of authority, *Administrative Science Quarterly* 4(3): 463–76

Berggren, C (1993) Lean production – the end of history? *Work, Employment and Society* 7(2): 44–58

Berlo, D K (1960) *The Process of Communication*, New York: Holt, Rinehart and Winston

Bernardin, H J and K Alvares (1976) The managerial grid as a predictor of conflict resolution and managerial effectiveness, *Administrative Science Quarterly* 21(1): 72–91

Berridge, J, C L Cooper and C Highley-Marchington (1997) *Employee Assistance Programmes and Workplace Counselling*, Chichester: Wiley

Berry, A J, J Broadbent and D Otley (1995) *Management Control: Themes, Issues and Practices*, London: Macmillan

Berry, J W (1969) On cross-cultural comparability, *International Journal of Psychology* 14(2): 119–28

Bertin, I and A Denbigh (1996) *The Teleworking Handbook: New Ways of Working in the Information Society*, London: The Telecottage Association

Beyer, J M and H M Trice (1987) How an organization's rites reveal its culture, *Organizational Dynamics* Spring: 13–21

Binet, A and T Simon (1908) Le developpement de l'intelligence chez les enfants, *L'Année Psychologique* 14(1): 1–94

Birchall, D and L Lyons (1995) *Creating Tomorrow's Organisation: Unlocking the Benefits of Future Work*, London: Pitman

Black, B (1999) National culture and high commitment management, *Employee Relations* 21(4): 389–404

Blackhurst, C (1996) Whatever happened to Sid? *Management Today* July: 36–9

Blair, H, S G Taylor and K Randle (1998) A pernicious panacea – a critical appraisal of business re-engineering, *New Technology, Work and Employment* 13(2): 116–28

Blake, R R and A A McCanse (1991) *Leadership Dilemmas: Grid Solutions*, Houston, TX: Gulf

Blake, R R and J Mouton (1964) *The Managerial Grid*, Houston, TX: Gulf

Blau, P (1964) *Exchange and Power in Social Life*, New York: Wiley

Blinkhorn, S and C Johnson (1990) The insignificance of personality testing, *Nature* 34(8): 671–2

Blood, M R and C L Hulin (1967) Job enlargement, worker differences and worker responses, *Journal of Applied Psychology* 51(2): 284–90

Bloom, B S (1956) *Taxonomy of Educational Objectives, Handbook 1: The Cognitive Domain*, London: Longman

Boddy, D and N Gunson (1995) *Organisations in the Network Age*, London: Routledge

Boschken, H I (1990) Strategy and structure: reconceiving the relationship, *Journal of Management* March: 135–50

Bottger, P and P W Yetton (1988) An integration of process and decision scheme explanations of group problem solving performance, *Organizational Behaviour and Human Decision Processes* 42(2): 234–49

Bowditch, J L and A F Buono (1985) *A Primer in Organisational Behaviour*, New York: Wiley

Bowen, D E and E E Lawler (1992) The empowerment of service workers: why, how and when? *Sloan Management Review* Spring: 36–9

Bowen J and Z L Qui (1992) Satisficing when buying information, *Organisational Behaviour and Human Decision Processes* 60(3): 471–81

Bowers, D G and S E Seashore (1966) Predicting organisational effectiveness with a four-factor theory of leadership, *Administrative Science Quarterly* 11(2): 238–63

Bragganti, N and E Devine (1984) *The Traveler's Guide to European Customs and Manners*, St Paul, MN: Meadowbank

Bramlette, C A and J H Tucker (1981) Encounter groups: positive change or deterioration: more data and a partial replication, *Human Relations* 34(4): 303–14

Breckler, S J (1984) Empirical validation of affect, behaviour and cognition as distinct components of attitude, *Journal of Personality and Social Psychology* 47(8): 1191–205

Brehm, J W (1972) *Responses to Loss of Freedom: A Theory of Psychological Reactance*, New York: General Learning Press

Brewster, C, A Hegewisch, T Lockhart and L Mayne (1993) Flexible working patterns in Europe, *Issues in Personnel Management*, No. 6, London: Institute of Personnel Management

Brief, A P and H K Downey (1983) Cognitive and organisational structures: a conceptual analysis of organising features, *Human Relations* 36(12): 1065–90

Brodbeck, F C, M Frese, S Ackerblom, G Audia, G Bakacsi, H Bendova, D Bodega, M Bondur, S Booth, K Brenk, P Castel, D D Hartog, G Donnelly-Cox, M V Gratchev, I Holmberg, S Jarmuz, G C Jesuino, R Jorbenadse, H E Kabasakal, M Keating, G Kipiani, E Maczynski, G S Martin, J O'Connell, A Papalexandris, N Sabadin, J Schramm-Nielsen, M Schultz, C Sigfrids, E Szabo, H Thierry, M Vondrysova, J Weibler, C Wilderom, S Witkowski and R Wunderer (2000) Cultural variation of leadership prototypes across 22 European countries, *Journal of Occupational and Organisational Psychology*, 73(1): 1–29

Brownell, J (1986) *Building Active Listening Skills*, Englewood Cliffs, NJ: Prentice Hall

Bruner, J S (1973) *The Relevance of Education*, New York: Norton

Bruner, J S and L Postman (1947) Emotional selectivity in perception and reaction, *Journal of Personality* 16(1): 69–77

Bryman, A (1992) *Charisma and Leadership in Organisations*, London: Sage

Bryman, A (1996) Leadership in organisations. In S R Clegg, C Hardy and W R Nord (eds), *Handbook of Organisational Studies*, London: Sage

Buchanan, D and J Storey (1997) Role-taking and role-switching in organisational change: the four

pluralities. In I McLoughlin and M Harris (eds), *Innovation, Organisational Change and Technology*, London: Thompson

Buitendam, A (1987) The horizontal perspective of organization design and new technology. In J M Pennings and A Buitendam (eds), *New Technology as Organizational Innovation*, Cambridge, MA: Ballinger

Buller, P F and C H Bell Jr (1986) Effects of team building and goal setting on productivity: a field experiment, *Academy of Management Journal* 29(2): 305–28

Bunce, D and M A West (1996) Stress management and innovative interventions at work, *Human Relations* 49(2): 209–32

Burke, W W (1987) *Organisation Development: A Normative View*, Reading, MA: Addison-Wesley

Burkeman, O (2000) Waiting for the revolution, *The Guardian* 5 December: 2

Burnes, B (1998) Understanding organisational change. In J Arnold, C L Cooper and I T Robertson (eds), *Work Psychology: Understanding Human Behaviour in the Workplace*, 3rd edn, Harlow: Financial Times/Prentice Hall

Burnes, B (2000) *Managing Change: A Strategic Approach to Organisational Dynamics*, 3rd edn, Harlow: Financial Times/Prentice Hall

Burns, J M (1978) *Leadership*, New York: Harper and Row

Burns, T and G M Stalker (1994) *The Management of Innovation*, Oxford: Oxford University Press

Burt, C (1955) The evidence for the concept of intelligence, *British Journal of Educational Psychology* 25(2): 158–77

C

Callaghan, G and P Thompson (2002) We recruit 'attitude': the selection and shaping of routine call centre labour, *Journal of Management Studies* 39(2): 233–54

Callan, V J (1993) Subordinate–manager communication in different sex dyads: consequences for job satisfaction, *Journal of Occupational and Organisational Psychology* 66(1): 13–27

Campbell, D T (1965) Ethnocentrism and other altruistic motives. In D Levine (ed.), *Nebraska Symposium on Motivation*, Vol. 13, Lincoln, NB: University of Nebraska Press

Cannon, T (1994) *Corporate Responsibility*, London: Pitman

Carey, A (1967) The Hawthorne studies: a radical criticism, *American Sociological Review* 32(2): 403–16

Carlisle, Y M and D J Manning (1996) The domain of professional business ethics, *Organization* 3(3): 341–60

Cartwright, S and C L Cooper (1996) *Managing Workplace Stress*, London: Sage

Carysforth, C (1998) *Communication for Work*, Oxford: Butterworth-Heinemann

Casey, C (1999) Come join our family: discipline and integration in corporate organisational culture, *Human Relations* 52(2): 155–78

Cassidy, T and R Lynn (1989) A multifactorial approach to achievement motivation: the development of a comprehensive measure, *Journal of Occupational Psychology* 63(4): 301–12

Cattell, R B (1965) *The Scientific Analysis of Personality*, Harmondsworth: Penguin

Cavanagh, G F, D J Moberg and M Velasquez (1981) The ethics of organizational politics, *Academy of Management Review* 8(2): 363–74

Cavanaugh, M A, W R Boswell, M V Roehling and J W Boudreau (2000) An empirical examination of self-reported work stress among US managers, *Journal of Applied Psychology* 85(1): 65–74

Chaikin, A L and J Cooper (1973) Evaluation as a function of correspondence and hedonic relevance, *Journal of Experimental Social Psychology* 9(2): 257–64

Chandler, A E Jr (1962) *Strategy and Structure: Chapters in the History of the American Enterprise*, Cambridge, MA: MIT Press

Chapman, M (2001) Emotional intelligence – critical competence or passing fad? Beyond the rhetoric, *The Occupational Psychologist*, Vol. 43 August: 3–5

Chen, P Y and P E Spector (1992) Relationships of work stressors with aggression, withdrawal, theft and substance use: an exploratory study, *Journal of Occupational and Organisational Psychology* 65(3): 177–84

Chen, X Z, A S Tsui and J L Farh (2002) Loyalty to supervisor vs. organisational commitment: relationships to employee performance in China, *Journal of Occupational and Organisational Psychology* 73(3): 339–56

Cherns, A (1987) Principles of socio-technical design revisited, *Human Relations* 40(2): 153–62

Chia, R (1995) From modern to postmodern organisational analysis, *Organization Studies* 16(4): 579–604

Child, J (1981) Culture, contingency and capitalism in the cross-national study of organization. In L L Cummings and B M Staw (eds), *Research in Organizational Behaviour*, Vol. 3, Greenwich, CT: JAI Press

Child, J (1984) *Organization: A Guide to Problems and Practice*, London: Harper and Row

Child, J (1997) Strategic choice in the analysis of action, structure organisations and environment: retrospect and prospect, *Organisation Studies* 18(1): 43–76

Ciborra, C and G Patriotta (1996) Groupware and teamwork in new product development. In C Ciborra (ed.), *Groupware and Teamwork*, Chichester: Wiley

Clark, A E (1996) Job satisfaction in Britain, *British Journal of Industrial Relations* 34(2): 189–217

Clark, R D (1971) Group-induced shift towards risk: a critical appraisal, *Psychological Bulletin* 76: 251–70

Claydon, T and M Doyle (1996) Trusting me trusting you? The ethics of employee empowerment, *Personnel Review* 25(6): 13–25

Clegg, B (2003) Junk That Mail, *Professional Manager* March: 22–23

Clegg, S R (1989) *Frameworks of Power*, London: Sage

Cohen, A (2000) The relationship between commitment forms and work outcomes: a comparison of three models, *Human Relations* 53(3): 387–417

Cohen, M D, J G March and J P Olsen (1972) A garbage can model of decision making, *Administrative Science Quarterly* 17(1): 1–25

Cohen, S (1980) After effects of stress on human behaviour and performance: a review of research and theory, *Psychological Bulletin* 88(1): 92–108

Colehart, M, C D Lea and K Thompson (1974) In defense of iconic memory, *Quarterly Journal of Experimental Psychology* 26(4): 633–41

Colenso, M (1997) *High Performing Teams*, London: Butterworth-Heinemann

Collins, A M and M R Quillian (1969) Retrieval time from semantic memory, *Journal of Verbal Learning and Verbal Behaviour* 8(2): 240–7

Collins, D (1998) *Organisational Change: Sociological Perspectives*, London: Routledge

Collins, P D and F Hull (1986) Technology and span of control: Woodward revisited, *Journal of Management Studies* 23(2): 143–64

Collinson, D L (1994) Strategies of resistance: power, knowledge and subjectivity in the workplace. In J M Jermier, D Knights and W R Nord (eds), *Resistance and Power in Organisations*, London: Routledge

Conger, J A (1993) Leadership: the art of empowering others. In J R Gordon (ed.), *A Diagnostic Approach to Organisational Behaviour*, Boston, MA: Allyn and Bacon

Conger, J A and R N Kanugo (1987) Towards a behaviourial theory of charismatic leadership in organisational settings, *Academy of Management Review* 12(4): 637–74

Conner, M and C J Armitage (1998) Extending the theory of planned behaviour: a review and avenues for further research, *Journal of Applied Social Psychology* 28(6): 1430–64

Connolly, T, E J Conlon and S J Deutsch (1980) Organisational effectiveness: a multiple-constituency approach, *Academy of Management Review* 5(2): 211–17

Conrad, R (1964) Acoustic confusion in immediate memory, *British Journal of Psychology* 55(1): 75–84

Cook, M (1971) *Interpersonal Perception*, Harmondsworth: Penguin

Cook, S (2003) Who cares wins, *Management Today*, January: 40–47

Cook, S and H Slack (1991) *Making Management Decisions*, 2nd edn, London: Prentice Hall

Cooley, C H (1964) *Human Nature and the Social Order*, New York: Schocken

Cooper, C L (1996) *Handbook of Stress, Medicine and Health*, Boca Raton, FL: CRC Press

Cooper, C L (1998) Working in a short-term culture, *Management Today*, February: 5

Cooper, C L and S Cartwright (1994) Healthy mind: healthy organisation – a proactive approach to occupational stress, *Human Relations* 47(4): 455–71

Cooper, C L and M J Davidson (1991) *The Stress Survivors*, London: Grafton Publishing

Cooper, C L and R Payne (1988) *Causes, Coping and Consequences of Stress at Work*, Chichester: Wiley

Cooper, C L and G Sadri (1991) The impact of stress counselling at work. In P L Perrewe (ed.), *Handbook of Job Stress* (Special Issue), *Journal of Social Behaviour and Personality* 6(7): 411–23

Cooper, C L, J Watts, A J Baglioni and M Kelly (1988) Stress amongst general practice dentists, *Journal of Occupational Psychology* 61(2): 163–74

Cooper, C L and B White (1995) Organisational behaviour. In S Tyson (ed.), *Strategic Prospects for Human Resource Management*, London: Institute of Personnel and Development

Cooper, R and G Burrell (1988) Modernism, postmodernism and organisational analysis: an introduction, *Organization Studies* 9(1): 91–112

Cordery, J L, W S Mueller and L M Smith (1991) Attitudinal and behavioural outcomes of autonomous group working: a longitudinal field study, *Academy of Management Journal* 31(2): 464–76

Cordes, C L and T W Dougherty (1993) A review and integration of research on job burnout, *Academy of Management Review* 18(3): 621–56

Cosier, R A and D R Dalton (1983) Equity theory and time: a reformulation, *Academy of Management Review* 4(2): 311–19

Covaleski, M A , M W Dirsmith, J B Heian and S Samuel (1998) The calculated and the avowed: techniques of discipline and struggles over identity in the six big public accounting firms, *Administrative Science Quarterly* 43(2): 293–327

Cowe R (1996) BT won over by argument for ethical audit, *The Guardian*, 25 November: 14

Craik, F I M and R S Lockheart (1972) Levels of processing: a framework for memory research, *Journal of Verbal Learning and Verbal Behaviour* 11(5): 671–84

Crawley, R and P Spurgeon (1979) Computer assistance and the air traffic controller's job satisfaction. In R G Sell and P Shipley (eds), *Satisfaction in Work Design: Ergonomics and Other Approaches*, London: Taylor and Francis

Cray, D and G R Mallory (1997) *Making Sense of Managing Culture*, London: Thomson

Cressey, P and P Scott (1992) Employment, technology and industrial relations in the clearing banks: is the honeymoon over? *New Technology, Work and Employment* 7(2): 83–96

Crozier, M (1964) *The Bureaucratic Phenomenon*, Chicago, IL: University of Chicago Press

CSO (1996) JUVOS Cohort Database, Central Statistical Office, as reported in the *Financial Times*, 4 March 1996

Cullen, D (1997) Maslow, monkeys and motivation theory, *Organization* 4(3): 355–73

Cummings, T G (1978) Self-regulating work groups: a socio-technical synthesis, *Academy of Management Review* 3(3): 625–34

Cummings, T G and C Worley (1997) *Organisation Development and Change*, 7th edn, St Paul, MN: West Publishing

Cunningham, I and J Hyman (1999) The poverty of empowerment? A critical case study, *Personnel Review* 28(3): 192–207

Cunningham, I, J Hyman and C Baldry (1996) Empowerment: the power to do what? *Industrial Relations Journal* 27(2): 143–54

Cunningham, J B (1978) A systems-resource approach for evaluating organisational effectiveness, *Human Relations* 31(7): 631–56

Curran, K (2003) Make time for flexibility, *People Management* 24 August: 19

Cyert, R M and J C March (1963) *A Behavioural Theory of the Firm*, Englewood Cliffs, NJ: Prentice Hall

D

Daft, R L (1996) *Organization Theory and Design*, 3rd edn, St Paul, MN: West Publishing

Danford, A (1998) Teamworking and labour regulation in the autocomponents industry, *Work, Employment and Society* 12(3): 409–43

Danserau, F D, G Graen and W J Haga (1975) A vertical dyad linkage approach to leadership within formal organizations: a longitudinal investigation of the role making process, *Organisational Behaviour and Human Performance* 13(1): 46–78

Dastmalchian, A (1986) Environmental characteristics and organizational climate: an exploratory study, *Journal of Management Studies* 23(6): 609–33

Dastmalchian, A and R Mansfield (1980) Payment systems in smaller companies: relationships with size and climate, *Personnel Review* 9(2): 27–32

Davenport, T (1992) *Process Innovation: Re-engineering Work through Information Technology*, Cambridge, MA: Harvard Business School Press

Davidow, W and T Malone (1992) *The Virtual Organisation*, New York: Harper and Row

Davidson, E (2003) Counter terrorism, *People Management* 26 June: 38–40

Davidson, M J and C L Cooper (1992) *Shattering the Glass Ceiling: The Woman Manager*, London: Chapman

Davis, S M and P R Lawrence (1977) *Matrix*, Reading, MA: Addison-Wesley

De Dreu, C and E Van de Vliert (eds) (1977) *Using Conflict in Organisations*, London: Sage

De Fruyt, F and I Mervielde (1999) Riasec types and big five traits as predictors of employment status and nature of employment, *Personnel Psychology* 52(3): 701–27

Deal, T E and A A Kennedy (1982) *Corporate Culture: The Rites and Rituals of Corporate Life*, Reading, MA: Addison-Wesley

Deary, I J and G Matthews (1993) Personality traits are alive and well, *The Psychologist* July: 299–311

DeBrabander, B and C Boone (1990) Sex differences in perceived locus of control, *Journal of Social Psychology* 61(2): 271–6

DeCotis, T A and T P Summers (1987) A path analysis of the antecedents and consequences of organisational commitment, *Human Relations* 40(6): 445–70

Deery S J, R D Iverson and P J Erwin (1994) Predicting organisational and union commitment: the effects of industrial relations climate, *British Journal of Industrial Relations* 32(4): 581–97

Delbridge, R, J Lowe and N Oliver (2000) Shopfloor responsibilities under lean teamworking, *Human Relations* 53(11): 1549–79

Denison, D R (1996) What is the difference between organisational culture and organisational climate? A native's point of view on a decade of paradigm wars, *Academy of Management Review* 21(3): 619–54

Denison, D R and A K Mishra (1995) Towards a theory of organisational culture and effectiveness, *Organisation Science* 6(2): 204–23

Dent, E B and S G Goldberg (1999) Challenging resistance to change, *Journal of Applied Behavioural Science* 35(1): 25–41

Dewe, P (1991) Primary appraisal, secondary appraisal and coping: their role in stressful work encounters, *Journal of Occupational Psychology* 64(4): 331–51

Dewe, P J (1992) Applying the concept of appraisal to work stressors: some exploratory analysis, *Human Relations* 46(2): 143–64

Dewe, P and M O'Driscoll (2002) Stress management interventions: what do managers actually do? *Personnel Review* 31(2): 143–65

Diehl, C and M Donnelly (2001) *How Did They Manage? Leadership Secrets of History*, London: Spiro Press

Digman, J M (1990) Personality structure: emergence of the five-factor model, *Annual Review of Psychology*, 41: 417–46

Dill, W (1958) Environment as an influence on managerial autonomy, *Administrative Science Quarterly* 2(3): 409–33

Dion, K L (1973) Cohesiveness as a determinant of ingroup–outgroup bias, *Journal of Personality and Social Psychology* 28(2): 163–71

Dixon, N M (2000) *Common Knowledge: How Companies Thrive by Sharing What They Know*, Boston: Harvard Business School Press

Doane, D (2003) Lip service brings no solutions, *The Guardian* 3 February: 25

Doherty, N and J Horsted (1995) Helping survivors stay on board, *People Management* January: 26–9

Donaldson, T and L E Preston (1995) The stakeholder theory of the corporation: concepts, evidence and implications, *Academy of Management Review* 20(1): 65–91

Donnelly, M and D Scholarios (1998) Workers' experiences of redundancy: evidence from Scottish defence-dependent companies, *Personnel Review* 27(4): 325–42

Dornbusch, S M, A H Hastorf, S A Richardson, R E Muzzy and R S Vreeland (1965) The perceivers and the perceived: their influence on categories of interpersonal perception, *Journal of Personality and Social Psychology* 1(3): 434–40

Doyle, C (2003) *Work and Organisational Psychology: An Introduction With Attitude*, Hove: Psychology Press

Drever, J (1964) *A Dictionary of Psychology*, Harmondsworth: Penguin

Drucker, P (1984) *The Practice of Management*, London: Heinemann

Drucker, P (1988) The coming of the new organisation, *Harvard Business Review*, January–February: 45–53

Dulewicz, S V and M J Higgs (1999) Can emotional intelligence be measured and developed? *Leadership and Organisational Development* 20(5): 242–52

Dulewicz, S V and M J Higgs (2000) 360 degree assessment of emotional intelligence, *Selection and Development Review* 16(3): 3–8

Dunegan, K, D Duchon and M Uhl-Bien (1992) Examining the link between leader–member exchange and subordinate performance: the role of task analyzability and variety as moderators, *Academy of Management Journal* 35(1): 59–76

Dunning, J N (1993) *The Globalisation of Business*, London: Thompson

Durkheim, E (1966) *The Division of Labour in Society*, New York: Free Press

E

Easton, G S (1993) The 1993 state of US Total Quality Management, *California Management Review* Spring: 32–54

Eaton, S C (2003) If you can use them: flexibility policies, organisational commitment and perceived performance, *Industrial Relations* 42(2): 145–67

EC (1996) *People First: Challenges of Living and Working in the European Information Society*, Brussels: European Commission

Eckman, P and W V Friesen (1975) *Unmasking the Face*, New York: Prentice Hall

Edwards, J E (1997) *How to Conduct Organisational Surveys*, Thousand Oaks, CA: Sage

Edwards, P K (1986) *Conflict at Work*, Oxford: Blackwell

Edwards, P K and C Whitston (1989) Industrial discipline, the control of attendance and subordination of labour: towards an integrated perspective, *Work, Employment and Society* 3(1): 1–28

Edwards, R (1979) *Contested Terrain: The Transformation of the Workplace in the Twentieth Century*, London: Heinemann

Ekstrand, B R (1972) To sleep, perchance to dream: about why we forget. In C P Duncan, L Sechrest and A W Melton (eds), *Human Memory*, New York: Appleton Century Crofts

Elkin, A J and P J Rosch (1990) Promoting mental health at the workplace: the prevention side of stress management, *Occupational Medicine: State of the Art Review* 5(4): 739–54

Epstein, S (1980) The stability of behaviour: implications for psychological research, *American Psychologist* 35: 790–806

Erera-Weatherley, P I (1996) Coping with stress: public welfare supervisors doing their best, *Human Relations* 49(2): 157–69

Erez, M (1992) Interpersonal communication systems in organisations and their relationship to cultural values, productivity and innovation: the case of Japanese corporations, *Applied Psychology: An International Review* 41(1): 43–64

Erez, M, C Early and C L Hulin (1985) The impact of participation on goal acceptance and performance: a two-step model, *Academy of Management Journal* 28(1): 50–66

Erlenmeyer-Kimling, I and L F Jarvik (1963) Genetics and intelligence: a review, *Science* 142(10): 1477–9

ESRC (2002) *Britain's World of Work – Myths and Realities*, London: Economic and Social Research Council

Etzioni, A (1964) *Modern Organizations*, Englewood Cliffs, NJ: Prentice Hall

Etzioni, A (1975) *A Comparative Analysis of Complex Organisations: On Power, Involvement and their Correlates*, rev. edn, New York: Free Press

Evans, B K and D G Fischer (1993) The nature of burnout: a study of the three-factor model of burnout in human service and non-human service samples, *Journal of Occupational and Organisational Psychology* 66(1): 29–38

Evans, M, H Gunz and M Jalland (1996) The aftermath of downsizing: a cautionary tale about restructuring and careers, *Business Horizons* May–June: 1–5

Eysenck, H J (1947) *Dimensions of Personality*, London: Routledge and Kegan Paul

Eysenck, H J (1970) *The Structure of Human Personality*, 3rd edn, London: Methuen

Eysenck, H J (1991) Dimensions of personality: 16, 5 or 3? – criteria for a taxonomic paradigm, *Personality and Individual Differences* 12(4): 773–90

F

Fagley, N S and P M Miller (1987) The effects of framing on choice of risks vs. certain options, *Organisational Behaviour and Human Decision Processes* 39(2): 264–77

Fang, T (1998) Reflection on Hofstede's 5th dimension: a critique of Confucian Dynamism, Paper presented at annual meeting of Academy of Management, San Diego, CA, August

Fayol, H (1916) *General and Industrial Management*, Trans. C Storrs (1946), London: Pitman

Fazio, R H and M P Zanna (1978) On the predictive validity of attitudes, *Journal of Personality* 46(2): 228–43

Feldman, D C (1984) The development and enforcement of group norms, *Academy of Management Review* 9(1): 47–53

Feldman, D C and H B Thompson (1992) Entry shock, culture shock; socialising the new breed of global managers, *Human Resource Management* Winter: 345–62

Feldman, J M (1981) Beyond attribution theory: cognitive processes in performance appraisal, *Journal of Applied Psychology* 66(2): 127–48

Feldman, M S and B T Pentland (2003) Reconceptualising organisational routines as a source of flexibility and change, *Administrative Science Quarterly* 48(1): 94–118

Feldman, M S and A Rafaeli (2002) Organisational routines as sources of connections and understandings, *Journal of Management Studies* 39(3): 309–31

Felstead, A, N Jewson and S Walters (2003) Managerial control of employees working at home, *British Journal of Industrial Relations* 41(2): 241–64

Fenton-O'Creevy, M (1995) Moderators of differences in job satisfaction between full-time and part-time female employees: a research note, *Human Resource Management Journal* 5(5): 75–81

Ferner, A and M Varul (2000) Vanguard subsidiaries and the diffusion of new practices: a case study of German multinationals, *British Journal of Industrial Relations* 38(1): 115–40

Ferris, G R, D D Frink, M C Galang, J Zhou, M C Kacmar and J L Howard (1996) Perceptions of organisational politics: prediction, stress-related implications and outcomes, *Human Relations* 49(2): 233–66

Ferris, G R, D D Frink, D C Gilmore, M C Kacmar (1994) Understanding as an antidote for the dysfunctional consequences of organisational politics as a stressor, *Journal of Applied Social Psychology* 24(6): 1204–20

Festinger, L (1957) *A Theory of Cognitive Dissonance*, Evanston, IL: Row Peterson

Fiedler, F E (1965) Engineering the job to fit the manager, *Harvard Business Review* September–October: 115–22

Fiedler, F E (1967) *A Theory of Leadership Effectiveness*, New York: McGraw-Hill

Fiedler, F E and J E Garcia (1987) *New Approaches to Effective Leadership: Cognitive Resources and Organisational Performance*, New York: Wiley

Finholt, T and I Sproull (1990) Electronic groups at work, *Organisation Science* 1(1): 41–64

Finkelstein, S and D C Hambrick (1996) *Strategic Leadership: Top Executives and Their Effects on Organisations*, St Paul, MN: West Publishing

Firth-Cozens, J and G E Hardy (1992) Occupational stress, clinical treatment and changes in job perceptions, *Journal of Occupational and Organisational Psychology* 65(2): 81–8

Fishbein, M and I Ajzen (1975) *Belief, Attitude, Intention and Behaviour*, Reading, MA: Addison-Wesley

Fisher, C D and R Gitelson (1983) A meta-analysis of the correlates of role conflict and ambiguity, *Journal of Applied Psychology* 63(3): 320–33

Fisher, S G, T A Hunter and W D K Macrosson (1998) The structure of Belbin's team roles, *Journal of Occupational and Organisational Psychology* 71(3): 283–8

Flach, F F (1974) *The Secret Strength of Depression*, Philadelphia, PA: Lippincott

Fleishman, E A (1953) The measurement of leadership attitudes in industry, *Journal of Applied Psychology* 38(1): 153–8

Fontana, D (1990) *Managing Stress*, New York: Routledge

Ford, J D and L W Ford (1995) The role of conversation in producing intentional change in organisations, *Academy of Management Review* 20(2): 541–70

Fox, A (1973) Industrial relations: a social critique of pluralist ideology. In J Child (ed.), *Man and Organisation*, New York: Halstead

Fox, M L, D J Dwyer and D C Ganster (1993) Effects of stressful job demands and control on physiological and attitudinal outcomes in a hospital setting, *Academy of Management Journal* 31(2): 289–318

Foy, N (1983) Networks of the world unite, *Personnel Management* March: 16–19

French, J and B Raven (1959) The bases of social power. In D Cartwright (ed.), *Studies in Social Power*, Ann Arbor, MI: Institute for Social Research

French, J R P and R D Caplan (1973) Organisational stress and individual strain. In A J Marrow (ed.), *The Failure of Success*, New York: AMACOM

French, W L and C H Bell (1999) *Organisation Development: Behavioural Science Interventions for Organisational Improvement*, 6th edn, Englewood Cliffs, NJ: Prentice Hall

Freud, S (1901a) *The Psychopathology of Everyday Life*, Trans. A Tyson (1975), Harmondsworth: Penguin

Freud, S (1901b) *The Ego Mechanisms of Defence*, Trans. A Tyson (1975), Harmondsworth: Penguin

Freud, S (1940) *An Outline of Psyhcoanalysis*, Trans. J Strachey (1969), London: Hogarth Press

Friedman, A (1977) *Industry and Labour*, London: Macmillan

Friedman, M and R Rosenman (1974) *Type A Behaviour and Your Heart*, New York: Knopf

Fromm, E (1942) *The Fear of Freedom*, London: Routledge and Kegan Paul

Frooman, J (1999) Stakeholder influence strategies, *Academy of Management Review* 24(2): 191–205

Fryer, D and R Payne (1986) Being unemployed: a review of the literature on the psychological experience of unemployment. In C L Cooper and I T Robertson (eds), *International Review of Industrial and Organisational Psychology*, Chichester: Wiley

Furnham, A (1990) Faking personality questionnaires: fabricating different profiles for different purposes, *Current Psychology: Research and Reviews* Spring: 45–55

Furnham, A (2000) Work in 2020: prognostications about the world of work 20 years into the millennium, *Journal of Managerial Psychology* 15(3): 1–10

Furnham, A and B Gunter (1993) Corporate culture: diagnosis and change. In C L Cooper and I T Robertson (eds), *International Review of Industrial and Organisational Psychology*, Chichester: Wiley

Furnham, A, H Steele and D Pendleton (1993) A psychometric assessment of the Belbin team-role self-perception inventory, *Journal of Occupational and Organisational Psychology* 66(3): 245–57

G

Gabriel, Y (1999) Beyond happy families: a critical re-evaluation of the control–resistance–identity triangle, *Human Relations* 52(2): 179–203

Gaines, J and J M Jermier (1983) Emotional exhaustion in high stress organisation, *Academy of Management Journal* 26(3): 567–86

Gandz, J and V V Murray (1980) The experience of workplace politics, *Academy of Management Journal* 15(2): 237–51

Gangé, R M (1974) *Essentials of Learning for Instruction*, Hinsdale, IL: Dryden

Ganzach, Y (1998) Intelligence and job satisfaction, *Academy of Management Journal* 41(5): 526–39

Garland, H (1990) Throwing good money after bad: the effect of sunk costs on the decision to escalate commitment to an ongoing project, *Journal of Applied Psychology* 74(6): 728–32

Garrett, T M and R J Klonoski (1992) *Business Ethics*, 3rd edn, Englewood Cliffs, NJ: Prentice Hall

Garten, J E (1992) *A Cold Peace*, New York: Times Books

Garton, L and B Wellman (1995) Social impacts of electronic mail in organisations: a review of the research literature. In B Burleston (ed.), *Communication Yearbook*, Vol. 18, Thousand Oaks, CA: Sage

Geary, J F and A Dobbins (2001) Teamworking: a new dynamic in the pursuit of management control, *Human Resource Management Journal* 11(1): 3–23

Geller, P A and S E Hobfall (1994) Gender differences in job stress, tedium and social support in the workplace, *Journal of Social and Personality Relationships* 11(4): 555–72

Gemmil, G R and W J Heiser (1972) Machiavellianism as a factor in managerial job strain, job satisfaction and upward mobility, *Academy of Management Journal* 15(1): 53–67

George, J M (1990) Personality, affect and behaviour in groups, *Journal of Applied Psychology* 75(2): 101–17

George J M and G R Jones (1997) Experiencing work: values, attitudes and moods, *Human Relations* 50(4): 393–416

Georgopoulos, B S and A S Tannenbaum (1957) A study of organisational effectiveness, *Sociological Review* 22(4): 534–40

Gibson, C B and M E Zellmer-Bruhn (2001) Metaphors and meanings: an intercultural analysis of the concept of teamwork, *Administrative Science Quarterly* 46(2): 274–303

Gibson, J L, J M Ivancevich and J H Donnelly (1994) *Organisations: Behaviour, Structure, Process*, 8th edn, Boston, MA: Irwin

Gilmore, T N, G P Shea and M Useem (1997) Side effects of corporate cultural transformations, *Journal of Applied Behavioural Science* 33(2): 174–89

Ginnett, R C (1990) The airline cockpit crew. In J R Hackman (ed.), *Groups That Work (and Those That Don't)*, San Francisco, CA: Jossey-Bass

Gist, M E and T R Mitchell (1992) Self-efficacy: a theoretical analysis of its determinism and malleability, *Academy of Management Review* 17(2): 183–211

Gleick, J (2003) Get out of my inbox, *Observer Review* 2 March: 1–2

Gleitman, H (1991) *Psychology*, 3rd edn, New York: Norton

Glick, W H, G D Jenkins and N Gupta (1986) Method versus substance: how strong are underlying relationships between job characteristics and attitudinal outcomes, *Academy of Management Journal* 29(3): 441–64

Godin, G and G Kok (1996) The theory of planned behaviour: a review of its application to health-related behaviours, *American Journal of Health Promotion* 11(1): 87–98

Goffee, R and G Jones (1998) *The Character of a Corporation: How Your Company's Culture Can Make or Break Your Business*, London: HarperCollins

Goffman, I (1971) *The Presentation of Self in Everyday Life*, Harmondsworth: Penguin

Goldberg, L R (1993) The structure of phenotypic personality traits, *American Psychologist* 48(1): 26–34

Goldstein, E (1998) *Sensation and Perception*, San Francisco: Jossey-Bass

Goldthorpe, J H, D Lockwood, F Bechofer and J Platt (1968) *The Affluent Worker: Industrial Attitudes and Behaviour*, Cambridge: Cambridge University Press

Goleman, D (1998) *Working With Emotional Intelligence*, London: Bloomsbury

Gordon, G G and N DiTomaso (1992) Predicting corporate performance from organisational culture, *Journal of Management Studies* 29(6): 783–96

Gordon, I E (1997) *Theories of Visual Perception*, 2nd edn, Chichester: Wiley

Gottesman, I I and J Shields (1972) *Schizophrenia and Genetics: A Twin Study Vantage Point*, New York: Academic Press

Gouldner, A W (1954) *Patterns of Industrial Bureaucracy*, New York: Free Press

Graen, G J, J B Orris and K Alvares (1971) The contingency model of leadership effectiveness: some experimental results, *Journal of Applied Psychology* 55(1): 196–201

Gray, M J (2003) Personality and performance, *Selection and Development Review* 19(1): 3–5

Green, C (1975) The reciprocal nature of influence between leader and subordinate, *Journal of Applied Psychology* 60(2): 187–93

Green, C (1979) Questions of causality in the path–goal theory of leadership, *Academy of Management Journal* 22(1): 22–41

Green, F (2001) It's been a hard day's night: the concentration and intensification of work in late twentieth century Britain, *British Journal of Industrial Relations* 39(1): 53–80

Greenberg, J (1996) 'Forgive me. I'm new': three experimental demonstrations of the effects of attempts to excuse poor performance, *Organizational Behaviour and Human Decision Processes* 66(2): 167–78

Greenley, G E and G R Foxall (1996) Consumer and nonconsumer stakeholder orientations in UK companies, *Journal of Business Research* 35(1): 105–16

Greenley, G E and G R Foxall (1997) Multiple stakeholder orientation in UK companies and the implications for company performance, *Journal of Management Studies* 34(2): 258–82

Greenwood, D J, W F Whyte and I Harkavy (1993) Participatory action research as a process and as a goal, *Human Relations* 46(2): 175–92

Grey, C and M Mitev (1995) Re-engineering organisations: a critical appraisal, *Personnel Review* 24(1): 6–18

Grey, R J and T J F Thone (1990) Differences between North American and European corporate cultures, *Canadian Business Review* Autumn: 26–30

Griffin, R W and G C McMahan (1994) Motivation through job design. In J Greenberg (ed.), *Organisational Behaviour: State of Science*, New York: Lawrence Erlbaum Associates

Grinyear, P H and M Yasai-Ardekani (1980) Dimensions of organizational structure: a critical replication, *Academy of Management Journal* 22(3): 405–21

Gross, B (1968) *Organisations and their Managing*, New York: Free Press

Guest, D (1992) Employee commitment and control. In J F Hartley and G M Stephenson (eds), *Employment Relations*, Oxford: Blackwell

Guest, D and C Conway (2002) Communicating the psychological contract: an employer perspective, *Human Resource Management Journal* 12(2): 22–38

Guzzo, R A and W Dickson (1998) Teams in organisations: recent research on performance and effectiveness, *Annual Review of Psychology*, Vol. 49: 307–38

Gwyther, M (1999) Voicemail hell, *Management Today*, 76–7

H

Hackman, J R and G R Oldham (1975) Development of the job diagnostic survey, *Journal of Applied Psychology* 60(2): 159–70

Hackman, J R and G R Oldham (1980) *Work Redesign*, New York: Addison-Wesley

Haire, M and W F Grunes (1950) Perceptual defenses: processes protection and organized perception of another personality, *Human Relations* 3(3): 403–12

Hakim, K (1990) Core and periphery in employers workforce strategies: evidence from the 1987 ELUS Survey, *Work, Employment and Society* 4(2): 157–88

Halaby, C H (2003) Where job values come from: family and schooling background, cognitive ability and gender, *American Sociological Review* 68(2): 251–78

Hall, D T (1987) Careers and socialization, *Journal of Management* 13(3): 291–308

Hall, D T and K E Nougain (1968) An examination of Maslow's need hierarchy in an organisational setting, *Organisational Behaviour and Human Performance* 3(1): 12–35

Hall, E (1966) *The Hidden Dimensions*, New York: Doubleday

Hall, E T and M R Hall (1990) *Understanding Cultural Differences*, Yarmouth, ME: Intercultural Press

Hall, J (1973) Communication revisited, *California Management Review* Fall: 56–67

Hall, R H (1980) Effectiveness theory and organisational effectiveness, *Journal of Applied Behaviourial Science* 16(2): 536–49

Hall, R H (1987) *Organisations: Structures, Processes and Outcomes*, Englewood Cliffs, NJ: Prentice-Hall

Hammer, M and J Champey (1993) *Reengineering the Corporation: A Manifesto for Business Transformation*, New York: Brearley

Hancock, P (1999) Baudrillard and the metaphysics of motivation: a reappraisal of corporate culturalism in the light of the work and ideas of Jean Baudrillard, *Journal of Management Studies* 36(2): 155–75

Handy, C (1995) Trust and the virtual organisation, *Harvard Business Review* May–June; 40–50

Hardy, C (ed.) (1995) *Power and Politics in Organisations*, Aldershot: Dartmouth Publishing

Hargie, O and D Tourish (eds) (2000) *Handbook of Communication Audits for Organisations*, London: Routledge

Harley, B (1999) The myth of empowerment: work organisation, hierarchy and employee autonomy in contemporary Australian workplaces, *Work, Employment and Society* 13(1): 41–68

Harris, L C (1996) Benchmarking against the theory of market orientation, *Management Decision* 34(2): 34–9

Harris, L C and E Ogbonna (1998) A three-perspective approach to understanding culture in retail organisations, *Personnel Review* 27(1/2): 104–23

Harris, L C and E Ogbonna (1999) Developing a market-oriented culture: a critical evaluation, *Journal of Management Studies* 36(2): 177–96

Harris, L C and E Ogbonna (2002) The unintended consequences of culture interventions: a study of unexpected outcomes, *British Journal of Management* 13(1): 31–49

Harrison, E F (1999) *The Managerial Decision-making Process*, 5th edn, Chicago: Houghton Mifflin

Harrison, R (1972) Understanding your organisation's character, *Harvard Business Review* May–June: 119–28

Harrison, R (2000) *Employee Development*, London: Institute of Personnel and Development

Harrison, R, H M Trice and J M Beyer (1984) Studying organizational cultures through rites and ceremonials, *Academy of Management Review* 9(4): 633–69

Hartley, J, J Bennington and P Binns (1997) Researching the roles of internal change agents in the management of organisational change, *British Journal of Management* 8(1): 61–73

Harvey, E (1968) Technology and the structure of organisations, *American Sociological Review* 33(2): 341–54

Harzing, A W and J V Ruysseveldt (1995) *International Human Resource Management*, London: Sage

Harzing, A W and A Sorge (2003) The relative impact of country of origin and universal contingencies on internationalisation strategies and corporate control in multinational enterprises: worldwide and European perspectives, *Organisation Studies* 24(2): 187–214

Hatch, M J (1997) *Organisation Theory: Symbolic and Postmodern Perspectives*, Oxford: Oxford University Press

Hayes, N (1997) *Successful Team Management*, London: Thompson

Heather, N (1976) *Radical Perspectives in Psychology*, London: Methuen

Hebb, D O (1949) *The Organization of Behaviour*, New York: Wiley

Hebden, J E (1986) Adopting an organization's culture: the socialisation of graduate trainees, *Organizational Dynamics* Summer: 54–72

Heider, F (1958) *The Psychology of Interpersonal Relations*, New York: Wiley

Heller, J F, M S Pallak and J M Picek (1973) The interactive effects of intent and threat on boomerang attitude change, *Journal of Personality and Social Psychology* 26(2): 273–9

Herbert, I C (1988) How Coke markets to the world: an interview with a marketing executive, *Journal of Business Strategy* September/October: 5–6

Hernstein, R J (1973) *IQ in the Meritocracy*, London: Allen Lane

Hersey, P and K H Blanchard (1988) *Management of Organizational Behaviour: Utilizing Human Resources*, 5th edn, Englewood Cliffs, NJ: Prentice Hall

Herzberg, F (1968) One more time: how do you motivate employees, *Harvard Business Review* 46(1): 53–62

Herzberg, F, B Mausner and B Synderman (1959) *The Motivation to Work*, London: Granada

Hewstone, M (1989) *Causal Attribution: From Cognitive Processes to Collective Beliefs*, Oxford: Blackwell

Hickman, G R (ed) (1998) *Leading Organisations: Perspectives for a New Era*, Thousand Oaks CA: Sage

Hickson, D J, C R Hinings, C A Lee, R E Schneck and J M Pennings (1971) A strategic contingencies theory of intraorganizational power, *Administrative Science Quarterly* 16(2): 216–29

Hickson D J and C J McMillan (1981) *Organisation and Nation: The Aston Programme IV*, Aldershot: Gower

Hinings, C R and R Greenwood (2002) Disconnects and consequences in organisation theory, *Administrative Science Quarterly* 47(3): 411–21

Hinings, C R, D J Hickson, J M Pennings and R E Schneck (1974) Structural conditions of intraorganizational power, *Administrative Science Quarterly* 19(1): 22–44

Hinings, C R, L Thibault, T Slack and L M Kikulis (1996) Values and organisational structure, *Human Relations* 49(7): 885–916

Hitt, M A and R D Ireland (1987) Peters and Waterman revisited: the unended quest for excellence, *Academy of Management Executive* 1: 91–8

Hodgetts, R M (1991) *Organisational Behaviour: Theory and Practice*, New York: Macmillan

Hodgetts, R M and F Luthans (1991) *International Management*, New York: McGraw-Hill

Hodgetts, R M and F Luthans (1994) *International Management*, 2nd edn, New York: McGraw-Hill

Hofstede, G (1980) *Culture's Consequences: International Differences in Work-related Values*, Beverly Hills, CA: Sage

Hofstede, G (1991) *Cultures and Organisations: Softwares of the Mind*, London: McGraw-Hill

Hofstede, G (1998) Identifying organisational subcultures: an empirical approach, *Journal of Management Studies* 35(1): 1–12

Hofstede, G (2001) *Culture's Consequences: Comparing Values, Behaviours, Institutions and Organisations*, 2nd edn, Thousand Oaks, CA: Sage

Hogg, M A and G M Vaughan (1998) *Social Psychology*, Hemel Hempstead: Prentice-Hall

Holbeche, L (1995) Peering into the future of careers, *People Management* May: 26–8

Holbeche, L (1997) *Motivating People in Lean Organisations*, London: Butterworth-Heinemann

Holden, L (1999) The perception gap in employee empowerment: a comparative study of banks in Sweden and Britain, *Personnel Review* 28(3): 222–41

Hollyforde, S and S Whiddett (2002) How to nurture motivation, *People Management* 11 July: 52–53

Holmes, T H and R H Rahe (1967) The social readjustment rating scale, *Journal of Psychosomatic Research* 26(2): 213–18

Homans, G C (1950) *The Human Group*, New York: Harcourt Brace and World

Honey, P and A Mumford (1992) *The Manual of Learning Styles*, Maidenhead: Peter Honey

Hope, V and J Hendry (1995) Corporate cultural change – is it relevant for organisations of the 1990s? *Human Resource Management Journal* 5(1): 61–73

Horner, M S (1970) Femininity and successful achievement: a basic inconsistency. In J Bardwich (ed.), *Feminine Personality and Conflict*, Belmont, CA: Brooks-Cole

House, R J (1971) A path–goal theory of leadership, *Administrative Science Quarterly* 16(2): 321–38

House, R J and M L Baetz (1979) Leadership: some empirical generalisations and new research directions. In B M Staw (ed.), *Research in Organisational Behaviour*, Vol. 1, Greenwich, CT: JAI Press

House, R J and L A Wigdor (1967) Herzberg's dual-factor theory of job satisfaction and motivation: a review of the evidence and a criticism, *Personnel Psychology* 20(4): 369–89

Howell, J P, D E Bowen, P W Dorfman, S Kerr and P M Podsakoff (1990) Substitutes for leadership: effective alternatives to ineffective leadership, *Organizational Dynamics* Summer: 20–38

Hsia, H J (1977) Redundancy: is it the lost key to better communication? *AV Communication Review* 25(1): 63–85

Huczynski, A and D Buchanan (2001) *Organisational Behaviour: An Introductory Text*, 4th edn, London: Prentice Hall

Hulse, S H, J Deese and N Egeth (1980) *The Psychology of Learning*, 5th edn, New York: McGraw-Hill

Hussein, R T (1989) Informal groups, leadership and productivity, *Leadership and Organization Development Journal* 10(1): 9–16

Hutton, W (1995) *The State We're In*, London: Vintage

I

Ingram, P N (1991) Changes in working practices in British manufacturing in the 1980s: a study of employee concessions made during wage negotiations, *British Journal of Industrial Relations* 29(1): 1–13

IPD (1998) *Stress at Work: Key Facts*, London: Institute of Personnel and Development, October

Ivancevich, J M and J H Donnelly (1975) Relations of organisational structure to job satisfaction, *Administrative Science Quarterly* 20(2): 272–80

Ivancevich, J M and M T Matteson (1993) *Organisational Behaviour and Management*, 3rd edn, Homewood, IL: Irwin

Ivancevich, J M, M T Matteson, S M Freedman and J S Phillips (1990) Worksite stress management interventions, *American Psychologist* 45(2): 252–61

Iverson, R D and D M Buttigieg (1999) Affective, normative and continuance commitment: can the 'right kind' of commitment be managed? *Journal of Management Studies* 36(3): 307–33

J

Jackson, C (1996) *Understanding Psychological Testing*, Leicester: BPS Books

Jackson, S E (1983) Participation in decision making as a strategy for reducing job-related strain, *Journal of Applied Psychology* 68(1): 3–19

Jago, A G (1982) Leadership: perspectives in theory and research, *Management Science* 28(3): 297–318

James, L R and A P Jones (1974) Organisational climate: a review of theory and research, *Psychological Bulletin* 83(8): 1096–1112

Janis, I L (1972) *Victims of Groupthink*, Boston, MA: Houghton Mifflin

Janis, I L and S Feshback (1953) Effects of fear-arousing communications, *Journal of Abnormal and Social Psychology* 48(1): 78–92

Jaques, E (1952) *The Changing Culture of a Factory*, London: Tavistock

Jaques, E (1990) In praise of hierarchy, *Harvard Business Review* January–February: 127–33

Jehn, K A (1997) A qualitative analysis of conflict types and dimensions in organisational groups, *Administrative Science Quarterly* 42(3): 530–7

Jermier, J M, D Knights and W R Nord (1994) *Resistance and Power in Organisations*, London: Routledge

Jex, S M, G A Adams, T C Elacqua and D G Bachrach (2002) Type 'A' as a moderator of stressors and job complexity: a comparison of achievement striving and impatience-irritability, *Journal of Applied Social Psychology* 32(5): 977–96

John, R, G I Gillies, H Cox and N Grimswade (1997) *Global Business Strategy: An Introduction*, London: Thomson

Johnson, G and K Scholes (1999) *Exploring Corporate Strategy: Text and Cases*, 5th edn, Hemel Hempstead: Prentice Hall

Johnson, P and J Gill (1993) *Management Control and Organisational Behaviour*, London: Sage

Jones, E E and R E Nisbett (1972) The actor and the observer: divergent perceptions of the causes of behaviour. In E E Jones, D H Kanouse, H H Kelly, R E Nisbett, S Valins and B Weiner (eds), *Attribution: Perceiving the Causes of Behaviour*, Morristown, NJ: General Learning Press

Jones, F and B C Fletcher (1993) An empirical study of occupational stress transmission in working couples, *Human Relations* 46(7): 881–903

Jones, G R (1995) *Organisation Theory: Text and Cases*, Reading, MA: Addison-Wesley

Jones, R (2000) Grounded by the fiasco in cyberspace, *The Guardian* 5 August: 2–3

Jordan, P C (1986) Effects of extrinsic reward on intrinsic motivation: a field experiment, *Academy of Management Journal* 29(2): 405–12

Judge, T A, J E Bono, R Illes and M W Gerhardt (2002) Personality and leadership: a qualitative and quantitative review, *Journal of Applied Psychology* 87(4): 765–80

Judge, T A, C A Higgins, C J Thoresen and M R Barrick (1999) The Big Five personality traits, general mental ability and career success across life span, *Personnel Psychology* 52(3): 621–52

Judge, T A and E A Locke (1993) Effect of dysfunctional thought processes on subjective wellbeing and job satisfaction, *Journal of Applied Psychology* 78(3): 475–90

Jung, C G (1960) The structure and dynamics of the psyche. In H Read *et al.* (eds) *The Collected Works of C G Jung*, Vol. 8, London: Routledge and Kegan Paul

K

Kahn, R L, D M Wolfe, R P Quinn, J D Snoek and R A Rosenthal (1964) *Organisational Stress*, New York: Wiley

Kahneman, D and A Tversky (2000) *Choices, Values and Frames*, Cambridge: Cambridge University Press

Kallenberg, A L (2001) Organising flexibility: the flexible firm in a new century, *British Journal of Industrial Relations* 39(4): 479–504

Kamin, L (1977) *The Science and Politics of IQ*, Harmondsworth: Penguin

Kanfer, R (1992) Work motivation: new directions in theory and research. In I Robertson and C L Cooper (eds) *International Review of Industrial and Organisational Psychology*, Vol. 74, Chichester: Wiley

Kanter, R M (1995) *The Change Masters: Corporate Entrepreneurs at Work*, London: Unwin-Hyman

Kanter, R M, B A Stein and T Jick (1992) *The Challenge of Organisational Change: How Companies Experience It and Leaders Guide It*, New York: Free Press

Katz, D (1960) The functional approach to the study of attitudes, *Public Opinion Quarterly* 24(2): 163–204

Katz, D and R L Kahn (1978) *The Social Psychology of Organisations*, 2nd edn, New York: Wiley

Katzenbach, J R and D K Smith (1993) *The Wisdom of Teams: Creating the High Performance Organisation*, Boston, MA: Harvard Business School Press

Keeley, M (1984) Impartiality and participant interest theories of organisational effectiveness, *Administrative Science Quarterly* 28(1): 1–23

Keller, R T (1986) Predictors of the performance of project groups in research and development organisations, *Academy of Management Review* 11(4): 715–26

Kelley, H H (1967) Attribution theory in social psychology. In D Levine (ed.), *Nebraska Symposium on Motivation*, Vol. 15, Lincoln, NB: University of Nebraska Press

Kellner, P (1996) Don't bash the unions, *The Observer*, 4 August: 17

Kelly, G A (1955) *The Psychology of Personal Constructs*, Vols 1 and 2, New York: Norton

Kelly, J (1992) Does job re-design theory explain job re-design outcomes, *Human Relations* 45(8): 753–74

Kelly, J and N Nicholson (1980) The causation of strikes: a review of theoretical approaches and the potential contribution of social psychology, *Human Relations* 33(12): 853–83

Kenny, D A and S J Zaccaro (1983) An estimate of variance due to traits in leadership, *Journal of Applied Psychology* 68(4): 678–85

Kenyon, W (2003) How to create a policy for whistle-blowing, *People Management* 20 February: 56–7

Kerr, S and J M Jermier (1978) Substitutes for leadership: their meaning and measurement, *Organisational Behaviour and Human Performance* 22(3): 375–403

Kets de Vries, M F (1998) Charisma in action: the transformational abilities of Virgin's Richard Branson and ABB's Percy Barnevik, *Organisational Dynamics* 26(3): 7–21

Kets de Vries, M F R and D Miller (1984) *The Neurotic Organisation*, San Francisco, CA: Jossey-Bass

Kets de Vries, M F R and K Balazs (1997) The downside of downsizing, *Human Relations* 50(1): 11–50

Khandwalla, R N (1981) Properties of competing organizations. In W H Starbuck and P C Nystrom (eds), *Handbook of Organizational Design, Vol. 1: Adapting Organizations to their Environments*, New York: Oxford University Press

Kiecolt-Glaser, J and R Glaser (1987) Psychosocial moderators of immune function, *Annals of Behaviour Medicine* Summer: 16–20

Kiev, A and V Kohn (1979) *Executive Stress: An AMA Survey Report*, New York: American Management Association

Kilmann, R H, M J Saxton and R Serpa (1985) *Gaining Control of the Corporate Culture*, San Francisco, CA: Jossey-Bass

Kinnie, N, S Hutchinson and J Purcell (1998) Downsizing: is it always lean and mean? *Personnel Review* 27(4): 296–311

Kinnie, N and J Purcell (1998) Side effects, *People Management* April: 34–6

Kipnis, D, S M Schmidt, C Swaffin-Smith and I Wilkinson (1984) Patterns of managerial influence: shotgun managers, tacticians and bystanders, *Organizational Dynamics* Winter: 58–67

Kirkpatrick, S A and E A Locke (1991) Leadership: do traits matter? *Academy of Management Executive* May: 48–60

Knights, D and D McCabe (2000) Ain't misbehavin'? Opportunities for resistance under new forms of quality management, *Sociology* 34(3): 421–36

Kobasa, S C, S R Maddi and S Kahn (1982) Hardiness and health: a perspective study, *Journal of Personality and Social Psychology* 42(2): 168–77

Koch, R (2002) *The 80/20 Revolution*, London: Nicholas Brearley

Koffman, F and P Senge (1993) Communities of commitment: the heart of learning organisation, *Organisational Dynamics* Autumn: 5–23

Kohlberg, L (1968) The child as a moral philosopher, *Psychology Today* 2(1): 25–30

Kolb, D A and R Fry (1975) Towards an applied theory of experiential learning. In C L Cooper (ed.), *Theories of Group Processes*, Chichester: Wiley (pp. 33–57)

Kolb, D A, J M Rubin and J McIntyre (1974) *Organizational Psychology: An Experimental Approach*, 2nd edn, Englewood Cliffs, NJ: Prentice-Hall

Kotter, J P (1988) *The Leadership Process*, New York: Free Press

Kotter, J P (1990) What do leaders really do? *Harvard Business Review* 68: 103–11

Kotter, J P (1995) Leading change: why transformation efforts fail, *Harvard Business Review*, March/April: 59–67

Kotter, J P and J L Heskett (1992) *Corporate Culture and Performance*, New York: Macmillan

Kotter, J P and L A Schlesinger (1979) Choosing strategies for change, *Harvard Business Review*, March/April: 106–14

Kotter, J P, L A Schlesinger and V Sathe (1986) *Organisation: Text Cases and Readings in Organizational Design and Change*, 2nd edn, Homewood, IL: Irwin

Koys, D J and T A DeCotis (1991) Inductive measures of psychological climate, *Human Relations* 44(3): 265–85

Kozlowski, S W, G T Chao, E M Smith and J Hedlund (1993) Organisational downsizing strategies, interventions and research implications. In C L Cooper and I T Robertson (eds), *International Review of Industrial and Organizational Psychology*, New York: Wiley

Kozlowski, S W J and M Doherty (1989) Integration of climate and leadership: examination of a neglected issue, *Journal of Applied Psychology* 74(5): 546–53

Krantz, J (1999) Comment on challenging resistance to change, *Journal of Applied Behavioural Science* 35(1): 42–4

Kraut, R and R Fish (1997) Prospects for videotelephony. In K Finn, A Sellen and S Wilbur (eds), *Video-mediated Communication*, Mahwah, NJ: Lawrence Erlbaum Associates

Kreitner, R and A Kinicki (1995) *Organisational Behaviour*, 3rd edn, Chicago, IL: Irwin

Kremer, J M D and J Marks (1992) Sexual harassment: the response of management and trade unions, *Journal of Occupational and Organizational Psychology* 65(1): 5–15

Kren, L (1992) The moderating effects of locus of control on performance incentives and participation, *Human Relations* 45(9): 991–1012

Kvale, S (ed.) (1992) *Psychology and Postmodernism*, London: Sage

L

Laing, R D (1972) *Knots*, Harmondsworth: Penguin

Lang, J R, J E Dittrich and S E White (1978) Management problem-solving models: a review and proposals, *Academy of Management Review* 3(4): 854–65

Larwood, L, P Rand and A Der Hovanessian (1979) Sex difference in response to simulated disciplinary cases, *Personnel Psychology* 32(4): 539–50

Latham, G P and E A Locke (1979) Goal-setting: a motivational technique that works, *Organisational Dynamics* Autumn: 68–80

Latham, G P and T P Steele (1983) The motivational effects of participation versus goal setting on performance, *Academy of Management Journal* 26(3): 406–17

Lawrence, P R and J W Lorsch (1969) *Organisation and Environment: Managing Differentiation and Integration*, Homewood, IL: Irwin

Lazarus, R S (1966) *Psychological Stress and the Coping Process*, New York: McGraw-Hill

Lazarus, R S (1971) *Personality*, New York: Prentice Hall

Lazarus, R S and S Folkman (1984) Coping and adaptation. In W D Gentry (ed.), *Handbook of Behavioural Medicine*, New York: Guilford Press

Leavitt, H J (1951) Some effects of certain patterns on group performance, *Journal of Abnormal and Social Psychology* 46(1): 38–50

Lee, R and P Lawrence (1985) *Organisational Behaviour: Politics at Work*, London: Hutchinson

Legge, K (1995) *Human Resource Management: Rhetorics and Realities*, London: Macmillan

Lengel, R H and R L Daft (1988) The selection of communication media as an executive skill, *Academy of Management Executive* August: 225–32

Lenway, S A and K Rehbein (1991) Leaders, followers and free riders: an empirical test of variation in corporate political involvement, *Academy of Management Journal* 26(6): 893–905

Leonard, N H, L L Beauvais and R W Scholl (1999) Work motivation: the incorporation of self-based processes, *Human Relations* 52(8): 969–97

Levitt, B and C Nass (1984) The lid on the garbage can: institutional constraints on decision making in the technical core of college text publishers, *Administrative Science Quarterly* 29(2): 190–207

Lewin, K (1951) *Field Theory in Social Science*, New York: Harper and Row

Lewin, K, R Lippit and R K White (1939) Patterns of aggressive behaviour in experimentally created social climates, *Journal of Social Psychology* 10(2): 271–99

Lewis, P S, S H Goodman and P M Fandt (1995) *Management: Challenges in the 21st Century*, St Paul, MN: West Publishing

Lewis, S N and C L Cooper (1987) Stress in two-earner couples and stage in the life cycle, *Journal of Occupational Psychology* 60(4): 289–304

Likert, R (1932) A technique for the measurement of attitudes, *Archives of Psychology* 22(1): 1–55

Likert, R (1961) *New Patterns in Management*, New York: McGraw-Hill

Lim, V K G (1996) Job insecurity and its outcomes: moderating effects of work-based and nonwork-based social support, *Human Relations* 40(2): 171–94

Lind, J S (1990) Improving process consultation on business and organisations, *International Journal of Technology Management* 5(6): 742–5

Lipshitz, R and O Strauss (1997) Coping with uncertainty: a naturalistic decision-making analysis, *Organisational Behaviour and Human Decision Processes* 69(2): 149–63

Little, B R (1969) Sex differences and comparability of three measures of cognitive complexity, *Psychological Reports* 24(5): 607–9

Littlefield, D (1996) Oxfam calls on firms to adopt labour code, *People Management* June: 6

Litwin, G H and R A Stringer (1968) *Motivation and Organizational Climate*, Boston, MA: Harvard University Graduate School of Business Administration

Locke, E A (1968) Towards a theory of task performance and incentives, *Organisational Behaviour and Human Performance* 3(2): 157–89

Locke, E A (1976) The nature and cause of job satisfaction. In M D Dunnette (ed.), *Handbook of Industrial and Organizational Psychology*, Chicago, IL: Rand McNally

Locke, E A (1977) The myths of behaviour mod. in organisations, *Academy of Management Review* 2(3): 543–53

Locke, E A and G P Latham (1990) *A Theory of Goal Setting and Task Performance*, Englewood Cliffs, NJ: Prentice-Hall

Locke, E A, K N Shaw, L M Saari and G P Latham (1981) Goal setting and task performance 1969–1980, *Psychological Bulletin* 82(2): 127–40

Long, P (1986) *Performance Appraisal Revisited*, London: Institute of Personnel Management

Lord, R G, C L De Valder and G M Allinger (1986) A meta-analysis of the relation between personality traits and leadership perceptions: an application of validity generalisation procedures, *Journal of Applied Psychology* 71(3): 396–419

Lord, W and J Rust (2003) The big five revisited: where are we now? *Selection and Development Review* 19(4): 15–18

Lowe, R and P Bennett (2003) Exploring coping reactions to work stress: application of an appraisal theory, *Journal of Occupational and Organisational Psychology* 76(3): 393–400

Lucas, E (2002) The feelgood factor, *Professional Manager* July: 19–20

Luchak, A A (2003) What kind of voice do employees use? *British Journal of Industrial Relations* 41(1): 115–41

Lukes, S (1974) *Power*, London: Macmillan

Luthans, F (1995) *Organizational Behaviour*, 7th edn, New York: McGraw-Hill

Luthans, F and R Kreitner (1985) *Organizational Behaviour Modification and Beyond*, Glenview, IL: Scott Foresman

Luthans, F and J K Larsen (1986) How managers really communicate, *Human Relations* 39(2): 161–78

M

Maccoby, M (2000) Narcissistic leaders: incredible pros and the inevitable cons, *Harvard Business Review*, Vol. 78: 69–77

MacCrimmon, K R (1974) Managerial decision making. In J W McGuire (ed.), *Contemporary Management*, Englewood Cliffs, NJ: Prentice-Hall

MacCrimmon, K R and D Wehrung (1986) *Taking Risks*, New York: Free Press

Macduffie, J P (1995) Human resource bundles and manufacturing performance: organizational logic and flexible production systems in the world auto industry, *Industrial and Labor Relations Review* 48(2): 107–21

Machiavelli, N (1958) *The Prince* (English translation), London: Everyman

Mackay, C and T Cox (1984) Occupational stress associated with visual display unit operation. In B G Pearce (ed.), *Health Hazards and VDUs*, Chichester: Wiley

Madison, D L, R W Allen, L W Porter, P A Renwick and B T Mayes (1980) Organizational politics: an exploration of manager's perceptions, *Human Relations* 33(2): 79–100

Mahoney, T A and P J Frost (1974) The role of technology in models of organizational effectiveness, *Organizational Behaviour and Human Performance* 11(1): 126–38

Malnight, T W (2001) Emerging structural patterns within multinational corporations: towards process based structures, *Academy of Management Journal* 44(6): 1187–1210

Makin, P, C L Cooper and C Cox (1996) *Organisations and the Psychological Contract*, Leicester: British Psychological Society

Manocha, R (2002) Code allows for closer monitoring of staff, *People Management* 27 June: 7

Mansfield, R and R L Payne (1977) Correlates of variance in perceptions of organizational climate. In D S Pugh and R L Payne (eds), *Organizational Behaviour in its Context: The Aston Programme III*, Farnborough: Saxon House

Manz, C C and H P Simms (1981) Vicarious learning: the influence of modelling on organisational behaviour, *Academy of Management Review* 6(1): 105–13

March, J G (1982) Theories of choice and making decisions, *Social Science and Modern Society* 20(1): 29–39

March, J G and H A Simon (1958) *Organizations*, New York: Wiley

Marchington, M and A Wilkinson (1996) *Core Personnel and Development*, London: Institute of Personnel and Development

Marginson, P, P Armstrong, P K Edwards and J Purcell (1995) Extending beyond borders: multinational companies in the international management of labour, *International Journal of Human Resource Management* 6(3): 702–19

Marshall, A (1891) *Principles of Economics*, 2nd edn, London: Macmillan

Martin, J (1992) *Cultures and Organisations: Three Perspectives*, Oxford: Oxford University Press

Martin, J and M Power (1983) Truth or corporate propaganda: the value of a good war story. In L Pondy, P J Frost, G Morgan and T C Dandridge (eds), *Organisational Symbolism*, Greenwich, CT: JAI Press

Martin, X, A Swaminathan and W Mitchell (1998) Organisational evolution in the international environment: incentives and constraints in international expansion strategy, *Administrative Science Quarterly* 43(3): 566–601

Marx, K (1894/1972) *Capital*, Vol. 3, London: Lawrence Wishart

Maslow, A H (1954) *Motivation and Personality*, New York: Harper and Row

Mathieu, J E and D M Zanjoc (1990) A review and meta-analysis of the antecedents, correlates and consequences of organisational commitment, *Psychological Bulletin* 108(2): 171–99

Maurice, M, A Sorge and M Warner (1980) Societal differences in organising manufacturing units: a comparison of France, West Germany and Britain, *Organization Studies* 1(1): 59–86

Mayo, E (1933) *The Human Problems of Industrial Civilization*, New York: Macmillan

McAndrew, F T, A Akande, R Bridgstock, L Mealy, S C Gordon, J E Scheibe, B E Akande-Adetoun, F Odewale, A Morakinyo, P Nyahete and G M Mubavakane (2000) A multicultural study of stereotyping in English speaking countries, *Journal of Social Psychology* 140(4): 487–502

McCabe, D (1996) The best laid schemes O'TQM: strategy, politics and power, *New Technology, Work and Employment* 11(1): 28–38

McCall, G J and J L Simmons (1966) *Identities and Interactions*, New York: Free Press

McClelland, D C (1967) *The Achieving Society*, New York: Free Press

McClelland, D C (1971) *Motivational Trends in Society*, Morristown, NJ: General Learning Press

McClelland, D C and R E Boyatzis (1982) Leadership motive pattern and long-term success in management, *Journal of Applied Psychology* 67(4): 737–43

McCrae, R R and P T Costa (1990) *Personality in Adulthood*, New York: Guilford Press

McGill, M E and J W Slocum (1993) Unlearning the organisation, *Organisational Dynamics* Autmn: 82–91

McGinnies, E (1949) *Social Behaviour: A Functional Analysis*, Boston, MA: Houghton Mifflin

McNeill, D (2000) *The Face*, London: Penguin

Mehrabian, A (1971) *Silent Messages*, Belmont, CA: Wadsworth

Meindl, J R, S R Ehrlich and J M Dukerich (1987) The romance of leadership and the evaluation of organisational performance, *Academy of Management Review* 12(1): 91–109

Mendenhall, M E, B J Punnett and D Ricks (1995) *Global Management*, Cambridge, MA: Blackwell

Merrick, N (1997) Business chiefs take to stakeholding ideal, *People Management* May: 12

Merton, R K (1957) *Social Theory and Social Structure*, Glencoe, IL: Free Press

Meyer, J P and N J Allen (1997) *Commitment in the Workplace: Theory, Research and Application*, London: Sage

Miceli, M P, M Rehg, J P Near and K C Ryan (1999) Can laws protect whistle-blowers? Results of a naturally occurring field experiment, *Work and Occupations* 26(1): 129–51

Michaelsen, L K, W E Watson and R H Black (1989) A realistic test of individual versus group consensus decision making, *Journal of Applied Psychology* 69(4): 834–9

Middleton, R (1983) *A Briefer's Guide to Team Briefing*, London: The Industrial Society

Miles, R E and C Snow (1978) *Organizational Strategy, Structure and Process*, New York: McGraw-Hill

Miles, R E and C Snow (1986) Network organisations: new concepts for new forms, *California Management Review* 28(1): 62–73

Miles, R H (1980) *Macro Organisational Behaviour*, Santa Monica, CA: Goodyear

Miles, R H (1982) *Coffin Nails and Corporate Strategies*, Englewood Cliffs, NJ: Prentice-Hall

Miles, T R (1957) Contributions to intelligence testing and the theory of intelligence: on defining intelligence, *British Journal of Educational Psychology* 27(2): 153–65

Milgram, S (1965) Some conditions of obedience and disobedience to authority, *Human Relations* 18(1): 57–76

Miller, D (1994) What happens after success: the perils of excellence, *Journal of Management Studies* 31(3): 325–58

Miller, G A (1956) The magical number seven, plus or minus two: some limits on our capacity for processing information, *Psychological Review* 63(1): 81–97

Miner, F C (1984) Group versus individual decision making: an investigation of performance measures, decision strategies and process losses and gains, *Organisational Behaviour and Human Performance* February: 112–24

Mintzberg, H (1979) *The Structuring of Organizations*, Englewood Cliffs, NJ: Prentice Hall

Mintzberg, H (1983) *Power In and Around Organizations*, Englewood Cliffs, NJ: Prentice Hall

Mintzberg, H (1985) The organisation as political arena, *Journal of Management Studies* 22(2): 133–54

Mischel, W (1977) The interaction of person and situation. In D Magnusson and N S Endler (eds), *Personality at the Crossroads: Current Issues in Interactional Psychology*, Hillsdale, NJ: Lawrence Erlbaum Associates

Mishra, J (1990) Managing the grapevine, *Public Personnel Management* Summer: 213–28

Mitchell, D (1979) *Control without Bureaucracy*, London: McGraw-Hill

Mitchell, R K, B R Agle and D J Wood (1997) Toward a theory of stakeholder identification and salience: defining the principles of who and what really counts, *Academy of Management Review* 22(4): 853–86

Mitchell, T R (1982) Motivation: new directions for theory, research and practice, *Academy of Management Review* 7(1): 80–8

Mitchell, T R (1973) Motivation and participation: an integration, *Academy of Management Journal* 16(2): 160–79

Mitchell, T R, S G Green and R Wood (1981) An attributional model of leadership and the poor performing subordinate. In L L Cummings and B M Staw (eds), *Research in Organizational Behaviour*, Vol. 3, Greenwich CT: JAI Press

Mitchell, T R and L S Kalb (1982) Effects of job experience on supervisor's attributions for poor performance, *Journal of Applied Psychology* 62(2): 181–8

Mitchell, T R and R E Wood (1980) Supervisors' responses to subordinate poor performance: a test of an attributional model, *Organisational Behaviour and Human Performance* 25(2): 123–38

Monk, T and D Tepas (1985) Shift work. In C L Cooper and M J Smith (eds), *Job Stress and Blue-collar Work*, Chichester: Wiley

Monks, J (1999) Ready, willing and able, *People Management* May: 29

Monson, T C, J W Hesley and L Chernick (1982) Specifying when personality traits cannot predict behaviour: an alternative to abandoning the attempt to predict single action criteria, *Journal of Personality and Social Psychology* 43(3): 358–65

Moore, J D (1997) *Visions of Culture: An Introduction to Anthropological Theories and Theorists*, London: Sage

Moorhead, G and R W Griffin (1995) *Organizational Behaviour*, 4th edn, Boston, MA: Houghton Mifflin

Moreland, R L and R B Zajonc (1979) Exposure effects may not depend on stimulus recognition, *Journal of Personality and Social Psychology* 37(5): 1085–9

Morgan, G (1989) *Creative Organisation Theory: A Resourcebook*, London: Sage

Morgan, G (1997) *Images of Organisation*, London: Sage

Morris, J R, W F Cascio and C E Young (1999) Downsizing after all these years: questions and answers about who did it, how many did it, and who benefited from it, *Organisational Dynamics* Winter: 78–87

Morris, T, H Lydka and M Fenton-O'Creevy (1993) Can commitment be managed? A longitudinal analysis of employee commitment and human resource policies, *Human Resource Management Journal* 3(3): 21–42

Moss, L (1981) *Management Stress*, Reading, MA: Addison-Wesley

Mowday, R T, R M Steers and L W Porter (1979) The measure of organisational commitment, *Journal of Vocational Behaviour* 14(3): 224–47

Mulholland, K (2002) Gender, emotional labour and teamworking in a call centre, *Personnel Review* 31(3): 283–303

Mulinge, M M (2001) Employer control of employees: extending the Lincoln–Kallenberg corporatist model of satisfaction and attachment, *Human Relations* 54(3): 285–318

Mullins, L J (1999) *Management and Organisational Behaviour*, 5th edn, London: Pitman

Mullins, L J (2002) *Management and Organisational Behaviour*, 6th edn, Harlow: Financial Times/Prentice Hall

Mumford, E and R Hendricks (1996) Business process re-engineering RIP, *People Management* 2 May: 22–9

Muna, F A (1980) *The Arab Executive*, London: St Martin's Press

Murdoch, A (1998) Human re-engineering, *Management Today* March: 66–70

Murphy, K R, R A Jako and R L Anhalt (1993) Nature and consequences of halo error: a critical analysis, *Journal of Applied Psychology* 77(2): 215–29

Murphy, M G and K M Davey (2002) Ambiguity, ambivalence and indifference in organisational values, *Human Resource Management Journal* 12(1): 3–16

Murray, F and H Willmott (1997) Putting information technology in its place: towards flexible integration in the network age? In B Bloomfield, R Coombs, D Knights and D Littler (eds), *Information Technology and Organisations*, Oxford: Oxford University Press

N

Nadler, D and M Tushman (1986) *Managing Strategic Organisational Change: Frame Binding and Frame Breaking*, New York: Delta Consulting Group

Natvany, I (1996) *Putting Pressure to Work*, London: IPD and Pitman

Naughton, J (2000) Any fool can create their own e-commerce site: many do so, *The Observer* 23 July: 10

Naylor, K (1994) Part-time working in Great Britain – an historical analysis, *Employment Gazette* December: 473–85

Neck, C P, M L Connerley, C A Zuniga and S Goel (1999) Family therapy meets self-managing teams: explaining self-managing team performance through team member perceptions, *Journal of Applied Behavioural Science* 35(2): 245–59

Negroponte, N (1995) *Being Digital*, London: Hodder and Stoughton

Neisser, U (1976) *Cognition and Reality*, San Francisco, CA: Freeman

Nelson, R E and S Gopalan (2003) Do organisational cultures replicate national cultures? Isomorphism, rejection and reciprocal opposition in the corporate values of three countries, *Organisation Studies* 24(7): 1115–51

Nemetz, P L and S L Christensen (1996) The challenge of cultural diversity: harnessing a diversity of views to understand multiculturalism, *Academy of Management Review* 21(2): 434–62

Newby, H (1977) *The Deferential Worker*, Harmondsworth: Penguin

Newman, K L and S D Nollen (1996) Culture and congruence: the fit beween management practice and national culture, *Journal of International Business Studies* 27(4): 753–79

Newton, T J (1994) Discourse and agency: the example of personnel psychology and assessment centres, *Organization Studies* 15(6): 879–902

Nichols, R G (1962) Listening is good business, *Management of Personnel Quarterly* 1(2): 2–10

Nichols, T and P Armstrong (1976) *Workers Divided*, London: Fontana

Nohria, N and J Berkley (1994) The virtual organisation: bureacracy, technology and the implosion of control. In C Heckscher and A Donnelon (eds), *The Post-bureaucratic Organisation*, Thousand Oaks, CA: Sage

Nohria, N and R Eccles (1992) Face-to-face: making nework organisations work. In N Nohria and R Eccles (eds), *Networks and Organisation*, Boston, MA: Harvard Business Press

Nonaka, I and H Takeuchi (1995) *The Knowledge Creating Company*, New York: Oxford University Press

Noon, M and R Delbridge (1993) News from behind my hand: gossip in organisations, *Organisation Studies* 14(1): 23–36

Northouse, P G (1997) *Leadership: Theory and Practice*, London: Sage

Nunamaker, J (1997) Future research in group support systems: needs, some questions and possible directions, *International Journal of Human-Computer Studies* 47(3): 357–85

O

O'Connor, E S (1999) The politics of management thought: a case study of the Harvard Business School and the Human Relations School, *Academy of Management Review* 24(1): 117–31

O'Leary, A (1990) Stress, emotion and human immune functioning, *Psychological Bulletin* 99(3): 363–82

O'Reilly, C A (1977) Supervisors and peers as information sources, group supportiveness and individual performance, *Journal of Applied Psychology* 62(5): 632–5

O'Reilly, C A and L R Pondy (1979) Organisational communication. In S Kerr (ed.), *Organisational Behaviour*, Columbus, OH: Grid

O'Reilly, C A and K H Roberts (1977) Task group structure, communication and effectiveness in three organisations, *Journal of Applied Psychology* 62(6): 674–81

Oakland, S and A Ostell (1996) Measuring coping: a review and critique, *Human Relations* 49(2): 133–55

Oborne, D J (1994) *Computers at Work: A Behaviourial Approach*, 3rd edn, Chichester: Wiley

Ogbonna, E (1993) Managing organisational culture: fantasy or reality? *Human Resource Management Journal* 3(2): 42–53

Orbell, S (2003) Personality systems interaction theory and the theory of planned behaviour: evidence that self-regulatory volitional components enhance enactment of studying behaviour, *British Journal of Social Psychology* 42(1): 95–112

Organ, D W and T S Bateman (1991) *Organisational Behaviour*, 4th edn, Homewood, IL: Irwin

Osgood, C E, W H May and M S Miron (1975) *Cross-cultural Universals of Affective Meaning*, Urbana, IL: University of Illinois Press

Osgood, C E, G J Suci and P H Tannenbaum (1957) *The Measurement of Meaning*, Urbana, IL: University of Illinois Press

Ostell, A, I Macfarlane and A Jackson (1980) Evaluating the impact of a communication exercise in an industrial works, *Industrial Relations Journal* 11(2): 37–48

Osterman, P (1994) How common is workplace transformation and who adopts it? *Industrial and Labor Relations Review* 47(2): 185–201

Ott, J S (1989) *The Organizational Culture Perspective*, Pacific Grove, CA: Brooks-Cole

Ouchi, W G (1979) A conceptual framework for the design of organisational control mechanisms, *Management Science* 25(6): 833–48

Ouchi, W G (1981) *Theory Z*, Reading, MA: Addison-Wesley

Overell, S (1996) Firms take on social ills, *People Management* June: 7–8

Oxman, J A and B D Smith (2003) The limits of structural change, *MIT Sloan Management Review* Fall: 77–82

P

Park, S H and G R Ungson (1997) The effect of national culture, organisational complementarity and economic motivation on joint venture dissolution, *Academy of Management Journal* 40(2): 279–307

Parker, M (2000) *Organisational Culture and Identity*, London: Sage

Parker, M (2003) Introduction. Ethics, politics and organizing, *Organisation* 10(2): 187–203

Parker, M and J Slaughter (1988) Management by stress, *Technology Review* October: 27–31

Parker, S, T D Wall and P R Jackson (1997) 'That's not my job': developing flexible employee work orientations, *Academy of Management Journal* 40(4): 899–929

Parker, S M, S Mullarkey and P Jackson (1993) Dimensions of performance effectiveness in high-involvement work organisations, *Human Resource Management Journal* 4(3): 1–21

Parnell, J A and T Hatem (1999) Cultural antecedents of behavioural differences between American and Egyptian managers, *Journal of Management Studies* 36(3): 399–415

Parry, R (2003) *Enterprise – The Leadership Role*, London: Profile Press

Pascale, R (1985) The paradox of corporate culture: reconciling ourselves to socialisation, *California Management Review* Winter: 120–1

Pascale, R and A Athos (1981) *The Art of Japanese Management*, New York: Simon and Schuster

Pasmore, W A and M R Fagans (1992) Participation, individual development and organisational change: a review and synthesis, *Journal of Management* June: 375–97

Paton, R (1983) Powers visible and invisible. In R Paton, S Brown, R Spear, J Chapman, M Floyd and J Hamwee (eds), *Organizations: Cases, Issues and Concepts*, London: Harper and Row

Patti, R J (1974) Organisational resistance and change: the view from below, *Social Service Review* 48(4): 371–2

Pavlov, I P (1927) *Conditioned Reflexes*, Oxford: Oxford University Press

Payne, R and C Cooper (eds) (2001) *Emotions at Work*, Chichester: Wiley

Payne, R L and D C Phesey (1971) G G Stern's organizational climate index: a conceptualisation and application to business organizations, *Organizational Behaviour and Human Performance* 6(1): 77–98

Pease, A (1997) *Body Language: How to Read Other's Thoughts by Their Gestures*, 3rd edn, London: Sheldon Press

Peck, D and D Whitlow (1975) *Approaches to Personality Theory*, London: Methuen

Pedler, M J, J G Burgoyne and T Boydell (1997) *The Learning Company: A Strategy for Sustainable Development*, 2nd edn, London: McGraw-Hill

Perkins, D V (1982) The assessment of stress using life events scales. In L Goldberger and S Breznitz (eds), *Handbook of Stress*, New York: Free Press

Perlow, L A, G A Okhuyysen and N P Repenning (2002) The speed trap: exploring the relationship between decision making and temporal context, *Academy of Management Journal* 45(5): 931–55

Perrow, C (1961) The analysis of goals in complex organisations, *American Sociological Review* 26: 55–67

Perrow, C (1970) *Organizational Analysis*, London: Tavistock

Perrow, C (1972) *Organisational Analysis: A Sociological View*, London: Tavistock

Pervin, A and O P John (1996) *Personality: Theories and Research*, 7th edn, Chichester: Wiley

Pervin, L A (1980) *Personality: Theory, Assessment and Research*, New York: Wiley

Peters, T J (1985) *Thriving on Chaos: Handbook for a Management Revolution*, New York: Knopf

Peters, T (1987) A world turned upside down, *Academy of Management Executive* 1: 231–41

Peters, T J and R H Waterman (1982) *In Search of Excellence: Lessons from America's Best-Run Companies*, New York: Harper and Row

Petri, H L (1996) *Motivation: Theory, Research and Application*, London: Thompson

Pettigrew, A M (1973) *The Politics of Organizational Decision Making*, London: Tavistock

Pettigrew, A M (1987) Context and action in the transformation of the firm, *Journal of Management Studies* 24(6): 649–70

Pettigrew, A M and R Whipp (1993) Understanding the environment. In C Mabey and B Mayon-White (eds), *Managing Change*, 2nd edn, London: Open University Press/Paul Chapman

Pfeffer, J (1977) The ambiguity of leadership, *Academy of Management Review* 2(1): 104–12

Pfeffer, J (1981) *Power in Organizations*, Marchfield, MA: Pitman

Pfeffer, J (1992) *Managing with Power: Politics and Influence in Organisations*, Boston, MA: Harvard Business School Press

Pfeffer, J (1996) *Competitive Advantage Through People: Unleashing the Power of the Workforce*, Boston: Harvard Business School Press

Pfeffer, J and G R Salanick (1978) *The External Control of Organizations: A Resource-Dependence Perspective*, London: Harper and Row

Phares, E J (1987) *Introduction to Personality*, 2nd edn, Glenview, IL: Scott Foresman

Philpott, R (2003) Time to tackle the age-old problem, *People Management* 27 June: 22

Pickard, J (1993) The real meaning of empowerment, *Personnel Management* November: 28–33

Pinkley, R L (1990) Dimensions of conflict frame: disputant interpretations of conflict, *Journal of Applied Psychology* 75(1): 117–26

Piore, M J and C F Sabel (1984) *The Second Industrial Divide: Possibilities for Prosperity*, New York: Basic Books

Piper, W E, M Marrache, R Lacroix, A M Richardson and B D Jones (1983) Cohesion as a basic bond in groups, *Human Relations* 26(2): 93–108

Plomin, R (1994) *Genetics and Experience: The Interplay between Nature and Nurture*, Thousand Oaks, CA: Sage

Podsakoff, P M and L J Williams (1986) The relationship between job performance and job satisfaction. In E A Locke (ed.), *Generalizing from Laboratory to Field Settings*, Lexington, MA: Lexington Books

Polsky, H W (1971) Notes on personal feedback in sensitivity training, *Sociological Enquiry* 41(2): 175–82

Pondy, L (1967) Organisational conflict: concepts and models, *Administrative Science Quarterly* 12(2): 296–320

Poole, M and R Mansfield (1993) Patterns of continuity and change in managerial attitudes and behaviour in industrial relations, *British Journal of Industrial Relations* 31(1): 11–33

Porras, J I and P O Berg (1978) Evaluation methodology in organisational development: analysis and critique, *Journal of Applied Behavioural Science* 14(2): 151–73

Porras, J I and P J Robertson (1992) Organisational development: theory, practice and research. In M D Dunnette and L M Hugh (eds), *Handbook of Industrial and Organisational Psychology*, 2nd edn, Palo Alto, CA: Consulting Psychologists Press

Porras, J I and R Silvers (1991) Organisation development and transformation, *Annual Review of Psychology* 42: 51–78

Porter, L W (1996) Forty years of organisation studies: reflections from a micro perspective, *Administrative Science Quarterly* 41(2): 262–9

Porter, L W and E E Lawler (1968) *Managerial Attitudes and Performance*, Homewood, IL: Irwin

Porter, L W and L E McKibbin (1988) *Management Education and Development: Drift or Thrust into the 21st Century*, New York: McGraw-Hill

Porter, M E (1986) Competition in global industries. In M E Porter (ed.), *Competition in Global Industries*, Boston: Harvard Business School Press

Porter, M E (1990) *The Competitive Advantage of Nations*, New York: Free Press

Poster, M (1990) *The Mode of Information: Poststructuralism and Social Context*, Cambridge: Polity Press

Powell, G N and D A Butterfield (1978) The case for sub-system climate in organizations, *Academy of Management Review* 3(2): 151–7

Prickett, R (1998) Littlewoods takes ethical supply stand, *People Management* November: 13

Pritchard, R D and P J DeLeo (1973) Experimental test of the valence–instrumentality relationships in job performance, *Journal of Applied Psychology* 57(2): 264–79

Proctor, S and F Mueller (eds) (2000) *Teamworking*, London: Macmillan

Pugh, D S (ed.) (1971) *Organisation Theory: Selected Readings*, Harmondsworth: Penguin

Pugh, D S and D J Hickson (1976) *Organizational Structure in its Context: The Aston Programme I*, Aldershot: Gower

Purcell, J (1987) Mapping management styles in industrial relations, *Journal of Management Studies* 24(5): 535–48

Purcell, J (1993) The end of institutional industrial relations, *British Journal of Industrial Relations* 31(1): 6–23

Purcell, J and R Smith (eds) (1979) *The Control of Work*, London: Macmillan

Q

Quinn, J B (1977) Strategic goals: process and politics, *Sloan Management Review*, 19: 21–37

Quinn, R E (1988) *Beyond Rational Management: Mastering the Paradoxes and Competing Demands of High Performance*, San Francisco, CA: Jossey-Bass

Quinn, R E and J Rohrbaugh (1983) A spatial model of effectiveness criteria, *Management Science* 29: 363–77

R

Rajan, A, E Lank and K Chapple (1999) *Good Practice in Knowledge Creation and Exchange*, London: Focus/London Training and Enterprise Council

Ramamoorthy, N and S J Carroll (1998) Individualism/collectivism orientations and reactions toward alternative human resource management practices, *Human Relations* 52(5): 571–88

Ray, C A (1986) Corporate culture: the last frontier of control, *Journal of Management Studies* 23(3): 287–97

Redman, T and Grieves (1999) Managing strategic change through TQM: learning from failure, *New Technology, Work and Employment* 14(1): 45–61

Reed, E W and S C Reed (1964) *Mental Retardation: A Family Study*, Philadelphia, PA: Saunders

Reeves, R (2002) Reality bites, *Management Today* September: 35

Reeves, R (2003) Reality bites, *Management Today* May: 37

Reich, R (1985) The executive's new clothes, *The New Republic* 13(1): 23–8

Reichers, A E (1987) An interactionist perspective on newcomer socialisation rates, *Academy of Management Review* 12(3): 278–87

Renn, R W and R J Vandberg (1995) The critical psychological states; an underrepresented component in job characteristics model research, *Journal of Management* 21(2): 279–303

Revil, J (2003) Life makes you sick, *The Observer* 12 October: 19

Ricardo, D (1817) *The Principles of Political Economy and Taxation*, London: Dent and Son

Ricks, D A (1983) *Big Business Blunders: Mistakes in Multinational Marketing*, Homewood, IL: Dow Jones-Irwin

Robbins, S P (1974) *Managing Organisational Conflict*, New York: Prentice Hall

Robbins, S P (1998) *Organisational Behaviour: Concepts, Controversies, Applications*, 8th edn, New York: Prentice Hall

Roberts, J (2003) The manufacture of corporate social responsibility: constructing corporate sensibility, *Organisation* 10(2): 249–65

Roberts, N C (1986) Organisational power styles: competitive power under varying organisational conditions, *Journal of Applied Behaviourial Science* 22(3): 443–58

Roberts, Z (2003) Pressure group, *People Management* 28 August: 1

Robertson, I (2001) Undue diligence, *People Management* 22 November: 42–43

Robertson, I, M Smith and D Cooper (1992) *Motivation: Strategies, Theory and Practice*, 2nd edn, London: Institute of Personnel and Development

Robinson, A L and A M O'Leary-Kelly (1998) Monkey see, monkey do: the influence of work groups on the antisocial behaviour of employees, *Academy of Management Journal* 41(6): 658–72

Robinson, O (1985) The changing labour market: the phenomenon of part-time employment in Britain, *National Westminster Bank Quarterly Review* November

Roethlisberger, F J and W J Dickson (1939) *Management and the Worker*, Cambridge, MA: Harvard University Press

Rogelberg, S G and A Luong (1998) Nonresponse to mailed surveys: a review and guide, *Current Directions in Psychological Science* 7: 60–5

Rogelberg, S G, A Luong, M E Sederburg and D S Cristol (2000) Employees, attitude surveys: examining the attitudes of noncompliant employees, *Journal of Applied Psychology* 85(2): 284–93

Rogers, C R (1951) *Client Centred Therapy*, Boston, MA: Houghton Mifflin

Rogers, C R (1961) *On Becoming a Person*, Boston, MA: Houghton Mifflin

Rollinson, D J (1993) *Understanding Employee Relations: A Behavioural Approach*, Wokingham: Addison-Wesley

Rollinson, D J, J Handley, C Hook and M Foot (1997) The disciplinary experience and its effects on behaviour: an exploratory study, *Work, Employment and Society* 11(2): 283–311

Romm, C and N Pilskin (1998) Electronic mail as a coalition building information technology, *ACM Transactions on Information Systems* 16(1): 82–100

Ronen, S (1986) *Comparative and Multinational Management*, New York: Wiley

Roney, A and C L Cooper (1997) *Professionals on Workplace Stress*, Chichester: Wiley

Rosen, B and T Jerdee (1974) Factors influencing disciplinary judgements, *Journal of Applied Psychology* 59(3): 327–31

Rosen, M and J Baroundi (1992) Computer-based technology and the emergence of new forms of control. In A Sturdy, D Knights and H Willmott (eds), *Skill and Consent: Contemporary Studies in the Labour Process*, London: Routledge

Rosenberg, M J (1960) An analysis of affective-cognitive consistency. In I Hovland and M J Rosenberg (eds), *Attitude, Organizational and Change*, New Haven, CT: Yale University Press

Rosenfeld, P, R A Gicalone and C A Riorden (1995) *Impression Management in Organisations*, London: Routledge

Rosenthal, R and L Jacobsen (1968) *Pygmalion in the Classroom*, New York: Holt, Rinehart and Winston

Ross, J and B M Staw (1993) Organisational escalation and exit: lessons from the Shoreham nuclear power plant, *Academy of Management Journal* 36(3): 701–32

Ross, L (1977) The intuitive psychologist and his shortcomings: distortions in the attribution process. In L Berkowitz (ed.), *Advances in Experimental Social Psychology*, New York: Academic Press

Rothschild, J and T D Miethe (1999) Whistleblower disclosures and management retaliation, *Work and Occupations* 26(1): 107–28

Rotter, J B (1966) Generalised expectancies for internal versus external control of reinforcement, *Psychological Monographs* 80(1), Whole No. 609

Rouillard, L A (1994) *Goals and Goal Setting*, London: Kogan Page

Rousseau, D M (1979) Assessment of technology in organisations: closed versus open systems approaches, *Academy of Management Review* 4(4): 527–41

Rousseau, D M and J Parks (1993) The contracts of individuals and organisations, *Organisational Behaviour* 15(1): 1–43

Rowlinson, S (1996) Low inflation is bringing out ageism in employers, *People Management* 7 March: 19

RSA (1995) *Tomorrow's Company*, London: Royal Society for the Encouragement of Arts, Manufactures and Commerce

Rubin, D C (1995) *Remembering Our Past: Studies in Autobiographical Memory*, Cambridge: Cambridge University Press

Runciman, W G (1966) *Relative Deprivation and Social Justice*, London: Routledge and Kegan Paul

S

Sackman, S A (1992) Culture and sub-culture: an analysis of organisational knowledge, *Administrative Science Quarterly* 37(2): 140–61

Sackman, S A (ed.) (1997) *Cultural Complexity in Organisations*, London: Sage

Salaman, G (1978) Management development and organisation theory, *Journal of European Industrial Training* 2(7): 7–11

Salancik, G and J Pfeffer (1977) An examination of need-satisfaction models of job attitudes, *Administrative Science Quarterly* 22(3): 427–56

Sarafino, E P (1997) *Principles of Behaviour Change*, Chichester: Wiley

Sathe, V (1985) *Culture and Related Corporate Realities: Text, Cases and Readings on Organizational Entry, Establishment and Change*, Homewood, IL: Irwin

Savery, L K, A Travaglione and I G J Firns (1998) The links between absenteeism and commitment during downsizing, *Personnel Review* 27(4): 312–24

Scarborough, H and J Swan (1999) *Case Studies in Knowledge Management*, London: Institute of Personnel and Development

Schaunbroeck, J and D C Ganster (1993) Chronic demands and responsivity to challenge, *Journal of Applied Psychology* 78(1): 73–85

Schaunbroeck, J, D C Ganster and M L Fox (1992) Dispositional affect and work related stress, *Journal of Applied Psychology* 77(4): 322–35

Schein, E H (1969) *Process Consultation: Its Role in Organisational Development*, Reading, MA: Addison-Wesley

Schein, E H (1980) *Organizational Psychology*, 3rd edn, Englewood Cliffs, NJ: Prentice Hall

Schein, E H (1983) The role of the founder in creating organizational culture, *Organizational Dynamics* Summer: 13–28

Schein, E H (1990) Organizational culture, *American Psychologist* 45: 109–19

Schein, E H (1992) *Organizational Culture and Leadership*, San Francisco, CA: Jossey-Bass

Schein, V S (1977) Individual power and political behaviour in organisations: an inadequately explored reality, *Academy of Management Review* 2(1): 64–72

Schemerhorn, J R Jr, J G Hunt and R N Osborn (2000) *Organizational Behaviour*, 7th edn, New York: Wiley

Schick, F (1997) *Making Choices: A Recasting of Decision Theory*, Cambridge: Cambridge University Press

Schmidt, S M and T Kochan (1972) Conflict: towards conceptual clarity, *Administrative Science Quarterly* 17(3): 359–70

Schneider, B (1983) Work climates: an interactionist perspective. In N W Feimer and E S Geller (eds), *Environmental Psychology: Directions and Perspectives*, New York: Praeger

Schneider, L and E Locke (1971) A critique of Herzberg's classification system and a suggested revision, *Organizational Behaviour and Human Performance* 6(3): 441–58

Schneider, S C and J L Barsoux (1997) *Managing across Cultures*, London: Prentice Hall

Schonberger, R J (1982) *Japanese Manufacturing Techniques: Nine Hidden Lessons in Simplicity*, New York: Free Press

Schonfeld, I S (1990) Coping with job-related stress: the case of teachers, *Journal of Occupational Psychology* 63(2): 141–90

Schriesheim, C and A S DeNisi (1981) Task dimensions as moderators of the effects of instrumental leadership: a two-sample replicated test of path–goal leadership theory, *Journal of Applied Psychology* 66(3): 589–97

Schriesheim, C and S Kerr (1977) Theories and measures of leadership: a critical reappraisal of current and future directions. In J G Hunt and L L Larson (eds), *Leadership: The Cutting Edge*, Carbondale, IL: Southern Illinois University Press

Scott, W E and P M Podsakoff (1982) Leadership, supervision and behavioural control: perspectives from an experimental analysis. In L W Fredericksen (ed.), *Handbook of Organizational Behaviour Management*, New York: Wiley

Seashore, S (1954) *Group Cohesiveness in the Industrial Workgroup*, Ann Arbor, MI: University of Michigan

Segall, M W, D T Campbell and M S Herskovits (1966) *The Influence of Culture on Visual Perception*, Indianapolis, IN: Bobbs-Merrill

Seligman, M P P (1975) *Helplessness: On Depression, Development and Death*, San Francisco, CA: Freeman

Selnes, F, B J Jaworski and A K Kohli (1996) Market orientation in United States and Scandinavian companies: a cross-cultural view, *Scandinavian Journal of Management* 12(2): 139–57

Selye, H (1974) *Stress without Distress*, Philadelphia, PA: Lippincott

Selye, H (1976) *The Stress of Life*, New York: McGraw-Hill

Selznick, P (1966) *TVA and the Grassroots*, New York: Harper and Row

Selznick, P (1957) *Leadership in Administration, A Sociological Interpretation*, New York: Harper and Row

Selznick, P (1984) *Leadership in Administration*, Berkeley, CA: University of California Press

Senge, P (1991) *The Fifth Discipline: The Art and Practice of the Learning Organisation*, New York: Random House

Senge, P (1993) Transforming the practice of management, *Human Resource Development Quarterly* Spring: 3–17

Senge, P (1994) The leader's new work: building learning organisations. In C Mabey and P Iles (eds), *Managing Learning*, London: Pitman

Senior, B (1997a) *Organisational Change*, London: Pitman

Senior, B (1997b) Team roles and team performance: is there really a link? *Journal of Occupational and Organisational Psychology* 70(3): 241–58

Sewell, G (1998) The discipline of teams: the control of team-based industrial work through electronic and peer surveillance, *Administrative Science Quarterly* 43(4): 397–428

Shapira, Z (1997) *Organisational Decision Making*, Cambridge: Cambridge University Press

Shaw, J B (1990) A cognitive categorisation model for the study of intercultural management, *Academy of Management Review* 15(3): 626–45

Shaw, J B and E Barrett-Power (1997) A conceptual framework for assessing organisation, workgroup and individual effectiveness during and after downsizing, *Human Relations* 50(2): 109–27

Shaw, M (1981) *Group Dynamics: The Psychology of Small Group Behaviour*, New York: McGraw-Hill

Sheldon, W H (1954) *A Guide for Somatyping the Adult Male at All Ages*, New York: Harper and Row

Sherif, M (1936) *The Social Psychology of Group Norms*, New York: Harper and Row

Shostak, A B (1980) *Blue Collar Stress*, Reading, MA: Addison-Wesley

Silver, J (1987) The ideology of excellence: management and neo-conservatism, *Studies in Political Economy* 24(1): 5–29

Silverzweig, S and R F Allen (1976) Changing the corporate culture, *Sloan Management Review* 17(3): 33–49

Simon, H A (1957) *Administrative Behaviour*, 2nd edn, New York: Macmillan

Simon, H A (1960) *The New Science of Management Decision*, New York: Harper and Row

Simon, H A (1964) On the concept of organisational goal, *Administrative Science Quarterly* 10(1): 1–22

Simon, H A (1976) *Administrative Behaviour: A Study of Decision Making Processes in Administrative Organisations*, 3rd edn, New York: Free Press

Simon, H A (1978) Rational decision making in business organisations, *American Economic Review* September: 510–22

Simonson, I and B M Staw (1992) De-escalation strategies: a comparison of techniques for reducing commitment to losing courses of action, *Journal of Applied Psychology* 76(3): 419–26

Sinclair, A (1992) The tyranny of a team ideology, *Organisation Studies* 13(4): 611–26

Singh, J V (1986) Performance, slack and risk-taking in organisational decision making, *Academy of Management Journal* 29(3): 562–83

Singh, R (1996) Commentary on the Disability Discrimination Act 1995, *Industrial Relations Journal* 27(2): 175–80

Skinner, B F (1974) *About Behaviourism*, London: Jonathan Cape

Smethhurst, S (2003) A slice of the cake, *People Management* 6 February: 32–34

Smircich, L (1983) Concepts of culture and organisational analysis, *Administrative Science Quarterly* 28(3): 339–58

Smircich, L and G Morgan (1982) Leadership: the management of meaning, *Journal of Applied Behaviourial Science* 18(2): 2–73

Smith, A (1776) *An Enquiry into the Nature and Causes of the Wealth of Nations*, New York: Modern Library

Smith, W (2002) Whistling while you work, *The Guardian* 21 September: 22

Smith, W (2000) Pity the poor employees, *The Guardian* 19 June: 5

Smulders, P G W, M A J Kompier and P Paoli (1996) The work environment in the twelve EU countries: differences and similarities, *Human Relations* 49(10): 1291–313

Sparks, K, C L Cooper, Y Fried and A Shirom (1997) The effects of hours of work on health: a meta-analytic review, *Journal of Occupational and Organisational Psychology* 70(4): 391–408

Spearman, C E (1904) General intelligence objectively determined and measured, *American Journal of Psychology* 15(1): 72–101

Spector, P (1982) Behaviour in organisations as a function of employees' locus of control, *Psychological Bulletin* 91(3): 482–97

Spector, P (1995) *Industrial and Organisational Psychology: Research and Practice*, Chichester: Wiley

Sperling, G (1960) The information available in brief visual presentation, *Psychological Monographs* 74, No. 498

Spreitzer, G M and R E Quinn (1996) Empowering middle managers to be transformational leaders, *Journal of Applied Behavioural Science* 32(3): 237–61

Stahelski, A J, D E Frost and M E Patch (1989) Uses of socially dependent bases of power: French and Raven's theory applied to workgroup leadership, *Journal of Applied Social Psychology* 69(2): 283–97

Stahl, M J and A M Harrell (1982) Evolution and validation of a behaviourial decision theory measurement approach to achievement, power and affiliation, *Journal of Applied Psychology* 67(4): 744–51

Stajkovic, A D and F Luthans (1997) A meta-analysis of the effects of organisational behaviour modification on task performance 1975–95, *Academy of Management Journal* 40(5): 1122–49

Stanworth, C (1998) Telework and the information age, *New Technology, Work and Employment* 13(1): 51–62

Staw, B M (1975) Attribution of the causes of performance: a new alternative interpretation of cross-sectional research on organisations, *Organisational Behaviour and Human Performance* 13(3): 414–32

Staw, B M (1980) The escalation of commitment to a course of action, *Academy of Management Review* 6(3): 577–87

Staw, B M and S G Barsade (1993) Affect and managerial performance: a test of the sadder-but-wiser vs. happier-and-smarter hypothesis, *Administrative Science Quarterly* 38(3): 304–31

Staw, B M, N E Bell and J A Clausen (1986) The dispositional approach to job attitudes, *Administrative Science Quarterly* 27(1): 49–72

Staw, B M and J Ross (1987) Behaviour in escalation situations: antecedents, prototypes and solutions. In E E Cummings and B M Staw (eds), *Research in Organisational Behaviour*, Vol. 9, Greenwich, CT: JAI Press (pp. 39–78)

Staw, B M and J Ross (1989) Understanding behaviour in escalation situations, *Science* October: 216–20

Steele, R P and J R Rentsch (1995) Influence of cumulative strategies on the long-range prediction of absenteeism, *Academy of Management Journal* 38(6): 1616–34

Steers, R and L Porter (1991) *Motivation and Work Behaviour*, New York: McGraw-Hill

Steers, R M and S R Rhodes (1978) Major influences on employee attendance: a process model, *Journal of Applied Psychology* 63(3): 391–407

Stein, H (2001) *Nothing Personal, Just Business: A Guided Journey Into Organisational Darkness*, Westport: Quorum Books

Stephenson, T (1985) *Management: A Political Activity*, Basingstoke: Macmillan

Stewart, R (1991) *Managing Today and Tomorrow*, London: Macmillan

Stiles, P, L Gratton, K Truss, V Hope-Hailey and P McGovern (1997) Performance management and the psychological contract, *Human Resource Management Journal* 7(1): 57–66

Stinchcombe, A L (1965) Social structure and organisations. In J March (ed.), *Handbook of Organisations*, Chicago, IL: Rand McNally

Stogdill, R M (1948) Personal factors associated with leadership: a survey of the literature, *Journal of Psychology* 25(1): 35–71

Stogdill, R M (1974) *Handbook of Leadership: A Survey of Theory and Research*, New York: Free Press

Stoner, J A F (1961) A comparison of individual and group decisions involving risk. In R Brown (ed.), *Social Psychology*, New York: Free Press

Strasser, S, J D Eveland, G Cunnins, O L Denitson and J H Romani (1981) Conceptualising the goal and systems models of organisational effectiveness: implications for comparative evaluation research, *Journal of Management Studies* 18(3): 321–40

Symon, G (2000) Information and communication technologies and the networked organisation: a critical analysis, *Journal of Occupational and Organisational Psychology* 73(4): 389–414

T

Taggar, S, R Hackett and S Saha (1999) Leadership emergence in autonomous work teams: antecedents and outcomes, *Personnel Psychology* 52(4): 899–926

Tagiuri, R (1969) Person perception. In G Lindzey and E Aronson (eds), *Handbook of Social Psychology*, Vol. 3, Reading, MA: Addison-Wesley

Tajfel, H (1969) Cultural factors in perception. In G Lindzey and E Aronson (eds), *Handbook of Social Psychology*, Vol. 3, Reading, MA: Addison-Wesley

Tannenbaum, R (1962) Control in organisations: individual adjustment and performance, *Administrative Science Quarterly* 7(2): 236–57

Tannenbaum, R and W H Schmidt (1958) How to choose a leadership pattern, *Harvard Business Review* March/April: 95–102

Tawney, R H (1931) *Equality*, London: Allen and Unwin

Taylor, F W (1911) *Scientific Management*, New York: Wiley

Taylor, P, C Baldry, P Bain and V Ellis (2003) A unique working environment: health, sickness and absence management in UK call centres, *Work, Employment and Society* 17(3): 435–50

Taylor, S (1998) Emotional labour and the new workplace. In P Thompson and C Warhurst (eds), *Workplaces of the Future*, London: Macmillan

Taylor, S W, P T Hertel, M C McCallum and H C Ellis (1979) Cognitive effort and memory, *Human Learning and Memory* 5(3): 607–17

Terborg, J (1981) Interactional psychology and research on human behaviour in organisations, *Academy of Management Review* 6(4): 569–76

Terpstra, D E (1981) Relationship between methodological rigour and reported outcomes in organisational development research, *Journal of Applied Psychology* 66(3): 541–3

Terry, D J, M A Hogg and K M White (1999) The theory of planned behaviour: self-identity, social identity and group norms, *British Journal of Social Psychology* 38(2): 225–44

Terry, D T (1994) Determinants of coping: the role of stable and situational factors, *Journal of Personality and Social Psychology* 56(4): 895–910

Tett, R P and J P Meyer (1993) Job satisfaction, organisational commitment, turnover intention and turnover: path analyses based on meta-analytic findings, *Personnel Psychology* 46(3): 259–94

Thomas, K W (1976) Conflict and conflict management. In M Dunette (ed.), *Handbook of Industrial and Organisational Psychology*, Stol, IL: Rand McNally

Thomas, K W (1977) Towards multi-dimensional values in teaching: the example of conflict behaviours, *Academy of Management Review* 2(3): 484–90

Thomas, R R (1990) From affirmative action to affirmative diversity, *Harvard Business* Review March/April: 107–17

Thompson, J D (1967) *Organisations in Action*, New York: McGraw-Hill

Thompson, P and S Ackroyd (1995) All quiet on the workplace front? A critique of recent trends in British industrial sociology, *Sociology* 29(4): 615–33

Thompson, P and D McHugh (1995) *Work Organisations: A Critical Introduction*, 2nd edn, Basingstoke: Macmillan

Thorndike, E L (1911) *Animal Intelligence*, New York: Macmillan

Thornhill, A and M N K Saunders (1998) The meanings, consequences and implications of downsizing and redundancy: a review, *Personnel Review* 27(4): 271–95

Thurstone, I I (1938) Primary mental abilities, *Psychometric Monographs* 1: 1–121

Timmons, S (2003) A failed panoptican: surveillance of nursing practice via new technology, *New Technology, Work and Employment* 18(2): 143–53

Tjosvold, D (1991) *Team Organisation: An Enduring Competitive Advantage*, London: Wiley

Tolman, E C, B E Ritchie and D Kalsh (1946) Studies in spatial learning 1: orientation and shortcut, *Journal of Experimental Psychology* 36(1): 13–24

Tourish, D and A Pinnington (2002) Transformational leadership, corporate cultism and the spirituality paradigm: an unholy trinity in the workplace, *Human Relations* 55(2): 147–72

Tower, R K, C Kelly and A Richards (1997) Individualism, collectivism and reward allocation: a cross-cultural study in Russia and Britain, *British Journal of Social Psychology* 36(4): 331–45

Tracy, L (1987) Consideration and initiating structure: are they basic dimensions of leader behaviour? *Social Behaviour and Personality* 15(1): 21–33

Trevino, L and V Bart (1992) Peer reporting of unethical behaviour: a social context perspective, *Academy of Management Journal* 35(1): 38–64

Trist, E L, G W Higgin, H Murray and A B Pollock (1963) *Organisational Choice*, London: Tavistock

Tsui, A S (1989) An empirical examination of the multiple constituency model of organisational effectiveness, *Proceedings of the Academy of Management* April: 188–92

Tuckman, B W (1965) Development sequence in small groups, *Psychological Bulletin* 63(3): 384–99

Tuckman, B W and N Jensen (1977) Stages of group development revisited, *Group and Organisation Studies* 2(3): 419–27

Tulving, E (1974) Theoretical issues in free recall. In T R Dixon and D L Horton (eds), *Verbal Behaviour and General Behaviour Theory*, Englewood Cliffs, NJ: Prentice Hall

Turner, A N and P R Lawrence (1965) *Industrial Jobs and the Worker*, Boston, MA: Harvard School of Business

Tversky, A and D Kahneman (1974) Judgement under uncertainty: heuristic and bias, *Science* 185: 1124–32

Tyson, S and T Jackson (1992) *The Essence of Organisational Behaviour*, Hemel Hempstead: Prentice Hall

V

Vaill, P B (1982) The purpose of high performing systems, *Organizational Dynamics* Autumn: 23–9

Valle, M and P L Perrewe (2000) Do politics perceptions relate to political behaviour? Tests of an implicit assumption and expanded model, *Human Relations* 53(3): 359–86

Van de Vliert, E and C De Dreu (1994) Optimising performance by conflict simulation, *International Journal of Conflict Management* 5(2): 211–22

Van Eynde, D F and J A Bledsoe (1990) The changing practice of organisational development, *Leadership and Organisational Development Journal* 11(2): 25–30

Van Vianen, A E M and A H Fischer (2002) Illuminating the glass ceiling: the role of organisational culture preferences, *Journal of Occupational and Organisational Psychology* 75(3): 315–37

Varey, R (1999) What the world needs now is . . . , *Professional Manager* September: 16–18

Vecchio, R (1987) Situational leadership theory: an examination of a prescriptive theory, *Journal of Applied Psychology* 72(3): 444–51

Vecchio, R (1991) *Organisational Behaviour*, 2nd edn, Orlando, FL: Dryden

Vecchio, R and B C Gobdel (1984) The vertical dyad linkage model of leadership: problems and prospects, *Organizational Behaviour and Human Performance* 34(1): 3–20

Vernon, P E (1955) The assessment of children. In *The Bearings of Recent Advances in Psychology on Educational Problems: Studies in Education*, 7, University of London Institute of Education (pp. 189–215)

Vernon, P E (1969) *Intelligence and Cultural Environment*, London: Methuen

Von Neuman, J and O Morgenstern (1947) *Theory of Games and Economic Behaviour*, Princeton, NJ: Princeton University Press

Vroom, V H (1964) *Work and Motivation*, New York: Wiley

Vroom, V H (1977) Leadership revisited. In H L Tosti and W C Hammer (eds), *Psychological Foundations of Organisational Behaviour*, Chicago, IL: St Clair Press

Vroom, V H and A G Jago (1978) On the validity of the Vroom–Yetton model, *Journal of Applied Psychology* 63(1): 151–62

Vroom, V H and A G Jago (1988) *The New Leadership*, Englewood Cliffs, NJ: Prentice Hall

Vroom, V H and P W Yetton (1973) *Leadership and Decision Making*, Pittsburg, PA: University of Pittsburg Press

W

Wahaba, M A and L G Bridewell (1976) A review of research on the need hierarchy theory, *Organizational Behaviour and Human Performance* 15(2): 212–40

Walker, C R and R H Guest (1957) *Man on the Assembly Line*, New Haven, CT: Yale University Press

Walsh, J (1999) Union movement stems its membership haemorrage, *People Management* May: 18

Walton, C C (1988) *The Moral Manager*, Cambridge, MA: Ballinger

Walton, E J and S Dawson (2001) Managers' perceptions of criteria of effectiveness, *Journal of Management Studies* 38(2): 173–99

Walton, R E (1977) Work innovations at Topeka: after six years, *Journal of Applied Behavioural Science* 13(4): 422–31

Walton, R E (1985) From control to commitment in the workplace, *Harvard Business Review* March–April: 77–84

Wanous, J P, T L Keon and J C Latack (1983) Expectancy theory and occupational/organisational choices: a review and test, *Organisational Behaviour and Human Performance* 22(1): 66–86

Wanous, J P, A E Reichers and S D Malik (1984) Organisational socialisation and group development: towards an integrated perspective, *Academy of Management Review* 9(4): 670–83

Warr, P B (1996) *Psychology at Work*, 4th edn, Harmondsworth: Penguin

Watson, K M (1982) An analysis of communication patterns: a method for discriminating leader and subordinate roles, *Academy of Management Journal* 25(1): 107–22

Waugh, H C and D A Norman (1965) Primary memory, *Psychological Review* 72(1): 89–104

Wayne, S J, L M Shore and R C Linden (1997) Perceived organisational support and leader–member exchange: a social exchange perspective, *Academy of Management Journal* 40(1): 82–111

Weber, E U, C J Anderson and M H Birnbaum (1992) A theory of perceived risk and attractiveness, *Organisational Behaviour and Human Decision Processes* 60(3): 492–523

Weber, M (1947) *The Theory of Social and Economic Organisation*, London: Hodge

Weber, M (1948) *From Max Weber. Essays in Sociology*, Trans., edited and introduction H H Gerth and C W Mills, London: Routledge and Kegan Paul

Weick, K (1979) *The Social Psychology of Organizing*, 2nd edn, Reading, MA: Addison-Wesley

Weick, K E and L D Browning (1986) Argument and narration in organisational communication, *Journal of Management* Summer: 243–59

Weierter, S J M (1997) Who wants to play 'follow the leader'? A theory of charismatic relationships based on routinised charisma and follower characteristics, *Leadership Quarterly* 8(2): 161–86

Weiner, B (1992) *Human Motivation: Metaphors, Theories and Research*, London: Sage

Welch, J (1999) ROM with a view, *People Management* 17 June: 34–40

Wernimont, P (1966) Intrinsic and extrinsic factors in job satisfaction, *Journal of Applied Psychology* 50(1): 41–50

Wesley, F and H Mintzberg (1989) Visionary leadership and strategic management, *Strategic Management Journal* 10(1): 17–32

West, M (1994) *Effective Teamwork*, Leicester: BPS Books

Wheeler, H M (1976) Punishment theory and industrial discipline, *Industrial Relations* 15(2): 235–43

White, R P, P Hodgson and S Crainer (1996) *The Future of Leadership: A White Water Revolution*, London: Pitman

Whitehead, A N (1985) *Science and the Modern World*, London: Free Association Books

Whitehead, M (1999) Churning questions, *People Management* 30 September: 46–9

Whitsett, D A and L Yorks (1983) Looking back at Topeka: General Foods and the quality-of-work-life experiment, *California Management Review* 15: 93–100

Whorf, B L (1940) Science and linguistics, *Technology Review* 42(2): 229–48

Wilkinson, A, M Marchington, T Redman and E Snape (1997) *Total Quality Management: Organisational Change and Human Resource Management*, London: Macmillan

Williams, A (1999) The truth will out, *People Management* May: 23–4

Williams, D R and J S House (1985) Social support and stress reduction. In C L Cooper and M J Smith (eds), *Job Stress and Blue-collar Work*, Chichester: Wiley

Williams, S D (2002) Self-esteem and the self-censorship of creative ideas, *Personnel Review* 31(4): 495–503

Willmott, H (1993) Strength is ignorance: slavery is freedom: managing culture in modern organisation, *Journal of Management Studies* 30(4): 515–51

Willmott, H (1997) Rethinking managerial work: capitalism, control and subjectivity, *Human Relations* 50(11): 1329–59

Wilson, D C and R H Rosenfeld (1990) *Managing Organisations: Text, Readings and Cases*, London: McGraw-Hill

Wilson, D S, D Near and R R Miller (1996) Machiavellianism: a synthesis of evolutionary and psychological literatures, *Psychological Bulletin*, 119(2): 285–99

Windahl, S, B Signitzer and T J Olson (1992) *Using Communication Theory: An Introduction to Planned Communication*, London: Sage

Winter, S G (2003) Mistaken perceptions: cases and consequences, *British Journal of Management* 14(1): 39–44

Wittgenstein, L (1953) *Philosophical Investigations*, Trans. G E M Anscombe (1968), Oxford: Blackwell

Womak, J P, D T Jones and D Roos (1990) *The Machine that Changed the World: The Triumph of Lean Production*, New York: Macmillan

Wood, S and M T Albanese (1995) Can we speak of high commitment management on the shop floor? *Journal of Management Studies* 32(2): 215–47

Woodall, J (1996) Managing culture change: can it ever be ethical? *Personnel Review* 25(6): 28–40

Woodman, R W and J J Sherwood (1980) The role of team development in organisational effectiveness: a critical review, *Psychological Bulletin* 92(2): 166–86

Woodruffe, C (2000) Emotional intelligence: time for time out, *Selection and Development Review* 16(4): 3–9

Woodruffe, C (2001) Promotional intelligence, *People Management* 11 January: 26–29

Woodward, J (1965) *Industrial Organisation: Theory and Practice*, Oxford: Oxford University Press

Wooldridge, E (1995) Time to stand Maslow's hierarchy on its head, *People Management* 21 December: 17

Word, C O, M P Zanna and J Cooper (1974) The nonverbal mediation of self-fulfilling prophecies in interracial interaction, *Journal of Experimental Social Psychology* 10(1): 109–20

Worren, A M, K Ruddle and K Moor (1999) From organisational development to change management, *Journal of Applied Behavioural Science* 35(3): 273–86

Wright, D (1971) *The Psychology of Moral Behaviour*, Harmondsworth: Penguin

Wright, D S, A Taylor, D R Davies, W Sluckin, S G Lee and J T Reason (1970) *Introducing Psychology: An Experimental Approach*, Harmondsworth: Penguin

Wright, P (1995) *Managerial Leadership*, London: Thompson

Y

Yearta, S K, S Maitlis and R B Briner (1995) An exploratory study of goal-setting theory and practice: a motivational technique that works? *Journal of Occupational and Organisational Psychology* 68(4): 237–52

Yorks, L and D A Whitsett (1985) Hawthorne, Topeka and the issue of science versus advocacy in organisational behaviour, *Academy of Management Review* 10(1): 21–30

Yukl, G (1994) *Leadership in Organisations*, 3rd edn, Englewood Cliffs, NJ: Prentice-Hall

Z

Zack, M and J McKenney (1995) Social context and interaction in ongoing computer-supported management groups, *Organisation Science* 6(3): 394–422

Zaremba, A (1988) Working with the organisational grapevine, *Personnel Journal* July: 38–42

Ziera, Y and J Avedisian (1989) Organisational planned change: assessing the chances for success, *Organisational Dynamics* Spring: 31–45

Zimbardo, P G (1973) *Proceedings of the American Psychological Association Conference*, Montreal, Canada: American Psychological Association

Zimmerman, F M (1991) *The Turnaround Experience: Real-world Lessons in Revitalising Organisations*, New York: McGraw-Hill

Author index

C

D

G

H

L

M

Q

R

Subject index

References in **bold** indicate that a 'key concept' explanation is included in the margin.